CFA Institute®
CFA Program

AF886045

FINANCIAL REPORTING AND ANALYSIS

CFA® Program Curriculum
2020 • LEVEL I • VOLUME 3

WILEY

© 2019, 2018, 2017, 2016, 2015, 2014, 2013, 2012, 2011, 2010, 2009, 2008, 2007, 2006 by CFA Institute. All rights reserved.

This copyright covers material written expressly for this volume by the editor/s as well as the compilation itself. It does not cover the individual selections herein that first appeared elsewhere. Permission to reprint these has been obtained by CFA Institute for this edition only. Further reproductions by any means, electronic or mechanical, including photocopying and recording, or by any information storage or retrieval systems, must be arranged with the individual copyright holders noted.

CFA®, Chartered Financial Analyst®, AIMR-PPS®, and GIPS® are just a few of the trademarks owned by CFA Institute. To view a list of CFA Institute trademarks and the Guide for Use of CFA Institute Marks, please visit our website at www.cfainstitute.org.

This publication is designed to provide accurate and authoritative information in regard to the subject matter covered. It is sold with the understanding that the publisher is not engaged in rendering legal, accounting, or other professional service. If legal advice or other expert assistance is required, the services of a competent professional should be sought.

All trademarks, service marks, registered trademarks, and registered service marks are the property of their respective owners and are used herein for identification purposes only.

ISBN 978-1-946442-78-9 (paper)
ISBN 978-1-950157-02-0 (ebk)

SKYA191FD45-7987-4D88-8929-68F15EE20912_091620

Please visit our website at
www.WileyGlobalFinance.com.

WILEY

FSC
www.fsc.org
MIX
Paper from responsible sources
FSC® C084269

CONTENTS

How to Use the CFA Program Curriculum ix
Background on the CBOK ix
Organization of the Curriculum x
Features of the Curriculum x
Designing Your Personal Study Program xii
Feedback xiii

Financial Reporting and Analysis

Study Session 6 **Financial Reporting and Analysis (1)** 3

Reading 19 **Introduction to Financial Statement Analysis** 5
Introduction 6
Roles of Financial Reporting and Financial Statement Analysis 6
Primary Financial Statements and Other Information Sources 13
Financial Statements and Supplementary Information 13
Other Sources of Information 31
Financial Statement Analysis Framework 32
Articulate the Purpose and Context of Analysis 33
Collect Data 34
Process Data 35
Analyze/Interpret the Processed Data 35
Develop and Communicate Conclusions/Recommendations 35
Follow-Up 36
Summary 36
Practice Problems 39
Solutions 42

Reading 20 **Financial Reporting Standards** 45
Introduction 46
The Objective of Financial Reporting 46
Standard-Setting Bodies and Regulatory Authorities 47
Accounting Standards Boards 48
Regulatory Authorities 49
The International Financial Reporting Standards Framework 54
Qualitative Characteristics of Financial Reports 54
Constraints on Financial Reports 55
The Elements of Financial Statements 56
General Requirements for Financial Statements 58
Comparison of IFRS with Alternative Reporting Systems 61
Monitoring Developments in Financial Reporting Standards 62
New Products or Types of Transactions 63
Evolving Standards and the Role of CFA Institute 63

◘ indicates an optional segment

	Summary	64
	Practice Problems	66
	Solutions	68
Study Session 7	**Financial Reporting and Analysis (2)**	69
Reading 21	**Understanding Income Statements**	71
	Introduction	72
	Components and Format of the Income Statement	72
	Revenue Recognition	78
	General Principles	79
	Accounting Standards for Revenue Recognition	80
	Expense Recognition	84
	General Principles	84
	Issues in Expense Recognition	88
	Implications for Financial Analysis	93
	Non-Recurring Items and Non-Operating Items	93
	Discontinued Operations	94
	Unusual or Infrequent Items	94
	Changes in Accounting Policies	96
	Non-Operating Items	98
	Earnings per Share	99
	Simple versus Complex Capital Structure	100
	Basic EPS	101
	Diluted EPS	102
	Changes in EPS	109
	Analysis of the Income Statement	109
	Common-Size Analysis of the Income Statement	109
	Income Statement Ratios	111
	Comprehensive Income	113
	Summary	116
	Practice Problems	119
	Solutions	124
Reading 22	**Understanding Balance Sheets**	127
	Introduction	128
	Components and Format of the Balance Sheet	128
	Balance Sheet Components	129
	Current and Non-Current Classification	131
	Liquidity-Based Presentation	132
	Current Assets and Current Liabilities	133
	Current Assets	133
	Current Liabilities	138
	Non-Current Assets	142
	Property, Plant, and Equipment	143
	Investment Property	144
	Intangible Assets	145
	Goodwill	148
	Financial Assets	150

	Deferred Tax Assets	154
	Non-Current Liabilities	154
	Long-term Financial Liabilities	156
	Deferred Tax Liabilities	156
	Equity	157
	Components of Equity	157
	Statement of Changes in Equity	160
	Analysis of the Balance Sheet	161
	Common-Size Analysis of the Balance Sheet	161
	Balance Sheet Ratios	169
	Summary	171
	Practice Problems	174
	Solutions	179
Reading 23	**Understanding Cash Flow Statements**	**183**
	Introduction	184
	Components and Format of the Cash Flow Statement	185
	Classification of Cash Flows and Non-Cash Activities	185
	A Summary of Differences between IFRS and US GAAP	187
	Direct and Indirect Methods for Reporting Cash Flow from Operating Activities	188
	The Cash Flow Statement: Linkages and Preparation	198
	Linkages of the Cash Flow Statement with the Income Statement and Balance Sheet	198
	Steps in Preparing the Cash Flow Statement	199
	Conversion of Cash Flows from the Indirect to the Direct Method	211
	Cash Flow Statement Analysis	212
	Evaluation of the Sources and Uses of Cash	212
	Common-Size Analysis of the Statement of Cash Flows	216
	Free Cash Flow to the Firm and Free Cash Flow to Equity	222
	Cash Flow Ratios	223
	Summary	225
	Practice Problems	226
	Solutions	232
Reading 24	**Financial Analysis Techniques**	**235**
	Introduction	236
	The Financial Analysis Process	237
	The Objectives of the Financial Analysis Process	237
	Distinguishing between Computations and Analysis	238
	Analytical Tools and Techniques	241
	Ratios	243
	Common-Size Analysis	248
	The Use of Graphs as an Analytical Tool	254
	Regression Analysis	256
	Common Ratios Used in Financial Analysis	256
	Interpretation and Context	257
	Activity Ratios	258
	Liquidity Ratios	264

	Solvency Ratios	269
	Profitability Ratios	273
	Integrated Financial Ratio Analysis	276
	Equity Analysis	284
	Valuation Ratios	284
	Industry-Specific Ratios	287
	Historical Research on Ratios in Equity Analysis	289
	Credit Analysis	290
	The Credit Rating Process	290
	Historical Research on Ratios in Credit Analysis	291
	Business and Geographic Segments	292
	Segment Reporting Requirements	292
	Segment Ratios	293
	Model Building and Forecasting	296
	Summary	297
	Practice Problems	299
	Solutions	305
Study Session 8	**Financial Reporting and Analysis (3)**	309
Reading 25	**Inventories**	311
	Introduction	312
	Cost of Inventories	313
	Inventory Valuation Methods	314
	Specific Identification	315
	First-In, First-Out (FIFO)	315
	Weighted Average Cost	315
	Last-In, First-Out (LIFO)	316
	Calculation of Cost of Sales, Gross Profit, and Ending Inventory	316
	Periodic versus Perpetual Inventory Systems	318
	Comparison of Inventory Valuation Methods	320
	The LIFO Method	323
	LIFO Reserve	323
	LIFO Liquidations	324
	Inventory Method Changes	331
	Inventory Adjustments	332
	Evaluation of Inventory Management	339
	Presentation and Disclosure	339
	Inventory Ratios	340
	Financial Analysis Illustrations	341
	Summary	350
	Practice Problems	353
	Solutions	369
Reading 26	**Long-Lived Assets**	377
	Introduction	378
	Acquisition of Long-Lived Assets	379
	Property, Plant, and Equipment	379
	Intangible Assets	382

Capitalising versus Expensing: Impact on Financial Statements and Ratios 386
Capitalisation of Interest Costs 391
Capitalisation of Internal Development Costs 394
Depreciation and Amortisation of Long-Lived Assets 398
Depreciation Methods and Calculation of Depreciation Expense 398
Amortisation Methods and Calculation of Amortisation Expense 406
The Revaluation Model 407
Impairment of Assets 411
Impairment of Property, Plant, and Equipment 412
Impairment of Intangible Assets with a Finite Life 414
Impairment of Intangibles with Indefinite Lives 414
Impairment of Long-Lived Assets Held for Sale 414
Reversals of Impairments of Long-Lived Assets 414
Derecognition 415
Sale of Long-Lived Assets 415
Long-Lived Assets Disposed of Other Than by a Sale 416
Presentation and Disclosures 417
Investment Property 428
Summary 432
Practice Problems 434
Solutions 446

Reading 27 **Income Taxes** 451
Introduction 452
Differences between Accounting Profit and Taxable Income 452
Current Tax Assets and Liabilities 453
Deferred Tax Assets and Liabilities 454
Determining the Tax Base of Assets and Liabilities 457
Determining the Tax Base of an Asset 457
Determining the Tax Base of a Liability 459
Changes in Income Tax Rates 461
Temporary and Permanent Differences Between Taxable and Accounting Profit 462
Taxable Temporary Differences 463
Deductible Temporary Differences 463
Examples of Taxable and Deductible Temporary Differences 464
Temporary Differences at Initial Recognition of Assets and Liabilities 466
Business Combinations and Deferred Taxes 466
Investments in Subsidiaries, Branches, Associates and Interests in Joint Ventures 467
Unused Tax Losses and Tax Credits 467
Recognition and Measurement of Current and Deferred Tax 468
Recognition of a Valuation Allowance 469
Recognition of Current and Deferred Tax Charged Directly to Equity 469
Presentation and Disclosure 471
Comparison of IFRS and US GAAP 477

	Summary	**479**
	Practice Problems	**481**
	Solutions	**486**
Reading 28	**Non-Current (Long-Term) Liabilities**	**489**
	Introduction	**490**
	Bonds Payable	**490**
	Accounting for Bond Issuance	**490**
	Accounting for Bond Amortisation, Interest Expense, and Interest Payments	**494**
	Current Market Rates and Fair Value Reporting Option	**498**
	Derecognition of Debt	**502**
	Debt Covenants	**504**
	Presentation and Disclosure of Long-Term Debt	**506**
	Leases	**509**
	Lessee accounting	**510**
	Lessor accounting	**511**
	Introduction to Pensions and Other Post-Employment Benefits	**513**
	Evaluating Solvency: Leverage and Coverage Ratios	**516**
	Summary	**520**
	Practice Problems	**523**
	Solutions	**529**
Study Session 9	**Financial Reporting and Analysis (4)**	**537**
Reading 29	**Financial Reporting Quality**	**539**
	Introduction	**540**
	Conceptual Overview	**540**
	GAAP, Decision-Useful, Sustainable, and Adequate Returns	**542**
	GAAP, Decision-Useful, but Sustainable?	**542**
	Biased Accounting Choices	**543**
	Departures from GAAP	**552**
	Differentiate between Conservative and Aggressive Accounting	**554**
	Context for Assessing Financial Reporting Quality	**557**
	Motivations	**557**
	Conditions Conducive to Issuing Low-Quality Financial Reports	**558**
	Mechanisms That Discipline Financial Reporting Quality	**559**
	Detection of Financial Reporting Quality Issues	**566**
	Presentation Choices	**567**
	Accounting Choices and Estimates	**573**
	Warning Signs	**591**
	Summary	**596**
	Practice Problems	**599**
	Solutions	**603**

Reading 30 **Applications of Financial Statement Analysis** **607**
Introduction **608**
Application: Evaluating Past Financial Performance **609**
Application: Projecting Future Financial Performance **612**
Projecting Performance: An Input to Market-Based Valuation **613**
Projecting Multiple-Period Performance **618**
Application: Assessing Credit Risk **622**
Application: Screening for Potential Equity Investments **624**
Analyst Adjustments to Reported Financials **627**
A Framework for Analyst Adjustments **627**
Analyst Adjustments Related to Investments **628**
Analyst Adjustments Related to Inventory **628**
Analyst Adjustments Related to Property, Plant, and Equipment **632**
Analyst Adjustments Related to Goodwill **634**
Summary **636**
Practice Problems **638**
Solutions **640**

Glossary **G-1**

▣ indicates an optional segment

How to Use the CFA Program Curriculum

Congratulations on your decision to enter the Chartered Financial Analyst (CFA®) Program. This exciting and rewarding program of study reflects your desire to become a serious investment professional. You are embarking on a program noted for its high ethical standards and the breadth of knowledge, skills, and abilities (competencies) it develops. Your commitment to the CFA Program should be educationally and professionally rewarding.

The credential you seek is respected around the world as a mark of accomplishment and dedication. Each level of the program represents a distinct achievement in professional development. Successful completion of the program is rewarded with membership in a prestigious global community of investment professionals. CFA charterholders are dedicated to life-long learning and maintaining currency with the ever-changing dynamics of a challenging profession. The CFA Program represents the first step toward a career-long commitment to professional education.

The CFA examination measures your mastery of the core knowledge, skills, and abilities required to succeed as an investment professional. These core competencies are the basis for the Candidate Body of Knowledge (CBOK™). The CBOK consists of four components:

- A broad outline that lists the major topic areas covered in the CFA Program (https://www.cfainstitute.org/programs/cfa/curriculum/cbok);
- Topic area weights that indicate the relative exam weightings of the top-level topic areas (https://www.cfainstitute.org/programs/cfa/curriculum/overview);
- Learning outcome statements (LOS) that advise candidates about the specific knowledge, skills, and abilities they should acquire from readings covering a topic area (LOS are provided in candidate study sessions and at the beginning of each reading); and
- The CFA Program curriculum that candidates receive upon examination registration.

Therefore, the key to your success on the CFA examinations is studying and understanding the CBOK. The following sections provide background on the CBOK, the organization of the curriculum, features of the curriculum, and tips for designing an effective personal study program.

BACKGROUND ON THE CBOK

The CFA Program is grounded in the practice of the investment profession. Beginning with the Global Body of Investment Knowledge (GBIK), CFA Institute performs a continuous practice analysis with investment professionals around the world to determine the competencies that are relevant to the profession. Regional expert panels and targeted surveys are conducted annually to verify and reinforce the continuous feedback about the GBIK. The practice analysis process ultimately defines the CBOK. The

© 2019 CFA Institute. All rights reserved.

CBOK reflects the competencies that are generally accepted and applied by investment professionals. These competencies are used in practice in a generalist context and are expected to be demonstrated by a recently qualified CFA charterholder.

The CFA Institute staff, in conjunction with the Education Advisory Committee and Curriculum Level Advisors, who consist of practicing CFA charterholders, designs the CFA Program curriculum in order to deliver the CBOK to candidates. The examinations, also written by CFA charterholders, are designed to allow you to demonstrate your mastery of the CBOK as set forth in the CFA Program curriculum. As you structure your personal study program, you should emphasize mastery of the CBOK and the practical application of that knowledge. For more information on the practice analysis, CBOK, and development of the CFA Program curriculum, please visit www.cfainstitute.org.

ORGANIZATION OF THE CURRICULUM

The Level I CFA Program curriculum is organized into 10 topic areas. Each topic area begins with a brief statement of the material and the depth of knowledge expected. It is then divided into one or more study sessions. These study sessions—19 sessions in the Level I curriculum—should form the basic structure of your reading and preparation. Each study session includes a statement of its structure and objective and is further divided into assigned readings. An outline illustrating the organization of these 19 study sessions can be found at the front of each volume of the curriculum.

The readings are commissioned by CFA Institute and written by content experts, including investment professionals and university professors. Each reading includes LOS and the core material to be studied, often a combination of text, exhibits, and in-text examples and questions. A reading typically ends with practice problems followed by solutions to these problems to help you understand and master the material. The LOS indicate what you should be able to accomplish after studying the material. The LOS, the core material, and the practice problems are dependent on each other, with the core material and the practice problems providing context for understanding the scope of the LOS and enabling you to apply a principle or concept in a variety of scenarios.

The entire readings, including the practice problems at the end of the readings, are the basis for all examination questions and are selected or developed specifically to teach the knowledge, skills, and abilities reflected in the CBOK.

You should use the LOS to guide and focus your study because each examination question is based on one or more LOS and the core material and practice problems associated with the LOS. As a candidate, you are responsible for the entirety of the required material in a study session.

We encourage you to review the information about the LOS on our website (www.cfainstitute.org/programs/cfa/curriculum/study-sessions), including the descriptions of LOS "command words" on the candidate resources page at www.cfainstitute.org.

FEATURES OF THE CURRICULUM

OPTIONAL SEGMENT

Required vs. Optional Segments You should read all of an assigned reading. In some cases, though, we have reprinted an entire publication and marked certain parts of the reading as "optional." The CFA examination is based only on the required segments, and the optional segments are included only when it is determined that they might help you to better understand the required segments (by seeing the required material in its full context). When an optional segment begins, you will see an icon and a dashed vertical bar in the outside margin that will continue until the optional segment ends, accompanied by another icon. *Unless the material is specifically marked as optional, you should assume it is required.* You should rely on the required segments and the reading-specific LOS in preparing for the examination.

END OPTIONAL SEGMENT

Practice Problems/Solutions *All practice problems at the end of the readings as well as their solutions are part of the curriculum and are required material for the examination.* In addition to the in-text examples and questions, these practice problems should help demonstrate practical applications and reinforce your understanding of the concepts presented. Some of these practice problems are adapted from past CFA examinations and/or may serve as a basis for examination questions.

Glossary For your convenience, each volume includes a comprehensive glossary. Throughout the curriculum, a **bolded** word in a reading denotes a term defined in the glossary.

Note that the digital curriculum that is included in your examination registration fee is searchable for key words, including glossary terms.

LOS Self-Check We have inserted checkboxes next to each LOS that you can use to track your progress in mastering the concepts in each reading.

Source Material The CFA Institute curriculum cites textbooks, journal articles, and other publications that provide additional context or information about topics covered in the readings. As a candidate, you are not responsible for familiarity with the original source materials cited in the curriculum.

Note that some readings may contain a web address or URL. The referenced sites were live at the time the reading was written or updated but may have been deactivated since then.

Some readings in the curriculum cite articles published in the *Financial Analysts Journal*®, which is the flagship publication of CFA Institute. Since its launch in 1945, the *Financial Analysts Journal* has established itself as the leading practitioner-oriented journal in the investment management community. Over the years, it has advanced the knowledge and understanding of the practice of investment management through the publication of peer-reviewed practitioner-relevant research from leading academics and practitioners. It has also featured thought-provoking opinion pieces that advance the common level of discourse within the investment management profession. Some of the most influential research in the area of investment management has appeared in the pages of the *Financial Analysts Journal*, and several Nobel laureates have contributed articles.

Candidates are not responsible for familiarity with *Financial Analysts Journal* articles that are cited in the curriculum. But, as your time and studies allow, we strongly encourage you to begin supplementing your understanding of key investment management issues by reading this practice-oriented publication. Candidates have full online access to the *Financial Analysts Journal* and associated resources. All you need is to log in on www.cfapubs.org using your candidate credentials.

Errata The curriculum development process is rigorous and includes multiple rounds of reviews by content experts. Despite our efforts to produce a curriculum that is free of errors, there are times when we must make corrections. Curriculum errata are periodically updated and posted on the candidate resources page at www.cfainstitute.org.

DESIGNING YOUR PERSONAL STUDY PROGRAM

Create a Schedule An orderly, systematic approach to examination preparation is critical. You should dedicate a consistent block of time every week to reading and studying. Complete all assigned readings and the associated problems and solutions in each study session. Review the LOS both before and after you study each reading to ensure that you have mastered the applicable content and can demonstrate the knowledge, skills, and abilities described by the LOS and the assigned reading. Use the LOS self-check to track your progress and highlight areas of weakness for later review.

Successful candidates report an average of more than 300 hours preparing for each examination. Your preparation time will vary based on your prior education and experience, and you will probably spend more time on some study sessions than on others. As the Level I curriculum includes 19 study sessions, a good plan is to devote 15–20 hours per week for 19 weeks to studying the material and use the final four to six weeks before the examination to review what you have learned and practice with practice questions and mock examinations. This recommendation, however, may underestimate the hours needed for appropriate examination preparation depending on your individual circumstances, relevant experience, and academic background. You will undoubtedly adjust your study time to conform to your own strengths and weaknesses and to your educational and professional background.

You should allow ample time for both in-depth study of all topic areas and additional concentration on those topic areas for which you feel the least prepared.

As part of the supplemental study tools that are included in your examination registration fee, you have access to a study planner to help you plan your study time. The study planner calculates your study progress and pace based on the time remaining until examination. For more information on the study planner and other supplemental study tools, please visit www.cfainstitute.org.

As you prepare for your examination, we will e-mail you important examination updates, testing policies, and study tips. Be sure to read these carefully.

CFA Institute Practice Questions Your examination registration fee includes digital access to hundreds of practice questions that are additional to the practice problems at the end of the readings. These practice questions are intended to help you assess your mastery of individual topic areas as you progress through your studies. After each practice question, you will be able to receive immediate feedback noting the correct responses and indicating the relevant assigned reading so you can identify areas of weakness for further study. For more information on the practice questions, please visit www.cfainstitute.org.

CFA Institute Mock Examinations Your examination registration fee also includes digital access to three-hour mock examinations that simulate the morning and afternoon sessions of the actual CFA examination. These mock examinations are intended to be taken after you complete your study of the full curriculum and take practice questions so you can test your understanding of the curriculum and your readiness for the examination. You will receive feedback at the end of the mock examination, noting the correct responses and indicating the relevant assigned readings so you can assess areas of weakness for further study during your review period. We recommend that you take mock examinations during the final stages of your preparation for the actual CFA examination. For more information on the mock examinations, please visit www.cfainstitute.org.

Preparatory Providers After you enroll in the CFA Program, you may receive numerous solicitations for preparatory courses and review materials. When considering a preparatory course, make sure the provider belongs to the CFA Institute Approved Prep Provider Program. Approved Prep Providers have committed to follow CFA Institute guidelines and high standards in their offerings and communications with candidates. For more information on the Approved Prep Providers, please visit www.cfainstitute.org/programs/cfa/exam/prep-providers.

Remember, however, that there are no shortcuts to success on the CFA examinations; reading and studying the CFA curriculum *is* the key to success on the examination. The CFA examinations reference only the CFA Institute assigned curriculum—no preparatory course or review course materials are consulted or referenced.

SUMMARY

Every question on the CFA examination is based on the content contained in the required readings and on one or more LOS. Frequently, an examination question is based on a specific example highlighted within a reading or on a specific practice problem and its solution. To make effective use of the CFA Program curriculum, please remember these key points:

1 All pages of the curriculum are required reading for the examination except for occasional sections marked as optional. You may read optional pages as background, but you will not be tested on them.

2 All questions, problems, and their solutions—found at the end of readings—are part of the curriculum and are required study material for the examination.

3 You should make appropriate use of the practice questions and mock examinations as well as other supplemental study tools and candidate resources available at www.cfainstitute.org.

4 Create a schedule and commit sufficient study time to cover the 19 study sessions, using the study planner. You should also plan to review the materials and take practice questions and mock examinations.

5 Some of the concepts in the study sessions may be superseded by updated rulings and/or pronouncements issued after a reading was published. Candidates are expected to be familiar with the overall analytical framework contained in the assigned readings. Candidates are not responsible for changes that occur after the material was written.

FEEDBACK

At CFA Institute, we are committed to delivering a comprehensive and rigorous curriculum for the development of competent, ethically grounded investment professionals. We rely on candidate and investment professional comments and feedback as we work to improve the curriculum, supplemental study tools, and candidate resources.

Please send any comments or feedback to info@cfainstitute.org. You can be assured that we will review your suggestions carefully. Ongoing improvements in the curriculum will help you prepare for success on the upcoming examinations and for a lifetime of learning as a serious investment professional.

Financial Reporting and Analysis

STUDY SESSIONS

Study Session 6	Financial Reporting and Analysis (1)
Study Session 7	Financial Reporting and Analysis (2)
Study Session 8	Financial Reporting and Analysis (3)
Study Session 9	Financial Reporting and Analysis (4)

TOPIC LEVEL LEARNING OUTCOME

The candidate should be able to demonstrate a thorough knowledge of financial reporting procedures and the standards that govern financial reporting disclosure. Emphasis is on basic financial statements and how alternative accounting methods affect those statements and the analysis of them.

Financial statement analysis is critical in assessing a company's overall financial position and associated risks over time. Security and business valuation, credit risk assessment, and acquisition due diligence all require an understanding of the major financial statements including general principles and reporting approaches. Because no set of accounting standards has universal acceptance, companies around the world may differ in reporting treatment based on their jurisdiction.

Financial statement analysis requires the ability to analyze a company's reported results with its economic reality, normalize differences in accounting treatment to make valid cross company comparisons, identify quality issues that may exist in reported financial statements, and discern evidence of financial statement manipulation by management.

Note: Changes in accounting standards as well as new rulings and/or pronouncements issued after the publication of the readings on financial reporting and analysis may cause some of the information in these readings to become dated. Candidates are *not* responsible for anything that occurs after the readings were published. In addition, candidates are expected to be familiar with the analytical frameworks contained in the readings, as well as the implications of alternative accounting methods for financial analysis and valuation discussed in the readings. Candidates are also responsible for the content of accounting standards, but not for the actual reference numbers. Finally, candidates should be aware that certain ratios may be defined and calculated differently. When alternative ratio definitions exist and no specific definition is given, candidates should use the ratio definitions emphasized in the readings.

© 2019 CFA Institute. All rights reserved.

Candidates should be familiar with the material covered in the following prerequisite reading available in Candidate Resources on the CFA Institute website:

- **Financial Reporting Mechanics**

FINANCIAL REPORTING AND ANALYSIS

STUDY SESSION

6

Financial Reporting and Analysis (1)

This study session introduces the principal information sources used to evaluate a company's financial performance. Primary financial statements (income statement, balance sheet, cash flow statement, and statement of changes in equity) in addition to notes to these statements and management reporting are examined. A general framework for conducting financial statement analysis is provided. The session also includes a description of the roles played by financial reporting standard-setting bodies and regulatory authorities.

READING ASSIGNMENTS

Reading 19	Introduction to Financial Statement Analysis by Elaine Henry, PhD, CFA, and Thomas R. Robinson, PhD, CFA
Reading 20	Financial Reporting Standards by Elaine Henry, PhD, CFA, Jan Hendrik van Greuning, DCom, CFA, and Thomas R. Robinson, PhD, CFA

Note: Changes in accounting standards as well as new rulings and/or pronouncements issued after the publication of the readings on financial reporting and analysis may cause some of the information in these readings to become dated. Candidates are *not* responsible for anything that occurs after the readings were published. In addition, candidates are expected to be familiar with the analytical frameworks contained in the readings, as well as the implications of alternative accounting methods for financial analysis and valuation discussed in the readings. Candidates are also responsible for the content of accounting standards, but not for the actual reference numbers. Finally, candidates should be aware that certain ratios may be defined and calculated differently. When alternative ratio definitions exist and no specific definition is given, candidates should use the ratio definitions emphasized in the readings.

© 2019 CFA Institute. All rights reserved.

READING

19

Introduction to Financial Statement Analysis

by Elaine Henry, PhD, CFA, and Thomas R. Robinson, PhD, CFA

Elaine Henry, PhD, CFA, is at Stevens Institute of Technology (USA). Thomas R. Robinson, PhD, CFA, is at AACSB International (USA).

LEARNING OUTCOMES

Mastery	*The candidate should be able to:*
☐	**a.** describe the roles of financial reporting and financial statement analysis;
☐	**b.** describe the roles of the statement of financial position, statement of comprehensive income, statement of changes in equity, and statement of cash flows in evaluating a company's performance and financial position;
☐	**c.** describe the importance of financial statement notes and supplementary information—including disclosures of accounting policies, methods, and estimates—and management's commentary;
☐	**d.** describe the objective of audits of financial statements, the types of audit reports, and the importance of effective internal controls;
☐	**e.** identify and describe information sources that analysts use in financial statement analysis besides annual financial statements and supplementary information;
☐	**f.** describe the steps in the financial statement analysis framework.

Note: Changes in accounting standards as well as new rulings and/or pronouncements issued after the publication of the readings on financial reporting and analysis may cause some of the information in these readings to become dated. Candidates are *not* responsible for anything that occurs after the readings were published. In addition, candidates are expected to be familiar with the analytical frameworks contained in the readings, as well as the implications of alternative accounting methods for financial analysis and valuation discussed in the readings. Candidates are also responsible for the content of accounting standards, but not for the actual reference numbers. Finally, candidates should be aware that certain ratios may be defined and calculated differently. When alternative ratio definitions exist and no specific definition is given, candidates should use the ratio definitions emphasized in the readings.

© 2019 CFA Institute. All rights reserved.

1 INTRODUCTION

Financial analysis is the process of examining a company's performance in the context of its industry and economic environment in order to arrive at a decision or recommendation. Often, the decisions and recommendations addressed by financial analysts pertain to providing capital to companies—specifically, whether to invest in the company's debt or equity securities and at what price. An investor in debt securities is concerned about the company's ability to pay interest and to repay the principal lent. An investor in equity securities is an owner with a residual interest in the company and is concerned about the company's ability to pay dividends and the likelihood that its share price will increase.

Overall, a central focus of financial analysis is evaluating the company's ability to earn a return on its capital that is at least equal to the cost of that capital, to profitably grow its operations, and to generate enough cash to meet obligations and pursue opportunities.

Fundamental financial analysis starts with the information found in a company's financial reports. These financial reports include audited financial statements, additional disclosures required by regulatory authorities, and any accompanying (unaudited) commentary by management. Basic financial statement analysis—as presented in this reading—provides a foundation that enables the analyst to better understand other information gathered from research beyond the financial reports.

This reading is organized as follows: Section 2 discusses the scope of financial statement analysis. Section 3 describes the sources of information used in financial statement analysis, including the primary financial statements (statement of financial position or balance sheet, statement of comprehensive income, statement of changes in equity, and cash flow statement). Section 4 provides a framework for guiding the financial statement analysis process. A summary of the key points conclude the reading.

2 ROLES OF FINANCIAL REPORTING AND FINANCIAL STATEMENT ANALYSIS

The role of financial statements issued by companies is to provide information about a company's performance, financial position, and changes in financial position that is useful to a wide range of users in making economic decisions. The role of financial statement analysis is to use financial reports prepared by companies, combined with other information, to evaluate the past, current, and potential performance and financial position of a company for the purpose of making investment, credit, and other economic decisions. Managers within a company perform financial analysis to make operating, investing, and financing decisions but do not necessarily rely on analysis of related financial statements. They have access to additional financial information that can be reported in whatever format is most useful to their decision.

In evaluating financial reports, analysts typically have a specific economic decision in mind. Examples of these decisions include the following:

- Evaluating an equity investment for inclusion in a portfolio.
- Evaluating a merger or acquisition candidate.
- Evaluating a subsidiary or operating division of a parent company.
- Deciding whether to make a venture capital or other private equity investment.
- Determining the creditworthiness of a company in order to decide whether to extend a loan to the company and if so, what terms to offer.

- Extending credit to a customer.
- Examining compliance with debt covenants or other contractual arrangements.
- Assigning a debt rating to a company or bond issue.
- Valuing a security for making an investment recommendation to others.
- Forecasting future net income and cash flow.

These decisions demonstrate certain themes in financial analysis. In general, analysts seek to examine the past and current performance and financial position of a company in order to form expectations about its future performance and financial position. Analysts are also concerned about factors that affect risks to a company's future performance and financial position. An examination of performance can include an assessment of a company's profitability (the ability to earn a profit from delivering goods and services) and its ability to generate positive cash flows (cash receipts in excess of cash disbursements). Profit and cash flow are not equivalent. Profit (or loss) represents the difference between the prices at which goods or services are provided to customers and the expenses incurred to provide those goods and services.

In addition, profit (or loss) includes other income (such as investing income or income from the sale of items other than goods and services) minus the expenses incurred to earn that income. Overall, profit (or loss) equals income minus expenses, and its recognition is mostly independent from when cash is received or paid. Example 1 illustrates the distinction between profit and cash flow.

EXAMPLE 1

Profit versus Cash Flow

Sennett Designs (SD) sells furniture on a retail basis. SD began operations during December 2017 and sold furniture for €250,000 in cash. The furniture sold by SD was purchased on credit for €150,000 and delivered by the supplier during December. The credit terms granted by the supplier required SD to pay the €150,000 in January for the furniture it received during December. In addition to the purchase and sale of furniture, in December, SD paid €20,000 in cash for rent and salaries.

1 How much is SD's profit for December 2017 if no other transactions occurred?

2 How much is SD's cash flow for December 2017?

3 If SD purchases and sells exactly the same amount in January 2018 as it did in December and under the same terms (receiving cash for the sales and making purchases on credit that will be due in February), how much will the company's profit and cash flow be for the month of January?

Solution to 1:

SD's profit for December 2017 is the excess of the sales price (€250,000) over the cost of the goods that were sold (€150,000) and rent and salaries (€20,000), or €80,000.

Solution to 2:

The December 2017 cash flow is €230,000, the amount of cash received from the customer (€250,000) less the cash paid for rent and salaries (€20,000).

Solution to 3:

SD's profit for January 2018 will be identical to its profit in December: €80,000, calculated as the sales price (€250,000) minus the cost of the goods that were sold (€150,000) and minus rent and salaries (€20,000). SD's cash flow in January 2018 will also equal €80,000, calculated as the amount of cash received from the customer (€250,000) minus the cash paid for rent and salaries (€20,000) *and* minus the €150,000 that SD owes for the goods it had purchased on credit in the prior month.

Although profitability is important, so is a company's ability to generate positive cash flow. Cash flow is important because, ultimately, the company needs cash to pay employees, suppliers, and others in order to continue as a going concern. A company that generates positive cash flow from operations has more flexibility in funding needed for investments and taking advantage of attractive business opportunities than an otherwise comparable company without positive operating cash flow. Additionally, a company needs cash to pay returns (interest and dividends) to providers of debt and equity capital.

The expected magnitude of future cash flows is important in valuing corporate securities and in determining the company's ability to meet its obligations. The ability to meet short-term obligations is generally referred to as **liquidity**, and the ability to meet long-term obligations is generally referred to as **solvency**. Cash flow in any given period is not, however, a complete measure of performance for that period because, as shown in Example 1, a company may be obligated to make future cash payments as a result of a transaction that generates positive cash flow in the current period.

Profits may provide useful information about cash flows, past and future. If the transaction of Example 1 were repeated month after month, the long-term average monthly cash flow of SD would equal €80,000, its monthly profit. Analysts typically not only evaluate past profitability but also forecast future profitability.

Exhibit 1 shows how news coverage of corporate earnings announcements places corporate results in the context of analysts' expectations. Panel A shows the earnings announcement, and Panel B shows a sample of the news coverage of the announcement. Earnings are also frequently used by analysts in valuation. For example, an analyst may value shares of a company by comparing its price-to-earnings ratio (P/E) to the P/Es of peer companies and/or may use forecasted future earnings as direct or indirect inputs into discounted cash flow models of valuation.

Exhibit 1 An Earnings Release and News Media Comparison with Analysts' Expectations

Panel A: Excerpt from Apple Earnings Release

Apple Reports Second Quarter Results

Revenue Grows 16 Percent and EPS Grows 30 Percent to New March Quarter Records
New $100 Billion Share Repurchase Authorization Announced, Dividend Raised by 16 Percent

> Cupertino, California—May 1, 2018—Apple today announced financial results for its fiscal 2018 second quarter ended March 31, 2018. The Company posted quarterly revenue of $61.1 billion, an increase of 16 percent from the year-ago quarter, and quarterly earnings per diluted share of $2.73, up 30 percent. International sales accounted for 65 percent of the quarter's revenue.

Exhibit 1 (Continued)

"We're thrilled to report our best March quarter ever, with strong revenue growth in iPhone, Services and Wearables," said Tim Cook, Apple's CEO. "Customers chose iPhone X more than any other iPhone each week in the March quarter, just as they did following its launch in the December quarter. We also grew revenue in all of our geographic segments, with over 20% growth in Greater China and Japan."

"Our business performed extremely well during the March quarter, as we grew earnings per share by 30 percent and generated over $15 billion in operating cash flow," said Luca Maestri, Apple's CFO. "With the greater flexibility we now have from access to our global cash, we can more efficiently invest in our US operations and work toward a more optimal capital structure. Given our confidence in Apple's future, we are very happy to announce that our Board has approved a new $100 billion share repurchase authorization and a 16 percent increase in our quarterly dividend."

The Company will complete the execution of the previous $210 billion share repurchase authorization during the third fiscal quarter.

Reflecting the approved increase, the Board has declared a cash dividend of $0.73 per share of Apple's common stock payable on May 17, 2018 to shareholders of record as of the close of business on May 14, 2018.

The Company also expects to continue to net-share-settle vesting restricted stock units.

From the inception of its capital return program in August 2012 through March 2018, Apple has returned $275 billion to shareholders, including $200 billion in share repurchases. The management team and the Board will continue to review each element of the capital return program regularly and plan to provide an update on the program on an annual basis.

Apple is providing the following guidance for its fiscal 2018 third quarter:

- revenue between $51.5 billion and $53.5 billion
- gross margin between 38 percent and 38.5 percent
- operating expenses between $7.7 billion and $7.8 billion
- other income/(expense) of $400 million
- tax rate of approximately 14.5 percent

Apple will provide live streaming of its Q2 2018 financial results conference call beginning at 2:00 p.m. PDT on May 1, 2018 at www.apple.com/investor/earnings-call/. This webcast will also be available for replay for approximately two weeks thereafter.

Source: https://www.apple.com/newsroom/2018/05/apple-reports-second-quarter-results/ (retrieved 3 November 2018)

Panel B: Excerpt from News Article: Apple Second Quarter 2018 Earnings Release

Apple reported quarterly earnings and revenue on Tuesday that beat expectations, but sold fewer iPhones than expected.

(continued)

Exhibit 1 (Continued)

Shares rose as much 5 percent after hours, as investors digested the company's better-than-expected outlook for the current quarter, and a hefty capital return program.

The soft iPhone sales were still up from a year ago, and Apple CEO Tim Cook said in a statement that customers "chose iPhone X more than any other iPhone each week in the March quarter."

- Earnings per share: \$2.73 vs. \$2.67, adjusted, expected by a Thomson Reuters consensus estimate
- Revenue: \$61.1 billion vs. \$60.82 billion expected by Thomson Reuters consensus
- iPhone unit sales: 52.2 million vs. 52.54 million expected by a StreetAccount estimate
- Fiscal Q3 revenue guidance: \$51.5 billion to \$53.5 billion vs. \$51.61 billion expected by Thomson Reuters consensus

Net income was \$13.82 billion, up from \$11.03 billion a year ago. A year ago, Apple earned \$2.10 a share on revenue of \$52.9 billion.

Source: https://cnbc.com/2018/05/01/apple-earnings-q2-2018.html (retrieved 3 November 2018)

Analysts are also interested in the financial position of a company. The financial position can be measured by comparing the resources controlled by the company (**assets**) in relation to the claims against those resources (**liabilities** and **equity**). The combination of liabilities and equity used to finance its assets represents the capital structure of the company. An example of a resource is cash. In Example 1, if no other transactions occur, the company should have €230,000 more in cash at 31 December 2017 than at the start of the period. The cash can be used by the company to pay its obligation to the supplier (a claim against the company) and may also be used to make distributions to the owner (who has a residual claim against the company's assets, net of liabilities).

Financial position and capital structure are particularly important in credit analysis, as depicted in Exhibit 2. Panel A of the exhibit is an excerpt from the company's annual earnings release highlighting the cumulative profitability, strong cash flow, strong balance sheet, and strong return on invested capital. Panel B of the exhibit is an excerpt from an August 2017 news article about an increase in the credit rating of Southwest Airlines due to a long history of profitability and a conservative capital structure.

Exhibit 2

Panel A: Excerpt from Earnings Announcement by Southwest Airlines

Southwest Airlines Reports Fourth Quarter and Record Annual Profit; 44th Consecutive Year of Profitability

DALLAS, Jan. 26, 2017 /PRNewswire/ -- Southwest Airlines Co. (NYSE:LUV) (the "Company") today reported its fourth quarter and annual 2016 results:

Exhibit 2 (Continued)

Fourth quarter net income of $522 million, or $.84 per diluted share, compared with fourth quarter 2015 net income of $536 million, or $.82 per diluted share.

Excluding special items, fourth quarter net income of $463 million, or $.75 per diluted share, compared with fourth quarter 2015 net income of $591 million, or $.90 per diluted share. This exceeded the First Call fourth quarter 2016 consensus estimate of $.70 per diluted share.

Record annual net income of $2.24 billion, or $3.55 per diluted share, compared with 2015 net income of $2.18 billion, or $3.27 per diluted share.

Excluding special items, record annual net income of $2.37 billion, or $3.75 per diluted share, compared with 2015 net income of $2.36 billion, or $3.52 per diluted share.

Annual operating income of $3.76 billion, resulting in an operating margin of 18.4 percent.

Excluding special items, annual operating income of $3.96 billion, resulting in an operating margin of 19.4 percent.

Record annual operating cash flow of $4.29 billion, and record annual free cash flow1 of $2.25 billion.

Returned $1.97 billion to Shareholders in 2016, through a combination of $222 million in dividends and $1.75 billion in share repurchases.

Annual return on invested capital (ROIC)1 of 30.0 percent.

Gary C. Kelly, Chairman of the Board and Chief Executive Officer, stated, "We are delighted to report record annual profits for 2016, our 44th consecutive year of profitability. Our total operating revenues reached a record $20.4 billion, with sustained demand for our legendary low fares and superior Customer Service. Our profit margins were very strong, and our ROIC was a near-record 30.0 percent. Our record profits and balance sheet discipline generated record free cash flow, allowing us to return significant value to our Shareholders. Operationally, our performance was also very solid. We carried a record number of Customers while improving our ontime performance, baggage delivery rate, and net promoter score. My thanks and congratulations to the superb People of Southwest for these outstanding results, which earned them $586 million in profit sharing during 2016.

"We ended the year with a solid fourth quarter 2016 performance. Total operating revenues grew 2.0 percent, year-over-year, to a fourth quarter record $5.1 billion, exceeding our expectations as of the beginning of the fourth quarter. Travel demand and close-in yields improved post-election. In addition, December business travel was stronger than anticipated leading up to the holiday period. Based on current bookings and revenue trends, we estimate first quarter 2017 operating unit revenues will be flat to down one percent, year-over-year. This represents a continued and sequential improvement from the 2.9 percent operating unit revenue year-over-year decline in fourth quarter 2016, which is an encouraging start to the year.

"As expected, our fourth quarter unit costs increased, year-over-year, due to higher fuel costs, pay increases from amended union contracts, and additional depreciation expense associated with the accelerated retirement of our Boeing 737-300 aircraft. While

(continued)

Exhibit 2 (Continued)

inflationary cost pressures are expected in 2017 due to the union contract pay increases, we are continuing our efforts to drive offsetting cost efficiencies through fleet modernization and ongoing technology investments in our operations.

..."As we close out a year of record results, we begin 2017 with momentum and enthusiasm. We are on track to open a new international terminal in Fort Lauderdale, along with the launch of new service, this June. We are on track to launch the new Boeing 737-8 in the fall. And, we are encouraged by recent revenue trends, as well as the prospects for continued economic growth and moderate fuel prices. We are excited about our current outlook for another strong year with opportunities to win more Customers and reward our People and our Shareholders."

Source: http://www.southwestairlinesinvestorrelations.com/news-and-events/news-releases/2017/01-26-2017-111504198 (retrieved November 3, 2018)

Panel B: Excerpt from News Article About Southwest Airlines

Southwest Wins Another Credit Rating Upgrade

Citing its "consistent record of profitability," S&P Global Ratings upgraded Southwest Airlines (LUV) on Monday to a triple-B-plus rating from triple-B.

This line from the report sums up the rationale for the upgrade nicely:

Southwest is the only U.S. airline that has recorded 44 consecutive years of profitability and remains the largest low-cost airline in the world.

The credit rating agency commends the airline for its record despite headwinds including, "multiple industry cycles, the evolution of the large U.S. hub-and-spoke airlines into more efficient and financially secure competitors, the emergence of ultra-low-cost airlines, the acquisition and integration of AirTran Holdings Inc. in 2011, and the company's entry into more congested but lucrative metropolitan airports such as New York's LaGuardia Airport."

In June, Moody's upgraded Southwest to A3, one notch higher than S&P's new rating on its credit scale. Moody's Senior Credit Officer Jonathan Root wrote then, "the upgrade to A3 reflects Moody's expectation that Southwest will continue to conservatively manage its capital structure, allowing it to sustain credit metrics supportive of the A3 rating category."

Source: https://www.barrons.com/articles/southwest-wins-another-credit-rating-upgrade-1502747699 (retrieved November 3, 2018)

In conducting financial analysis of a company, the analyst will regularly refer to the company's financial statements, financial notes, and supplementary schedules and a variety of other information sources. The next section introduces the primary financial statements and some commonly used information sources.

PRIMARY FINANCIAL STATEMENTS AND OTHER INFORMATION SOURCES

3

In order to perform an equity or credit analysis of a company, an analyst collects a great deal of information. The nature of the information collected will vary on the basis of the individual decision to be made (or the specific purpose of the analysis) but will typically include information about the economy, industry, and company, as well as information about comparable peer companies. Information from outside the company will likely include economic statistics, industry reports, trade publications, and databases containing information on competitors. The company itself provides core information for analysis in its financial reports, press releases, investor conference calls, and webcasts.

Companies prepare financial reports at regular intervals (annually, semiannually, and/or quarterly depending on the applicable regulatory requirements). Financial reports include financial statements along with supplemental disclosures necessary to assess the company's financial position and periodic performance.

Financial statements are the result of an accounting process that records a company's economic activities, following the applicable accounting standards and principles. These statements summarize the accounting information, mainly for users outside the company (such as investors, creditors, analysts, and others) because insiders have direct access to the underlying financial data summarized in the financial statements and to other information that is not included in the financial reporting process.

Financial statements are almost always audited by independent accountants, who provide an opinion on whether the financial statements present fairly the company's performance and financial position, in accordance with a specified, applicable set of accounting standards and principles.

3.1 Financial Statements and Supplementary Information

A complete set of financial statements include a statement of financial position (i.e., a balance sheet), a statement of comprehensive income (i.e., a single statement of comprehensive income or an income statement and a statement of comprehensive income), a statement of changes in equity, and a statement of cash flows.[1] The balance sheet portrays the company's financial position at a given point in time. The statement of comprehensive income and statement of cash flows present different aspects of a company's performance over a period of time. The statement of changes in equity provides additional information regarding the changes in a company's financial position. In addition, the accompanying required notes, or footnotes, are considered an integral part of a complete set of financial statements.

Along with the required financial statements, a company typically provides additional information in its financial reports. In many jurisdictions, some or all of this additional information is mandated by regulators or accounting standards boards. The additional information provided may include a letter from the chairman of the company, a report from management discussing the results (typically called management discussion and analysis [MD&A] or management commentary), an external auditor's report providing assurances, a governance report describing the structure of the company's board of directors, and a corporate responsibility report. As part of his or

1 The names of the financial statements are those in IAS 1. Commonly used terms for these financial statements are indicated in parentheses. Later readings will elaborate on each of these financial statements.

her analysis, the financial analyst should read and assess this additional information along with the financial statements. The following sections describe and illustrate each financial statement and some of the additional information.

3.1.1 *Balance Sheet (Statement of Financial Position)*

The **balance sheet** (also called the **statement of financial position** or **statement of financial condition**) presents a company's financial position by disclosing the resources the company controls (assets) and its obligations to lenders and other creditors (liabilities) at a specific point in time. **Owners' equity** (sometimes called "net assets") represents the excess of assets over liabilities. This amount is attributable to the company's owners or shareholders. Owners' equity is the owners' residual interest in (i.e., residual claim on) the company's assets after deducting its liabilities.

The relationship among the three parts of the balance sheet (assets, liabilities, and owners' equity) can be expressed in the following equation form: Assets = Liabilities + Owners' equity. This equation (sometimes called the accounting equation or the balance sheet equation) shows that the total amount of assets must equal or *balance* with the combined total amounts of liabilities and owners' equity. Alternatively, the equation may be rearranged as follows: Assets − Liabilities = Owners' equity. This formulation emphasizes the residual claim aspect of owners' equity. Depending on the form of the organization, owners' equity may be referred to as "partners' capital" or "shareholders' equity" or "shareholders' funds."

Exhibit 3 presents the balance sheet of the Volkswagen Group from its Annual Report 2017.

Exhibit 3 Balance Sheet of the Volkswagen Group (Excerpt)

€ million	31 Dec. 2017	31 Dec. 2016
Assets		
Noncurrent assets		
Intangible assets	63,419	62,599
Property, plant and equipment	55,243	54,033
Lease assets	39,254	38,439
Investment property	468	512
Equity-accounted investments	8,205	8,616
Other equity investments	1,318	996
Financial services receivables	73,249	68,402
Other financial assets	8,455	8,256
Other receivables	2,252	2,009
Tax receivables	407	392
Deferred tax assets	9,810	9,756
	262,081	**254,010**
Current assets		
Inventories	40,415	38,978
Trade receivables	13,357	12,187
Financial services receivables	53,145	49,673
Other financial assets	11,998	11,844
Other receivables	5,346	5,130
Tax receivables	1,339	1,126

Exhibit 3 (Continued)

€ million	31 Dec. 2017	31 Dec. 2016
Marketable securities	15,939	17,520
Cash, cash equivalents and time deposits	18,457	19,265
Assets held for sale	115	–
	160,112	**155,722**
Total assets	**422,193**	**409,732**
Equity and Liabilities		
Equity		
Subscribed capital	1,283	1,283
Capital reserves	14,551	14,551
Retained earnings	81,367	70,446
Other reserves	560	(1,158)
Equity attributable to Volkswagen AG hybrid capital investors	11,088	7,567
Equity attributable to Volkswagen AG shareholders and hybrid capital investors	108,849	92,689
Noncontrolling interests	229	221
	109,077	**92,910**
Noncurrent liabilities		
Financial liabilities	81,628	66,358
Other financial liabilities	2,665	4,488
Other liabilities	6,199	5,664
Deferred tax liabilities	5,636	4,745
Provisions for pensions	32,730	33,012
Provisions for taxes	3,030	3,556
Other provisions	20,839	21,482
	152,726	**139,306**
Current liabilities		
Put options and compensation rights granted to non-controlling interest shareholders	3,795	3,849
Financial liabilities	81,844	88,461
Trade payables	23,046	22,794
Tax payables	430	500
Other financial liabilities	8,570	9,438
Other liabilities	15,961	15,461
Provisions for taxes	1,397	1,301
Other provisions	25,347	35,711
	160,389	**177,515**
Total equity and liabilities	**422,193**	**409,732**

Note: Numbers are as shown in the annual report and may not precisely add because of rounding.
Source: Volkswagen 2017 annual report

In Exhibit 3, the balance sheet is presented with the most recent year in the left column and the earlier year in the right column. Although this is a common presentation, analysts should be careful when reading financial statements. In some cases, the ordering may be reversed, with the earlier year(s) on the left and the most recent year on the far right.

At 31 December 2017, Volkswagen's total resources or assets were €422 billion. This number is the sum of non-current assets of €262 billion and current assets of €160 billion.[2] Total equity was €109 billion. Although Volkswagen does not give a total amount for all the balance sheet liabilities, it can be determined by adding the non-current and current liabilities, €153 billion + €160 billion = €313 billion.[3]

Referring back to the basic accounting equation, Assets = Liabilities + Equity, we have €422billion = €313 billion + €109 billion. In other words, Volkswagen has assets of €422 billion, owes €313 billion, and thus has equity of €109 billion. Using the balance sheet and applying financial statement analysis, the analyst can answer such questions as

- Has the company's liquidity (ability to meet short-term obligations) improved?
- Is the company solvent (does it have sufficient resources to cover its obligations)?
- What is the company's financial position relative to the industry?

Volkswagen, a German-based automobile manufacturer, prepares its financial statements in accordance with International Financial Reporting Standards (IFRS). IFRS require companies to present balance sheets that show current and non-current assets and current and non-current liabilities as separate classifications. However, IFRS do not prescribe a particular ordering or format, and the order in which companies present their balance sheet items is largely a function of tradition.

As shown, Volkswagen presents non-current assets before current assets, owners' equity before liabilities, and non-current liabilities before current liabilities. This method generally reflects a presentation from least liquid to most liquid. In other countries, the typical order of presentation may differ. For example, in the United States, Australia, and Canada, companies usually present their assets and liabilities from most liquid to least liquid. Cash is typically the first asset shown, and equity is presented after liabilities.

As a basis for comparison, Exhibit 4 presents the balance sheet of Walmart, Inc. (Walmart) from its 2018 annual report, with a fiscal year end of 31 January.

Exhibit 4 Walmart Consolidated Balance Sheet

	As of 31 January	
(Amounts in $ millions)	**2018**	**2017**
ASSETS		
Current assets:		
Cash and cash equivalents	6,756	6,867
Receivables, net	5,614	5,835
Inventories	43,783	43,046

2 Current assets are defined, in general, as those assets that are cash or cash equivalents; are held for trading; or are expected to be converted to cash (realized), sold, or consumed within 12 months or the company's normal operating cycle. All other assets are classified as non-current.

3 Current liabilities are defined, in general, as those that are expected to be settled within 12 months or the company's normal operating cycle. All other liabilities are classified as non-current.

Exhibit 4 (Continued)

(Amounts in $ millions)	**As of 31 January 2018**	**2017**
Prepaid expenses and other	3,511	1,941
Total current assets	59,664	57,689
Property and equipment:		
Property and equipment	185,154	179,492
Less accumulated depreciation	(77,479)	(71,782)
Property and equipment, net	107,675	107,710
Property under capital lease and financing obligations:		
Property under capital lease and financing obligations	12,703	11,637
Less accumulated amortization	(5,560)	(5,169)
Property under capital lease and financing obligations, net	7,143	6,468
Goodwill	18,242	17,037
Other assets and deferred charges	11,798	9,921
Total assets	204,522	198,825
LIABILITIES AND EQUITY		
Current liabilities:		
Short-term borrowings	5,257	1,099
Accounts payable	46,092	41,433
Accrued liabilities	22,122	20,654
Accrued income taxes	645	921
Long-term debt due within one year	3,738	2,256
Capital lease and financing obligations due within one year	667	565
Total current liabilities	78,521	66,928
Long-term debt	30,045	36,015
Long-term capital lease and financing obligations	6,780	6,003
Deferred income taxes and other	8,354	9,344
Commitments and contingencies		
Equity:		
Common stock	295	305
Capital in excess of par value	2,648	2,371
Retained earnings	85,107	89,354
Accumulated other comprehensive loss	(10,181)	(14,232)
Total Walmart shareholders' equity	77,869	77,798
Noncontrolling interest	2,953	2,737

(continued)

Exhibit 4 (Continued)

(Amounts in $ millions)	As of 31 January 2018	2017
Total equity	80,822	80,535
Total liabilities and equity	204,522	198,825

Source: Walmart 2018 annual report.

As of 31 January 2018, Walmart has total assets of $205 billion. Liabilities and other non-equity claims total $124 billion, and equity is $81 billion.

3.1.2 *Statement of Comprehensive Income*

The statement of comprehensive income can be presented as a single statement of comprehensive income or as two statements, an income statement and a statement of comprehensive income that begins with profit or loss from the income statement. The Volkswagen Group chose the latter form of presentation.

3.1.2.1 Income Statement The income statement presents information on the financial performance of a company's business activities over a period of time. It communicates how much **revenue** and other income the company generated during a period and the expenses it incurred to generate that revenue and other income. Revenue typically refers to amounts charged for the delivery of goods or services in the ordinary activities of a business. Other income may include gains that may or may not arise in the ordinary activities of the business, such as profit on a business disposal. **Expenses** reflect outflows, depletions of assets, and incurrences of liabilities that decrease equity. Expenses typically include such items as cost of sales (cost of goods sold), administrative expenses, and income tax expenses and may be defined to include losses. Net income (revenue plus other income minus expenses) on the income statement is often referred to as the "bottom line" because of its proximity to the bottom of the income statement. Net income may also be referred to as "net earnings," "net profit," and "profit or loss." In the event that expenses exceed revenues and other income, the result is referred to as "net loss."

Income statements are reported on a consolidated basis, meaning that they include the income and expenses of subsidiary companies under the control of the parent (reporting) company. The income statement is sometimes referred to as a **statement of operations** or **profit and loss (P&L) statement**. The basic equation underlying the income statement is Revenue + Other income – Expenses = Income – Expenses = Net income.

In general terms, when one company (the parent) controls another company (the subsidiary), the parent presents its own financial statement information consolidated with that of the subsidiary. (When a parent company owns more than 50 percent of the voting shares of a subsidiary company, it is presumed to control the subsidiary and thus presents consolidated financial statements.) Each line item of the consolidated income statement includes the entire amount from the relevant line item on the subsidiary's income statement (after removing any intercompany transactions). However, if the parent does not own 100 percent of the subsidiary, it is necessary for the parent to present an allocation of net income to the minority interests. Minority interests, also called non-controlling interests, refer to owners of the remaining shares of the subsidiary that are not owned by the parent. The share of consolidated net income attributable to minority interests is shown at the bottom of the income statement along with the net income attributable to shareholders of the parent company. Exhibit 5 presents the income statements of the Volkswagen Group from its 2017 annual report.

Exhibit 5 Income Statement of the Volkswagen Group (Excerpt)

€ million	2017	2016
Sales revenue	**230,682**	**217,267**
Cost of sales	(188,140)	(176,270)
Gross result	**42,542**	**40,997**
Distribution expenses	(22,710)	(22,700)
Administrative expenses	(8,254)	(7,336)
Other operating income	14,500	13,049
Other operating expenses	(12,259)	(16,907)
Operating result	**13,818**	**7,103**
Share of the result of equity-accounted investments	3,482	3,497
Interest income	951	1,285
Interest expenses	(2,317)	(2,955)
Other financial result	(2,022)	(1,638)
Financial result	**94**	**189**
Earnings before tax	**13,913**	**7,292**
Income tax income/expense	(2,275)	(1,912)
Current	(3,205)	(3,273)
Deferred	930	1,361
Earnings after tax	**11,638**	**5,379**
of which attributable to		
Noncontrolling interests	10	10
Volkswagen AG hybrid capital investors	274	225
Volkswagen AG shareholders	11,354	5,144
Basic earnings per ordinary share in €	**22.63**	**10.24**
Diluted earnings per ordinary share in €	**22.63**	**10.24**
Basic earnings per preferred share in €	**22.69**	**10.30**
Diluted earnings per preferred share in €	**22.69**	**10.30**

Note: The numbers are as shown in the annual report and may not add because of rounding.
Source: 2017 Volkswagen annual report.

Exhibit 5 shows that Volkswagen's sales revenue for the year ended 31 December 2017 was €231 billion. Subtracting cost of sales from revenue gives gross profit (called "gross results" by Volkswagen) of €43 billion. After subtracting operating costs and expenses and adding other operating income, the company's operating profit (called "operating result" by Volkswaen) totals €14 billion. Operating profit represents the results of the company's usual business activities before deducting interest expense or taxes. Operating profit (also called operating income in addition to operating result) is thus often referred to as earnings before interest and taxes (EBIT).

Next, operating profit is increased by Volkswagen's share of the profits generated by certain of its investments (€3.5 billion) plus interest income of €1.0 billion, and decreased by losses from its other financial activities (€2.0 billion) and by interest expense of €2.3 million, resulting in profit (earnings) before tax of €13.9 billion. Total income tax expense for 2017 was €2.3 billion, resulting in profit after tax (net income) of €11.6 billion. After allocating the profits attributable to minority interest ownership in Volkswagen subsidiary companies, the profit attributable to shareholders of Volkswagen for 2017 was €11.4 billion.

Companies present both basic and diluted earnings per share on the face of the income statement. Earnings per share numbers represent net income attributable to the class of shareholders divided by the relevant number of shares outstanding during the period. Basic earnings per share is calculated using the weighted-average number of common (ordinary) shares that were actually outstanding during the period and the profit or loss attributable to the common shareowners. Diluted earnings per share uses **diluted shares**—the number of shares that would hypothetically be outstanding if potentially dilutive claims on common shares (e.g., stock options or convertible bonds) were exercised or converted by their holders—and an appropriately adjusted profit or loss attributable to the common shareowners.

Volkswagen has two types of shareholders, ordinary and preferred, and presents earnings per share information for both, although there is no requirement to present earnings per share information for preferred shareowners. Volkswagen's basic earnings per ordinary share was €22.63. A note to the company's financial statements explains that this number was calculated as follows: €11.4 billion profit attributable to shareholders of Volkswagen, of which €6.8 billion is attributable to ordinary shareholders and the balance is attributable to preferred shareholders. The €6.8 billion attributable to ordinary shareholders divided by the weighted-average number of ordinary shares of 0.295 billion shares equals basic earnings per share of €22.63. Similar detail is provided in the notes for each of the earnings per share numbers.

An analyst examining the income statement might note that Volkswagen was profitable in both years. The company's profits increased substantially in 2017, primarily because of higher sales and lower other operating expenses (footnotes reveal this was largely due to $4 billion less in litigation expenses in 2017). The analyst might formulate questions related to profitability, such as the following:

- Is the change in revenue related to an increase in units sold, an increase in prices, or some combination?
- If the company has multiple business segments (for example, Volkswagen's segments include passenger cars, light commercial vehicles, and financial services, among others), how are the segments' revenue and profits changing?
- How does the company compare with other companies in the industry?

Answering such questions requires the analyst to gather, analyze, and interpret information from a number of sources, including, but not limited to, the income statement.

3.1.2.2 Other Comprehensive Income Comprehensive income includes all items that impact owners' equity but are not the result of transactions with shareowners. Some of these items are included in the calculation of net income, and some are included in other comprehensive income (OCI). When comprehensive income is presented in two statements, the statement of comprehensive income begins with the profit or loss from the income statement and then presents the components of OCI.

Exhibit 6 presents an excerpt from the statement of comprehensive income of the Volkswagen Group from its 2017 annual report.

Exhibit 6 Statement of Comprehensive Income of the Volkswagen Group (Excerpt)

€ million	Fiscal Year Ended 31 December 2017
Earnings after tax	**11,638**
Pension plan remeasurements recognized in other comprehensive income	
Pension plan remeasurements recognized in other comprehensive income, before tax	785
Deferred taxes relating to pension plan remeasurements recognized in other comprehensive income	(198)
Pension plan remeasurements recognized in other comprehensive income, net of tax	588
Share of other comprehensive income of equity-accounted investments that will not be reclassified to profit or loss, net of tax	96
Items that will not be reclassified to profit or loss	**683**
Exchange differences on translating foreign operations	
Unrealized currency translation gains/losses	(2,095)
Transferred to profit or loss	(4)
Exchange differences on translating foreign operations, before tax	(2,099)
Deferred taxes relating to exchange differences on translating foreign operations	(8)
Exchange differences on translating foreign operations, net of tax	(2,107)
Cash flow hedges	
Fair value changes recognized in other comprehensive income	6,137
Transferred to profit or loss	(558)
Cash flow hedges, before tax	5,579
Deferred taxes relating to cash flow hedges	(1,597)
Cash flow hedges, net of tax	3,982
Available-for-sale financial assets	
Fair value changes recognized in other comprehensive income	56
Transferred to profit or loss	62
Available-for-sale financial assets, before tax	118
Deferred taxes relating to available-for-sale financial assets	(25)
Available-for-sale financial assets, net of tax	93
Share of other comprehensive income of equity-accounted investments that may be reclassified subsequently to profit or loss, net of tax	(346)
Items that may be reclassified subsequently to profit or loss	**1,622**
Other comprehensive income, before tax	4,133
Deferred taxes relating to other comprehensive income	(1,828)
Other comprehensive income, net of tax	**2,305**
Total comprehensive income	**13,943**

Source: Volkswagen 2017 annual report.

Exhibit 6 shows total comprehensive income for 2017 was €13.9 billion, which is the sum of earnings after tax of €11.6 billion, reported on the income statement, and other comprehensive income of €2.3 billion. The items in OCI reflect changes in the company's equity that are not considered to be profit or loss, some of which may be reclassified as such in the future such as unrealized currency translation gains and losses. The statement of comprehensive income will be discussed in greater detail in a later reading.

3.1.3 *Statement of Changes in Equity*

The statement of changes in equity, sometimes called the "statement of changes in owners' equity" or "statement of changes in shareholders' equity," primarily serves to report changes in the owners' investment in the business over time. The basic components of owners' equity are paid-in capital and retained earnings. Retained earnings include the cumulative amount of the company's profits that have been retained in the company. In addition, non-controlling or minority interests and reserves that represent accumulated OCI items are included in equity. The latter items may be shown separately or included in retained earnings. Volkswagen includes reserves as components of retained earnings.

The statement of changes in equity is organized to present, for each component of equity, the beginning balance, any increases during the period, any decreases during the period, and the ending balance. For paid-in capital, an example of an increase is a new issuance of equity and an example of a decrease is a repurchase of previously issued stock. For retained earnings, income (both net income as reported on the income statement and OCI) is the most common increase and a dividend payment is the most common decrease.

Volkswagen's balance sheet in Exhibit 3 shows that equity at the end of 2017 totaled €109 billion, compared with €93 billion at the end of 2016. The company's statement of changes in equity presents additional detail on the change in each line item. Exhibit 7 presents an excerpt of the statement of changes in equity of the Volkswagen Group from its 2017 annual report. For purposes of brevity, several interim columns were excluded from the presentation.

Exhibit 7 Statement of Changes in Equity of the Volkswagen Group (Excerpt)

€ million	Subscribed capital	Capital reserves	Retained earnings	Total equity
Balance at 1 January 2017	1,283	14,551	70,446	92,910
Earnings after tax	–	–	11,354	11,638
Other comprehensive income, net of tax	–	–	586	2,305
Total comprehensive income	–	–	11,940	13,943
Capital increases	–	–	–	3,481
Dividends payment	–	–	–1,015	–1,332
Capital transactions involving a change in ownership interest	–	–	–	–
Other changes	–	–	–4	75
Balance at 31 December 2017	1,283	14,551	81,367	109,077

Note: Numbers are as shown in the annual report and may not add and cross-add because of the exclusion of columns and due to rounding.

In Exhibit 7, as shown in the far right column, total equity is increased during the year by total comprehensive income of €13.9 billion and by capital infusions of €3.5 billion; it is decreased by dividends of €1.3 billion; and finally, slightly increased by €75 million of other changes. Explanatory notes on equity are included in the notes to the consolidated financial statements.

3.1.4 *Cash Flow Statement*

Although the income statement and balance sheet provide measures of a company's success in terms of performance and financial position, cash flow is also vital to a company's long-term success. Disclosing the sources and uses of cash helps creditors, investors, and other statement users evaluate the company's liquidity, solvency, and financial flexibility. **Financial flexibility** is the ability of the company to react and adapt to financial adversity and opportunities.

The cash flow statement classifies all cash flows of the company into three categories: operating, investing, and financing. Cash flows from **operating activities** generally involve the cash effects of transactions involved in the determination of net income and, hence, comprise the day-to-day operations of the company. Cash flows from **investing activities** are associated with the acquisition and disposal of long-term assets, such as property and equipment. Cash flows from **financing activities** relate to obtaining or repaying capital to be used in the business. IFRS permit more flexibility than US GAAP in classifying dividend and interest receipts and payments within these categories.

Exhibit 8 presents Volkswagen's statement of cash flows for the fiscal years ended 31 December 2017 and 2016.

Exhibit 8 Cash Flow Statement of the Volkswagen Group: 1 January to 31 December

€ million	2017	2016
Cash and cash equivalents at beginning of period	**18,833**	**20,462**
Earnings before tax	13,913	7,292
Income taxes paid	(3,664)	(3,315)
Depreciation and amortization of, and impairment losses on, intangible assets, property, plant and equipment, and investment property	10,562	10,100
Amortization of and impairment losses on capitalized development costs	3,734	3,586
Impairment losses on equity investments	136	130
Depreciation of and impairment losses on lease assets	7,734	7,107
Gain/loss on disposal of noncurrent assets and equity investments	(25)	(222)
Share of the result of equity-accounted investments	274	377
Other noncash expense/income	(480)	716
Change in inventories	(4,198)	(3,637)
Change in receivables (excluding financial services)	(1,660)	(2,155)
Change in liabilities (excluding financial liabilities)	5,302	5,048
Change in provisions	(9,443)	5,966
Change in lease assets	(11,478)	(12,074)
Change in financial services receivables	(11,891)	(9,490)
Cash flows from operating activities	**(1,185)**	**9,430**
Investments in intangible assets (excluding development costs), property, plant and equipment, and investment property	(13,052)	(13,152)
Additions to capitalized development costs	(5,260)	(5,750)
Acquisition of subsidiaries	(277)	(119)
Acquisition of other equity investments	(561)	(309)
Disposal of subsidiaries	496	(7)
Disposal of other equity investments	24	2,190
Proceeds from disposal of intangible assets, property, plant and equipment, and investment property	411	351

(continued)

Exhibit 8 (Continued)

€ million	2017	2016
Change in investments in securities	1,376	(1,245)
Change in loans and time deposits	335	(2,638)
Cash flows from investing activities	**(16,508)**	**(20,679)**
Capital contributions	3,473	–
Dividends paid	(1,332)	(364)
Capital transactions with noncontrolling interest shareholders	–	(3)
Proceeds from issuance of bonds	30,279	14,262
Repayments of bonds	(17,877)	(23,601)
Changes in other financial liabilities	3,109	19,455
Lease payments	(28)	(36)
Cash flows from financing activities	**17,625**	**9,712**
Effect of exchange rate changes on cash and cash equivalents	(727)	(91)
Net change in cash and cash equivalents	**(796)**	**(1,628)**
Cash and cash equivalents at end of period	**18,038**	**18,833**

After showing the beginning cash balance, the operating activities section starts with profit before tax,[4] €13.9 billion for 2017, subtracts actual income tax payments, and then adjusts for the effects of non-cash transactions, accruals and deferrals, and transactions of an investing and financing nature to arrive at the amount of cash generated from operating activities: a negative €1.2 billion (a net use of cash). This approach to reporting cash flow from operating activities is termed the indirect method. The direct method of reporting cash flows from operating activities discloses major classes of gross cash receipts and gross cash payments. Examples are cash received from customers and cash paid to suppliers and employees.

The indirect method emphasizes the different perspectives of the income statement and cash flow statement. On the income statement, income is reported when earned, not necessarily when cash is received, and expenses are reported when incurred, not necessarily when paid. The cash flow statement presents another aspect of performance: the ability of a company to generate cash flow from running its business. Ideally, for an established company, the analyst would like to see that the primary source of cash flow is from operating activities as opposed to investing or financing activities.

The sum of the net cash flows from operating, investing, and financing activities and the effect of exchange rates on cash equals the net change in cash during the fiscal year. For Volkswagen, the sum of these four items was a negative €796 million in 2017, decreasing the company's cash and cash equivalents from €18.8 billion at the beginning of the period to €18.0 billion at the end of the period.

3.1.5 *Financial Notes and Supplementary Schedules*

The notes (also sometimes referred to as footnotes) that accompany the four financial statements are required and are an integral part of the complete set of financial statements. The notes provide information that is essential to understanding the information provided in the primary statements. Volkswagen's 2017 financial statements, for example, include more than 100 pages of notes.

4 Other companies may choose to begin with net income.

The notes disclose the basis of preparation for the financial statements. For example, Volkswagen discloses that its fiscal year corresponds to the calendar year; its financial statements are prepared in accordance with IFRS as adopted by the European Union; the statements are prepared in compliance with German law; the statements are denominated in millions of euros unless otherwise specified; and the figures have been rounded, which might give rise to minor discrepancies when they are added. Volkswagen also states that its financial statements are on a consolidated basis—that is, including Volkswagen AG and all of the subsidiary companies it controls.

The notes also disclose information about the accounting policies, methods, and estimates used to prepare the financial statements. As will be discussed in later readings, both IFRS and US GAAP allow some flexibility in choosing among alternative policies and methods when accounting for certain items. This flexibility aims to meet the divergent needs of many businesses for reporting a variety of economic transactions. In addition to differences in accounting policies and methods, differences arise as a result of estimates needed to record and measure transactions, events, and financial statement line items.

Overall, flexibility in accounting choices is necessary because, ideally, a company will select those policies, methods, and estimates that are allowable and most relevant and that fairly reflect the unique economic environment of the company's business and industry. Flexibility can, however, create challenges for the analyst because the use of different policies, methods, and estimates reduces comparability across different companies' financial statements. Comparability occurs when different companies' information is measured and reported in a similar manner over time. Comparability helps the analyst identify and analyze the real economic differences across companies, rather than differences that arise solely from different accounting choices. Because comparability of financial statements is a critical requirement for objective financial analysis, an analyst should be aware of the potential for differences in accounting choices even when comparing two companies that use the same set of accounting standards.

For example, if a company acquires a piece of equipment to use in its operations, accounting standards require that the cost of the equipment be reported as an expense by allocating its cost, less any residual value, in a systematic manner over the equipment's useful life. This allocation of the cost is known as **depreciation**. Accounting standards permit flexibility, however, in determining the manner in which each year's expense is determined. Two companies may acquire similar equipment but use different methods and assumptions to record the expense over time. An analyst's ability to compare the companies' performance is hindered by the difference. Analysts must understand reporting choices in order to make appropriate adjustments when comparing companies' financial positions and performance.

A company's significant accounting choices (policies, methods, and estimates) must be discussed in the notes to the financial statements. For example, a note containing a summary of significant accounting policies includes how the company recognizes its revenues and depreciates its non-current tangible assets. Analysts must understand the accounting choices a company makes and determine whether they are similar to those of other companies identified and used as benchmarks or comparables. If the policies of the companies being compared are different, the analyst who understands accounting and financial reporting can often make necessary adjustments so that the financial statement data used are more comparable.

For many companies, the financial notes and supplemental schedules provide explanatory information about every line item (or almost every line item) on the balance sheet and income statement, as illustrated by the note references in Volkswagen's balance sheet and income statement in Exhibits 3 and 5. In addition, note disclosures include information about the following (this is not an exhaustive list):

- financial instruments and risks arising from financial instruments,

- commitments and contingencies,
- legal proceedings,
- related-party transactions,
- subsequent events (i.e., events that occur after the balance sheet date),
- business acquisitions and disposals, and
- operating segments' performance.

Exhibit 9 Notes to the Consolidated Financial Statements of the Volkswagen Group: Selected Data on Operating Segments (Excerpt)

€ million	Passenger Cars	Commercial Vehicles	Power Engineering	Financial Services	Total segments	Reconciliation	Volkswagen Group
Sales revenue from external customers	169,513	27,632	3,280	30,191	230,618	64	230,682
Intersegment sales revenue	18,892	7,568	3	3,541	30,004	–30,004	–
Total sales revenue	188,405	35,200	3,283	33,733	260,621	–29,939	230,682
Depreciation and amortization	11,363	2,557	371	6,797	21,089	-147	20,941
Impairment losses	704	2	0	574	1,280	0	1,280
Reversal of impairment losses	14	1	–	41	56	–	56
Segment result (operating result)	12,644	1,892	–55	2,673	17,153	–3,335	13,818
Share of the result of equity-accounted investments	3,390	83	1	9	3,482	–	3,482
Net interest result and other financial result	–1,920	–220	–2	–180	–2,321	–1,067	–3,388
Equity-accounted investments	6,724	753	18	710	8,205	–	8,205
Investments in intangible assets, property, plant and equipment, and investment property	15,713	1,915	159	421	18,208	104	18,313

An analyst uses a significant amount of judgment in deciding how to incorporate information from note disclosures into the analysis. For example, such information as financial instrument risk, contingencies, and legal proceedings can alert an analyst to risks that can affect a company's financial position and performance in the future and that require monitoring over time. As another example, information about a company's operating segments can be useful as a means of quickly understanding what a company does and how and where it earns money. The operating segment data shown in Exhibit 9 appear in the notes to the financial statements for Volkswagen. (The totals of the segment data do not equal the amounts reported in the company's financial statements because the financial statement data are adjusted for intersegment activities and unallocated items. The notes provide a complete reconciliation of the segment data to the reported data.) From the data in Exhibit 9, an analyst can quickly see that most of the company's revenues and operating profits come from the sale of passenger cars. Over 80 percent of the company's revenues was generated by this segment This segment accounted for over 90 percent of the company's total segment operating profits.

Experience using the disclosures made by a company and its competitors typically enhances an analyst's judgment about the relative importance of different disclosures and the ways in which they can be helpful.

3.1.6 *Management Commentary or Management's Discussion and Analysis*

Publicly held companies typically include a section in their annual reports where management discusses a variety of issues, including the nature of the business, past results, and future outlook. This section is referred to by a variety of names, including management report(ing), management commentary, operating and financial review, and management's discussion and analysis. Inclusion of a management report is recommended by the International Organization of Securities Commissions and frequently required by regulatory authorities, such as the US Securities and Exchange Commission (SEC) or the UK Financial Reporting Council (FRC). In Germany, management reporting has been required since 1931 and is audited.

The discussion by management is arguably one of the most useful parts of a company's annual report besides the financial statements themselves; however, other than excerpts from the financial statements, information included in the management commentary is typically unaudited. When using information from the management report, an analyst should be aware of whether the information is audited or unaudited.

To help improve the quality of the discussion by management, the International Accounting Standards Board (IASB) issued an IFRS Practice Statement "Management Commentary" includes a framework for the preparation and presentation of management commentary. The framework provides guidance rather than sets forth requirements in a standard. The framework identifies five content elements of a "decision-useful management commentary:" 1) the nature of the business; 2) management's objectives and strategies; 3) the company's significant resources, risks, and relationships; 4) results of operations; and 5) critical performance measures.

In the United States, the SEC requires listed companies to provide an MD&A and specifies the content.[5] Management must highlight any favorable or unfavorable trends and identify significant events and uncertainties that affect the company's liquidity, capital resources, and results of operations. The MD&A must also provide information about the effects of inflation, changing prices, or other material events and uncertainties that may cause the future operating results and financial condition to materially depart from the current reported financial information. In addition, the MD&A must provide information about off-balance-sheet obligations and about contractual commitments such as purchase obligations. Management should also discuss the critical accounting policies that require them to make subjective judgments and that have a significant impact on reported financial results.

The management commentary, or MD&A, is a good starting place for understanding information in the financial statements. In particular, the forward-looking disclosures, such as those about planned capital expenditures, new store openings, or divestitures, can be useful in projecting a company's future performance. However, the commentary is only one input for the analyst seeking an objective and independent perspective on a company's performance and prospects.

5 Relevant sections of SEC requirements are included for reference in the FASB ASC. The FASB ASC does not include sections of SEC requirements that deal with matters outside the basic financial statements, such as the MD&A.

The management report in Volkswagen's 2017 annual report includes much information of potential interest to an analyst. The lengthy report contains sections such as Goals and Strategies, Internal Management and Key Performance Indicators, Structure and Business Activities, Corporate Governance, Remuneration, Executive Bodies, Disclosures Required under Takeover Law, Diesel Issue, Business Development, Shares and Bonds, Results of Operations, and Report on Risks and Opportunities.

3.1.7 *Auditor's Reports*

Financial statements presented in companies' annual reports are generally required to be audited (examined) by an independent accounting firm in accordance with specified auditing standards. The independent auditor then provides a written opinion on the financial statements. This opinion is referred to as the audit report. Audit reports may vary in different jurisdictions, but the minimum components, including a specific statement of the auditor's opinion, are similar. Audits of financial statements may be required by contractual arrangement, law, or regulation.

International standards on auditing (ISAs) have been developed by the International Auditing and Assurance Standards Board (IAASB). This body has emerged from the International Federation of Accountants. ISAs have been adopted by many countries and are referenced in audit reports issued in those countries. Other countries, such as the United States, specify their own auditing standards. With the enactment of the Sarbanes–Oxley Act of 2002 in the United States, auditing standards for public companies are promulgated by the Public Company Accounting Oversight Board.

Under international standards for auditing (ISAs), the overall objectives of an auditor in conducting an audit of financial statements are

A To obtain reasonable assurance about whether the financial statements as a whole are free from material misstatement, whether due to fraud or error, thereby enabling the auditor to express an opinion on whether the financial statements are prepared, in all material respects, in accordance with an applicable financial reporting framework; and

B To report on the financial statements, and communicate as required by the ISAs, in accordance with the auditor's findings.[6]

Publicly traded companies may also have requirements set by regulators or stock exchanges, such as appointing an independent audit committee within its board of directors to oversee the audit process. The audit process provides a basis for the independent auditor to express an opinion on whether the information in the audited financial statements presents fairly the financial position, performance, and cash flows of the company in accordance with a specified set of accounting standards.

Audits are designed and conducted using sampling techniques, and financial statement line items may be based on estimates and assumptions. This means that the auditors cannot express an opinion that provides absolute assurance about the accuracy or precision of the financial statements. Instead, the independent audit report provides *reasonable assurance* that the financial statements are *fairly presented*, meaning that there is a high probability that the audited financial statements are free from *material* error, fraud, or illegal acts that have a direct effect on the financial statements.

The independent audit report expresses the auditor's opinion on the fairness of the audited financial statements, and specifies which financial statements were audited, the reporting entity, and the date. An *unqualified* audit opinion states that the financial statements give a "true and fair view" (international) or are "fairly presented" (international and US) in accordance with applicable accounting standards. This is

6 See the International Auditing and Assurance Standards Board (IAASB) *Handbook of International Quality Control, Auditing, Review, Other Assurance, and Related Services Pronouncements.*

also referred to as an "unmodified" or a "clean" opinion and is the one that analysts would like to see in a financial report. There are several other types of modified opinions. A *qualified* audit opinion is one in which there is some scope limitation or exception to accounting standards. Exceptions are described in the audit report with additional explanatory paragraphs so that the analyst can determine the importance of the exception. An *adverse* audit opinion is issued when an auditor determines that the financial statements materially depart from accounting standards and are not fairly presented. Finally, a *disclaimer of opinion* occurs when, for some reason, such as a scope limitation, the auditors are unable to issue an opinion.

The audit report also describes the basis for the auditor's opinion and, for listed companies, includes a discussion of Key Audit Matters (international) and Critical Audit Matters (US).[7] Key Audit Matters are defined as issues that the auditor considers to be most important, such as those that have a higher risk of misstatement, involve significant management judgment, or report the effects of significant transactions during the period. Critical Audit Matters are defined as issues that involve "especially challenging, subjective, or complex auditor judgment" and similarly include areas with higher risk of misstatement or involving significant management judgement and estimates.

Exhibit 10 presents the independent auditor's report for Volkswagen. Note that Volkswagen received an unqualified audit opinion (i.e., clean or unmodified opinion) from PricewaterhouseCoopers for the company's fiscal year ended 31 December 2017.

Exhibit 10 Volkswagen's Independent Audit Report

On completion of our audit, we issued the following unqualified auditor's report dated February 23, 2018. This report was originally prepared in German. In case of ambiguities the German version takes precedence:

To VOLKSWAGEN AKTIENGESELLSCHAFT, Wolfsburg

REPORT ON THE AUDIT OF THE CONSOLIDATED FINANCIAL STATEMENTS AND OF THE GROUP MANAGEMENT REPORT

AUDIT OPINIONS

We have audited the consolidated financial statements of VOLKSWAGEN AKTIENGESELLSCHAFT, Wolfsburg, and its subsidiaries (the Group), which comprise the income statement and the statement of comprehensive income, the balance sheet, the statement of changes in equity and the cash flow statement for the financial year from January 1 to December 31, 2017, and notes to the consolidated financial statements, including a summary of significant accounting policies. In addition, we have audited the group management report of VOLKSWAGEN AKTIENGESELLSCHAFT, which is combined with the Company's management report, for the financial year from January 1 to December 31, 2017. We have not audited the content of those parts of the group management report listed in the "Other Information" section of our auditor's report in accordance with the German legal requirements.

In our opinion, on the basis of the knowledge obtained in the audit,

- the accompanying consolidated financial statements comply, in all material respects, with the IFRSs as adopted by the EU, and the additional requirements of German commercial law pursuant to § [Article] 315e

(continued)

7 Discussion of Key Audit Matters in the auditor's report is required by the International Standard on Auditing (ISA) ISA 701, effective in 2017, issued by the International Audit and Assurance Standards Board. Discussion of Critical Audit Matters in the auditor's report is required by the Auditor Reporting Standard AS 3101, effective for large filers' fiscal years ending on or after June 30,2019, issued by the Public Company Accounting Oversight Board.

Exhibit 10 (Continued)

Abs. [paragraph] 1 HGB [Handelsgesetzbuch: German Commercial Code] and, in compliance with these requirements, give a true and fair view of the assets, liabilities, and financial position of the Group as at December 31, 2017, and of its financial performance for the financial year from January 1 to December 31, 2017, and

- the accompanying group management report as a whole provides an appropriate view of the Group's position. In all material respects, this group management report is consistent with the consolidated financial statements, complies with German legal requirements and appropriately presents the opportunities and risks of future development. Our audit opinion on the group management report does not cover the content of those parts of the group management report listed in the "Other Information" section of our auditor's report.

Pursuant to § 322 Abs. 3 Satz [sentence] 1 HGB, we declare that our audit has not led to any reservations relating to the legal compliance of the consolidated financial statements and of the group management report.

BASIS FOR THE AUDIT OPINIONS

We conducted our audit of the consolidated financial statements and of the group management report in accordance with § 317 HGB and the EU Audit Regulation (No. 537/2014, referred to subsequently as "EU Audit Regulation") and in compliance with German Generally Accepted Standards for Financial Statement Audits promulgated by the Institut der Wirtschaftsprüfer [Institute of Public Auditors in Germany] (IDW). Our responsibilities under those requirements and principles are further described in the "Auditor's Responsibilities for the Audit of the Consolidated Financial Statements and of the Group Management Report" section of our auditor's report. We are independent of the group entities in accordance with the requirements of European law and German commercial and professional law, and we have fulfilled our other German professional responsibilities in accordance with these requirements. In addition, in accordance with Article 10 (2) point (f) of the EU Audit Regulation, we declare that we have not provided non-audit services prohibited under Article 5 (1) of the EU Audit Regulation. We believe that the audit evidence we have obtained is sufficient and appropriate to provide a basis for our audit opinions on the consolidated financial statements and on the group management report.

EMPHASIS OF MATTER – DIESEL ISSUE

We draw attention to the information provided and statements made in section "Key Events" of the notes to the consolidated financial statements and in section "Diesel Issue" of the group management report with regard to the diesel issue including information about the underlying causes, the noninvolvement of members of the board of management as well as the impact on these financial statements.

Based on the results of the various measures taken to investigate the issue presented so far, which underlie the consolidated financial statements and the group management report, there is still no evidence that members of the Company's board of management were aware of the deliberate manipulation of engine management software before summer 2015. Nevertheless, should as a result of the ongoing investigation new solid knowledge be obtained showing that members of the board of management were informed earlier about the

Exhibit 10 (Continued)

diesel issue, this could eventually have an impact on the consolidated financial statements and on the group management report for financial year 2017 and prior years.

The provisions for warranties and legal risks recorded so far are based on the presented state of knowledge. Due to the inevitable uncertainties associated with the current and expected litigation it cannot be excluded that a future assessment of the risks may be different.

Our opinions on the consolidated financial statements and on the group management report are not modified in respect of this matter.

Source: Volkswagen 2017 annual report

In the United States, under the Sarbanes–Oxley Act, the auditors must also express an opinion on the company's internal control systems. This information may be provided in a separate opinion or incorporated as a paragraph in the opinion related to the financial statements. The internal control system is the company's internal system that is designed, among other things, to ensure that the company's process for generating financial reports is sound. Although management has always been responsible for maintaining effective internal control, the Sarbanes–Oxley Act greatly increases management's responsibility for demonstrating that the company's internal controls are effective. Management of publicly traded companies in the United States are now required by securities regulators to explicitly accept responsibility for the effectiveness of internal control, evaluate the effectiveness of internal control using suitable control criteria, support the evaluation with sufficient competent evidence, and provide a report on internal control.

Although these reports and attestations provide some assurances to analysts, they are not infallible. The analyst must always use a degree of healthy skepticism when analyzing financial statements.

3.2 Other Sources of Information

The information described in Section 3.1 is generally provided to shareholders at least annually. In addition, companies also provide information on management and director compensation, company stock performance, and any potential conflicts of interest that may exist between management, the board, and shareholders. This information may appear in the company's annual report or other publicly available documents. Public companies often provide this information in proxy statements, which are distributed to shareholders about matters that are to be put to a vote at the annual (or special) meeting of shareholders.

Interim reports are also provided by the company either semiannually or quarterly, depending on the applicable regulatory requirements. Interim reports generally present the four primary financial statements and condensed notes but are not audited. These interim reports provide updated information on a company's performance and financial position since the last annual period.

Companies also provide relevant current information on their websites, in press releases, and in conference calls with analysts and investors. One type of press release, which analysts often consider to be particularly important, is the periodic earnings announcement. The earnings announcement often happens well before the company files its formal financial statements. Such earnings announcements are often followed by a conference call in which the company's senior executives describe the company's performance and answer questions posed by conference call participants. Following the earnings conference call, the investor relations portion of the company's website may post a recording of the call accompanied by slides and supplemental information that was discussed.

When performing financial statement analysis, analysts should review all these company sources of information as well as information from external sources regarding the economy, the industry, the company, and peer (comparable) companies. Information on the economy, industry, and peer companies is useful in putting the company's financial performance and position in perspective and in assessing the company's future. In most cases, information from sources apart from the company is crucial to an analyst's effectiveness. For example, an analyst studying a consumer-oriented company will typically seek direct experience with the products (taste the food or drink, use the shampoo or soap, visit the stores or hotels). An analyst following a highly regulated industry will study the existing and expected relevant regulations. An analyst following a highly technical industry will gain relevant expertise personally or seek input from a technical specialist. In sum, thorough research goes beyond financial reports.

The next section presents a framework for using all this information in financial statement analysis.

4 FINANCIAL STATEMENT ANALYSIS FRAMEWORK

Analysts work in a variety of positions within the investment management industry. Some are equity analysts whose main objective is to evaluate potential investments in a company's equity securities (i.e., the shares or stock it issues) as a basis for deciding whether a prospective investment is attractive and what an appropriate purchase price might be. Others are credit analysts who evaluate the credit-worthiness of a company to decide whether (and on what terms) a loan should be made or what credit rating should be assigned. Analysts may also be involved in a variety of other tasks, such as evaluating the performance of a subsidiary company, evaluating a private equity investment, or finding stocks that are overvalued for purposes of taking a short position.

This section presents a generic framework for financial statement analysis that can be used in these various tasks. The framework is summarized in Exhibit 11.[8]

8 Components of this framework have been adapted from van Greuning and Bratanovic (2003, p. 300) and from Benninga and Sarig (1997, pp. 134–156).

Exhibit 11 Financial Statement Analysis Framework

Phase	Sources of Information	Output
1 Articulate the purpose and context of the analysis.	■ The nature of the analyst's function, such as evaluating an equity or debt investment or issuing a credit rating. ■ Communication with client or supervisor on needs and concerns. ■ Institutional guidelines related to developing specific work product.	■ Statement of the purpose or objective of analysis. ■ A list (written or unwritten) of specific questions to be answered by the analysis. ■ Nature and content of report to be provided. ■ Timetable and budgeted resources for completion.
2 Collect input data.	■ Financial statements, other financial data, questionnaires, and industry/economic data. ■ Discussions with management, suppliers, customers, and competitors. ■ Company site visits (e.g., to production facilities or retail stores).	■ Organized financial statements. ■ Financial data tables. ■ Completed questionnaires, if applicable.
3 Process data.	■ Data from the previous phase.	■ Adjusted financial statements. ■ Common-size statements. ■ Ratios and graphs. ■ Forecasts.
4 Analyze/interpret the processed data.	■ Input data as well as processed data.	■ Analytical results.
5 Develop and communicate conclusions and recommendations (e.g., with an analysis report).	■ Analytical results and previous reports. ■ Institutional guidelines for published reports.	■ Analytical report answering questions posed in Phase 1. ■ Recommendation regarding the purpose of the analysis, such as whether to make an investment or grant credit.
6 Follow-up.	■ Information gathered by periodically repeating above steps as necessary to determine whether changes to holdings or recommendations are necessary.	■ Updated reports and recommendations.

The following sections discuss the individual phases of financial statement analysis.

4.1 Articulate the Purpose and Context of Analysis

Prior to undertaking any analysis, it is essential to understand the purpose of the analysis. An understanding of the purpose is particularly important in financial statement analysis because of the numerous available techniques and the substantial amount of data.

Some analytical tasks are well defined, in which case articulating the purpose of the analysis requires little decision making by the analyst. For example, a periodic credit review of an investment-grade debt portfolio or an equity analyst's report on a particular company may be guided by institutional norms such that the purpose of the analysis is given. Furthermore, the format, procedures, and/or sources of information may also be given.

For other analytical tasks, articulating the purpose of the analysis requires the analyst to make decisions. The purpose of an analysis guides further decisions about the approach, the tools, the data sources, the format in which to report the results of the analysis, and the relative importance of different aspects of the analysis.

When facing a substantial amount of data, a less experienced analyst may be tempted to just start making calculations and generating financial ratios without considering what is relevant for the decision at hand. It is generally advisable to resist this temptation and thus avoid unnecessary or pointless efforts. Consider the questions: If you could have all the calculations and ratios completed instantly, what conclusion would you be able to draw? What question would you be able to answer? What decision would your answer support?

The analyst should also define the context at this stage. Who is the intended audience? What is the end product—for example, a final report explaining conclusions and recommendations? What is the time frame (i.e., when is the report due)? What resources and resource constraints are relevant to completion of the analysis? Again, the context may be predefined (i.e., standard and guided by institutional norms).

Having clarified the purpose and context of the financial statement analysis, the analyst should next compile the specific questions to be answered by the analysis. For example, if the purpose of the financial statement analysis (or, more likely, the particular stage of a larger analysis) is to compare the historical performance of three companies operating in a particular industry, specific questions would include the following: What has been the relative growth rate of the companies, and what has been their relative profitability?

4.2 Collect Data

Next, the analyst obtains the data required to answer the specific questions. A key part of this step is obtaining an understanding of the company's business, financial performance, and financial position (including trends over time and in comparison with peer companies). For historical analyses, financial statement data alone are adequate in some cases. For example, to screen a large number of companies to find those with a minimum level of profitability, financial statement data alone would be adequate. But to address more in-depth questions, such as why and how one company performed better or worse than its competitors, additional information would be required. As another example, to compare the historical performance of two companies in a particular industry, the historical financial statements would be sufficient to determine which had faster-growing sales or earnings and which was more profitable. However, a broader comparison with overall industry growth and profitability would obviously require industry data.

Furthermore, information on the economy and industry is necessary to understand the environment in which the company operates. Analysts often take a top-down approach whereby they 1) gain an understanding of the macroeconomic environment, such as prospects for growth in the economy and inflation, 2) analyze the prospects of the industry in which the company operates, based on the expected macroeconomic environment, and 3) determine the prospects for the company given the expected industry and macroeconomic environments. For example, an analyst may need to forecast future growth in earnings for a company. Past company data provide the platform for statistical forecasting; however, an understanding of economic and industry conditions can improve the analyst's ability to forecast earnings.

4.3 Process Data

After obtaining the requisite financial statement and other information, the analyst processes these data using appropriate analytical tools. For example, processing the data may involve computing ratios or growth rates; preparing common-size financial statements; creating charts; performing statistical analyses, such as regressions or Monte Carlo simulations; performing equity valuation; performing sensitivity analyses; or using any other analytical tools or combination of tools that are available and appropriate for the task. A comprehensive financial analysis at this stage would include the following:

- Reading and evaluating financial statements for each company being analyzed. This includes reading the notes and understanding what accounting standards have been used (for example, IFRS or US GAAP), what accounting choices have been made (for example, when to report revenue on the income statement), and what operating decisions have been made that affect reported financial statements (for example, leasing versus purchasing equipment).
- Making any needed adjustments to the financial statements to facilitate comparison when the unadjusted statements of the subject companies reflect differences in accounting standards, accounting choices, or operating decisions. Note that commonly used databases do not always make such analyst adjustments.
- Preparing or collecting common-size financial statement data (which scale data to directly reflect percentages [e.g., of sales] or changes [e.g., from the prior year]) and financial ratios (which are measures of various aspects of corporate performance based on financial statement elements). On the basis of common-size financial statements and financial ratios, analysts can evaluate a company's relative profitability, liquidity, leverage, efficiency, and valuation in relation to past results and/or peers' results.

4.4 Analyze/Interpret the Processed Data

Once the data have been processed, the next step—critical to any analysis—is to interpret the output. The answer to a specific question is seldom the numerical answer alone. Rather, the answer relies on the analyst's interpretation of the output, and the use of this interpreted output to support a conclusion or recommendation. The answers to the specific analytical questions may themselves achieve the underlying purpose of the analysis, but usually, a conclusion or recommendation is required. For example, an equity analysis may require a buy, hold, or sell recommendation or a conclusion about the value of a share of stock. In support of the decision, the analysis would cite such information as target value, relative performance, expected future performance given a company's strategic position, quality of management, and whatever other information influenced the decision.

4.5 Develop and Communicate Conclusions/ Recommendations

Communicating the conclusion or recommendation in an appropriate format is the next step. The appropriate format will vary by analytical task, by institution, and/ or by audience. For example, an equity analyst's report would typically include the following components:

- summary and investment conclusion;
- earnings projections;

- valuation;
- business summary;
- risk, industry, and competitive analysis;
- historical performance; and
- forecasts.

The contents of reports may also be specified by regulatory agencies or professional standards. For example, the CFA Institute *Standards of Practice Handbook* (*Handbook*) dictates standards that must be followed in communicating recommendations. According to the *Handbook*:

> Standard V(B) states that members and candidates should communicate in a recommendation the factors that were instrumental in making the investment recommendation. A critical part of this requirement is to distinguish clearly between opinions and facts. In preparing a research report, the member or candidate must present the basic characteristics of the security(ies) being analyzed, which will allow the reader to evaluate the report and incorporate information the reader deems relevant to his or her investment decision making process.[9]

The *Handbook* requires that limitations to the analysis and any risks inherent to the investment be disclosed. Furthermore, it requires that any report include elements important to the analysis and conclusions so that readers can evaluate the conclusions themselves.

4.6 Follow-Up

The process does not end with the report. If an equity investment is made or a credit rating is assigned, periodic review is required to determine if the original conclusions and recommendations are still valid. In the case of a rejected investment, follow-up may not be necessary but may be useful in determining whether the analytical process is adequate or should be refined (for example, if a rejected investment turns out to be successful in the market, perhaps the rejection was due to inadequate analysis). Follow-up may involve repeating all the previous steps in the process on a periodic basis.

SUMMARY

The information presented in financial and other reports, including the financial statements, notes, and management's commentary, help the financial analyst to assess a company's performance and financial position. An analyst may be called on to perform a financial analysis for a variety of reasons, including the valuation of equity securities, the assessment of credit risk, the performance of due diligence on an acquisition, and the evaluation of a subsidiary's performance relative to other business units. Major considerations in both equity analysis and credit analysis are evaluating a company's financial position, its ability to generate profits and cash flow, and its potential to generate future growth in profits and cash flow.

9 *Standards of Practice Handbook* (2014, p. 169).

This reading has presented an overview of financial statement analysis. Among the major points covered are the following:

- The primary purpose of financial reports is to provide information and data about a company's financial position and performance, including profitability and cash flows. The information presented in the reports —including the financial statements and notes and management's commentary or management's discussion and analysis—allows the financial analyst to assess a company's financial position and performance and trends in that performance.
- The primary financial statements are the statement of financial position (i.e., the balance sheet), the statement of comprehensive income (or two statements consisting of an income statement and a statement of comprehensive income), the statement of changes in equity, and the statement of cash flows.
- The balance sheet discloses what resources a company controls (assets) and what it owes (liabilities) at a specific point in time. Owners' equity represents the net assets of the company; it is the owners' residual interest in, or residual claim on, the company's assets after deducting its liabilities. The relationship among the three parts of the balance sheet (assets, liabilities, and owners' equity) may be shown in equation form as follows: Assets = Liabilities + Owners' equity.
- The income statement presents information on the financial results of a company's business activities over a period of time. The income statement communicates how much revenue and other income the company generated during a period and what expenses, including losses, it incurred in connection with generating that revenue and other income. The basic equation underlying the income statement is Revenue + Other income – Expenses = Net income.
- The statement of comprehensive income includes all items that change owners' equity except transactions with owners. Some of these items are included as part of net income, and some are reported as other comprehensive income (OCI).
- The statement of changes in equity provides information about increases or decreases in the various components of owners' equity.
- Although the income statement and balance sheet provide measures of a company's success, cash and cash flow are also vital to a company's long-term success. Disclosing the sources and uses of cash helps creditors, investors, and other statement users evaluate the company's liquidity, solvency, and financial flexibility.
- The notes (also referred to as footnotes) that accompany the financial statements are an integral part of those statements and provide information that is essential to understanding the statements. Analysts should evaluate note disclosures regarding the use of alternative accounting methods, estimates, and assumptions.
- In addition to the financial statements, a company provides other sources of information that are useful to the financial analyst. As part of his or her analysis, the financial analyst should read and assess this additional information, particularly that presented in the management commentary (also called management report[ing], operating and financial review, and management's discussion and analysis [MD&A]).
- A publicly traded company must have an independent audit performed on its annual financial statements. The auditor's report expresses an opinion on the financial statements and provides some assurance about whether the financial

statements fairly present a company's financial position, performance, and cash flows. In addition, for US publicly traded companies, auditors must also express an opinion on the company's internal control systems.

- Information on the economy, industry, and peer companies is useful in putting the company's financial performance and position in perspective and in assessing the company's future. In most cases, information from sources apart from the company are crucial to an analyst's effectiveness.
- The financial statement analysis framework provides steps that can be followed in any financial statement analysis project. These steps are:
  - articulate the purpose and context of the analysis;
  - collect input data;
  - process data;
  - analyze/interpret the processed data;
  - develop and communicate conclusions and recommendations; and
  - follow up.

REFERENCES

Benninga, Simon Z., and Oded H. Sarig. 1997. *Corporate Finance: A Valuation Approach*. New York: McGraw-Hill Publishing.

International Auditing and Assurance Standards Board (IAASB). *Handbook of International Quality Control, Auditing, Review, Other Assurance, and Related Services Pronouncements*, Standard 200, available at www.ifac.org/IAASB.

van Greuning, Hennie, and Sonja Brajovic Bratanovic. 2003. *Analyzing and Managing Banking Risk: A Framework for Assessing Corporate Governance and Financial Risk*. Washington, DC: World Bank.

PRACTICE PROBLEMS

1 Providing information about the performance and financial position of companies so that users can make economic decisions *best* describes the role of:

- **A** auditing.
- **B** financial reporting.
- **C** financial statement analysis.

2 Which of the following *best* describes the role of financial statement analysis?

- **A** To provide information about a company's performance
- **B** To provide information about a company's changes in financial position
- **C** To form expectations about a company's future performance and financial position

3 The role of financial statement analysis is *best* described as:

- **A** providing information useful for making investment decisions.
- **B** evaluating a company for the purpose of making economic decisions.
- **C** using financial reports prepared by analysts to make economic decisions.

4 A company's financial position would *best* be evaluated using the:

- **A** balance sheet.
- **B** income statement.
- **C** statement of cash flows.

5 A company's profitability for a period would *best* be evaluated using the:

- **A** balance sheet.
- **B** income statement.
- **C** statement of cash flows.

6 The financial statement that presents a shareholder's residual claim on assets is the:

- **A** balance sheet.
- **B** income statement.
- **C** cash flow statement.

7 A company's profitability over a period of time is *best* evaluated using the:

- **A** balance sheet.
- **B** income statement.
- **C** cash flow statement.

8 The income statement is *best* used to evaluate a company's:

- **A** financial position.
- **B** sources of cash flow.
- **C** financial results from business activities.

9 Accounting policies, methods, and estimates used in preparing financial statements are *most likely* to be found in the:

- **A** auditor's report.
- **B** management commentary.
- **C** notes to the financial statements.

© 2017 CFA Institute. All rights reserved.

10 Information about management and director compensation are *least likely* to be found in the:

A auditor's report.

B proxy statement.

C notes to the financial statements.

11 Information about a company's objectives, strategies, and significant risks are *most likely* to be found in the:

A auditor's report.

B management commentary.

C notes to the financial statements.

12 Which of the following *best* describes why the notes that accompany the financial statements are required? The notes:

A permit flexibility in statement preparation.

B standardize financial reporting across companies.

C provide information necessary to understand the financial statements.

13 What type of audit opinion is preferred when analyzing financial statements?

A Qualified.

B Adverse.

C Unqualified.

14 An auditor determines that a company's financial statements are prepared in accordance with applicable accounting standards except with respect to inventory reporting. This exception is *most likely* to result in an audit opinion that is:

A adverse.

B qualified.

C unqualified.

15 An independent audit report is *most likely* to provide:

A absolute assurance about the accuracy of the financial statements.

B reasonable assurance that the financial statements are fairly presented.

C a qualified opinion with respect to the transparency of the financial statements.

16 Interim financial reports released by a company are *most likely* to be:

A monthly.

B unaudited.

C unqualified.

17 Which of the following sources of information used by analysts is found outside a company's annual report?

A Auditor's report

B Peer company analysis

C Management's discussion and analysis

18 Ratios are an input into which step in the financial statement analysis framework?

A Process data.

B Collect input data.

C Analyze/interpret the processed data.

19 Which phase in the financial statement analysis framework is *most likely* to involve producing updated reports and recommendations?

A Follow-up

B Analyze/interpret the processed data

C Develop and communicate conclusions and recommendations

SOLUTIONS

1 B is correct. This is the role of financial reporting. The role of financial statement analysis is to evaluate the financial reports.

2 C is correct. In general, analysts seek to examine the past and current performance and financial position of a company in order to form expectations about its future performance and financial position.

3 B is correct. The primary role of financial statement analysis is to use financial reports prepared by companies to evaluate their past, current, and potential performance and financial position for the purpose of making investment, credit, and other economic decisions.

4 A is correct. The balance sheet portrays the company's financial position on a specified date. The income statement and statement of cash flows present different aspects of performance during the period.

5 B is correct. Profitability is the performance aspect measured by the income statement. The balance sheet portrays the financial position. The statement of cash flows presents a different aspect of performance.

6 A is correct. Owners' equity is the owners' residual interest in (i.e., residual claim on) the company's assets after deducting its liabilities, which is information presented on the balance sheet.

7 B is correct. A company's profitability is best evaluated using the income statement. The income statement presents information on the financial results of a company's business activities over a period of time by communicating how much revenue was generated and the expenses incurred to generate that revenue.

8 C is correct. A company's revenues and expenses are presented on the income statement, which is used to evaluate a company's financial results (or profitability) from business activities over a period of time. A company's financial position is best evaluated by using the balance sheet. A company's sources of cash flow are best evaluated using the cash flow statement.

9 C is correct. The notes disclose choices in accounting policies, methods, and estimates.

10 A is correct. Information about management and director compensation is not found in the auditor's report. Disclosure of management compensation is required in the proxy statement, and some aspects of management compensation are disclosed in the notes to the financial statements.

11 B is correct. These are components of management commentary.

12 C is correct. The notes provide information that is essential to understanding the information provided in the primary statements.

13 C is correct. An unqualified opinion is a "clean" opinion and indicates that the financial statements present the company's performance and financial position fairly in accordance with a specified set of accounting standards.

14 B is correct. A qualified audit opinion is one in which there is some scope limitation or exception to accounting standards. Exceptions are described in the audit report with additional explanatory paragraphs so that the analyst can determine the importance of the exception.

15 B is correct. The independent audit report provides reasonable assurance that the financial statements are fairly presented, meaning that there is a high probability that the audited financial statements are free from material error, fraud, or illegal acts that have a direct effect on the financial statements.

16 B is correct. Interim reports are typically provided semiannually or quarterly and present the four basic financial statements and condensed notes. They are not audited. Unqualified is a type of audit opinion

17 B is correct. When performing financial statement analysis, analysts should review all company sources of information as well as information from external sources regarding the economy, the industry, the company, and peer (comparable) companies.

18 C is correct. Ratios are an output of the process data step but are an input into the analyze/interpret data step.

19 A is correct. The follow-up phase involves gathering information and repeating the analysis to determine whether it is necessary to update reports and recommendations.

READING

20

Financial Reporting Standards

by Elaine Henry, PhD, CFA, Jan Hendrik van Greuning, DCom, CFA, and Thomas R. Robinson, PhD, CFA

Elaine Henry, PhD, CFA, is at Stevens Institute of Technology (USA). Jan Hendrik van Greuning, DCom, CFA, is at BIBD (Brunei). Thomas R. Robinson, PhD, CFA, is at AACSB International (USA).

LEARNING OUTCOMES

Mastery	The candidate should be able to:
☐	**a.** describe the objective of financial reporting and the importance of financial reporting standards in security analysis and valuation;
☐	**b.** describe the roles of financial reporting standard-setting bodies and regulatory authorities in establishing and enforcing reporting standards;
☐	**c.** describe the International Accounting Standards Board's conceptual framework, including qualitative characteristics of financial reports, constraints on financial reports, and required reporting elements;
☐	**d.** describe general requirements for financial statements under International Financial Reporting Standards (IFRS);
☐	**e.** describe implications for financial analysis of alternative financial reporting systems and the importance of monitoring developments in financial reporting standards.

Note: Changes in accounting standards as well as new rulings and/or pronouncements issued after the publication of the readings on financial reporting and analysis may cause some of the information in these readings to become dated. Candidates are *not* responsible for anything that occurs after the readings were published. In addition, candidates are expected to be familiar with the analytical frameworks contained in the readings, as well as the implications of alternative accounting methods for financial analysis and valuation discussed in the readings. Candidates are also responsible for the content of accounting standards, but not for the actual reference numbers. Finally, candidates should be aware that certain ratios may be defined and calculated differently. When alternative ratio definitions exist and no specific definition is given, candidates should use the ratio definitions emphasized in the readings.

© 2019 CFA Institute. All rights reserved.

1 INTRODUCTION

Financial reporting standards provide principles for preparing financial reports and determine the types and amounts of information that must be provided to users of financial statements, including investors and creditors, so that they may make informed decisions. This reading focuses on the context within which these standards are created. An understanding of the underlying framework of financial reporting standards, which is broader than knowledge of specific accounting rules, will allow an analyst to assess the valuation implications of financial statement elements and transactions—including transactions, such as those that represent new developments, which are not specifically addressed by the standards.

Section 2 of this reading discusses the objective of financial reporting and the importance of financial reporting standards in security analysis and valuation. Section 3 describes the roles of financial reporting standard-setting bodies and regulatory authorities and several of the financial reporting standard-setting bodies and regulatory authorities. Section 4 describes the International Financial Reporting Standards (IFRS) framework[1] and general requirements for financial statements. Section 5 compares IFRS and alternative reporting systems, and Section 6 discusses the importance of monitoring developments in financial reporting standards. A summary of the key points concludes the reading.

2 THE OBJECTIVE OF FINANCIAL REPORTING

The financial reports of a company include financial statements and other supplemental disclosures necessary to assess a company's financial position and periodic financial performance. Financial reporting is based on a simple premise. The International Accounting Standards Board (IASB), which sets financial reporting standards that have been adopted in many countries, said in its *Conceptual Framework for Financial Reporting* (*Conceptual Framework*) that the objective of financial reporting is to provide financial information that is useful to users in making decisions about providing resources to the reporting entity, where those decisions relate to equity and debt instruments, or loans or other forms of credit, and in influencing management's actions that affect the use of the entity's economic resources.[2]

A fully articulated framework is an essential first step to guide the development of a set of standards. Previously, financial reporting standards were primarily developed independently by each country's standard-setting body. This independent standard setting process created a wide range of standards, some of which were quite comprehensive and complex (rules-based standards), and others that were more general (principles-based standards). The globalization of capital flows and various accounting scandals increased awareness of the need for more uniform, high quality global financial reporting standards and provided the impetus for stronger coordination among the major standard-setting bodies. Such coordination is also a natural outgrowth of the increased globalization of capital markets.

Developing financial reporting standards is complicated because the underlying economic reality is complicated. The financial transactions and financial position that companies aim to present in their financial reports are also complex. Furthermore,

1 The body of standards issued by the International Accounting Standards Board (IASB) is referred to as International Financial Reporting Standards.

2 In March 2018, the IASB updated the *Conceptual Framework for Financial Reporting* originally adopted in 2010.

uncertainty about various aspects of transactions often results in the need for accruals and estimates, both of which necessitate judgment. Judgment varies from one preparer to the next. Accordingly, standards are needed to achieve some amount of consistency in these judgments. Even with such standards, there usually will be no single correct answer to the question of how to reflect economic reality in financial reports. Nevertheless, financial reporting standards try to limit the range of acceptable answers to increase consistency in financial reports.

The IASB and the US-based Financial Accounting Standards Board (FASB) have developed similar financial reporting frameworks which specify the overall objective and qualities of information to be provided. Financial reports are intended to provide information to many users, including investors, creditors, employees, customers, and others. As a result, financial reports are *not* designed solely with asset valuation in mind. However, financial reports provide important inputs into the process of valuing a company or the securities a company issues. Understanding the financial reporting framework—including how and when judgments and estimates can affect the numbers reported—enables an analyst to evaluate the information reported and to use the information appropriately when assessing a company's financial performance. Clearly, such an understanding is also important in assessing the financial impact of business decisions by, and in making comparisons across, entities.

STANDARD-SETTING BODIES AND REGULATORY AUTHORITIES

3

A distinction must be made between standard-setting bodies and regulatory authorities. Standard-setting bodies, such as the IASB and FASB, are typically private sector, self-regulated organizations with board members who are experienced accountants, auditors, users of financial statements, and academics. The requirement to prepare financial reports in accordance with specified accounting standards is the responsibility of regulatory authorities. Regulatory authorities, such as the Accounting and Corporate Regulatory Authority in Singapore, the Securities and Exchange Commission (SEC) in the United States, and the Securities and Exchange Commission of Brazil have the legal authority to enforce financial reporting requirements and exert other controls over entities that participate in the capital markets within their jurisdiction.

In other words, *generally*, standard-setting bodies set the standards and regulatory authorities recognise and enforce the standards. Without the recognition of the standards by the regulatory authorities, the private sector standard-setting bodies would have no authority. Note, however, that regulators often retain the legal authority to establish financial reporting standards in their jurisdiction and can overrule the private sector standard-setting bodies.

This section provides a brief overview of the IASB and the FASB. The overview is followed by descriptions of the International Organization of Securities Commissions, the US Securities and Exchange Commission, and capital markets regulation in the European Union. The topics covered in these overviews were chosen to serve as examples of standard-setting boards, securities commissions, and capital market regulation. After reading these descriptions, the reader should be able to describe the functioning and roles of standard-setting bodies and regulatory authorities in more detail than is given in the introduction to this section.

3.1 Accounting Standards Boards

Accounting standards boards exist in virtually every national market. These boards are typically independent, private, not-for-profit organizations. There are certain attributes that are typically common to these standard setters—the IASB and the FASB are discussed in this section as primary examples.

3.1.1 *International Accounting Standards Board*

The IASB is the independent standard-setting body of the IFRS Foundation, an independent, not-for-profit private sector organization. The Trustees of the IFRS Foundation reflect a diversity of geographical and professional backgrounds. The Trustees appoint the members of the IASB and are accountable to a monitoring board composed of public authorities that include representatives from the European Commission, IOSCO, the Japan Financial Services Agency, and the US SEC, with the chairman of the Basel Committee on Banking Supervision as an observer.

The Trustees of the IFRS Foundation make a commitment to act in the public interest. The principle objectives of the IFRS Foundation are to develop and promote the use and adoption of a single set of high quality financial standards; to ensure the standards result in transparent, comparable, and decision-useful information while taking into account the needs of a range of sizes and types of entities in diverse economic settings; and to promote the convergence of national accounting standards and IFRS. The Trustees are responsible for ensuring that the IASB is and is perceived as independent.

The members of the IASB are appointed by the Trustees on the basis of professional competence and practical experience and reflect a diversity of geographical and professional backgrounds. The members deliberate, develop, and issue international financial reporting standards,[3] assisted by advice on the standards, and their application, from advisory bodies whose members represent a wide range of organizations and individuals that are affected by and interested in international financial reporting.

The IASB has a basic process that it goes through when deliberating, developing, and issuing international financial reporting standards. A simplified version of the typical process is as follows. An issue is identified as a priority for consideration and placed on the IASB's agenda. After considering an issue, which may include soliciting advice from others including national standard-setters, the IASB may publish an exposure draft for public comment. After reviewing the input of others, the IASB may issue a new or revised financial reporting standard. These standards are authoritative to the extent that they are recognised and adopted by regulatory authorities.

3.1.2 *Financial Accounting Standards Board*

The FASB and its predecessor organizations have been issuing financial reporting standards in the United States since the 1930s. The FASB operates within a structure similar to that of the IASB. The Financial Accounting Foundation oversees, administers, and finances the organization. The Foundation ensures the independence of the standard-setting process and appoints members to the FASB and related advisory entities.

The FASB issues new and revised standards to improve standards of financial reporting so that decision-useful information is provided to users of financial reports. This is done through a thorough and independent process that seeks input from stakeholders

3 Although the name of the IASB incorporates "Accounting Standards" and early standards were titled International Accounting Standards (IAS), the term "International Financial Reporting Standards" (IFRS) is being used for new standards. The use of the words "financial reporting" recognizes the importance of disclosures outside of the core financial statements, such as management discussion of the business, risks, and future plans.

and is overseen by the Financial Accounting Foundation. The steps in the process are similar to those described for the IASB. The outputs of the standard-setting process are contained in the FASB Accounting Standards Codification™ (Codification).[4] The Codification, organized by topic, is the source of authoritative US generally accepted accounting principles to be applied to non-governmental entities.

US GAAP, as established by the FASB, is officially recognized as authoritative by the SEC, however the SEC retains the authority to establish standards. Although it has rarely overruled the FASB, the SEC does issue authoritative financial reporting guidance including Staff Accounting Bulletins. These bulletins reflect the SEC's views regarding accounting-related disclosure practices and can be found on the SEC website. Certain portions—but not all portions—of the SEC regulations, releases, interpretations, and guidance are included for reference in the FASB Codification.

3.2 Regulatory Authorities

The requirement to prepare financial reports in accordance with specified accounting standards is the responsibility of regulatory authorities. Regulatory authorities are governmental entities that have the legal authority to enforce financial reporting requirements and exert other controls over entities that participate in the capital markets within their jurisdiction. Regulatory authorities may require that financial reports be prepared in accordance with one specific set of accounting standards or may specify acceptable accounting standards. For example in Switzerland, Swiss-based companies listed on the main board of the Swiss Exchange have to prepare their financial statements in accordance with either IFRS or US GAAP if they are multinational.[5] Other registrants in Switzerland could use IFRS, US GAAP, or Swiss GAAP.

3.2.1 *International Organization of Securities Commissions*

While technically not a regulatory authority, the International Organization of Securities Commissions (IOSCO) regulate a significant portion of the world's financial capital markets. This organization has established objectives and principles to guide securities and capital market regulation.

IOSCO was formed in 1983 and consists of ordinary members, associate members, and affiliate members. Ordinary members are the securities commission or similar governmental regulatory authority with primary responsibility for securities regulation in the member country.[6] The members regulate more than 95 percent of the world's financial capital markets in more than 115 jurisdictions, and securities regulators in emerging markets account for 75% of its ordinary membership.

IOSCO's comprehensive set of *Objectives and Principles of Securities Regulation* is updated as required and is recognized as an international benchmark for all markets. The principles of securities regulation are based upon three core objectives:[7]

- protecting investors;
- ensuring that markets are fair, efficient, and transparent; and
- reducing systemic risk.

4 The Codification combines literature issued by various standard setters, including the FASB, the Emerging Issues Task Force (EITF), the Derivative Implementation Group (DIG), and the American Institute of Certified Public Accountants (AICPA).

5 https://www.iasplus.com/en/jurisdictions/europe/switzerland.

6 The names of the primary securities regulator vary from country to country. For example: China Securities Regulatory Commission, Egyptian Financial Supervisory Authority, Securities and Exchange Board of India, Kingdom of Saudi Arabia Capital Market Authority, and Banco Central del Uruguay.

7 *Objectives and Principles of Securities Regulation*, IOSCO, May 2017.

IOSCO's principles are grouped into ten categories, including principles for regulators, for enforcement, for auditing, and for issuers, among others. Within the category "Principles for Issuers," two principles relate directly to financial reporting:

- There should be full, accurate, and timely disclosure of financial results, risk, and other information which is material to investors' decisions.
- Accounting standards used by issuers to prepare financial statements should be of a high and internationally acceptable quality.

Historically, regulation and related financial reporting standards were developed within individual countries and were often based on the cultural, economic, and political norms of each country. As financial markets have become more global, it has become desirable to establish comparable financial reporting standards internationally. Ultimately, laws and regulations are established by individual jurisdictions, so this also requires cooperation among regulators. Another IOSCO principle deals with the use of self-regulatory organizations (SROs), which exercise some direct oversight for their areas of competence and should be subject to the oversight of the relevant regulator and observe fairness and confidentiality[8].

To ensure consistent application of international financial standards (such as the Basel Committee on Banking Supervision's standards and IFRS), it is important to have uniform regulation and enforcement across national boundaries. IOSCO assists in attaining this goal of uniform regulation as well as cross-border co-operation in combating violations of securities and derivatives laws.

3.2.2 *The Securities and Exchange Commission (US)*

The US SEC has primary responsibility for securities and capital markets regulation in the United States and is an ordinary member of IOSCO. Any company issuing securities within the United States, or otherwise involved in US capital markets, is subject to the rules and regulations of the SEC. The SEC, one of the oldest and most developed regulatory authorities, originated as a result of reform efforts made after the stock market crash of 1929, sometimes referred to as simply the "Great Crash."

A number of laws affect reporting companies, broker/dealers, and other market participants. From a financial reporting and analysis perspective, the most significant pieces of legislation are the Securities Acts of 1933 and 1934 and the Sarbanes–Oxley Act of 2002.

- **Securities Act of 1933** (The 1933 Act): This act specifies the financial and other significant information that investors must receive when securities are sold, prohibits misrepresentations, and requires initial registration of all public issuances of securities.
- **Securities Exchange Act of 1934** (The 1934 Act): This act created the SEC, gave the SEC authority over all aspects of the securities industry, and empowered the SEC to require periodic reporting by companies with publicly traded securities.
- **Sarbanes–Oxley Act of 2002**: This act created the Public Company Accounting Oversight Board (PCAOB) to oversee auditors. The SEC is responsible for carrying out the requirements of the act and overseeing the PCAOB. The act addresses auditor independence (it prohibits auditors from providing certain non-audit services to the companies they audit); strengthens corporate responsibility for financial reports (it requires executive management to certify that the company's financial reports fairly present the company's condition); and

8 *Objectives and Principles of Securities Regulation*, IOSCO, May 2017.

requires management to report on the effectiveness of the company's internal control over financial reporting (including obtaining external auditor confirmation of the effectiveness of internal control).

Companies comply with these acts principally through the completion and submission (i.e., filing) of standardized forms issued by the SEC. There are more than 50 different types of SEC forms that are used to satisfy reporting requirements; the discussion herein will be limited to those forms most relevant for financial analysts.

Most of the SEC filings are required to be made electronically, so filings that an analyst would be interested in can be retrieved online from one of many websites, including the SEC's own website. Some filings are required on the initial offering of securities, whereas others are required on a periodic basis thereafter. The following are some of the more common information sources used by analysts.

- **Securities Offerings Registration Statement**: The 1933 Act requires companies offering securities to file a registration statement. New issuers as well as previously registered companies that are issuing new securities are required to file these statements. Required information and the precise form vary depending upon the size and nature of the offering. Typically, required information includes: 1) disclosures about the securities being offered for sale, 2) the relationship of these new securities to the issuer's other capital securities, 3) the information typically provided in the annual filings, 4) recent audited financial statements, and 5) risk factors involved in the business.
- **Forms 10-K, 20-F, and 40-F**: These are forms that companies are required to file *annually*. Form 10-K is for US registrants, Form 40-F is for certain Canadian registrants, and Form 20-F is for all other non-US registrants. These forms require a comprehensive overview, including information concerning a company's business, financial disclosures, legal proceedings, and information related to management. The financial disclosures include a historical summary of financial data (usually 10 years), management's discussion and analysis (MD&A) of the company's financial condition and results of operations, and audited financial statements.
- **Annual Report**: In addition to the SEC's annual filings (e.g., Form 10-K), most companies prepare an annual report to shareholders. This is not a requirement of the SEC. The annual report is usually viewed as one of the most significant opportunities for a company to present itself to shareholders and other external parties; accordingly, it is often a highly polished marketing document with photographs, an opening letter from the chief executive officer, financial data, market segment information, research and development activities, and future corporate goals. In contrast, the Form 10-K is a more legal type of document with minimal marketing emphasis. Although the perspectives vary, there is considerable overlap between a company's annual report and its Form 10-K. Some companies elect to prepare just the Form 10-K or a document that integrates both the 10-K and annual report.
- **Proxy Statement/Form DEF-14A**: The SEC requires that shareholders of a company receive a proxy statement prior to a shareholder meeting. A proxy is an authorization from the shareholder giving another party the right to cast its vote. Shareholder meetings are held at least once a year, but any special meetings also require a proxy statement. Proxies, especially annual meeting proxies, contain information that is often useful to financial analysts. Such information typically includes proposals that require a shareholder vote, details of security ownership by management and principal owners, biographical information on directors, and disclosure of executive compensation. Proxy statement information is filed with the SEC as Form DEF-14A.

- **Forms 10-Q and 6-K**: These are forms that companies are required to submit for interim periods (quarterly for US companies on Form 10-Q, semiannually for many non-US companies on Form 6-K). The filing requires certain financial information, including unaudited financial statements and a MD&A for the interim period covered by the report. Additionally, if certain types of non-recurring events—such as the adoption of a significant accounting policy, commencement of significant litigation, or a material limitation on the rights of any holders of any class of registered securities—take place during the period covered by the report, these events must be included in the Form 10-Q report. Companies may provide the 10-Q report to shareholders or may prepare a separate, abbreviated, quarterly report to shareholders.

EXAMPLE 1

Initial Registration Statement

In 2004, Google filed a registration statement with the US SEC to register its initial public offering of securities (Class A Common Stock). In addition to a large amount of financial and business information, the registration statement provided a 20-page discussion Google's business and industry.

Which of the following is *most likely* to have been included in Google's registration statement?

A Interim unaudited financial statements.

B Assessment of risk factors involved in the business.

C Projected cash flows and earnings for the business.

Solution:

B is correct. Information provided by companies in registration statements typically includes disclosures about the securities being offered for sale; the relationship of these new securities to the issuer's other capital securities; the information typically provided in the annual filings; recent audited financial statements; and risk factors involved in the business.. Companies provide information useful in developing projected cash flows and earnings but do not typically include these in the registration statement, nor do they provide unaudited interim statements in the initial registration statement.

A company or its officers make other SEC filings—either periodically, or, if significant events or transactions have occurred, in between the periodic reports noted above. By their nature, these forms sometimes contain the most interesting and timely information and may have significant valuation implications.

- **Form 8-K:** In addition to filing annual and interim reports, SEC registrants must report material corporate events on a more current basis. Form 8-K (6-K for non-US registrants) is the "current report" companies must file with the SEC to announce such major events as acquisitions or disposals of corporate assets, changes in securities and trading markets, matters related to accountants and financial statements, corporate governance and management changes, and Regulation FD disclosures.[9]

- **Forms 3, 4, 5 and 144**: Forms 3, 4 and 5 are required to report beneficial ownership of securities. These filings are required for any director or officer of a registered company as well as beneficial owners of greater than 10 percent of a class of registered equity securities. Form 3 is the initial statement, Form 4 reports changes, and Form 5 is the annual report. Form 144 is notice of the proposed sale of restricted securities or securities held by an affiliate of the issuer. These forms can be used to examine purchases and sales of securities by officers, directors, and other affiliates of the company, who collectively are regarded as corporate insiders.
- **Form 11-K**: This is the annual report of employee stock purchase, savings, and similar plans. It might be of interest to analysts for companies with significant employee benefit plans because it contains more information than that disclosed in the company's financial statements.

In jurisdictions other than the United States, similar legislation exists for the purpose of regulating securities and capital markets. Regulatory authorities are responsible for enforcing regulation, and securities regulation is intended to be consistent with the IOSCO objectives described in the previous section. Within each jurisdiction, regulators will either establish or, more typically, recognize and adopt a specified set or sets of accounting standards. The regulators will also establish reporting and filing requirements. IOSCO members have agreed to cooperate in the development, implementation, and enforcement of internationally recognised and consistent standards of regulation.

3.2.3 *Capital Markets Regulation in Europe*

Each individual member state of the European Union (EU) regulates capital markets in its jurisdiction. There are, however, certain regulations that have been adopted at the EU level. Importantly the EU agreed that from 2005 consolidated accounts of EU listed companies would use International Financial Reporting Standards. The endorsement process by which newly issued IFRS are adopted by the EU reflects the balance between the individual member state's autonomy and the need for cooperation and convergence. When the IASB issues a new standard, the European Financial Reporting Advisory Group advises the European Commission on the standard, and the Standards Advice Review Group provides the Commission an opinion about that advice. Based on the input from these two entities, the Commission prepares a draft endorsement regulation. The Accounting Regulatory Committee votes on the proposal; and if the vote is favorable, the proposal proceeds to the European Parliament and the Council of the European Union for approval.[10]

Two bodies related to securities regulation established by the European Commission are the European Securities Committee (ESC) and the European Securities and Market Authority (ESMA). The ESC consists of high-level representatives of member states and advises the European Commission on securities policy issues. ESMA is an EU cross-border supervisor established to co-ordinate supervision of the EU market. As noted earlier, regulation still rests with the individual member states and, therefore,

9 Regulation Fair Disclosure (FD) provides that when an issuer discloses material non-public information to certain individuals or entities—generally, securities market professionals such as stock analysts or holders of the issuer's securities who may trade on the basis of the information—the issuer must make public disclosure of that information. In this way, the rule aims to promote full and fair disclosure.

10 Source: European Commission. http://ec.europa.eu/internal_market/accounting/legal_framework/ias_regulation_en.htm.

requirements for registering shares and filing periodic financial reports vary from country to country. ESMA is one of three European supervisory authorities; the two others supervise the banking and insurance industries.

4 THE INTERNATIONAL FINANCIAL REPORTING STANDARDS FRAMEWORK

As previously discussed, the IASB *Conceptual Framework for Financial Reporting* sets forth the concepts that underlie the preparation and presentation of financial statements for external users. The framework is designed to: assist standard setters in developing and reviewing standards; assist preparers of financial statements in applying standards and in dealing with issues not specifically covered by standard; assist auditors in forming an opinion on financial statements; and assist users in interpreting financial statement information. The objective of financial reporting is the provision of financial information that is useful to current and potential providers of resources in making decisions and all other aspects of the framework flow from that central objective.

The providers of resources are considered to be the primary users of financial reports and include investors, lenders, and other creditors. The purpose of providing the financial information is to be useful in making decisions about providing resources. Other users may find the financial information useful for making economic decisions. The types of economic decisions differ by users, so the specific information needed differs as well. However, although these users may have unique information needs, some information needs are common across all users. Information is needed about the company's financial position: its resources and its financial obligations. Information is needed about a company's financial performance; this information explains how and why the company's financial position changed in the past and can be useful in evaluating potential changes in the future. The third common information need is the need for information about a company's cash. How did the company obtain cash (by selling its products and services, borrowing, other)? How did the company use cash (by paying expenses, investing in new equipment, paying dividends, other)?

Information that is helpful to users in assessing future net cash inflows to the entity includes information about the economic resources of (assets) and claims against (liabilities and equity) the entity, and about how well the management and governing board have utilized the resources of the entity. Users need to consider information from other sources as well in making their decisions. Although financial reports do not show the value of an entity they are useful in estimating the value of an entity.

4.1 Qualitative Characteristics of Financial Reports

Flowing from the central objective of providing information that is *useful* to providers of resources, the *Conceptual Framework* identifies two fundamental qualitative characteristics that make financial information useful: relevance and faithful representation.[11] The concept of materiality is discussed within the context of relevance.

1 *Relevance*: Information is relevant if it would potentially affect or make a difference in users' decisions. The information can have predictive value (useful in making forecasts), confirmatory value (useful to evaluate past decisions or forecasts), or both. In other words, relevant information helps users of

11 *Conceptual Framework for Financial Reporting.*

financial information to evaluate past, present, and future events, or to confirm or correct their past evaluations in a decision-making context. *Materiality:* Information is considered to be material if omission or misstatement of the information could influence users' decisions. Materiality is a function of the nature and/or magnitude of the information.

2 *Faithful representation*: Information that faithfully represents an economic phenomenon that it purports to represent is ideally complete, neutral, and free from error. Complete means that all information necessary to understand the phenomenon is depicted. Neutral means that information is selected and presented without bias. In other words, the information is not presented in such a manner as to bias the users' decisions. Free from error means that there are no errors of commission or omission in the description of the economic phenomenon, and that an appropriate process to arrive at the reported information was selected and was adhered to without error. Faithful representation maximizes the qualities of complete, neutral, and free from error to the extent possible.

Relevance and faithful representation are the fundamental, most critical characteristics of useful financial information. In addition the *Conceptual Framework* identifies four enhancing qualitative characteristics: comparability, verifiability, timeliness, and understandability.

1 *Comparability*: Comparability allows users "to identify and understand similarities and differences of items." Information presented in a consistent manner over time and across entities enables users to make comparisons more easily than information with variations in how similar economic phenomena are represented.
2 *Verifiability*: Verifiability means that different knowledgeable and independent observers would agree that the information presented faithfully represents the economic phenomena it purports to represent.
3 *Timeliness*: Timely information is available to decision makers prior to their making a decision.
4 *Understandability*: Clear and concise presentation of information enhances understandability. Information should be prepared for and be understandable by users who have a reasonable knowledge of business and economic activities, and who are willing to study the information with diligence. Information that is useful should not be excluded simply because it is difficult to understand and it may be necessary for users to seek assistance to understand information about complex economic phenomena.

Financial information exhibiting these qualitative characteristics—fundamental and enhancing—should be useful for making economic decisions.

4.2 Constraints on Financial Reports

Although it would be ideal for financial statements to exhibit all of these qualitative characteristics and thus achieve maximum usefulness, it may be necessary to make tradeoffs across the enhancing characteristics. The application of the enhancing characteristics follows no set order of priority and each enhancing characteristic may take priority over the others. The aim is an appropriate balance among the enhancing characteristics.

A pervasive constraint on useful financial reporting is the cost of providing and using this information. Optimally, benefits derived from information should exceed the costs of providing and using it. Again, the aim is a balance between costs and benefits.

A limitation of financial reporting involves information that is not included. Financial statements, by necessity, omit information that is non-quantifiable. For example, the creativity, innovation, and competence of a company's work force are not directly captured in the financial statements. Similarly, customer loyalty, a positive corporate culture, environmental responsibility, and many other aspects about a company may not be directly reflected in the financial statements. Of course, to the extent that these items result in superior financial performance, a company's financial reports will reflect the results.

EXAMPLE 2

Balancing Qualitative Characteristics of Useful Information

A tradeoff between enhancing qualitative characteristics often occurs. For example, when a company records sales revenue, it is required to simultaneously estimate and record an expense for potential bad debts (uncollectible accounts). Including this estimated expense is considered to represent the economic event faithfully and to provide relevant information about the net profits for the accounting period. The information is timely and understandable; but because bad debts may not be known with certainty until a later period, inclusion of this estimated expense involves a sacrifice of verifiability. The bad debt expense is simply an estimate. It is apparent that it is not always possible to simultaneously fulfill all qualitative characteristics.

Companies are *most likely* to make tradeoffs between which of the following when preparing financial reports?

A Relevance and materiality.

B Timeliness and verifiability.

C Relevance and faithful representation.

Solution:

B is correct. Providing timely information implies a shorter time frame between the economic event and the information preparation; however, fully verifying information may require a longer time frame. Relevance and faithful representation are fundamental qualitative characteristics that make financial information useful. Both characteristics are required; there is no tradeoff between these. Materiality is an aspect of relevance.

4.3 The Elements of Financial Statements

Financial statements portray the financial effects of transactions and other events by grouping them into broad classes (elements) according to their economic characteristics. Three elements of financial statements are directly related to the measurement of financial position: assets, liabilities, and equity.

- **Assets**: A present economic resource controlled by the entity as a result of past events. An economic resource is a right that has the potential to produce economic benefits. Assets are what a company owns (e.g., inventory and equipment).

- **Liabilities**:. A present obligation of the entity to transfer an economic resource as a result of past events. An obligation is a duty or responsibility that the entity has no practical ability to avoid. Liabilities are what a company owes (e.g., bank borrowings).
- **Equity** (for public companies, also known as "shareholders' equity" or "stockholders' equity"): Assets less liabilities. Equity is the residual interest in the assets after subtracting the liabilities.

The elements of financial statements directly related to the measurement of performance (profit and related measures) are income and expenses.

- **Income**: Increases in assets, or decreases in liabilities, that result in increases in equity, other than those relating to contributions from holders of equity claims. Income includes both revenues and gains. Revenues represent income from the ordinary activities of the enterprise (e.g., the sale of products or provision of services). Gains may result from ordinary activities or other activities (the sale of surplus equipment).
- **Expenses**: Decreases in assets, or increases in liabilities, that result in decreases in equity, other than those relating to distributions to holders of equity claims. Expenses include those related to operating activities such as cost of good sold and operating expenses including wages, rents and other items. Losses are also considered expenses and can result from the sale of assets at less than their carrying values, impairments of asset values and a variety of other items.

4.3.1 *Underlying Assumptions in Financial Statements*

Two important assumptions underlie financial statements: accrual accounting and going concern. These assumptions determine how financial statement elements are recognized and measured.

The use of "accrual accounting" assumes that financial statements should reflect transactions in the period when they actually occur, not necessarily when cash movements occur. For example, a company reports revenues *when they are earned (when the performance obligations have been satisfied),* regardless of whether the company received cash before or after delivering the product, at the time of delivery.

"Going concern" refers to the assumption that the company will continue in business for the foreseeable future. To illustrate, consider the value of a company's inventory if it is assumed that the inventory can be sold over a normal period of time versus the value of that same inventory if it is assumed that the inventory must all be sold in a day (or a week). Companies with the intent to liquidate or materially curtail operations would require different information for a fair presentation.

4.3.2 *Recognition of Financial Statement Elements*

Recognition means that an item is included in the balance sheet or income statement. Recognition occurs if the item meets the definition of an element and satisfies the criteria for recognition. Recognition is appropriate if it results in both relevant information about assets, liabilities, equity, income and expenses and a faithful representation of those items, because the aim is to provide information that is useful to investors, lenders and other creditors.

4.3.3 *Measurement of Financial Statement Elements*

Measurement is the process of determining the monetary amounts at which the elements of the financial statements are to be recognized and carried in the balance sheet and income statement. The following alternative bases of measurement are used to different degrees and in varying combinations to measure assets and liabilities:

- **Historical cost**: Historical cost is simply the amount of cash or cash equivalents paid to purchase an asset, including any costs of acquisition and/or preparation. If the asset was not bought for cash, historical cost is the fair value of whatever was given in order to buy the asset. When referring to liabilities, the historical cost basis of measurement means the amount of proceeds received in exchange for the obligation.
- **Amortised cost**: Historical cost adjusted for amortisation, depreciation, or depletion and/or impairment.
- **Current cost**: In reference to assets, current cost is the amount of cash or cash equivalents that would have to be paid to buy the same or an equivalent asset today. In reference to liabilities, the current cost basis of measurement means the undiscounted amount of cash or cash equivalents that would be required to settle the obligation today.
- **Realizable (settlement) value**: In reference to assets, realizable value is the amount of cash or cash equivalents that could currently be obtained by selling the asset in an orderly disposal. For liabilities, the equivalent to realizable value is called "settlement value"—that is, settlement value is the undiscounted amount of cash or cash equivalents expected to be paid to satisfy the liabilities in the normal course of business.
- **Present value (PV)**: For assets, present value is the present discounted value of the future net cash inflows that the asset is expected to generate in the normal course of business. For liabilities, present value is the present discounted value of the future net cash outflows that are expected to be required to settle the liabilities in the normal course of business.
- **Fair value**: is defined as an exit price, the price that would be received to sell an asset or paid to transfer a liability in an orderly transaction between market participants at the measurement date. This may involve either market measures or present value measures depending on the availability of information.

4.4 General Requirements for Financial Statements

The *Conceptual Framework* provides a basis for establishing standards and the elements of financial statements. However, the framework does not address the general contents of the financial statements, which are addressed in International Accounting Standard (IAS) No. 1, *Presentation of Financial Statements.* IAS No. 1 specifies the required financial statements, general features of financial statements, and structure and content of financial statements.[12] These general requirements are illustrated in Exhibit 1 and described in the subsections below.

12 For US GAAP, financial statement presentation is covered in Sections 205 through 280 of the Accounting Standards Codification.

Exhibit 1 IASB General Requirements for Financial Statements

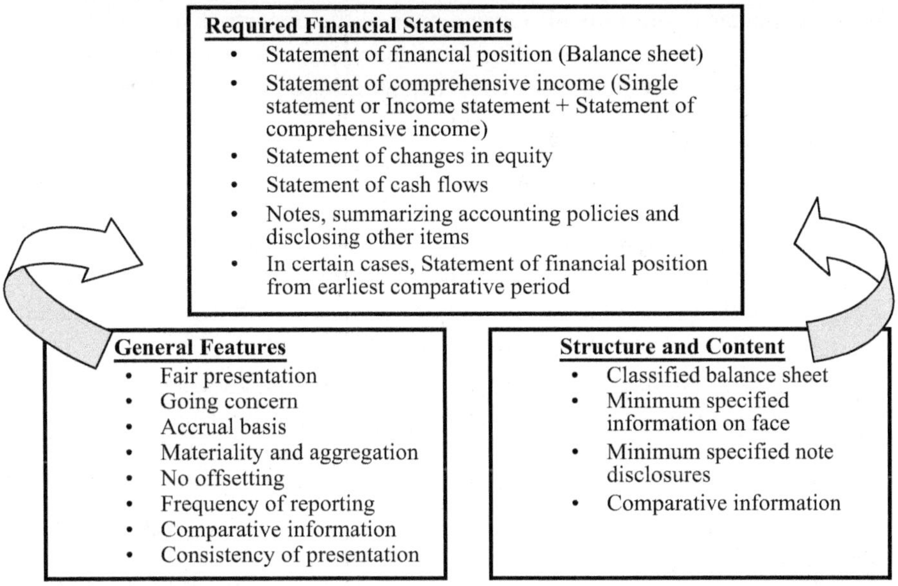

In the following sections, we discuss the required financial statements, the general features underlying the preparation of financial statements, and the specified structure and content in greater detail.

4.4.1 *Required Financial Statements*

Under IAS No. 1, a complete set of financial statements includes:[13]

- a statement of financial position (balance sheet);
- a statement of comprehensive income (a single statement of comprehensive income or two statements, an income statement and a statement of comprehensive income that begins with profit or loss from the income statement);
- a statement of changes in equity, separately showing changes in equity resulting from profit or loss, each item of other comprehensive income, and transactions with owners in their capacity as owners;[14]
- a statement of cash flows; and
- notes comprising a summary of significant accounting policies and other explanatory notes that disclose information required by IFRS and not presented elsewhere and that provide information relevant to an understanding of the financial statements.

Entities are encouraged to furnish other related financial and non-financial information in addition to that required. Financial statements need to present fairly the financial position, financial performance, and cash flows of an entity.

4.4.2 *General Features of Financial Statements*

A company that applies IFRS is required to state explicitly in the notes to its financial statements that it is in compliance with the standards. Such a statement is only made when a company is in compliance with *all* requirements of IFRS. In extremely rare

13 IAS No. 1, *Presentation of Financial Statements*, paragraph 10.

14 Examples of transactions with owners acting in their capacity as owners include sale of equity securities to investors, distributions of earnings to investors, and repurchases of equity securities from investors.

circumstances, a company may deviate from a requirement of IFRS if management concludes that complying with IFRS would result in misleading financial statements. In this case, management must disclose details of the departure from IFRS.

IAS No. 1 specifies a number of general features underlying the preparation of financial statements. These features clearly reflect the *Conceptual Framework*.

- *Fair Presentation*: The application of IFRS is presumed to result in financial statements that achieve a fair presentation. The IAS describes fair presentation as follows:

  > Fair presentation requires the faithful representation of the effects of transactions, other events and conditions in accordance with the definitions and recognition criteria for assets, liabilities, income and expenses set out in the *Framework*.[15]

- *Going Concern*: Financial statements are prepared on a going concern basis unless management either intends to liquidate the entity or to cease trading, or has no realistic alternative but to do so. If not presented on a going concern basis, the fact and rationale should be disclosed.
- *Accrual Basis*: Financial statements (except for cash flow information) are to be prepared using the accrual basis of accounting.
- *Materiality and Aggregation*: Omissions or misstatements of items are material if they could, individually or collectively, influence the economic decisions that users make on the basis of the financial statements. Each material class of similar items is presented separately. Dissimilar items are presented separately unless they are immaterial.
- *No Offsetting*: Assets and liabilities, and income and expenses, are not offset unless required or permitted by an IFRS.
- *Frequency of Reporting*: Financial statements must be prepared at least annually.
- *Comparative Information*: Financial statements must include comparative information from the previous period. The comparative information of prior periods is disclosed for all amounts reported in the financial statements, unless an IFRS requires or permits otherwise.
- *Consistency*: The presentation and classification of items in the financial statements are usually retained from one period to the next.

4.4.3 *Structure and Content Requirements*

IAS No. 1 also specifies structure and content of financial statements. These requirements include the following:

- *Classified Statement of Financial Position (Balance Sheet)*: requires the balance sheet to distinguish between current and non-current assets, and between current and non-current liabilities unless a presentation based on liquidity provides more relevant and reliable information (e.g., in the case of a bank or similar financial institution).
- *Minimum Information on the Face of the Financial Statements*: specifies the minimum line item disclosures on the face of, or in the notes to, the financial statements. For example, companies are specifically required to disclose the amount of their plant, property, and equipment as a line item on the face of the balance sheet. The major line items included in financial statements are covered in other readings.

---

15 IAS No. 1, *Presentation of Financial Statements*, paragraph 15.

- *Minimum Information in the Notes* (or on the face of financial statements): specifies disclosures about information to be presented in the financial statements. This information must be provided in a systematic manner and cross-referenced from the face of the financial statements to the notes. The required information is summarized in Exhibit 2.
- *Comparative Information*: For all amounts reported in a financial statement, comparative information should be provided for the previous period unless another standard requires or permits otherwise. Such comparative information allows users to better understand reported amounts.

Exhibit 2 Summary of IFRS Required Disclosures in the Notes to the Financial Statements

Disclosure of Accounting Policies	■ Measurement bases used in preparing financial statements ■ Significant accounting policies used ■ Judgments made in applying accounting policies that have the most significant effect on the amounts recognized in the financial statements
Sources of Estimation Uncertainty	■ Key assumptions about the future and other key sources of estimation uncertainty that have a significant risk of causing material adjustment to the carrying amount of assets and liabilities within the next year
Other Disclosures	■ Information about capital and about certain financial instruments classified as equity ■ Dividends not recognized as a distribution during the period, including dividends declared before the financial statements were issued and any cumulative preference dividends ■ Description of the entity, including its domicile, legal form, country of incorporation, and registered office or business address ■ Nature of operations and principal activities ■ Name of parent and ultimate parent

COMPARISON OF IFRS WITH ALTERNATIVE REPORTING SYSTEMS

5

The adoption of IFRS as the required financial reporting standard by the EU and other countries has advanced the goal of global convergence. Nevertheless, there are still significant differences in financial reporting in the global capital markets. Arguably, the most critical are the differences that exist between IFRS and US GAAP. Following the EU adoption of IFRS (in 2005), a significant number of the world's listed companies use one of these two reporting standards.

In general, the IASB and FASB work together to coordinate changes to accounting standards and reduce differences between the standards. A joint IASB/FASB project initiated in 2004 aimed to develop an improved, common conceptual framework. In late 2010, convergence of the conceptual frameworks was put on hold. In December 2012, the IASB reactivated the conceptual framework as an IASB project. As of year-end 2018, there are no new projects on the convergence agenda.

As more countries adopt IFRS, the need for analysts to consider other financial reporting systems will be reduced. Analysts are likely to encounter financial statements that are prepared on a basis other than IFRS. Differences between IFRS and US GAAP remain and affect the framework as well as numerous financial reporting standards. Curriculum readings on individual financial statements and specific topics provide a more detailed review of related differences in IFRS and US GAAP.

Exhibit 3 Differences between IFRS and US GAAP

Basis for Comparison	US GAAP	IFRS
Developed by	Financial Accounting Standard Board (FASB).	International Accounting Standard Board (IASB).
Based on	Rules	Principles
Inventory valuation	FIFO, LIFO and Weighted Average Method.	FIFO and Weighted Average Method.
Extraordinary items	Shown below (at the bottom of the income statement).	Not segregated in the income statement.
Development cost	Treated as an expense	Capitalized, only if certain conditions are satisfied.
Reversal of Inventory	Prohibited	Permissible, if specified conditions are met.

Source: https://keydifferences.com/difference-between-gaap-and-ifrs.html

For analyzing financial statements created under different standards, reconciliation schedules and disclosures regarding the significant differences between the reporting bases—historically available in some jurisdictions—were particularly helpful. For example, the SEC historically required reconciliation for foreign private issuers that did not prepare financial statements in accordance with US GAAP. In 2007, however, the SEC eliminated the reconciliation requirement for companies that prepared their financial statements according to IFRS. Although the disclosures related to any such differences were sometimes dauntingly long, the numerical reconciliations of net income and shareholders' equity appeared in charts that were relatively easy to use. Because reconciliation disclosures are no longer generally available, an analyst comparing two companies that use different reporting standards must be aware of areas where accounting standards have not converged. In many cases, a user of financial statements prepared under different accounting standards does not have enough information to make specific adjustments required to achieve comparability. Instead, an analyst must maintain caution in interpreting comparative financial measures produced under different accounting standards and monitor significant developments in financial reporting standards, as this can have important implications for comparing the performance of companies and security valuation.

6 MONITORING DEVELOPMENTS IN FINANCIAL REPORTING STANDARDS

In studying financial reporting and financial statement analysis in general, the analyst must be aware that reporting standards are evolving. Analysts need to monitor ongoing developments in financial reporting and assess their implications for security analysis and valuation. The need to monitor developments in financial reporting standards does not mean that analysts should be accountants. An accountant monitors these developments from a preparer's perspective; an analyst needs to monitor from a user's perspective. More specifically, analysts need to know how these developments will affect financial reports.

Analysts can remain aware of developments in financial reporting standards by monitoring new products or transactions, actions of standard setters and other groups representing users of financial statements (such as CFA Institute), and company disclosures regarding critical accounting policies and estimates.

6.1 New Products or Types of Transactions

New products and new types of transactions can have unusual or unique elements to them such that no explicit guidance in the financial reporting standards exists. New products or transactions typically arise from economic events, such as new businesses (e.g., fintech), or from a newly developed financial instrument or financial structure. Financial instruments, whether exchange traded or not, are typically designed to enhance a company's business or to mitigate inherent risks. However, at times, financial instruments or structured transactions have been developed primarily for purposes of financial report "window dressing."

Although companies might discuss new products and transactions in their financial reports, the analyst can also monitor business journals and the capital markets to identify such items. Additionally, when one company in an industry develops a new product or transaction, other companies in the industry often do the same. Once new products, financial instruments, or structured transactions are identified, it is helpful to gain an understanding of the business purpose. If necessary, an analyst can obtain further information from a company's management, which should be able to describe the economic purpose, the financial statement reporting, significant estimates, judgments applied in determining the reporting, and future cash flow implications for these items.

6.2 Evolving Standards and the Role of CFA Institute

The actions of standard setters and regulators are unlikely to be helpful in identifying new products and transactions, given the lag between new product development and regulatory action. Monitoring the actions of these authorities is nonetheless important for another reason: Changes in regulations can affect companies' financial reports and, thus, valuations. This is particularly true if the financial reporting standards change to require more explicit identification of matters affecting asset/liability valuation or financial performance. For example, one regulatory change required companies to include a provision for expenses associated with the grant and vesting of employee stock option grants as an expense in the income statement. Prior to the required expensing, an analyst could only assess the dilutive effect to shareholders associated with stock option grants by reviewing information disclosed in the notes to the financial statements.

To the extent that some market participants do not examine financial statement details and thus ignore some items when valuing a company's securities, more explicit identification could affect the value of the company's securities. Additionally, it is plausible to believe that management is more attentive to and rigorous in any calculations/estimates of items that appear in the financial statements, compared to items that are only disclosed in the notes.

The IASB (www.iasb.org) and FASB (www.fasb.org) provide a great deal of information on their websites regarding new standards and proposals for future changes in standards. In addition, the IASB and FASB seek input from the financial analyst community—those who regularly use financial statements in making investment and credit decisions. When a new standard is proposed, an exposure draft is made available and users of financial statements can draft comment letters and position papers for submission to the IASB and FASB in order to evaluate the proposal.

CFA Institute is active in supporting improvements to financial reporting. Volunteer members of CFA Institute serve on several liaison committees that meet regularly to make recommendations to the IASB and FASB on proposed standards and to draft comment letters and position papers. The comment letters and position papers of these groups on financial reporting issues are available at www.cfainstitute.org/advocacy.

In 2007, CFA Institute issued a position paper titled *A Comprehensive Business Reporting Model: Financial Reporting for Investors*, which provides a suggested model for significantly improving financial reporting. The position paper remains relevant in stating:

> Corporate financial statements and their related disclosures are fundamental to sound investment decision making. The well-being of the world's financial markets, and of the millions of investors who entrust their financial present and future to those markets, depends directly on the information financial statements and disclosures provide. Consequently, the quality of the information drives global financial markets. The quality, in turn, depends directly on the principles and standards managers apply when recognizing and measuring the economic activities and events affecting their companies' operations....
>
> Investors require timeliness, transparency, comparability, and consistency in financial reporting. Investors have a preference for decision relevance over reliability..."analysts need to know economic reality—what is really going on—to the greatest extent it can be depicted by accounting numbers." Corporate financial statements that fail to reflect this economic reality undermine the investment decision-making process.[16]

Among other principles, the proposed model stresses the importance of information regarding the current fair value of assets and liabilities, of neutrality in financial reporting, and of providing detailed information on cash flows to investors through the choice of the so-called direct format for the cash flow statement.

In summary, analysts can improve their investment decision making by keeping current on financial reporting standards. In addition, analysts can contribute to improving financial reporting by sharing their perspective as users with standard-setting bodies, which typically invite comments concerning proposed changes.

SUMMARY

An awareness of financial reporting and underlying financial reporting standards can assist in security valuation and other financial analysis. This reading describes the conceptual objectives of financial reporting standards, the parties involved in standard-setting processes, and the implication for analysts in monitoring developments in reporting standards.

16 *A Comprehensive Business Reporting Model: Financial Reporting for Investors*, CFA Institute Centre for Financial Market Integrity, July 2007, p. 1, 2.

Some key points of the reading are summarized below:

- The objective of financial reporting is to provide financial information about the reporting entity that is useful to existing and potential investors, lenders, and other creditors in making decisions about providing resources to the entity.
- Financial reporting requires policy choices and estimates. These choices and estimates require judgment, which can vary from one preparer to the next. Accordingly, standards are needed to ensure increased consistency in these judgments.
- Private sector standard setting bodies and regulatory authorities play significant but different roles in the standard setting process. In general, standard setting bodies make the rules, and regulatory authorities enforce the rules. However, regulators typically retain legal authority to establish financial reporting standards in their jurisdiction.
- The IFRS framework sets forth the concepts that underlie the preparation and presentation of financial statements for external users.
- The objective of fair presentation of useful information is the center of the IASB's *Conceptual Framework*. The qualitative characteristics of useful information include fundamental and enhancing characteristics. Information must exhibit the fundamental characteristics of relevance and faithful representation to be useful. The enhancing characteristics identified are comparability, verifiability, timeliness, and understandability.
- *IFRS Financial Statements*: IAS No. 1 prescribes that a complete set of financial statements includes a statement of financial position (balance sheet), a statement of comprehensive income (either two statements—one for net income and one for comprehensive income—or a single statement combining both net income and comprehensive income), a statement of changes in equity, a cash flow statement, and notes. The notes include a summary of significant accounting policies and other explanatory information.
- Financial statements need to reflect certain basic features: fair presentation, going concern, accrual basis, materiality and aggregation, and no offsetting.
- Financial statements must be prepared at least annually, must include comparative information from the previous period, and must be consistent.
- Financial statements must follow certain presentation requirements including a classified statement of financial position (balance sheet) and minimum information on both the face of the financial statements and in the notes.
- A significant number of the world's listed companies report under either IFRS or US GAAP.
- In many cases, a user of financial statements will lack the information necessary to make specific adjustments required to achieve comparability between companies that use IFRS and companies that use US GAAP. Instead, an analyst must maintain general caution in interpreting comparative financial measures produced under different accounting standards and monitor significant developments in financial reporting standards.
- Analysts can remain aware of ongoing developments in financial reporting by monitoring new products or types of transactions; actions of standard setters, regulators, and other groups; and company disclosures regarding critical accounting policies and estimates.

PRACTICE PROBLEMS

1 Which of the following is *most likely* not an objective of financial statements?
  - **A** To provide information about the performance of an entity.
  - **B** To provide information about the financial position of an entity.
  - **C** To provide information about the users of an entity's financial statements.

2 International financial reporting standards are currently developed by which entity?
  - **A** The IFRS Foundation.
  - **B** The International Accounting Standards Board.
  - **C** The International Organization of Securities Commissions.

3 US generally accepted accounting principles are currently developed by which entity?
  - **A** The Securities and Exchange Commission.
  - **B** The Financial Accounting Standards Board.
  - **C** The Public Company Accounting Oversight Board.

4 A core objective of the International Organization of Securities Commissions is to:
  - **A** eliminate systemic risk.
  - **B** protect users of financial statements.
  - **C** ensure that markets are fair, efficient, and transparent.

5 According to the *Conceptual Framework for Financial Reporting*, which of the following is *not* an enhancing qualitative characteristic of information in financial statements?
  - **A** Accuracy.
  - **B** Timeliness.
  - **C** Comparability.

6 Which of the following is *not* a constraint on the financial statements according to the *Conceptual Framework*?
  - **A** Understandability.
  - **B** Benefit versus cost.
  - **C** Balancing of qualitative characteristics.

7 The assumption that an entity will continue to operate for the foreseeable future is called:
  - **A** accrual basis.
  - **B** comparability.
  - **C** going concern.

8 The assumption that the effects of transactions and other events are recognized when they occur, not when the cash flows occur, is called:
  - **A** relevance.
  - **B** accrual basis.
  - **C** going concern.

© 2019 CFA Institute. All rights reserved.

9 Neutrality of information in the financial statements most closely contributes to which qualitative characteristic?

  A Relevance.

  B Understandability.

  C Faithful representation.

10 Valuing assets at the amount of cash or equivalents paid or the fair value of the consideration given to acquire them at the time of acquisition most closely describes which measurement of financial statement elements?

  A Current cost.

  B Historical cost.

  C Realizable value.

11 The valuation technique under which assets are recorded at the amount that would be received in an orderly disposal is:

  A current cost.

  B present value.

  C realizable value.

12 Which of the following is *not* a required financial statement according to IAS No. 1?

  A Statement of financial position.

  B Statement of changes in income.

  C Statement of comprehensive income.

13 Which of the following elements of financial statements is *most* closely related to measurement of performance?

  A Assets.

  B Expenses.

  C Liabilities.

14 Which of the following elements of financial statements is *most* closely related to measurement of financial position?

  A Equity.

  B Income.

  C Expenses.

15 Which of the following disclosures regarding new accounting standards provides the *most* meaningful information to an analyst?

  A The impact of adoption is discussed.

  B The standard will have no material impact.

  C Management is still evaluating the impact.

SOLUTIONS

1 C is correct. Financial statements provide information, including information about the entity's financial position, performance, and changes in financial position, to users. They do not typically provide information about users.

2 B is correct. The IASB is currently charged with developing International Financial Reporting Standards.

3 B is correct. The FASB is responsible for the Accounting Standards Codification™, the single source of nongovernmental authoritative US generally accepted accounting principles.

4 C is correct. A core objective of IOSCO is to ensure that markets are fair, efficient, and transparent. The other core objectives are to reduce, not eliminate, systemic risk and to protect investors, not all users of financial statements.

5 A is correct. Accuracy is not an enhancing qualitative characteristic. Faithful representation, not accuracy, is a fundamental qualitative characteristic.

6 A is correct. Understandability is an enhancing qualitative characteristic of financial information—not a constraint.

7 C is correct. The *Conceptual Framework* identifies two important underlying assumptions of financial statements: accrual basis and going concern. Going concern is the assumption that the entity will continue to operate for the foreseeable future. Enterprises with the intent to liquidate or materially curtail operations would require different information for a fair presentation.

8 B is correct. Accrual basis reflects the effects of transactions and other events being recognized when they occur, not when the cash flows. These effects are recorded and reported in the financial statements of the periods to which they relate.

9 C is correct. The fundamental qualitative characteristic of faithful representation is contributed to by completeness, neutrality, and freedom from error.

10 B is correct. Historical cost is the consideration paid to acquire an asset.

11 C is correct. The amount that would be received in an orderly disposal is realizable value.

12 B is correct. There is no statement of changes in income. Under IAS No. 1, a complete set of financial statements includes a statement of financial position, a statement of comprehensive income, a statement of changes in equity, a statement of cash flows, and notes comprising a summary of significant accounting policies and other explanatory information.

13 B is correct. The elements of financial statements related to the measure of performance are income and expenses.

14 A is correct. The elements of financial statements related to the measurement of financial position are assets, liabilities, and equity.

15 A is correct. A discussion of the impact would be the most meaningful, although B would also be useful.

FINANCIAL REPORTING AND ANALYSIS

STUDY SESSION 7

Financial Reporting and Analysis (2)

This study session addresses the three major financial statements—the income statement, the balance sheet, and the cash flow statement—by examining each in turn. The purpose, elements of, construction, pertinent ratios, and common-size analysis are presented for each major financial statement. The session concludes with a discussion of financial analysis techniques including the use of ratios to evaluate corporate financial health.

READING ASSIGNMENTS

Reading 21	Understanding Income Statements by Elaine Henry, PhD, CFA, and Thomas R. Robinson, PhD, CFA
Reading 22	Understanding Balance Sheets by Elaine Henry, PhD, CFA, and Thomas R. Robinson, PhD, CFA
Reading 23	Understanding Cash Flow Statements by Elaine Henry, PhD, CFA, Thomas R. Robinson, PhD, CFA, Jan Hendrik van Greuning, DCom, CFA, and Michael A. Broihahn, CPA, CIA, CFA
Reading 24	Financial Analysis Techniques by Elaine Henry, PhD, CFA, Thomas R. Robinson, PhD, CFA, and Jan Hendrik van Greuning, DCom, CFA

Note: Changes in accounting standards as well as new rulings and/or pronouncements issued after the publication of the readings on financial reporting and analysis may cause some of the information in these readings to become dated. Candidates are *not* responsible for anything that occurs after the readings were published. In addition, candidates are expected to be familiar with the analytical frameworks contained in the readings, as well as the implications of alternative accounting methods for financial analysis and valuation discussed in the readings. Candidates are also responsible for the content of accounting standards, but not for the actual reference numbers. Finally, candidates should be aware that certain ratios may be defined and calculated differently. When alternative ratio definitions exist and no specific definition is given, candidates should use the ratio definitions emphasized in the readings.

© 2019 CFA Institute. All rights reserved.

READING

21

Understanding Income Statements

by Elaine Henry, PhD, CFA, and Thomas R. Robinson, PhD, CFA

Elaine Henry, PhD, CFA, is at Stevens Institute of Technology (USA). Thomas R. Robinson, PhD, CFA, is at AACSB International (USA).

LEARNING OUTCOMES

Mastery	*The candidate should be able to:*
☐	**a.** describe the components of the income statement and alternative presentation formats of that statement;
☐	**b.** Describe general principles of revenue recognition and accounting standards for revenue recognition;
☐	**c.** calculate revenue given information that might influence the choice of revenue recognition method;
☐	**d.** describe general principles of expense recognition, specific expense recognition applications, and implications of expense recognition choices for financial analysis;
☐	**e.** describe the financial reporting treatment and analysis of non-recurring items (including discontinued operations, unusual or infrequent items) and changes in accounting policies;
☐	**f.** distinguish between the operating and non-operating components of the income statement;
☐	**g.** describe how earnings per share is calculated and calculate and interpret a company's earnings per share (both basic and diluted earnings per share) for both simple and complex capital structures;
☐	**h.** distinguish between dilutive and antidilutive securities and describe the implications of each for the earnings per share calculation;
☐	**i.** convert income statements to common-size income statements;
☐	**j.** evaluate a company's financial performance using common-size income statements and financial ratios based on the income statement;
☐	**k.** describe, calculate, and interpret comprehensive income;
☐	**l.** describe other comprehensive income and identify major types of items included in it.

Note: Changes in accounting standards as well as new rulings and/or pronouncements issued after the publication of the readings on financial reporting and analysis may cause some of the information in these readings to become dated. Candidates are *not* responsible for anything that occurs after the readings were published. In addition, candidates are expected to be familiar with the analytical frameworks contained in the readings, as well as the implications of alternative accounting methods for financial analysis and valuation discussed in the readings. Candidates are also responsible for the content of accounting standards, but not for the actual reference numbers. Finally, candidates should be aware that certain ratios may be defined and calculated differently. When alternative ratio definitions exist and no specific definition is given, candidates should use the ratio definitions emphasized in the readings.

© 2019 CFA Institute. All rights reserved.

1 INTRODUCTION

The income statement presents information on the financial results of a company's business activities over a period of time. The income statement communicates how much revenue the company generated during a period and what costs it incurred in connection with generating that revenue. The basic equation underlying the income statement, ignoring gains and losses, is Revenue minus Expenses equals Net income. The income statement is also sometimes referred to as the "statement of operations," "statement of earnings," or "profit and loss (P&L) statement." Under both International Financial Reporting Standards (IFRS) and US generally accepted accounting principles (US GAAP), the income statement may be presented as a separate statement followed by a statement of comprehensive income that begins with the profit or loss from the income statement or as a section of a single statement of comprehensive income.[1] This reading focuses on the income statement, and the term *income statement* will be used to describe either the separate statement that reports profit or loss used for earnings per share calculations or that section of a statement of comprehensive income that reports the same profit or loss. The reading also includes a discussion of comprehensive income (profit or loss from the income statement plus other comprehensive income).

Investment analysts intensely scrutinize companies' income statements. Equity analysts are interested in them because equity markets often reward relatively high- or low-earnings growth companies with above-average or below-average valuations, respectively, and because inputs into valuation models often include estimates of earnings. Fixed-income analysts examine the components of income statements, past and projected, for information on companies' abilities to make promised payments on their debt over the course of the business cycle. Corporate financial announcements frequently emphasize information reported in income statements, particularly earnings, more than information reported in the other financial statements.

This reading is organized as follows: Section 2 describes the components of the income statement and its format. Section 3 describes basic principles and selected applications related to the recognition of revenue, and Section 4 describes basic principles and selected applications related to the recognition of expenses. Section 5 covers non-recurring items and non-operating items. Section 6 explains the calculation of earnings per share. Section 7 introduces income statement analysis, and Section 8 explains comprehensive income and its reporting. A summary of the key points and practice problems in the CFA Institute multiple choice format complete the reading.

2 COMPONENTS AND FORMAT OF THE INCOME STATEMENT

Exhibits 1, 2, and 3 show the income statements for Anheuser-Busch InBev SA/NV (AB InBev), a multinational beverage company based in Belgium, Molson Coors Brewing Company (Molson Coors), a US-based multinational brewing company, and Groupe

1 International Accounting Standard (IAS) 1, *Presentation of Financial Statements*, establishes the presentation and minimum content requirements of financial statements and guidelines for the structure of financial statements under IFRS. Under US GAAP, the Financial Accounting Standards Board Accounting Standards Codification ASC Section 220-10-45 [Comprehensive Income–Overall–Other Presentation Matters] discusses acceptable formats in which to present income, other comprehensive income, and comprehensive income.

Danone (Danone), a French food manufacturer.[2] AB InBev and Danone report under IFRS, and Molson Coors reports under US GAAP. Note that both AB InBev and Molson Coors show three years' income statements and list the years in chronological order with the most recent year listed in the left-most column. In contrast, Danone shows two years of income statements and lists the years in chronological order from left to right with the most recent year in the right-most column. Different orderings of chronological information are common.

On the top line of the income statement, companies typically report revenue. **Revenue** generally refers to the amount charged for the delivery of goods or services in the *ordinary activities* of a business. Revenue may also be called sales or turnover.[3] For the year ended 31 December 2017, AB InBev reports $56.44 billion of revenue, Molson Coors reports $13.47 billion of revenue (labeled "sales"), and Danone reports €24.68 billion of revenue (labeled "sales").

Revenue is reported after adjustments (e.g., for cash or volume discounts, or for other reductions), and the term **net revenue** is sometimes used to specifically indicate that the revenue has been adjusted (e.g., for estimated returns). For all three companies in Exhibits 1 through 3, footnotes to their financial statements (not shown here) state that revenues are stated net of such items as returns, customer rebates, trade discounts, or volume-based incentive programs for customers.

In a comparative analysis, an analyst may need to reference information disclosed elsewhere in companies' annual reports—typically the notes to the financial statements and the Management Discussion and Analysis (MD&A)—to identify the appropriately comparable revenue amounts. For example, excise taxes represent a significant expenditure for brewing companies. On its income statement, Molson Coors reports $13.47 billion of revenue (labeled "sales") and $11.00 billion of net revenue (labeled "net sales"), which equals sales minus $2.47 billion of excise taxes. Unlike Molson Coors, AB InBev does not show the amount of excise taxes on its income statement. However, in its disclosures, AB InBev notes that excise taxes (amounting to $15.4 billion in 2017) have been deducted from the revenue amount shown on its income statement. Thus, the amount on AB InBev's income statement labeled "revenue" is more comparable to the amount on Molson Coors' income statement labeled "net sales."

Exhibit 1 Anheuser-Busch InBev SA/NV Consolidated Income Statement (in Millions of US Dollars) [Excerpt]

	12 Months Ended December 31		
	2017	**2016**	**2015**
Revenue	$56,444	$45,517	$43,604
Cost of sales	(21,386)	(17,803)	(17,137)
Gross profit	35,058	27,715	26,467
Distribution expenses	(5,876)	(4,543)	(4,259)
Sales and marketing expenses	(8,382)	(7,745)	(6,913)
Administrative expenses	(3,841)	(2,883)	(2,560)
Other operating income/(expenses)	854	732	1,032

(continued)

2 Following net income, the income statement also presents **earnings per share**, the amount of earnings per common share of the company. Earnings per share will be discussed in detail later in this reading, and the per-share display has been omitted from these exhibits to focus on the core income statement.

3 **Sales** is sometimes understood to refer to the sale of goods, whereas *revenue* can include the sale of goods or services; however, the terms are often used interchangeably. In some countries, the term "turnover" may be used in place of revenue.

Exhibit 1 (Continued)

	12 Months Ended December 31		
	2017	2016	2015
Restructuring	(468)	(323)	(171)
Business and asset disposal	(39)	377	524
Acquisition costs business combinations	(155)	(448)	(55)
Impairment of assets	—	—	(82)
Judicial settlement	—	—	(80)
Profit from operations	17,152	12,882	13,904
Finance cost	(6,885)	(9,216)	(3,142)
Finance income	378	652	1,689
Net finance income/(cost)	(6,507)	(8,564)	(1,453)
Share of result of associates and joint ventures	430	16	10
Profit before tax	11,076	4,334	12,461
Income tax expense	(1,920)	(1,613)	(2,594)
Profit from continuing operations	9,155	2,721	9,867
Profit from discontinued operations	28	48	
Profit of the year	9,183	2,769	9,867
Profit from continuing operations attributable to:			
Equity holders of AB InBev	7,968	1,193	8,273
Non-controlling interest	1,187	1,528	1,594
Profit of the year attributable to:			
Equity holders of AB InBev	7,996	1,241	8,273
Non-controlling interest	$1,187	$1,528	$1,594

Note: reported total amounts may have slight discrepancies due to rounding

Exhibit 2 Molson Coors Brewing Company Consolidated Statement of Operations (in Millions of US Dollars) [Excerpt]

	12 Months Ended		
	Dec. 31, 2017	Dec. 31, 2016	Dec. 31, 2015
Sales	$13,471.5	$6,597.4	$5,127.4
Excise taxes	(2,468.7)	(1,712.4)	(1,559.9)
Net sales	11,002.8	4,885.0	3,567.5
Cost of goods sold	(6,217.2)	(2,987.5)	(2,131.6)
Gross profit	4,785.6	1,897.5	1,435.9
Marketing, general and administrative expenses	(3,032.4)	(1,589.8)	(1,038.3)
Special items, net	(28.1)	2,522.4	(346.7)
Equity Income in MillerCoors	0	500.9	516.3
Operating income (loss)	1,725.1	3,331.0	567.2
Other income (expense), net			
Interest expense	(349.3)	(271.6)	(120.3)

Exhibit 2 (Continued)

	12 Months Ended		
	Dec. 31, 2017	Dec. 31, 2016	Dec. 31, 2015
Interest income	6.0	27.2	8.3
Other income (expense), net	(0.1)	(29.7)	0.9
Total other income (expense), net	(343.4)	(274.1)	(111.1)
Income (loss) from continuing operations before income taxes	1,381.7	3,056.9	456.1
Income tax benefit (expense)	53.2	(1,055.2)	(61.5)
Net income (loss) from continuing operations	1,434.9	2,001.7	394.6
Income (loss) from discontinued operations, net of tax	1.5	(2.8)	3.9
Net income (loss) including noncontrolling interests	1,436.4	1,998.9	398.5
Net (income) loss attributable to noncontrolling interests	(22.2)	(5.9)	(3.3)
Net income (loss) attributable to Molson Coors Brewing Company	$1,414.2	$1,993.0	$395.2

Exhibit 3 Groupe Danone Consolidated Income Statement (in Millions of Euros) [Excerpt]

	Year Ended 31 December	
	2016	2017
Sales	21,944	24,677
Cost of goods sold	(10,744)	(12,459)
Selling expense	(5,562)	(5,890)
General and administrative expense	(2,004)	(2,225)
Research and development expense	(333)	(342)
Other income (expense)	(278)	(219)
Recurring operating income	**3,022**	**3,543**
Other operating income (expense)	(99)	192
Operating income	**2,923**	**3,734**
Interest income on cash equivalents and short-term investments	130	151
Interest expense	(276)	(414)
Cost of net debt	(146)	(263)
Other financial income	67	137
Other financial expense	(214)	(312)
Income before tax	**2,630**	**3,296**
Income tax expense	(804)	(842)
Net income from fully consolidated companies	**1,826**	**2,454**
Share of profit of associates	1	109
Net income	1,827	2,563

(continued)

Exhibit 3 (Continued)

	Year Ended 31 December	
	2016	2017
Net income – Group share	**1,720**	**2,453**
Net income – Non-controlling interests	107	110

Differences in presentations of items, such as expenses, are also common. **Expenses** reflect outflows, depletions of assets, and incurrences of liabilities in the course of the activities of a business. Expenses may be grouped and reported in different formats, subject to some specific requirements.

At the bottom of the income statement, companies report net income (companies may use other terms such as "net earnings" or "profit or loss"). For 2017, AB InBev reports $9,183 million "Profit of the year", Molson Coors reports $1,436.4 million of net income including noncontrolling interests, and Danone reports €2,563 million of net income. Net income is often referred to as the "bottom line." The basis for this expression is that net income is the final—or bottom—line item in an income statement. Because net income is often viewed as the single most relevant number to describe a company's performance over a period of time, the term "bottom line" sometimes is used in business to refer to any final or most relevant result.

Despite this customary terminology, note that each company presents additional items below net income: information about how much of that net income is attributable to the company itself and how much of that income is attributable to noncontrolling interests, also known as minority interests. The companies consolidate subsidiaries over which they have control. Consolidation means that they include all of the revenues and expenses of the subsidiaries even if they own less than 100 percent. Noncontrolling interest represents the portion of income that "belongs" to the minority shareholders of the consolidated subsidiaries, as opposed to the parent company itself. For AB InBev, $7,996 million of the total profit is attributable to the shareholders of AB InBev, and $1,187 million is attributable to noncontrolling interests. For Molson Coors, $1,414.2 million is attributable to the shareholders of Molson Coors, and $22.2 million is attributable to noncontrolling interests. For Danone, €2,453 million of the net income amount is attributable to shareholders of Groupe Danone and €110 million is attributable to noncontrolling interests.

Net income also includes **gains** and **losses,** which are increases and decreases in economic benefits, respectively, which may or may not arise in the ordinary activities of the business. For example, when a manufacturing company sells its products, these transactions are reported as revenue, and the costs incurred to generate these revenues are expenses and are presented separately. However, if a manufacturing company sells surplus land that is not needed, the transaction is reported as a gain or a loss. The amount of the gain or loss is the difference between the carrying value of the land and the price at which the land is sold. For example, in Exhibit 1, AB InBev reports a loss (proceeds, net of carrying value) of $39 million on disposals of businesses and assets in fiscal 2017, and gains of $377 million and $524 million in 2016 and 2015, respectively. Details on these gains and losses can typically be found in the companies' disclosures. For example, AB InBev discloses that the $377 million gain in 2016 was mainly from selling one of its breweries in Mexico.

The definition of income encompasses both revenue and gains and the definition of expenses encompasses both expenses that arise in the ordinary activities of the business and losses.[4] Thus, **net income** (profit or loss) can be defined as: a) income minus expenses, or equivalently b) revenue plus other income plus gains minus expenses, or equivalently c) revenue plus other income plus gains minus expenses in the ordinary activities of the business minus other expenses, and minus losses. The last definition can be rearranged as follows: net income equals (i) revenue minus expenses in the ordinary activities of the business, plus (ii) other income minus other expenses, plus (iii) gains minus losses.

In addition to presenting the net income, income statements also present items, including subtotals, which are significant to users of financial statements. Some of the items are specified by IFRS but other items are not specified.[5] Certain items, such as revenue, finance costs, and tax expense, are required to be presented separately on the face of the income statement. IFRS additionally require that line items, headings, and subtotals relevant to understanding the entity's financial performance should be presented even if not specified. Expenses may be grouped together either by their nature or function. Grouping together expenses such as depreciation on manufacturing equipment and depreciation on administrative facilities into a single line item called "depreciation" is an example of a **grouping by nature** of the expense. An example of **grouping by function** would be grouping together expenses into a category such as cost of goods sold, which may include labour and material costs, depreciation, some salaries (e.g., salespeople's), and other direct sales related expenses.[6] All three companies in Exhibits 1 through 3 present their expenses by function, which is sometimes referred to "cost of sales" method.

One subtotal often shown in an income statement is **gross profit** or **gross margin** (that is revenue less cost of sales). When an income statement shows a gross profit subtotal, it is said to use a **multi-step format** rather than a **single-step format**. The AB InBev and Molson Coors income statements are examples of the multi-step format, whereas the Groupe Danone income statement is in a single-step format. For manufacturing and merchandising companies, gross profit is a relevant item and is calculated as revenue minus the cost of the goods that were sold. For service companies, gross profit is calculated as revenue minus the cost of services that were provided. In summary, gross profit is the amount of revenue available after subtracting the costs of delivering goods or services. Other expenses related to running the business are subtracted after gross profit.

Another important subtotal which may be shown on the income statement is **operating profit** (or, synonymously, operating income). Operating profit results from deducting operating expenses such as selling, general, administrative, and research and development expenses from gross profit. Operating profit reflects a company's profits on its business activities before deducting taxes, and for non-financial companies, before deducting interest expense. For financial companies, interest expense would be included in operating expenses and subtracted in arriving at operating profit because it relates to the operating activities for such companies. For some companies composed of a number of separate business segments, operating profit can be useful in evaluating the performance of the individual business segments, because interest and tax expenses may be more relevant at the level of the overall company rather than an individual segment level. The specific calculations of gross profit and operating profit may vary by company, and a reader of financial statements can consult the notes to the statements to identify significant variations across companies.

4 IASB *Conceptual Framework for Financial Reporting (2010)*, paragraphs 4.29 to 4.32.

5 Requirements are presented in IAS 1, *Presentation of Financial Statements.*

6 Later readings will provide additional information about alternative methods to calculate cost of goods sold.

Operating profit is sometimes referred to as EBIT (earnings before interest and taxes). However, operating profit and EBIT are not necessarily the same. Note that in each of the Exhibits 1 through 3, interest and taxes do not represent the only differences between earnings (net income, net earnings) and operating income. For example, AB InBev separately reports its share of associates' and joint ventures' income and Molson Coors separately reports some income from discontinued operations.

Exhibit 4 shows an excerpt from the income statement of CRA International, a company providing management consulting services. Accordingly, CRA deducts cost of services (rather than cost of goods) from revenues to derive gross profit. CRA's fiscal year ends on the Saturday nearest December 31st. Because of this fiscal year timeframe, CRA's fiscal year occasionally comprises 53 weeks rather than 52 weeks. Although the extra week is likely immaterial in computing year-to-year growth rates, it may have a material impact on a quarter containing the extra week. In general, an analyst should be alert to the effect of an extra week when making historical comparisons and forecasting future performance.

Exhibit 4 CRA International Inc. Consolidated Statements of Operations (Excerpt) (in Thousands of Dollars)

	Fiscal Year Ended		
	Dec. 30, 2017	**Dec. 31, 2016**	**Jan. 02, 2016**
Revenues	$370,075	$324,779	$303,559
Costs of services (exclusive of depreciation and amortization)	258,829	227,380	207,650
Selling, general and administrative expenses	86,537	70,584	72,439
Depreciation and amortization	8,945	7,896	6,552
GNU goodwill impairment	—	—	4,524
Income from operations	15,764	18,919	12,394

Note: Remaining items omitted

Exhibits 1 through 4 illustrate basic points about the income statement, including variations across the statements—some of which depend on the industry and/or country, and some of which reflect differences in accounting policies and practices of a particular company. In addition, some differences within an industry are primarily differences in terminology, whereas others are more fundamental accounting differences. Notes to the financial statements are helpful in identifying such differences.

Having introduced the components and format of an income statement, the next objective is to understand the actual reported numbers in it. To accurately interpret reported numbers, the analyst needs to be familiar with the principles of revenue and expense recognition—that is, how revenue and expenses are measured and attributed to a given accounting reporting period.

3 REVENUE RECOGNITION

Revenue is the top line in an income statement, so we begin the discussion of line items in the income statement with revenue recognition. Accounting standards for revenue recognition (which we discuss later in this section) became effective at the beginning of 2018 and are nearly identical under IFRS and US GAAP. The revenue recognition standards for IFRS and US GAAP (IFRS 15 and ASC Topic 606, respectively) were issued in 2014 and resulted from an effort to achieve convergence, consistency, and transparency in revenue recognition globally.

A first task is to explain some relevant accounting terminology. The terms revenue, sales, gains, losses, and net income (profit, net earnings) have been briefly defined. The IASB *Conceptual Framework for Financial Reporting* (2010),[7] referred to hereafter as the *Conceptual Framework*, further defines and discusses these income statement items. The *Conceptual Framework* explains that profit is a frequently used measure of performance and is composed of income and expenses.[8] It defines **income** as follows:

> Income is increases in economic benefits during the accounting period in the form of inflows or enhancements of assets or decreases of liabilities that result in increases in equity, other than those relating to contributions from equity participants.[9]

In IFRS, the term "income" includes revenue and gains. Gains are similar to revenue, but they typically arise from secondary or peripheral activities rather than from a company's primary business activities. For example, for a restaurant, the sale of surplus restaurant equipment for more than its carrying value is referred to as a gain rather than as revenue. Similarly, a loss typically arises from secondary activities. Gains and losses may be considered part of operating activities (e.g., a loss due to a decline in the value of inventory) or may be considered part of non-operating activities (e.g., the sale of non-trading investments).

In the following simple hypothetical scenario, revenue recognition is straightforward: a company sells goods to a buyer for cash and does not allow returns, so the company recognizes revenue when the exchange of goods for cash takes place and measures revenue at the amount of cash received. In practice, however, determining when revenue should be recognized and at what amount is considerably more complex for reasons discussed in the following sections.

3.1 General Principles

An important aspect concerning revenue recognition is that it can occur independently of cash movements. For example, assume a company sells goods to a buyer on credit, so does not actually receive cash until some later time. A fundamental principle of accrual accounting is that revenue is recognized (reported on the income statement) when it is earned, so the company's financial records reflect revenue from the sale when the risk and reward of ownership is transferred; this is often when the company delivers the goods or services. If the delivery was on credit, a related asset, such as trade or accounts receivable, is created. Later, when cash changes hands, the company's financial records simply reflect that cash has been received to settle an account receivable. Similarly, there are situations when a company receives cash in advance and actually delivers the product or service later, perhaps over a period of time. In this case, the company would record a liability for **unearned revenue** when the cash is initially received, and revenue would be recognized as being earned over time as products and services are delivered. An example would be a subscription payment received for a publication that is to be delivered periodically over time.

---

7 The IASB is currently in the process of updating its *Conceptual Framework for Financial Reporting*.

8 *Conceptual Framework*, paragraph 4.24. The text on the elements of financial statements and their recognition and measurement is the same in the IASB *Conceptual Framework for Financial Reporting* (2010) and the IASB *Framework for the Preparation and Presentation of Financial Statements* (1989).

9 Ibid., paragraph 4.25(a).

3.2 Accounting Standards for Revenue Recognition

The converged accounting standards issued by the IASB and FASB in May 2014 introduced some changes to the basic principles of revenue recognition and should enhance comparability.[10] The content of the two standards is nearly identical, and this discussion pertains to both, unless specified otherwise. Issuance of this converged standard is significant because of the differences between IFRS and US GAAP on revenue recognition prior to the converged standard. The converged standard aims to provide a principles-based approach to revenue recognition that can be applied to many types of revenue-generating activities.

The core principle of the converged standard is that revenue should be recognized to "depict the transfer of promised goods or services to customers in an amount that reflects the consideration to which the entity expects to be entitled in an exchange for those goods or services." To achieve the core principle, the standard describes the application of five steps in recognizing revenue:

1 Identify the contract(s) with a customer
2 Identify the separate or distinct performance obligations in the contract
3 Determine the transaction price
4 Allocate the transaction price to the performance obligations in the contract
5 Recognize revenue when (or as) the entity satisfies a performance obligation

According to the standard, a contract is an agreement and commitment, with commercial substance, between the contacting parties. It establishes each party's *obligations* and *rights*, including payment terms. In addition, a contract exists only if collectability is probable. Each standard uses the same wording, but the threshold for probable collectability differs. Under IFRS, probable means more likely than not, and under US GAAP it means likely to occur. As a result, economically similar contracts may be treated differently under IFRS and US GAAP.

The performance obligations within a contract represent promises to transfer distinct good(s) or service(s). A good or service is distinct if the customer can benefit from it on its own or in combination with readily available resources and if the promise to transfer it can be separated from other promises in the contract. Each identified performance obligation is accounted for separately.

The transaction price is what the seller estimates will be received in exchange for transferring the good(s) or service(s) identified in the contract. The transaction price is then allocated to each identified performance obligation. Revenue is recognized when a performance obligation is fulfilled. Steps three and four address amount, and step five addresses timing of recognition. The amount recognized reflects expectations about collectability and (if applicable) an allocation to multiple obligations within the same contract. Revenue is recognized when the obligation-satisfying transfer is made.

Revenue should only be recognized when it is highly probable that it will not be subsequently reversed. This may result in the recording of a minimal amount of revenue upon sale when an estimate of total revenue is not reliable. The balance sheet will be required to reflect the entire refund obligation as a liability and will include an asset for the "right to returned goods" based on the carrying amount of inventory less costs of recovery.

When revenue is recognized, a contract asset is presented on the balance sheet. It is only at the point when all performance obligations have been met except for payment that a receivable appears on the seller's balance sheet. If consideration is received in advance of transferring good(s) or service(s), the seller presents a contract liability.

---

10 *IFRS 15 Revenue from Contracts with Customers* and FASB ASC Topic 606 (Revenue from Contracts with Customers).

The entity will recognize revenue when it is able to satisfy the performance obligation by transferring control to the customer. Factors to consider when assessing whether the customer has obtained control of an asset at a point in time:

- Entity has a present right to payment,
- Customer has legal title,
- Customer has physical possession,
- Customer has the significant risks and rewards of ownership, and
- Customer has accepted the asset.

For a simple contract with only one deliverable at a single point in time, completing the five steps is straight-forward. For more complex contracts—such as when the performance obligations are satisfied over time, when the terms of the multi-period contracts change, when the performance obligation includes various components of goods and services, or when the compensation is "variable"—accounting choices can be less obvious. The steps in the standards are intended to provide guidance that can be generalized to most situations.

In addition, the standard provides many specific examples. These examples are intended to provide guidance as to how to approach more complex contracts. Some of these examples are summarized in Exhibit 5. Note that the end result for many examples may not differ substantially from that under revenue recognition standards that were in effect prior to the adoption of the converged standard; instead it is the conceptual approach and, in some cases, the terminology that will differ.

Exhibit 5 Applying the Converged Revenue Recognition Standard

The references in this exhibit are to Examples in IFRS 15 *Revenue from Contracts with Customers* (and ASU 2014-09 (FASB ASC Topic 606)), on which these summaries are based.

Part 1 (*ref. Example 10*).

Builder Co. enters into a contract with Customer Co. to construct a commercial building. Builder Co. identifies various goods and services to be provided, such as pre-construction engineering, construction of the building's individual components, plumbing, electrical wiring, and interior finishes. With respect to "Identifying the Performance Obligation," should Builder Co. treat each specific item as a separate performance obligation to which revenue should be allocated?

The standard provides two criteria, which must be met, to determine if a good or service is distinct for purposes of identifying performance obligations. First, the customer can benefit from the good or service either on its own or together with other readily available resources. Second, the seller's "promise to transfer the good or service to the customer is separately identifiable from other promises in the contract." In this example, the second criterion is not met because it is the building for which the customer has contracted, not the separate goods and services. The seller will integrate all the goods and services into a combined output and each specific item should not be treated as a distinct good or service but accounted for together as a single performance obligation.

Part 2 (*ref. Example 8*).

Builder Co.'s contract with Customer Co. to construct the commercial building specifies consideration of $1 million. Builder Co.'s expected total costs are $700,000. The Builder incurs $420,000 in costs in the first year. Assuming that costs incurred provide an appropriate measure of progress toward completing the contract, how much revenue should Builder Co. recognize for the first year?

(continued)

Exhibit 5 (Continued)

The standard states that for performance obligations satisfied over time (e.g., where there is a long-term contract), revenue is recognized over time by measuring progress toward satisfying the obligation. In this case, the Builder has incurred 60% of the total expected costs ($420,000/$700,000) and will thus recognize $600,000 (60% × $1 million) in revenue for the first year.

This is the same amount of revenue that would be recognized using the "percentage-of-completion" method under previous accounting standards, but that term is not used in the converged standard. Instead, the standard refers to performance obligations satisfied over time and requires that progress toward complete satisfaction of the performance obligation be measured based on input method such as the one illustrated here (recognizing revenue based on the proportion of total costs that have been incurred in the period) or an output method (recognizing revenue based on units produced or milestones achieved).

Part 3 (*ref. Example 8*).

Assume that Builder Co.'s contract with Customer Co. to construct the commercial building specifies consideration of $1 million *plus* a bonus of $200,000 if the building is completed within 2 years. Builder Co. has only limited experience with similar types of contracts and knows that many factors outside its control (e.g., weather, regulatory requirements) could cause delay. Builder Co.'s expected total costs are $700,000. The Builder incurs $420,000 in costs in the first year. Assuming that costs incurred provide an appropriate measure of progress toward completing the contract, how much revenue should Builder Co. recognize for the first year?

The standard addresses so-called "variable consideration" as part of determining the transaction price. A company is only allowed to recognize variable consideration if it can conclude that it will not have to reverse the cumulative revenue in the future. In this case, Builder Co. does not recognize any of the bonus in year one because it cannot reach the non-reversible conclusion given its limited experience with similar contracts and potential delays from factors outside its control.

Part 4 (*ref. Example 8*).

Assume all facts from Part 3. In the beginning of year two, Builder Co. and Customer Co. agree to change the building floor plan and modify the contract. As a result the consideration will increase by $150,000, and the allowable time for achieving the bonus is extended by 6 months. Builder expects its costs will increase by $120,000. Also, given the additional 6 months to earn the completion bonus, Builder concludes that it now meets the criteria for including the $200,000 bonus in revenue. How should Builder account for this change in the contract?

Note that previous standards did not provide a general framework for contract modifications. The converged standard provides guidance on whether a change in a contract is a new contract or a modification of an existing contract. To be considered a new contract, the change would need to involve goods and services that are distinct from the goods and services already transferred.

In this case, the change does not meet the criteria of a new contract and is therefore considered a modification of the existing contract, which requires the company to reflect the impact on a cumulative catch-up basis. Therefore, the company must update its transaction price and measure of progress. Builder's total revenue on the transaction (transaction price) is now $1.35 million ($1 million original plus the $150,000 new consideration plus $200,000 for the completion bonus). Builder Co.'s progress toward completion is now 51.2% ($420,000 costs

Exhibit 5 (Continued)

incurred divided by total expected costs of $820,000). Based on the changes in the contract, the amount of additional revenue to be recognized is $91,200, calculated as (51.2% × $1.35 million) minus the $600,000 already recognized. The additional $91,200 of revenue would be recognized as a "cumulative catch-up adjustment" on the date of the contract modification.

Part 5 (*ref. Example 45*).

Assume a Company operates a website that enables customers to purchase goods from various suppliers. The customers pay the Company in advance, and orders are nonrefundable. The *suppliers* deliver the goods directly to the customer, and the Company receives a 10% commission. Should the Company report Total Revenues equal to 100% of the sales amount (gross) or Total Revenues equal to 10% of the sales amount (net)? Revenues are reported gross if the Company is acting as a Principal and net if the Company is acting as an Agent.

In this example, the Company is an Agent because it isn't primarily responsible for fulfilling the contract, doesn't take any inventory risk or credit risk, doesn't have discretion in setting the price, and receives compensation in the form of a commission. Because the Company is acting as an Agent, it should report only the amount of commission as its revenue.

Some related costs require specific accounting treatment under the new standards. In particular, incremental costs of obtaining a contract and certain costs incurred to fulfill a contract must be capitalized under the new standards (i.e., reported as an asset on the balance sheet rather than as an expense on the income statement). If a company had previously expensed these incremental costs in the years prior to adopting the converged standard, all else equal, its profitability will initially appear higher under the converged standards.

The disclosure requirements are quite extensive. Companies are required at year end[11] to disclose information about contracts with customers disaggregated into different categories of contracts. The categories might be based on the type of product, the geographic region, the type of customer or sales channel, the type of contract pricing terms, the contract duration, or the timing of transfers. Companies are also required to disclose balances of any contract-related assets and liabilities and significant changes in those balances, remaining performance obligations and transaction price allocated to those obligations, and any significant judgments and changes in judgments related to revenue recognition. Significant judgments are those used in determining timing and amounts of revenue to be recognized.

The converged standard is expected to affect some industries more than others. For example, industries where bundled sales are common, such as the telecommunications and software industries, are expected to be significantly affected by the converged standard.

11 Interim period disclosures are required under IFRS and US GAAP but differ between them.

4 EXPENSE RECOGNITION

Expenses are deducted against revenue to arrive at a company's net profit or loss. Under the IASB *Conceptual Framework*, **expenses** are "decreases in economic benefits during the accounting period in the form of outflows or depletions of assets or incurrences of liabilities that result in decreases in equity, other than those relating to distributions to equity participants."[12]

The IASB *Conceptual Framework* also states:

> The definition of expenses encompasses losses as well as those expenses that arise in the course of the ordinary activities of the enterprise. Expenses that arise in the course of the ordinary activities of the enterprise include, for example, cost of sales, wages and depreciation. They usually take the form of an outflow or depletion of assets such as cash and cash equivalents, inventory, property, plant and equipment.
>
> Losses represent other items that meet the definition of expenses and may, or may not, arise in the course of the ordinary activities of the enterprise. Losses represent decreases in economic benefits and as such they are no different in nature from other expenses. Hence, they are not regarded as a separate element in this *Conceptual Framework*.
>
> Losses include, for example, those resulting from disasters such as fire and flood, as well as those arising on the disposal of non-current assets.[13]

Similar to the issues with revenue recognition, in a simple hypothetical scenario, expense recognition would not be an issue. For instance, assume a company purchased inventory for cash and sold the entire inventory in the same period. When the company paid for the inventory, absent indications to the contrary, it is clear that the inventory cost has been incurred and when that inventory is sold, it should be recognized as an expense (cost of goods sold) in the financial records. Assume also that the company paid all operating and administrative expenses in cash within each accounting period. In such a simple hypothetical scenario, no issues of expense recognition would arise. In practice, however, as with revenue recognition, determining when expenses should be recognized can be somewhat more complex.

4.1 General Principles

In general, a company recognizes expenses in the period that it consumes (i.e., uses up) the economic benefits associated with the expenditure, or loses some previously recognized economic benefit.[14]

A general principle of expense recognition is the **matching principle.** Strictly speaking, IFRS do not refer to a "matching principle" but rather to a "matching concept" or to a process resulting in "matching of costs with revenues."[15] The distinction is relevant in certain standard setting deliberations. Under matching, a company recognizes some expenses (e.g., cost of goods sold) when associated revenues are recognized and thus, expenses and revenues are matched. Associated revenues and expenses are those that result directly and jointly from the same transactions or events. Unlike the simple scenario in which a company purchases inventory and sells all of the inventory within the same accounting period, in practice, it is more likely that some of the current period's sales are made from inventory purchased in a previous

12 IASB *Conceptual Framework*, paragraph 4.25(b).
13 Ibid., paragraphs 4.33–4.35.
14 Ibid., paragraph 4.49.
15 Ibid., paragraph 4.50.

period or previous periods. It is also likely that some of the inventory purchased in the current period will remain unsold at the end of the current period and so will be sold in a following period. Matching requires that a company recognizes cost of goods sold in the same period as revenues from the sale of the goods.

Period costs, expenditures that less directly match revenues, are reflected in the period when a company makes the expenditure or incurs the liability to pay. Administrative expenses are an example of period costs. Other expenditures that also less directly match revenues relate more directly to future expected benefits; in this case, the expenditures are allocated systematically with the passage of time. An example is depreciation expense.

Examples 1 and 2 demonstrate matching applied to inventory and cost of goods sold.

EXAMPLE 1

The Matching of Inventory Costs with Revenues

Kahn Distribution Limited (KDL), a hypothetical company, purchases inventory items for resale. At the beginning of 2018, Kahn had no inventory on hand. During 2018, KDL had the following transactions:

Inventory Purchases		
First quarter	2,000	units at $40 per unit
Second quarter	1,500	units at $41 per unit
Third quarter	2,200	units at $43 per unit
Fourth quarter	1,900	units at $45 per unit
Total	7,600	units at a total cost of $321,600

KDL sold 5,600 units of inventory during the year at $50 per unit, and received cash. KDL determines that there were 2,000 remaining units of inventory and specifically identifies that 1,900 were those purchased in the fourth quarter and 100 were purchased in the third quarter. What are the revenue and expense associated with these transactions during 2018 based on specific identification of inventory items as sold or remaining in inventory? (Assume that the company does not expect any products to be returned.)

Solution:

The revenue for 2018 would be $280,000 (5,600 units × $50 per unit). Initially, the total cost of the goods purchased would be recorded as inventory (an asset) in the amount of $321,600. During 2018, the cost of the 5,600 units sold would be expensed (matched against the revenue) while the cost of the 2,000 remaining unsold units would remain in inventory as follows:

Cost of Goods Sold		
From the first quarter	2,000 units at $40 per unit =	$80,000
From the second quarter	1,500 units at $41 per unit =	$61,500
From the third quarter	2,100 units at $43 per unit =	$90,300
Total cost of goods sold		$231,800
Cost of Goods Remaining in Inventory		
From the third quarter	100 units at $43 per unit =	$4,300
From the fourth quarter	1,900 units at $45 per unit =	$85,500
Total remaining (or ending) inventory cost		$89,800

To confirm that total costs are accounted for: $231,800 + $89,800 = $321,600. The cost of the goods sold would be expensed against the revenue of $280,000 as follows:

Revenue	$280,000
Cost of goods sold	231,800
Gross profit	$48,200

An alternative way to think about this is that the company created an asset (inventory) of $321,600 as it made its purchases. At the end of the period, the value of the company's inventory on hand is $89,800. Therefore, the amount of the Cost of goods sold expense recognized for the period should be the difference: $231,800.

The remaining inventory amount of $89,800 will be matched against revenue in a future year when the inventory items are sold.

EXAMPLE 2

Alternative Inventory Costing Methods

In Example 1, KDL was able to specifically identify which inventory items were sold and which remained in inventory to be carried over to later periods. This is called the **specific identification method** and inventory and cost of goods sold are based on their physical flow. It is generally not feasible to specifically identify which items were sold and which remain on hand, so accounting standards permit the assignment of inventory costs to costs of goods sold and to ending inventory using cost formulas (IFRS terminology) or cost flow assumptions (US GAAP). The cost formula or cost flow assumption determines which goods are assumed to be sold and which goods are assumed to remain in inventory. Both IFRS and US GAAP permit the use of the first in, first out (FIFO) method, and the weighted average cost method to assign costs.

Under the **FIFO method**, the oldest goods purchased (or manufactured) are assumed to be sold first and the newest goods purchased (or manufactured) are assumed to remain in inventory. Cost of goods in beginning inventory and costs of the first items purchased (or manufactured) flow into cost of goods sold first, as if the earliest items purchased sold first. Ending inventory would, therefore, include the most recent purchases. It turns out that those items specifically identified as sold in Example 1 were also the first items purchased, so in this example, under FIFO, the cost of goods sold would also be $231,800, calculated as above.

The **weighted average cost method** assigns the average cost of goods available for sale to the units sold and remaining in inventory. The assignment is based on the average cost per unit (total cost of goods available for sale/total units available for sale) and the number of units sold and the number remaining in inventory.

For KDL, the weighted average cost per unit would be

$321,600/7,600 units = $42.3158 per unit

Cost of goods sold using the weighted average cost method would be

5,600 units at $42.3158 = $236,968

Ending inventory using the weighted average cost method would be

2,000 units at $42.3158 = $84,632

Another method is permitted under US GAAP but is not permitted under IFRS. This is the last in, first out (LIFO) method. Under the **LIFO method**, the newest goods purchased (or manufactured) are assumed to be sold first and the oldest goods purchased (or manufactured) are assumed to remain in inventory. Costs of the latest items purchased flow into cost of goods sold first, as if the most recent items purchased were sold first. Although this may seem contrary to common sense, it is logical in certain circumstances. For example, lumber in a lumberyard may be stacked up with the oldest lumber on the bottom. As lumber is sold, it is sold from the top of the stack, so the last lumber purchased and put in inventory is the first lumber out. Theoretically, a company should choose a method linked to the physical inventory flows.[16] Under the LIFO method, in the KDL example, it would be assumed that the 2,000 units remaining in ending inventory would have come from the first quarter's purchases:[17]

Ending inventory 2,000 units at $40 per unit = $80,000

The remaining costs would be allocated to cost of goods sold under LIFO:

Total costs of $321,600 less $80,000 remaining in ending inventory = $241,600

Alternatively, the cost of the last 5,600 units purchased is allocated to cost of goods sold under LIFO:

1,900 units at $45 per unit + 2,200 units at $43 per unit + 1,500 units at $41 per unit = $241,600

An alternative way to think about expense recognition is that the company created an asset (inventory) of $321,600 as it made its purchases. At the end of the period, the value of the company's inventory is $80,000. Therefore, the amount of the Cost of goods sold expense recognized for the period should be the difference: $241,600.

Exhibit 6 summarizes and compares inventory costing methods.

(continued)

16 Practically, the reason some companies choose to use LIFO in the United States is to reduce taxes. When prices and inventory quantities are rising, LIFO will normally result in higher cost of goods sold and lower income and hence lower taxes. US tax regulations require that if LIFO is used on a company's tax return, it must also be used on the company's GAAP financial statements.

17 If data on the precise timing of quarterly sales were available, the answer would differ because the cost of goods sold would be determined during the quarter rather than at the end of the quarter.

Exhibit 6 Summary Table on Inventory Costing Methods

Method	Description	Cost of Goods Sold When Prices Are Rising, Relative to Other Two Methods	Ending Inventory When Prices Are Rising, Relative to Other Two Methods
FIFO (first in, first out)	Costs of the earliest items purchased flow to cost of goods sold first	Lowest	Highest
LIFO (last in, first out)	Costs of the most recent items purchased flow to cost of goods sold first	Highest*	Lowest*
Weighted average cost	Averages total costs over total units available	Middle	Middle

*Assumes no LIFO layer liquidation. **LIFO layer liquidation** occurs when the volume of sales exceeds the volume of purchases in the period so that some sales are assumed to be made from existing, relatively low-priced inventory rather than from more recent purchases.

4.2 Issues in Expense Recognition

The following sections cover applications of the principles of expense recognition to certain common situations.

4.2.1 *Doubtful Accounts*

When a company sells its products or services on credit, it is likely that some customers will ultimately default on their obligations (i.e., fail to pay). At the time of the sale, it is not known which customer will default. (If it were known that a particular customer would ultimately default, presumably a company would not sell on credit to that customer.) One possible approach to recognizing credit losses on customer receivables would be for the company to wait until such time as a customer defaulted and only then recognize the loss (**direct write-off method**). Such an approach would usually not be consistent with generally accepted accounting principles.

Under the matching principle, at the time revenue is recognized on a sale, a company is required to record an estimate of how much of the revenue will ultimately be uncollectible. Companies make such estimates based on previous experience with uncollectible accounts. Such estimates may be expressed as a proportion of the overall amount of sales, the overall amount of receivables, or the amount of receivables overdue by a specific amount of time. The company records its estimate of uncollectible amounts as an expense on the income statement, not as a direct reduction of revenues.

4.2.2 *Warranties*

At times, companies offer warranties on the products they sell. If the product proves deficient in some respect that is covered under the terms of the warranty, the company will incur an expense to repair or replace the product. At the time of sale, the company does not know the amount of future expenses it will incur in connection with its warranties. One possible approach would be for a company to wait until actual expenses are incurred under the warranty and to reflect the expense at that time. However, this would not result in a matching of the expense with the associated revenue.

Under the matching principle, a company is required to estimate the amount of future expenses resulting from its warranties, to recognize an estimated warranty expense in the period of the sale, and to update the expense as indicated by experience over the life of the warranty.

4.2.3 *Depreciation and Amortisation*

Companies commonly incur costs to obtain long-lived assets. **Long-lived assets** are assets expected to provide economic benefits over a future period of time greater than one year. Examples are land (property), plant, equipment, and **intangible assets** (assets lacking physical substance) such as trademarks. The costs of most long-lived assets are allocated over the period of time during which they provide economic benefits. The two main types of long-lived assets whose costs are *not* allocated over time are land and those intangible assets with indefinite useful lives.

Depreciation is the process of systematically allocating costs of long-lived assets over the period during which the assets are expected to provide economic benefits. "Depreciation" is the term commonly applied to this process for physical long-lived assets such as plant and equipment (land is not depreciated), and **amortisation** is the term commonly applied to this process for intangible long-lived assets with a finite useful life.[18] Examples of intangible long-lived assets with a finite useful life include an acquired mailing list, an acquired patent with a set expiration date, and an acquired copyright with a set legal life. The term "amortisation" is also commonly applied to the systematic allocation of a premium or discount relative to the face value of a fixed-income security over the life of the security.

IFRS allow two alternative models for valuing property, plant, and equipment: the cost model and the revaluation model.[19] Under the cost model, the depreciable amount of that asset (cost less residual value) is allocated on a systematic basis over the remaining useful life of the asset. Under the cost model, the asset is reported at its cost less any accumulated depreciation. Under the revaluation model, the asset is reported at its fair value. The revaluation model is not permitted under US GAAP. Although the revaluation model is permitted under IFRS, as noted earlier, it is not as widely used and thus we focus on the cost model here. There are two other differences between IFRS and US GAAP to note: IFRS require each component of an asset to be depreciated separately and US GAAP do not require component depreciation; and IFRS require an annual review of residual value and useful life, and US GAAP do not explicitly require such a review.

The method used to compute depreciation should reflect the pattern over which the economic benefits of the asset are expected to be consumed. IFRS do not prescribe a particular method for computing depreciation but note that several methods are commonly used, such as the straight-line method, diminishing balance method (accelerated depreciation), and the units of production method (depreciation varies depending upon production or usage).

The **straight-line method** allocates evenly the cost of long-lived assets less estimated residual value over the estimated useful life of an asset. (The term "straight line" derives from the fact that the annual depreciation expense, if represented as a line graph over time, would be a straight line. In addition, a plot of the cost of the asset minus the cumulative amount of annual depreciation expense, if represented as a line graph over time, would be a straight line with a negative downward slope.) Calculating depreciation and amortisation requires two significant estimates: the estimated useful life of an asset and the estimated residual value (also known as "salvage value") of an asset. Under IFRS, the residual value is the amount that the company expects to receive upon sale of the asset at the end of its useful life. Example 3 assumes that an item of equipment is depreciated using the straight-line method and illustrates how

---

18 Intangible assets with indefinite life are not amortised. Instead, they are reviewed each period as to the reasonableness of continuing to assume an indefinite useful life and are tested at least annually for impairment (i.e., if the recoverable or fair value of an intangible asset is materially lower than its value in the company's books, the value of the asset is considered to be impaired and its value must be decreased). IAS 38, *Intangible Assets* and FASB ASC Topic 350 [Intangibles–Goodwill and Other].

19 IAS No. 16, *Property, Plant, and Equipment.*

the annual depreciation expense varies under different estimates of the useful life and estimated residual value of an asset. As shown, annual depreciation expense is sensitive to both the estimated useful life and to the estimated residual value.

EXAMPLE 3

Sensitivity of Annual Depreciation Expense to Varying Estimates of Useful Life and Residual Value

Using the straight-line method of depreciation, annual depreciation expense is calculated as:

$$\frac{\text{Cost} - \text{Residual value}}{\text{Estimated useful life}}$$

Assume the cost of an asset is $10,000. If, for example, the residual value of the asset is estimated to be $0 and its useful life is estimated to be 5 years, the annual depreciation expense under the straight-line method would be ($10,000 – $0)/5 years = $2,000. In contrast, holding the estimated useful life of the asset constant at 5 years but increasing the estimated residual value of the asset to $4,000 would result in annual depreciation expense of only $1,200 [calculated as ($10,000 – $4,000)/5 years]. Alternatively, holding the estimated residual value at $0 but increasing the estimated useful life of the asset to 10 years would result in annual depreciation expense of only $1,000 [calculated as ($10,000 – $0)/10 years]. Exhibit 7 shows annual depreciation expense for various combinations of estimated useful life and residual value.

Exhibit 7 Annual Depreciation Expense (in Dollars)

Estimated Useful Life (Years)	Estimated Residual Value					
	0	1,000	2,000	3,000	4,000	5,000
2	5,000	4,500	4,000	3,500	3,000	2,500
4	2,500	2,250	2,000	1,750	1,500	1,250
5	2,000	1,800	1,600	1,400	1,200	1,000
8	1,250	1,125	1,000	875	750	625
10	1,000	900	800	700	600	500

Generally, alternatives to the straight-line method of depreciation are called **accelerated methods** of depreciation because they accelerate (i.e., speed up) the timing of depreciation. Accelerated depreciation methods allocate a greater proportion of the cost to the early years of an asset's useful life. These methods are appropriate if the plant or equipment is expected to be used up faster in the early years (e.g., an automobile). A commonly used accelerated method is the **diminishing balance method**, (also known as the declining balance method). The diminishing balance method is demonstrated in Example 4.

EXAMPLE 4

An Illustration of Diminishing Balance Depreciation

Assume the cost of computer equipment was $11,000, the estimated residual value is $1,000, and the estimated useful life is five years. Under the diminishing or declining balance method, the first step is to determine the straight-line rate, the rate at which the asset would be depreciated under the straight-line method. This rate is measured as 100 percent divided by the useful life or 20 percent for a five-year useful life. Under the straight-line method, 1/5 or 20 percent of the depreciable cost of the asset (here, $11,000 – $1,000 = $10,000) would be expensed each year for five years: The depreciation expense would be $2,000 per year.

The next step is to determine an acceleration factor that approximates the pattern of the asset's wear. Common acceleration factors are 150 percent and 200 percent. The latter is known as **double declining balance depreciation** because it depreciates the asset at double the straight-line rate. Using the 200 percent acceleration factor, the diminishing balance rate would be 40 percent (20 percent × 2.0). This rate is then applied to the remaining undepreciated balance of the asset each period (known as the **net book value**).

At the beginning of the first year, the net book value is $11,000. Depreciation expense for the first full year of use of the asset would be 40 percent of $11,000, or $4,400. Under this method, the residual value, if any, is generally not used in the computation of the depreciation each period (the 40 percent is applied to $11,000 rather than to $11,000 minus residual value). However, the company will stop taking depreciation when the salvage value is reached.

At the beginning of Year 2, the net book value is measured as

Asset cost	$11,000
Less: Accumulated depreciation	(4,400)
Net book value	$6,600

For the second full year, depreciation expense would be $6,600 × 40 percent, or $2,640. At the end of the second year (i.e., beginning of the third year), a total of $7,040 ($4,400 + $2,640) of depreciation would have been recorded. So, the remaining net book value at the beginning of the third year would be

Asset cost	$11,000
Less: Accumulated depreciation	(7,040)
Net book value	$3,960

For the third full year, depreciation would be $3,960 × 40 percent, or $1,584. At the end of the third year, a total of $8,624 ($4,400 + $2,640 + $1,584) of depreciation would have been recorded. So, the remaining net book value at the beginning of the fourth year would be

Asset cost	$11,000
Less: Accumulated depreciation	(8,624)
Net book value	$2,376

For the fourth full year, depreciation would be $2,376 × 40 percent, or $950. At the end of the fourth year, a total of $9,574 ($4,400 + $2,640 + $1,584 + $950) of depreciation would have been recorded. So, the remaining net book value at the beginning of the fifth year would be

Asset cost	$11,000
Less: Accumulated depreciation	(9,574)
Net book value	$1,426

For the fifth year, if deprecation were determined as in previous years, it would amount to $570 ($1,426 × 40 percent). However, this would result in a remaining net book value of the asset below its estimated residual value of $1,000. So, instead, only $426 would be depreciated, leaving a $1,000 net book value at the end of the fifth year.

Asset cost	$11,000
Less: Accumulated depreciation	(10,000)
Net book value	$1,000

Companies often use a zero or small residual value, which creates problems for diminishing balance depreciation because the asset never fully depreciates. In order to fully depreciate the asset over the initially estimated useful life when a zero or small residual value is assumed, companies often adopt a depreciation policy that combines the diminishing balance and straight-line methods. An example would be a deprecation policy of using double-declining balance depreciation and switching to the straight-line method halfway through the useful life.

Under accelerated depreciation methods, there is a higher depreciation expense in early years relative to the straight-line method. This results in higher expenses and lower net income in the early depreciation years. In later years, there is a reversal with accelerated depreciation expense lower than straight-line depreciation. Accelerated depreciation is sometimes referred to as a conservative accounting choice because it results in lower net income in the early years of asset use.

For those intangible assets that must be amortised (those with an identifiable useful life), the process is the same as for depreciation; only the name of the expense is different. IFRS state that if a pattern cannot be determined over the useful life, then the straight-line method should be used.[20] In most cases under IFRS and US GAAP, amortisable intangible assets are amortised using the straight-line method with no residual value. **Goodwill**[21] and intangible assets with indefinite life are not amortised. Instead, they are tested at least annually for impairment (i.e., if the current value of an intangible asset or goodwill is materially lower than its value in the company's books, the value of the asset is considered to be impaired and its value in the company's books must be decreased).

In summary, to calculate depreciation and amortisation, a company must choose a method, estimate the asset's useful life, and estimate residual value. Clearly, different choices have a differing effect on depreciation or amortisation expense and, therefore, on reported net income.

20 IAS 38, *Intangible Assets*.

21 Goodwill is recorded in acquisitions and is the amount by which the price to purchase an entity exceeds the amount of net identifiable assets acquired (the total amount of identifiable assets acquired less liabilities assumed).

4.3 Implications for Financial Analysis

A company's estimates for doubtful accounts and/or for warranty expenses can affect its reported net income. Similarly, a company's choice of depreciation or amortisation method, estimates of assets' useful lives, and estimates of assets' residual values can affect reported net income. These are only a few of the choices and estimates that affect a company's reported net income.

As with revenue recognition policies, a company's choice of expense recognition can be characterized by its relative conservatism. A policy that results in recognition of expenses later rather than sooner is considered less conservative. In addition, many items of expense require the company to make estimates that can significantly affect net income. Analysis of a company's financial statements, and particularly comparison of one company's financial statements with those of another, requires an understanding of differences in these estimates and their potential impact.

If, for example, a company shows a significant year-to-year change in its estimates of uncollectible accounts as a percentage of sales, warranty expenses as a percentage of sales, or estimated useful lives of assets, the analyst should seek to understand the underlying reasons. Do the changes reflect a change in business operations (e.g., lower estimated warranty expenses reflecting recent experience of fewer warranty claims because of improved product quality)? Or are the changes seemingly unrelated to changes in business operations and thus possibly a signal that a company is manipulating estimates in order to achieve a particular effect on its reported net income?

As another example, if two companies in the same industry have dramatically different estimates for uncollectible accounts as a percentage of their sales, warranty expenses as a percentage of sales, or estimated useful lives as a percentage of assets, it is important to understand the underlying reasons. Are the differences consistent with differences in the two companies' business operations (e.g., lower uncollectible accounts for one company reflecting a different, more creditworthy customer base or possibly stricter credit policies)? Another difference consistent with differences in business operations would be a difference in estimated useful lives of assets if one of the companies employs newer equipment. Or, alternatively, are the differences seemingly inconsistent with differences in the two companies' business operations, possibly signaling that a company is manipulating estimates?

Information about a company's accounting policies and significant estimates are described in the notes to the financial statements and in the management discussion and analysis section of a company's annual report.

When possible, the monetary effect of differences in expense recognition policies and estimates can facilitate more meaningful comparisons with a single company's historical performance or across a number of companies. An analyst can use the monetary effect to adjust the reported expenses so that they are on a comparable basis.

Even when the monetary effects of differences in policies and estimates cannot be calculated, it is generally possible to characterize the relative conservatism of the policies and estimates and, therefore, to qualitatively assess how such differences might affect reported expenses and thus financial ratios.

NON-RECURRING ITEMS AND NON-OPERATING ITEMS 5

From a company's income statements, we can see its earnings from last year and in the previous year. Looking forward, the question is: What will the company earn next year and in the years after?

To assess a company's future earnings, it is helpful to separate those prior years' items of income and expense that are likely to continue in the future from those items that are less likely to continue.[22] Some items from prior years are clearly not expected to continue in the future periods and are separately disclosed on a company's income statement. This is consistent with "An entity shall present additional line items, headings, and subtotals ... when such presentation is relevant to an understanding of the entity's financial performance."[23] IFRS describe considerations that enter into the decision to present information other than that explicitly specified by a standard. Both IFRS and US GAAP specify that the results of discontinued operations should be reported separately from continuing operations. Other items that may be reported separately on a company's income statement, such as unusual items, items that occur infrequently, effects due to accounting changes, and non-operating income, require the analyst to make some judgments.

5.1 Discontinued Operations

When a company disposes of or establishes a plan to dispose of one of its component operations and will have no further involvement in the operation, the income statement reports separately the effect of this disposal as a "discontinued" operation under both IFRS and US GAAP. Financial standards provide various criteria for reporting the effect separately, which are generally that the discontinued component must be separable both physically and operationally.[24]

In Exhibit 1, AB InBev reported profit from discontinued operations of $28 million in 2017 and $48 million in 2016. In Exhibit 2, Molson Coors reported income from discontinued operations of $1.5 million and $3.9 million in 2017 and 2015, respectively, and a loss from discontinued operations of $2.8 million in 2016.

Because the discontinued operation will no longer provide earnings (or cash flow) to the company, an analyst may eliminate discontinued operations in formulating expectations about a company's future financial performance.

5.2 Unusual or Infrequent Items

IFRS require that items of income or expense that are material and/or relevant to the understanding of the entity's financial performance should be disclosed separately. Unusual or infrequent items are likely to meet these criteria. Under US GAAP, material items that are unusual or infrequent, and that are both as of reporting periods beginning after December 15, 2015, are shown as part of a company's continuing operations but are presented separately. For example, restructuring charges, such as costs to close plants and employee termination costs, are considered part of a company's ordinary activities. As another example, gains and losses arising when a company sells an asset or part of a business, for more or less than its carrying value, are also disclosed separately on the income statement. These sales are considered ordinary business activities.

Highlighting the unusual or infrequent nature of these items assists an analyst in judging the likelihood that such items will reoccur. This meets the IFRS criteria of disclosing items that are relevant to the understanding of an entity's financial performance. In Exhibit 2, Molson Coors' income statement showed a separate line item for "Special Items, net." The company's footnotes provide details on the amount and

---

22 In business writing, items expected to continue in the future are often described as "persistent" or "permanent," whereas those not expected to continue are described as "transitory."

23 IAS No. 1, *Presentation of Financial Statements*, paragraph 85.

24 IFRS No. 5, *Non-Current Assets Held for Sale and Discontinued Operations*, paragraphs 31–33.

explain that this line includes revenues or expenses that either they "do not believe to be indicative of [their] core operations, or they believe are significant to [their] current operating results warranting separate classification". In Exhibit 3, the income statement of Danone shows an amount for "Recurring operating income" followed by a separate line item for "other operating income (expense)", which is not included as a component of recurring income. Exhibit 8 presents an excerpt from Danone's additional disclosure about this non-recurring amount.

Exhibit 8 Highlighting Infrequent Nature of Items—Excerpt from Groupe Danone footnotes to its 2017 financial statements

NOTE 6. Events and Transactions Outside the Group's Ordinary Activities [Excerpt]

"Other operating income (expense) is defined under Recommendation 2013-03 of the French CNC relating to the format of consolidated financial statements prepared under international accounting standards, and comprises significant items that, because of their exceptional nature, cannot be viewed as inherent to Danone's current activities. These mainly include capital gains and losses on disposals of fully consolidated companies, impairment charges on goodwill, significant costs related to strategic restructuring and major external growth transactions, and incurred or estimated costs related to major crises and major litigation. Furthermore, in connection with Revised IFRS 3 and Revised IAS 27, Danone also classifies in Other operating income (expense) (i) acquisition costs related to business combinations, (ii) revaluation profit or loss accounted for following a loss of control, and (iii) changes in earn-outs related to business combinations and subsequent to the acquisition date.

"In 2017, the net Other operating income of €192 million consisted mainly of the following items:

(in € millions)	**Related income (expense)**
Capital gain on disposal of Stonyfield	628
Compensation received following the decision of the Singapore arbitration court in the Fonterra case	105
Territorial risks, mainly in certain countries in the ALMA region	(148)
Costs associated with the integration of WhiteWave	(118)
Impairment of several intangible assets in Waters and Specialized Nutrition Reporting entities	(115)
Remainder of table omitted	

In Exhibit 8, Danone provides details on items considered to be "exceptional" items and not "inherent" to the company's current activities. The exceptional items include gains on asset disposals, receipts from a legal case, costs of integrating an acquisition, and impairment of intangible assets, among others. Generally, in forecasting future operations, an analyst would assess whether the items reported are likely to reoccur and also possible implications for future earnings. It is generally not advisable simply to ignore all unusual items.

5.3 Changes in Accounting Policies

At times, standard setters issue new standards that require companies to change accounting policies. Depending on the standard, companies may be permitted to adopt the standards prospectively (in the future) or retrospectively (restate financial statements as though the standard existed in the past). In other cases, changes in accounting policies (e.g., from one acceptable inventory costing method to another) are made for other reasons, such as providing a better reflection of the company's performance. Changes in accounting policies are reported through retrospective application[25] unless it is impractical to do so.

Retrospective application means that the financial statements for all fiscal years shown in a company's financial report are presented as if the newly adopted accounting principle had been used throughout the entire period. Notes to the financial statements describe the change and explain the justification for the change. Because changes in accounting principles are retrospectively applied, the financial statements that appear within a financial report are comparable.

Example 5 presents an excerpt from Microsoft Corporation's Form 10-K for the fiscal year ended 30 June 2018 describing a change in accounting principle resulting from the new revenue recognition standard. Microsoft elected to adopt the new standard 1 July 2017, earlier than the required adoption date. Microsoft also elected to use the "full retrospective method," which requires companies to restate prior periods' results. On its income statement, both 2016 and 2017 are presented as if the new standard had been used throughout both years. In the footnotes to its financial statements, Microsoft discloses the impact of the new standard.

EXAMPLE 5

Microsoft Corporation Excerpt from Footnotes to the Financial Statements

> The most significant impact of the [new revenue recognition] standard relates to our accounting for software license revenue. Specifically, for Windows 10, we recognize revenue predominantly at the time of billing and delivery rather than ratably over the life of the related device. For certain multi-year commercial software subscriptions that include both distinct software licenses and SA, we recognize license revenue at the time of contract execution rather than over the subscription period. Due to the complexity of certain of our commercial license subscription contracts, the actual revenue recognition treatment required under the standard depends on contract-specific terms and in some instances may vary from recognition at the time of billing. Revenue recognition related to our hardware, cloud offerings (such as Office 365), LinkedIn, and professional services remains substantially unchanged. Refer to Impacts to Previously Reported Results below for the impact of adoption of the standard in our consolidated financial statements.

25 IAS No. 8, *Accounting Policies, Changes in Accounting Estimates and Errors*, and FASB ASC Topic 250 [Accounting Changes and Error Corrections].

(In $ millions, except per share amounts)	As Previously Reported	New Revenue Standard Adjustment	As Restated
Income Statements			
Year Ended June 30, 2017			
Revenue	89,950	6,621	96,571
Provision for income taxes	1,945	2,467	4,412
Net income	21,204	4,285	25,489
Diluted earnings per share	2.71	0.54	3.25
Year Ended June 30, 2016			
Revenue	85,320	5,834	91,154
Provision for income taxes	2,953	2,147	5,100
Net income	16,798	3,741	20,539
Diluted earnings per share	2.1	0.46	2.56

Question: Based on the above information, describe whether Microsoft's results appear better or worse under the new revenue recognition standard.

Solution:

Microsoft's results appear better under the new revenue recognition standard. Revenues and income are higher under the new standard. The net profit margin is higher under the new standard. For 2017, the net profit margin is 26.4% (= 25,489/96,571) under the new standard versus 23.6% (= 21,204/89,950) under the old standard. Reported revenue grew faster under the new standard. Revenue growth under the new standard was 5.9% [= (96,571/91,154) – 1] compared to 5.4% [= (89,950/85,320) – 1)] under the old standard.

Microsoft's presentation of the effects of the new revenue recognition enables an analyst to identify the impact of the change in accounting standards.

Note that the new revenue recognition standard also offered companies the option of using a "modified retrospective" method of adoption. Under the modified retrospective approach, companies were not required to revise previously reported financial statements. Instead, they adjusted opening balances of retained earnings (and other applicable accounts) for the cumulative impact of the new standard.

In contrast to changes in accounting policies (such as whether to expense the cost of employee stock options), companies sometimes make *changes in accounting estimates* (such as the useful life of a depreciable asset). Changes in accounting estimates are handled prospectively, with the change affecting the financial statements for the period of change and future periods. No adjustments are made to prior statements, and the adjustment is not shown on the face of the income statement. Significant changes should be disclosed in the notes. Exhibit 9 provides an excerpt from the annual Form 10-K of Catalent Inc., a US-based biotechnology company, that illustrates a change in accounting estimate.

Exhibit 9 Change in Accounting Estimate

Catalent Inc. discloses a change in the method it uses to calculate both annual expenses related to its defined benefit pension plans. Rather than use a single, weighted-average discount rate in its calculations, the company will use the spot rates applicable to each projected cash flow.

> **Post-Retirement and Pension Plans**
>
> ...The measurement of the related benefit obligations and the net periodic benefit costs recorded each year are based upon actuarial computations, which require management's judgment as to certain assumptions. These assumptions include the discount rates used in computing the present value of the benefit obligations and the net periodic benefit costs...
>
> Effective June 30, 2016, the approach used to estimate the service and interest components of net periodic benefit cost for benefit plans was changed to provide a more precise measurement of service and interest costs. Historically, the Company estimated these service and interest components utilizing a single weighted-average discount rate derived from the yield curve used to measure the benefit obligation at the beginning of the period. Going forward, the Company has elected to utilize an approach that discounts the individual expected cash flows using the applicable spot rates derived from the yield curve over the projected cash flow period. The Company has accounted for this change as a change in accounting estimate that is inseparable from a change in accounting principle and accordingly has accounted for it prospectively.

Another possible adjustment is a *correction of an error for a prior period* (e.g., in financial statements issued for an earlier year). This cannot be handled by simply adjusting the current period income statement. Correction of an error for a prior period is handled by restating the financial statements (including the balance sheet, statement of owners' equity, and cash flow statement) for the prior periods presented in the current financial statements.[26] Note disclosures are required regarding the error. These disclosures should be examined carefully because they may reveal weaknesses in the company's accounting systems and financial controls.

5.4 Non-Operating Items

Non-operating items are typically reported separately from operating income because they are material and/or relevant to the understanding of the entity's financial performance. Under IFRS, there is no definition of operating activities, and companies that choose to report operating income or the results of operating activities should ensure that these represent activities that are normally regarded as operating. Under US GAAP, operating activities generally involve producing and delivering goods and providing services and include all transactions and other events that are not defined as investing or financing activities.[27] For example, if a non-financial service company invests in equity or debt securities issued by another company, any interest, dividends, or profits from sales of these securities will be shown as non-operating income. In

26 Ibid.
27 FASB ASC *Master Glossary.*

general, for non-financial services companies,[28] non-operating income that is disclosed separately on the income statement (or in the notes) includes amounts earned through investing activities.

Among non-operating items on the income statement (or accompanying notes), non-financial service companies also disclose the interest expense on their debt securities, including amortisation of any discount or premium. The amount of interest expense is related to the amount of a company's borrowings and is generally described in the notes to the financial statements. For financial service companies, interest income and expense are likely components of operating activities. (Note that the characterization of interest and dividends as non-operating items on the income statement is not necessarily consistent with the classification on the statement of cash flows. Specifically, under IFRS, interest and dividends received can be shown either as operating or as investing on the statement of cash flows, while under US GAAP interest and dividends received are shown as operating cash flows. Under IFRS, interest and dividends paid can be shown either as operating or as financing on the statement of cash flows, while under US GAAP, interest paid is shown as operating and dividends paid are shown as financing.)

In practice, companies often disclose the interest expense and income separately, along with a net amount. For example, in Exhibit 1, ABN InBev's 2017 income statement shows finance cost of $6,885 million, finance income of $378 million, and net finance cost of $6,507 million. Similarly, in Exhibit 3, Danone's 2017 income statement shows interest income of €130, interest expense of €276, and cost of net debt of €146.

For purposes of assessing a company's future performance, the amount of financing expense will depend on the company's financing policy (target capital structure) and borrowing costs. The amount of investing income will depend on the purpose and success of investing activities. For a non-financial company, a significant amount of financial income would typically warrant further exploration. What are the reasons underlying the company's investments in the securities of other companies? Is the company simply investing excess cash in short-term securities to generate income higher than cash deposits, or is the company purchasing securities issued by other companies for strategic reasons, such as access to raw material supply or research?

EARNINGS PER SHARE

6

One metric of particular importance to an equity investor is earnings per share (EPS). EPS is an input into ratios such as the price/earnings ratio. Additionally, each shareholder in a company owns a different number of shares. IFRS require the presentation of EPS on the face of the income statement for net profit or loss (net income) and profit or loss (income) from continuing operations.[29] Similar presentation is required under US GAAP.[30] This section outlines the calculations for EPS and explains how the calculation differs for a simple versus complex capital structure.

28 Examples of financial services companies are insurance companies, banks, brokers, dealers, and investment companies.
29 IAS No. 33, *Earnings Per Share.*
30 FASB ASC Topic 260 [Earnings Per Share].

6.1 Simple versus Complex Capital Structure

A company's capital is composed of its equity and debt. Some types of equity have preference over others, and some debt (and other instruments) may be converted into equity. Under IFRS, the type of equity for which EPS is presented is referred to as ordinary. **Ordinary shares** are those equity shares that are subordinate to all other types of equity. The ordinary shareholders are basically the owners of the company—the equity holders who are paid last in a liquidation of the company and who benefit the most when the company does well. Under US GAAP, this ordinary equity is referred to as **common stock** or **common shares**, reflecting US language usage. The terms "ordinary shares," "common stock," and "common shares" are used interchangeably in the following discussion.

When a company has issued any financial instruments that are potentially convertible into common stock, it is said to have a complex capital structure. Examples of financial instruments that are potentially convertible into common stock include convertible bonds, convertible preferred stock, employee stock options, and warrants.[31] If a company's capital structure does not include such potentially convertible financial instruments, it is said to have a simple capital structure.

The distinction between simple versus complex capital structure is relevant to the calculation of EPS because financial instruments that are potentially convertible into common stock could, as a result of conversion or exercise, potentially dilute (i.e., decrease) EPS. Information about such a potential dilution is valuable to a company's current and potential shareholders; therefore, accounting standards require companies to disclose what their EPS would be if all dilutive financial instruments were converted into common stock. The EPS that would result if all dilutive financial instruments were converted is called **diluted EPS**. In contrast, **basic EPS** is calculated using the reported earnings available to common shareholders of the parent company and the weighted average number of shares outstanding.

Companies are required to report both basic and diluted EPS as well as amounts for continuing operations. Exhibit 10 shows the per share amounts reported by AB InBev at the bottom of its income statement that was presented in Exhibit 1. The company's basic EPS ("before dilution") was $4.06, and diluted EPS ("after dilution") was $3.98 for 2017. In addition, in the same way that AB InBev's income statement shows income from continuing operations separately from total income, EPS from continuing operations is also shown separately from total EPS. For 2017, the basic and diluted EPS from continuing operations were $4.04 and $3.96, respectively. Across all measures, AB InBev's EPS was much higher in 2017 than in 2016. An analyst would seek to understand the causes underlying the changes in EPS, a topic we will address following an explanation of the calculations of both basic and diluted EPS.

Exhibit 10 AB InBev's Earnings Per Share

	12 Months Ended December 31		
	2017	**2016**	**2015**
Basic earnings per share	$4.06	$0.72	$5.05
Diluted earnings per share	3.98	0.71	4.96

31 A warrant is a call option typically attached to securities issued by a company, such as bonds. A warrant gives the holder the right to acquire the company's stock from the company at a specified price within a specified time period. IFRS and US GAAP standards regarding earnings per share apply equally to call options, warrants, and equivalent instruments.

Exhibit 10 (Continued)

	12 Months Ended December 31		
	2017	2016	2015
Basic earnings per share from continuing operations	4.04	0.69	5.05
Diluted earnings per share from continuing operations	$3.96	$0.68	$4.96

6.2 Basic EPS

Basic EPS is the amount of income available to common shareholders divided by the weighted average number of common shares outstanding over a period. The amount of income available to common shareholders is the amount of net income remaining after preferred dividends (if any) have been paid. Thus, the formula to calculate basic EPS is:

$$\text{Basic EPS} = \frac{\text{Net income} - \text{Preferred dividends}}{\text{Weighted average number of shares outstanding}} \quad (1)$$

The weighted average number of shares outstanding is a time weighting of common shares outstanding. For example, assume a company began the year with 2,000,000 common shares outstanding and repurchased 100,000 common shares on 1 July. The weighted average number of common shares outstanding would be the sum of 2,000,000 shares × 1/2 year + 1,900,000 shares × 1/2 year, or 1,950,000 shares. So the company would use 1,950,000 shares as the weighted average number of shares in calculating its basic EPS.

If the number of shares of common stock increases as a result of a stock dividend or a stock split, the EPS calculation reflects the change retroactively to the beginning of the period.

Examples 6, 7, and 8 illustrate the computation of basic EPS.

EXAMPLE 6

A Basic EPS Calculation (1)

For the year ended 31 December 2018, Shopalot Company had net income of $1,950,000. The company had 1,500,000 shares of common stock outstanding, no preferred stock, and no convertible financial instruments. What is Shopalot's basic EPS?

Solution:

Shopalot's basic EPS is $1.30 ($1,950,000 divided by 1,500,000 shares).

EXAMPLE 7

A Basic EPS Calculation (2)

For the year ended 31 December 2018, Angler Products had net income of $2,500,000. The company declared and paid $200,000 of dividends on preferred stock. The company also had the following common stock share information:

Shares outstanding on 1 January 2018	1,000,000
Shares issued on 1 April 2018	200,000
Shares repurchased (treasury shares) on 1 October 2018	(100,000)
Shares outstanding on 31 December 2018	1,100,000

1 What is the company's weighted average number of shares outstanding?

2 What is the company's basic EPS?

Solution to 1:

The weighted average number of shares outstanding is determined by the length of time each quantity of shares was outstanding:

1,000,000 × (3 months/12 months) =	250,000
1,200,000 × (6 months/12 months) =	600,000
1,100,000 × (3 months/12 months) =	275,000
Weighted average number of shares outstanding	1,125,000

Solution to 2:

Basic EPS = (Net income – Preferred dividends)/Weighted average number of shares = ($2,500,000 – $200,000)/1,125,000 = $2.04

EXAMPLE 8

A Basic EPS Calculation (3)

Assume the same facts as Example 7 except that on 1 December 2018, a previously declared 2-for-1 stock split took effect. Each shareholder of record receives two shares in exchange for each current share that he or she owns. What is the company's basic EPS?

Solution:

For EPS calculation purposes, a stock split is treated as if it occurred at the beginning of the period. The weighted average number of shares would, therefore, be 2,250,000, and the basic EPS would be $1.02 [= ($2,500,000 – $200,000)/2,250,000].

6.3 Diluted EPS

If a company has a simple capital structure (in other words, one that includes no potentially dilutive financial instruments), then its basic EPS is equal to its diluted EPS. However, if a company has potentially dilutive financial instruments, its diluted EPS may differ from its basic EPS. Diluted EPS, by definition, is always equal to or less than basic EPS. The sections below describe the effects of three types of potentially dilutive financial instruments on diluted EPS: convertible preferred, convertible debt, and employee stock options. The final section explains why not all potentially dilutive financial instruments actually result in a difference between basic and diluted EPS.

6.3.1 *Diluted EPS When a Company Has Convertible Preferred Stock Outstanding*

When a company has convertible preferred stock outstanding, diluted EPS is calculated using the **if-converted method**. The if-converted method is based on what EPS would have been if the convertible preferred securities had been converted at the beginning of the period. In other words, the method calculates what the effect would have been if the convertible preferred shares converted at the beginning of the period. If the convertible shares had been converted, there would be two effects. First, the convertible preferred securities would no longer be outstanding; instead, additional common stock would be outstanding. Thus, under the if-converted method, the weighted average number of shares outstanding would be higher than in the basic EPS calculation. Second, if such a conversion had taken place, the company would not have paid preferred dividends. Thus, under the if-converted method, the net income available to common shareholders would be higher than in the basic EPS calculation.

Diluted EPS using the if-converted method for convertible preferred stock is equal to net income divided by the weighted average number of shares outstanding from the basic EPS calculation plus the additional shares of common stock that would be issued upon conversion of the preferred. Thus, the formula to calculate diluted EPS using the if-converted method for preferred stock is:

$$\text{Diluted EPS} = \frac{(\text{Net income})}{\left(\begin{array}{l}\text{Weighted average number of shares}\\ \text{outstanding + New common shares that}\\ \text{would have been issued at conversion}\end{array}\right)} \tag{2}$$

A diluted EPS calculation using the if-converted method for preferred stock is provided in Example 9.

EXAMPLE 9

A Diluted EPS Calculation Using the If-Converted Method for Preferred Stock

For the year ended 31 December 2018, Bright-Warm Utility Company (fictitious) had net income of $1,750,000. The company had an average of 500,000 shares of common stock outstanding, 20,000 shares of convertible preferred, and no other potentially dilutive securities. Each share of preferred pays a dividend of $10 per share, and each is convertible into five shares of the company's common stock. Calculate the company's basic and diluted EPS.

Solution:

If the 20,000 shares of convertible preferred had each converted into 5 shares of the company's common stock, the company would have had an additional 100,000 shares of common stock (5 shares of common for each of the 20,000 shares of preferred). If the conversion had taken place, the company would not have paid preferred dividends of $200,000 ($10 per share for each of the 20,000 shares of preferred). As shown in Exhibit 11, the company's basic EPS was $3.10 and its diluted EPS was $2.92.

Exhibit 11 Calculation of Diluted EPS for Bright-Warm Utility Company Using the If-Converted Method: Case of Preferred Stock

	Basic EPS	Diluted EPS Using If-Converted Method
Net income	$1,750,000	$1,750,000
Preferred dividend	–200,000	0
Numerator	$1,550,000	$1,750,000

(continued)

Exhibit 11 (Continued)

	Basic EPS	Diluted EPS Using If-Converted Method
Weighted average number of shares outstanding	500,000	500,000
Additional shares issued if preferred converted	0	100,000
Denominator	500,000	600,000
EPS	**$3.10**	**$2.92**

6.3.2 *Diluted EPS When a Company Has Convertible Debt Outstanding*

When a company has convertible debt outstanding, the diluted EPS calculation also uses the if-converted method. Diluted EPS is calculated as if the convertible debt had been converted at the beginning of the period. If the convertible debt had been converted, the debt securities would no longer be outstanding; instead, additional shares of common stock would be outstanding. Also, if such a conversion had taken place, the company would not have paid interest on the convertible debt, so the net income available to common shareholders would increase by the after-tax amount of interest expense on the debt converted.

Thus, the formula to calculate diluted EPS using the if-converted method for convertible debt is:

$$\text{Diluted EPS} = \frac{\left(\begin{array}{l}\text{Net income} + \text{After-tax interest on}\\ \text{convertible debt} - \text{Preferred dividends}\end{array}\right)}{\left(\begin{array}{l}\text{Weighted average number of shares}\\ \text{outstanding} + \text{Additional common}\\ \text{shares that would have been}\\ \text{issued at conversion}\end{array}\right)} \quad (3)$$

A diluted EPS calculation using the if-converted method for convertible debt is provided in Example 10.

EXAMPLE 10

A Diluted EPS Calculation Using the If-Converted Method for Convertible Debt

Oppnox Company (fictitious) reported net income of $750,000 for the year ended 31 December 2018. The company had a weighted average of 690,000 shares of common stock outstanding. In addition, the company has only one potentially dilutive security: $50,000 of 6 percent convertible bonds, convertible into a total of 10,000 shares. Assuming a tax rate of 30 percent, calculate Oppnox's basic and diluted EPS.

Solution:

If the debt securities had been converted, the debt securities would no longer be outstanding and instead, an additional 10,000 shares of common stock would be outstanding. Also, if the debt securities had been converted, the company would not have paid interest of $3,000 on the convertible debt, so net income available to common shareholders would have increased by $2,100 [= $3,000(1 – 0.30)] on an after-tax basis. Exhibit 12 illustrates the calculation of diluted EPS using the if-converted method for convertible debt.

Exhibit 12 Calculation of Diluted EPS for Oppnox Company Using the If-Converted Method: Case of a Convertible Bond

	Basic EPS	Diluted EPS Using If-Converted Method
Net income	$750,000	$750,000
After-tax cost of interest		2,100
Numerator	$750,000	$752,100
Weighted average number of shares outstanding	690,000	690,000
If converted	0	10,000
Denominator	690,000	700,000
EPS	**$1.09**	**$1.07**

6.3.3 *Diluted EPS When a Company Has Stock Options, Warrants, or Their Equivalents Outstanding*

When a company has stock options, warrants, or their equivalents[32] outstanding, diluted EPS is calculated as if the financial instruments had been exercised and the company had used the proceeds from exercise to repurchase as many shares of common stock as possible at the average market price of common stock during the period. The weighted average number of shares outstanding for diluted EPS is thus increased by the number of shares that would be issued upon exercise minus the number of shares that would have been purchased with the proceeds. This method is called the **treasury stock method** under US GAAP because companies typically hold repurchased shares as treasury stock. The same method is used under IFRS but is not named.

For the calculation of diluted EPS using this method, the assumed exercise of these financial instruments would have the following effects:

- The company is assumed to receive cash upon exercise and, in exchange, to issue shares.
- The company is assumed to use the cash proceeds to repurchase shares at the weighted average market price during the period.

32 Hereafter, options, warrants, and their equivalents will be referred to simply as "options" because the accounting treatment for EPS calculations is interchangeable for these instruments under IFRS and US GAAP.

As a result of these two effects, the number of shares outstanding would increase by the incremental number of shares issued (the difference between the number of shares issued to the holders and the number of shares assumed to be repurchased by the company). For calculating diluted EPS, the incremental number of shares is weighted based upon the length of time the financial instrument was outstanding in the year. If the financial instrument was issued prior to the beginning of the year, the weighted average number of shares outstanding increases by the incremental number of shares. If the financial instruments were issued during the year, then the incremental shares are weighted by the amount of time the financial instruments were outstanding during the year.

The assumed exercise of these financial instruments would not affect net income. For calculating EPS, therefore, no change is made to the numerator. The formula to calculate diluted EPS using the treasury stock method (same method as used under IFRS but not named) for options is:

$$\text{Diluted EPS} = \frac{(\text{Net income} - \text{Preferred dividends})}{\begin{array}{l}[\text{Weighted average number of shares} \\ \text{outstanding} + (\text{New shares that would} \\ \text{have been issued at option exercise} - \\ \text{Shares that could have been purchased} \\ \text{with cash received upon exercise}) \times \\ (\text{Proportion of year during which the} \\ \text{financial instruments were outstanding})]\end{array}} \quad (4)$$

A diluted EPS calculation using the treasury stock method for options is provided in Example 11.

EXAMPLE 11

A Diluted EPS Calculation Using the Treasury Stock Method for Options

Hihotech Company (fictitious) reported net income of $2.3 million for the year ended 30 June 2018 and had a weighted average of 800,000 common shares outstanding. At the beginning of the fiscal year, the company has outstanding 30,000 options with an exercise price of $35. No other potentially dilutive financial instruments are outstanding. Over the fiscal year, the company's market price has averaged $55 per share. Calculate the company's basic and diluted EPS.

Solution:

Using the treasury stock method, we first calculate that the company would have received $1,050,000 ($35 for each of the 30,000 options exercised) if all the options had been exercised. The options would no longer be outstanding; instead, 30,000 shares of common stock would be outstanding. Under the treasury stock method, we assume that shares would be repurchased with the cash received upon exercise of the options. At an average market price of $55 per share, the $1,050,000 proceeds from option exercise, the company could have repurchased 19,091 shares. Therefore, the incremental number of shares issued is 10,909 (calculated as 30,000 minus 19,091). For the diluted EPS calculation, no change is made to the numerator. As shown in Exhibit 13, the company's basic EPS was $2.88 and the diluted EPS was $2.84.

Exhibit 13 Calculation of Diluted EPS for Hihotech Company Using the Treasury Stock Method: Case of Stock Options

	Basic EPS	Diluted EPS Using Treasury Stock Method
Net income	$2,300,000	$2,300,000
Numerator	$2,300,000	$2,300,000
Weighted average number of shares outstanding	800,000	800,000
If converted	0	10,909
Denominator	800,000	810,909
EPS	**$2.88**	**$2.84**

As noted, IFRS require a similar computation but does not refer to it as the "treasury stock method." The company is required to consider that any assumed proceeds are received from the issuance of new shares at the average market price for the period. These new "inferred" shares would be disregarded in the computation of diluted EPS, but the excess of the new shares that would be issued under options contracts minus the new inferred shares would be added to the weighted average number of shares outstanding. The results are the same as the treasury stock method, as shown in Example 12.

EXAMPLE 12

Diluted EPS for Options under IFRS

Assuming the same facts as in Example 11, calculate the weighted average number of shares outstanding for diluted EPS under IFRS.

Solution:

If the options had been exercised, the company would have received $1,050,000. If this amount had been received from the issuance of new shares at the average market price of $55 per share, the company would have issued 19,091 shares. IFRS refer to the 19,091 shares the company would have issued at market prices as the inferred shares. The number of shares issued under options (30,000) minus the number of inferred shares (19,091) equals 10,909. This amount is added to the weighted average number of shares outstanding of 800,000 to get diluted shares of 810,909. Note that this is the same result as that obtained under US GAAP; it is just derived in a different manner.

6.3.4 *Other Issues with Diluted EPS*

It is possible that some potentially convertible securities could be **antidilutive** (i.e., their inclusion in the computation would result in an EPS higher than the company's basic EPS). Under IFRS and US GAAP, antidilutive securities are not included in the calculation of diluted EPS. Diluted EPS should reflect the maximum potential dilution from conversion or exercise of potentially dilutive financial instruments. Diluted EPS will always be less than or equal to basic EPS. Example 13 provides an illustration of an antidilutive security.

EXAMPLE 13

An Antidilutive Security

For the year ended 31 December 2018, Dim-Cool Utility Company (fictitious) had net income of $1,750,000. The company had an average of 500,000 shares of common stock outstanding, 20,000 shares of convertible preferred, and no other potentially dilutive securities. Each share of preferred pays a dividend of $10 per share, and each is convertible into three shares of the company's common stock. What was the company's basic and diluted EPS?

Solution:

If the 20,000 shares of convertible preferred had each converted into 3 shares of the company's common stock, the company would have had an additional 60,000 shares of common stock (3 shares of common for each of the 20,000 shares of preferred). If the conversion had taken place, the company would not have paid preferred dividends of $200,000 ($10 per share for each of the 20,000 shares of preferred). The effect of using the if-converted method would be EPS of $3.13, as shown in Exhibit 14. Because this is greater than the company's basic EPS of $3.10, the securities are said to be antidilutive and the effect of their conversion would not be included in diluted EPS. Diluted EPS would be the same as basic EPS (i.e., $3.10).

Exhibit 14 Calculation for an Antidilutive Security

	Basic EPS	Diluted EPS Using If-Converted Method	
Net income	$1,750,000	$1,750,000	
Preferred dividend	–200,000	0	
Numerator	$1,550,000	$1,750,000	
Weighted average number of shares outstanding	500,000	500,000	
If converted	0	60,000	
Denominator	500,000	560,000	
EPS	**$3.10**	$3.13	←Exceeds basic EPS; security is antidilutive and, therefore, **not** included. **Reported diluted EPS = $3.10.**

6.4 Changes in EPS

Having explained the calculations of both basic and diluted EPS, we return to an examination of changes in EPS. As noted above, AB InBev's fully diluted EPS from continuing operations increased from \$0.68 in 2016 to \$3.96 in 2017. In general, an increase in EPS results from an increase in net income, a decrease in the number of shares outstanding, or a combination of both. In the notes to its financial statements (not shown), AB InBev discloses that the weighted average number of shares for both the basic and fully-diluted calculations was greater in 2017 than in 2016. Thus, for AB InBev, the improvement in EPS from 2016 to 2017 was driven by an increase in net income. Changes in the numerator and denominator explain the changes in EPS arithmetically. To understand the business drivers of those changes requires further research. The next section presents analytical tools that an analyst can use to highlight areas for further examination.

ANALYSIS OF THE INCOME STATEMENT

7

In this section, we apply two analytical tools to analyze the income statement: common-size analysis and income statement ratios. The objective of this analysis is to assess a company's performance over a period of time—compared with its own past performance or the performance of another company.

7.1 Common-Size Analysis of the Income Statement

Common-size analysis of the income statement can be performed by stating each line item on the income statement as a percentage of revenue.[33] Common-size statements facilitate comparison across time periods (time series analysis) and across companies (cross-sectional analysis) because the standardization of each line item removes the effect of size.

To illustrate, Panel A of Exhibit 15 presents an income statement for three hypothetical companies in the same industry. Company A and Company B, each with \$10 million in sales, are larger (as measured by sales) than Company C, which has only \$2 million in sales. In addition, Companies A and B both have higher operating profit: \$2 million and \$1.5 million, respectively, compared with Company C's operating profit of only \$400,000.

How can an analyst meaningfully compare the performance of these companies? By preparing a common-size income statement, as illustrated in Panel B, an analyst can readily see that the percentages of Company C's expenses and profit relative to its sales are exactly the same as for Company A. Furthermore, although Company C's operating profit is lower than Company B's in absolute dollars, it is higher in percentage terms (20 percent for Company C compared with only 15 percent for Company B). For each \$100 of sales, Company C generates \$5 more operating profit than Company B. In other words, Company C is relatively more profitable than Company B based on this measure.

The common-size income statement also highlights differences in companies' strategies. Comparing the two larger companies, Company A reports significantly higher gross profit as a percentage of sales than does Company B (70 percent compared

33 This format can be distinguished as "vertical common-size analysis." As the reading on financial statement analysis discusses, there is another type of common-size analysis, known as "horizontal common-size analysis," that states items in relation to a selected base year value. Unless otherwise indicated, text references to "common-size analysis" refer to vertical analysis.

with 25 percent). Given that both companies operate in the same industry, why can Company A generate so much higher gross profit? One possible explanation is found by comparing the operating expenses of the two companies. Company A spends significantly more on research and development and on advertising than Company B. Expenditures on research and development likely result in products with superior technology. Expenditures on advertising likely result in greater brand awareness. So, based on these differences, it is likely that Company A is selling technologically superior products with a better brand image. Company B may be selling its products more cheaply (with a lower gross profit as a percentage of sales) but saving money by not investing in research and development or advertising. In practice, differences across companies are more subtle, but the concept is similar. An analyst, noting significant differences, would do more research and seek to understand the underlying reasons for the differences and their implications for the future performance of the companies.

Exhibit 15

Panel A: Income Statements for Companies A, B, and C ($)

	A	B	C
Sales	$10,000,000	$10,000,000	$2,000,000
Cost of sales	3,000,000	7,500,000	600,000
Gross profit	7,000,000	2,500,000	1,400,000
Selling, general, and administrative expenses	1,000,000	1,000,000	200,000
Research and development	2,000,000	—	400,000
Advertising	2,000,000	—	400,000
Operating profit	2,000,000	1,500,000	400,000

Panel B: Common-Size Income Statements for Companies A, B, and C (%)

	A	B	C
Sales	100%	100%	100%
Cost of sales	30	75	30
Gross profit	70	25	70
Selling, general, and administrative expenses	10	10	10
Research and development	20	0	20
Advertising	20	0	20
Operating profit	20	15	20

Note: Each line item is expressed as a percentage of the company's sales.

For most expenses, comparison to the amount of sales is appropriate. However, in the case of taxes, it is more meaningful to compare the amount of taxes with the amount of pretax income. Using note disclosure, an analyst can then examine the causes for differences in effective tax rates. To project the companies' future net income, an analyst would project the companies' pretax income and apply an estimated effective tax rate determined in part by the historical tax rates.

Vertical common-size analysis of the income statement is particularly useful in cross-sectional analysis—comparing companies with each other for a particular time period or comparing a company with industry or sector data. The analyst could select individual peer companies for comparison, use industry data from published sources, or compile data from databases based on a selection of peer companies or broader industry data. For example, Exhibit 16 presents median common-size income statement data compiled for the components of the S&P 500 classified into the 10 S&P/MSCI Global Industrial Classification System (GICS) sectors using 2017 data. Note that when compiling aggregate data such as this, some level of aggregation is necessary and less detail may be available than from peer company financial statements. The performance of an individual company can be compared with industry or peer company data to evaluate its relative performance.

Exhibit 16 Median Common-Size Income Statement Statistics for the S&P 500 Classified by S&P/MSCI GICS Sector Data for 2017

	Energy	Materials	Industrials	Consumer Discretionary	Consumer Staples	Health Care
Number of observations	34	27	69	81	34	59
Gross Margin	37.7%	33.0%	36.8%	37.6%	43.4%	59.0%
Operating Margin	6.4%	14.9%	13.5%	11.0%	17.2%	17.4%
Net Profit Margin	4.9%	9.9%	8.8%	6.0%	10.9%	7.2%

	Financials	Information Technology	Telecommunication Services	Utilities	Real Estate
Number of observations	63	64	4	29	29
Gross Margin	40.5%	62.4%	56.4%	34.3%	39.8%
Operating Margin	36.5%	21.1%	15.4%	21.7%	30.1%
Net Profit Margin	18.5%	11.3%	13.1%	10.1%	21.3%

Source: Based on data from Compustat. Operating margin based on EBIT (earnings before interest and taxes.)

7.2 Income Statement Ratios

One aspect of financial performance is profitability. One indicator of profitability is **net profit margin,** also known as **profit margin** and **return on sales,** which is calculated as net income divided by revenue (or sales).[34]

$$\text{Net profit margin} = \frac{\text{Net income}}{\text{Revenue}}$$

Net profit margin measures the amount of income that a company was able to generate for each dollar of revenue. A higher level of net profit margin indicates higher profitability and is thus more desirable. Net profit margin can also be found directly on the common-size income statements.

For AB InBev, net profit margin based on continuing operations for 2017 was 16.2 percent (calculated as profit from continuing operations of $9,155 million, divided by revenue of $56,444 million). To judge this ratio, some comparison is needed. AB InBev's profitability can be compared with that of another company or with its own previous performance. Compared with previous years, AB InBev's profitability is higher than in 2016 but lower than 2015. In 2016, net profit margin based on continuing operations was 6.0 percent, and in 2015, it was 22.9 percent.

34 In the definition of margin ratios of this type, "sales" is often used interchangeably with "revenue." "Return on sales" has also been used to refer to a class of profitability ratios having revenue in the denominator.

Another measure of profitability is the gross profit margin. Gross profit (gross margin) is calculated as revenue minus cost of goods sold, and the **gross profit margin** is calculated as the gross profit divided by revenue.

$$\text{Gross profit margin} = \frac{\text{Gross profit}}{\text{Revenue}}$$

The gross profit margin measures the amount of gross profit that a company generated for each dollar of revenue. A higher level of gross profit margin indicates higher profitability and thus is generally more desirable, although differences in gross profit margins across companies reflect differences in companies' strategies. For example, consider a company pursuing a strategy of selling a differentiated product (e.g., a product differentiated based on brand name, quality, superior technology, or patent protection). The company would likely be able to sell the differentiated product at a higher price than a similar, but undifferentiated, product and, therefore, would likely show a higher gross profit margin than a company selling an undifferentiated product. Although a company selling a differentiated product would likely show a higher gross profit margin, this may take time. In the initial stage of the strategy, the company would likely incur costs to create a differentiated product, such as advertising or research and development, which would not be reflected in the gross margin calculation.

AB InBev's gross profit (shown in Exhibit 1) was \$35,058 million in 2017, \$27,715 million in 2016, and \$26,467 million in 2015. Expressing gross profit as a percentage of revenues, we see that the gross profit margin was 62.1 percent in 2017, 60.9 percent in 2016, and 60.7 percent in 2015. In absolute terms, AB InBev's gross profit was higher in 2016 than in 2015. However, AB InBev's gross profit *margin* was lower in 2016 than in 2015.

Exhibit 17 presents a common-size income statement for AB InBev, and highlights certain profitability ratios. The net profit margin and gross profit margin described above are just two of the many subtotals that can be generated from common-size income statements. Other "margins" used by analysts include the **operating profit margin** (profit from operations divided by revenue) and the **pretax margin** (profit before tax divided by revenue).

Exhibit 17 AB InBev's Margins: Abbreviated Common-Size Income Statement

	12 Months Ended December 31					
	2017		2016		2015	
	$	%	$	%	$	%
Revenue	56,444	100.0	45,517	100.0	43,604	100.0
Cost of sales	(21,386)	(37.9)	(17,803)	(39.1)	(17,137)	(39.3)
Gross profit	**35,058**	**62.1**	**27,715**	**60.9**	**26,467**	**60.7**
Distribution expenses	(5,876)	(10.4)	(4,543)	(10.0)	(4,259)	(9.8)
Sales and marketing expenses	(8,382)	(14.9)	(7,745)	(17.0)	(6,913)	(15.9)
Administrative expenses	(3,841)	(6.8)	(2,883)	(6.3)	(2,560)	(5.9)
		Portions omitted				
Profit from operations	**17,152**	**30.4**	**12,882**	**28.3**	**13,904**	**31.9**
Finance cost	(6,885)	(12.2)	(9,382)	(20.6)	(3,142)	(7.2)
Finance income	378	0.7	818	1.8	1,689	3.9
Net finance income/(cost)	(6,507)	(11.5)	(8,564)	(18.8)	(1,453)	(3.3)
Share of result of associates and joint ventures	430	0.8	16	0.0	10	0.0

Exhibit 17 (Continued)

	12 Months Ended December 31					
	2017		2016		2015	
	$	%	$	%	$	%
Profit before tax	**11,076**	**19.6**	**4,334**	**9.5**	**12,461**	**28.6**
Income tax expense	(1,920)	(3.4)	(1,613)	(3.5)	(2,594)	(5.9)
Profit from continuing operations	**9,155**	**16.2**	**2,721**	**6.0**	**9,867**	**22.6**
Profit from discontinued operations	28	0.0	48	0.1		—
Profit of the year	**9,183**	**16.3**	**2,769**	**6.1**	**9,867**	**22.6**

The profitability ratios and the common-size income statement yield quick insights about changes in a company's performance. For example, AB InBev's decrease in profitability in 2016 was not driven by a decrease in gross profit margin. Gross profit margin in 2016 was actually slightly higher than in 2015. The company's decrease in profitability in 2016 was driven in part by higher operating expenses and, in particular, by a significant increase in finance costs. The increased finance costs resulted from the 2016 merger with SABMiller. Valued at more than $100 billion, the acquisition was one of the largest in history. The combination of AB InBev and SABMiller also explains the increase in revenue from around $45 billion to over $56 billion. The profitability ratios and the common-size income statement thus serve to highlight areas about which an analyst might wish to gain further understanding.

COMPREHENSIVE INCOME

8

The general expression for net income is revenue minus expenses. There are, however, certain items of revenue and expense that, by accounting convention, are excluded from the net income calculation. To understand how reported shareholders' equity of one period links with reported shareholders' equity of the next period, we must understand these excluded items, known as **other comprehensive income**. Under IFRS, other comprehensive income includes items of income and expense that are "not recognized in profit or loss as required or permitted by other IFRS." **Total comprehensive income** is "the change in equity during a period resulting from transaction and other events, other than those changes resulting from transactions with owners in their capacity as owners."[35]

Under US GAAP, **comprehensive income** is defined as "the change in equity [net assets] of a business enterprise during a period from transactions and other events and circumstances from non-owner sources. It includes all changes in equity during a period except those resulting from investments by owners and distributions to owners."[36] While the wording differs, comprehensive income is conceptually the same under IFRS and US GAAP.

Comprehensive income includes *both* net income and other revenue and expense items that are excluded from the net income calculation (collectively referred to as Other Comprehensive Income). Assume, for example, a company's beginning shareholders' equity is €110 million, its net income for the year is €10 million, its cash

35 IAS 1, *Presentation of Financial Statements.*

36 FASB ASC Section 220-10-05 [Comprehensive Income–Overall–Overview and Background].

dividends for the year are €2 million, and there was no issuance or repurchase of common stock. If the company's actual ending shareholders' equity is €123 million, then €5 million [€123 – (€110 + €10 – €2)] has bypassed the net income calculation by being classified as other comprehensive income. If the company had no other comprehensive income, its ending shareholders' equity would have been €118 million [€110 + €10 – €2].

Four types of items are treated as other comprehensive income under both IFRS and US GAAP. (The specific treatment of some of these items differs between the two sets of standards, but these types of items are common to both.)

- Foreign currency translation adjustments. In consolidating the financial statements of foreign subsidiaries, the effects of translating the subsidiaries' balance sheet assets and liabilities at current exchange rates are included as other comprehensive income.
- Unrealized gains or losses on derivatives contracts accounted for as hedges. Changes in the fair value of derivatives are recorded each period, but certain changes in value are treated as other comprehensive income and thus bypass the income statement.
- Unrealized holding gains and losses on a certain category of investment securities, namely, available-for-sale debt securities under US GAAP and securities designated as "fair value through other comprehensive income" under IFRS. (Note: IFRS, but not US GAAP, also includes a category of equity investments designated at fair value through other comprehensive income.)
- Certain costs of a company's defined benefit post-retirement plans that are not recognized in the current period.

In addition, under IFRS, other comprehensive income includes certain changes in the value of long-lived assets that are measured using the revaluation model rather than the cost model. Also, under IFRS, companies are not permitted to reclassify certain items of other comprehensive income to profit or loss, and companies must present separately the items of other comprehensive income that will and will not be reclassified subsequently to profit or loss.

The third type of item listed above is perhaps the simplest to illustrate. Holding gains on securities arise when a company owns securities over an accounting period, during which time the securities' value increases. Similarly, holding losses on securities arise when a company owns securities over a period during which time the securities' value decreases. If the company has not sold the securities (i.e., has not realized the gain or loss), its holding gain or loss is said to be unrealized. The question is: Should the company exclude unrealized gains and losses from income; reflect these unrealized holding gains and losses in its income statement (i.e., statement of profit and loss); or reflect these unrealized holding gains as other comprehensive income?

According to accounting standards, the answer depends on how the company has categorized the securities. Categorization depends on what the company intends to do with the securities (i.e., the business model for managing the asset) and on the cash flows of the security. Unrealized gains and losses are excluded from income for debt securities that the company intends to hold to maturity. These held-to-maturity debt securities are reported at their amortized cost, so no unrealized gains or losses are reported. For other securities reported at fair value, the unrealized gains or losses are reflected either in the income statement or as other comprehensive income.

Under US GAAP, unrealized gains and losses are reflected in the income statement for: (a) debt securities designated as **trading securities**; and (b) all investments in equity securities (other than investments giving rise to ownership positions that confer significant influence over the investee). The trading securities category pertains to a debt security that is acquired with the intent of selling it rather than holding it to collect the interest and principal payments. Also, under US GAAP, unrealized gains and losses are reflected as other comprehensive income for debt securities designated as **available-for-sale** securities. Available-for-sale debt securities are those not designated as either held-to-maturity or trading.

Under IFRS, unrealized gains and losses are reflected in the income statement for: (a) investments in equity investments, unless the company makes an irrevocable election otherwise; and (b) debt securities, if the securities do not fall into the other measurement categories or if the company makes an irrevocable election to show gains and losses on the income statement. These debt and equity investments are referred to as being measured at *fair value through profit or loss.* Also under IFRS, unrealized gains and losses are reflected as other comprehensive income for: (a) "debt securities held within a business model whose objective is achieved both by collecting contractual cash flows and selling financial assets"; and (b) equity investments for which the company makes an irrevocable election at initial recognition to show gains and losses as part of other comprehensive income. These debt and equity investments are referred to as being measured at *fair value through other comprehensive income.* Accounting for these securities is similar to accounting for US GAAP's available-for-sale debt securities.

Even where unrealized holding gains and losses are excluded from a company's net income (profit and loss), they are *included* in other comprehensive income and thus form a part of a company's comprehensive income.

EXAMPLE 14

Other Comprehensive Income

Assume a company's beginning shareholders' equity is €200 million, its net income for the year is €20 million, its cash dividends for the year are €3 million, and there was no issuance or repurchase of common stock. The company's actual ending shareholders' equity is €227 million.

1 What amount has bypassed the net income calculation by being classified as other comprehensive income?

   A €0.

   B €7 million.

   C €10 million.

2 Which of the following statements *best* describes other comprehensive income?

   A Income earned from diverse geographic and segment activities.

   B Income that increases stockholders' equity but is not reflected as part of net income.

   C Income earned from activities that are not part of the company's ordinary business activities.

Solution to 1:

C is correct. If the company's actual ending shareholders' equity is €227 million, then €10 million [€227– (€200 + €20 – €3)] has bypassed the net income calculation by being classified as other comprehensive income.

Solution to 2:

B is correct. Answers A and C are not correct because they do not specify whether such income is reported as part of net income and shown in the income statement.

EXAMPLE 15

Other Comprehensive Income in Analysis

An analyst is looking at two comparable companies. Company A has a lower price/earnings (P/E) ratio than Company B, and the conclusion that has been suggested is that Company A is undervalued. As part of examining this conclusion, the analyst decides to explore the question: What would the company's P/E look like if total comprehensive income per share—rather than net income per share—were used as the relevant metric?

	Company A	Company B
Price	$35	$30
EPS	$1.60	$0.90
P/E ratio	21.9×	33.3×
Other comprehensive income (loss) $ million	($16.272)	$(1.757)
Shares (millions)	22.6	25.1

Solution:

As shown in the following table, part of the explanation for Company A's lower P/E ratio may be that its significant losses—accounted for as other comprehensive income (OCI)—are not included in the P/E ratio.

	Company A	Company B
Price	$35	$30
EPS	$1.60	$0.90
OCI (loss) $ million	($16.272)	$(1.757)
Shares (millions)	22.6	25.1
OCI (loss) per share	$(0.72)	$(0.07)
Comprehensive EPS = EPS + OCI per share	$ 0.88	$0.83
Price/Comprehensive EPS ratio	39.8×	36.1×

Both IFRS and US GAAP allow companies two alternative presentations. One alternative is to present two statements—a separate income statement and a second statement additionally including other comprehensive income. The other alternative is to present a single statement of other comprehensive income. Particularly in comparing financial statements of two companies, it is relevant to examine significant differences in comprehensive income.

SUMMARY

This reading has presented the elements of income statement analysis. The income statement presents information on the financial results of a company's business activities over a period of time; it communicates how much revenue the company generated during a period and what costs it incurred in connection with generating that revenue. A company's net income and its components (e.g., gross margin, operating earnings, and pretax earnings) are critical inputs into both the equity and credit analysis processes. Equity analysts are interested in earnings because equity markets often reward relatively high- or low-earnings growth companies with above-average or below-average valuations, respectively. Fixed-income analysts examine the components of income statements, past and projected, for information on companies' abilities to make promised payments on their debt over the course of the business cycle. Corporate financial announcements frequently emphasize income statements more than the other financial statements.

Key points to this reading include the following:

- The income statement presents revenue, expenses, and net income.
- The components of the income statement include: revenue; cost of sales; sales, general, and administrative expenses; other operating expenses; non-operating income and expenses; gains and losses; non-recurring items; net income; and EPS.
- An income statement that presents a subtotal for gross profit (revenue minus cost of goods sold) is said to be presented in a multi-step format. One that does not present this subtotal is said to be presented in a single-step format.
- Revenue is recognized in the period it is earned, which may or may not be in the same period as the related cash collection. Recognition of revenue when earned is a fundamental principal of accrual accounting.
- An analyst should identify differences in companies' revenue recognition methods and adjust reported revenue where possible to facilitate comparability. Where the available information does not permit adjustment, an analyst can characterize the revenue recognition as more or less conservative and thus qualitatively assess how differences in policies might affect financial ratios and judgments about profitability.
- As of the beginning of 2018, revenue recognition standards have converged. The core principle of the converged standards is that revenue should be recognized to "depict the transfer of promised goods or services to customers in an amount that reflects the consideration to which the entity expects to be entitled in an exchange for those goods or services."
- To achieve the core principle, the standard describes the application of five steps in recognizing revenue. The standard also specifies the treatment of some related contract costs and disclosure requirements.
- The general principles of expense recognition include a process to match expenses either to revenue (such as, cost of goods sold) or to the time period in which the expenditure occurs (period costs such as, administrative salaries) or to the time period of expected benefits of the expenditures (such as, depreciation).
- In expense recognition, choice of method (i.e., depreciation method and inventory cost method), as well as estimates (i.e., uncollectible accounts, warranty expenses, assets' useful life, and salvage value) affect a company's reported income. An analyst should identify differences in companies' expense recognition methods and adjust reported financial statements where possible to facilitate comparability. Where the available information does not permit adjustment, an analyst can characterize the policies and estimates as more or less conservative and thus qualitatively assess how differences in policies might affect financial ratios and judgments about companies' performance.
- To assess a company's future earnings, it is helpful to separate those prior years' items of income and expense that are likely to continue in the future from those items that are less likely to continue.

- Under IFRS, a company should present additional line items, headings, and subtotals beyond those specified when such presentation is relevant to an understanding of the entity's financial performance. Some items from prior years clearly are not expected to continue in future periods and are separately disclosed on a company's income statement. Under US GAAP, unusual and/or infrequently occurring items, which are material, are presented separately within income from continuing operations.
- Non-operating items are reported separately from operating items on the income statement. Under both IFRS and US GAAP, the income statement reports separately the effect of the disposal of a component operation as a "discontinued" operation.
- Basic EPS is the amount of income available to common shareholders divided by the weighted average number of common shares outstanding over a period. The amount of income available to common shareholders is the amount of net income remaining after preferred dividends (if any) have been paid.
- If a company has a simple capital structure (i.e., one with no potentially dilutive securities), then its basic EPS is equal to its diluted EPS. If, however, a company has dilutive securities, its diluted EPS is lower than its basic EPS.
- Diluted EPS is calculated using the if-converted method for convertible securities and the treasury stock method for options.
- Common-size analysis of the income statement involves stating each line item on the income statement as a percentage of sales. Common-size statements facilitate comparison across time periods and across companies of different sizes.
- Two income-statement-based indicators of profitability are net profit margin and gross profit margin.
- Comprehensive income includes *both* net income and other revenue and expense items that are excluded from the net income calculation.

PRACTICE PROBLEMS

1 Expenses on the income statement may be grouped by:

A nature, but not by function.

B function, but not by nature.

C either function or nature.

2 An example of an expense classification by function is:

A tax expense.

B interest expense.

C cost of goods sold.

3 Denali Limited, a manufacturing company, had the following income statement information:

Revenue	$4,000,000
Cost of goods sold	$3,000,000
Other operating expenses	$500,000
Interest expense	$100,000
Tax expense	$120,000

Denali's gross profit is equal to:

A $280,000.

B $500,000.

C $1,000,000.

4 Under IFRS, income includes increases in economic benefits from:

A increases in liabilities not related to owners' contributions.

B enhancements of assets not related to owners' contributions.

C increases in owners' equity related to owners' contributions.

5 Fairplay had the following information related to the sale of its products during 2009, which was its first year of business:

Revenue	$1,000,000
Returns of goods sold	$100,000
Cash collected	$800,000
Cost of goods sold	$700,000

Under the accrual basis of accounting, how much net revenue would be reported on Fairplay's 2009 income statement?

A $200,000.

B $900,000.

C $1,000,000.

6 Apex Consignment sells items over the internet for individuals on a consignment basis. Apex receives the items from the owner, lists them for sale on the internet, and receives a 25 percent commission for any items sold. Apex collects the full amount from the buyer and pays the net amount after commission to the owner. Unsold items are returned to the owner after 90 days. During 2009, Apex had the following information:

© 2019 CFA Institute. All rights reserved.

- Total sales price of items sold during 2009 on consignment was €2,000,000.
- Total commissions retained by Apex during 2009 for these items was €500,000.

How much revenue should Apex report on its 2009 income statement?

A €500,000.

B €2,000,000.

C €1,500,000.

7 A company previously expensed the incremental costs of obtaining a contract. All else being equal, adopting the May 2014 IASB and FASB converged accounting standards on revenue recognition makes the company's profitability initially appear:

A lower.

B unchanged.

C higher.

8 During 2009, Accent Toys Plc., which began business in October of that year, purchased 10,000 units of a toy at a cost of £10 per unit in October. The toy sold well in October. In anticipation of heavy December sales, Accent purchased 5,000 additional units in November at a cost of £11 per unit. During 2009, Accent sold 12,000 units at a price of £15 per unit. Under the first in, first out (FIFO) method, what is Accent's cost of goods sold for 2009?

A £120,000.

B £122,000.

C £124,000.

9 Using the same information as in Question 8, what would Accent's cost of goods sold be under the weighted average cost method?

A £120,000.

B £122,000.

C £124,000.

10 Which inventory method is least likely to be used under IFRS?

A First in, first out (FIFO).

B Last in, first out (LIFO).

C Weighted average.

11 At the beginning of 2009, Glass Manufacturing purchased a new machine for its assembly line at a cost of $600,000. The machine has an estimated useful life of 10 years and estimated residual value of $50,000. Under the straight-line method, how much depreciation would Glass take in 2010 for financial reporting purposes?

A $55,000.

B $60,000.

C $65,000.

12 Using the same information as in Question 16, how much depreciation would Glass take in 2009 for financial reporting purposes under the double-declining balance method?

A $60,000.

B $110,000.

C $120,000.

13 Which combination of depreciation methods and useful lives is most conservative in the year a depreciable asset is acquired?

A Straight-line depreciation with a short useful life.

B Declining balance depreciation with a long useful life.

C Declining balance depreciation with a short useful life.

14 Under IFRS, a loss from the destruction of property in a fire would most likely be classified as:

A continuing operations.

B discontinued operations.

C other comprehensive income.

15 A company chooses to change an accounting policy. This change requires that, if practical, the company restate its financial statements for:

A all prior periods.

B current and future periods.

C prior periods shown in a report.

16 For 2009, Flamingo Products had net income of $1,000,000. At 1 January 2009, there were 1,000,000 shares outstanding. On 1 July 2009, the company issued 100,000 new shares for $20 per share. The company paid $200,000 in dividends to common shareholders. What is Flamingo's basic earnings per share for 2009?

A $0.80.

B $0.91.

C $0.95.

17 For its fiscal year-end, Calvan Water Corporation (CWC) reported net income of $12 million and a weighted average of 2,000,000 common shares outstanding. The company paid $800,000 in preferred dividends and had 100,000 options outstanding with an average exercise price of $20. CWC's market price over the year averaged $25 per share. CWC's diluted EPS is *closest* to:

A $5.33.

B $5.54.

C $5.94.

18 A company with no debt or convertible securities issued publicly traded common stock three times during the current fiscal year. Under both IFRS and US GAAP, the company's:

A basic EPS equals its diluted EPS.

B capital structure is considered complex at year-end.

C basic EPS is calculated by using a simple average number of shares outstanding.

19 Laurelli Builders (LB) reported the following financial data for year-end 31 December:

Common shares outstanding, 1 January	2,020,000
Common shares issued as stock dividend, 1 June	380,000
Warrants outstanding, 1 January	500,000
Net income	$3,350,000
Preferred stock dividends paid	$430,000
Common stock dividends paid	$240,000

Which statement about the calculation of LB's EPS is *most* accurate?

A LB's basic EPS is $1.12.

B LB's diluted EPS is equal to or less than its basic EPS.

C The weighted average number of shares outstanding is 2,210,000.

20 Cell Services Inc. (CSI) had 1,000,000 average shares outstanding during all of 2009. During 2009, CSI also had 10,000 options outstanding with exercise prices of $10 each. The average stock price of CSI during 2009 was $15. For purposes of computing diluted earnings per share, how many shares would be used in the denominator?

A 1,003,333.

B 1,006,667.

C 1,010,000.

21 For its fiscal year-end, Sublyme Corporation reported net income of $200 million and a weighted average of 50,000,000 common shares outstanding. There are 2,000,000 convertible preferred shares outstanding that paid an annual dividend of $5. Each preferred share is convertible into two shares of the common stock. The diluted EPS is *closest to*:

A $3.52.

B $3.65.

C $3.70.

22 When calculating diluted EPS, which of the following securities in the capital structure increases the weighted average number of common shares outstanding without affecting net income available to common shareholders?

A Stock options

B Convertible debt that is dilutive

C Convertible preferred stock that is dilutive

23 Which statement is *most* accurate? A common size income statement:

A restates each line item of the income statement as a percentage of net income.

B allows an analyst to conduct cross-sectional analysis by removing the effect of company size.

C standardizes each line item of the income statement but fails to help an analyst identify differences in companies' strategies.

24 Selected year-end financial statement data for Workhard are shown below.

	$ millions
Beginning shareholders' equity	475
Ending shareholders' equity	493
Unrealized gain on available-for-sale securities	5
Unrealized loss on derivatives accounted for as hedges	–3
Foreign currency translation gain on consolidation	2
Dividends paid	1
Net income	15

Workhard's comprehensive income for the year:

A is $18 million.

B is increased by the derivatives accounted for as hedges.

C includes $4 million in other comprehensive income.

25 When preparing an income statement, which of the following items would *most likely* be classified as other comprehensive income?

- **A** A foreign currency translation adjustment
- **B** An unrealized gain on a security held for trading purposes
- **C** A realized gain on a derivative contract not accounted for as a hedge

SOLUTIONS

1 C is correct. IAS No. 1 states that expenses may be categorized by either nature or function.

2 C is correct. Cost of goods sold is a classification by function. The other two expenses represent classifications by nature.

3 C is correct. Gross margin is revenue minus cost of goods sold. Answer A represents net income and B represents operating income.

4 B is correct. Under IFRS, income includes increases in economic benefits from increases in assets, enhancement of assets, and decreases in liabilities.

5 B is correct. Net revenue is revenue for goods sold during the period less any returns and allowances, or \$1,000,000 minus \$100,000 = \$900,000.

6 A is correct. Apex is not the owner of the goods and should only report its net commission as revenue.

7 C is correct. Under the converged accounting standards, the incremental costs of obtaining a contract and certain costs incurred to fulfill a contract must be capitalized. If a company expensed these incremental costs in the years prior to adopting the converged standards, all else being equal, its profitability will appear higher under the converged standards.

8 B is correct. Under the first in, first out (FIFO) method, the first 10,000 units sold came from the October purchases at £10, and the next 2,000 units sold came from the November purchases at £11.

9 C is correct. Under the weighted average cost method:

October purchases	10,000 units	\$100,000
November purchases	5,000 units	\$55,000
Total	15,000 units	\$155,000

\$155,000/15,000 units = \$10.3333 × 12,000 units = \$124,000.

10 B is correct. The last in, first out (LIFO) method is not permitted under IFRS. The other two methods are permitted.

11 A is correct. Straight-line depreciation would be (\$600,000 – \$50,000)/10, or \$55,000.

12 C is correct. Double-declining balance depreciation would be \$600,000 × 20 percent (twice the straight-line rate). The residual value is not subtracted from the initial book value to calculate depreciation. However, the book value (carrying amount) of the asset will not be reduced below the estimated residual value.

13 C is correct. This would result in the highest amount of depreciation in the first year and hence the lowest amount of net income relative to the other choices.

14 A is correct. A fire may be infrequent, but it would still be part of continuing operations and reported in the profit and loss statement. Discontinued operations relate to a decision to dispose of an operating division.

15 C is correct. If a company changes an accounting policy, the financial statements for all fiscal years shown in a company's financial report are presented, if practical, as if the newly adopted accounting policy had been used throughout the entire period; this retrospective application of the change makes the

financial results of any prior years included in the report comparable. Notes to the financial statements describe the change and explain the justification for the change.

16 C is correct. The weighted average number of shares outstanding for 2009 is 1,050,000. Basic earnings per share would be \$1,000,000 divided by 1,050,000, or \$0.95.

17 B is correct. The formula to calculate diluted EPS is as follows:

Diluted EPS = (Net income – Preferred dividends)/[Weighted average number of shares outstanding + (New shares that would have been issued at option exercise – Shares that could have been purchased with cash received upon exercise) × (Proportion of year during which the financial instruments were outstanding)].

The underlying assumption is that outstanding options are exercised, and then the proceeds from the issuance of new shares are used to repurchase shares already outstanding:

Proceeds from option exercise = 100,000 × \$20 = \$2,000,000

Shares repurchased = \$2,000,000/\$25 = 80,000

The net increase in shares outstanding is thus 100,000 – 80,000 = 20,000. Therefore, the diluted EPS for CWC = (\$12,000,000 – \$800,000)/2,020,000 = \$5.54.

18 A is correct. Basic and diluted EPS are equal for a company with a simple capital structure. A company that issues only common stock, with no financial instruments that are potentially convertible into common stock has a simple capital structure. Basic EPS is calculated using the weighted average number of shares outstanding.

19 B is correct. LB has warrants in its capital structure; if the exercise price is less than the weighted average market price during the year, the effect of their conversion is to increase the weighted average number of common shares outstanding, causing diluted EPS to be lower than basic EPS. If the exercise price is equal to the weighted average market price, the number of shares issued equals the number of shares repurchased. Therefore, the weighted average number of common shares outstanding is not affected and diluted EPS equals basic EPS. If the exercise price is greater than the weighted average market price, the effect of their conversion is anti-dilutive. As such, they are not included in the calculation of basic EPS. LB's basic EPS is \$1.22 [= (\$3,350,000 – \$430,000)/2,400,000]. Stock dividends are treated as having been issued retroactively to the beginning of the period.

20 A is correct. With stock options, the treasury stock method must be used. Under that method, the company would receive \$100,000 (10,000 × \$10) and would repurchase 6,667 shares (\$100,000/\$15). The shares for the denominator would be:

Shares outstanding	1,000,000
Options exercises	10,000
Treasury shares purchased	(6,667)
Denominator	1,003,333

21 C is correct.

Diluted EPS = (Net income)/(Weighted average number of shares outstanding + New common shares that would have been issued at conversion)
= $200,000,000/[50,000,000 + (2,000,000 × 2)]
= $3.70

The diluted EPS assumes that the preferred dividend is not paid and that the shares are converted at the beginning of the period.

22 A is correct. When a company has stock options outstanding, diluted EPS is calculated as if the financial instruments had been exercised and the company had used the proceeds from the exercise to repurchase as many shares possible at the weighted average market price of common stock during the period. As a result, the conversion of stock options increases the number of common shares outstanding but has no effect on net income available to common shareholders. The conversion of convertible debt increases the net income available to common shareholders by the after-tax amount of interest expense saved. The conversion of convertible preferred shares increases the net income available to common shareholders by the amount of preferred dividends paid; the numerator becomes the net income.

23 B is correct. Common size income statements facilitate comparison across time periods (time-series analysis) and across companies (cross-sectional analysis) by stating each line item of the income statement as a percentage of revenue. The relative performance of different companies can be more easily assessed because scaling the numbers removes the effect of size. A common size income statement states each line item on the income statement as a percentage of revenue. The standardization of each line item makes a common size income statement useful for identifying differences in companies' strategies.

24 C is correct. Comprehensive income includes both net income and other comprehensive income.

Other comprehensive income = Unrealized gain on available-for-sale securities – Unrealized loss on derivatives accounted for as hedges + Foreign currency translation gain on consolidation
= $5 million – $3 million + $2 million
= $4 million

Alternatively,

Comprehensive income – Net income = Other comprehensive income

Comprehensive income = (Ending shareholders equity – Beginning shareholders equity) + Dividends
= ($493 million – $475 million) + $1 million
= $18 million + $1 million = $19 million

Net income is $15 million so other comprehensive income is $4 million.

25 A is correct. Other comprehensive income includes items that affect shareholders' equity but are not reflected in the company's income statement. In consolidating the financial statements of foreign subsidiaries, the effects of translating the subsidiaries' balance sheet assets and liabilities at current exchange rates are included as other comprehensive income.

READING

22

Understanding Balance Sheets

by Elaine Henry, PhD, CFA, and Thomas R. Robinson, PhD, CFA

Elaine Henry, PhD, CFA, is at Stevens Institute of Technology (USA). Thomas R. Robinson, PhD, CFA, is at AACSB International (USA).

LEARNING OUTCOMES

Mastery	*The candidate should be able to:*
☐	**a.** describe the elements of the balance sheet: assets, liabilities, and equity;
☐	**b.** describe uses and limitations of the balance sheet in financial analysis;
☐	**c.** describe alternative formats of balance sheet presentation;
☐	**d.** distinguish between current and non-current assets and current and non-current liabilities;
☐	**e.** describe different types of assets and liabilities and the measurement bases of each;
☐	**f.** describe the components of shareholders' equity;
☐	**g.** convert balance sheets to common-size balance sheets and interpret common-size balance sheets;
☐	**h.** calculate and interpret liquidity and solvency ratios.

Note: Changes in accounting standards as well as new rulings and/or pronouncements issued after the publication of the readings on financial reporting and analysis may cause some of the information in these readings to become dated. Candidates are *not* responsible for anything that occurs after the readings were published. In addition, candidates are expected to be familiar with the analytical frameworks contained in the readings, as well as the implications of alternative accounting methods for financial analysis and valuation discussed in the readings. Candidates are also responsible for the content of accounting standards, but not for the actual reference numbers. Finally, candidates should be aware that certain ratios may be defined and calculated differently. When alternative ratio definitions exist and no specific definition is given, candidates should use the ratio definitions emphasized in the readings.

© 2011 CFA Institute. All rights reserved.

1 INTRODUCTION

The balance sheet provides information on a company's resources (assets) and its sources of capital (equity and liabilities/debt). This information helps an analyst assess a company's ability to pay for its near-term operating needs, meet future debt obligations, and make distributions to owners. The basic equation underlying the balance sheet is Assets = Liabilities + Equity.

Analysts should be aware that different types of assets and liabilities may be measured differently. For example, some items are measured at historical cost or a variation thereof and others at fair value.[1] An understanding of the measurement issues will facilitate analysis. The balance sheet measurement issues are, of course, closely linked to the revenue and expense recognition issues affecting the income statement. Throughout this reading, we describe and illustrate some of the linkages between the measurement issues affecting the balance sheet and the revenue and expense recognition issues affecting the income statement.

This reading is organized as follows: In Section 2, we describe and give examples of the elements and formats of balance sheets. Section 3 discusses current assets and current liabilities. Section 4 focuses on assets, and Section 5 focuses on liabilities. Section 6 describes the components of equity and illustrates the statement of changes in shareholders' equity. Section 7 introduces balance sheet analysis. A summary of the key points and practice problems in the CFA Institute multiple-choice format conclude the reading.

2 COMPONENTS AND FORMAT OF THE BALANCE SHEET

The **balance sheet** (also called the **statement of financial position** or **statement of financial condition**) discloses what an entity owns (or controls), what it owes, and what the owners' claims are at a specific point in time.[2]

The financial position of a company is described in terms of its basic elements (assets, liabilities, and equity):

- **Assets** (A) are what the company owns (or controls). More formally, assets are resources controlled by the company as a result of past events and from which future economic benefits are expected to flow *to* the entity.
- **Liabilities** (L) are what the company owes. More formally, liabilities represent obligations of a company arising from past events, the settlement of which is expected to result in a future outflow of economic benefits *from* the entity.
- **Equity** (E) represents the owners' residual interest in the company's assets after deducting its liabilities. Commonly known as **shareholders' equity** or **owners' equity**, equity is determined by subtracting the liabilities from the assets of a company, giving rise to the accounting equation: **A − L = E** or **A = L + E**.

1 IFRS and US GAAP define "fair value" as an exit price, i.e., the price that would be received to sell an asset or paid to transfer a liability in an orderly transaction between market participants at the measurement date (IFRS 13, FASB ASC Topic 820).

2 IFRS uses the term "statement of financial position" (IAS 1 *Presentation of Financial Statements*), and US GAAP uses the terms "balance sheet" and "statement of financial position" interchangeably (ASC 210-10-05 [Balance Sheet–Overall–Overview and Background]).

The equation A = L + E is sometimes summarized as follows: The left side of the equation reflects the resources controlled by the company and the right side reflects how those resources were financed. For all financial statement items, an item should only be recognized in the financial statements if it is probable that any future economic benefit associated with the item will flow to or from the entity and if the item has a cost or value that can be measured with reliability.[3]

The balance sheet provides important information about a company's financial condition, but the balance sheet amounts of equity (assets, net of liabilities) should not be viewed as a measure of either the market or intrinsic value of a company's equity for several reasons. First, the balance sheet under current accounting standards is a mixed model with respect to measurement. Some assets and liabilities are measured based on historical cost, sometimes with adjustments, whereas other assets and liabilities are measured based on a fair value, which represents its current value as of the balance sheet date. The measurement bases may have a significant effect on the amount reported. Second, even the items measured at current value reflect the value that was current at the end of the reporting period. The values of those items obviously can change after the balance sheet is prepared. Third, the value of a company is a function of many factors, including future cash flows expected to be generated by the company and current market conditions. Important aspects of a company's ability to generate future cash flows—for example, its reputation and management skills—are not included in its balance sheet.

2.1 Balance Sheet Components

To illustrate the components and formats of balance sheets, we show the major subtotals from two companies' balance sheets. Exhibit 1 and Exhibit 2 are based on the balance sheets of SAP Group and Apple Inc. SAP Group is a leading business software company based in Germany and prepares its financial statements in accordance with IFRS. Apple is a technology manufacturer based in the United States and prepares its financial statements in accordance with US GAAP. For purposes of discussion, Exhibits 1 and 2 show only the main subtotals and totals of these companies' balance sheets. Additional exhibits throughout this reading will expand on these subtotals.

Exhibit 1 SAP Group Consolidated Statements of Financial Position (Excerpt) (in millions of €)

	31 December	
Assets	**2017**	**2016***
Total current assets	11,930	11,564
Total non-current assets	30,567	32,713
Total assets	42,497	44,277
Equity and liabilities		
Total current liabilities	10,210	9,675
Total non-current liabilities	6,747	8,205
Total liabilities	16,957	17,880

(continued)

3 *Conceptual Framework for Financial Reporting (2018).*

Exhibit 1 (Continued)

Assets	31 December 2017	2016*
Total equity	25,540	26,397
Equity and liabilities	42,497	44,277

Source: SAP Group 2017 annual report.
Notes: Numbers exactly from the annual report as prepared by the company, which reflects some rounding.
* *Numbers are the reclassified numbers from the SAP Group 2017 annual report.*

Exhibit 2 Apple Inc. Consolidated Balance Sheets (Excerpt)* (in millions of $)

Assets	30 September 2017	24 September 2016
Total current assets	128,645	106,869
[All other assets]	*246,674*	*214,817*
Total assets	375,319	321,686
Liabilities and shareholders' equity		
Total current liabilities	100,814	79,006
[Total non-current liabilities]	*140,458*	*114,431*
Total liabilities	241,272	193,437
Total shareholders' equity	134,047	128,249
Total liabilities and shareholders' equity	375,319	321,686

**Note*: The italicized subtotals presented in this excerpt are not explicitly shown on the face of the financial statement as prepared by the company.
Source: Apple Inc. 2017 annual report (Form 10K).

SAP Group uses the title Statement of Financial Position and Apple uses the title Balance Sheet. Despite their different titles, both statements report the three basic elements: assets, liabilities, and equity. Both companies are reporting on a consolidated basis, i.e., including all their controlled subsidiaries. The numbers in SAP Group's balance sheet are in millions of euro, and the numbers in Apple's balance sheet are in millions of dollars.

Balance sheet information is as of a specific point in time. These exhibits are from the companies' annual financial statements, so the balance sheet information is as of the last day of their respective fiscal years. SAP Group's fiscal year is the same as the calendar year and the balance sheet information is as of 31 December. Apple's fiscal year ends on the last Saturday of September, so the actual date changes from year to year. About every six years, Apple's fiscal year will include 53 weeks rather than 52 weeks. This feature of Apple's fiscal year should be noted, but in general, the extra week is more relevant to evaluating statements spanning a period of time (the income and cash flow statements) rather than the balance sheet which captures information as of a specific point in time.

A company's ability to pay for its short term operating needs relates to the concept of **liquidity**. With respect to a company overall, liquidity refers to the availability of cash to meet those short-term needs. With respect to a particular asset or liability, liquidity refers to its "nearness to cash." A liquid asset is one that can be easily converted into cash in a short period of time at a price close to fair market value. For example, a small holding of an actively traded stock is much more liquid than an investment in an asset such as a commercial real estate property, particularly in a weak property market.

The separate presentation of current and non-current assets and liabilities facilitates analysis of a company's liquidity position (at least as of the end of the fiscal period). Both IFRS and US GAAP require that the balance sheet distinguish between current and non-current assets and between current and non-current liabilities and present these as separate classifications. An exception to this requirement, under IFRS, is that the current and non-current classifications are not required if a liquidity-based presentation provides reliable and more relevant information. Presentations distinguishing between current and non-current elements are shown in Exhibits 1 and 2. Exhibit 3 in Section 2.3 shows a liquidity-based presentation.

2.2 Current and Non-Current Classification

Assets that are held primarily for the purpose of trading or that are expected to be sold, used up, or otherwise realized in cash within one year or one operating cycle of the business, whichever is greater, after the reporting period are classified as **current assets**. A company's operating cycle is the average amount of time that elapses between acquiring inventory and collecting the cash from sales to customers. (When the entity's normal operating cycle is not clearly identifiable, its duration is assumed to be one year.) For a manufacturer, the operating cycle is the average amount of time between acquiring raw materials and converting these into cash from a sale. Examples of companies that might be expected to have operating cycles longer than one year include those operating in the tobacco, distillery, and lumber industries. Even though these types of companies often hold inventories longer than one year, the inventory is classified as a current asset because it is expected to be sold within an operating cycle. Assets not expected to be sold or used up within one year or one operating cycle of the business, whichever is greater, are classified as **non-current assets** (long-term, long-lived assets).

Current assets are generally maintained for operating purposes, and these assets include—in addition to cash—items expected to be converted into cash (e.g., trade receivables), used up (e.g., office supplies, prepaid expenses), or sold (e.g., inventories) in the current operating cycle. Current assets provide information about the operating activities and the operating capability of the entity. For example, the item "trade receivables" or "accounts receivable" would indicate that a company provides credit to its customers. Non-current assets represent the infrastructure from which the entity operates and are not consumed or sold in the current period. Investments in such assets are made from a strategic and longer term perspective.

Similarly, liabilities expected to be settled within one year or within one operating cycle of the business, whichever is greater, after the reporting period are classified as **current liabilities**. The specific criteria for classification of a liability as current include the following:

- It is expected to be settled in the entity's normal operating cycle;
- It is held primarily for the purpose of being traded;[4]

4 Examples of these are financial liabilities classified as held for trading in accordance with IAS 39, which is replaced by IFRS 9 effective for periods beginning on or after 1 January 2018.

- It is due to be settled within one year after the balance sheet date; or
- The entity does not have an unconditional right to defer settlement of the liability for at least one year after the balance sheet date.[5]

IFRS specify that some current liabilities, such as trade payables and some accruals for employee and other operating costs, are part of the working capital used in the entity's normal operating cycle. Such operating items are classified as current liabilities even if they will be settled more than one year after the balance sheet date. All other liabilities are classified as **non-current liabilities**. Non-current liabilities include financial liabilities that provide financing on a long-term basis.

The excess of current assets over current liabilities is called **working capital**. The level of working capital provides analysts with information about the ability of an entity to meet liabilities as they fall due. Although adequate working capital is essential, excessive working capital should be so that funds that could be used more productively elsewhere are not inappropriately tied up.

A balance sheet with separately classified current and non-current assets and liabilities is referred to as a **classified balance sheet**. Classification also refers generally to the grouping of accounts into subcategories. Both companies' balance sheets that are summarized in Exhibits 1 and 2 are classified balance sheets. Although both companies' balance sheets present current assets before non-current assets and current liabilities before non-current liabilities, this is not required. IFRS does not specify the order or format in which a company presents items on a current/non-current classified balance sheet.

2.3 Liquidity-Based Presentation

A liquidity-based presentation, rather than a current/non-current presentation, is used when such a presentation provides information that is reliable and more relevant. With a liquidity-based presentation, all assets and liabilities are presented broadly in order of liquidity.

Entities such as banks are candidates to use a liquidity-based presentation. Exhibit 3 presents the assets portion of the balance sheet of HSBC Holdings plc (HSBC), a global financial services company that reports using IFRS. HSBC's balance sheet is ordered using a liquidity-based presentation. As shown, the asset section begins with cash and balances at central banks. Less liquid items such as "Interest in associates and joint ventures" appear near the bottom of the asset listing.

Exhibit 3 HSBC Holdings plc Consolidated Statement of Financial Position (Excerpt: Assets Only) as of 31 December (in millions of US $)

Consolidated balance sheet - USD ($) $ in Millions	Dec. 31, 2017	Dec. 31, 2016
Assets		
Cash and balances at central banks	$180,624	$128,009
Items in the course of collection from other banks	6,628	5,003
Hong Kong Government certificates of indebtedness	34,186	31,228
Trading assets	287,995	235,125
Financial assets designated at fair value	29,464	24,756
Derivatives	219,818	290,872

5 IAS 1, *Presentation of Financial Statements*, paragraph 69.

Exhibit 3 (Continued)

Consolidated balance sheet - USD ($) $ in Millions	Dec. 31, 2017	Dec. 31, 2016
Loans and advances to banks	90,393	88,126
Loans and advances to customers	962,964	861,504
Reverse repurchase agreements – non-trading	201,553	160,974
Financial investments	389,076	436,797
Prepayments, accrued income and other assets	67,191	63,909
Current tax assets	1,006	1,145
Interests in associates and joint ventures	22,744	20,029
Goodwill and intangible assets	23,453	21,346
Deferred tax assets	4,676	6,163
Total assets	2,521,771	2,374,986

Source: HSBC Holdings plc 2017 Annual Report and Accounts.

CURRENT ASSETS AND CURRENT LIABILITIES

3

This section examines current assets and current liabilities in greater detail.

3.1 Current Assets

Accounting standards require that certain specific line items, if they are material, must be shown on a balance sheet. Among the current assets' required line items are cash and cash equivalents, trade and other receivables, inventories, and financial assets (with short maturities). Companies present other line items as needed, consistent with the requirements to separately present each material class of similar items. As examples, Exhibit 4 and Exhibit 5 present balance sheet excerpts for SAP Group and Apple Inc. showing the line items for the companies' current assets.

Exhibit 4 SAP Group Consolidated Statements of Financial Position (Excerpt: Current Assets Detail) (in millions of €)

	As of 31 December	
Assets	**2017**	**2016**
Cash and cash equivalents	€4,011	€3,702
Other financial assets	990	1,124
Trade and other receivables	5,899	5,924
Other non-financial assets	725	581
Tax assets	306	233
Total current assets	11,930	11,564
Total non-current assets	30,567	32,713
Total assets	**42,497**	**44,277**
Total current liabilities	10,210	9,674
Total non-current liabilities	6,747	8,205

(continued)

Exhibit 4 (Continued)

Assets	As of 31 December 2017	2016
Total liabilities	16,958	17,880
Total equity	25,540	26,397
Total equity and liabilities	**€42,497**	**€44,277**

Source: SAP Group 2017 annual report.

Exhibit 5 Apple Inc. Consolidated Balance Sheet (Excerpt: Current Assets Detail) * (in millions of $)

Assets	30 September, 2017	24 September, 2016
Cash and cash equivalents	$20,289	$20,484
Short-term marketable securities	53,892	46,671
Accounts receivable, less allowances of $58 and $53, respectively	17,874	15,754
Inventories	4,855	2,132
Vendor non-trade receivables	17,799	13,545
Other current assets	13,936	8,283
Total current assets	128,645	106,869
[All other assets]	*246,674*	*214,817*
Total assets	**375,319**	**321,686**
Total current liabilities	100,814	79,006
[Total non-current liabilities]	*140,458*	*114,431*
Total liabilities	241,272	193,437
Total shareholders' equity	134,047	128,249
Total liabilities and shareholders' equity	**$375,319**	**$321,686**

**Note*: The italicized subtotals presented in this excerpt are not explicitly shown on the face of the financial statement as prepared by the company.
Source: Apple Inc. 2017 annual report (Form 10K).

3.1.1 *Cash and Cash Equivalents*

Cash equivalents are highly liquid, short-term investments that are so close to maturity,[6] the risk is minimal that their value will change significantly with changes in interest rates. Cash and cash equivalents are financial assets. Financial assets, in general, are measured and reported at either **amortised cost** or **fair value**. Amortised cost is the historical cost (initially recognised cost) of the asset adjusted for amortisation and

6 Generally, three months or less.

impairment. Under IFRS and US GAAP, fair value is based on an exit price, the price received to sell an asset or paid to transfer a liability in an orderly transaction between two market participants at the measurement date.

For cash and cash equivalents, amortised cost and fair value are likely to be immaterially different. Examples of cash equivalents are demand deposits with banks and highly liquid investments (such as US Treasury bills, commercial paper, and money market funds) with original maturities of three months or less. Cash and cash equivalents excludes amounts that are restricted in use for at least 12 months. For all companies, the Statement of Cash Flows presents information about the changes in cash over a period. For the fiscal year 2017, SAP Group's cash and cash equivalents increased from €3,702 million to €4,011 million, and Apple's cash and cash equivalents decreased from $20,484 million to $20,289 million.

3.1.2 *Marketable Securities*

Marketable securities are also financial assets and include investments in debt or equity securities that are traded in a public market, and whose value can be determined from price information in a public market. Examples of marketable securities include treasury bills, notes, bonds, and equity securities, such as common stocks and mutual fund shares. Companies disclose further detail in the notes to their financial statements about their holdings. For example, SAP Group discloses that its other financial assets consist of items such as time deposits, other receivables, and loans to employees and third parties. Apple's short-term marketable securities, totaling $53.9 billion and $46.7 billion at the end of fiscal 2017 and 2016, respectively, include holdings of US treasuries, corporate securities, commercial paper, and time deposits. Financial assets such as investments in debt and equity securities involve a variety of measurement issues and will be addressed in Section 4.5.

3.1.3 *Trade Receivables*

Trade receivables, also referred to as accounts receivable, are another type of financial asset. These are amounts owed to a company by its customers for products and services already delivered. They are typically reported at net realizable value, an approximation of fair value, based on estimates of collectability. Several aspects of accounts receivable are usually relevant to an analyst. First, the overall level of accounts receivable relative to sales (a topic to be addressed further in ratio analysis) is important because a significant increase in accounts receivable relative to sales could signal that the company is having problems collecting cash from its customers.

A second relevant aspect of accounts receivable is the allowance for doubtful accounts. The allowance for doubtful accounts reflects the company's estimate of the amount of receivables that will ultimately be uncollectible. Additions to the allowance in a particular period are reflected as bad debt expenses, and the balance of the allowance for doubtful accounts reduces the gross receivables amount to a net amount that is an estimate of net realizable value. When specific receivables are deemed to be uncollectible, they are written off by reducing accounts receivable and the allowance for doubtful accounts. The allowance for doubtful accounts is called a **contra account** because it is netted against (i.e., reduces) the balance of accounts receivable, which is an asset account. SAP Group's balance sheet, for example, reports current net trade and other receivables of €5,899 million as of 31 December 2017. The amount of the allowance for doubtful accounts (€74 million) is disclosed in the notes[7] to the financial statements. Apple discloses the allowance for doubtful accounts on the face of the balance sheet; as of 30 September 2017, the allowance was $58 million. The $17,874 million of accounts receivable on that date is net of the allowance. Apple's

7 Note 13 SAP Group 2017 Annual report

disclosures state that the allowance is based on "historical experience, the age of the accounts receivable balances, credit quality of the Company's customers, current economic conditions, and other factors that may affect customers' abilities to pay." The age of an accounts receivable balance refers to the length of time the receivable has been outstanding, including how many days past the due date.

Another relevant aspect of accounts receivable is the concentration of credit risk. For example, SAP Group's annual report discloses that concentration of credit risk is limited because they have a large customer base diversified across various industries, company sizes, and countries. Similarly, Apple's annual report notes that no single customer accounted for 10 percent or more of its revenues. However, Apple's disclosures for 2017 indicate that two customers individually represented 10% or more of its total trade receivables and its cellular network carriers accounted for 59% of trade receivables. Of its vendor non-trade receivables, three vendors represent 42%, 19%, and 10% of the total. [8]

EXAMPLE 1

Analysis of Accounts Receivable

1 Based on the balance sheet excerpt for Apple Inc. in Exhibit 5, what percentage of its total accounts receivable in 2017 and 2016 does Apple estimate will be uncollectible?

2 In general, how does the amount of allowance for doubtful accounts relate to bad debt expense?

3 In general, what are some factors that could cause a company's allowance for doubtful accounts to decrease?

Solution to 1:

($ millions) The percentage of 2017 accounts receivable estimated to be uncollectible is 0.32 percent, calculated as $58/($17,874 + $58). Note that the $17,874 is net of the $58 allowance, so the gross amount of accounts receivable is determined by adding the allowance to the net amount. The percentage of 2016 accounts receivable estimated to be uncollectible is 0.34 percent [$53/($15,754 + $53)].

Solution to 2:

Bad debt expense is an expense of the period, based on a company's estimate of the percentage of credit sales in the period, for which cash will ultimately not be collected. The allowance for bad debts is a contra asset account, which is netted against the asset accounts receivable.

To record the estimated bad debts, a company recognizes a bad debt expense (which affects net income) and increases the balance in the allowance for doubtful accounts by the same amount. To record the write off of a particular account receivable, a company reduces the balance in the allowance for doubtful accounts and reduces the balance in accounts receivable by the same amount.

Solution to 3:

In general, a decrease in a company's allowance for doubtful accounts in absolute terms could be caused by a decrease in the amount of credit sales.

8 Page 53, Apple Inc 2017 10-K

Some factors that could cause a company's allowance for doubtful accounts to decrease as a percentage of accounts receivable include the following:

- Improvements in the credit quality of the company's existing customers (whether driven by a customer-specific improvement or by an improvement in the overall economy);
- Stricter credit policies (for example, refusing to allow less creditworthy customers to make credit purchases and instead requiring them to pay cash, to provide collateral, or to provide some additional form of financial backing); and/or
- Stricter risk management policies (for example, buying more insurance against potential defaults).

In addition to the business factors noted above, because the allowance is based on management's estimates of collectability, management can potentially bias these estimates to manipulate reported earnings. For example, a management team aiming to increase reported income could intentionally over-estimate collectability and under-estimate the bad debt expense for a period. Conversely, in a period of good earnings, management could under-estimate collectability and over-estimate the bad debt expense with the intent of reversing the bias in a period of poorer earnings.

3.1.4 *Inventories*

Inventories are physical products that will eventually be sold to the company's customers, either in their current form (finished goods) or as inputs into a process to manufacture a final product (raw materials and work-in-process). Like any manufacturer, Apple holds inventories. The 2017 balance sheet of Apple Inc. shows $4,855 million of inventories. SAP Group's balance sheet does not include a line item for inventory, consistent with the fact that SAP Group is primarily a software and services provider.

Inventories are measured at the lower of cost and net realizable value (NRV) under IFRS. The cost of inventories comprises all costs of purchase, costs of conversion, and other costs incurred in bringing the inventories to their present location and condition. NRV is the estimated selling price less the estimated costs of completion and costs necessary to complete the sale. NRV is applicable for all inventories under IFRS. Under US GAAP, inventories are also measured at the lower of cost and NRV unless they are measured using the last-in, first-out (LIFO) or retail inventory methods. When using LIFO or the retail inventory methods, inventories are measured at the lower of cost or market value. US GAAP defines market value as current replacement cost but with upper and lower limits; the recorded value cannot exceed NRV and cannot be lower than NRV less a normal profit margin.

If the net realizable value or market value (under US GAAP, in certain cases) of a company's inventory falls below its carrying amount, the company must write down the value of the inventory. The loss in value is reflected in the income statement. For example, within its Management's Discussion and Analysis and notes, Apple indicates that the company reviews its inventory each quarter and records write-downs of inventory that has become obsolete, exceeds anticipated demand, or is carried at a value higher than its market value. Under IFRS, if inventory that was written down in a previous period subsequently increases in value, the amount of the original write-down is reversed. Subsequent reversal of an inventory write-down is not permitted under US GAAP.

When inventory is sold, the cost of that inventory is reported as an expense, "cost of goods sold." Accounting standards allow different valuation methods for determining the amounts that are included in cost of goods sold on the income statement and thus the amounts that are reported in inventory on the balance sheet. (Inventory valuation methods are referred to as cost formulas and cost flow assumptions under IFRS and US GAAP, respectively.) IFRS allows only the first-in, first-out (FIFO), weighted average cost, and specific identification methods. Some accounting standards (such as US GAAP) also allow last-in, first-out (LIFO) as an additional inventory valuation method. The LIFO method is not allowed under IFRS.

3.1.5 *Other Current Assets*

The amounts shown in "other current assets" reflect items that are individually not material enough to require a separate line item on the balance sheet and so are aggregated into a single amount. Companies usually disclose the components of other assets in a note to the financial statements. A typical item included in other current assets is prepaid expenses. **Prepaid expenses** are normal operating expenses that have been paid in advance. Because expenses are recognized in the period in which they are incurred—and not necessarily the period in which the payment is made—the advance payment of a future expense creates an asset. The asset (prepaid expenses) will be recognized as an expense in future periods as it is used up. For example, consider prepaid insurance. Assume a company pays its insurance premium for coverage over the next calendar year on 31 December of the current year. At the time of the payment, the company recognizes an asset (prepaid insurance expense). The expense is not incurred at that date; the expense is incurred as time passes (in this example, one-twelfth, 1/12, in each following month). Therefore, the expense is recognized and the value of the asset is reduced in the financial statements over the course of the year.

SAP's notes to the financial statements disclose components of the amount shown as other non-financial assets on the balance sheet. The largest portion pertains to prepaid expenses, primarily prepayments for operating leases, support services, and software royalties. Apple's notes do not disclose components of other current assets.

3.2 Current Liabilities

Current liabilities are those liabilities that are expected to be settled in the entity's normal operating cycle, held primarily for trading, or due to be settled within 12 months after the balance sheet date. Exhibit 6 and Exhibit 7 present balance sheet excerpts for SAP Group and Apple Inc. showing the line items for the companies' current liabilities. Some of the common types of current liabilities, including trade payables, financial liabilities, accrued expenses, and deferred income, are discussed below.

Exhibit 6 SAP Group Consolidated Statements of Financial Position (Excerpt: Current Liabilities Detail) (in millions of €)

	As of 31 December	
	2017	**2016**
Assets		
Total current assets	11,930	11,564
Total non-current assets	30,567	32,713
Total assets	42,497	44,277
Equity and liabilities		
Trade and other payables	1,151	1,281
Tax liabilities	597	316
Financial liabilities	1,561	1,813

Exhibit 6 (Continued)

	As of 31 December	
	2017	**2016**
Other non-financial liabilities	3,946	3,699
Provisions	184	183
Deferred income	2,771	2,383
Total current liabilities	10,210	9,674
Total non-current liabilities	6,747	8,205
Total liabilities	16,958	17,880
Total equity	25,540	26,397
Total equity and liabilities	€42,497	€44,277

Source: SAP Group 2017 annual report.

Exhibit 7 Apple Inc. Consolidated Balance Sheet (Excerpt: Current Liabilities Detail)* (in millions of $)

Assets	**30 September 2017**	**24 September 2016**
Total current assets	128,645	106,869
[All other assets]	*246,674*	*214,817*
Total assets	375,319	321,686
Liabilities and shareholders' equity		
Accounts payable	49,049	37,294
Accrued expenses	25,744	22,027
Deferred revenue	7,548	8,080
Commercial paper	11,977	8,105
Current portion of long-term debt	6,496	3,500
Total current liabilities	100,814	79,006
[Total non-current liabilities]	*140,458*	*114,431*
Total liabilities	241,272	193,437
Total shareholders' equity	134,047	128,249
Total liabilities and shareholders' equity	375,319	321,686

**Note:* The italicized subtotals presented in this excerpt are not explicitly shown on the face of the financial statement as prepared by the company.
Source: Apple Inc. 2017 annual report (Form 10K).

Trade payables, also called **accounts payable**, are amounts that a company owes its vendors for purchases of goods and services. In other words, these represent the unpaid amount as of the balance sheet date of the company's purchases on credit. An issue relevant to analysts is the trend in overall levels of trade payables relative to purchases (a topic to be addressed further in ratio analysis). Significant changes in accounts payable relative to purchases could signal potential changes in the company's credit relationships with its suppliers. The general term "trade credit" refers to credit provided to a company by its vendors. Trade credit is a source of financing that allows the company to make purchases and then pay for those purchases at a later date.

Financial liabilities that are due within one year or the operating cycle, whichever is longer, appear in the current liability section of the balance sheet. Financial liabilities include borrowings such as bank loans, notes payable (which refers to financial liabilities owed by a company to creditors, including trade creditors and banks, through a formal loan agreement), and commercial paper. In addition, any portions of long-term liabilities that are due within one year (i.e., the current portion of long-term liabilities) are also shown in the current liability section of the balance sheet. According to its footnote disclosures, most of SAP's €1,561 million of current financial liabilities is for bonds payable due in the next year. Apple shows $11,977 million of commercial paper borrowing (short-term promissory notes issued by companies) and $6,496 million of long-term debt due within the next year.

Accrued expenses (also called accrued expenses payable, accrued liabilities, and other non-financial liabilities) are expenses that have been recognized on a company's income statement but not yet been paid as of the balance sheet date. For example, SAP's 2017 balance sheet shows €597 million of tax liabilities. In addition to income taxes payable, other common examples of accrued expenses are accrued interest payable, accrued warranty costs, and accrued employee compensation (i.e., wages payable). SAP's notes disclose that the €3,946 million line item of other non-financial liabilities in 2017, for example, includes €2,565 million of employee-related liabilities.

Deferred income (also called **deferred revenue** or **unearned revenue**) arises when a company receives payment in advance of delivery of the goods and services associated with the payment. The company has an obligation either to provide the goods or services or to return the cash received. Examples include lease payments received at the beginning of a lease, fees for servicing office equipment received at the beginning of the service period, and payments for magazine subscriptions received at the beginning of the subscription period. SAP's balance sheet shows deferred income of €2,771 million at the end of 2017, up slightly from €2,383 million at the end of 2016. Apple's balance sheet shows deferred revenue of $7,548 million at the end of fiscal 2017, down slightly from $8,080 million at the end of fiscal 2016. Example 3 presents each company's disclosures about deferred revenue and discusses some of the implications.

EXAMPLE 2

Analysis of Deferred Revenue

In the notes to its 2017 financial statements, SAP describes its deferred income as follows:

> Deferred income consists mainly of prepayments made by our customers for cloud subscriptions and support; software support and services; fees from multiple-element arrangements allocated to undelivered elements; and amounts ... for obligations to perform under acquired customer contracts in connection with acquisitions.

Apple's deferred revenue also arises from sales involving multiple elements, some delivered at the time of sale and others to be delivered in the future. In addition, Apple recognizes deferred revenue in connection with sales of gifts cards as well as service contracts. In the notes to its 2017 financial statements, Apple describes its deferred revenue as follows:

> The Company records deferred revenue when it receives payments in advance of the delivery of products or the performance of services. This includes amounts that have been deferred for unspecified and specified software upgrade rights and non-software services that are attached to hardware and software products. The Company sells gift cards redeemable at its retail and online stores ... The Company records deferred revenue upon the sale of the card, which is relieved upon redemption of the card by the customer. Revenue from AppleCare service and support contracts is deferred and recognized over the service coverage periods. AppleCare service and support contracts typically include extended phone support, repair services, web-based support resources and diagnostic tools offered under the Company's standard limited warranty.

1. In general, in the period a transaction occurs, how would a company's balance sheet reflect \$100 of deferred revenue resulting from a sale? (Assume, for simplicity, that the company receives cash for all sales, the company's income tax payable is 30 percent based on cash receipts, and the company pays cash for all relevant income tax obligations as they arise. Ignore any associated deferred costs.)
2. In general, how does deferred revenue impact a company's financial statements in the periods following its initial recognition?
3. Interpret the amounts shown by SAP as deferred income and by Apple as deferred revenue.
4. Both accounts payable and deferred revenue are classified as current liabilities. Discuss the following statements:
   - **A** When assessing a company's liquidity, the implication of amounts in accounts payable differs from the implication of amounts in deferred revenue.
   - **B** Some investors monitor amounts in deferred revenue as an indicator of future revenue growth.

Solution to 1:

In the period that deferred revenue arises, the company would record a \$100 increase in the asset Cash and a \$100 increase in the liability Deferred Revenues. In addition, because the company's income tax payable is based on cash receipts and is paid in the current period, the company would record a \$30 decrease in the asset Cash and a \$30 increase in the asset Deferred Tax Assets. Deferred tax assets increase because the company has paid taxes on revenue it has not yet recognized for accounting purposes. In effect, the company has prepaid taxes from an accounting perspective.

Solution to 2:

In subsequent periods, the company will recognize the deferred revenue as it is earned. When the revenue is recognized, the liability Deferred Revenue will decrease. In addition, the tax expense is recognized on the income statement as the revenue is recognized and thus the associated amounts of Deferred Tax Assets will decrease.

Solution to 3:

The deferred income on SAP's balance sheet and deferred revenue on Apple's balance sheet at the end of their respective 2017 fiscal years will be recognized as revenue, sales, or a similar item in income statements subsequent to the 2017 fiscal year, as the goods or services are provided or the obligation is reduced. The costs of delivering the goods or services will also be recognised.

Solution to 4A:

The amount of accounts payable represents a future obligation to pay cash to suppliers. In contrast, the amount of deferred revenue represents payments that the company has already received from its customers, and the future obligation is to deliver the related services. With respect to liquidity, settling accounts payable will require cash outflows whereas settling deferred revenue obligations will not.

Solution to 4B:

Some investors monitor amounts in deferred revenue as an indicator of future growth because the amounts in deferred revenue will be recognized as revenue in the future. Thus, growth in the amount of deferred revenue implies future growth of that component of a company's revenue.

4 NON-CURRENT ASSETS

This section provides an overview of assets other than current assets, sometimes collectively referred to as non-current, long-term, or long-lived assets. The categories discussed are property, plant, and equipment; investment property; intangible assets; goodwill; financial assets; and deferred tax assets. Exhibit 8 and Exhibit 9 present balance sheet excerpts for SAP Group and Apple Inc. showing the line items for the companies' non-current assets.

Exhibit 8 SAP Group Consolidated Statements of Financial Position (Excerpt: Non-Current Assets Detail) (in millions of €)

	As of 31 December	
Assets	**2017**	**2016**
Total current assets	11,930	11,564
Goodwill	21,274	23,311
Intangible assets	2,967	3,786
Property, plant and equipment	2,967	2,580
Other financial assets	1,155	1,358
Trade and other receivables	118	126
Other non-financial assets	621	532
Tax assets	443	450
Deferred tax assets	1,022	571
Total non-current assets	30,567	32,713
Total assets	**42,497**	**44,277**
Total current liabilities	10,210	9,674
Total non-current liabilities	6,747	8,205

Exhibit 8 (Continued)

Assets	As of 31 December 2017	2016
Total liabilities	**16,958**	**17,880**
Total equity	**25,540**	**26,397**
Total equity and liabilities	**€42,497**	**€44,277**

Source: SAP Group 2017 annual report.

Exhibit 9 Apple Inc. Consolidated Balance Sheet (Excerpt: Non-Current Assets Detail)* (in millions of $)

Assets	30 September 2017	24 September 2016
Total current assets	128,645	106,869
Long-term marketable securities	194,714	170,430
Property, plant and equipment, net	33,783	27,010
Goodwill	5,717	5,414
Acquired intangible assets, net	2,298	3,206
Other non-current assets	10,162	8,757
[All other assets]	*246,674*	*214,817*
Total assets	375,319	321,686
Liabilities and shareholders' equity		
Total current liabilities	100,814	79,006
[Total non-current liabilities]	*140,458*	*114,431*
Total liabilities	241,272	193,437
Total shareholders' equity	134,047	128,249
Total liabilities and shareholders' equity	375,319	321,686

**Note*: The italicized subtotals presented in this excerpt are not explicitly shown on the face of the financial statement as prepared by the company.
Source: Apple Inc. 2017 annual report (Form 10K).

4.1 Property, Plant, and Equipment

Property, plant, and equipment (PPE) are tangible assets that are used in company operations and expected to be used (provide economic benefits) over more than one fiscal period. Examples of tangible assets treated as property, plant, and equipment, include land, buildings, equipment, machinery, furniture, and natural resources such as mineral and petroleum resources. IFRS permits companies to report PPE using either a cost model or a revaluation model.[9] While IFRS permits companies to use the cost model for some classes of assets and the revaluation model for others, the company must apply the same model to all assets within a particular class of assets. US GAAP permits only the cost model for reporting PPE.

9 IAS 16, *Property, Plant and Equipment,* paragraphs 29-31.

Under the cost model, PPE is carried at amortised cost (historical cost less any accumulated depreciation or accumulated depletion, and less any impairment losses). Historical cost generally consists of an asset's purchase price, plus its delivery cost, and any other additional costs incurred to make the asset operable (such as costs to install a machine). Depreciation and depletion refer to the process of allocating (recognizing as an expense) the cost of a long-lived asset over its useful life. Land is not depreciated. Because PPE is presented on the balance sheet net of depreciation and depreciation expense is recognised in the income statement, the choice of depreciation method and the related estimates of useful life and salvage value impact both a company's balance sheet and income statement.

Whereas depreciation is the systematic allocation of cost over an asset's useful life, impairment losses reflect an unanticipated decline in value. Impairment occurs when the asset's recoverable amount is less than its carrying amount, with terms defined as follows under IFRS:[10]

- Recoverable amount: The higher of an asset's fair value less cost to sell, and its value in use.
- Fair value less cost to sell: The amount obtainable in a sale of the asset in an arms-length transaction between knowledgeable willing parties, less the costs of the sale.
- Value in use: The present value of the future cash flows expected to be derived from the asset.

When an asset is considered impaired, the company recognizes the impairment loss in the income statement in the period the impairment is identified. Reversals of impairment losses are permitted under IFRS but not under US GAAP.

Under the revaluation model, the reported and carrying value for PPE is the fair value at the date of revaluation less any subsequent accumulated depreciation. Changes in the value of PPE under the revaluation model affect equity directly or profit and loss depending upon the circumstances.

In Exhibits 8 and 9, SAP reports €2,967 million of PPE and Apple reports $33,783 million of PPE at the end of fiscal year 2017. For SAP, PPE represents approximately 7 percent of total assets and for Apple, PPE represents approximately 9 percent of total assets. Both companies disclose in the notes that PPE are generally depreciated over their expected useful lives using the straight-line method.

4.2 Investment Property

Some property is not used in the production of goods or services or for administrative purposes. Instead, it is used to earn rental income or capital appreciation (or both). Under IFRS, such property is considered to be **investment property**.[11] US GAAP does not include a specific definition for investment property. IFRS provides companies with the choice to report investment property using either a cost model or a fair value model. In general, a company must apply its chosen model (cost or fair value) to all of its investment property. The cost model for investment property is identical to the cost model for PPE: In other words, investment property is carried at cost less any accumulated depreciation and any accumulated impairment losses. Under the fair value model, investment property is carried at its fair value. When a company

---

10 IAS 36, *Impairment of Assets*, paragraph 6. US GAAP uses a different approach to impairment.
11 IAS 40, *Investment Property*.

uses the fair value model to measure the value of its investment property, any gain or loss arising from a change in the fair value of the investment property is recognized in profit and loss, i.e., on the income statement, in the period in which it arises.[12]

Neither SAP Group nor Apple disclose ownership of investment property. The types of companies that typically hold investment property are real estate investment companies or property management companies. Entities such as life insurance companies and endowment funds may also hold investment properties as part of their investment portfolio.

4.3 Intangible Assets

Intangible assets are identifiable non-monetary assets without physical substance.[13] An identifiable asset can be acquired singly (can be separated from the entity) or is the result of specific contractual or legal rights or privileges. Examples include patents, licenses, and trademarks. The most common asset that is not a separately identifiable asset is accounting goodwill, which arises in business combinations and is discussed further in Section 4.4.

IFRS allows companies to report intangible assets using either a cost model or a revaluation model. The revaluation model can only be selected when there is an active market for an intangible asset. These measurement models are essentially the same as described for PPE. US GAAP permits only the cost model.

For each intangible asset, a company assesses whether the useful life of the asset is finite or indefinite. Amortisation and impairment principles apply as follows:

- An intangible asset with a finite useful life is amortised on a systematic basis over the best estimate of its useful life, with the amortisation method and useful life estimate reviewed at least annually.
- Impairment principles for an intangible asset with a finite useful life are the same as for PPE.
- An intangible asset with an indefinite useful life is not amortised. Instead, at least annually, the reasonableness of assuming an indefinite useful life for the asset is reviewed and the asset is tested for impairment.

Financial analysts have traditionally viewed the values assigned to intangible assets, particularly goodwill, with caution. Consequently, in assessing financial statements, analysts often exclude the book value assigned to intangibles, reducing net equity by an equal amount and increasing pretax income by any amortisation expense or impairment associated with the intangibles. An arbitrary assignment of zero value to intangibles is not advisable; instead, an analyst should examine each listed intangible and assess whether an adjustment should be made. Note disclosures about intangible assets may provide useful information to the analyst. These disclosures include information about useful lives, amortisation rates and methods, and impairment losses recognised or reversed.

Further, a company may have developed intangible assets internally that can only be recognised in certain circumstances. Companies may also have assets that are never recorded on a balance sheet because they have no physical substance and are non-identifiable. These assets might include management skill, name recognition, a good reputation, and so forth. Such assets are valuable and are, in theory, reflected in the price at which the company's equity securities trade in the market (and the

12 IAS 40, *Investment Property*, paragraph 35.
13 IAS 38, *Intangible Assets*, paragraph 8.

price at which the entirety of the company's equity would be sold in an acquisition transaction). Such assets may be recognised as goodwill if a company is acquired, but are not recognised until an acquisition occurs.

4.3.1 *Identifiable Intangibles*

Under IFRS, identifiable intangible assets are recognised on the balance sheet if it is probable that future economic benefits will flow to the company and the cost of the asset can be measured reliably. Examples of identifiable intangible assets include patents, trademarks, copyrights, franchises, licenses, and other rights. Identifiable intangible assets may have been created internally or purchased by a company. Determining the cost of internally created intangible assets can be difficult and subjective. For these reasons, under IFRS and US GAAP, the general requirement is that internally created identifiable intangibles are expensed rather than reported on the balance sheet.

IFRS provides that for internally created intangible assets, the company must separately identify the research phase and the development phase.[14] The research phase includes activities that seek new knowledge or products. The development phase occurs after the research phase and includes design or testing of prototypes and models. IFRS require that costs to internally generate intangible assets during the research phase must be expensed on the income statement. Costs incurred in the development stage can be capitalized as intangible assets if certain criteria are met, including technological feasibility, the ability to use or sell the resulting asset, and the ability to complete the project.

US GAAP prohibits the capitalization as an asset of most costs of internally developed intangibles and research and development. All such costs usually must be expensed. Costs related to the following categories are typically expensed under IFRS and US GAAP. They include:

- internally generated brands, mastheads, publishing titles, customer lists, etc.;
- start-up costs;
- training costs;
- administrative and other general overhead costs;
- advertising and promotion;
- relocation and reorganization expenses; and
- redundancy and other termination costs.

Generally, acquired intangible assets are reported as separately identifiable intangibles (as opposed to goodwill) if they arise from contractual rights (such as a licensing agreement), other legal rights (such as patents), or have the ability to be separated and sold (such as a customer list).

EXAMPLE 3

Measuring Intangible Assets

Alpha Inc., a motor vehicle manufacturer, has a research division that worked on the following projects during the year:

Project 1	Research aimed at finding a steering mechanism that does not operate like a conventional steering wheel but reacts to the impulses from a driver's fingers.

14 IAS 38, *Intangible Assets*, paragraphs 51–67.

Project 2 The design of a prototype welding apparatus that is controlled electronically rather than mechanically. The apparatus has been determined to be technologically feasible, salable, and feasible to produce.

The following is a summary of the expenses of the research division (in thousands of €):

	General	Project 1	Project 2
Material and services	128	935	620
Labor			
• Direct labor	—	630	320
• Administrative personnel	720	—	—
Design, construction, and testing	270	450	470

Five percent of administrative personnel costs can be attributed to each of Projects 1 and 2. Explain the accounting treatment of Alpha's costs for Projects 1 and 2 under IFRS and US GAAP.

Solution:

Under IFRS, the capitalization of development costs for Projects 1 and 2 would be as follows:

		Amount Capitalized as an Asset (€'000)
Project 1:	Classified as in the research stage, so all costs are recognized as expenses	NIL
Project 2:	Classified as in the development stage, so costs may be capitalized. Note that administrative costs are not capitalized.	(620 + 320 + 410 + 60) = 1,410

Under US GAAP, the costs of Projects 1 and 2 are expensed.

As presented in Exhibits 8 and 9, SAP's 2017 balance sheet shows €2,967 million of intangible assets, and Apple's 2017 balance sheet shows acquired intangible assets, net of $2,298 million. SAP's notes disclose the types of intangible assets (software and database licenses, purchased software to be incorporated into its products, customer contracts, and acquired trademark licenses) and notes that all of its purchased intangible assets other than goodwill have finite useful lives and are amortised either based on expected consumption of economic benefits or on a straight-line basis over their estimated useful lives which range from two to 20 years. Apple's notes disclose that its acquired intangible assets consist primarily of patents and licenses, and almost the entire amount represents definite-lived and amortisable assets for which the remaining weighted-average amortisation period is 3.4 years as of 2017.

4.4 Goodwill

When one company acquires another, the purchase price is allocated to all the identifiable assets (tangible and intangible) and liabilities acquired, based on fair value. If the purchase price is greater than the acquirer's interest in the fair value of the identifiable assets and liabilities acquired, the excess amount is recognized as an asset, described as **goodwill**. To understand why an acquirer would pay more to purchase a company than the fair value of the target company's identifiable assets net of liabilities, consider the following three observations. First, as noted, certain items not recognized in a company's own financial statements (e.g., its reputation, established distribution system, trained employees) have value. Second, a target company's expenditures in research and development may not have resulted in a separately identifiable asset that meets the criteria for recognition but nonetheless may have created some value. Third, part of the value of an acquisition may arise from strategic positioning versus a competitor or from perceived synergies. The purchase price might not pertain solely to the separately identifiable assets and liabilities acquired and thus may exceed the value of those net assets due to the acquisition's role in protecting the value of all of the acquirer's existing assets or to cost savings and benefits from combining the companies.

The subject of recognizing goodwill in financial statements has found both proponents and opponents among professionals. The proponents of goodwill recognition assert that goodwill is the present value of excess returns that a company is expected to earn. This group claims that determining the present value of these excess returns is analogous to determining the present value of future cash flows associated with other assets and projects. Opponents of goodwill recognition claim that the prices paid for acquisitions often turn out to be based on unrealistic expectations, thereby leading to future write-offs of goodwill.

Analysts should distinguish between accounting goodwill and economic goodwill. Economic goodwill is based on the economic performance of the entity, whereas accounting goodwill is based on accounting standards and is reported only in the case of acquisitions. Economic goodwill is important to analysts and investors, and it is not necessarily reflected on the balance sheet. Instead, economic goodwill is reflected in the stock price (at least in theory). Some financial statement users believe that goodwill should not be listed on the balance sheet, because it cannot be sold separately from the entity. These financial statement users believe that only assets that can be separately identified and sold should be reflected on the balance sheet. Other financial statement users analyze goodwill and any subsequent impairment charges to assess management's performance on prior acquisitions.

Under both IFRS and US GAAP, accounting goodwill arising from acquisitions is capitalized. Goodwill is not amortised but is tested for impairment annually. If goodwill is deemed to be impaired, an impairment loss is charged against income in the current period. An impairment loss reduces current earnings. An impairment loss also reduces total assets, so some performance measures, such as return on assets (net income divided by average total assets), may actually increase in future periods. An impairment loss is a non-cash item.

Accounting standards' requirements for recognizing goodwill can be summarized by the following steps:

A The total cost to purchase the target company (the acquiree) is determined.

B The acquiree's identifiable assets are measured at fair value. The acquiree's liabilities and contingent liabilities are measured at fair value. The difference between the fair value of identifiable assets and the fair value of the liabilities and contingent liabilities equals the net identifiable assets acquired.

C Goodwill arising from the purchase is the excess of a) the cost to purchase the target company over b) the net identifiable assets acquired. Occasionally, a transaction will involve the purchase of net identifiable assets with a value greater than the cost to purchase. Such a transaction is called a "bargain purchase." Any gain from a bargain purchase is recognized in profit and loss in the period in which it arises.[15]

Companies are also required to disclose information that enables users to evaluate the nature and financial effect of business combinations. The required disclosures include, for example, the acquisition date fair value of the total cost to purchase the target company, the acquisition date amount recognized for each major class of assets and liabilities, and a qualitative description of the factors that make up the goodwill recognized.

Despite the guidance incorporated in accounting standards, analysts should be aware that the estimations of fair value involve considerable management judgment. Values for intangible assets, such as computer software, might not be easily validated when analyzing acquisitions. Management judgment about valuation in turn impacts current and future financial statements because identifiable intangible assets with definite lives are amortised over time. In contrast, neither goodwill nor identifiable intangible assets with indefinite lives are amortised; instead, as noted, both are tested annually for impairment.

The recognition and impairment of goodwill can significantly affect the comparability of financial statements between companies. Therefore, analysts often adjust the companies' financial statements by removing the impact of goodwill. Such adjustments include:

- excluding goodwill from balance sheet data used to compute financial ratios, and
- excluding goodwill impairment losses from income data used to examine operating trends.

In addition, analysts can develop expectations about a company's performance following an acquisition by taking into account the purchase price paid relative to the net assets and earnings prospects of the acquired company. Example 4 provides an historical example of goodwill impairment.

EXAMPLE 4

Goodwill Impairment

Safeway, Inc., is a North American food and drug retailer. On 25 February 2010, Safeway issued a press release that included the following information:

> Safeway Inc. today reported a net loss of $1,609.1 million ($4.06 per diluted share) for the 16-week fourth quarter of 2009. Excluding a non-cash goodwill impairment charge of $1,818.2 million, net of tax ($4.59 per diluted share), net income would have been $209.1 million ($0.53 per diluted share). Net income was $338.0 million ($0.79 per diluted share) for the 17-week fourth quarter of 2008.

15 IFRS 3 *Business Combinations* and FASB ASC 805 [Business Combinations].

In the fourth quarter of 2009, Safeway recorded a non-cash goodwill impairment charge of $1,974.2 million ($1,818.2 million, net of tax). The impairment was due primarily to Safeway's reduced market capitalization and a weak economy....The goodwill originated from previous acquisitions.

Safeway's balance sheet as of 2 January 2010 showed goodwill of $426.6 million and total assets of $14,963.6 million. The company's balance sheet as of 3 January 2009 showed goodwill of $2,390.2 million and total assets of $17,484.7 million.

1 How significant is this goodwill impairment charge?

2 With reference to acquisition prices, what might this goodwill impairment indicate?

Solution to 1:

The goodwill impairment was more than 80 percent of the total value of goodwill and 11 percent of total assets, so it was clearly significant. (The charge of $1,974.2 million equals 82.6 percent of the $2,390.2 million of goodwill at the beginning of the year and 11.3 percent of the $17,484.7 million total assets at the beginning of the year.)

Solution to 2:

The goodwill had originated from previous acquisitions. The impairment charge implies that the acquired operations are now worth less than the price that was paid for their acquisition.

As presented in Exhibits 8 and 9, SAP's 2017 balance sheet shows €21,274 million of goodwill, and Apple's 2017 balance sheet shows goodwill of $5,717 million. Goodwill represents 50.1 percent of SAP's total assets and only 1.5 percent of Apple's total assets. An analyst may be concerned that goodwill represents such a high proportion of SAP's total assets.

4.5 Financial Assets

IFRS define a financial instrument as a contract that gives rise to a financial asset of one entity, and a financial liability or equity instrument of another entity.[16] This section will focus on financial assets such as a company's investments in stocks issued by another company or its investments in the notes, bonds, or other fixed-income instruments issued by another company (or issued by a governmental entity). Financial liabilities such as notes payable and bonds payable issued by the company itself will be discussed in the liability portion of this reading. Some financial instruments may be classified as either an asset or a liability depending on the contractual terms and current market conditions. One example of such a financial instrument is a derivative. **Derivatives** are financial instruments for which the value is derived based on some underlying factor (interest rate, exchange rate, commodity price, security price, or credit rating) and for which little or no initial investment is required.

Financial instruments are generally recognized when the entity becomes a party to the contractual provisions of the instrument. In general, there are two basic alternative ways that financial instruments are measured subsequent to initial acquisition: fair value or amortised cost. Recall that fair value is the price that would be received

16 IAS 32, *Financial Instruments: Presentation*, paragraph 11.

to sell an asset or paid to transfer a liability in an orderly market transaction.[17] The **amortised cost** of a financial asset (or liability) is the amount at which it was initially recognized, minus any principal repayments, plus or minus any amortisation of discount or premium, and minus any reduction for impairment.

Under IFRS, financial assets are subsequently measured at amortised cost if the asset's cash flows occur on specified dates and consist solely of principal and interest, and if the business model is to hold the asset to maturity. The concept is similar in US GAAP, where this category of asset is referred to as **held-to-maturity**. An example is an investment in a long-term bond issued by another company or by a government; the value of the bond will fluctuate, for example with interest rate movements, but if the bond is classified as a held-to-maturity investment, it will be measured at amortised cost on the balance sheet of the investing company. Other types of financial assets measured at historical cost are loans to other companies.

Financial assets not measured at amortised cost subsequent to acquisition are measured at fair value as of the reporting date. For financial instruments measured at fair value, there are two basic alternatives in how net changes in fair value are recognized: as profit or loss on the income statement, or as other comprehensive income (loss) which bypasses the income statement. Note that these alternatives refer to *un*realized changes in fair value, i.e., changes in the value of a financial asset that has not been sold and is still owned at the end of the period. Unrealized gains and losses are also referred to as holding period gains and losses. If a financial asset is sold within the period, a gain is realized if the selling price is greater than the carrying value and a loss is realized if the selling price is less than the carrying value. When a financial asset is sold, any realized gain or loss is reported on the income statement.

Under IFRS, financial assets are subsequently measured at fair value through other comprehensive income (i.e., any unrealized holding gains or losses are recognized in other comprehensive income) if the business model's objective involves both collecting contractual cash flows and selling the financial assets. This IFRS category applies specifically to debt investments, namely assets with cash flows occurring on specified dates and consisting solely of principal and interest. However, IFRS also permits equity investments to be measured at fair value through other comprehensive income if, at the time a company buys an equity investment, the company decides to make an irrevocable election to measure the asset in this manner.[18] The concept is similar to the US GAAP investment category **available-for-sale** in which assets are measured at fair value, with any unrealized holding gains or losses recognized in other comprehensive income. However, unlike IFRS, the US GAAP category available-for-sale applies only to debt securities and is not permitted for investments in equity securities.[19]

Under IFRS, financial assets are subsequently measured at fair value through profit or loss (i.e., any unrealized holding gains or losses are recognized in the income statement) if they are not assigned to either of the other two measurement categories described above. In addition, IFRS allows a company to make an irrevocable election at acquisition to measure a financial asset in this category. Under US GAAP, all investments in equity securities (other than investments giving rise to ownership positions that confer significant influence over the investee) are measured at fair value with unrealized holding gains or losses recognized in the income statement. Under US GAAP, debt securities designated as trading securities are also measured at fair value with unrealized holding gains or losses recognized in the income statement. The trading securities category pertains to a debt security that is acquired with the intent of selling it rather than holding it to collect the interest and principal payments.

17 IFRS 13 *Fair Value Measurement* and US GAAP ASC 820 *Fair Value Measurement.*

18 IFRS 7 *Financial Instruments: Disclosures*, paragraph 8(h) and IFRS 9 *Financial Instruments*, paragraph 5.7.5.

19 US GAAP ASU 2016-01 and ASC 32X *Investments.*

Exhibit 10 summarizes how various financial assets are classified and measured subsequent to acquisition.

Exhibit 10 Measurement of Financial Assets

Measured at Cost or Amortised Cost	Measured at Fair Value through Other Comprehensive Income	Measured at Fair Value through Profit and Loss
■ Debt securities that are to be held to maturity. ■ Loans and notes receivable ■ Unquoted equity instruments (in limited circumstances where the fair value is not reliably measurable, cost may serve as a proxy (estimate) for fair value)	■ "Available-for-sale" debt securities (US GAAP); Debt securities where the business model involves both collecting interest and principal and selling the security (IFRS); ■ Equity investments for which the company irrevocably elects this measurement at acquisition (IFRS only)	■ All equity securities unless the investment gives the investor significant influence (US GAAP only) ■ "Trading" debt securities (US GAAP) ■ Securities not assigned to either of the other two categories, or investments for which the company irrevocably elects this measurement at acquisition (IFRS only)

To illustrate the different accounting treatments of the gains and losses on financial assets, consider an entity that invests €100,000,000 on 1 January 200X in a fixed-income security investment, with a 5 percent coupon paid semi-annually. After six months, the company receives the first coupon payment of €2,500,000. Additionally, market interest rates have declined such that the value of the fixed-income investment has increased by €2,000,000 as of 30 June 200X. Exhibit 11 illustrates how this situation will be portrayed in the balance sheet and income statement (ignoring taxes) of the entity concerned, under each of the following three measurement categories of financial assets: assets held for trading purposes, assets available for sale, and held-to-maturity assets.

Exhibit 11 Accounting for Gains and Losses on Marketable Securities

IFRS Categories	**Measured at Cost or Amortised Cost**	**Measured at Fair Value through Other Comprehensive Income**	**Measured at Fair Value through Profit and Loss**
US GAAP Comparable Categories	***Held to Maturity***	***Available-for-Sale Debt Securities***	***Trading Debt Securities***
Income Statement For period 1 January–30 June 200X			
Interest income	2,500,000	2,500,000	2,500,000
Unrealized gains	—	—	2,000,000
Impact on profit and loss	2,500,000	2,500,000	4,500,000

Exhibit 11 (Continued)

Balance Sheet As of 30 June 200X

Assets			
Cash and cash equivalents	2,500,000	2,500,000	2,500,000
Cost of securities	100,000,000	100,000,000	100,000,000
Unrealized gains on securities	—	2,000,000	2,000,000
	102,500,000	104,500,000	104,500,000
Liabilities			
Equity			
Paid-in capital	100,000,000	100,000,000	100,000,000
Retained earnings	2,500,000	2,500,000	4,500,000
Accumulated other comprehensive income	—	2,000,000	—
	102,500,000	104,500,000	104,500,000

In the case of held-to-maturity securities, the income statement shows only the interest income (which is then reflected in retained earnings of the ending balance sheet). Because the securities are measured at cost rather than fair value, no unrealized gain is recognized. On the balance sheet, the investment asset is shown at its amortised cost of €100,000,000. In the case of securities classified as Measured at Fair Value through Other Comprehensive Income (IFRS) or equivalently as Available-for-sale debt securities (US GAAP), the income statement shows only the interest income (which is then reflected in retained earnings of the balance sheet). The unrealized gain does not appear on the income statement; instead, it would appear on a Statement of Comprehensive Income as Other Comprehensive Income. On the balance sheet, the investment asset is shown at its fair value of €102,000,000. (Exhibit 11 shows the unrealized gain on a separate line solely to highlight the impact of the change in value. In practice, the investments would be shown at their fair value on a single line.) In the case of securities classified as Measured at Fair Value through Profit and Loss (IFRS) or equivalently as trading debt securities (US GAAP), both the interest income and the unrealized gain are included on the income statement and thus reflected in retained earnings on the balance sheet.

In Exhibits 4 and 8, SAP's 2017 balance sheet shows other financial assets of €990 million (current) and €1,155 million (non-current). The company's notes disclose that the largest component of the current financial assets are loans and other financial receivables (€793 million) and the largest component of the non-current financial assets is €827 million of available-for-sale equity investments.

In Exhibits 5 and 9, Apple's 2017 balance sheet shows $53,892 million of short-term marketable securities and $194,714 million of long-term marketable securities. In total, marketable securities represent more than 66 percent of Apple's $375.3 billion in total assets. Marketable securities plus cash and cash equivalents represent around 72 percent of the company's total assets. Apple's notes disclose that most of the company's marketable securities are fixed-income securities issued by the US government or its agencies ($60,237 million) and by other companies including commercial paper ($153,451 million). In accordance with its investment policy, Apple invests in highly rated securities (which the company defines as investment grade) and limits

its credit exposure to any one issuer. The company classifies its marketable securities as available for sale and reports them on the balance sheet at fair value. Unrealized gains and losses are reported in other comprehensive income.

4.6 Deferred Tax Assets

Portions of the amounts shown as **deferred tax assets** on SAP's balance sheet represent income taxes incurred prior to the time that the income tax expense will be recognized on the income statement. Deferred tax assets may result when the actual **income tax payable** based on income for tax purposes in a period exceeds the amount of income tax expense based on the reported financial statement income due to temporary timing differences. For example, a company may be required to report certain income for tax purposes in the current period but to defer recognition of that income for financial statement purposes to subsequent periods. In this case, the company will pay income tax as required by tax laws, and the difference between the taxes payable and the tax expense related to the income for which recognition was deferred on the financial statements will be reported as a deferred tax asset. When the income is subsequently recognized on the income statement, the related tax expense is also recognized which will reduce the deferred tax asset.

Also, a company may claim certain expenses for financial statement purposes that it is only allowed to claim in subsequent periods for tax purposes. In this case, as in the previous example, the financial statement income before taxes is less than taxable income. Thus, income taxes payable based on taxable income exceeds income tax expense based on accounting net income before taxes. The difference is expected to reverse in the future when the income reported on the financial statements exceeds the taxable income as a deduction for the expense becomes allowed for tax purposes. Deferred tax assets may also result from carrying forward unused tax losses and credits (these are not temporary timing differences). Deferred tax assets are only to be recognized if there is an expectation that there will be taxable income in the future, against which the temporary difference or carried forward tax losses or credits can be applied to reduce taxes payable.

5 NON-CURRENT LIABILITIES

All liabilities that are not classified as current are considered to be non-current or long-term. Exhibits 12 and 13 present balance sheet excerpts for SAP Group and Apple Inc. showing the line items for the companies' non-current liabilities.

Both companies' balance sheets show non-current unearned revenue (deferred income for SAP Group and deferred revenue for Apple). These amounts represent the amounts of unearned revenue relating to goods and services expected to be delivered in periods beyond twelve months following the reporting period. The sections that follow focus on two common types of non-current (long-term) liabilities: long-term financial liabilities and deferred tax liabilities.

Exhibit 12 SAP Group Consolidated Statements of Financial Position (Excerpt: Non-Current Liabilities Detail) (in millions of €)

	as of 31 December	
	2017	**2016**
Assets		
Total current assets	11,930	11,564
Total non-current assets	30,567	32,713
Total assets	42,497	44,277
Total current liabilities	10,210	9,674
Trade and other payables	119	127
Tax liabilities	470	365
Financial liabilities	5,034	6,481
Other non-financial liabilities	503	461
Provisions	303	217
Deferred tax liabilities	240	411
Deferred income	79	143
Total non-current liabilities	6,747	8,205
Total liabilities	16,958	17,880
Total equity	25,540	26,397
Total equity and liabilities	€42,497	€44,277

Source: SAP Group 2017 annual report.

Exhibit 13 Apple Inc. Consolidated Balance Sheet (Excerpt: Non-Current Liabilities Detail)* (in millions of $)

Assets	**30 September 2017**	**24 September 2016**
Total current assets	128,645	106,869
[All other assets]	*246,674*	*214,817*
Total assets	375,319	321,686
Liabilities and shareholders' equity		
Total current liabilities	100,814	79,006
Deferred revenue, non-current	2,836	2,930
Long-term debt	97,207	75,427
Other non-current liabilities	40,415	36,074
[Total non-current liabilities]	*140,458*	*114,431*
Total liabilities	241,272	193,437
Total shareholders' equity	134,047	128,249
Total liabilities and shareholders' equity	375,319	321,686

**Note:* The italicized subtotals presented in this excerpt are not explicitly shown on the face of the financial statement as prepared by the company.
Source: Apple Inc. 2017 annual report (Form 10K).

5.1 Long-term Financial Liabilities

Typical long-term financial liabilities include loans (i.e., borrowings from banks) and notes or bonds payable (i.e., fixed-income securities issued to investors). Liabilities such as loans payable and bonds payable are usually reported at amortised cost on the balance sheet. At maturity, the amortised cost of the bond (carrying amount) will be equal to the face value of the bond. For example, if a company issues $10,000,000 of bonds at par, the bonds are reported as a long-term liability of $10 million. The carrying amount (amortised cost) from the date of issue to the date of maturity remains at $10 million. As another example, if a company issues $10,000,000 of bonds at a price of 97.50 (a discount to par), the bonds are reported as a liability of $9,750,000 at issue date. Over the bond's life, the discount of $250,000 is amortised so that the bond will be reported as a liability of $10,000,000 at maturity. Similarly, any bond premium would be amortised for bonds issued at a price in excess of face or par value.

In certain cases, liabilities such as bonds issued by a company are reported at fair value. Those cases include financial liabilities held for trading, derivatives that are a liability to the company, and some non-derivative instruments such as those which are hedged by derivatives.

SAP's balance sheet in Exhibit 12 shows €5,034 million of financial liabilities, and the notes disclose that these liabilities are mostly for bonds payable. Apple's balance sheet shows $97,207 million of long-term debt, and the notes disclose that this debt includes floating- and fixed-rate notes with varying maturities.

5.2 Deferred Tax Liabilities

Deferred tax liabilities result from temporary timing differences between a company's income as reported for tax purposes (taxable income) and income as reported for financial statement purposes (reported income). Deferred tax liabilities result when taxable income and the actual income tax payable in a period based on it is less than the reported financial statement income before taxes and the income tax expense based on it. Deferred tax liabilities are defined as the amounts of income taxes payable in future periods in respect of taxable temporary differences.[20] In contrast, in the previous discussion of unearned revenue, inclusion of revenue in taxable income in an earlier period created a deferred tax asset (essentially prepaid tax).

Deferred tax liabilities typically arise when items of expense are included in taxable income in earlier periods than for financial statement net income. This results in taxable income being less than income before taxes in the earlier periods. As a result, taxes payable based on taxable income are less than income tax expense based on accounting income before taxes. The difference between taxes payable and income tax expense results in a deferred tax liability—for example, when companies use accelerated depreciation methods for tax purposes and straight-line depreciation methods for financial statement purposes. Deferred tax liabilities also arise when items of income are included in taxable income in later periods—for example, when a company's subsidiary has profits that have not yet been distributed and thus have not yet been taxed.

SAP's balance sheet in Exhibit 12 shows €240 million of deferred tax liabilities. Apple's balance sheet in Exhibit 13 does not show a separate line item for deferred tax liabilities, however, note disclosures indicate that most of the $40,415 million of other non-current liabilities reported on Apple's balance sheet represents deferred tax liabilities, which totaled $31,504 million.

20 IAS 12, *Income Taxes*, paragraph 5.

EQUITY

6

Equity is the owners' residual claim on a company's assets after subtracting its liabilities.[21] It represents the claim of the owner against the company. Equity includes funds directly invested in the company by the owners, as well as earnings that have been reinvested over time. Equity can also include items of gain or loss that are not recognized on the company's income statement.

6.1 Components of Equity

Six main components typically comprise total owners' equity. The first five components listed below comprise equity attributable to owners of the parent company. The sixth component is the equity attributable to non-controlling interests.

1 *Capital contributed by owners* (or common stock, or issued capital). The amount contributed to the company by owners. Ownership of a corporation is evidenced through the issuance of common shares. Common shares may have a par value (or stated value) or may be issued as no par shares (depending on regulations governing the incorporation). Where par or stated value requirements exist, it must be disclosed in the equity section of the balance sheet. In addition, the number of shares authorized, issued, and outstanding must be disclosed for each class of share issued by the company. The number of authorized shares is the number of shares that may be sold by the company under its articles of incorporation. The number of issued shares refers to those shares that have been sold to investors. The number of outstanding shares consists of the issued shares less treasury shares.

2 *Preferred shares.* Classified as equity or financial liabilities based upon their characteristics rather than legal form. For example, perpetual, non-redeemable preferred shares are classified as equity. In contrast, preferred shares with mandatory redemption at a fixed amount at a future date are classified as financial liabilities. Preferred shares have rights that take precedence over the rights of common shareholders—rights that generally pertain to receipt of dividends and receipt of assets if the company is liquidated.

3 *Treasury shares* (or treasury stock or own shares repurchased). Shares in the company that have been repurchased by the company and are held as treasury shares, rather than being cancelled. The company is able to sell (reissue) these shares. A company may repurchase its shares when management considers the shares undervalued, needs shares to fulfill employees' stock options, or wants to limit the effects of dilution from various employee stock compensation plans. A repurchase of previously issued shares reduces shareholders' equity by the amount of the cost of repurchasing the shares and reduces the number of total shares outstanding. If treasury shares are subsequently reissued, a company does not recognize any gain or loss from the reissuance on the income statement. Treasury shares are non-voting and do not receive any dividends declared by the company.

4 *Retained earnings.* The cumulative amount of earnings recognized in the company's income statements which have not been paid to the owners of the company as dividends.

21 IASB *Conceptual Framework (2018)*, paragraph 4.4 (c) and FASB ASC 505-10-05-3 [Equity–Overview and Background].

5 *Accumulated other comprehensive income* (or other reserves). The cumulative amount of *other* comprehensive income or loss. The term comprehensive income includes both a) net income, which is recognized on the income statement and is reflected in retained earnings, and b) other comprehensive income which is not recognized as part of net income and is reflected in accumulated other comprehensive income.[22]

6 *Noncontrolling interest* (or minority interest). The equity interests of minority shareholders in the subsidiary companies that have been consolidated by the parent (controlling) company but that are not wholly owned by the parent company.

Exhibits 14 and 15 present excerpts of the balance sheets of SAP Group and Apple Inc., respectively, with detailed line items for each company's equity section. SAP's balance sheet indicates that the company has €1,229 million issued capital, and the notes to the financial statements disclose that the company has issued 1,229 million no-par common stock with a nominal value of €1 per share. SAP's balance sheet also indicates that the company has €1,591 of treasury shares, and the notes to the financial statements disclose that the company holds 35 million of its shares as treasury shares. The line item share premium of €570 million includes amounts from treasury share transactions (and certain other transactions). The amount of retained earnings, €24,794 million, represents the cumulative amount of earnings that the company has recognized in its income statements, net of dividends. SAP's €508 million of "Other components of equity" includes the company's accumulated other comprehensive income. The notes disclose that this is composed of €330 million gains on exchange differences in translation, €157 million gains on remeasuring available-for-sale financial assets, and €21 million gains on cash flow hedges. The balance sheet next presents a subtotal for the amount of equity attributable to the parent company €25,509 million followed by the amount of equity attributable to non-controlling interests €31 million. Total equity includes both equity attributable to the parent company and equity attributable to non-controlling interests.

The equity section of Apple's balance sheet consists of only three line items: common stock, retained earnings, and accumulated other comprehensive income/(loss). Although Apple's balance sheet shows no treasury stock, the company does repurchase its own shares but cancels the repurchased shares rather than holding the shares in treasury. Apple's balance sheet shows that 5,126,201 thousand shares were issued and outstanding at the end of fiscal 2017 and 5,336,166 thousand shares were issued and outstanding at the end of fiscal 2016. Details on the change in shares outstanding is presented on the Statement of Shareholders' Equity in Exhibit 15, which shows that in 2017 Apple repurchased 246,496 thousand shares of its previously issued common stock and issued 36,531 thousand shares to employees.

---

22 IFRS defines Total comprehensive income as "the change in equity during a period resulting from transactions and other events, other than those changes resulting from transactions with owners in their capacity as owners. (IAS 1, Presentation of Financial Statements, paragraph 7. Similarly, US GAAP defines comprehensive income as "the change in equity [net assets] of a business entity during a period from transactions and other events and circumstances from nonowner sources. It includes all changes in equity during a period except those resulting from investments by owners and distributions to owners." (FASB ASC *Master Glossary*.)

Exhibit 14 SAP Group Consolidated Statements of Financial Position (Excerpt: Equity Detail) (in millions of €)

Assets	as of 31 December 2017	2016
Total current assets	11,930	11,564
Total non-current assets	30,567	32,713
Total assets	42,497	44,277
Total current liabilities	10,210	9,674
Total non-current liabilities	6,747	8,205
Total liabilities	16,958	17,880
Issued capital	1,229	1,229
Share premium	570	599
Retained earnings	24,794	22,302
Other components of equity	508	3,346
Treasury shares	(1,591)	(1,099)
Equity attributable to owners of parent	25,509	26,376
Non-controlling interests	31	21
Total equity	25,540	26,397
Total equity and liabilities	€42,497	€44,277

Source: SAP Group 2017 annual report.

Exhibit 15 Apple Inc. Consolidated Balance Sheet (Excerpt: Equity Detail) (in millions of $) (Number of shares are reflected in thousands)

Assets	30 September 2017	24 September 2016
Total current assets	128,645	106,869
[All other assets]	*246,674*	*214,817*
Total assets	375,319	321,686
Liabilities and shareholders' equity		
Total current liabilities	100,814	79,006
[Total non-current liabilities]	*140,458*	*114,431*
Total liabilities	241,272	193,437
Common stock and additional paid-in capital, $0.00001 par value: 12,600,000 shares authorized; 5,126,201 and 5,336,166 shares issued and outstanding, respectively	35,867	31,251
Retained earnings	98,330	96,364
Accumulated other comprehensive income/(loss)	(150)	634

(continued)

Exhibit 15 (Continued)

Assets	30 September 2017	24 September 2016
Total shareholders' equity	134,047	128,249
Total liabilities and shareholders' equity	375,319	321,686

Source: Apple Inc. 2017 annual report (10K).

6.2 Statement of Changes in Equity

The **statement of changes in equity** (or statement of shareholders' equity) presents information about the increases or decreases in a company's equity over a period. IFRS requires the following information in the statement of changes in equity:

- total comprehensive income for the period;
- the effects of any accounting changes that have been retrospectively applied to previous periods;
- capital transactions with owners and distributions to owners; and
- reconciliation of the carrying amounts of each component of equity at the beginning and end of the year.[23]

Under US GAAP, the requirement as specified by the SEC is for companies to provide an analysis of changes in each component of stockholders' equity that is shown in the balance sheet.[24]

Exhibit 16 presents an excerpt from Apple's Consolidated Statements of Changes in Shareholders' Equity. The excerpt shows only one of the years presented on the actual statement. It begins with the balance as of 24 September 2016 (i.e., the beginning of fiscal 2017) and presents the analysis of changes to 30 September 2017 in each component of equity that is shown on Apple's balance sheet. As noted above, the number of shares outstanding decreased from 5,336,166 thousand to 5,126,201 thousand as the company repurchased 246,496 thousand shares of its common stock and issued 36,531 thousand new shares which reduced the dollar balance of Paid-in Capital and Retained earnings by $913 million and $581 million, respectively. The dollar balance in common stock also increased by $ 4,909 million in connection with share-based compensation. Retained earnings increased by $48,351 million net income, minus $12,803 million dividends, $33,001 million for the share repurchase and $581 million adjustment in connection with the stock issuance. For companies that pay dividends, the amount of dividends are shown separately as a deduction from retained earnings. The statement also provides details on the $784 million change in Apple's Accumulated other comprehensive income. Note that the statement provides a subtotal for total comprehensive income that includes net income and each of the components of other comprehensive income.

23 IAS 1, *Presentation of Financial Statements*, paragraph 106.

24 FASB ASC 505-10-S99 [Equity–Overall–SEC materials] indicates that a company can present the analysis of changes in stockholders' equity either in the notes or in a separate statement.

Exhibit 16 Excerpt from Apple Inc.'s Consolidated Statements of Changes in Shareholders' Equity (in millions, except share amounts which are reflected in thousands)

	Common Stock and Additional Paid-In Capital		Retained Earnings	Accumulated Other Comprehensive Income/(Loss)	Total Shareholders' Equity
	Shares	Amount			
Balances as of September 24, 2016	5,336,166	31,251	96,364	634	128,249
Net income	—	—	48,351	—	48,351
Other comprehensive income/(loss)	—	—	—	(784)	(784)
Dividends and dividend equivalents declared	—	—	(12,803)	—	(12,803)
Repurchase of common stock	(246,496)	—	(33,001)	—	(33,001)
Share-based compensation	—	4,909	—	—	4,909
Common stock issued, net of shares withheld for employee taxes	36,531	(913)	(581)	—	(1,494)
Tax benefit from equity awards, including transfer pricing adjustments		620	—	—	620
Balances as of September 30, 2017	5,126,201	35,867	98,330	(150)	134,047

ANALYSIS OF THE BALANCE SHEET

7

This section describes two tools for analyzing the balance sheet: common-size analysis and balance sheet ratios. Analysis of a company's balance sheet can provide insight into the company's liquidity and solvency—as of the balance sheet date—as well as the economic resources the company controls. **Liquidity** refers to a company's ability to meet its short-term financial commitments. Assessments of liquidity focus a company's ability to convert assets to cash and to pay for operating needs. **Solvency** refers to a company's ability to meet its financial obligations over the longer term. Assessments of solvency focus on the company's financial structure and its ability to pay long-term financing obligations.

7.1 Common-Size Analysis of the Balance Sheet

The first technique, vertical common-size analysis, involves stating each balance sheet item as a percentage of total assets.[25] Common-size statements are useful in comparing a company's balance sheet composition over time (time-series analysis) and across companies in the same industry. To illustrate, Panel A of Exhibit 17 presents a balance sheet for three hypothetical companies. Company C, with assets of $9.75 million is

25 As discussed in the curriculum reading on financial statement analysis, another type of common-size analysis, known as "horizontal common-size analysis," states quantities in terms of a selected base-year value. Unless otherwise indicated, text references to "common-size analysis" refer to vertical analysis.

much larger than Company A and Company B, each with only $3.25 million in assets. The common-size balance sheet presented in Panel B facilitates a comparison of these different sized companies.

Exhibit 17

Panel A: Balance Sheets for Companies A, B, and C

($ Thousands)	A	B	C
ASSETS			
Current assets			
Cash and cash equivalents	1,000	200	3,000
Short-term marketable securities	900	—	300
Accounts receivable	500	1,050	1,500
Inventory	100	950	300
Total current assets	2,500	2,200	5,100
Property, plant, and equipment, net	750	750	4,650
Intangible assets	—	200	—
Goodwill	—	100	—
Total assets	3,250	3,250	9,750
LIABILITIES AND SHAREHOLDERS' EQUITY			
Current liabilities			
Accounts payable	—	2,500	600
Total current liabilities	—	2,500	600
Long term bonds payable	10	10	9,000
Total liabilities	10	2,510	9,600
Total shareholders' equity	3,240	740	150
Total liabilities and shareholders' equity	3,250	3,250	9,750

Panel B: Common-Size Balance Sheets for Companies A, B, and C

(Percent)	A	B	C
ASSETS			
Current assets			
Cash and cash equivalents	30.8	6.2	30.8
Short-term marketable securities	27.7	0.0	3.1
Accounts receivable	15.4	32.3	15.4
Inventory	3.1	29.2	3.1
Total current assets	76.9	67.7	52.3
Property, plant and equipment, net	23.1	23.1	47.7
Intangible assets	0.0	6.2	0.0
Goodwill	0.0	3.1	0.0
Total assets	100.0	100.0	100.0
LIABILITIES AND SHAREHOLDERS' EQUITY			

Exhibit 17 (Continued)

Panel B: Common-Size Balance Sheets for Companies A, B, and C

(Percent)	**A**	**B**	**C**
Current liabilities			
Accounts payable	0.0	76.9	6.2
Total current liabilities	0.0	76.9	6.2
Long term bonds payable	0.3	0.3	92.3
Total liabilities	0.3	77.2	98.5
Total shareholders' equity	99.7	22.8	1.5
Total liabilities and shareholders' equity	100.0	100.0	100.0

Most of the assets of Company A and B are current assets; however, Company A has nearly 60 percent of its total assets in cash and short-term marketable securities while Company B has only 6 percent of its assets in cash. Company A is more liquid than Company B. Company A shows no current liabilities (its current liabilities round to less than $10 thousand), and it has cash on hand of $1.0 million to meet any near-term financial obligations it might have. In contrast, Company B has $2.5 million of current liabilities which exceed its available cash of only $200 thousand. To pay those near-term obligations, Company B will need to collect some of its accounts receivables, sell more inventory, borrow from a bank, and/or raise more long-term capital (e.g., by issuing more bonds or more equity). Company C also appears more liquid than Company B. It holds over 30 percent of its total assets in cash and short-term marketable securities, and its current liabilities are only 6.2 percent of the amount of total assets.

Company C's $3.3 million in cash and short-term marketable securities is substantially more than its current liabilities of $600 thousand. Turning to the question of solvency, however, note that 98.5 percent of Company C's assets are financed with liabilities. If Company C experiences significant fluctuations in cash flows, it may be unable to pay the interest and principal on its long-term bonds. Company A is far more solvent than Company C, with less than one percent of its assets financed with liabilities.

Note that these examples are hypothetical only. Other than general comparisons, little more can be said without further detail. In practice, a wide range of factors affect a company's liquidity management and capital structure. The study of optimal **capital structure** is a fundamental issue addressed in corporate finance. Capital refers to a company's long-term debt and equity financing; capital structure refers to the proportion of debt versus equity financing.

Common-size balance sheets can also highlight differences in companies' strategies. Comparing the asset composition of the companies, Company C has made a greater proportional investment in property, plant, and equipment—possibly because it manufactures more of its products in-house. The presence of goodwill on Company B's balance sheet signifies that it has made one or more acquisitions in the past. In contrast, the lack of goodwill on the balance sheets of Company A and Company C suggests that these two companies may have pursued a strategy of internal growth rather than growth by acquisition. Company A may be in either a start-up or liquidation stage of operations as evidenced by the composition of its balance sheet. It has relatively little inventory and no accounts payable. It either has not yet established trade credit or it is in the process of paying off its obligations in the process of liquidating.

EXAMPLE 5

Common-Size Analysis

Applying common-size analysis to the excerpts of SAP Group's balance sheets presented in Exhibits 4, 6, 8, and 12, answer the following: In 2017 relative to 2016, which of the following line items increased as a percentage of assets?

A Cash and cash equivalents.

B Total current assets.

C Total financial liabilities

D Total deferred income.

Solution:

A, B, and D are correct. The following items increased as a percentage of total assets:

- Cash and cash equivalents increased from 8.4 percent of total assets in 2016 (€3,702 ÷ €44,277) to 9.4 percent in 2017 (€4,011 ÷ €42,497).
- Total current assets increased from 26.1 percent of total assets in 2016 (€11,564 ÷ €44,277) to 28.1 percent in 2017 (€11,930 ÷ €42,497).
- Total deferred income increased from 5.7 percent of total assets in 2016 ((€ 2,383 +€143) ÷ €44,277) to 6.7 percent in 2017 ((€ 2,771 +€79) ÷ €42,497).

Total financial liabilities decreased both in absolute Euro amounts and as a percentage of total assets when compared with the previous year.

Note that some amounts of the company's deferred income and financial liabilities are classified as current liabilities (shown in Exhibit 6) and some amounts are classified as non-current liabilities (shown in Exhibit 12). The total amounts—current and non-current—of deferred income and financial liabilities, therefore, are obtained by summing the amounts in Exhibits 6 and 12.

Overall, aspects of the company's liquidity position are somewhat stronger in 2017 compared to 2016. The company's cash balances as a percentage of total assets increased. While current liabilities increased as a percentage of total assets and total liabilities remained approximately the same percentage, the mix of liabilities shifted. Financial liabilities, which represent future cash outlays, decreased as a percentage of total assets, while deferred revenues, which represent cash received in advance of revenue recognition, increased.

Common-size analysis of the balance sheet is particularly useful in cross-sectional analysis—comparing companies to each other for a particular time period or comparing a company with industry or sector data. The analyst could select individual peer companies for comparison, use industry data from published sources, or compile data from databases. When analyzing a company, many analysts prefer to select the peer companies for comparison or to compile their own industry statistics.

Exhibit 18 Common-Size Balance Sheet Statistics for the S&P 500 Grouped by S&P/MSCI GICS Sector (in percent except No. of Observations; data for 2017)

Panel A. Median Data

	10 Energy	15 Materials	20 Industrials	25 Consumer Discretionary	30 Consumer Staples	35 Health Care	40 Financials	45 Information Technology	50 Telecommunication Services	55 Utilities	60 Real Estate
Number of observation	34	27	68	81	33	59	64	64	4	29	30
Cash and short-term investments	6.8%	6.3%	8.1%	8.3%	4.1%	11.2%	6.2%	22.7%	1.2%	0.7%	1.4%
Receivables	5.8%	8.8%	12.9%	6.8%	6.5%	9.7%	20.4%	9.6%	3.7%	3.6%	2.0%
Inventories	1.6%	8.9%	6.9%	14.9%	9.6%	4.3%	0.0%	1.3%	0.3%	1.7%	0.0%
Total current assets	16.1%	26.0%	30.5%	41.5%	29.1%	31.4%	N.A.	48.7%	8.6%	7.3%	10.8%
PPE	73.3%	36.3%	12.5%	19.8%	17.2%	8.1%	0.9%	6.2%	35.0%	72.0%	33.4%
Intangibles	1.6%	27.9%	33.3%	16.8%	41.9%	37.6%	2.8%	26.4%	49.6%	6.2%	1.0%
Goodwill	*0.7%*	*20.0%*	*28.3%*	*11.3%*	*26.2%*	*22.8%*	*2.2%*	*22.3%*	*26.0%*	*4.8%*	*0.0%*
Accounts payable	5.7%	7.3%	6.2%	8.0%	8.0%	3.1%	27.0%	2.7%	2.5%	3.0%	1.3%
Current liabilities	10.9%	16.5%	22.5%	25.8%	25.0%	16.5%	N.A.	21.2%	11.5%	11.5%	7.1%
LT debt	27.3%	31.4%	28.0%	28.7%	32.3%	24.3%	6.4%	22.9%	46.8%	32.5%	43.4%
Total liabilities	49.3%	64.2%	65.5%	64.9%	63.8%	59.2%	86.7%	59.9%	75.8%	71.8%	53.3%
Common equity	47.3%	33.8%	34.5%	34.7%	36.2%	39.4%	12.6%	39.3%	23.9%	27.7%	40.4%
Preferred stock	0.0%	0.0%	0.0%	0.0%	0.0%	0.0%	0.0%	0.0%	0.0%	0.0%	0.0%
Total equity	47.3%	33.8%	34.5%	34.7%	36.2%	39.4%	13.2%	39.3%	23.9%	28.0%	41.8%

Exhibit 18 (Continued)

Panel B. Mean Data

	10 Energy	15 Materials	20 Industrials	25 Consumer Discretionary	30 Consumer Staples	35 Health Care	40 Financials	45 Information Technology	50 Telecommunication Services	55 Utilities	60 Real Estate
Number of observations	34	27	68	81	33	59	64	64	4	29	30
Cash and short-term investments	6.9%	7.4%	9.2%	12.9%	7.3%	15.4%	11.2%	28.3%	3.6%	1.3%	2.9%
Receivables	6.6%	10.5%	15.2%	9.0%	7.7%	11.2%	31.5%	11.8%	5.0%	3.8%	3.8%
Inventories	3.4%	9.3%	7.8%	18.3%	10.6%	6.3%	3.8%	4.1%	0.3%	1.6%	0.1%
Total current assets	17.7%	28.8%	32.9%	40.6%	27.8%	36.4%	N.A.	49.4%	10.1%	8.6%	16.1%
PPE	68.0%	36.9%	24.5%	25.1%	21.6%	11.2%	2.1%	10.3%	39.0%	69.9%	34.9%
Intangibles	7.8%	26.6%	35.6%	23.0%	43.6%	43.9%	11.4%	31.1%	48.2%	6.8%	10.3%
Goodwill	5.4%	18.4%	26.8%	14.6%	24.6%	27.3%	7.7%	24.5%	25.9%	5.7%	5.7%
Accounts payable	5.9%	8.1%	7.1%	11.8%	9.8%	8.1%	35.9%	5.1%	3.1%	2.9%	2.0%
Current liabilities	11.8%	17.0%	23.0%	26.8%	24.6%	21.2%	N.A.	26.1%	11.9%	11.8%	12.8%
LT debt	28.3%	31.2%	29.4%	31.3%	32.4%	28.5%	10.3%	24.8%	47.5%	35.0%	44.8%
Total liabilities	50.3%	63.4%	67.1%	67.5%	68.3%	60.1%	80.1%	61.8%	77.6%	73.9%	54.5%
Common equity	46.4%	34.2%	32.3%	32.3%	30.9%	38.9%	18.2%	37.5%	22.2%	24.7%	40.2%
Preferred stock	0.0%	0.0%	0.1%	0.0%	0.0%	0.1%	0.4%	0.3%	0.0%	0.3%	2.2%
Total equity	46.4%	34.2%	32.4%	32.3%	30.9%	39.0%	18.5%	37.8%	22.2%	25.0%	42.3%

PPE = Property, plant, and equipment, LT = Long term.
Source: Based on data from Compustat.

Exhibit 18 presents common-size balance sheet data compiled for the 10 sectors of the S&P 500 using 2017 data. The sector classification follows the S&P/MSCI Global Industrial Classification System (GICS). The exhibit presents mean and median common-size balance sheet data for those companies in the S&P 500 for which 2017 data was available in the Compustat database.[26]

Some interesting general observations can be made from these data:

- Energy and utility companies have the largest amounts of property, plant, and equipment (PPE). Telecommunication services, followed by utilities, have the highest level of long-term debt. Utilities also use some preferred stock.
- Financial companies have the greatest percentage of total liabilities. Financial companies typically have relatively high financial leverage.
- Telecommunications services and utility companies have the lowest level of receivables.
- Inventory levels are highest for consumer discretionary. Materials and consumer staples have the next highest inventories.
- Information technology companies use the least amount of leverage as evidenced by the lowest percentages for long-term debt and total liabilities and highest percentages for common and total equity.

Example 6 discusses an analyst using cross-sectional common-size balance sheet data.

EXAMPLE 6

Cross-Sectional Common-Size Analysis

Jason Lu is comparing two companies in the computer industry to evaluate their relative financial position as reflected on their balance sheets. He has compiled the following vertical common-size data for Apple and Microsoft.

Cross-Sectional Analysis: Consolidated Balance Sheets (as Percent of Total Assets)

	Apple	Microsoft
ASSETS:	**30 September 2017**	**30 June 2017**
Current assets:		
Cash and cash equivalents	5.4	3.2
Short-term marketable securities	14.4	52.0
Accounts receivable	4.8	8.2
Inventories	1.3	0.9
Vendor non-trade receivables	4.7	0.0
Other current assets	3.7	2.0
Total current assets	34.3	66.3
Long-term marketable securities	51.9	2.5
Property, plant and equipment, net	9.0	9.8
Goodwill	1.5	14.6

(continued)

26 An entry of zero for an item (e.g., current assets) was excluded from the data, except in the case of preferred stock. Note that most financial institutions did not provide current asset or current liability data, so these are reported as not available in the database.

(Continued)

ASSETS:	Apple 30 September 2017	Microsoft 30 June 2017
Acquired intangible assets, net	0.6	4.2
Other assets	2.7	2.6
Total assets	100.0	100.0
LIABILITIES AND SHAREHOLDERS' EQUITY:		
Current liabilities:		
Accounts payable	13.1	3.1
Short-term debt	3.2	3.8
Current portion of long-term debt	1.7	0.4
Accrued expenses	6.9	2.7
Deferred revenue	2.0	14.1
Other current liabilities	0.0	2.6
Total current liabilities	26.9	26.8
Long-term debt	25.9	31.6
Deferred revenue non-current	0.8	4.3
Other non-current liabilities	10.8	7.3
Total liabilities	64.3	70.0
Commitments and contingencies		
Total shareholders' equity	35.7	30.0
Total liabilities and shareholders' equity	100.0	100.0

Source: Based on data from companies' annual reports.

From this data, Lu learns the following:

- Apple and Microsoft have high levels of cash and short-term marketable securities, consistent with the information technology sector as reported in Exhibit 18. Apple also has a high balance in long-term marketable securities. This may reflect the success of the company's business model, which has generated large operating cash flows in recent years.
- Apple's level of accounts receivable is lower than Microsoft's and lower than the industry average. Further research is necessary to learn the extent to which this is related to Apple's cash sales through its own retail stores. An alternative explanation would be that the company has been selling/factoring receivables to a greater degree than the other companies; however, that explanation is unlikely given Apple's cash position. Additionally, Apple shows vendor non-trade receivables, reflecting arrangements with its contract manufacturers.
- Apple and Microsoft both have low levels of inventory, similar to industry medians as reported in Exhibit 18. Apple uses contract manufacturers and can rely on suppliers to hold inventory until needed. Additionally, in the Management Discussion and Analysis section of their annual report, Apple discloses $38 billion of noncancelable manufacturing purchase obligations, $33 billion of which is due within twelve months. These amounts are not currently recorded as inventory and reflect the use of contract manufacturers to assemble and test some finished products. The use of

purchase commitments and contract manufacturers implies that inventory may be "understated." Microsoft's low level of inventory is consistent with its business mix which is more heavily weighted to software than to hardware.

- Apple and Microsoft have a level of property, plant, and equipment that is relatively close to the sector median as reported in Exhibit 18.
- Apple has a very low amount of goodwill, reflecting its strategy to grow organically rather than through acquisition. Microsoft's level of goodwill, while higher than Apple's, is lower than the industry median and mean. Microsoft made a number of major acquisitions (for example, Nokia in 2014) but subsequently (in 2015) wrote off significant amounts of goodwill as an impairment charge.
- Apple's level of accounts payable is higher than the industry, but given the company's high level of cash and investments, it is unlikely that this is a problem.
- Apple's and Microsoft's levels of long-term debt are slightly higher than industry averages. Again, given the companies' high level of cash and investments, it is unlikely that this is a problem.

7.2 Balance Sheet Ratios

Ratios facilitate time-series and cross-sectional analysis of a company's financial position. **Balance sheet ratios** are those involving balance sheet items only. Each of the line items on a vertical common-size balance sheet is a ratio in that it expresses a balance sheet amount in relation to total assets. Other balance sheet ratios compare one balance sheet item to another. For example, the current ratio expresses current assets in relation to current liabilities as an indicator of a company's liquidity. Balance sheet ratios include **liquidity ratios** (measuring the company's ability to meet its short-term obligations) and **solvency ratios** (measuring the company's ability to meet long-term and other obligations). These ratios and others are discussed in a later reading. Exhibit 19 summarizes the calculation and interpretation of selected balance sheet ratios.

Exhibit 19 Balance Sheet Ratios

Liquidity Ratios	Calculation	Indicates
Current	Current assets ÷ Current liabilities	Ability to meet current liabilities
Quick (acid test)	(Cash + Marketable securities + Receivables) ÷ Current liabilities	Ability to meet current liabilities
Cash	(Cash + Marketable securities) ÷ Current liabilities	Ability to meet current liabilities

(continued)

Exhibit 19 (Continued)

Solvency Ratios		
Long-term debt-to-equity	Total long-term debt ÷ Total equity	Financial risk and financial leverage
Debt-to-equity	Total debt ÷ Total equity	Financial risk and financial leverage
Total debt	Total debt ÷ Total assets	Financial risk and financial leverage
Financial leverage	Total assets ÷ Total equity	Financial risk and financial leverage

EXAMPLE 7

Ratio Analysis

For the following ratio questions, refer to the balance sheet information for the SAP Group presented in Exhibits 1, 4, 6, 8, and 12.

1 The current ratio for SAP Group at 31 December 2017 is *closest* to:
   A 1.17.
   B 1.20.
   C 2.00.
2 Which of the following liquidity ratios decreased in 2017 relative to 2016?
   A Cash.
   B Quick.
   C Current.
3 Which of the following leverage ratios decreased in 2017 relative to 2016?
   A Debt-to-equity.
   B Financial leverage.
   C Long-term debt-to-equity.

Solution to 1:

A is correct. SAP Group's current ratio (Current assets ÷ Current liabilities) at 31 December 2017 is 1.17 (€11,930 million ÷ €10,210 million).

Solution to 2:

B and C are correct. The ratios are shown in the table below. The quick ratio and current ratio are lower in 2017 than in 2016. The cash ratio is slightly higher.

Liquidity Ratios	Calculation	2017 € in millions	2016 € in millions
Current	Current assets ÷ Current liabilities	€11,930 ÷ €10,210 = **1.17**	€11,564 ÷ €9,674 = **1.20**
Quick (acid test)	(Cash + Marketable securities + Receivables) ÷ Current liabilities	(€4,011 + €990 + €5,899) ÷ €10,210 = **1.07**	(€3,702 + €1,124 + €5,924) ÷ €9,674 = **1.11**
Cash	(Cash + Marketable securities) ÷ Current liabilities	€4,011 ÷ €10,210 = **0.39**	€3,702 ÷ €9,674 = **0.38**

Solution to 3:

A, B, and C are correct. The ratios are shown in the table below. All three leverage ratios decreased in 2017 relative to 2016.

Solvency Ratios			
Long-term debt-to-equity	Total long-term debt ÷ Total equity	€5,034 ÷ €25,540 =**19.7%**	€6,481 ÷ €26,397 = **24.6%**
Debt-to-equity	Total debt ÷ Total equity	(€1,561 + €5,034) ÷ €25,540 = **25.8%**	(€ 1,813 + €6,481) ÷ €26,397 = **31.4%**
Financial Leverage	Total assets ÷ Total equity	€42,497 ÷ €25,540 = **1.66**	€44,277 ÷ €26,397 = **1.68**

Cross-sectional financial ratio analysis can be limited by differences in accounting methods. In addition, lack of homogeneity of a company's operating activities can limit comparability. For diversified companies operating in different industries, using industry-specific ratios for different lines of business can provide better comparisons. Companies disclose information on operating segments. The financial position and performance of the operating segments can be compared to the relevant industry.

Ratio analysis requires a significant amount of judgment. One key area requiring judgment is understanding the limitations of any ratio. The current ratio, for example, is only a rough measure of liquidity at a specific point in time. The ratio captures only the amount of current assets, but the components of current assets differ significantly in their nearness to cash (e.g., marketable securities versus inventory). Another limitation of the current ratio is its sensitivity to end-of-period financing and operating decisions that can potentially impact current asset and current liability amounts. Another overall area requiring judgment is determining whether a ratio for a company is within a reasonable range for an industry. Yet another area requiring judgment is evaluating whether a ratio signifies a persistent condition or reflects only a temporary condition. Overall, evaluating specific ratios requires an examination of the entire operations of a company, its competitors, and the external economic and industry setting in which it is operating.

SUMMARY

The balance sheet (also referred to as the statement of financial position) discloses what an entity owns (assets) and what it owes (liabilities) at a specific point in time. Equity is the owners' residual interest in the assets of a company, net of its liabilities. The amount of equity is increased by income earned during the year, or by the issuance of new equity. The amount of equity is decreased by losses, by dividend payments, or by share repurchases.

An understanding of the balance sheet enables an analyst to evaluate the liquidity, solvency, and overall financial position of a company.

- The balance sheet distinguishes between current and non-current assets and between current and non-current liabilities unless a presentation based on liquidity provides more relevant and reliable information.

- The concept of liquidity relates to a company's ability to pay for its near-term operating needs. With respect to a company overall, liquidity refers to the availability of cash to pay those near-term needs. With respect to a particular asset or liability, liquidity refers to its "nearness to cash."
- Some assets and liabilities are measured on the basis of fair value and some are measured at historical cost. Notes to financial statements provide information that is helpful in assessing the comparability of measurement bases across companies.
- Assets expected to be liquidated or used up within one year or one operating cycle of the business, whichever is greater, are classified as current assets. Assets not expected to be liquidated or used up within one year or one operating cycle of the business, whichever is greater, are classified as non-current assets.
- Liabilities expected to be settled or paid within one year or one operating cycle of the business, whichever is greater, are classified as current liabilities. Liabilities not expected to be settled or paid within one year or one operating cycle of the business, whichever is greater, are classified as non-current liabilities.
- Trade receivables, also referred to as accounts receivable, are amounts owed to a company by its customers for products and services already delivered. Receivables are reported net of the allowance for doubtful accounts.
- Inventories are physical products that will eventually be sold to the company's customers, either in their current form (finished goods) or as inputs into a process to manufacture a final product (raw materials and work-in-process). Inventories are reported at the lower of cost or net realizable value. If the net realizable value of a company's inventory falls below its carrying amount, the company must write down the value of the inventory and record an expense.
- Inventory cost is based on specific identification or estimated using the first-in, first-out or weighted average cost methods. Some accounting standards (including US GAAP but not IFRS) also allow last-in, first-out as an additional inventory valuation method.
- Accounts payable, also called trade payables, are amounts that a business owes its vendors for purchases of goods and services.
- Deferred revenue (also known as unearned revenue) arises when a company receives payment in advance of delivery of the goods and services associated with the payment received.
- Property, plant, and equipment (PPE) are tangible assets that are used in company operations and expected to be used over more than one fiscal period. Examples of tangible assets include land, buildings, equipment, machinery, furniture, and natural resources such as mineral and petroleum resources.
- IFRS provide companies with the choice to report PPE using either a historical cost model or a revaluation model. US GAAP permit only the historical cost model for reporting PPE.
- Depreciation is the process of recognizing the cost of a long-lived asset over its useful life. (Land is not depreciated.)
- Under IFRS, property used to earn rental income or capital appreciation is considered to be an investment property. IFRS provide companies with the choice to report an investment property using either a historical cost model or a fair value model.

- Intangible assets refer to identifiable non-monetary assets without physical substance. Examples include patents, licenses, and trademarks. For each intangible asset, a company assesses whether the useful life is finite or indefinite.
- An intangible asset with a finite useful life is amortised on a systematic basis over the best estimate of its useful life, with the amortisation method and useful-life estimate reviewed at least annually. Impairment principles for an intangible asset with a finite useful life are the same as for PPE.
- An intangible asset with an indefinite useful life is not amortised. Instead, it is tested for impairment at least annually.
- For internally generated intangible assets, IFRS require that costs incurred during the research phase must be expensed. Costs incurred in the development stage can be capitalized as intangible assets if certain criteria are met, including technological feasibility, the ability to use or sell the resulting asset, and the ability to complete the project.
- The most common intangible asset that is not a separately identifiable asset is goodwill, which arises in business combinations. Goodwill is not amortised; instead it is tested for impairment at least annually.
- Financial instruments are contracts that give rise to both a financial asset of one entity and a financial liability or equity instrument of another entity. In general, there are two basic alternative ways that financial instruments are measured: fair value or amortised cost. For financial instruments measured at fair value, there are two basic alternatives in how net changes in fair value are recognized: as profit or loss on the income statement, or as other comprehensive income (loss) which bypasses the income statement.
- Typical long-term financial liabilities include loans (i.e., borrowings from banks) and notes or bonds payable (i.e., fixed-income securities issued to investors). Liabilities such as bonds issued by a company are usually reported at amortised cost on the balance sheet.
- Deferred tax liabilities arise from temporary timing differences between a company's income as reported for tax purposes and income as reported for financial statement purposes.
- Six potential components that comprise the owners' equity section of the balance sheet include: contributed capital, preferred shares, treasury shares, retained earnings, accumulated other comprehensive income, and non-controlling interest.
- The statement of changes in equity reflects information about the increases or decreases in each component of a company's equity over a period.
- Vertical common-size analysis of the balance sheet involves stating each balance sheet item as a percentage of total assets.
- Balance sheet ratios include liquidity ratios (measuring the company's ability to meet its short-term obligations) and solvency ratios (measuring the company's ability to meet long-term and other obligations).

PRACTICE PROBLEMS

1 Resources controlled by a company as a result of past events are:

A equity.

B assets.

C liabilities.

2 Equity equals:

A Assets – Liabilities.

B Liabilities – Assets.

C Assets + Liabilities.

3 Distinguishing between current and non-current items on the balance sheet and presenting a subtotal for current assets and liabilities is referred to as:

A a classified balance sheet.

B an unclassified balance sheet.

C a liquidity-based balance sheet.

4 Shareholders' equity reported on the balance sheet is *most likely* to differ from the market value of shareholders' equity because:

A historical cost basis is used for all assets and liabilities.

B some factors that affect the generation of future cash flows are excluded.

C shareholders' equity reported on the balance sheet is updated continuously.

5 The information provided by a balance sheet item is limited because of uncertainty regarding:

A measurement of its cost or value with reliability.

B the change in current value following the end of the reporting period.

C the probability that any future economic benefit will flow to or from the entity.

6 Which of the following is *most likely* classified as a current liability?

A Payment received for a product due to be delivered at least one year after the balance sheet date

B Payments for merchandise due at least one year after the balance sheet date but still within a normal operating cycle

C Payment on debt due in six months for which the company has the unconditional right to defer settlement for at least one year after the balance sheet date

7 The *most likely* company to use a liquidity-based balance sheet presentation is a:

A bank.

B computer manufacturer holding inventories.

C software company with trade receivables and payables.

8 All of the following are current assets *except*:

A cash.

B goodwill.

C inventories.

© 2019 CFA Institute. All rights reserved.

9 The *most* likely costs included in both the cost of inventory and property, plant, and equipment are:

A selling costs.

B storage costs.

C delivery costs.

10 Debt due within one year is considered:

A current.

B preferred.

C convertible.

11 Money received from customers for products to be delivered in the future is recorded as:

A revenue and an asset.

B an asset and a liability.

C revenue and a liability.

12 An example of a contra asset account is:

A depreciation expense.

B sales returns and allowances.

C allowance for doubtful accounts.

13 The carrying value of inventories reflects:

A their historical cost.

B their current value.

C the lower of historical cost or net realizable value.

14 When a company pays its rent in advance, its balance sheet will reflect a reduction in:

A assets and liabilities.

B assets and shareholders' equity.

C one category of assets and an increase in another.

15 Accrued expenses (accrued liabilities) are:

A expenses that have been paid.

B created when another liability is reduced.

C expenses that have been reported on the income statement but not yet paid.

16 The initial measurement of goodwill is *most likely* affected by:

A an acquisition's purchase price.

B the acquired company's book value.

C the fair value of the acquirer's assets and liabilities.

17 Defining total asset turnover as revenue divided by average total assets, all else equal, impairment write-downs of long-lived assets owned by a company will *most likely* result in an increase for that company in:

A the debt-to-equity ratio but not the total asset turnover.

B the total asset turnover but not the debt-to-equity ratio.

C both the debt-to-equity ratio and the total asset turnover.

18 A company has total liabilities of £35 million and total stockholders' equity of £55 million. Total liabilities are represented on a vertical common-size balance sheet by a percentage *closest* to:

A 35%.

B 39%.

C 64%.

19 For financial assets classified as trading securities, how are unrealized gains and losses reflected in shareholders' equity?

A They are not recognized.

B They flow through income into retained earnings.

C They are a component of accumulated other comprehensive income.

20 For financial assets classified as available for sale, how are unrealized gains and losses reflected in shareholders' equity?

A They are not recognized.

B They flow through retained earnings.

C They are a component of accumulated other comprehensive income.

21 For financial assets classified as held to maturity, how are unrealized gains and losses reflected in shareholders' equity?

A They are not recognized.

B They flow through retained earnings.

C They are a component of accumulated other comprehensive income.

22 The non-controlling (minority) interest in consolidated subsidiaries is presented on the balance sheet:

A as a long-term liability.

B separately, but as a part of shareholders' equity.

C as a mezzanine item between liabilities and shareholders' equity.

23 The item "retained earnings" is a component of:

A assets.

B liabilities.

C shareholders' equity.

24 When a company buys shares of its own stock to be held in treasury, it records a reduction in:

A both assets and liabilities.

B both assets and shareholders' equity.

C assets and an increase in shareholders' equity.

25 Which of the following would an analyst *most likely* be able to determine from a common-size analysis of a company's balance sheet over several periods?

A An increase or decrease in sales.

B An increase or decrease in financial leverage.

C A more efficient or less efficient use of assets.

26 An investor concerned whether a company can meet its near-term obligations is *most likely* to calculate the:

A current ratio.

B return on total capital.

C financial leverage ratio.

27 The most stringent test of a company's liquidity is its:

A cash ratio.

B quick ratio.

C current ratio.

28 An investor worried about a company's long-term solvency would *most likely* examine its:

- **A** current ratio.
- **B** return on equity.
- **C** debt-to-equity ratio.

29 Using the information presented in Exhibit 4, the quick ratio for SAP Group at 31 December 2017 is *closest* to:

- **A** 1.00.
- **B** 1.07.
- **C** 1.17.

30 Using the information presented in Exhibit 14, the financial leverage ratio for SAP Group at 31 December 2017 is *closest* to:

- **A** 1.50.
- **B** 1.66.
- **C** 2.00.

Questions 31 through 34 refer to Exhibit 1.

Exhibit 1 Common-Size Balance Sheets for Company A, Company B, and Sector Average

	Company A	Company B	Sector Average
ASSETS			
Current assets			
Cash and cash equivalents	5	5	7
Marketable securities	5	0	2
Accounts receivable, net	5	15	12
Inventories	15	20	16
Prepaid expenses	5	15	11
Total current assets	35	55	48
Property, plant, and equipment, net	40	35	37
Goodwill	25	0	8
Other assets	0	10	7
Total assets	100	100	100
LIABILITIES AND SHAREHOLDERS' EQUITY			
Current liabilities			
Accounts payable	10	10	10
Short-term debt	25	10	15
Accrued expenses	0	5	3
Total current liabilities	35	25	28

(continued)

Exhibit 1 (Continued)

LIABILITIES AND SHAREHOLDERS' EQUITY			
Long-term debt	45	20	28
Other non-current liabilities	0	10	7
Total liabilities	80	55	63
Total shareholders' equity	20	45	37
Total liabilities and shareholders' equity	100	100	100

31 Based on Exhibit 1, which statement is *most likely* correct?

A Company A has below-average liquidity risk.

B Company B has above-average solvency risk.

C Company A has made one or more acquisitions.

32 The quick ratio for Company A is *closest* to:

A 0.43.

B 0.57.

C 1.00.

33 Based on Exhibit 1, the financial leverage ratio for Company B is *closest* to:

A 0.55.

B 1.22.

C 2.22.

34 Based on Exhibit 1, which ratio indicates lower liquidity risk for Company A compared with Company B?

A Cash ratio

B Quick ratio

C Current ratio

SOLUTIONS

1 B is correct. Assets are resources controlled by a company as a result of past events.

2 A is correct. Assets = Liabilities + Equity and, therefore, Assets – Liabilities = Equity.

3 A is correct. A classified balance sheet is one that classifies assets and liabilities as current or non-current and provides a subtotal for current assets and current liabilities. A liquidity-based balance sheet broadly presents assets and liabilities in order of liquidity.

4 B is correct. The balance sheet omits important aspects of a company's ability to generate future cash flows, such as its reputation and management skills. The balance sheet measures some assets and liabilities based on historical cost and measures others based on current value. Market value of shareholders' equity is updated continuously. Shareholders' equity reported on the balance sheet is updated for reporting purposes and represents the value that was current at the end of the reporting period.

5 B is correct. Balance sheet information is as of a specific point in time, and items measured at current value reflect the value that was current at the end of the reporting period. For all financial statement items, an item should be recognized in the financial statements only if it is probable that any future economic benefit associated with the item will flow to or from the entity and if the item has a cost or value that can be measured with reliability.

6 B is correct. Payments due within one operating cycle of the business, even if they will be settled more than one year after the balance sheet date, are classified as current liabilities. Payment received in advance of the delivery of a good or service creates an obligation or liability. If the obligation is to be fulfilled at least one year after the balance sheet date, it is recorded as a non-current liability, such as deferred revenue or deferred income. Payments that the company has the unconditional right to defer for at least one year after the balance sheet may be classified as non-current liabilities.

7 A is correct. A liquidity-based presentation, rather than a current/non-current presentation, may be used by such entities as banks if broadly presenting assets and liabilities in order of liquidity is reliable and more relevant.

8 B is correct. Goodwill is a long-term asset, and the others are all current assets.

9 C is correct. Both the cost of inventory and property, plant, and equipment include delivery costs, or costs incurred in bringing them to the location for use or resale.

10 A is correct. Current liabilities are those liabilities, including debt, due within one year. Preferred refers to a class of stock. Convertible refers to a feature of bonds (or preferred stock) allowing the holder to convert the instrument into common stock.

11 B is correct. The cash received from customers represents an asset. The obligation to provide a product in the future is a liability called "unearned income" or "unearned revenue." As the product is delivered, revenue will be recognized and the liability will be reduced.

12 C is correct. A contra asset account is netted against (i.e., reduces) the balance of an asset account. The allowance for doubtful accounts reduces the balance of accounts receivable. Accumulated depreciation, not depreciation expense, is a contra asset account. Sales returns and allowances create a contra account that reduce sales, not an asset.

13 C is correct. Under IFRS, inventories are carried at historical cost, unless net realizable value of the inventory is less. Under US GAAP, inventories are carried at the lower of cost or market.

14 C is correct. Paying rent in advance will reduce cash and increase prepaid expenses, both of which are assets.

15 C is correct. Accrued liabilities are expenses that have been reported on a company's income statement but have not yet been paid.

16 A is correct. Initially, goodwill is measured as the difference between the purchase price paid for an acquisition and the fair value of the acquired, not acquiring, company's net assets (identifiable assets less liabilities).

17 C is correct. Impairment write-downs reduce equity in the denominator of the debt-to-equity ratio but do not affect debt, so the debt-to-equity ratio is expected to increase. Impairment write-downs reduce total assets but do not affect revenue. Thus, total asset turnover is expected to increase.

18 B is correct. Vertical common-size analysis involves stating each balance sheet item as a percentage of total assets. Total assets are the sum of total liabilities (£35 million) and total stockholders' equity (£55 million), or £90 million. Total liabilities are shown on a vertical common-size balance sheet as (£35 million/£90 million) ≈ 39%.

19 B is correct. For financial assets classified as trading securities, unrealized gains and losses are reported on the income statement and flow to shareholders' equity as part of retained earnings.

20 C is correct. For financial assets classified as available for sale, unrealized gains and losses are not recorded on the income statement and instead are part of *other* comprehensive income. Accumulated other comprehensive income is a component of Shareholders' equity

21 A is correct. Financial assets classified as held to maturity are measured at amortised cost. Gains and losses are recognized only when realized.

22 B is correct. The non-controlling interest in consolidated subsidiaries is shown separately as part of shareholders' equity.

23 C is correct. The item "retained earnings" is a component of shareholders' equity.

24 B is correct. Share repurchases reduce the company's cash (an asset). Shareholders' equity is reduced because there are fewer shares outstanding and treasury stock is an offset to owners' equity.

25 B is correct. Common-size analysis (as presented in the reading) provides information about composition of the balance sheet and changes over time. As a result, it can provide information about an increase or decrease in a company's financial leverage.

26 A is correct. The current ratio provides a comparison of assets that can be turned into cash relatively quickly and liabilities that must be paid within one year. The other ratios are more suited to longer-term concerns.

27 A is correct. The cash ratio determines how much of a company's near-term obligations can be settled with existing amounts of cash and marketable securities.

28 C is correct. The debt-to-equity ratio, a solvency ratio, is an indicator of financial risk.

29 B is correct. The quick ratio ([Cash + Marketable securities + Receivables] ÷ Current liabilities) is 1.07 ([= €4,011 + €990 + €5,899] ÷ €10,210). As noted in the text, the largest component of the current financial assets are loans and other financial receivables. Thus, financial assets are included in the quick ratio but not the cash ratio.

30 B is correct. The financial leverage ratio (Total assets ÷ Total equity) is 1.66 (= €42,497 ÷ €25,540).

31 C is correct. The presence of goodwill on Company A's balance sheet signifies that it has made one or more acquisitions in the past. The current, cash, and quick ratios are lower for Company A than for the sector average. These lower liquidity ratios imply above-average liquidity risk. The total debt, long-term debt-to-equity, debt-to-equity, and financial leverage ratios are lower for Company B than for the sector average. These lower solvency ratios imply below-average solvency risk.

Current ratio is (35/35) = 1.00 for Company A, versus (48/28) = 1.71 for the sector average.

Cash ratio is (5 + 5)/35 = 0.29 for Company A, versus (7 + 2)/28 = 0.32 for the sector average.

Quick ratio is (5 + 5 + 5)/35 = 0.43 for Company A, versus (7 + 2 + 12)/28 = 0.75 for the sector average.

Total debt ratio is (55/100) = 0.55 for Company B, versus (63/100) = 0.63 for the sector average.

Long-term debt-to-equity ratio is (20/45) = 0.44 for Company B, versus (28/37) = 0.76 for the sector average.

Debt-to-equity ratio is (55/45) = 1.22 for Company B, versus (63/37) = 1.70 for the sector average.

Financial leverage ratio is (100/45) = 2.22 for Company B, versus (100/37) = 2.70 for the sector average.

32 A is correct. The quick ratio is defined as (Cash and cash equivalents + Marketable securities + receivables) ÷ Current liabilities. For Company A, this calculation is (5 + 5 + 5)/35 = 0.43.

33 C is correct. The financial leverage ratio is defined as Total assets ÷ Total equity. For Company B, total assets are 100 and total equity is 45; hence, the financial leverage ratio is 100/45 = 2.22.

34 A is correct. The cash ratio is defined as (Cash + Marketable securities)/Current liabilities. Company A's cash ratio, (5 + 5)/35 = 0.29, is higher than (5 + 0)/25 = 0.20 for Company B.

READING

23

Understanding Cash Flow Statements

**by Elaine Henry, PhD, CFA, Thomas R. Robinson, PhD, CFA,
J Hennie van Greuning, DCom, CFA, and
Michael A. Broihahn, CPA, CIA, CFA**

Elaine Henry, PhD, CFA, is at Stevens Institute of Technology (USA). Thomas R. Robinson, PhD, CFA, is at AACSB International (USA). J. Hennie van Greuning, DCom, CFA, is at BIBD (Brunei). Michael A. Broihahn, CPA, CIA, CFA, is at Barry University (USA).

LEARNING OUTCOMES

Mastery	*The candidate should be able to:*
☐	a. compare cash flows from operating, investing, and financing activities and classify cash flow items as relating to one of those three categories given a description of the items;
☐	b. describe how non-cash investing and financing activities are reported;
☐	c. contrast cash flow statements prepared under International Financial Reporting Standards (IFRS) and US generally accepted accounting principles (US GAAP);
☐	d. distinguish between the direct and indirect methods of presenting cash from operating activities and describe arguments in favor of each method;
☐	e. describe how the cash flow statement is linked to the income statement and the balance sheet;
☐	f. describe the steps in the preparation of direct and indirect cash flow statements, including how cash flows can be computed using income statement and balance sheet data;
☐	g. convert cash flows from the indirect to direct method;
☐	h. analyze and interpret both reported and common-size cash flow statements;
☐	i. calculate and interpret free cash flow to the firm, free cash flow to equity, and performance and coverage cash flow ratios.

Note: Changes in accounting standards as well as new rulings and/or pronouncements issued after the publication of the readings on financial reporting and analysis may cause some of the information in these readings to become dated. Candidates are *not* responsible for anything that occurs after the readings were published. In addition, candidates are expected to be familiar with the analytical frameworks contained in the readings, as well as the implications of alternative accounting methods for financial analysis and valuation discussed in the readings. Candidates are also responsible for the content of accounting standards, but not for the actual reference numbers. Finally, candidates should be aware that certain ratios may be defined and calculated differently. When alternative ratio definitions exist and no specific definition is given, candidates should use the ratio definitions emphasized in the readings.

© 2019 CFA Institute. All rights reserved.

1 INTRODUCTION

The cash flow statement provides information about a company's *cash receipts* and *cash payments* during an accounting period. The cash-based information provided by the cash flow statement contrasts with the accrual-based information from the income statement. For example, the income statement reflects revenues when earned rather than when cash is collected; in contrast, the cash flow statement reflects cash receipts when collected as opposed to when the revenue was earned. A reconciliation between reported income and cash flows from operating activities provides useful information about when, whether, and how a company is able to generate cash from its operating activities. Although income is an important measure of the results of a company's activities, cash flow is also essential. As an extreme illustration, a hypothetical company that makes all sales on account, without regard to whether it will ever collect its accounts receivable, would report healthy sales on its income statement and might well report significant income; however, with zero cash inflow, the company would not survive. The cash flow statement also provides a reconciliation of the beginning and ending cash on the balance sheet.

In addition to information about cash generated (or, alternatively, cash used) in operating activities, the cash flow statement provides information about cash provided (or used) in a company's investing and financing activities. This information allows the analyst to answer such questions as:

- Does the company generate enough cash from its operations to pay for its new investments, or is the company relying on new debt issuance to finance them?
- Does the company pay its dividends to common stockholders using cash generated from operations, from selling assets, or from issuing debt?

Answers to these questions are important because, in theory, generating cash from operations can continue indefinitely, but generating cash from selling assets, for example, is possible only as long as there are assets to sell. Similarly, generating cash from debt financing is possible only as long as lenders are willing to lend, and the lending decision depends on expectations that the company will ultimately have adequate cash to repay its obligations. In summary, information about the sources and uses of cash helps creditors, investors, and other statement users evaluate the company's liquidity, solvency, and financial flexibility.

This reading explains how cash flow activities are reflected in a company's cash flow statement. The reading is organized as follows. Section 2 describes the components and format of the cash flow statement, including the classification of cash flows under International Financial Reporting Standards (IFRS) and US generally accepted accounting principles (GAAP) and the direct and indirect formats for presenting the cash flow statement. Section 3 discusses the linkages of the cash flow statement with the income statement and balance sheet and the steps in the preparation of the cash flow statement. Section 4 demonstrates the analysis of cash flow statements, including the conversion of an indirect cash flow statement to the direct method and how to use common-size cash flow analysis, free cash flow measures, and cash flow ratios used in security analysis. A summary of the key points and practice problems in the CFA Institute multiple-choice format conclude the reading.

COMPONENTS AND FORMAT OF THE CASH FLOW STATEMENT

2

The analyst needs to be able to extract and interpret information on cash flows from financial statements. The basic components and allowable formats of the cash flow statement are well established.

- The cash flow statement has subsections relating specific items to the operating, investing, and financing activities of the company.
- Two presentation formats for the operating section are allowable: direct and indirect.

The following discussion presents these topics in greater detail.

2.1 Classification of Cash Flows and Non-Cash Activities

All companies engage in operating, investing, and financing activities. These activities are the classifications used in the cash flow statement under both IFRS and US GAAP and are described as follows:[1]

- **Operating activities** include the company's day-to-day activities that create revenues, such as selling inventory and providing services, and other activities not classified as investing or financing. Cash inflows result from cash sales and from collection of accounts receivable. Examples include cash receipts from the provision of services and royalties, commissions, and other revenue. To generate revenue, companies undertake such activities as manufacturing inventory, purchasing inventory from suppliers, and paying employees. Cash outflows result from cash payments for inventory, salaries, taxes, and other operating-related expenses and from paying accounts payable. Additionally, operating activities include cash receipts and payments related to **dealing securities** or **trading securities** (as opposed to buying or selling securities as investments, as discussed below).
- **Investing activities** include purchasing and selling long-term assets and other investments. These long-term assets and other investments include property, plant, and equipment; intangible assets; other long-term assets; and both long-term and short-term investments in the equity and debt (bonds and loans) issued by other companies. For this purpose, investments in equity and debt securities exclude a) any securities considered cash equivalents (very short-term, highly liquid securities) and b) securities held for dealing or trading purposes, the purchase and sale of which are considered operating activities even for companies where this is not a primary business activity. Cash inflows in the investing category include cash receipts from the sale of non-trading securities; property, plant, and equipment; intangibles; and other long-term assets. Cash outflows include cash payments for the purchase of these assets.
- **Financing activities** include obtaining or repaying capital, such as equity and long-term debt. The two primary sources of capital are shareholders and creditors. Cash inflows in this category include cash receipts from issuing stock (common or preferred) or bonds and cash receipts from borrowing. Cash outflows include cash payments to repurchase stock (e.g., treasury stock) and to repay bonds and other borrowings. Note that indirect borrowing using accounts payable is not considered a financing activity—such borrowing is classified as

1 IAS 7 *Statement of Cash Flows*.

an operating activity. The new IFRS standard relating to lease accounting (IFRS 16) affects how operating leases are represented in the cash flow statement.[2] Under IFRS 16, operating leases are treated similarly to finance leases—that is, the interest component of lease payments will be reflected in either the operating or financing section, and the principal component of lease payments is included in the financing section.

EXAMPLE 1

Net Cash Flow from Investing Activities

A company recorded the following in Year 1:

Proceeds from issuance of long-term debt	€300,000
Purchase of equipment	€200,000
Loss on sale of equipment	€70,000
Proceeds from sale of equipment	€120,000
Equity in earnings of affiliate	€10,000

On the Year 1 statement of cash flows, the company would report net cash flow from investing activities *closest* to:

A (€150,000).

B (€80,000).

C €200,000.

Solution:

B is correct. The only two items that would affect the investing section are the purchase of equipment and the proceeds from sale of equipment: (€200,000) + €120,000 = (€80,000). The loss on sale of equipment and the equity in earnings of affiliate affect net income but are not cash flows. The issuance of debt is a financing cash flow.

IFRS provide companies with choices in reporting some items of cash flow, particularly interest and dividends. IFRS explain that although for a financial institution interest paid and received would normally be classified as operating activities, for other entities, alternative classifications may be appropriate. For this reason, under IFRS, interest received may be classified either as an operating activity or as an investing activity. Under IFRS, interest paid may be classified as either an operating activity or a financing activity. Furthermore, under IFRS, dividends received may be classified as either an operating activity or an investing activity and dividends paid may be classified as either an operating activity or a financing activity. Companies must use a consistent classification from year to year and disclose separately the amounts of interest and dividends received and paid and where the amounts are reported.

Under US GAAP, discretion is not permitted in classifying interest and dividends. Interest received and interest paid are reported as operating activities for all companies.[3] Under US GAAP, dividends received are always reported as operating activities and dividends paid are always reported as financing activities.

2 IFRS 16 is effective for fiscal years beginning 1 January 2019, with earlier voluntary adoption allowed.
3 FASB ASC Topic 230 [Statement of Cash Flows].

EXAMPLE 2

Operating versus Financing Cash Flows

On 31 December 2018, a company issued a £30,000 180-day note at 8 percent and used the cash received to pay for inventory and issued £110,000 long-term debt at 11 percent annually and used the cash received to pay for new equipment. Which of the following *most* accurately reflects the combined effect of both transactions on the company's cash flows for the year ended 31 December 2018 under IFRS? Cash flows from:

A operations are unchanged.

B financing increase £110,000.

C operations decrease £30,000.

Solution:

C is correct. The payment for inventory would decrease cash flows from operations. The issuance of debt (both short-term and long-term debt) is part of financing activities and would increase cash flows from financing activities by £140,000. The purchase of equipment is an investing activity. Note that the treatment under US GAAP would be the same for these transactions.

Companies may also engage in non-cash investing and financing transactions. A non-cash transaction is any transaction that does not involve an inflow or outflow of cash. For example, if a company exchanges one non-monetary asset for another non-monetary asset, no cash is involved. Similarly, no cash is involved when a company issues common stock either for dividends or in connection with conversion of a convertible bond or convertible preferred stock. Because no cash is involved in non-cash transactions (by definition), these transactions are not incorporated in the cash flow statement. However, because such transactions may affect a company's capital or asset structures, any significant non-cash transaction is required to be disclosed, either in a separate note or a supplementary schedule to the cash flow statement.

2.2 A Summary of Differences between IFRS and US GAAP

As highlighted in the previous section, there are some differences in cash flow statements prepared under IFRS and US GAAP that the analyst should be aware of when comparing the cash flow statements of companies prepared in accordance with different sets of standards. The key differences are summarized in Exhibit 1. Most significantly, IFRS allow more flexibility in the reporting of such items as interest paid or received and dividends paid or received and in how income tax expense is classified.

US GAAP classify interest and dividends received from investments as operating activities, whereas IFRS allow companies to classify those items as either operating or investing cash flows. Likewise, US GAAP classify interest expense as an operating activity, even though the principal amount of the debt issued is classified as a financing activity. IFRS allow companies to classify interest expense as either an operating activity or a financing activity. US GAAP classify dividends paid to stockholders as a financing activity, whereas IFRS allow companies to classify dividends paid as either an operating activity or a financing activity.

US GAAP classify all income tax expenses as an operating activity. IFRS also classify income tax expense as an operating activity, unless the tax expense can be specifically identified with an investing or financing activity (e.g., the tax effect of the sale of a discontinued operation could be classified under investing activities).

Exhibit 1 Cash Flow Statements: Differences between IFRS and US GAAP

Topic	IFRS	US GAAP
Classification of cash flows:		
■ Interest received	Operating or investing	Operating
■ Interest paid	Operating or financing	Operating
■ Dividends received	Operating or investing	Operating
■ Dividends paid	Operating or financing	Financing
■ Bank overdrafts	Considered part of cash equivalents	Not considered part of cash and cash equivalents and classified as financing
■ Taxes paid	Generally operating, but a portion can be allocated to investing or financing if it can be specifically identified with these categories	Operating
Format of statement	Direct or indirect; direct is encouraged	Direct or indirect; direct is encouraged. A reconciliation of net income to cash flow from operating activities must be provided regardless of method used

Sources: IAS 7; FASB ASC Topic 230; and "IFRS and US GAAP: Similarities and Differences," PricewaterhouseCoopers (November 2017), available at www.pwc.com.

Under either set of standards, companies currently have a choice of formats for presenting cash flow statements, as discussed in the next section.

2.3 Direct and Indirect Methods for Reporting Cash Flow from Operating Activities

There are two acceptable formats for reporting **cash flow from operating activities** (also known as **cash flow from operations** or **operating cash flow**), defined as the net amount of cash provided from operating activities: the direct and the indirect methods. The *amount* of operating cash flow is identical under both methods; only the *presentation format* of the operating cash flow section differs. The presentation format of the cash flows from investing and financing is exactly the same, regardless of which method is used to present operating cash flows.

The **direct method** shows the specific cash inflows and outflows that result in reported cash flow from operating activities. It shows each cash inflow and outflow related to a company's cash receipts and disbursements. In other words, the direct method eliminates any impact of accruals and shows only cash receipts and cash payments. The primary argument in favor of the direct method is that it provides information on the specific sources of operating cash receipts and payments. This is in contrast to the indirect method, which shows only the net result of these receipts and payments. Just as information on the specific sources of revenues and expenses is more useful than knowing only the net result—net income—the analyst gets additional information from a direct-format cash flow statement. The additional information is useful in understanding historical performance and in predicting future operating cash flows.

The **indirect method** shows how cash flow from operations can be obtained from reported net income as the result of a series of adjustments. The **indirect format** begins with net income. To reconcile net income with operating cash flow, adjustments are made for non-cash items, for non-operating items, and for the net changes in operating accruals. The main argument for the indirect approach is that it shows the reasons for differences between net income and operating cash flows. (However, the differences between net income and operating cash flows are equally visible on an indirect-format cash flow statement and in the supplementary reconciliation required under US GAAP if the company uses the direct method.) Another argument for the indirect method is that it mirrors a forecasting approach that begins by forecasting future income and then derives cash flows by adjusting for changes in balance sheet accounts that occur because of the timing differences between accrual and cash accounting.

IFRS and US GAAP both encourage the use of the direct method but permit either method. US GAAP encourage the use of the direct method but also require companies to present a reconciliation between net income and cash flow (which is equivalent to the indirect method).[4] If the indirect method is chosen, no direct-format disclosures are required. The majority of companies, reporting under IFRS or US GAAP, present using the indirect method for operating cash flows.

Many users of financial statements prefer the **direct format**, particularly analysts and commercial lenders, because of the importance of information about operating receipts and payments in assessing a company's financing needs and capacity to repay existing obligations. Preparers argue that adjusting net income to operating cash flow, as in the indirect format, is easier and less costly than reporting gross operating cash receipts and payments, as in the direct format. With advances in accounting systems and technology, it is not clear that gathering the information required to use the direct method is difficult or costly. CFA Institute has advocated that standard setters require the use of the direct format for the main presentation of the cash flow statement, with indirect cash flows as supplementary disclosure.[5]

2.3.1 *An Indirect-Format Cash Flow Statement Prepared under IFRS*

Exhibit 2 presents the consolidated cash flow statement prepared under IFRS from Unilever Group's 2017 annual report. The statement, covering the fiscal years ended 31 December 2017, 2016, and 2015, shows the use of the indirect method. Unilever is an Anglo-Dutch consumer products company with headquarters in the United Kingdom and the Netherlands.[6]

Exhibit 2 Unilever Group Consolidated Cash Flow Statement (€ millions)

	For the year ended 31 December		
	2017	2016	2015
Cash flow from operating activities			
Net profit	6,486	5,547	5,259
Taxation	1,667	1,922	1,961
Share of net profit of joint ventures/associates and other income (loss) from non-current investments and associates	(173)	(231)	(198)
Net finance costs:	877	563	493
Operating profit	8,857	7,801	7,515

(continued)

4 FASB ASC Section 230-10-45 [Statement of Cash Flows–Overall–Other Presentation Matters].

5 *A Comprehensive Business Reporting Model: Financial Reporting for Investors*, CFA Institute Centre for Financial Market Integrity (July 2007), p. 13.

6 Unilever NV and Unilever PLC have independent legal structures, but a series of agreements enable the companies to operate as a single economic entity.

Exhibit 2 (Continued)

	For the year ended 31 December		
	2017	**2016**	**2015**
Depreciation, amortisation and impairment	1,538	1,464	1,370
Changes in working capital:	(68)	51	720
Inventories	(104)	190	(129)
Trade and other current receivables	(506)	142	2
Trade payables and other liabilities	542	(281)	847
Pensions and similar obligations less payments	(904)	(327)	(385)
Provisions less payments	200	65	(94)
Elimination of (profits)/losses on disposals	(298)	127	26
Non-cash charge for share-based compensation	284	198	150
Other adjustments	(153)	(81)	49
Cash flow from operating activities	**9,456**	**9,298**	**9,351**
Income tax paid	(2,164)	(2,251)	(2,021)
Net cash flow from operating activities	**7,292**	**7,047**	**7,330**
Interest received	154	105	119
Purchase of intangible assets	(158)	(232)	(334)
Purchase of property, plant and equipment	(1,509)	(1,804)	(1,867)
Disposal of property, plant and equipment	46	158	127
Acquisition of group companies, joint ventures and associates	(4,896)	(1,731)	(1,897)
Disposal of group companies, joint ventures and associates	561	30	199
Acquisition of other non-current investments	(317)	(208)	(78)
Disposal of other non-current investments	251	173	127
Dividends from joint ventures, associates and other non-current investments	138	186	176
(Purchase)/sale of financial assets	(149)	135	(111)
Net cash flow (used in)/from investing activities	**(5,879)**	**(3,188)**	**(3,539)**
Dividends paid on ordinary share capital	(3,916)	(3,609)	(3,331)
Interest and preference dividends paid	(470)	(472)	(579)
Net change in short-term borrowings	2,695	258	245
Additional financial liabilities	8,851	6,761	7,566
Repayment of financial liabilities	(2,604)	(5,213)	(6,270)
Capital element of finance lease rental payments	(14)	(35)	(14)
Buy back of preference shares	(448)	—	—
Repurchase of shares	(5,014)	—	—
Other movements on treasury stock	(204)	(257)	(276)
Other financing activities	(309)	(506)	(373)
Net cash flow (used in)/from financing activities	**(1,433)**	**(3,073)**	**(3,032)**
Net increase/(decrease) in cash and cash equivalents	**(20)**	**786**	**759**
Cash and cash equivalents at the beginning of the year	**3,198**	**2,128**	**1,910**

Exhibit 2 (Continued)

	For the year ended 31 December		
	2017	**2016**	**2015**
Effect of foreign exchange rate changes	(9)	284	(541)
Cash and cash equivalents at the end of the year	3,169	3,198	2,128

Beginning first at the bottom of the statement, we note that cash increased from €1,910 million at the beginning of 2015 to €3,169 million at the end of 2017, with the largest increase occurring in 2016. To understand the changes, we next examine the sections of the statement. In each year, the primary cash inflow derived from operating activities, as would be expected for a mature company in a relatively stable industry. In each year, the operating cash flow was more than the reported net profit, again, as would be expected from a mature company, with the largest differences primarily arising from the add-back of depreciation. Also, in each year, the operating cash flow was more than enough to cover the company's capital expenditures. For example, in 2017, the company generated €7,292 million in net cash from operating activities and—as shown in the investing section—spent €1,509 million on property, plant, and equipment. The operating cash flow was also sufficient to cover acquisitions of other companies.

The financing section of the statement shows that each year the company returned more than €3.3 billion to its common shareholders through dividends and around €500 million to its debt holders and preferred shareholders via interest and dividends. In 2017, the company used cash to repurchase about €5 billion in common stock in and generated cash from increased borrowing. The increase in short-term borrowings (€2,695 million) and additional financial liabilities (€8,851 million) exceeded the cash repayment of liabilities (€2,604 million).

Having examined each section of the statement, we return to the operating activities section of Unilever's cash flow statement, which presents a reconciliation of net profit to net cash flow from operating activities (i.e., uses the indirect method). The following discussion of certain adjustments to reconcile net profit to operating cash flows explains some of the main reconciliation adjustments and refers to the amounts in 2017. The first adjustment adds back the €1,667 million income tax expense (labeled "Taxation") that had been recognized as an expense in the computation of net profit. A €2,164 million deduction for the (cash) income taxes paid is then shown separately, as the last item in the operating activities section, consistent with the IFRS requirement that cash flows arising from income taxes be separately disclosed. The classification of taxes on income paid should be indicated. The classification is in operating activities unless the taxes can be specifically identified with financing or investing activities.

The next adjustment "removes" from the operating cash flow section the €173 million representing Unilever's share of joint ventures' income that had been included in the computation of net profit. A €138 million inflow of (cash) dividends received from those joint ventures is then shown in the investing activities section. Similarly, a €877 million adjustment removes the net finance costs from the operating activities section. Unilever then reports its €154 million (cash) interest received in the investing activities section and its €470 million (cash) interest paid (and preference dividends paid) in the financing activities section. The next adjustment in the operating section of this indirect-method statement adds back €1,538 million depreciation, amortisation, and impairment, all of which are expenses that had been deducted in the computation of net income but which did not involve any outflow of cash in the period. The €68 million adjustment for changes in working capital is necessary because these changes result from applying accrual accounting and thus do not necessarily correspond to the actual cash movement. These adjustments are described in greater detail in a later section.

In summary, some observations from an analysis of Unilever's cash flow statement include:

- Total cash increased from €1,910 million at the beginning of 2015 to €3,169 million at the end of 2017, with the largest increase occurring in 2016.
- In each year, the operating cash flow was more than the reported net profit, as would generally be expected from a mature company.
- In each year, the operating cash flow was more than enough to cover the company's capital expenditures.
- The company returned cash to its equity investors through dividends in each year and through share buybacks in 2017.

2.3.2 *A Direct-Format Cash Flow Statement Prepared under IFRS*

In the direct format of the cash flow statement, the cash received from customers, as well as other operating items, is clearly shown.

Exhibit 3 presents a direct-method format cash flow statement prepared under IFRS for Telefónica Group, a diversified telecommunications company based in Madrid.[7]

Exhibit 3 Telefónica Group Consolidated Statement of Cash Flows (€ millions)

for the years ended 31 December	2017	2016	2015
Cash flows from operating activities			
Cash received from operations	63,456	63,514	67,582
Cash paid from operations	(46,929)	(47,384)	(50,833)
Net interest and other financial expenses net of dividends received	(1,726)	(2,143)	(2,445)
Taxes paid	(1,005)	(649)	(689)
Net cash flow provided by operating activities	**13,796**	**13,338**	**13,615**
Cash flows from investing activities			
(Payments on investments)/proceeds from the sale in property, plant and equipment and intangible assets, net	(8,992)	(9,187)	(10,256)
Proceeds on disposals of companies, net of cash and cash equivalents disposed	40	767	354
Payments on investments in companies, net of cash and cash equivalents acquired	(128)	(54)	(3,181)
Proceeds on financial investments not included under cash equivalents	296	489	1,142
Payments made on financial investments not included under cash equivalents	(1,106)	(265)	(426)
(Payments)/proceeds on placements of cash surpluses not included under cash equivalents	(357)	42	(557)

7 This statement excludes the supplemental cash flow reconciliation provided at the bottom of the original cash flow statement by the company.

Exhibit 3 (Continued)

Government grants received	2	-	7
Net cash used in investing activities	**(10,245)**	**(8,208)**	**(12,917)**
Cash flows from financing activities			
Dividends paid	(2,459)	(2,906)	(2,775)
Proceeds from share capital increase	2	-	4,255
Proceeds/(payments) of treasury shares and other operations with shareholders and with minority interests	1,269	(660)	(1,772)
Operations with other equity holders	646	656	83
Proceeds on issue of debentures and bonds, and other debts	8,390	5,693	1,602
Proceeds on loans, borrowings and promissory notes	4,844	10,332	8,784
Repayments of debentures and bonds and other debts	(6,687)	(6,873)	(3,805)
Repayments of loans, borrowings and promissory notes	(6,711)	(8,506)	(9,858)
Financed operating payments and investments in property, plant and equipment and intangible assets payments	(1,046)	(1,956)	(126)
Net cash flow used in financing activities	**(1,752)**	**(4,220)**	**(3,612)**
Effect of changes in exchange rates	(341)	185	(1,000)
Effect of changes in consolidation methods and others	(2)	26	—
Net increase (decrease) in cash and cash equivalents during the period	**1,456**	**1,121**	**(3,914)**
Cash and cash equivalents at 1 January	3,736	2,615	6,529
Cash and cash equivalents at 31 December	5,192	3,736	2,615

As shown at the bottom of the statement, cash and cash equivalents decreased from €6,529 million at the beginning of 2015 to €5,192 million at the end of 2017. The largest decrease in cash occurred in 2015. Cash from operations was the primary source of cash, consistent with the profile of a mature company in a relatively stable industry. Each year, the company generated significantly more cash from operations than it required for its capital expenditures. For example, in 2017, the company generated €13.8 billion cash from operations and spent—as shown in the investing section—only €9 billion on property, plant, and equipment, net of proceeds from sales. Another notable item from the investing section is the company's limited acquisition activity in 2017 and 2016 compared with 2015. In 2015, the company made over €3 billion of acquisitions. As shown in the financing section, cash flows from financing was negative in all three years, although the components of the negative cash flows differed. In 2015, for example, the company generated cash with an equity issuance of €4.2 billion but made significant net repayments of debts resulting in negative cash from financing activities.

In summary, some observations from an analysis of Telefónica's cash flow statement include

- Total cash and cash equivalents decreased over the three-year period, with 2015 showing the biggest decrease.
- Cash from operating activities was large enough in each year to cover the company's capital expenditures.
- The amount paid for property, plant, and equipment and intangible assets was the largest investing expenditure each year.

- The company had a significant amount of acquisition activity in 2015.
- The company paid dividends each year although the amount in 2017 is somewhat lower than in prior years.

2.3.3 *Illustrations of Cash Flow Statements Prepared under US GAAP*

Previously, we presented cash flow statements prepared under IFRS. In this section, we illustrate cash flow statements prepared under US GAAP. This section presents the cash flow statements of two companies, Tech Data Corporation and Walmart. Tech Data reports its operating activities using the direct method, whereas Walmart reports its operating activities using the more common indirect method.

Tech Data Corporation is a leading distributor of information technology products. Exhibit 4 presents comparative cash flow statements from the company's annual report for the fiscal years ended 31 January 2016 through 2018.

Exhibit 4 Tech Data Corporation and Subsidiaries Consolidated Cash Flow Statements (in Thousands)

Years Ended 31 January	2018	2017	2016
Cash flows from operating activities:			
Cash received from customers	$42,981,601	$29,427,357	$28,119,687
Cash paid to vendors and employees	(41,666,356)	(28,664,222)	(27,819,886)
Interest paid, net	(86,544)	(22,020)	(20,264)
Income taxes paid	(131,632)	(84,272)	(85,645)
Net cash provided by operating activities	**1,097,069**	**656,843**	**193,892**
Cash flows from investing activities:			
Acquisition of business, net of cash acquired	(2,249,849)	(2,916)	(27,848)
Expenditures for property and equipment	(192,235)	(24,971)	(20,917)
Software and software development costs	(39,702)	(14,364)	(13,055)
Proceeds from sale of subsidiaries	0	0	20,020
Net cash used in investing activities	**(2,481,786)**	**(42,251)**	**(41,800)**
Cash flows from financing activities:			
Borrowings on long-term debt	1,008,148	998,405	-
Principal payments on long-term debt	(861,394)	-	(319)
Cash paid for debt issuance costs	(6,348)	(21,581)	-
Net borrowings on revolving credit loans	(16,028)	3,417	5,912
Cash paid for purchase of treasury stock	-	-	(147,003)
Payments for employee withholdings on equity awards	(6,027)	(4,479)	(4,662)
Proceeds from the reissuance of treasury stock	1,543	733	561
Acquisition of earn-out payments	-	-	(2,736)
Net cash provided by (used in) financing activities	**119,894**	**976,495**	**(148,247)**
Effect of exchange rate changes on cash and cash equivalents	94,860	3,335	(15,671)
Net (decrease) increase in cash and cash equivalents	(1,169,963)	1,594,422	(11,826)

Exhibit 4 (Continued)

Years Ended 31 January	2018	2017	2016
Cash and cash equivalents at beginning of year	2,125,591	531,169	542,995
Cash and cash equivalents at end of year	$955,628	$2,125,591	$531,169
Reconciliation of net income to net cash provided by operating activities:			
Net income	$116,641	$195,095	$265,736
Adjustments to reconcile net income to net cash provided by operating activities:			
Depreciation and amortization	150,046	54,437	57,253
Provision for losses on accounts receivable	21,022	5,026	6,061
Stock-based compensation expense	29,381	13,947	14,890
Loss on disposal of subsidiaries	-	-	699
Accretion of debt discount and debt issuance costs	3,326	835	839
Deferred income taxes	(4,261)	(11,002)	2,387
Changes in operating assets and liabilities:			
Accounts receivable	(554,627)	(91,961)	(297,637)
Inventories	(502,352)	(20,838)	(219,482)
Prepaid expenses and other assets	32,963	66,027	(44,384)
Accounts payable	1,704,307	459,146	426,412
Accrued expenses and other liabilities	100,623	(13,869)	(18,882)
Total adjustments	980,428	461,748	(71,844)
Net cash provided by operating activities	$1,097,069	$656,843	$193,892

Tech Data Corporation prepares its cash flow statements under the direct method. The company's cash increased from $543 million at the beginning of 2016 to $956 million at the end of January 2018, with the biggest increase occurring in 2017. The 2017 increase was driven by changes in both operating cash flow and financing cash flow. In the cash flows from operating activities section of Tech Data's cash flow statements, the company identifies the amount of cash it received from customers, $43 billion for 2018, and the amount of cash that it paid to suppliers and employees, $41.7 billion for 2018. Cash receipts increased from $29.4 billion in the prior year and cash paid also increased substantially. Net cash provided by operating activities was adequate to cover the company's investing activities in 2016 and 2017 but not in 2018, primarily because of increased amounts of cash used for acquisition of business. Related to this investing cash outflow for an acquisition, footnotes disclose that the major acquisition in 2018 accounted for the large increase in cash receipts and cash payments in the operating section. Also related to the 2018 acquisition, the financing section shows that the company borrowed more debt that it repaid in both 2017 and 2018. In 2017, borrowings on long-term debt were $998.4 million, and net borrowings on revolving credit loans were $3.4 million. In 2018, the company generated cash by borrowing more long-term debt than it repaid but used cash to pay down its revolving credit loans. There are no dividend payments, although in 2016, the company paid $147 million to repurchase its common stock.

Whenever the direct method is used, US GAAP require a disclosure note and a schedule that reconciles net income with the net cash flow from operating activities. Tech Data shows this reconciliation at the bottom of its consolidated statements of cash flows. The disclosure note and reconciliation schedule are exactly the information that would have been presented in the body of the cash flow statement if the company had elected to use the indirect method rather than the direct method. For 2018, the reconciliation highlights an increase in the company's accounts receivable, inventory, and payables.

In summary, some observations from an analysis of Tech Data's cash flow statement include:

- The company's cash increased by over $412 million over the three years ending in January 2018, with the biggest increase occurring in 2017.
- The company's operating cash was adequate to cover the company's investments in 2016 and 2017, but not in 2018 primarily because of a major acquisition.
- Related to the 2018 acquisition, the financing section shows an increase in long-term borrowings in 2017 and 2018, including a $998 million increase in 2017.
- The company has not paid dividends in the past three years, but the financing section shows that in 2016 the company repurchased stock.

Walmart is a global retailer that conducts business under the names of Walmart and Sam's Club. Exhibit 5 presents the comparative cash flow statements from the company's annual report for the fiscal years ended 31 January 2018, 2017, and 2016.

Exhibit 5 Walmart Cash Flow Statements Fiscal Years Ended 31 January ($ millions)

Fiscal Year Ended 31 January	2018	2017	2016
Cash flows from operating activities:			
Consolidated net income	10,523	14,293	15,080
Adjustments to reconcile income from continuing operations to net cash provided by operating activities:			
Depreciation and amortization	10,529	10,080	9,454
Deferred income taxes	(304)	761	(672)
Loss on extinguishment of debt	3,136	-	-
Other operating activities	1,210	206	1,410
Changes in certain assets and liabilities, net of effects of acquisitions:			
Receivables, net	(1.074)	(402)	(19)
Inventories	(140)	1,021	(703)
Accounts payable	4,086	3,942	2,008
Accrued liabilities	928	1,280	1,466
Accrued income taxes	(557)	492	(472)
Net cash provided by operating activities	28,337	31,673	27,552
Cash flows from investing activities:			
Payments for property and equipment	(10,051)	(10,619)	(11,477)
Proceeds from disposal of property and equipment	378	456	635

Exhibit 5 (Continued)

Fiscal Year Ended 31 January	2018	2017	2016
Proceeds from the disposal of certain operations	1,046	662	246
Purchase of available for sale securities	-	(1,901)	-
Investment and business acquisitions, net of cash acquired	(375)	(2,463)	-
Other investing activities	(58)	(122)	(79)
Net cash used in investing activities	(9,060)	(13,987)	(10,675)
Cash flows from financing activities:			
Net change in short-term borrowings	4,148	(1,673)	1,235
Proceeds from issuance of long-term debt	7,476	137	39
Payments of long-term debt	(13,061)	(2,055)	(4,432)
Payment for debt extinguishment or debt prepayment cost	(3,059)	-	-
Dividends paid	(6,124)	(6,216)	(6,294)
Purchase of Company stock	(8,296)	(8,298)	(4,112)
Dividends paid to noncontrolling interest	(690)	(479)	(719)
Purchase of noncontrolling interest	(8)	(90)	(1,326)
Other financing activities	(261)	(398)	(676)
Net cash used in financing activities	(19,875)	(19,072)	(16,285)
Effect of exchange rates on cash and cash equivalents	487	(452)	(1,022)
Net increase (decrease) in cash and cash equivalents	(111)	(1,838)	(430)
Cash and cash equivalents at beginning of yea	6,867	8,705	9,135
Cash and cash equivalents at end of yea	**6,756**	**6,867**	**8,705**
Supplemental disclosure of cash flow information			
Income taxes paid	6,179	4,507	8,111
Interest paid	2,450	2,351	2,540

Walmart's cash flow statement indicates the following:

- Cash and cash equivalents declined over the three years, from \$9.1 billion at the beginning of fiscal 2016 to \$6.8 billion at the end of fiscal 2018.
- Operating cash flow was relatively steady at \$27.6 billion, \$31.7 billion, and \$28.3 billion in fiscal 2016, 2017, and 2018, respectively. Further, operating cash flow was significantly greater than the company's expenditures on property and equipment in every year.
- Over the three years, the company used significant amounts of cash to pay dividends and to repurchase its common stock. The company also repaid borrowing, particularly in fiscal 2018.

Walmart prepares its cash flow statements under the indirect method. In the cash flows from operating activities section of Walmart's cash flow statement, the company reconciles its net income for 2018 of \$10.5 billion to net cash provided by operating activities of \$28.3 billion. The largest adjustment is for depreciation and amortization of \$10.5 billion. Depreciation and amortization expense requires an adjustment because it was a non-cash expense on the income statement. As illustrated in previous examples, depreciation is the largest or one of the largest adjustments made by many companies in the reconciliation of net income to operating cash flow.

Whenever the indirect method is used, US GAAP mandate disclosure of how much cash was paid for interest and income taxes. Note that these are line items in cash flow statements using the direct method, so disclosure does not have to be mandated. Walmart discloses the amount of cash paid for income tax ($6.2 billion) and interest ($2.5 billion) at the bottom of its cash flow statements.

3 THE CASH FLOW STATEMENT: LINKAGES AND PREPARATION

The indirect format of the cash flow statement demonstrates that changes in balance sheet accounts are an important factor in determining cash flows. The next section addresses the linkages between the cash flow statement and other financial statements.

3.1 Linkages of the Cash Flow Statement with the Income Statement and Balance Sheet

Recall the accounting equation that summarizes the balance sheet:

Assets = Liabilities + Equity

Cash is an asset. The statement of cash flows ultimately shows the change in cash during an accounting period. The beginning and ending balances of cash are shown on the company's balance sheets for the previous and current years, and the bottom of the cash flow statement reconciles beginning cash with ending cash. The relationship, stated in general terms, is as shown below.

Beginning Balance Sheet at 31 December 20X8	**Statement of Cash Flows for Year Ended 31 December 20X9**		**Ending Balance Sheet at 31 December 20X9**
Beginning cash	Plus: Cash receipts (from operating, investing, and financing activities)	Less: Cash payments (for operating, investing, and financing activities)	Ending cash

In the case of cash held in foreign currencies, there would also be an impact from changes in exchange rates. For example, Walmart's cash flow statement for 2018, presented in Exhibit 5, shows overall cash flows from operating, investing, and financing activities that total $(111) million during the year, including $487 million net effect of exchange rates on cash and cash equivalents.

The body of Walmart's cash flow statement shows why the change in cash occurred; in other words, it shows the company's operating, investing, and financing activities (as well as the impact of foreign currency translation). The beginning and ending balance sheet values of cash and cash equivalents are linked through the cash flow statement.

The current assets and current liabilities sections of the balance sheet typically reflect a company's operating decisions and activities. Because a company's operating activities are reported on an accrual basis in the income statement, any differences between the accrual basis and the cash basis of accounting for an operating transaction result in an increase or decrease in some (usually) short-term asset or liability on the balance sheet. For example, if revenue reported using accrual accounting is higher than the cash actually collected, the result will typically be an increase in accounts receivable. If expenses reported using accrual accounting are lower than cash actually paid, the result will typically be a decrease in accounts payable or another accrued liability account[8]. As an example of how items on the balance sheet are related to the income statement and/or cash flow statement through the change in the beginning and ending balances, consider accounts receivable:

Beginning Balance Sheet at 31 December 20X8	Income Statement for Year Ended 31 December 20X9	Statement of Cash Flows for Year Ended 31 December 20X9	Ending Balance Sheet at 31 December 20X9
Beginning accounts receivable	Plus: Revenues	Minus: Cash collected from customers	Equals: Ending accounts receivable

Knowing any three of these four items makes it easy to compute the fourth. For example, if you know beginning accounts receivable, revenues, and cash collected from customers, you can compute ending accounts receivable. Understanding the interrelationships among the balance sheet, income statement, and cash flow statement is useful not only in evaluating the company's financial health but also in detecting accounting irregularities. Recall the extreme illustration of a hypothetical company that makes sales on account without regard to future collections and thus reports healthy sales and significant income on its income statement yet lacks cash inflow. Such a pattern would occur if a company improperly recognized revenue.

A company's investing activities typically relate to the long-term asset section of the balance sheet, and its financing activities typically relate to the equity and long-term debt sections of the balance sheet. The next section demonstrates the preparation of cash flow information based on income statement and balance sheet information.

3.2 Steps in Preparing the Cash Flow Statement

The preparation of the cash flow statement uses data from both the income statement and the comparative balance sheets.

As noted earlier, companies often only disclose indirect operating cash flow information, whereas analysts prefer direct-format information. Understanding how cash flow information is put together will enable you to take an indirect statement apart and reconfigure it in a more useful manner. The result is an approximation of a direct cash flow statement, which—while not perfectly accurate—can be helpful to an analyst. The following demonstration of how an approximation of a direct cash flow statement is prepared uses the income statement and the comparative balance sheets for Acme Corporation (a fictitious retail company) shown in Exhibits 6 and 7.

Exhibit 6 Acme Corporation Income Statement Year Ended 31 December 2018

Revenue (net)		$23,598
Cost of goods sold		11,456
Gross profit		12,142
Salary and wage expense	$4,123	
Depreciation expense	1,052	
Other operating expenses	3,577	
Total operating expenses		8,752

(continued)

8 There are other less typical explanations of the differences. For example, if revenue reported using accrual accounting is higher than the cash actually collected, it is possible that it is the result of a decrease in an unearned revenue liability account. If expenses reported using accrual accounting are lower than cash actually paid, it is possible that it is the result of an increase in prepaid expenses, inventory, or another asset account.

Exhibit 6 (Continued)

Operating profit		3,390
Other revenues (expenses):		
Gain on sale of equipment	205	
Interest expense	(246)	(41)
Income before tax		3,349
Income tax expense		1,139
Net income		$2,210

Exhibit 7 Acme Corporation Comparative Balance Sheets 31 December 2018 and 2017

	2018	2017	Net Change
Cash	$1,011	$1,163	$(152)
Accounts receivable	1,012	957	55
Inventory	3,984	3,277	707
Prepaid expenses	155	178	(23)
Total current assets	6,162	5,575	587
Land	510	510	—
Buildings	3,680	3,680	—
Equipment*	8,798	8,555	243
Less: accumulated depreciation	(3,443)	(2,891)	(552)
Total long-term assets	9,545	9,854	(309)
Total assets	$15,707	$15,429	$278
Accounts payable	$3,588	$3,325	$263
Salary and wage payable	85	75	10
Interest payable	62	74	(12)
Income tax payable	55	50	5
Other accrued liabilities	1,126	1,104	22
Total current liabilities	4,916	4,628	288
Long-term debt	3,075	3,575	(500)
Common stock	3,750	4,350	(600)
Retained earnings	3,966	2,876	1,090
Total liabilities and equity	$15,707	$15,429	$278

* During 2018, Acme purchased new equipment for a total cost of $1,300. No items impacted retained earnings other than net income and dividends.

The first step in preparing the cash flow statement is to determine the total cash flows from operating activities. The direct method of presenting cash from operating activities is illustrated in sections 3.2.1 through 3.2.4. Section 3.2.5 illustrates the indirect method of presenting cash flows from operating activities. Cash flows from investing activities and from financing activities are identical regardless of whether the direct or indirect method is used to present operating cash flows.

3.2.1 *Operating Activities: Direct Method*

We first determine how much cash Acme received from its customers, followed by how much cash was paid to suppliers and to employees as well as how much cash was paid for other operating expenses, interest, and income taxes.

3.2.1.1 Cash Received from Customers The income statement for Acme reported revenue of $23,598 for the year ended 31 December 2018. To determine the approximate cash receipts from its customers, it is necessary to adjust this revenue amount by the net change in accounts receivable for the year. If accounts receivable increase during the year, revenue on an accrual basis is higher than cash receipts from customers, and vice versa. For Acme Corporation, accounts receivable increased by $55, so cash received from customers was $23,543, as follows:

Revenue	$23,598
Less: Increase in accounts receivable	(55)
Cash received from customers	**$23,543**

Cash received from customers affects the accounts receivable account as follows:

Beginning accounts receivable	957
Plus revenue	23,598
Minus cash collected from customers	**(23,543)**
Ending accounts receivable	$1,012

The accounts receivable account information can also be presented as follows:

Beginning accounts receivable	$957
Plus revenue	23,598
Minus ending accounts receivable	(1,012)
Cash collected from customers	**$23,543**

EXAMPLE 3

Computing Cash Received from Customers

Blue Bayou, a fictitious advertising company, reported revenues of $50 million, total expenses of $35 million, and net income of $15 million in the most recent year. If accounts receivable decreased by $12 million, how much cash did the company receive from customers?

A $38 million.

B $50 million.

C $62 million.

Solution:

C is correct. Revenues of $50 million plus the decrease in accounts receivable of $12 million equals $62 million cash received from customers. The decrease in accounts receivable means that the company received more in cash than the amount of revenue it reported.

"Cash received from customers" is sometimes referred to as "cash collections from customers" or "cash collections."

3.2.1.2 Cash Paid to Suppliers For Acme, the cash paid to suppliers was $11,900, determined as follows:

Cost of goods sold	$11,456
Plus: Increase in inventory	707
Equals purchases from suppliers	$12,163
Less: Increase in accounts payable	(263)
Cash paid to suppliers	**$11,900**

There are two pieces to this calculation: the amount of inventory purchased and the amount paid for it. To determine purchases from suppliers, cost of goods sold is adjusted for the change in inventory. If inventory increased during the year, then purchases during the year exceeded cost of goods sold, and vice versa. Acme reported cost of goods sold of $11,456 for the year ended 31 December 2018. For Acme Corporation, inventory increased by $707, so purchases from suppliers was $12,163. Purchases from suppliers affect the inventory account, as shown below:

Beginning inventory	$3,277
Plus purchases	12,163
Minus cost of goods sold	(11,456)
Ending inventory	$3,984

Acme purchased $12,163 of inventory from suppliers in 2018, but is this the amount of cash that Acme paid to its suppliers during the year? Not necessarily. Acme may not have yet paid for all of these purchases and may yet owe for some of the purchases made this year. In other words, Acme may have paid less cash to its suppliers than the amount of this year's purchases, in which case Acme's liability (accounts payable) will have increased by the difference. Alternatively, Acme may have paid even more to its suppliers than the amount of this year's purchases, in which case Acme's accounts payable will have decreased.

Therefore, once purchases have been determined, cash paid to suppliers can be calculated by adjusting purchases for the change in accounts payable. If the company made all purchases with cash, then accounts payable would not change and cash outflows would equal purchases. If accounts payable increased during the year, then purchases on an accrual basis would be higher than they would be on a cash basis, and vice versa. In this example, Acme made more purchases than it paid in cash, so the balance in accounts payable increased. For Acme, the cash paid to suppliers was $11,900, determined as follows:

Purchases from suppliers	$12,163
Less: Increase in accounts payable	(263)
Cash paid to suppliers	**$11,900**

The amount of cash paid to suppliers is reflected in the accounts payable account, as shown below:

Beginning accounts payable	$3,325
Plus purchases	12,163
Minus cash paid to suppliers	**(11,900)**
Ending accounts payable	$3,588

EXAMPLE 4

Computing Cash Paid to Suppliers

Orange Beverages Plc., a fictitious manufacturer of tropical drinks, reported cost of goods sold for the year of $100 million. Total assets increased by $55 million, but inventory declined by $6 million. Total liabilities increased by $45 million, but accounts payable decreased by $2 million. How much cash did the company pay to its suppliers during the year?

A $96 million.

B $104 million.

C $108 million.

Solution:

A is correct. Cost of goods sold of $100 million less the decrease in inventory of $6 million equals purchases from suppliers of $94 million. The decrease in accounts payable of $2 million means that the company paid $96 million in cash ($94 million plus $2 million).

3.2.1.3 Cash Paid to Employees To determine the cash paid to employees, it is necessary to adjust salary and wages expense by the net change in salary and wages payable for the year. If salary and wages payable increased during the year, then salary and wages expense on an accrual basis would be higher than the amount of cash paid for this expense, and vice versa. For Acme, salary and wages payable increased by $10, so cash paid for salary and wages was $4,113, as follows:

Salary and wages expense	$4,123
Less: Increase in salary and wages payable	(10)
Cash paid to employees	**$4,113**

The amount of cash paid to employees is reflected in the salary and wages payable account, as shown below:

Beginning salary and wages payable	$75
Plus salary and wages expense	4,123
Minus cash paid to employees	**(4,113)**
Ending salary and wages payable	$85

3.2.1.4 Cash Paid for Other Operating Expenses To determine the cash paid for other operating expenses, it is necessary to adjust the other operating expenses amount on the income statement by the net changes in prepaid expenses and accrued expense liabilities for the year. If prepaid expenses increased during the year, other operating expenses on a cash basis would be higher than on an accrual basis, and vice versa. Likewise, if accrued expense liabilities increased during the year, other operating expenses on a cash basis would be lower than on an accrual basis, and vice versa. For Acme Corporation, the amount of cash paid for operating expenses in 2018 was $3,532, as follows:

Other operating expenses	$3,577
Less: Decrease in prepaid expenses	(23)
Less: Increase in other accrued liabilities	(22)
Cash paid for other operating expenses	**$3,532**

EXAMPLE 5

Computing Cash Paid for Other Operating Expenses

Black Ice, a fictitious sportswear manufacturer, reported other operating expenses of $30 million. Prepaid insurance expense increased by $4 million, and accrued utilities payable decreased by $7 million. Insurance and utilities are the only two components of other operating expenses. How much cash did the company pay in other operating expenses?

A $19 million.

B $33 million.

C $41 million.

Solution:

C is correct. Other operating expenses of $30 million plus the increase in prepaid insurance expense of $4 million plus the decrease in accrued utilities payable of $7 million equals $41 million.

3.2.1.5 Cash Paid for Interest The cash paid for interest is included in operating cash flows under US GAAP and may be included in operating or financing cash flows under IFRS. To determine the cash paid for interest, it is necessary to adjust interest expense by the net change in interest payable for the year. If interest payable increases during the year, then interest expense on an accrual basis will be higher than the amount of cash paid for interest, and vice versa. For Acme Corporation, interest payable decreased by $12, and cash paid for interest was $258, as follows:

Interest expense	$246
Plus: Decrease in interest payable	12
Cash paid for interest	**$258**

Alternatively, cash paid for interest may also be determined by an analysis of the interest payable account, as shown below:

Beginning interest payable	$74
Plus interest expense	246
Minus cash paid for interest	**(258)**
Ending interest payable	$62

3.2.1.6 Cash Paid for Income Taxes To determine the cash paid for income taxes, it is necessary to adjust the income tax expense amount on the income statement by the net changes in taxes receivable, taxes payable, and deferred income taxes for the year. If taxes receivable or deferred tax assets increase during the year, income taxes on a cash basis will be higher than on an accrual basis, and vice versa. Likewise, if taxes payable or deferred tax liabilities increase during the year, income tax expense on a cash basis will be lower than on an accrual basis, and vice versa. For Acme Corporation, the amount of cash paid for income taxes in 2018 was $1,134, as follows:

Income tax expense	$1,139
Less: Increase in income tax payable	(5)
Cash paid for income taxes	**$1,134**

3.2.2 *Investing Activities*

The second and third steps in preparing the cash flow statement are to determine the total cash flows from investing activities and from financing activities. The presentation of this information is identical, regardless of whether the direct or indirect method is used for operating cash flows.

Purchases and sales of equipment were the only investing activities undertaken by Acme in 2018, as evidenced by the fact that the amounts reported for land and buildings were unchanged during the year. An informational note in Exhibit 7 tells us that Acme *purchased* new equipment in 2018 for a total cost of $1,300. However, the amount of equipment shown on Acme's balance sheet increased by only $243 (ending balance of $8,798 minus beginning balance of $8,555); therefore, Acme must have also *sold or otherwise disposed of* some equipment during the year. To determine the cash inflow from the sale of equipment, we analyze the equipment and accumulated depreciation accounts as well as the gain on the sale of equipment from Exhibits 6 and 7. Assuming that the entire accumulated depreciation is related to equipment, the cash received from sale of equipment is determined as follows.

The historical cost of the equipment sold was $1,057. This amount is determined as follows:

Beginning balance equipment (from balance sheet)	$8,555
Plus equipment purchased (from informational note)	1,300
Minus ending balance equipment (from balance sheet)	(8,798)
Equals historical cost of equipment sold	$1,057

The accumulated depreciation on the equipment sold was $500, determined as follows:

Beginning balance accumulated depreciation (from balance sheet)	$2,891
Plus depreciation expense (from income statement)	1,052
Minus ending balance accumulated depreciation (from balance sheet)	(3,443)
Equals accumulated depreciation on equipment sold	$500

The historical cost information, accumulated depreciation information, and information from the income statement about the gain on the sale of equipment can be used to determine the cash received from the sale.

Historical cost of equipment sold (calculated above)	$1,057
Less accumulated depreciation on equipment sold (calculated above)	(500)
Equals book value of equipment sold	$557
Plus gain on sale of equipment (from the income statement)	205
Equals cash received from sale of equipment	**$762**

EXAMPLE 6

Computing Cash Received from the Sale of Equipment

Copper, Inc., a fictitious brewery and restaurant chain, reported a gain on the sale of equipment of $12 million. In addition, the company's income statement shows depreciation expense of $8 million and the cash flow statement shows capital expenditure of $15 million, all of which was for the purchase of new equipment.

Balance sheet item	12/31/2018	12/31/2017	Change
Equipment	$100 million	$109 million	$9 million
Accumulated depreciation—equipment	$30 million	$36 million	$6 million

Using the above information from the comparative balance sheets, how much cash did the company receive from the equipment sale?

A $12 million.

B $16 million.

C $18 million.

Solution:

B is correct. Selling price (cash inflow) minus book value equals gain or loss on sale; therefore, gain or loss on sale plus book value equals selling price (cash inflow). The amount of gain is given, $12 million. To calculate the book value of the equipment sold, find the historical cost of the equipment and the accumulated depreciation on the equipment.

- Beginning balance of equipment of $100 million plus equipment purchased of $15 million minus ending balance of equipment of $109 million equals historical cost of equipment sold, or $6 million.
- Beginning accumulated depreciation on equipment of $30 million plus depreciation expense for the year of $8 million minus ending balance of accumulated depreciation of $36 million equals accumulated depreciation on the equipment sold, or $2 million.
- Therefore, the book value of the equipment sold was $6 million minus $2 million, or $4 million.
- Because the gain on the sale of equipment was $12 million, the amount of cash received must have been $16 million.

3.2.3 *Financing Activities*

As with investing activities, the presentation of financing activities is identical, regardless of whether the direct or indirect method is used for operating cash flows.

3.2.3.1 Long-Term Debt and Common Stock The change in long-term debt, based on the beginning 2018 (ending 2017) and ending 2018 balances in Exhibit 7, was a decrease of $500. Absent other information, this indicates that Acme retired $500 of long-term debt. Retiring long-term debt is a cash outflow relating to financing activities.

Similarly, the change in common stock during 2018 was a decrease of $600. Absent other information, this indicates that Acme repurchased $600 of its common stock. Repurchase of common stock is also a cash outflow related to financing activity.

3.2.3.2 Dividends Recall the following relationship:

Beginning retained earnings + Net income – Dividends = Ending retained earnings

Based on this relationship, the amount of cash dividends paid in 2018 can be determined from an analysis of retained earnings, as follows:

Beginning balance of retained earnings (from the balance sheet)	$2,876
Plus net income (from the income statement)	2,210
Minus ending balance of retained earnings (from the balance sheet)	(3,966)
Equals dividends paid	**$1,120**

Note that dividends paid are presented in the statement of changes in equity.

3.2.4 *Overall Statement of Cash Flows: Direct Method*

Exhibit 8 summarizes the information about Acme's operating, investing, and financing cash flows in the statement of cash flows. At the bottom of the statement, the total net change in cash is shown to be a decrease of $152 (from $1,163 to $1,011). This decrease can also be seen on the comparative balance sheet in Exhibit 7. The cash provided by operating activities of $2,606 was adequate to cover the net cash used in investing activities of $538; however, the company's debt repayments, cash payments for dividends, and repurchase of common stock (i.e., its financing activities) of $2,220 resulted in an overall decrease in cash of $152.

Exhibit 8 Acme Corporation Cash Flow Statement (Direct Method) for Year Ended 31 December 2018

Cash flow from operating activities:	
Cash received from customers	$23,543
Cash paid to suppliers	(11,900)
Cash paid to employees	(4,113)
Cash paid for other operating expenses	(3,532)
Cash paid for interest	(258)
Cash paid for income tax	(1,134)
Net cash provided by operating activities	2,606
Cash flow from investing activities:	
Cash received from sale of equipment	762
Cash paid for purchase of equipment	(1,300)
Net cash used for investing activities	(538)
Cash flow from financing activities:	
Cash paid to retire long-term debt	(500)
Cash paid to retire common stock	(600)
Cash paid for dividends	(1,120)
Net cash used for financing activities	(2,220)
Net increase (decrease) in cash	(152)
Cash balance, 31 December 2017	1,163
Cash balance, 31 December 2018	$1,011

3.2.5 *Overall Statement of Cash Flows: Indirect Method*

Using the alternative approach to reporting cash from operating activities, the indirect method, we will present the same amount of cash provided by operating activities. Under this approach, we reconcile Acme's net income of $2,210 to its operating cash flow of $2,606.

To perform this reconciliation, net income is adjusted for the following: a) any non-operating activities, b) any non-cash expenses, and c) changes in operating working capital items.

The only non-operating activity in Acme's income statement, the sale of equipment, resulted in a gain of $205. This amount is removed from the operating cash flow section; the cash effects of the sale are shown in the investing section.

Acme's only non-cash expense was depreciation expense of $1,052. Under the indirect method, depreciation expense must be added back to net income because it was a non-cash deduction in the calculation of net income.

Changes in working capital accounts include increases and decreases in the current operating asset and liability accounts. The changes in these accounts arise from applying accrual accounting; that is, recognizing revenues when they are earned and expenses when they are incurred instead of when the cash is received or paid. To make the working capital adjustments under the indirect method, any increase in a current operating asset account is subtracted from net income and a net decrease is added to net income. As described above, the increase in accounts receivable, for example, resulted from Acme recording income statement revenue higher than the amount of cash received from customers; therefore, to reconcile back to operating cash flow, that increase in accounts receivable must be deducted from net income. For current operating liabilities, a net increase is added to net income and a net decrease is subtracted from net income. As described above, the increase in wages payable, for example, resulted from Acme recording income statement expenses higher than the amount of cash paid to employees.

Exhibit 9 presents a tabulation of the most common types of adjustments that are made to net income when using the indirect method to determine net cash flow from operating activities.

Exhibit 9 Adjustments to Net Income Using the Indirect Method

Additions	▪ Non-cash items • Depreciation expense of tangible assets • Amortisation expense of intangible assets • Depletion expense of natural resources • Amortisation of bond discount ▪ Non-operating losses • Loss on sale or write-down of assets • Loss on retirement of debt • Loss on investments accounted for under the equity method ▪ Increase in deferred income tax liability ▪ Changes in working capital resulting from accruing higher amounts for expenses than the amounts of cash payments or lower amounts for revenues than the amounts of cash receipts • Decrease in current operating assets (e.g., accounts receivable, inventory, and prepaid expenses) • Increase in current operating liabilities (e.g., accounts payable and accrued expense liabilities)

Exhibit 9 (Continued)	
Subtractions	■ Non-cash items (e.g., amortisation of bond premium) ■ Non-operating items • Gain on sale of assets • Gain on retirement of debt • Income on investments accounted for under the equity method ■ Decrease in deferred income tax liability ■ Changes in working capital resulting from accruing lower amounts for expenses than for cash payments or higher amounts for revenues than for cash receipts • Increase in current operating assets (e.g., accounts receivable, inventory, and prepaid expenses) • Decrease in current operating liabilities (e.g., accounts payable and accrued expense liabilities)

Accordingly, for Acme Corporation, the $55 increase in accounts receivable and the $707 increase in inventory are subtracted from net income and the $23 decrease in prepaid expenses is added to net income. For Acme's current liabilities, the increases in accounts payable, salary and wage payable, income tax payable, and other accrued liabilities ($263, $10, $5, and $22, respectively) are added to net income and the $12 decrease in interest payable is subtracted from net income. Exhibit 10 presents the cash flow statement for Acme Corporation under the indirect method by using the information that we have determined from our analysis of the income statement and the comparative balance sheets. Note that the investing and financing sections are identical to the statement of cash flows prepared using the direct method.

Exhibit 10 Acme Corporation Cash Flow Statement (Indirect Method) Year Ended 31 December 2018

Cash flow from operating activities:	
Net income	$2,210
Depreciation expense	1,052
Gain on sale of equipment	(205)
Increase in accounts receivable	(55)
Increase in inventory	(707)
Decrease in prepaid expenses	23
Increase in accounts payable	263
Increase in salary and wage payable	10
Decrease in interest payable	(12)
Increase in income tax payable	5
Increase in other accrued liabilities	22
Net cash provided by operating activities	2,606
Cash flow from investing activities:	
Cash received from sale of equipment	762
Cash paid for purchase of equipment	(1,300)
Net cash used for investing activities	(538)

(continued)

Exhibit 10 (Continued)

Cash flow from financing activities:	
Cash paid to retire long-term debt	(500)
Cash paid to retire common stock	(600)
Cash paid for dividends	(1,120)
Net cash used for financing activities	(2,220)
Net decrease in cash	(152)
Cash balance, 31 December 2017	1,163
Cash balance, 31 December 2018	$1,011

EXAMPLE 7

Adjusting Net Income to Compute Operating Cash Flow

Based on the following information for Pinkerly Inc., a fictitious company, what are the total adjustments that the company would make to net income in order to derive operating cash flow?

	Year Ended		
Income statement item		12/31/2018	
Net income		$30 million	
Depreciation		$7 million	
Balance sheet item	12/31/2017	12/31/2018	Change
Accounts receivable	$15 million	$30 million	$15 million
Inventory	$16 million	$13 million	($3 million)
Accounts payable	$10 million	$20 million	$10 million

A Add $5 million.

B Add $21 million.

C Subtract $9 million.

Solution:

A is correct. To derive operating cash flow, the company would make the following adjustments to net income: add depreciation (a non-cash expense) of $7 million; add the decrease in inventory of $3 million; add the increase in accounts payable of $10 million; and subtract the increase in accounts receivable of $15 million. Total additions of $20 million and total subtractions of $15 million result in net total additions of $5 million.

3.3 Conversion of Cash Flows from the Indirect to the Direct Method

An analyst may desire to review direct-format operating cash flow to review trends in cash receipts and payments (such as cash received from customers or cash paid to suppliers). If a direct-format statement is not available, cash flows from operating activities reported under the indirect method can be converted to the direct method. Accuracy of conversion depends on adjustments using data available in published financial reports. The method described here is sufficiently accurate for most analytical purposes.

The three-step conversion process is demonstrated for Acme Corporation in Exhibit 11. Referring again to Exhibits 6 and 7 for Acme Corporation's income statement and balance sheet information, begin by disaggregating net income of $2,210 into total revenues and total expenses (Step 1). Next, remove any non-operating and non-cash items (Step 2). For Acme, we therefore remove the non-operating gain on the sale of equipment of $205 and the non-cash depreciation expense of $1,052. Then, convert accrual amounts of revenues and expenses to cash flow amounts of receipts and payments by adjusting for changes in working capital accounts (Step 3). The results of these adjustments are the items of information for the direct format of operating cash flows. These line items are shown as the results of Step 3.

Exhibit 11 Conversion from the Indirect to the Direct Method

Step 1	Total revenues		$23,803
Aggregate all revenue and all expenses	Total expenses		21,593
	Net income		$2,210
Step 2	Total revenue less noncash item revenues:		
Remove all noncash items from aggregated revenues and expenses and break out remaining items into relevant cash flow items		($23,803 – $205) =	$23,598
		Revenue	$23,598
	Total expenses less noncash item expenses:		
		($21,593 – $1,052) =	$20,541
	Cost of goods sold		$11,456
	Salary and wage expenses		4,123
	Other operating expenses		3,577
	Interest expense		246
	Income tax expense		1,139
	Total		$20,541
Step 3	Cash received from customers[a]		$23,543
Convert accrual amounts to cash flow amounts by adjusting for working capital changes	Cash paid to suppliers[b]		(11,900)
	Cash paid to employees[c]		(4,113)
	Cash paid for other operating expenses[d]		(3,532)
	Cash paid for interest[e]		(258)
	Cash paid for income tax[f]		(1,134)
	Net cash provided by operating activities		$2,606

Calculations for Step 3:

[a] Revenue of $23,598 less increase in accounts receivable of $55.

(continued)

Exhibit 11 (Continued)

[b] Cost of goods sold of $11,456 plus increase in inventory of $707 less increase in accounts payable of $263.
[c] Salary and wage expense of $4,123 less increase in salary and wage payable of $10.
[d] Other operating expenses of $3,577 less decrease in prepaid expenses of $23 less increase in other accrued liabilities of $22.
[e] Interest expense of $246 plus decrease in interest payable of $12.
[f] Income tax expense of $1,139 less increase in income tax payable of $5.

4 CASH FLOW STATEMENT ANALYSIS

The analysis of a company's cash flows can provide useful information for understanding a company's business and earnings and for predicting its future cash flows. This section describes tools and techniques for analyzing the statement of cash flows, including the analysis of sources and uses of cash and cash flow, common-size analysis, and calculation of free cash flow measures and cash flow ratios.

4.1 Evaluation of the Sources and Uses of Cash

Evaluation of the cash flow statement should involve an overall assessment of the sources and uses of cash between the three main categories as well as an assessment of the main drivers of cash flow within each category, as follows:

1 Evaluate where the major sources and uses of cash flow are between operating, investing, and financing activities.
2 Evaluate the primary determinants of operating cash flow.
3 Evaluate the primary determinants of investing cash flow.
4 Evaluate the primary determinants of financing cash flow.

Step 1 The major sources of cash for a company can vary with its stage of growth. For a mature company, it is expected and desirable that operating activities are the primary source of cash flows. Over the long term, a company must generate cash from its operating activities. If operating cash flow were consistently negative, a company would need to borrow money or issue stock (financing activities) to fund the shortfall. Eventually, these providers of capital need to be repaid from operations or they will no longer be willing to provide capital. Cash generated from operating activities can be used in either investing or financing activities. If the company has good opportunities to grow the business or other investment opportunities, it is desirable to use the cash in investing activities. If the company does not have profitable investment opportunities, the cash should be returned to capital providers, a financing activity. For a new or growth stage company, operating cash flow may be negative for some period of time as it invests in such assets as inventory and receivables (extending credit to new customers) in order to grow the business. This situation is not sustainable over the long term, so eventually the cash must start to come primarily from operating activities so that capital can be returned to the providers of capital. Lastly, it is desirable that operating cash flows are sufficient to cover capital expenditures (in other words, the company has free cash flow as discussed further in Section 4.3). In summary, major points to consider at this step are:

- What are the major sources and uses of cash flow?
- Is operating cash flow positive and sufficient to cover capital expenditures?

Step 2 Turning to the operating section, the analysts should examine the most significant determinants of operating cash flow. Companies need cash for use in operations (for example, to hold receivables and inventory and to pay employees and suppliers) and receive cash from operating activities (for example, payments from customers). Under the indirect method, the increases and decreases in receivables, inventory, payables, and so on can be examined to determine whether the company is using or generating cash in operations and why. It is also useful to compare operating cash flow with net income. For a mature company, because net income includes non-cash expenses (depreciation and amortisation), it is expected and desirable that operating cash flow exceeds net income. The relationship between net income and operating cash flow is also an indicator of earnings quality. If a company has large net income but poor operating cash flow, it may be a sign of poor earnings quality. The company may be making aggressive accounting choices to increase net income but not be generating cash for its business. You should also examine the variability of both earnings and cash flow and consider the impact of this variability on the company's risk as well as the ability to forecast future cash flows for valuation purposes. In summary:

- What are the major determinants of operating cash flow?
- Is operating cash flow higher or lower than net income? Why?
- How consistent are operating cash flows?

Step 3 Within the investing section, you should evaluate each line item. Each line item represents either a source or use of cash. This enables you to understand where the cash is being spent (or received). This section will tell you how much cash is being invested for the future in property, plant, and equipment; how much is used to acquire entire companies; and how much is put aside in liquid investments, such as stocks and bonds. It will also tell you how much cash is being raised by selling these types of assets. If the company is making major capital investments, you should consider where the cash is coming from to cover these investments (e.g., is the cash coming from excess operating cash flow or from the financing activities described in Step 4). If assets are being sold, it is important to determine why and to assess the effects on the company.

Step 4 Within the financing section, you should examine each line item to understand whether the company is raising capital or repaying capital and what the nature of its capital sources are. If the company is borrowing each year, you should consider when repayment may be required. This section will also present dividend payments and repurchases of stock that are alternative means of returning capital to owners. It is important to assess why capital is being raised or repaid.

We now provide an example of a cash flow statement evaluation.

EXAMPLE 8

Analysis of the Cash Flow Statement

Derek Yee, CFA, is preparing to forecast cash flow for Groupe Danone as an input into his valuation model. He has asked you to evaluate the historical cash flow statement of Groupe Danone, which is presented in Exhibit 12. Groupe Danone prepares its financial statements in conformity with IFRS. Note that Groupe Danone presents the most recent period on the right. Exhibit 13 presents excerpts from Danone's 2017 Registration Document.

Yee would like answers to the following questions:

- What are the major sources of cash for Groupe Danone?
- What are the major uses of cash for Groupe Danone?

- Is cash flow from operating activities sufficient to cover capital expenditures?
- What is the relationship between net income and cash flow from operating activities?
- What types of financing cash flows does Groupe Danone have?

Exhibit 12 Groupe Danone Consolidated Financial Statements Consolidated Statements of Cash Flows (in € Millions)

Years Ended 31 December	2016	2017
Net income	1,827	2,563
Share of profits of associates net of dividends received	52	(54)
Depreciation, amortization and impairment of tangible and intangible assets	786	974
Increases in (reversals of) provisions	51	153
Change in deferred taxes	(65)	(353)
(Gains) losses on disposal of property, plant and equipment and financial investments	(74)	(284)
Expense related to Group performance shares	24	22
Cost of net financial debt	149	265
Net interest paid	(148)	(186)
Net change in interest income (expense)	—	80
Other components with no cash impact	13	(15)
Cash flows provided by operating activities, before changes in net working capital	**2,615**	**3,085**
(Increase) decrease in inventories	(24)	(122)
(Increase) decrease in trade receivables	(110)	(190)
Increase (decrease) in trade payables	298	145
Changes in other receivables and payables	(127)	40
Change in other working capital requirements	37	(127)
Cash flows provided by (used in) operating activities	**2,652**	**2,958**
Capital expenditure	(925)	(969)
Proceeds from the disposal of property, plant and equipment	27	45
Net cash outflows on purchases of subsidiaries and financial investments	(66)	(10,949)
Net cash inflows on disposal of subsidiaries and financial investments	110	441
(Increase) decrease in long-term loans and other long-term financial assets	6	(4)
Cash flows provided by (used in) investing activities	**(848)**	**(11,437)**
Increase in capital and additional paid-in capital	46	47
Purchases of treasury stock (net of disposals) and DANONE call options	32	13
Issue of perpetual subordinated debt securities	—	1,245
Interest on perpetual subordinated debt securities	—	—
Dividends paid to Danone shareholders	(985)	(279)
Buyout of non-controlling interests	(295)	(107)
Dividends paid	(94)	(86)
Contribution from non-controlling interests to capital increases	6	1
Transactions with non-controlling interests	(383)	(193)

Exhibit 12 (Continued)

Years Ended 31 December	2016	2017
Net cash flows on hedging derivatives	50	(52)
Bonds issued during the period	11,237	—
Bonds repaid during the period	(638)	(1,487)
Net cash flows from other current and non-current financial debt	(442)	(564)
Net cash flows from short-term investments	(10,531)	9,559
Cash flows provided by (used in) financing activities	**(1,616)**	**8,289**
Effect of exchange rate and other changes	(151)	272
Increase (decrease) in cash and cash equivalents	**38**	**81**
Cash and cash equivalents at beginning of period	519	557
Cash and cash equivalents at end of period	557	638
Supplemental disclosures		
Income tax payments during the year	(891)	(1,116)

Note: the numbers in the consolidated statement of cash flows were derived straight from company filings; some sub-totals may not sum exactly due to rounding by the company.

Exhibit 13 Groupe Danone Excerpt from 2017 Registration Statement

Excerpt from Footnote 2 to the financial statements:

... On July 7, 2016, Danone announced the signing of an agreement to acquire The WhiteWave Foods Company ("WhiteWave"), the global leader in plant-based foods and beverages and organic produce. The acquisition in cash, for USD 56.25 per share, represented, as of the date of the agreement, a total enterprise value of approximately USD 12.5 billion, including debt and certain other WhiteWave liabilities. ...

"Acquisition expenses recognized in Danone's consolidated financial statements totaled €51 million before tax, of which €48 million was recognized in 2016 in Other operating income (expense), with the balance recognized in 2017.

"WhiteWave's contribution to 2017 consolidated sales totaled €2.7 billion. Had the transaction been completed on January 1, 2017, the Group's 2017 consolidated sales would have been €25.7 billion, with recurring operating income of €3.6 billion.

"Meanwhile, integration expenses for the period totaled €91 million, recognized under Other operating income (expense)...

Excerpt from Overview of Activities:

"... As part of its transformation plan aimed at ensuring a safe journey to deliver strong, profitable and sustainable growth, Danone set objectives for 2020 that include like-for-like sales growth between 4% and 5% .... a recurring operating margin of over 16% in 2020 ... Finally, Danone will continue to focus on growing its free cash flow, which will contribute to financial deleverage with an objective of a ratio of Net debt/EBITDA below 3x in 2020. Danone is committed to reaching a ROIC level around 12% in 2020."

Solution:

The major categories of cash flows can be summarized as follows (in € millions):

	2016	2017
Cash flows provided by operating activities	2,615	3,085
Cash flows provided by (used in) investing activities	(848)	(11,437)
Cash flows provided by (used in) financing activities	(1,616)	8,289
Exchange rate effects on cash	(151)	272
Increase in cash	38	81

The primary source of cash for Groupe Danone in 2016 is operating activities. In both 2016 and 2017, there was sufficient operating cash flow to cover usual capital expenditures, and operating cash flow exceeded net income. Evaluating the five prior years [not shown in this Example], you confirm that Danone typically derives most of its cash from operating activities, reports operating cash flow greater than net income, and generates sufficient operating cash flow to cover capital expenditures.

The fact that the primary source of cash is from operations is positive and desirable for a mature company. Additionally, the fact that operating cash flow exceeds net income in both years is a positive sign. Finally, operating cash flows exceed normal capital expenditures, indicating that the company can fund capital expenditures from operations.

In 2017, however, the primary source of cash was financing activities, and the investing section shows significant use of cash for purchase of subsidiaries within investing activities. Footnotes disclose a major acquisition with an aggregate value of €12.5 billion, some of which was funded through proceeds from an earlier bond issuance, which appears as a financing cash flow in the financing section for 2016.

For purposes of Yee's cash flow forecast, the company's targets for free cash flow and debt reduction—as well as disclosures concerning the acquisition's impact on 2017 operating results—are potentially helpful.

4.2 Common-Size Analysis of the Statement of Cash Flows

In common-size analysis of a company's income statement, each income and expense line item is expressed as a percentage of net revenues (net sales). For the common-size balance sheet, each asset, liability, and equity line item is expressed as a percentage of total assets. For the common-size cash flow statement, there are two alternative approaches. The first approach is to express each line item of cash inflow (outflow) as a percentage of total inflows (outflows) of cash, and the second approach is to express each line item as a percentage of net revenue.

Exhibit 14 demonstrates the total cash inflows/total cash outflows method for Acme Corporation. Under this approach, each of the cash inflows is expressed as a percentage of the total cash inflows, whereas each of the cash outflows is expressed as a percentage of the total cash outflows. In Panel A, Acme's common-size statement is based on a cash flow statement using the direct method of presenting operating cash flows. Operating cash inflows and outflows are separately presented on the cash flow statement, and therefore, the common-size cash flow statement shows each of these operating inflows (outflows) as a percentage of total inflows (outflows). In Panel B, Acme's common-size statement is based on a cash flow statement using the indirect method of presenting operating cash flows. When a cash flow statement has been presented using the indirect method, operating cash inflows and outflows are not separately presented; therefore, the common-size cash flow statement shows only the net operating cash flow (net cash provided by or used in operating activities) as a percentage of total inflows or outflows, depending on whether the net amount was a cash inflow or outflow. Because Acme's net operating cash flow is positive, it is shown as a percentage of total inflows.

Exhibit 14 Acme Corporation Common-Size Cash Flow Statement Year Ended 31 December 2018

Panel A. Direct Format for Cash Flow

Inflows		Percentage of Total Inflows
Receipts from customers	$23,543	96.86%
Sale of equipment	762	3.14
Total	$24,305	100.00%

Outflows		Percentage of Total Outflows
Payments to suppliers	$11,900	48.66%
Payments to employees	4,113	16.82
Payments for other operating expenses	3,532	14.44
Payments for interest	258	1.05
Payments for income tax	1,134	4.64
Purchase of equipment	1,300	5.32
Retirement of long-term debt	500	2.04
Retirement of common stock	600	2.45
Dividend payments	1,120	4.58
Total	$24,457	100.00%
Net increase (decrease) in cash	($152)	

Panel B. Indirect Format for Cash Flow

Inflows		Percentage of Total Inflows
Net cash provided by operating activities	$2,606	77.38%
Sale of equipment	762	22.62
Total	$3,368	100.00%

(continued)

Exhibit 14 (Continued)

Outflows		Percentage of Total Outflows
Purchase of equipment	$1,300	36.93%
Retirement of long-term debt	500	14.20
Retirement of common stock	600	17.05
Dividend payments	1,120	31.82
Total	$3,520	100.00%
Net increase (decrease) in cash	($152)	

Exhibit 15 demonstrates the net revenue common-size cash flow statement for Acme Corporation. Under the net revenue approach, each line item in the cash flow statement is shown as a percentage of net revenue. The common-size statement in this exhibit has been developed based on Acme's cash flow statement using the indirect method for operating cash flows and using net revenue of $23,598 as shown in Exhibit 6. Each line item of the reconciliation between net income and net operating cash flows is expressed as a percentage of net revenue. The common-size format makes it easier to see trends in cash flow rather than just looking at the total amount. This method is also useful to the analyst in forecasting future cash flows because individual items in the common-size statement (e.g., depreciation, fixed capital expenditures, debt borrowing, and repayment) are expressed as a percentage of net revenue. Thus, once the analyst has forecast revenue, the common-size statement provides a basis for forecasting cash flows for those items with an expected relation to net revenue.

Exhibit 15 Acme Corporation Common-Size Cash Flow Statement: Indirect Format Year Ended 31 December 2018

		Percentage of Net Revenue
Cash flow from operating activities:		
Net income	$2,210	9.37%
Depreciation expense	1,052	4.46
Gain on sale of equipment	(205)	(0.87)
Increase in accounts receivable	(55)	(0.23)
Increase in inventory	(707)	(3.00)
Decrease in prepaid expenses	23	0.10
Increase in accounts payable	263	1.11
Increase in salary and wage payable	10	0.04
Decrease in interest payable	(12)	(0.05)
Increase in income tax payable	5	0.02
Increase in other accrued liabilities	22	0.09
Net cash provided by operating activities	$2,606	11.04%
Cash flow from investing activities:		
Cash received from sale of equipment	$762	3.23%

Exhibit 15 (Continued)

		Percentage of Net Revenue
Cash paid for purchase of equipment	(1,300)	(5.51)
Net cash used for investing activities	$(538)	(2.28)%
Cash flow from financing activities:		
Cash paid to retire long-term debt	$(500)	(2.12)%
Cash paid to retire common stock	(600)	(2.54)
Cash paid for dividends	(1,120)	(4.75)
Net cash used for financing activities	$(2,220)	(9.41)%
Net decrease in cash	$(152)	(0.64)%

EXAMPLE 9

Analysis of a Common-Size Cash Flow Statement

Andrew Potter is examining an abbreviated common-size cash flow statement for Apple Inc., a multinational technology company. The common-size cash flow statement was prepared by dividing each line item by total net sales for the same year.

Apple Inc. Common Size Statements OF Cash Flows as Percentage of Total Net Sales

	12 Months Ended		
	30 Sep. 2017	24 Sep. 2016	26 Sep. 2015
Statement of Cash Flows [Abstract]			
Operating activities:			
Net income	21.1%	21.2%	22.8%
Adjustments to reconcile net income to cash generated by operating activities:			
Depreciation and amortization	4.4%	4.9%	4.8%
Share-based compensation expense	2.1%	2.0%	1.5%
Deferred income tax expense	2.6%	2.3%	0.6%
Other	−0.1%	0.2%	0.2%
Changes in operating assets and liabilities:			
Accounts receivable, net	−0.9%	0.2%	0.2%
Inventories	−1.2%	0.1%	−0.1%

(continued)

(Continued)

	12 Months Ended		
	30 Sep. 2017	**24 Sep. 2016**	**26 Sep. 2015**
Vendor non-trade receivables	–1.9%	0.0%	–1.6%
Other current and non-current assets	–2.3%	0.5%	–0.1%
Accounts payable	4.2%	0.9%	2.1%
Deferred revenue	–0.3%	–0.7%	0.4%
Other current and non-current liabilities	–0.1%	–0.9%	3.9%
Cash generated by operating activities	27.7%	30.5%	34.8%
Investing activities:			
Purchases of marketable securities	–69.6%	–66.0%	–71.2%
Proceeds from maturities of marketable securities	13.9%	9.9%	6.2%
Proceeds from sales of marketable securities	41.3%	42.0%	46.0%
Payments made in connection with business acquisitions, net	–0.1%	–0.1%	–0.1%
Payments for acquisition of property, plant and equipment	–5.4%	–5.9%	–4.8%
Payments for acquisition of intangible assets	–0.2%	–0.4%	–0.1%
Payments for strategic investments, net	–0.2%	–0.6%	0.0%
Other	0.1%	–0.1%	0.0%
Cash used in investing activities	–20.3%	–21.3%	–24.1%
Financing activities:			
Proceeds from issuance of common stock	0.2%	0.2%	0.2%
Excess tax benefits from equity awards	0.3%	0.2%	0.3%
Payments for taxes related to net share settlement of equity awards	–0.8%	–0.7%	–0.6%
Payments for dividends and dividend equivalents	5.6%	5.6%	4.9%
Repurchases of common stock	–14.4%	–13.8%	–15.1%
Proceeds from issuance of term debt, net	12.5%	11.6%	—
Repayments of term debt	–1.5%	–1.2%	0.0%
Change in commercial paper, net	1.7%	–0.2%	0.9%
Cash used in financing activities	–7.6%	–9.5%	–7.6%

(Continued)

	12 Months Ended		
	30 Sep. 2017	24 Sep. 2016	26 Sep. 2015
Increase/(Decrease) in cash and cash equivalents	−0.1%	−0.3%	3.1%

Based on the information in the above exhibit:

1 Discuss the significance of
   A depreciation and amortization.
   B capital expenditures.
2 Compare Apple's operating cash flow as a percentage of revenue with Apple's net profit margin.
3 Discuss Apple's use of its positive operating cash flow.

Solution to 1:

A Apple's depreciation and amortization expense was consistently just less than 5% of total net revenue in 2015 and 2016, declining to 4.4% in 2017.

B Apple's level of capital expenditures is greater than depreciation and amortization in 2016 and 2017 whereas it was at about the same level as depreciation and amortization in 2015. In 2017 capital expenditures approached 6%. This is an indication that Apple is doing more than replacing property, plant, and equipment, and is expanding those investments. With cash generated from operating activities exceeding 27% of sales in every year, however, Apple has more than enough cash flow from operations to fund these expenditures.

Solution to 2:

Apple's operating cash flow as a percentage of sales is much higher than net profit margin in every year. This gap appears to be declining however over the three year period. In 2015 net profit margin was 22.8% while operating cash flow as a percentage of sales was 34.8%. By 2017 the net profit margin declined slightly to 21.1% while the operating cash flow as a percentage of sales declined more to 27.7%. The primary difference appears to have been an increase in the level of receivables and inventory purchases, somewhat offset by an increase in accounts payable.

Solution to 3:

Apple has a very strong cash flow statement. Apple generates a large amount of operating cash flow in every year, exceeding net income. This cash flow is used for relatively modest purchases of property, plant and equipment, substantial purchases of marketable securities (investments), dividend payments and repurchases of its own stock.

4.3 Free Cash Flow to the Firm and Free Cash Flow to Equity

It was mentioned earlier that it is desirable that operating cash flows are sufficient to cover capital expenditures. The excess of operating cash flow over capital expenditures is known generically as **free cash flow**. For purposes of valuing a company or its equity securities, an analyst may want to determine and use other cash flow measures, such as free cash flow to the firm (FCFF) or free cash flow to equity (FCFE).

FCFF is the cash flow available to the company's suppliers of debt and equity capital after all operating expenses (including income taxes) have been paid and necessary investments in working capital and fixed capital have been made. FCFF can be computed starting with net income as

$$\text{FCFF} = \text{NI} + \text{NCC} + \text{Int}(1 - \text{Tax rate}) - \text{FCInv} - \text{WCInv}$$

where

NI = Net income
NCC = Non-cash charges (such as depreciation and amortisation)
Int = Interest expense
FCInv = Capital expenditures (fixed capital, such as equipment)
WCInv = Working capital expenditures

The reason for adding back interest is that FCFF is the cash flow available to the suppliers of debt capital as well as equity capital. Conveniently, FCFF can also be computed from cash flow from operating activities as

$$\text{FCFF} = \text{CFO} + \text{Int}(1 - \text{Tax rate}) - \text{FCInv}$$

CFO represents cash flow from operating activities under US GAAP or under IFRS where the company has included interest paid in operating activities. If interest paid was included in financing activities, then CFO does not have to be adjusted for Int(1 – Tax rate). Under IFRS, if the company has placed interest and dividends received in investing activities, these should be added back to CFO to determine FCFF. Additionally, if dividends paid were subtracted in the operating section, these should be added back in to compute FCFF.

The computation of FCFF for Acme Corporation (based on the data from Exhibits 6, 7, and 8) is as follows:

CFO	$2,606
Plus: Interest paid times (1 – income tax rate)	
{$258 [1 – 0.34[a]]}	170
Less: Net investments in fixed capital	
($1,300 – $762)	(538)
FCFF	$2,238

[a] Income tax rate of 0.34 = (Tax expense ÷ Pretax income) = ($1,139 ÷ $3,349).

FCFE is the cash flow available to the company's common stockholders after all operating expenses and borrowing costs (principal and interest) have been paid and necessary investments in working capital and fixed capital have been made. FCFE can be computed as

$$\text{FCFE} = \text{CFO} - \text{FCInv} + \text{Net borrowing}$$

When net borrowing is negative, debt repayments exceed receipts of borrowed funds. In this case, FCFE can be expressed as

$$\text{FCFE} = \text{CFO} - \text{FCInv} - \text{Net debt repayment}$$

The computation of FCFE for Acme Corporation (based on the data from Exhibits 6, 7, and 8) is as follows:

CFO	\$2,606
Less: Net investments in fixed capital (\$1,300 – \$762)	(538)
Less: Debt repayment	(500)
FCFE	\$1,568

Positive FCFE means that the company has an excess of operating cash flow over amounts needed for capital expenditures and repayment of debt. This cash would be available for distribution to owners.

4.4 Cash Flow Ratios

The statement of cash flows provides information that can be analyzed over time to obtain a better understanding of the past performance of a company and its future prospects. This information can also be effectively used to compare the performance and prospects of different companies in an industry and of different industries. There are several ratios based on cash flow from operating activities that are useful in this analysis. These ratios generally fall into cash flow performance (profitability) ratios and cash flow coverage (solvency) ratios. Exhibit 15 summarizes the calculation and interpretation of some of these ratios.

Exhibit 16 Cash Flow Ratios

Performance Ratios	Calculation	What It Measures
Cash flow to revenue	CFO ÷ Net revenue	Operating cash generated per dollar of revenue
Cash return on assets	CFO ÷ Average total assets	Operating cash generated per dollar of asset investment
Cash return on equity	CFO ÷ Average shareholders' equity	Operating cash generated per dollar of owner investment
Cash to income	CFO ÷ Operating income	Cash generating ability of operations
Cash flow per share[a]	(CFO – Preferred dividends) ÷ Number of common shares outstanding	Operating cash flow on a per-share basis

Coverage Ratios	Calculation	What It Measures
Debt coverage	CFO ÷ Total debt	Financial risk and financial leverage
Interest coverage[b]	(CFO + Interest paid + Taxes paid) ÷ Interest paid	Ability to meet interest obligations
Reinvestment	CFO ÷ Cash paid for long-term assets	Ability to acquire assets with operating cash flows
Debt payment	CFO ÷ Cash paid for long-term debt repayment	Ability to pay debts with operating cash flows

(continued)

Exhibit 16 (Continued)

Coverage Ratios	Calculation	What It Measures
Dividend payment	CFO ÷ Dividends paid	Ability to pay dividends with operating cash flows
Investing and financing	CFO ÷ Cash outflows for investing and financing activities	Ability to acquire assets, pay debts, and make distributions to owners

Notes:

[a] If the company reports under IFRS and includes total dividends paid as a use of cash in the operating section, total dividends should be added back to CFO as reported and then preferred dividends should be subtracted. Recall that CFO reported under US GAAP and IFRS may differ depending on the treatment of interest and dividends, received and paid.

[b] If the company reports under IFRS and included interest paid as a use of cash in the financing section, then interest paid should not be added back to the numerator.

EXAMPLE 10

A Cash Flow Analysis of Comparables

Andrew Potter is comparing the cash-flow-generating ability of Microsoft with that of Apple Inc. He collects information from the companies' annual reports and prepares the following table.

Cash Flow from Operating Activities as a Percentage of Total Net Revenue

	2017 (%)	2016 (%)	2015 (%)
Microsoft	43.9	39.1	31.7
Apple Inc.	27.7	30.5	34.8

As a Percentage of Average Total Assets

	2017 (%)	2016 (%)	2015 (%)
Microsoft	18.2	18.1	17.1
Apple Inc.	18.2	21.5	31.1

What is Potter likely to conclude about the relative cash-flow-generating ability of these two companies?

Solution:

On both measures—operating cash flow divided by revenue and operating cash flow divided by assets—both companies have overall strong results. However, Microsoft has higher cash flow from operating activities as a percentage of revenues in both 2016 and 2017. Further, Microsoft has an increasing trend. While Apple had a higher operating cash flow as a percent of revenue in 2015 compared to Microsoft, it has had a declining trend and was below Microsoft in the two more recent years. Microsoft's operating cash flow relative to assets is the same as Apple's in 2016 and relatively stable with a slight increase since 2015. Apple started the three years with a much stronger ratio but saw a declining trend such that its ratio is now at the same level as Microsoft. We should note that this ratio is heavily influenced by substantial investments in financial instruments that Apple has made over the years due to its strong historic cash flow.

SUMMARY

The cash flow statement provides important information about a company's cash receipts and cash payments during an accounting period as well as information about a company's operating, investing, and financing activities. Although the income statement provides a measure of a company's success, cash and cash flow are also vital to a company's long-term success. Information on the sources and uses of cash helps creditors, investors, and other statement users evaluate the company's liquidity, solvency, and financial flexibility. Key concepts are as follows:

- Cash flow activities are classified into three categories: operating activities, investing activities, and financing activities. Significant non-cash transaction activities (if present) are reported by using a supplemental disclosure note to the cash flow statement.
- Cash flow statements under IFRS and US GAAP are similar; however, IFRS provide companies with more choices in classifying some cash flow items as operating, investing, or financing activities.
- Companies can use either the direct or the indirect method for reporting their operating cash flow:
  - The direct method discloses operating cash inflows by source (e.g., cash received from customers, cash received from investment income) and operating cash outflows by use (e.g., cash paid to suppliers, cash paid for interest) in the operating activities section of the cash flow statement.
  - The indirect method reconciles net income to operating cash flow by adjusting net income for all non-cash items and the net changes in the operating working capital accounts.
- The cash flow statement is linked to a company's income statement and comparative balance sheets and to data on those statements.
- Although the indirect method is most commonly used by companies, an analyst can generally convert it to an approximation of the direct format by following a simple three-step process.
- An evaluation of a cash flow statement should involve an assessment of the sources and uses of cash and the main drivers of cash flow within each category of activities.
- The analyst can use common-size statement analysis for the cash flow statement. Two approaches to developing the common-size statements are the total cash inflows/total cash outflows method and the percentage of net revenues method.
- The cash flow statement can be used to determine free cash flow to the firm (FCFF) and free cash flow to equity (FCFE).
- The cash flow statement may also be used in financial ratios that measure a company's profitability, performance, and financial strength.

PRACTICE PROBLEMS

1 The three major classifications of activities in a cash flow statement are:
  A inflows, outflows, and net flows.
  B operating, investing, and financing.
  C revenues, expenses, and net income.

2 The sale of a building for cash would be classified as what type of activity on the cash flow statement?
  A Operating.
  B Investing.
  C Financing.

3 Under which section of a manufacturing company's cash flow statement are the following activities reported?

  Item 1: Purchases of securities held for trading

  Item 2: Sales of securities considered cash equivalents

  A Both items are investing activities.
  B Both items are operating activities.
  C Only Item 1 is an investing activity.

4 Which of the following is an example of a financing activity on the cash flow statement under US GAAP?
  A Payment of interest.
  B Receipt of dividends.
  C Payment of dividends.

5 A conversion of a face value \$1 million convertible bond for \$1 million of common stock would most likely be:
  A reported as a \$1 million investing cash inflow and outflow.
  B reported as a \$1 million financing cash outflow and inflow.
  C reported as supplementary information to the cash flow statement.

6 A company recently engaged in a non-cash transaction that significantly affected its property, plant, and equipment. The transaction is:
  A reported under the investing section of the cash flow statement.
  B reported differently in cash flow from operations under the direct and indirect methods.
  C disclosed as a separate note or in a supplementary schedule to the cash flow statement.

7 Interest paid is classified as an operating cash flow under:
  A US GAAP but may be classified as either operating or investing cash flows under IFRS.
  B IFRS but may be classified as either operating or investing cash flows under US GAAP.
  C US GAAP but may be classified as either operating or financing cash flows under IFRS.

8 Cash flows from taxes on income must be separately disclosed under:

© 2019 CFA Institute. All rights reserved.

A IFRS only.

B US GAAP only.

C both IFRS and US GAAP.

9 Which of the following components of the cash flow statement may be prepared under the indirect method under both IFRS and US GAAP?

A Operating.

B Investing.

C Financing.

10 Which of the following is *most likely* to appear in the operating section of a cash flow statement under the indirect method?

A Net income.

B Cash paid to suppliers.

C Cash received from customers.

11 A benefit of using the direct method rather than the indirect method when reporting operating cash flows is that the direct method:

A mirrors a forecasting approach.

B is easier and less costly.

C provides specific information on the sources of operating cash flows.

12 Mabel Corporation (MC) reported accounts receivable of $66 million at the end of its second fiscal quarter. MC had revenues of $72 million for its third fiscal quarter and reported accounts receivable of $55 million at the end of its third fiscal quarter. Based on this information, the amount of cash MC collected from customers during the third fiscal quarter is:

A $61 million.

B $72 million.

C $83 million.

13 When computing net cash flow from operating activities using the indirect method, an addition to net income is *most likely* to occur when there is a:

A gain on the sale of an asset.

B loss on the retirement of debt.

C decrease in a deferred tax liability.

14 Red Road Company, a consulting company, reported total revenues of $100 million, total expenses of $80 million, and net income of $20 million in the most recent year. If accounts receivable increased by $10 million, how much cash did the company receive from customers?

A $90 million.

B $100 million.

C $110 million.

15 In 2018, a company using US GAAP made cash payments of $6 million for salaries, $2 million for interest expense, and $4 million for income taxes. Additional information for the company is provided in the table:

($ millions)	2017	2018
Revenue	42	37
Cost of goods sold	18	16
Inventory	36	40

(continued)

($ millions)	2017	2018
Accounts receivable	22	19
Accounts payable	14	12

Based only on the information given, the company's operating cash flow for 2018 is *closest to*:

A $6 million.

B $10 million.

C $14 million.

16 Green Glory Corp., a garden supply wholesaler, reported cost of goods sold for the year of $80 million. Total assets increased by $55 million, including an increase of $5 million in inventory. Total liabilities increased by $45 million, including an increase of $2 million in accounts payable. The cash paid by the company to its suppliers is most likely *closest* to:

A $73 million.

B $77 million.

C $83 million.

17 Purple Fleur S.A., a retailer of floral products, reported cost of goods sold for the year of $75 million. Total assets increased by $55 million, but inventory declined by $6 million. Total liabilities increased by $45 million, and accounts payable increased by $2 million. The cash paid by the company to its suppliers is most likely *closest* to:

A $67 million.

B $79 million.

C $83 million.

18 White Flag, a women's clothing manufacturer, reported salaries expense of $20 million. The beginning balance of salaries payable was $3 million, and the ending balance of salaries payable was $1 million. How much cash did the company pay in salaries?

A $18 million.

B $21 million.

C $22 million.

19 An analyst gathered the following information from a company's 2018 financial statements (in $ millions):

Year ended 31 December	2017	2018
Net sales	245.8	254.6
Cost of goods sold	168.3	175.9
Accounts receivable	73.2	68.3
Inventory	39.0	47.8
Accounts payable	20.3	22.9

Based only on the information above, the company's 2018 statement of cash flows in the direct format would include amounts (in $ millions) for cash received from customers and cash paid to suppliers, respectively, that are *closest* to:

	cash received from customers	cash paid to suppliers
A	249.7	169.7
B	259.5	174.5
C	259.5	182.1

20 Golden Cumulus Corp., a commodities trading company, reported interest expense of $19 million and taxes of $6 million. Interest payable increased by $3 million, and taxes payable decreased by $4 million over the period. How much cash did the company pay for interest and taxes?

A $22 million for interest and $10 million for taxes.

B $16 million for interest and $2 million for taxes.

C $16 million for interest and $10 million for taxes.

21 An analyst gathered the following information from a company's 2018 financial statements (in $ millions):

Balances as of Year Ended 31 December	2017	2018
Retained earnings	120	145
Accounts receivable	38	43
Inventory	45	48
Accounts payable	36	29

In 2018, the company declared and paid cash dividends of $10 million and recorded depreciation expense in the amount of $25 million. The company considers dividends paid a financing activity. The company's 2018 cash flow from operations (in $ millions) was *closest* to

A 25.

B 45.

C 75.

22 Silverago Incorporated, an international metals company, reported a loss on the sale of equipment of $2 million in 2018. In addition, the company's income statement shows depreciation expense of $8 million and the cash flow statement shows capital expenditure of $10 million, all of which was for the purchase of new equipment. Using the following information from the comparative balance sheets, how much cash did the company receive from the equipment sale?

Balance Sheet Item	12/31/2017	12/31/2018	Change
Equipment	$100 million	$105 million	$5 million
Accumulated depreciation—equipment	$40 million	$46 million	$6 million

A $1 million.

B $2 million.

C $3 million.

23 Jaderong Plinkett Stores reported net income of $25 million. The company has no outstanding debt. Using the following information from the comparative balance sheets (in millions), what should the company report in the financing section of the statement of cash flows in 2018?

Balance Sheet Item	12/31/2017	12/31/2018	Change
Common stock	$100	$102	$2
Additional paid-in capital common stock	$100	$140	$40
Retained earnings	$100	$115	$15
Total stockholders' equity	$300	$357	$57

A Issuance of common stock of $42 million; dividends paid of $10 million.

B Issuance of common stock of $38 million; dividends paid of $10 million.

C Issuance of common stock of $42 million; dividends paid of $40 million.

24 Based on the following information for Star Inc., what are the total net adjustments that the company would make to net income in order to derive operating cash flow?

	Year Ended
Income Statement Item	12/31/2018
Net income	$20 million
Depreciation	$2 million

Balance Sheet Item	12/31/2017	12/31/2018	Change
Accounts receivable	$25 million	$22 million	($3 million)
Inventory	$10 million	$14 million	$4 million
Accounts payable	$8 million	$13 million	$5 million

A Add $2 million.

B Add $6 million.

C Subtract $6 million.

25 The first step in cash flow statement analysis should be to:

A evaluate consistency of cash flows.

B determine operating cash flow drivers.

C identify the major sources and uses of cash.

26 Which of the following would be valid conclusions from an analysis of the cash flow statement for Telefónica Group presented in Exhibit 3?

A The primary use of cash is financing activities.

B The primary source of cash is operating activities.

C Telefónica classifies dividends paid as an operating activity.

27 The following information is extracted from Sweetfall Incorporated's financial statements.

Income Statement		Balance Sheet Changes	
Revenue	$56,800	Decrease in accounts receivable	$1,324
Cost of goods sold	27,264	Decrease in inventory	501
Other operating expense	562	Increase in prepaid expense	6
Depreciation expense	2,500	Increase in accounts payable	1,063

The amount of cash Sweetfall Inc. paid to suppliers is:

A $25,700.

B $26,702.

C $27,826.

28 Which is an appropriate method of preparing a common-size cash flow statement?

A Show each item of revenue and expense as a percentage of net revenue.

B Show each line item on the cash flow statement as a percentage of net revenue.

C Show each line item on the cash flow statement as a percentage of total cash outflows.

29 Which of the following is an appropriate method of computing free cash flow to the firm?

A Add operating cash flows to capital expenditures and deduct after-tax interest payments.

B Add operating cash flows to after-tax interest payments and deduct capital expenditures.

C Deduct both after-tax interest payments and capital expenditures from operating cash flows.

30 An analyst has calculated a ratio using as the numerator the sum of operating cash flow, interest, and taxes and as the denominator the amount of interest. What is this ratio, what does it measure, and what does it indicate?

A This ratio is an interest coverage ratio, measuring a company's ability to meet its interest obligations and indicating a company's solvency.

B This ratio is an effective tax ratio, measuring the amount of a company's operating cash flow used for taxes and indicating a company's efficiency in tax management.

C This ratio is an operating profitability ratio, measuring the operating cash flow generated accounting for taxes and interest and indicating a company's liquidity.

SOLUTIONS

1 B is correct. Operating, investing, and financing are the three major classifications of activities in a cash flow statement. Revenues, expenses, and net income are elements of the income statement. Inflows, outflows, and net flows are items of information in the statement of cash flows.

2 B is correct. Purchases and sales of long-term assets are considered investing activities. Note that if the transaction had involved the exchange of a building for other than cash (for example, for another building, common stock of another company, or a long-term note receivable), it would have been considered a significant non-cash activity.

3 B is correct. The purchase and sale of securities considered cash equivalents and securities held for trading are considered operating activities even for companies in which this activity is not a primary business activity.

4 C is correct. Payment of dividends is a financing activity under US GAAP. Payment of interest and receipt of dividends are included in operating cash flows under US GAAP. Note that IFRS allow companies to include receipt of interest and dividends as either operating or investing cash flows and to include payment of interest and dividends as either operating or financing cash flows.

5 C is correct. Non-cash transactions, if significant, are reported as supplementary information, not in the investing or financing sections of the cash flow statement.

6 C is correct. Because no cash is involved in non-cash transactions, these transactions are not incorporated in the cash flow statement. However, non-cash transactions that significantly affect capital or asset structures are required to be disclosed either in a separate note or a supplementary schedule to the cash flow statement.

7 C is correct. Interest expense is always classified as an operating cash flow under US GAAP but may be classified as either an operating or financing cash flow under IFRS.

8 C is correct. Taxes on income are required to be separately disclosed under IFRS and US GAAP. The disclosure may be in the cash flow statement or elsewhere.

9 A is correct. The operating section may be prepared under the indirect method. The other sections are always prepared under the direct method.

10 A is correct. Under the indirect method, the operating section would begin with net income and adjust it to arrive at operating cash flow. The other two items would appear in the operating section under the direct method.

11 C is correct. The primary argument in favor of the direct method is that it provides information on the specific sources of operating cash receipts and payments. Arguments for the indirect method include that it mirrors a forecasting approach and it is easier and less costly

12 C is correct. The amount of cash collected from customers during the quarter is equal to beginning accounts receivable plus revenues minus ending accounts receivable: \$66 million + \$72 million – \$55 million = \$83 million. A reduction in accounts receivable indicates that cash collected during the quarter was greater than revenue on an accrual basis.

13 B is correct. An addition to net income is made when there is a loss on the retirement of debt, which is a non-operating loss. A gain on the sale of an asset and a decrease in deferred tax liability are both subtracted from net-income.

14 A is correct. Revenues of \$100 million minus the increase in accounts receivable of \$10 million equal \$90 million cash received from customers. The increase in accounts receivable means that the company received less in cash than it reported as revenue.

15 A is correct.

Operating cash flows = Cash received from customers – (Cash paid to suppliers + Cash paid to employees + Cash paid for other operating expenses + Cash paid for interest + Cash paid for income taxes)

Cash received from customers = Revenue + Decrease in accounts receivable
= \$37 + \$3 = \$40 million

Cash paid to suppliers = Cost of goods sold + Increase in inventory + Decrease in accounts payable
= \$16 + \$4 + \$2 = \$22 million

Therefore, the company's operating cash flow = \$40 – \$22 – Cash paid for salaries – Cash paid for interest – Cash paid for taxes = \$40 – \$22 – \$6 – \$2 – \$4 = \$6 million.

16 C is correct. Cost of goods sold of \$80 million plus the increase in inventory of \$5 million equals purchases from suppliers of \$85 million. The increase in accounts payable of \$2 million means that the company paid \$83 million in cash (\$85 million minus \$2 million) to its suppliers.

17 A is correct. Cost of goods sold of \$75 million less the decrease in inventory of \$6 million equals purchases from suppliers of \$69 million. The increase in accounts payable of \$2 million means that the company paid \$67 million in cash (\$69 million minus \$2 million).

18 C is correct. Beginning salaries payable of \$3 million plus salaries expense of \$20 million minus ending salaries payable of \$1 million equals \$22 million. Alternatively, the expense of \$20 million plus the \$2 million decrease in salaries payable equals \$22 million.

19 C is correct. Cash received from customers = Sales + Decrease in accounts receivable = 254.6 + 4.9 = 259.5. Cash paid to suppliers = Cost of goods sold + Increase in inventory – Increase in accounts payable = 175.9 + 8.8 – 2.6 = 182.1.

20 C is correct. Interest expense of \$19 million less the increase in interest payable of \$3 million equals interest paid of \$16 million. Tax expense of \$6 million plus the decrease in taxes payable of \$4 million equals taxes paid of \$10 million.

21 B is correct. All dollar amounts are in millions. Net income (NI) for 2018 is \$35. This amount is the increase in retained earnings, \$25, plus the dividends paid, \$10. Depreciation of \$25 is added back to net income, and the increases in accounts receivable, \$5, and in inventory, \$3, are subtracted from net income because they are uses of cash. The decrease in accounts payable is also a use of cash and, therefore, a subtraction from net income. Thus, cash flow from operations is \$25 + \$10 + \$25 – \$5 – \$3 – \$7 = \$45.

22 A is correct. Selling price (cash inflow) minus book value equals gain or loss on sale; therefore, gain or loss on sale plus book value equals selling price (cash inflow). The amount of loss is given—$2 million. To calculate the book value of the equipment sold, find the historical cost of the equipment and the accumulated depreciation on the equipment.

- Beginning balance of equipment of $100 million plus equipment purchased of $10 million minus ending balance of equipment of $105 million equals the historical cost of equipment sold, or $5 million.
- Beginning accumulated depreciation of $40 million plus depreciation expense for the year of $8 million minus ending balance of accumulated depreciation of $46 million equals accumulated depreciation on the equipment sold, or $2 million.
- Therefore, the book value of the equipment sold was $5 million minus $2 million, or $3 million.
- Because the loss on the sale of equipment was $2 million, the amount of cash received must have been $1 million.

23 A is correct. The increase of $42 million in common stock and additional paid-in capital indicates that the company issued stock during the year. The increase in retained earnings of $15 million indicates that the company paid $10 million in cash dividends during the year, determined as beginning retained earnings of $100 million plus net income of $25 million minus ending retained earnings of $115 million, which equals $10 million in cash dividends.

24 B is correct. To derive operating cash flow, the company would make the following adjustments to net income: Add depreciation (a non-cash expense) of $2 million; add the decrease in accounts receivable of $3 million; add the increase in accounts payable of $5 million; and subtract the increase in inventory of $4 million. Total additions would be $10 million, and total subtractions would be $4 million, which gives net additions of $6 million.

25 C is correct. An overall assessment of the major sources and uses of cash should be the first step in evaluating a cash flow statement.

26 B is correct. The primary source of cash is operating activities. Cash flow provided by operating activity totaled €13,796 million in the most recent year. The primary use of cash is investing activities (total of €10,245 million). Dividends paid are classified as a financing activity.

27 A is correct. The amount of cash paid to suppliers is calculated as follows:

= Cost of goods sold – Decrease in inventory – Increase in accounts payable
= $27,264 – $501 – $1,063
= $25,700.

28 B is correct. An appropriate method to prepare a common-size cash flow statement is to show each line item on the cash flow statement as a percentage of net revenue. An alternative way to prepare a statement of cash flows is to show each item of cash inflow as a percentage of total inflows and each item of cash outflows as a percentage of total outflows.

29 B is correct. Free cash flow to the firm can be computed as operating cash flows plus after-tax interest expense less capital expenditures.

30 A is correct. This ratio is an interest coverage ratio, measuring a company's ability to meet its interest obligations and indicating a company's solvency. This coverage ratio is based on cash flow information; another common coverage ratio uses a measure based on the income statement (earnings before interest, taxes, depreciation, and amortisation).

READING

24

Financial Analysis Techniques

by Elaine Henry, PhD, CFA, Thomas R. Robinson, PhD, CFA, and Jan Hendrik van Greuning, DCom, CFA

Elaine Henry, PhD, CFA, is at Stevens Institute of Technology (USA). Thomas R. Robinson, PhD, CFA, is at AACSB International (USA). Jan Hendrik van Greuning, DCom, CFA, is at BIBD (Brunei).

LEARNING OUTCOMES

Mastery	*The candidate should be able to:*
☐	**a.** describe tools and techniques used in financial analysis, including their uses and limitations;
☐	**b.** classify, calculate, and interpret activity, liquidity, solvency, profitability, and valuation ratios;
☐	**c.** describe relationships among ratios and evaluate a company using ratio analysis;
☐	**d.** demonstrate the application of DuPont analysis of return on equity and calculate and interpret effects of changes in its components;
☐	**e.** calculate and interpret ratios used in equity analysis and credit analysis;
☐	**f.** explain the requirements for segment reporting and calculate and interpret segment ratios;
☐	**g.** describe how ratio analysis and other techniques can be used to model and forecast earnings.

Note: Changes in accounting standards as well as new rulings and/or pronouncements issued after the publication of the readings on financial reporting and analysis may cause some of the information in these readings to become dated. Candidates are *not* responsible for anything that occurs after the readings were published. In addition, candidates are expected to be familiar with the analytical frameworks contained in the readings, as well as the implications of alternative accounting methods for financial analysis and valuation discussed in the readings. Candidates are also responsible for the content of accounting standards, but not for the actual reference numbers. Finally, candidates should be aware that certain ratios may be defined and calculated differently. When alternative ratio definitions exist and no specific definition is given, candidates should use the ratio definitions emphasized in the readings.

© 2019 CFA Institute. All rights reserved.

1 INTRODUCTION

Financial analysis tools can be useful in assessing a company's performance and trends in that performance. In essence, an analyst converts data into financial metrics that assist in decision making. Analysts seek to answer such questions as: How successfully has the company performed, relative to its own past performance and relative to its competitors? How is the company likely to perform in the future? Based on expectations about future performance, what is the value of this company or the securities it issues?

A primary source of data is a company's annual report, including the financial statements and notes, and management commentary (operating and financial review or management's discussion and analysis). This reading focuses on data presented in financial reports prepared under International Financial Reporting Standards (IFRS) and United States generally accepted accounting principles (US GAAP). However, financial reports do not contain all the information needed to perform effective financial analysis. Although financial statements do contain data about the *past* performance of a company (its income and cash flows) as well as its *current* financial condition (assets, liabilities, and owners' equity), such statements do not necessarily provide all the information useful for analysis nor do they forecast *future* results. The financial analyst must be capable of using financial statements in conjunction with other information to make projections and reach valid conclusions. Accordingly, an analyst typically needs to supplement the information found in a company's financial reports with other information, including information on the economy, industry, comparable companies, and the company itself.

This reading describes various techniques used to analyze a company's financial statements. Financial analysis of a company may be performed for a variety of reasons, such as valuing equity securities, assessing credit risk, conducting due diligence related to an acquisition, or assessing a subsidiary's performance. This reading will describe techniques common to any financial analysis and then discuss more specific aspects for the two most common categories: equity analysis and credit analysis.

Equity analysis incorporates an owner's perspective, either for valuation or performance evaluation. Credit analysis incorporates a creditor's (such as a banker or bondholder) perspective. In either case, there is a need to gather and analyze information to make a decision (ownership or credit); the focus of analysis varies because of the differing interest of owners and creditors. Both equity and credit analyses assess the entity's ability to generate and grow earnings, and cash flow, as well as any associated risks. Equity analysis usually places a greater emphasis on growth, whereas credit analysis usually places a greater emphasis on risks. The difference in emphasis reflects the different fundamentals of these types of investments: The value of a company's equity generally increases as the company's earnings and cash flow increase, whereas the value of a company's debt has an upper limit.[1]

The balance of this reading is organized as follows: Section 2 recaps the framework for financial statements and the place of financial analysis techniques within the framework. Section 3 provides a description of analytical tools and techniques. Section 4 explains how to compute, analyze, and interpret common financial ratios. Sections 5 through 8 explain the use of ratios and other analytical data in equity analysis, credit analysis, segment analysis, and forecasting, respectively. A summary of the key points and practice problems in the CFA Institute multiple-choice format conclude the reading.

1 The upper limit is equal to the undiscounted sum of the principal and remaining interest payments (i.e., the present value of these contractual payments at a zero percent discount rate).

THE FINANCIAL ANALYSIS PROCESS

2

In financial analysis, it is essential to clearly identify and understand the final objective and the steps required to reach that objective. In addition, the analyst needs to know where to find relevant data, how to process and analyze the data (in other words, know the typical questions to address when interpreting data), and how to communicate the analysis and conclusions.

2.1 The Objectives of the Financial Analysis Process

Because of the variety of reasons for performing financial analysis, the numerous available techniques, and the often substantial amount of data, it is important that the analytical approach be tailored to the specific situation. Prior to beginning any financial analysis, the analyst should clarify the purpose and context, and clearly understand the following:

- What is the purpose of the analysis? What questions will this analysis answer?
- What level of detail will be needed to accomplish this purpose?
- What data are available for the analysis?
- What are the factors or relationships that will influence the analysis?
- What are the analytical limitations, and will these limitations potentially impair the analysis?

Having clarified the purpose and context of the analysis, the analyst can select the set of techniques (e.g., ratios) that will best assist in making a decision. Although there is no single approach to structuring the analysis process, a general framework is set forth in Exhibit 1.[2] The steps in this process were discussed in more detail in an earlier reading; the primary focus of this reading is on Phases 3 and 4, processing and analyzing data.

2 Components of this framework have been adapted from van Greuning and Bratanovic (2003, p. 300) and Benninga and Sarig (1997, pp. 134–156).

Exhibit 1 A Financial Statement Analysis Framework

Phase	Sources of Information	Output
1 Articulate the purpose and context of the analysis.	■ The nature of the analyst's function, such as evaluating an equity or debt investment or issuing a credit rating. ■ Communication with client or supervisor on needs and concerns. ■ Institutional guidelines related to developing specific work product.	■ Statement of the purpose or objective of analysis. ■ A list (written or unwritten) of specific questions to be answered by the analysis. ■ Nature and content of report to be provided. ■ Timetable and budgeted resources for completion.
2 Collect input data.	■ Financial statements, other financial data, questionnaires, and industry/economic data. ■ Discussions with management, suppliers, customers, and competitors. ■ Company site visits (e.g., to production facilities or retail stores).	■ Organized financial statements. ■ Financial data tables. ■ Completed questionnaires, if applicable.
3 Process data.	■ Data from the previous phase.	■ Adjusted financial statements. ■ Common-size statements. ■ Ratios and graphs. ■ Forecasts.
4 Analyze/interpret the processed data.	■ Input data as well as processed data.	■ Analytical results.
5 Develop and communicate conclusions and recommendations (e.g., with an analysis report).	■ Analytical results and previous reports. ■ Institutional guidelines for published reports.	■ Analytical report answering questions posed in Phase 1. ■ Recommendation regarding the purpose of the analysis, such as whether to make an investment or grant credit.
6 Follow-up.	■ Information gathered by periodically repeating above steps as necessary to determine whether changes to holdings or recommendations are necessary.	■ Updated reports and recommendations.

2.2 Distinguishing between Computations and Analysis

An effective analysis encompasses both computations and interpretations. A well-reasoned analysis differs from a mere compilation of various pieces of information, computations, tables, and graphs by integrating the data collected into a cohesive whole. Analysis of past performance, for example, should address not only what happened but also why it happened and whether it advanced the company's strategy. Some of the key questions to address include:

- What aspects of performance are critical for this company to successfully compete in this industry?

- How well did the company's performance meet these critical aspects? (Established through computation and comparison with appropriate benchmarks, such as the company's own historical performance or competitors' performance.)
- What were the key causes of this performance, and how does this performance reflect the company's strategy? (Established through analysis.)

If the analysis is forward looking, additional questions include:

- What is the likely impact of an event or trend? (Established through interpretation of analysis.)
- What is the likely response of management to this trend? (Established through evaluation of quality of management and corporate governance.)
- What is the likely impact of trends in the company, industry, and economy on future cash flows? (Established through assessment of corporate strategy and through forecasts.)
- What are the recommendations of the analyst? (Established through interpretation and forecasting of results of analysis.)
- What risks should be highlighted? (Established by an evaluation of major uncertainties in the forecast and in the environment within which the company operates.)

Example 1 demonstrates how a company's financial data can be analyzed in the context of its business strategy and changes in that strategy. An analyst must be able to understand the "why" behind the numbers and ratios, not just what the numbers and ratios are.

EXAMPLE 1

Strategy Reflected in Financial Performance

Apple Inc. engages in the design, manufacture, and sale of computer hardware, mobile devices, operating systems and related products, and services. It also operates retail and online stores. Microsoft develops, licenses, and supports software products, services, and technology devices through a variety of channels including retail stores in recent years. Selected financial data for 2015 through 2017 for these two companies are given below. Apple's fiscal year (FY) ends on the final Saturday in September (for example, FY2017 ended on 30 September 2017). Microsoft's fiscal year ends on 30 June (for example, FY2017 ended on 30 June 2017).

Selected Financial Data for Apple (Dollars in Millions)

Fiscal year	2017	2016	2015
Net sales (or Revenue)	229,234	215,639	233,715
Gross margin	88,186	84,263	93,626
Operating income	61,344	60,024	71,230

Selected Financial Data for Microsoft (Dollars in Millions)*

Fiscal year	2017	2016	2015
Net sales (or Revenue)	89,950	85,320	93,580
Gross margin	55,689	52,540	60,542
Operating income	22,326	20,182	18,161

* Microsoft revenue for 2017 and 2016 were subsequently revised in the company's 2018 10-K report due to changes in revenue recognition and lease accounting standards.
Source: 10-K reports for Apple and Microsoft.

Apple reported a 7.7 percent decrease in net sales from FY2015 to FY2016 and an increase of 6.3 percent from FY2016 to FY2017 for an overall slight decline over the three-year period. Gross margin decreased 10.0 percent from FY2015 to FY2016 and increased 4.7 percent from FY2016 to FY2017. This also represented an overall decline in gross margin over the three-year period. The company's operating income exhibited similar trends.

Microsoft reported an 8.8 percent decrease in net sales from FY2015 to FY2016 and an increase of 5.4 percent from FY2016 to FY2017 for an overall slight decline over the three-year period. Gross margin decreased 13.2 percent from FY2015 to FY2016 and increased 6.0 percent from FY2016 to FY2017. Similar to Apple, this represented an overall decline in gross margin over the three-year period. Microsoft's operating income on the other hand exhibited growth each year and for the three-year period. Overall growth in operating income was 23%.

What caused Microsoft's growth in operating income while Apple and Microsoft had similar negative trends in sales and gross margin? Apple's decline in sales, gross margin, and operating income from FY2015 to FY2016 was caused by declines in iPhone sales and weakness in foreign currencies relative to the US dollar. FY2017 saw a rebound in sales of iPhones, Mac computers, and services offset somewhat by continued weaknesses in foreign currencies. Microsoft similarly had declines in revenue and gross margin from sales of its devices and Windows software in FY2016, as well as negative impacts from foreign currency weakness. Microsoft's increase in revenue and gross margin in FY2017 was driven by the acquisition of LinkedIn, higher sales of Microsoft Office software, and higher sales of cloud services. The driver in the continuous increase in operating income for Microsoft was a large decline over the three-year period in impairment, integration, and restructuring charges. Microsoft recorded a $10 billion charge in FY2015 related to its phone business, and there were further charges of $1.1 billion in FY2016 and $306 million in FY2017. Absent these large write-offs, Microsoft would have had a trend similar to Apple's in operating income over the three-year period.

Analysts often need to communicate the findings of their analysis in a written report. Their reports should communicate how conclusions were reached and why recommendations were made. For example, a report might present the following:

- the purpose of the report, unless it is readily apparent;
- relevant aspects of the business context:
  - economic environment (country/region, macro economy, sector);
  - financial and other infrastructure (accounting, auditing, rating agencies);

- legal and regulatory environment (and any other material limitations on the company being analyzed);
- evaluation of corporate governance and assessment of management strategy, including the company's competitive advantage(s);
- assessment of financial and operational data, including key assumptions in the analysis; and
- conclusions and recommendations, including limitations of the analysis and risks.

An effective narrative and well supported conclusions and recommendations are normally enhanced by using 3–10 years of data, as well as analytic techniques appropriate to the purpose of the report.

ANALYTICAL TOOLS AND TECHNIQUES

3

The tools and techniques presented in this section facilitate evaluations of company data. Evaluations require comparisons. It is difficult to say that a company's financial performance was "good" without clarifying the basis for comparison. In assessing a company's ability to generate and grow earnings and cash flow, and the risks related to those earnings and cash flows, the analyst draws comparisons to other companies (cross-sectional analysis) and over time (trend or time-series analysis).

For example, an analyst may wish to compare the profitability of companies competing in a global industry. If the companies differ significantly in size and/or report their financial data in different currencies, comparing net income as reported is not useful. Ratios (which express one number in relation to another) and common-size financial statements can remove size as a factor and enable a more relevant comparison. To achieve comparability across companies reporting in different currencies, one approach is to translate all reported numbers into a common currency using exchange rates at the end of a period. Others may prefer to translate reported numbers using the average exchange rates during the period. Alternatively, if the focus is primarily on ratios, comparability can be achieved without translating the currencies.

The analyst may also want to examine comparable performance over time. Again, the nominal currency amounts of sales or net income may not highlight significant changes. To address this challenge, horizontal financial statements (whereby quantities are stated in terms of a selected base year value) can make such changes more apparent. Another obstacle to comparison is differences in fiscal year end. To achieve comparability, one approach is to develop trailing twelve months data, which will be described in a section below. Finally, it should be noted that differences in accounting standards can limit comparability.

EXAMPLE 2

Ratio Analysis

An analyst is examining the profitability of two international companies with large shares of the global personal computer market: Acer Inc. and Lenovo Group Limited. Acer has pursued a strategy of selling its products at affordable prices. In contrast, Lenovo aims to achieve higher selling prices by stressing the high engineering quality of its personal computers for business use. Acer reports in TWD,[3] and Lenovo reports in USD. For Acer, fiscal year end is 31 December. For Lenovo, fiscal year end is 31 March; thus, FY2017 ended 31 March 2018.

The analyst collects the data shown in Exhibit 2 below. Use this information to answer the following questions:

1 Which company is larger based on the amount of revenue, in US$, reported in fiscal year 2017? For FY2017, assume the relevant, average exchange rate was 30.95 TWD/USD.

2 Which company had the higher revenue growth from FY2016 to FY2017? FY2013 to FY2017?

3 How do the companies compare, based on profitability?

Exhibit 2

Acer

TWD Millions	FY2013	FY2014	FY2015	FY2016	FY2017
Revenue	360,132	329,684	263,775	232,724	237,275
Gross profit	22,550	28,942	24,884	23,212	25,361
Net income	(20,519)	1,791	604	(4,901)	2,797

Lenovo

USD Millions	FY2013*	FY2014*	FY2015*	FY2016*	FY2017*
Revenue	38,707	46,296	44,912	43,035	45,350
Gross profit	5,064	6,682	6,624	6,105	6,272
Net income (Loss)	817	837	(145)	530	(127)

* Fiscal years for Lenovo end 31 March. Thus FY2017 represents the fiscal year ended 31 March 2018; the same applies respectively for prior years.

Solution to 1:

Lenovo is much larger than Acer based on FY2017 revenues in USD terms. Lenovo's FY2017 revenues of $USD45.35 billion are considerably higher than Acer's USD7.67 million (= TWD 237.275 million/30.95).

Acer: At the assumed average exchange rate of 30.95 TWD/USD, Acer's FY2017 revenues are equivalent to USD7.67 billion (= TWD237.275 billion ÷ 30.95 TWD/USD).

Lenovo: Lenovo's FY2017 revenues totaled USD45.35 billion.

Note: Comparing the size of companies reporting in different currencies requires translating reported numbers into a common currency using exchange rates at some point in time. This solution converts the revenues of Acer to billions of USD using the average exchange rate of the fiscal period. It would be equally informative (and would yield the same conclusion) to convert the revenues of Lenovo to TWD.

Solution to 2:

The growth in Lenovo's revenue was much higher than Acer's in the most recent fiscal year and for the five-year period.

3 TWD is the three-letter ISO 4217 currency code for Taiwan New Dollar.

	Change in Revenue FY2016 versus FY2017 (%)	Change in Revenue FY2013 to FY2017 (%)
Acer	1.96	(34.11)
Lenovo	5.38	17.16

The table shows two growth metrics. Calculations are illustrated using the revenue data for Acer:

The change in Acer's revenue for FY2016 versus FY2017 is 1.96% percent calculated as (237,275 – 232,724) ÷ 232,724 or equivalently (237,275 ÷ 232,724) – 1. The change in Acer's revenue from FY2013 to FY2017 is a decline of 34.11%.

Solution to 3:

Profitability can be assessed by comparing the amount of gross profit to revenue and the amount of net income to revenue. The following table presents these two profitability ratios—**gross profit margin** (gross profit divided by revenue) and **net profit margin** (net income divided by revenue)—for each year.

Acer	FY2013 (%)	FY2014 (%)	FY2015 (%)	FY2016 (%)	FY2017 (%)
Gross profit margin	6.26	8.78	9.43	9.97	10.69
Net profit margin	(5.70)	0.54	0.23	(2.11)	1.18

Lenovo	FY2013 (%)	FY2014 (%)	FY2015 (%)	FY2016 (%)	FY2017 (%)
Gross profit margin	13.08	14.43	14.75	14.19	13.83
Net profit margin	2.11	1.81	(0.32)	1.23	(0.28)

The net profit margins indicate that both companies' profitability is relatively low. Acer's net profit margin is lower than Lenovo's in three out of the five years. Acer's gross profit margin increased each year but remains significantly below that of Lenovo. Lenovo's gross profit margin grew from FY2013 to FY2015 and then declined in FY2016 and FY2017. Overall, Lenovo is the more profitable company, likely attributable to its larger size and commensurate economies of scale. (Lenovo has the largest share of the personal computer market relative to other personal computer companies.)

Section 3.1 describes the tools and techniques of ratio analysis in more detail. Sections 3.2 to 3.4 describe other tools and techniques.

3.1 Ratios

There are many relationships among financial accounts and various expected relationships from one point in time to another. Ratios are a useful way of expressing these relationships. Ratios express one quantity in relation to another (usually as a quotient).

Extensive academic research has examined the importance of ratios in predicting stock returns (Ou and Penman, 1989; Abarbanell and Bushee, 1998) or credit failure (Altman, 1968; Ohlson, 1980; Hopwood et al., 1994). This research has found that financial statement ratios are effective in selecting investments and in predicting financial distress. Practitioners routinely use ratios to derive and communicate the value of companies and securities.

Several aspects of ratio analysis are important to understand. First, the computed ratio is not "the answer." The ratio is an *indicator* of some aspect of a company's performance, telling what happened but not why it happened. For example, an analyst might want to answer the question: Which of two companies was more profitable? As demonstrated in the previous example, the net profit margin, which expresses profit relative to revenue, can provide insight into this question. Net profit margin is calculated by dividing net income by revenue:[4]

$$\frac{\text{Net income}}{\text{Revenue}}$$

Assume Company A has €100,000 of net income and Company B has €200,000 of net income. Company B generated twice as much income as Company A, but was it more profitable? Assume further that Company A has €2,000,000 of revenue, and thus a net profit margin of 5 percent, and Company B has €6,000,000 of revenue, and thus a net profit margin of 3.33 percent. Expressing net income as a percentage of revenue clarifies the relationship: For each €100 of revenue, Company A earns €5 in net income, whereas Company B earns only €3.33 for each €100 of revenue. So, we can now answer the question of which company was more profitable in percentage terms: Company A was more profitable, as indicated by its higher net profit margin of 5 percent. Note that Company A was more *profitable* despite the fact that Company B reported higher absolute amounts of net income and revenue. However, this ratio by itself does not tell us *why* Company A has a higher profit margin. Further analysis is required to determine the reason (perhaps higher relative sales prices or better cost control or lower effective tax rates).

Company size sometimes confers economies of scale, so the absolute amounts of net income and revenue are useful in financial analysis. However, ratios control for the effect of size, which enhances comparisons between companies and over time.

A second important aspect of ratio analysis is that differences in accounting policies (across companies and across time) can distort ratios, and a meaningful comparison may, therefore, involve adjustments to the financial data. Third, not all ratios are necessarily relevant to a particular analysis. The ability to select a relevant ratio or ratios to answer the research question is an analytical skill. Finally, as with financial analysis in general, ratio analysis does not stop with computation; interpretation of the result is essential. In practice, differences in ratios across time and across companies can be subtle, and interpretation is situation specific.

3.1.1 *The Universe of Ratios*

There are no authoritative bodies specifying exact formulas for computing ratios or providing a standard, comprehensive list of ratios. Formulas and even names of ratios often differ from analyst to analyst or from database to database. The number of different ratios that can be created is practically limitless. There are, however, widely accepted ratios that have been found to be useful. Section 4 of this reading will focus primarily on these broad classes and commonly accepted definitions of key ratios. However, the analyst should be aware that different ratios may be used in practice and that certain industries have unique ratios tailored to the characteristics of that

4 The term "sales" is often used interchangeably with the term "revenues." Other times it is used to refer to revenues derived from sales of products versus services. The income statement usually reflects "revenues" or "sales" after returns and allowances (e.g., returns of products or discounts offered after a sale to induce the customer to not return a product). Additionally, in some countries, including the United Kingdom and South Africa, the term "turnover" is used in the sense of "revenue."

industry. When faced with an unfamiliar ratio, the analyst can examine the underlying formula to gain insight into what the ratio is measuring. For example, consider the following ratio formula:

$$\frac{\text{Operating income}}{\text{Average total assets}}$$

Never having seen this ratio, an analyst might question whether a result of 12 percent is better than 8 percent. The answer can be found in the ratio itself. The numerator is operating income and the denominator is average total assets, so the ratio can be interpreted as the amount of operating income generated per unit of assets. For every €100 of average total assets, generating €12 of operating income is better than generating €8 of operating income. Furthermore, it is apparent that this particular ratio is an indicator of profitability (and, to a lesser extent, efficiency in use of assets in generating operating profits). When encountering a ratio for the first time, the analyst should evaluate the numerator and denominator to assess what the ratio is attempting to measure and how it should be interpreted. This is demonstrated in Example 3.

EXAMPLE 3

Interpreting a Financial Ratio

A US insurance company reports that its "combined ratio" is determined by dividing losses and expenses incurred by net premiums earned. It reports the following combined ratios:

Fiscal Year	5	4	3	2	1
Combined ratio	90.1%	104.0%	98.5%	104.1%	101.1%

Explain what this ratio is measuring and compare the results reported for each of the years shown in the chart. What other information might an analyst want to review before making any conclusions on this information?

Solution:

The combined ratio is a profitability measure. The ratio is explaining how much costs (losses and expenses) were incurred for every dollar of revenue (net premiums earned). The underlying formula indicates that a *lower* value for this ratio is better. The Year 5 ratio of 90.1 percent means that for every dollar of net premiums earned, the costs were $0.901, yielding a gross profit of $0.099. Ratios greater than 100 percent indicate an overall loss. A review of the data indicates that there does not seem to be a consistent trend in this ratio. Profits were achieved in Years 5 and 3. The results for Years 4 and 2 show the most significant costs at approximately 104 percent.

The analyst would want to discuss this data further with management and understand the characteristics of the underlying business. He or she would want to understand why the results are so volatile. The analyst would also want to determine what should be used as a benchmark for this ratio.

The Operating income/Average total assets ratio shown above is one of many versions of the **return on assets (ROA)** ratio. Note that there are other ways of specifying this formula based on how assets are defined. Some financial ratio databases compute ROA using the ending value of assets rather than average assets. In limited cases, one may also see beginning assets in the denominator. Which one is right? It depends on what you are trying to measure and the underlying company trends. If the company has a stable level of assets, the answer will not differ greatly under the three measures of assets (beginning, average, and ending). However, if the assets are growing (or shrinking), the results will differ among the three measures. When assets are growing, operating income divided by ending assets may not make sense because some of the income would have been generated before some assets were purchased, and this would understate the company's performance. Similarly, if beginning assets are used, some of the operating income later in the year may have been generated only because of the addition of assets; therefore, the ratio would overstate the company's performance. Because operating income occurs throughout the period, it generally makes sense to use some average measure of assets. A good general rule is that when an income statement or cash flow statement number is in the numerator of a ratio and a balance sheet number is in the denominator, then an average should be used for the denominator. It is generally not necessary to use averages when only balance sheet numbers are used in both the numerator and denominator because both are determined as of the same date. However, in some instances, even ratios that only use balance sheet data may use averages. For example, **return on equity (ROE)**, which is defined as net income divided by average shareholders' equity, can be decomposed into other ratios, some of which only use balance sheet data. In decomposing ROE into component ratios, if an average is used in one of the component ratios then it should be used in the other component ratios. The decomposition of ROE is discussed further in Section 4.6.2.

If an average is used, judgment is also required about what average should be used. For simplicity, most ratio databases use a simple average of the beginning and end-of-year balance sheet amounts. If the company's business is seasonal so that levels of assets vary by interim period (semiannual or quarterly), then it may be beneficial to take an average over all interim periods, if available. (If the analyst is working within a company and has access to monthly data, this can also be used.)

3.1.2 *Value, Purposes, and Limitations of Ratio Analysis*

The value of ratio analysis is that it enables a financial analyst to evaluate past performance, assess the current financial position of the company, and gain insights useful for projecting future results. As noted previously, the ratio itself is not "the answer" but is an indicator of some aspect of a company's performance. Financial ratios provide insights into:

- economic relationships within a company that help analysts project earnings and free cash flow;
- a company's financial flexibility, or ability to obtain the cash required to grow and meet its obligations, even if unexpected circumstances develop;
- management's ability;
- changes in the company and/or industry over time; and
- comparability with peer companies or the relevant industry(ies).

There are also limitations to ratio analysis. Factors to consider include:

- *The heterogeneity or homogeneity of a company's operating activities.* Companies may have divisions operating in many different industries. This can make it difficult to find comparable industry ratios to use for comparison purposes.
- *The need to determine whether the results of the ratio analysis are consistent.* One set of ratios may indicate a problem, whereas another set may indicate that the potential problem is only short term in nature.
- *The need to use judgment.* A key issue is whether a ratio for a company is within a reasonable range. Although financial ratios are used to help assess the growth potential and risk of a company, they cannot be used alone to directly value a company or its securities, or to determine its creditworthiness. The entire

operation of the company must be examined, and the external economic and industry setting in which it is operating must be considered when interpreting financial ratios.

- *The use of alternative accounting methods.* Companies frequently have latitude when choosing certain accounting methods. Ratios taken from financial statements that employ different accounting choices may not be comparable unless adjustments are made. Some important accounting considerations include the following:
  - FIFO (first in, first out), LIFO (last in, first out), or average cost inventory valuation methods (IFRS does not allow LIFO);
  - Cost or equity methods of accounting for unconsolidated affiliates;
  - Straight line or accelerated methods of depreciation; and
  - Operating or finance lease treatment for lessors (under US GAAP, the type of lease affects classifications of expenses; under IFRS, operating lease treatment for lessors is not applicable).

The expanding use of IFRS and past convergence efforts between IFRS and US GAAP make the financial statements of different companies more comparable and may overcome some of these difficulties. Nonetheless, there will remain accounting choices that the analyst must consider.

3.1.3 *Sources of Ratios*

Ratios may be computed using data obtained directly from companies' financial statements or from a database such as Bloomberg, Compustat, FactSet, or Thomson Reuters. The information provided by the database may include information as reported in companies' financial statements and ratios calculated based on the information. These databases are popular because they provide easy access to many years of historical data so that trends over time can be examined. They also allow for ratio calculations based on periods other than the company's fiscal year, such as for the trailing 12 months (TTM) or most recent quarter (MRQ).

EXAMPLE 4

Trailing Twelve Months

On 15 July, an analyst is examining a company with a fiscal year ending on 31 December. Use the following data to calculate the company's trailing 12 month earnings (for the period ended 30 June 2018):

- Earnings for the year ended 31 December, 2017: $1,200;
- Earnings for the six months ended 30 June 2017: $550; and
- Earnings for the six months ended 30 June 2018: $750.

Solution:

The company's trailing 12 months earnings is $1,400, calculated as $1,200 – $550 + $750.

Analysts should be aware that the underlying formulas for ratios may differ by vendor. The formula used should be obtained from the vendor, and the analyst should determine whether any adjustments are necessary. Furthermore, database providers often exercise judgment when classifying items. For example, operating income may not appear directly on a company's income statement, and the vendor may use judgment to classify income statement items as "operating" or "non-operating." Variation in such judgments would affect any computation involving operating income. It is therefore a good practice to use the same source for data when comparing different companies or when evaluating the historical record of a single company. Analysts should verify the consistency of formulas and data classifications by the data source. Analysts should also be mindful of the judgments made by a vendor in data classifications and refer back to the source financial statements until they are comfortable that the classifications are appropriate.

Collection of financial data from regulatory filings and calculation of ratios can be automated. The eXtensible Business Reporting Language (XBRL) is a mechanism that attaches "smart tags" to financial information (e.g., total assets), so that software can automatically collect the data and perform desired computations. The organization developing XBRL (www.xbrl.org) is an international nonprofit consortium of over 600 members from companies, associations, and agencies, including the International Accounting Standards Board. Many stock exchanges and regulatory agencies around the world now use XBRL for receiving and distributing public financial reports from listed companies.

Analysts can compare a subject company to similar (peer) companies in these databases or use aggregate industry data. For non-public companies, aggregate industry data can be obtained from such sources as Annual Statement Studies by the Risk Management Association or Dun & Bradstreet. These publications typically provide industry data with companies sorted into quartiles. By definition, twenty-five percent of companies' ratios fall within the lowest quartile, 25 percent have ratios between the lower quartile and median value, and so on. Analysts can then determine a company's relative standing in the industry.

3.2 Common-Size Analysis

Common-size analysis involves expressing financial data, including entire financial statements, in relation to a single financial statement item, or base. Items used most frequently as the bases are total assets or revenue. In essence, common-size analysis creates a ratio between every financial statement item and the base item.

Common-size analysis was demonstrated in readings for the income statement, balance sheet, and cash flow statement. In this section, we present common-size analysis of financial statements in greater detail and include further discussion of their interpretation.

3.2.1 *Common-Size Analysis of the Balance Sheet*

A vertical[5] common-size balance sheet, prepared by dividing each item on the balance sheet by the same period's total assets and expressing the results as percentages, highlights the composition of the balance sheet. What is the mix of assets being used? How is the company financing itself? How does one company's balance sheet composition compare with that of peer companies, and what are the reasons for any differences?

A horizontal common-size balance sheet, prepared by computing the increase or decrease in percentage terms of each balance sheet item from the prior year or prepared by dividing the quantity of each item by a base year quantity of the item, highlights changes in items. These changes can be compared to expectations. The section on trend analysis below will illustrate a horizontal common-size balance sheet.

5 The term **vertical analysis** is used to denote a common-size analysis using only one reporting period or one base financial statement, whereas **horizontal analysis** refers to an analysis comparing a specific financial statement with prior or future time periods or to a cross-sectional analysis of one company with another.

Exhibit 3 presents a vertical common-size (partial) balance sheet for a hypothetical company in two time periods. In this example, receivables have increased from 35 percent to 57 percent of total assets and the ratio has increased by 63 percent from Period 1 to Period 2. What are possible reasons for such an increase? The increase might indicate that the company is making more of its sales on a credit basis rather than a cash basis, perhaps in response to some action taken by a competitor. Alternatively, the increase in receivables as a percentage of assets may have occurred because of a change in another current asset category, for example, a decrease in the level of inventory; the analyst would then need to investigate why that asset category has changed. Another possible reason for the increase in receivables as a percentage of assets is that the company has lowered its credit standards, relaxed its collection procedures, or adopted more aggressive revenue recognition policies. The analyst can turn to other comparisons and ratios (e.g., comparing the rate of growth in accounts receivable with the rate of growth in sales) to help determine which explanation is most likely.

Exhibit 3 Vertical Common-Size (Partial) Balance Sheet for a Hypothetical Company

	Period 1 Percent of Total Assets	Period 2 Percent of Total Assets
Cash	25	15
Receivables	35	57
Inventory	35	20
Fixed assets, net of depreciation	5	8
Total assets	100	100

3.2.2 *Common-Size Analysis of the Income Statement*

A vertical common-size income statement divides each income statement item by revenue, or sometimes by total assets (especially in the case of financial institutions). If there are multiple revenue sources, a decomposition of revenue in percentage terms is useful. Exhibit 4 presents a hypothetical company's vertical common-size income statement in two time periods. Revenue is separated into the company's four services, each shown as a percentage of total revenue.

In this example, revenues from Service A have become a far greater percentage of the company's total revenue (30 percent in Period 1 and 45 percent in Period 2). What are possible reasons for and implications of this change in business mix? Did the company make a strategic decision to sell more of Service A, perhaps because it is more profitable? Apparently not, because the company's earnings before interest, taxes, depreciation, and amortisation (EBITDA) declined from 53 percent of sales to 45 percent, so other possible explanations should be examined. In addition, we note from the composition of operating expenses that the main reason for this decline in profitability is that salaries and employee benefits have increased from 15 percent to 25 percent of total revenue. Are more highly compensated employees required for Service A? Were higher training costs incurred in order to increase revenues from Service A? If the analyst wants to predict future performance, the causes of these changes must be understood.

In addition, Exhibit 4 shows that the company's income tax as a percentage of sales has declined dramatically (from 15 percent to 8 percent). Furthermore, taxes as a percentage of earnings before tax (EBT) (the effective tax rate, which is usually the more relevant comparison), have decreased from 36 percent (= 15/42) to 24 percent

(= 8/34). Is Service A, which in Period 2 is a greater percentage of total revenue, provided in a jurisdiction with lower tax rates? If not, what is the explanation for the change in effective tax rate?

The observations based on Exhibit 4 summarize the issues that can be raised through analysis of the vertical common-size income statement.

Exhibit 4 Vertical Common-Size Income Statement for Hypothetical Company

	Period 1 Percent of Total Revenue	Period 2 Percent of Total Revenue
Revenue source: Service A	30	45
Revenue source: Service B	23	20
Revenue source: Service C	30	30
Revenue source: Service D	17	5
Total revenue	**100**	**100**
Operating expenses (excluding depreciation)		
Salaries and employee benefits	15	25
Administrative expenses	22	20
Rent expense	10	10
EBITDA	**53**	**45**
Depreciation and amortisation	4	4
EBIT	**49**	**41**
Interest paid	7	7
EBT	**42**	**34**
Income tax provision	15	8
Net income	**27**	**26**

EBIT = earnings before interest and tax.

3.2.3 *Cross-Sectional Analysis*

As noted previously, ratios and common-size statements derive part of their meaning through comparison to some benchmark. **Cross-sectional analysis** (sometimes called "relative analysis") compares a specific metric for one company with the same metric for another company or group of companies, allowing comparisons even though the companies might be of significantly different sizes and/or operate in different currencies. This is illustrated in Exhibit 5.

Exhibit 5 Vertical Common-Size (Partial) Balance Sheet for Two Hypothetical Companies

Assets	Company 1 Percent of Total Assets	Company 2 Percent of Total Assets
Cash	38	12
Receivables	33	55
Inventory	27	24

Exhibit 5 (Continued)

Assets	Company 1 Percent of Total Assets	Company 2 Percent of Total Assets
Fixed assets net of depreciation	1	2
Investments	1	7
Total Assets	**100**	**100**

Exhibit 5 presents a vertical common-size (partial) balance sheet for two hypothetical companies at the same point in time. Company 1 is clearly more liquid (liquidity is a function of how quickly assets can be converted into cash) than Company 2, which has only 12 percent of assets available as cash, compared with the highly liquid Company 1, which has 38 percent of assets available as cash. Given that cash is generally a relatively low-yielding asset and thus not a particularly efficient use of excess funds, why does Company 1 hold such a large percentage of total assets in cash? Perhaps the company is preparing for an acquisition, or maintains a large cash position as insulation from a particularly volatile operating environment. Another issue highlighted by the comparison in this example is the relatively high percentage of receivables in Company 2's assets, which may indicate a greater proportion of credit sales, overall changes in asset composition, lower credit or collection standards, or aggressive accounting policies.

3.2.4 *Trend Analysis*[6]

When looking at financial statements and ratios, trends in the data, whether they are improving or deteriorating, are as important as the current absolute or relative levels. Trend analysis provides important information regarding historical performance and growth and, given a sufficiently long history of accurate seasonal information, can be of great assistance as a planning and forecasting tool for management and analysts.

Exhibit 6A presents a partial balance sheet for a hypothetical company over five periods. The last two columns of the table show the changes for Period 5 compared with Period 4, expressed both in absolute currency (in this case, dollars) and in percentages. A small percentage change could hide a significant currency change and vice versa, prompting the analyst to investigate the reasons despite one of the changes being relatively small. In this example, the largest percentage change was in investments, which decreased by 33.3 percent.[7] However, an examination of the absolute currency amount of changes shows that investments changed by only $2 million, and the more significant change was the $12 million increase in receivables.

Another way to present data covering a period of time is to show each item in relation to the same item in a base year (i.e., a horizontal common-size balance sheet). Exhibits 6B and 6C illustrate alternative presentations of horizontal common-size balance sheets. Exhibit 6B presents the information from the same partial balance sheet as in Exhibit 6A, but indexes each item relative to the same item in Period 1. For example, in Period 2, the company had $29 million cash, which is 74 percent or 0.74 of the amount of cash it had in Period 1. Expressed as an index relative to Period

6 In financial statement analysis, the term "trend analysis" usually refers to comparisons across time periods of 3–10 years not involving statistical tools. This differs from the use of the term in the quantitative methods portion of the CFA curriculum, where "trend analysis" refers to statistical methods of measuring patterns in time-series data.

7 Percentage change is calculated as (Ending value − Beginning value)/Beginning value, or equivalently, (Ending value/Beginning value) − 1.

1, where each item in Period 1 is given a value of 1.00, the value in Period 2 would be 0.74 ($29/$39 = 0.74). In Period 3, the company had $27 million cash, which is 69 percent of the amount of cash it had in Period 1 ($27/$39 = 0.69).

Exhibit 6C presents the percentage change in each item, relative to the previous year. For example, the change in cash from Period 1 to Period 2 was –25.6 percent ($29/$39 – 1 = –0.256), and the change in cash from Period 2 to Period 3 was –6.9 percent ($27/$29 – 1 = –0.069). An analyst will select the horizontal common-size balance that addresses the particular period of interest. Exhibit 6B clearly highlights that in Period 5 compared to Period 1, the company has less than half the amount of cash, four times the amount of investments, and eight times the amount of property, plant, and equipment. Exhibit 6C highlights year-to-year changes: For example, cash has declined in each period. Presenting data this way highlights significant changes. Again, note that a mathematically big change is not necessarily an important change. For example, fixed assets increased 100 percent, i.e., doubled between Period 1 and 2; however, as a proportion of total assets, fixed assets increased from 1 percent of total assets to 2 percent of total assets. The company's working capital assets (receivables and inventory) are a far higher proportion of total assets and would likely warrant more attention from an analyst.

An analysis of horizontal common-size balance sheets highlights structural changes that have occurred in a business. Past trends are obviously not necessarily an accurate predictor of the future, especially when the economic or competitive environment changes. An examination of past trends is more valuable when the macroeconomic and competitive environments are relatively stable and when the analyst is reviewing a stable or mature business. However, even in less stable contexts, historical analysis can serve as a basis for developing expectations. Understanding of past trends is helpful in assessing whether these trends are likely to continue or if the trend is likely to change direction.

Exhibit 6A Partial Balance Sheet for a Hypothetical Company over Five Periods

Assets ($ Millions)	Period 1	Period 2	Period 3	Period 4	Period 5	Change 4 to 5 ($ Million)	Change 4 to 5 (Percent)
Cash	39	29	27	19	16	–3	–15.8
Investments	1	7	7	6	4	–2	–33.3
Receivables	44	41	37	67	79	12	17.9
Inventory	15	25	36	25	27	2	8.0
Fixed assets net of depreciation	1	2	6	9	8	–1	–11.1
Total assets	100	104	113	126	134	8	6.3

Exhibit 6B Horizontal Common-Size (Partial) Balance Sheet for a Hypothetical Company over Five Periods, with Each Item Expressed Relative to the Same Item in Period One

	Period				
Assets	**1**	**2**	**3**	**4**	**5**
Cash	1.00	0.74	0.69	0.49	0.41
Investments	1.00	7.00	7.00	6.00	4.00
Receivables	1.00	0.93	0.84	1.52	1.80
Inventory	1.00	1.67	2.40	1.67	1.80
Fixed assets net of depreciation	1.00	2.00	6.00	9.00	8.00
Total assets	1.00	1.04	1.13	1.26	1.34

Exhibit 6C Horizontal Common-Size (Partial) Balance Sheet for a Hypothetical Company over Five Periods, with Percent Change in Each Item Relative to the Prior Period

	Period			
Assets	**2 (%)**	**3 (%)**	**4 (%)**	**5 (%)**
Cash	–25.6	–6.9	–29.6	–15.8
Investments	600.0	0.0	–14.3	–33.3
Receivables	–6.8	–9.8	81.1	17.9
Inventory	66.7	44.0	–30.6	8.0
Fixed assets net of depreciation	100.0	200.0	50.0	–11.1
Total assets	4.0	8.7	11.5	6.3

One measure of success is for a company to grow at a rate greater than the rate of the overall market in which it operates. Companies that grow slowly may find themselves unable to attract equity capital. Conversely, companies that grow too quickly may find that their administrative and management information systems cannot keep up with the rate of expansion.

3.2.5 *Relationships among Financial Statements*

Trend data generated by a horizontal common-size analysis can be compared across financial statements. For example, the growth rate of assets for the hypothetical company in Exhibit 6 can be compared with the company's growth in revenue over the same period of time. If revenue is growing more quickly than assets, the company may be increasing its efficiency (i.e., generating more revenue for every dollar invested in assets).

As another example, consider the following year-over-year percentage changes for a hypothetical company:

Revenue	+20%
Net income	+25%
Operating cash flow	–10%
Total assets	+30%

Net income is growing faster than revenue, which indicates increasing profitability. However, the analyst would need to determine whether the faster growth in net income resulted from continuing operations or from non-operating, non-recurring items. In addition, the 10 percent decline in operating cash flow despite increasing revenue and net income clearly warrants further investigation because it could indicate a problem with earnings quality (perhaps aggressive reporting of revenue). Lastly, the fact that assets have grown faster than revenue indicates the company's efficiency may be declining. The analyst should examine the composition of the increase in assets and the reasons for the changes. Example 5 illustrates a historical example of a company where comparisons of trend data from different financial statements were actually indicative of aggressive accounting policies.

EXAMPLE 5

Use of Comparative Growth Information[8]

In July 1996, Sunbeam, a US company, brought in new management to turn the company around. In the following year, 1997, using 1996 as the base, the following was observed based on reported numbers:

Revenue	+19%
Inventory	+58%
Receivables	+38%

It is generally more desirable to observe inventory and receivables growing at a slower (or similar) rate compared to revenue growth. Receivables growing faster than revenue can indicate operational issues, such as lower credit standards or aggressive accounting policies for revenue recognition. Similarly, inventory growing faster than revenue can indicate an operational problem with obsolescence or aggressive accounting policies, such as an improper overstatement of inventory to increase profits.

In this case, the explanation lay in aggressive accounting policies. Sunbeam was later charged by the US Securities and Exchange Commission with improperly accelerating the recognition of revenue and engaging in other practices, such as billing customers for inventory prior to shipment.

3.3 The Use of Graphs as an Analytical Tool

Graphs facilitate comparison of performance and financial structure over time, highlighting changes in significant aspects of business operations. In addition, graphs provide the analyst (and management) with a visual overview of risk trends in a business. Graphs may also be used effectively to communicate the analyst's conclusions regarding financial condition and risk management aspects.

Exhibit 7 presents the information from Exhibit 6A in a stacked column format. The graph makes the significant decline in cash and growth in receivables (both in absolute terms and as a percentage of assets) readily apparent. In Exhibit 7, the vertical axis shows US$ millions and the horizontal axis denotes the period.

Choosing the appropriate graph to communicate the most significant conclusions of a financial analysis is a skill. In general, pie graphs are most useful to communicate the composition of a total value (e.g., assets over a limited amount of time, say one or two periods). Line graphs are useful when the focus is on the change in amount for a

8 Adapted from Robinson and Munter (2004, pp. 2–15).

limited number of items over a relatively longer time period. When the composition and amounts, as well as their change over time, are all important, a stacked column graph can be useful.

Exhibit 7 Stacked Column Graph of Asset Composition of Hypothetical Company over Five Periods

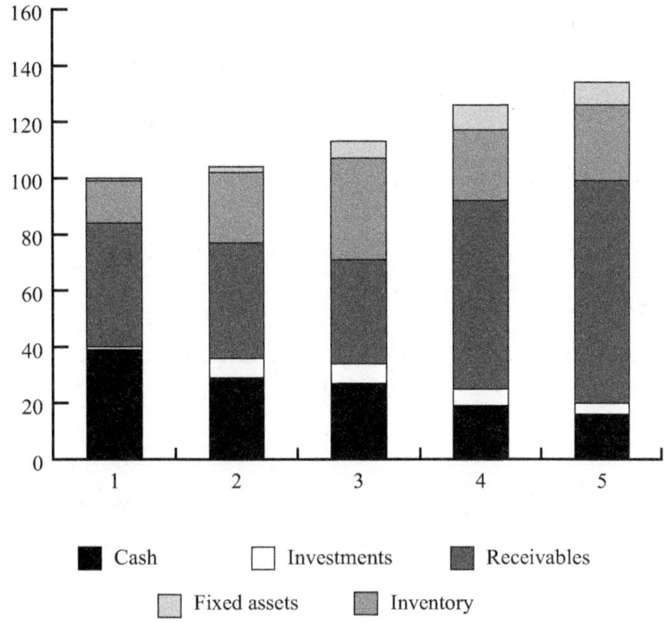

When comparing Period 5 with Period 4, the growth in receivables appears to be within normal bounds; but when comparing Period 5 with earlier periods, the dramatic growth becomes apparent. In the same manner, a simple line graph will also illustrate the growth trends in key financial variables. Exhibit 8 presents the information from Exhibit 6A as a line graph, illustrating the growth of assets of a hypothetical company over five periods. The steady decline in cash, volatile movements of inventory, and dramatic growth of receivables is clearly illustrated. Again, the vertical axis is shown in US$ millions and the horizontal axis denotes periods.

Exhibit 8 Line Graph of Growth of Assets of Hypothetical Company over Five Periods

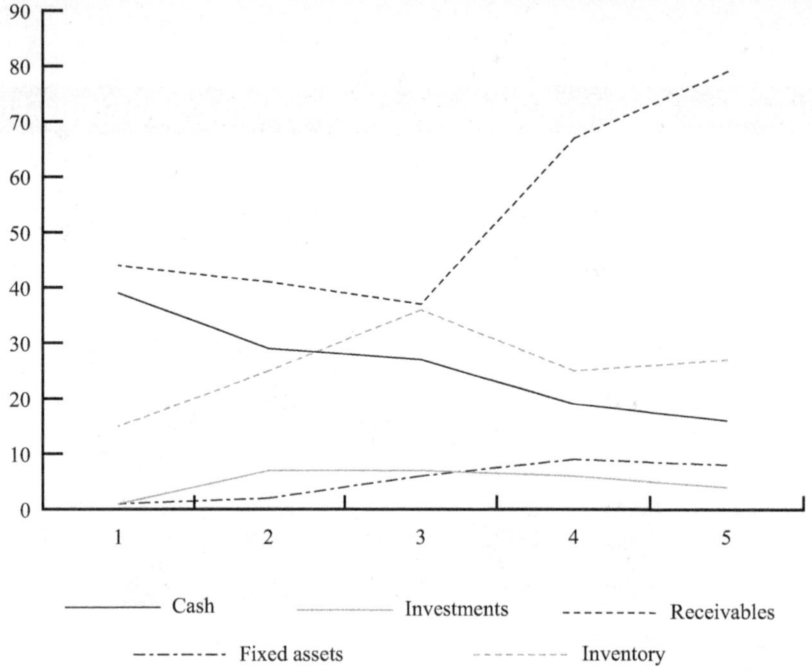

3.4 Regression Analysis

When analyzing the trend in a specific line item or ratio, frequently it is possible simply to visually evaluate the changes. For more complex situations, regression analysis can help identify relationships (or correlation) between variables. For example, a regression analysis could relate a company's sales to GDP over time, providing insight into whether the company is cyclical. In addition, the statistical relationship between sales and GDP could be used as a basis for forecasting sales.

Other examples where regression analysis may be useful include the relationship between a company's sales and inventory over time, or the relationship between hotel occupancy and a company's hotel revenues. In addition to providing a basis for forecasting, regression analysis facilitates identification of items or ratios that are not behaving as expected, given historical statistical relationships.

4 COMMON RATIOS USED IN FINANCIAL ANALYSIS

In the previous section, we focused on ratios resulting from common-size analysis. In this section, we expand the discussion to include other commonly used financial ratios and the broad classes into which they are categorized. There is some overlap with common-size financial statement ratios. For example, a common indicator of profitability is the net profit margin, which is calculated as net income divided by sales. This ratio appears on a vertical common-size income statement. Other ratios involve information from multiple financial statements or even data from outside the financial statements.

Because of the large number of ratios, it is helpful to think about ratios in terms of broad categories based on what aspects of performance a ratio is intended to detect. Financial analysts and data vendors use a variety of categories to classify ratios. The category names and the ratios included in each category can differ. Common ratio categories include activity, liquidity, solvency, profitability, and valuation. These categories are summarized in Exhibit 9. Each category measures a different aspect of the company's business, but all are useful in evaluating a company's overall ability to generate cash flows from operating its business and the associated risks.

Exhibit 9 Categories of Financial Ratios

Category	Description
Activity	**Activity ratios** measure how efficiently a company performs day-to-day tasks, such as the collection of receivables and management of inventory.
Liquidity	**Liquidity ratios** measure the company's ability to meet its short-term obligations.
Solvency	**Solvency ratios** measure a company's ability to meet long-term obligations. Subsets of these ratios are also known as "leverage" and "long-term debt" ratios.
Profitability	**Profitability ratios** measure the company's ability to generate profits from its resources (assets).
Valuation	**Valuation ratios** measure the quantity of an asset or flow (e.g., earnings) associated with ownership of a specified claim (e.g., a share or ownership of the enterprise).

These categories are not mutually exclusive; some ratios are useful in measuring multiple aspects of the business. For example, an activity ratio measuring how quickly a company collects accounts receivable is also useful in assessing the company's liquidity because collection of revenues increases cash. Some profitability ratios also reflect the operating efficiency of the business. In summary, analysts appropriately use certain ratios to evaluate multiple aspects of the business. Analysts also need to be aware of variations in industry practice in the calculation of financial ratios. In the text that follows, alternative views on ratio calculations are often provided.

4.1 Interpretation and Context

Financial ratios can only be interpreted in the context of other information, including benchmarks. In general, the financial ratios of a company are compared with those of its major competitors (cross-sectional and trend analysis) and to the company's prior periods (trend analysis). The goal is to understand the underlying causes of divergence between a company's ratios and those of the industry. Even ratios that remain consistent require understanding because consistency can sometimes indicate accounting policies selected to smooth earnings. An analyst should evaluate financial ratios based on the following:

1 *Company goals and strategy.* Actual ratios can be compared with company objectives to determine whether objectives are being attained and whether the results are consistent with the company's strategy.

2 *Industry norms* (*cross-sectional analysis*). A company can be compared with others in its industry by relating its financial ratios to industry norms or to a subset of the companies in an industry. When industry norms are used to make judgments, care must be taken because:
   - Many ratios are industry specific, and not all ratios are important to all industries.
   - Companies may have several different lines of business. This will cause aggregate financial ratios to be distorted. It is better to examine industry-specific ratios by lines of business.
   - Differences in accounting methods used by companies can distort financial ratios.
   - Differences in corporate strategies can affect certain financial ratios.

3 *Economic conditions*. For cyclical companies, financial ratios tend to improve when the economy is strong and weaken during recessions. Therefore, financial ratios should be examined in light of the current phase of the business cycle.

The following sections discuss activity, liquidity, solvency, and profitability ratios in turn. Selected valuation ratios are presented later in the section on equity analysis.

4.2 Activity Ratios

Activity ratios are also known as **asset utilization ratios** or **operating efficiency ratios**. This category is intended to measure how well a company manages various activities, particularly how efficiently it manages its various assets. Activity ratios are analyzed as indicators of ongoing operational performance—how effectively assets are used by a company. These ratios reflect the efficient management of both working capital and longer term assets. As noted, efficiency has a direct impact on liquidity (the ability of a company to meet its short-term obligations), so some activity ratios are also useful in assessing liquidity.

4.2.1 *Calculation of Activity Ratios*

Exhibit 10 presents the most commonly used activity ratios. The exhibit shows the numerator and denominator of each ratio.

Exhibit 10 Definitions of Commonly Used Activity Ratios

Activity Ratios	Numerator	Denominator
Inventory turnover	Cost of sales or cost of goods sold	Average inventory
Days of inventory on hand (DOH)	Number of days in period	Inventory turnover
Receivables turnover	Revenue	Average receivables
Days of sales outstanding (DSO)	Number of days in period	Receivables turnover
Payables turnover	Purchases	Average trade payables
Number of days of payables	Number of days in period	Payables turnover
Working capital turnover	Revenue	Average working capital

Exhibit 10 (Continued)

Activity Ratios	Numerator	Denominator
Fixed asset turnover	Revenue	Average net fixed assets
Total asset turnover	Revenue	Average total assets

Activity ratios measure how efficiently the company utilizes assets. They generally combine information from the income statement in the numerator with balance sheet items in the denominator. Because the income statement measures what happened *during* a period whereas the balance sheet shows the condition only at the end of the period, average balance sheet data are normally used for consistency. For example, to measure inventory management efficiency, cost of sales or cost of goods sold (from the income statement) is divided by average inventory (from the balance sheet). Most databases, such as Bloomberg and Baseline, use this averaging convention when income statement and balance sheet data are combined. These databases typically average only two points: the beginning of the year and the end of the year. The examples that follow based on annual financial statements illustrate that practice. However, some analysts prefer to average more observations if they are available, especially if the business is seasonal. If a semiannual report is prepared, an average can be taken over three data points (beginning, middle, and end of year). If quarterly data are available, a five-point average can be computed (beginning of year and end of each quarterly period) or a four-point average using the end of each quarterly period. Note that if the company's year ends at a low or high point for inventory for the year, there can still be bias in using three or five data points, because the beginning and end of year occur at the same time of the year and are effectively double counted.

Because cost of goods sold measures the cost of inventory that has been sold, this ratio measures how many times per year the entire inventory was theoretically turned over, or sold. (We say that the entire inventory was "theoretically" sold because in practice companies do not generally sell out their entire inventory.) If, for example, a company's cost of goods sold for a recent year was €120,000 and its average inventory was €10,000, the inventory turnover ratio would be 12. The company theoretically turns over (i.e., sells) its entire inventory 12 times per year (i.e., once a month). (Again, we say "theoretically" because in practice the company likely carries some inventory from one month into another.) Turnover can then be converted to days of inventory on hand (DOH) by dividing inventory turnover into the number of days in the accounting period. In this example, the result is a DOH of 30.42 (365/12), meaning that, on average, the company's inventory was on hand for about 30 days, or, equivalently, the company kept on hand about 30 days' worth of inventory, on average, during the period.

Activity ratios can be computed for any annual or interim period, but care must be taken in the interpretation and comparison across periods. For example, if the same company had cost of goods sold for the first quarter (90 days) of the following year of €35,000 and average inventory of €11,000, the inventory turnover would be 3.18 times. However, this turnover rate is 3.18 times per quarter, which is not directly comparable to the 12 times per year in the preceding year. In this case, we can annualize the quarterly inventory turnover rate by multiplying the quarterly turnover by 4 (12 months/3 months; or by 4.06, using 365 days/90 days) for comparison to the annual turnover rate. So, the quarterly inventory turnover is equivalent to a 12.72 annual inventory turnover (or 12.91 if we annualize the ratio using a 90-day quarter and a 365-day year). To compute the DOH using quarterly data, we can use the quarterly turnover rate and the number of days in the quarter for the numerator—or, we can use the annualized turnover rate and 365 days; either results in DOH of around 28.3, with slight differences due to rounding (90/3.18 = 28.30 and 365/12.91 = 28.27). Another time-related computational detail is that for companies using a 52/53-week annual period and for leap years, the actual days in the year should be used rather than 365.

In some cases, an analyst may want to know how many days of inventory are on hand at the end of the year rather than the average for the year. In this case, it would be appropriate to use the year-end inventory balance in the computation rather than the average. If the company is growing rapidly or if costs are increasing rapidly, analysts should consider using cost of goods sold just for the fourth quarter in this computation because the cost of goods sold of earlier quarters may not be relevant. Example 6 further demonstrates computation of activity ratios using Hong Kong Stock Exchange(HKEX)-listed Lenovo Group Limited.

EXAMPLE 6

Computation of Activity Ratios

An analyst would like to evaluate Lenovo Group's efficiency in collecting its trade accounts receivable during the fiscal year ended 31 March 2018 (FY2017). The analyst gathers the following information from Lenovo's annual and interim reports:

	US$ in Thousands
Trade receivables as of 31 March 2017	4,468,392
Trade receivables as of 31 March 2018	4,972,722
Revenue for year ended 31 March 2018	45,349,943

Calculate Lenovo's receivables turnover and number of days of sales outstanding (DSO) for the fiscal year ended 31 March 2018.

Solution:

Receivables turnover	=	Revenue/Average receivables
	=	45,349,943/[(4,468,392 + 4,972,722)/2]
	=	45,349,943/4,720,557
	=	9.6069 times, or 9.6 rounded
DSO	=	Number of days in period/Receivables turnover
	=	365/9.6
	=	38.0 days

On average, it took Lenovo 38 days to collect receivables during the fiscal year ended 31 March 2018.

4.2.2 *Interpretation of Activity Ratios*

In the following section, we further discuss the activity ratios that were defined in Exhibit 10.

Inventory Turnover and DOH Inventory turnover lies at the heart of operations for many entities. It indicates the resources tied up in inventory (i.e., the carrying costs) and can, therefore, be used to indicate inventory management effectiveness. A higher inventory turnover ratio implies a shorter period that inventory is held, and thus a lower DOH. In general, inventory turnover and DOH should be benchmarked against industry norms.

A high inventory turnover ratio relative to industry norms might indicate highly effective inventory management. Alternatively, a high inventory turnover ratio (and commensurately low DOH) could possibly indicate the company does not carry adequate inventory, so shortages could potentially hurt revenue. To assess which explanation is more likely, the analyst can compare the company's revenue growth with that of the industry. Slower growth combined with higher inventory turnover could indicate inadequate inventory levels. Revenue growth at or above the industry's growth supports the interpretation that the higher turnover reflects greater inventory management efficiency.

A low inventory turnover ratio (and commensurately high DOH) relative to the rest of the industry could be an indicator of slow-moving inventory, perhaps due to technological obsolescence or a change in fashion. Again, comparing the company's sales growth with the industry can offer insight.

Receivables Turnover and DSO. The number of DSO represents the elapsed time between a sale and cash collection, reflecting how fast the company collects cash from customers to whom it offers credit. Although limiting the numerator to sales made on credit in the receivables turnover would be more appropriate, credit sales information is not always available to analysts; therefore, revenue as reported in the income statement is generally used as an approximation.

A relatively high receivables turnover ratio (and commensurately low DSO) might indicate highly efficient credit and collection. Alternatively, a high receivables turnover ratio could indicate that the company's credit or collection policies are too stringent, suggesting the possibility of sales being lost to competitors offering more lenient terms. A relatively low receivables turnover ratio would typically raise questions about the efficiency of the company's credit and collections procedures. As with inventory management, comparison of the company's sales growth relative to the industry can help the analyst assess whether sales are being lost due to stringent credit policies. In addition, comparing the company's estimates of uncollectible accounts receivable and actual credit losses with past experience and with peer companies can help assess whether low turnover reflects credit management issues. Companies often provide details of receivables aging (how much receivables have been outstanding by age). This can be used along with DSO to understand trends in collection, as demonstrated in Example 7.

EXAMPLE 7

Evaluation of an Activity Ratio

An analyst has computed the average DSO for Lenovo for fiscal years ended 31 March 2018 and 2017:

	FY2017	FY2016
Days of sales outstanding	38.0	37.6

Revenue increased from US$43.035 billion for fiscal year ended 31 March 2017 (FY2016) to US$45.350 billion for fiscal year ended 31 March 2018 (FY2017). The analyst would like to better understand the change in the company's DSO from FY2016 to FY2017 and whether the increase is indicative of any issues with the customers' credit quality. The analyst collects accounts receivable aging information from Lenovo's annual reports and computes the percentage of accounts receivable by days outstanding. This information is presented in Exhibit 11:

Exhibit 11

	FY2017		FY2016		FY2015	
	US$000	Percent	US$000	Percent	US$000	Percent
Accounts receivable						
0–30 days	3,046,240	59.95	2,923,083	63.92	3,246,600	71.99
31–60 days	1,169,286	23.01	985,251	21.55	617,199	13.69
61–90 days	320,183	6.30	283,050	6.19	240,470	5.33
Over 90 days	545,629	10.74	381,387	8.34	405,410	8.99
Total	5,081,338	100.00	4,572,771	100.00	4,509,679	100.00
Less: Provision for impairment	−108,616	−2.14	−104,379	−2.28	−106,172	−2.35
Trade receivables, net	4,972,722	97.86	4,468,392	97.72	4,403,507	97.65
Total sales	*45,349,943*		*43,034,731*		*44,912,097*	

Note: Lenovo's footnotes disclose that general trade customers are provided with credit terms ranging from 0 to 120 days.

These data indicate that total accounts receivable increased by about 11.3% in FY2017 versus FY2016, while total sales increased by only 5.4%. Further, the percentage of receivables in all categories older than 30 days has increased over the three-year period, indicating that customers are indeed taking longer to pay. On the other hand, the provision for impairment (estimate of uncollectible accounts) has declined as a percent of total receivables. Considering all this information, the company may be increasing customer financing purposely to drive its sales growth. They also may be underestimating the impairment. This should be investigated further by the analyst.

Payables Turnover and the Number of Days of Payables The number of days of payables reflects the average number of days the company takes to pay its suppliers, and the payables turnover ratio measures how many times per year the company theoretically pays off all its creditors. For purposes of calculating these ratios, an implicit assumption is that the company makes all its purchases using credit. If the amount of purchases is not directly available, it can be computed as cost of goods sold plus ending inventory less beginning inventory. Alternatively, cost of goods sold is sometimes used as an approximation of purchases.

A payables turnover ratio that is high (low days payable) relative to the industry could indicate that the company is not making full use of available credit facilities; alternatively, it could result from a company taking advantage of early payment discounts. An excessively low turnover ratio (high days payable) could indicate trouble making payments on time, or alternatively, exploitation of lenient supplier terms. This is another example where it is useful to look simultaneously at other ratios. If liquidity ratios indicate that the company has sufficient cash and other short-term assets to pay obligations and yet the days payable ratio is relatively high, the analyst would favor the lenient supplier credit and collection policies as an explanation.

Working Capital Turnover **Working capital** is defined as current assets minus current liabilities. Working capital turnover indicates how efficiently the company generates revenue with its working capital. For example, a working capital turnover ratio of 4.0 indicates that the company generates €4 of revenue for every €1 of working capital. A high working capital turnover ratio indicates greater efficiency (i.e., the company is generating a high level of revenues relative to working capital). For some companies, working capital can be near zero or negative, rendering this ratio incapable of being interpreted. The following two ratios are more useful in those circumstances.

Fixed Asset Turnover This ratio measures how efficiently the company generates revenues from its investments in fixed assets. Generally, a higher fixed asset turnover ratio indicates more efficient use of fixed assets in generating revenue. A low ratio can indicate inefficiency, a capital-intensive business environment, or a new business not yet operating at full capacity—in which case the analyst will not be able to link the ratio directly to efficiency. In addition, asset turnover can be affected by factors other than a company's efficiency. The fixed asset turnover ratio would be lower for a company whose assets are newer (and, therefore, less depreciated and so reflected in the financial statements at a higher carrying value) than the ratio for a company with older assets (that are thus more depreciated and so reflected at a lower carrying value). The fixed asset ratio can be erratic because, although revenue may have a steady growth rate, increases in fixed assets may not follow a smooth pattern; so, every year-to-year change in the ratio does not necessarily indicate important changes in the company's efficiency.

Total Asset Turnover The total asset turnover ratio measures the company's overall ability to generate revenues with a given level of assets. A ratio of 1.20 would indicate that the company is generating €1.20 of revenues for every €1 of average assets. A higher ratio indicates greater efficiency. Because this ratio includes both fixed and current assets, inefficient working capital management can distort overall interpretations. It is therefore helpful to analyze working capital and fixed asset turnover ratios separately.

A low asset turnover ratio can be an indicator of inefficiency or of relative capital intensity of the business. The ratio also reflects strategic decisions by management—for example, the decision whether to use a more labor-intensive (and less capital-intensive) approach to its business or a more capital-intensive (and less labor-intensive) approach.

When interpreting activity ratios, the analysts should examine not only the individual ratios but also the collection of relevant ratios to determine the overall efficiency of a company. Example 8 demonstrates the evaluation of activity ratios, both narrow (e.g., days of inventory on hand) and broad (e.g., total asset turnover) for a hypothetical manufacturer.

EXAMPLE 8

Evaluation of Activity Ratios

ZZZ Company is a hypothetical manufacturing company. As part of an analysis of management's operating efficiency, an analyst collects the following activity ratios from a data provider:

Ratio	2018	2017	2016	2015
DOH	35.68	40.70	40.47	48.51
DSO	45.07	58.28	51.27	76.98
Total asset turnover	0.36	0.28	0.23	0.22

These ratios indicate that the company has improved on all three measures of activity over the four-year period. The company appears to be managing its inventory more efficiently, is collecting receivables faster, and is generating a higher level of revenues relative to total assets. The overall trend appears good, but thus far, the analyst has only determined *what* happened. A more important question is *why* the ratios improved, because understanding good changes as well as bad ones facilitates judgments about the company's future performance. To answer this question, the analyst examines company financial reports as well as external information about the industry and economy. In examining the annual report, the analyst notes that in the fourth quarter of 2018, the company experienced an "inventory correction" and that the company recorded an allowance for the decline in market value and obsolescence of inventory of about 15 percent of year-end inventory value (compared with about a 6 percent allowance in the prior year). This reduction in the value of inventory accounts for a large portion of the decline in DOH from 40.70 in 2017 to 35.68 in 2018. Management claims that this inventory obsolescence is a short-term issue; analysts can watch DOH in future interim periods to confirm this assertion. In any event, all else being equal, the analyst would likely expect DOH to return to a level closer to 40 days going forward.

More positive interpretations can be drawn from the total asset turnover. The analyst finds that the company's revenues increased more than 35 percent while total assets only increased by about 6 percent. Based on external information about the industry and economy, the analyst attributes the increased revenues both to overall growth in the industry and to the company's increased market share. Management was able to achieve growth in revenues with a comparatively modest increase in assets, leading to an improvement in total asset turnover. Note further that part of the reason for the increase in asset turnover is lower DOH and DSO.

4.3 Liquidity Ratios

Liquidity analysis, which focuses on cash flows, measures a company's ability to meet its short-term obligations. Liquidity measures how quickly assets are converted into cash. Liquidity ratios also measure the ability to pay off short-term obligations. In day-to-day operations, liquidity management is typically achieved through efficient use of assets. In the medium term, liquidity in the non-financial sector is also addressed by managing the structure of liabilities. (See the discussion on financial sector below.)

The level of liquidity needed differs from one industry to another. A particular company's liquidity position may vary according to the anticipated need for funds at any given time. Judging whether a company has adequate liquidity requires analysis of its historical funding requirements, current liquidity position, anticipated future funding needs, and options for reducing funding needs or attracting additional funds (including actual and potential sources of such funding).

Larger companies are usually better able to control the level and composition of their liabilities than smaller companies. Therefore, they may have more potential funding sources, including public capital and money markets. Greater discretionary access to capital markets also reduces the size of the liquidity buffer needed relative to companies without such access.

Contingent liabilities, such as letters of credit or financial guarantees, can also be relevant when assessing liquidity. The importance of contingent liabilities varies for the non-banking and banking sector. In the non-banking sector, contingent liabilities (usually disclosed in the footnotes to the company's financial statements) represent potential cash outflows, and when appropriate, should be included in an assessment of a company's liquidity. In the banking sector, contingent liabilities represent potentially significant cash outflows that are not dependent on the bank's financial condition. Although outflows in normal market circumstances typically may be low, a general macroeconomic or market crisis can trigger a substantial increase in cash outflows related to contingent liabilities because of the increase in defaults and business bankruptcies that often accompany such events. In addition, such crises are usually characterized by diminished levels of overall liquidity, which can further exacerbate funding shortfalls. Therefore, for the banking sector, the effect of contingent liabilities on liquidity warrants particular attention.

4.3.1 *Calculation of Liquidity Ratios*

Common liquidity ratios are presented in Exhibit 12. These liquidity ratios reflect a company's position at a point in time and, therefore, typically use data from the ending balance sheet rather than averages. The current, quick, and cash ratios reflect three measures of a company's ability to pay current liabilities. Each uses a progressively stricter definition of liquid assets.

The **defensive interval ratio** measures how long a company can pay its daily cash expenditures using only its existing liquid assets, without additional cash flow coming in. This ratio is similar to the "burn rate" often computed for start-up internet companies in the late 1990s or for biotechnology companies. The numerator of this ratio includes the same liquid assets used in the quick ratio, and the denominator is an estimate of daily cash expenditures. To obtain daily cash expenditures, the total of cash expenditures for the period is divided by the number of days in the period. Total cash expenditures for a period can be approximated by summing all expenses on the income statement—such as cost of goods sold; selling, general, and administrative expenses; and research and development expenses—and then subtracting any non-cash expenses, such as depreciation and amortisation. (Typically, taxes are not included.)

The **cash conversion cycle**, a financial metric not in ratio form, measures the length of time required for a company to go from cash paid (used in its operations) to cash received (as a result of its operations). The cash conversion cycle is sometimes expressed as the length of time funds are tied up in working capital. During this period of time, the company needs to finance its investment in operations through other sources (i.e., through debt or equity).

Exhibit 12 Definitions of Commonly Used Liquidity Ratios

Liquidity Ratios	Numerator	Denominator
Current ratio	Current assets	Current liabilities
Quick ratio	Cash + Short-term marketable investments + Receivables	Current liabilities
Cash ratio	Cash + Short-term marketable investments	Current liabilities
Defensive interval ratio	Cash + Short-term marketable investments + Receivables	Daily cash expenditures
Additional Liquidity Measure		
Cash conversion cycle (net operating cycle)	DOH + DSO – Number of days of payables	

4.3.2 *Interpretation of Liquidity Ratios*

In the following, we discuss the interpretation of the five basic liquidity measures presented in Exhibit 12.

Current Ratio This ratio expresses current assets in relation to current liabilities. A higher ratio indicates a higher level of liquidity (i.e., a greater ability to meet short-term obligations). A current ratio of 1.0 would indicate that the book value of its current assets exactly equals the book value of its current liabilities.

A lower ratio indicates less liquidity, implying a greater reliance on operating cash flow and outside financing to meet short-term obligations. Liquidity affects the company's capacity to take on debt. The current ratio implicitly assumes that inventories and accounts receivable are indeed liquid (which is presumably not the case when related turnover ratios are low).

Quick Ratio The quick ratio is more conservative than the current ratio because it includes only the more liquid current assets (sometimes referred to as "quick assets") in relation to current liabilities. Like the current ratio, a higher quick ratio indicates greater liquidity.

The quick ratio reflects the fact that certain current assets—such as prepaid expenses, some taxes, and employee-related prepayments—represent costs of the current period that have been paid in advance and cannot usually be converted back into cash. This ratio also reflects the fact that inventory might not be easily and quickly converted into cash, and furthermore, that a company would probably not be able to sell all of its inventory for an amount equal to its carrying value, especially if it were required to sell the inventory quickly. In situations where inventories are illiquid (as indicated, for example, by low inventory turnover ratios), the quick ratio may be a better indicator of liquidity than is the current ratio.

Cash Ratio The cash ratio normally represents a reliable measure of an entity's liquidity in a crisis situation. Only highly marketable short-term investments and cash are included. In a general market crisis, the fair value of marketable securities could decrease significantly as a result of market factors, in which case even this ratio might not provide reliable information.

Defensive Interval Ratio This ratio measures how long the company can continue to pay its expenses from its existing liquid assets without receiving any additional cash inflow. A defensive interval ratio of 50 would indicate that the company can continue to pay its operating expenses for 50 days before running out of quick assets, assuming no additional cash inflows. A higher defensive interval ratio indicates greater liquidity. If a company's defensive interval ratio is very low relative to peer companies or to the company's own history, the analyst would want to ascertain whether there is sufficient cash inflow expected to mitigate the low defensive interval ratio.

Cash Conversion Cycle (Net Operating Cycle) This metric indicates the amount of time that elapses from the point when a company invests in working capital until the point at which the company collects cash. In the typical course of events, a merchandising company acquires inventory on credit, incurring accounts payable. The company then sells that inventory on credit, increasing accounts receivable. Afterwards, it pays out cash to settle its accounts payable, and it collects cash in settlement of its accounts receivable. The time between the outlay of cash and the collection of cash is called the "cash conversion cycle." A shorter cash conversion cycle indicates greater liquidity. A short cash conversion cycle implies that the company only needs to finance its inventory and accounts receivable for a short period of time. A longer cash conversion cycle indicates lower liquidity; it implies that the company must finance its inventory and accounts receivable for a longer period of time, possibly indicating a need for a higher level of capital to fund current assets. Example 9 demonstrates the advantages of a short cash conversion cycle as well as how a company's business strategies are reflected in financial ratios.

EXAMPLE 9

Evaluation of Liquidity Measures

An analyst is evaluating the liquidity of Apple and calculates the number of days of receivables, inventory, and accounts payable, as well as the overall cash conversion cycle, as follows:

	FY2017	FY2016	FY2015
DSO	27	28	27
DOH	9	6	6
Less: Number of days of payables	112	101	86
Equals: Cash conversion cycle	(76)	(67)	(53)

The minimal DOH indicates that Apple maintains lean inventories, which is attributable to key aspects of the company's business model where manufacturing is outsourced. In isolation, the increase in number of days payable (from 86 days in FY2015 to 112 days in FY2017) might suggest an inability to pay suppliers; however, in Apple's case, the balance sheet indicates that the company has more than $70 billion of cash and short-term investments, which would be more than enough to pay suppliers sooner if Apple chose to do so. Instead, Apple takes advantage of the favorable credit terms granted by its suppliers. The overall effect is a negative cash cycle, a somewhat unusual result. Instead of requiring additional capital to fund working capital as is the case for most companies, Apple has excess cash to invest for over 50 days during that three-year period (reflected on the balance sheet as short-term investments) on which it is earning, rather than paying, interest.

EXAMPLE 10

Bounds and Context of Financial Measures

The previous example focused on the cash conversion cycle, which many companies identify as a key performance metric. The less positive the number of days in the cash conversion cycle, typically, the better it is considered to be. However, is this always true?

This example considers the following question: If a larger negative number of days in a cash conversion cycle is considered to be a desirable performance metric, does identifying a company with a large negative cash conversion cycle necessarily imply good performance?

Using a historical example, National Datacomputer, a technology company, had large negative number of days in its cash conversion cycle during the 2005 to 2009 period. In 2008 its cash conversion cycle was 275.5 days.

Exhibit 13 National Datacomputer Inc. ($ millions)

Fiscal year	2004	2005	2006	2007	2008	2009
Sales	3.248	2.672	2.045	1.761	1.820	1.723
Cost of goods sold	1.919	1.491	0.898	1.201	1.316	1.228
Receivables, Total	0.281	0.139	0.099	0.076	0.115	0.045
Inventories, Total	0.194	0.176	0.010	0.002	0.000	0.000
Accounts payable	0.223	0.317	0.366	1.423	0.704	0.674
DSO		28.69	21.24	18.14	19.15	16.95
DOH		45.29	37.80	1.82	0.28	0.00
*Less: Number of days of payables**		66.10	138.81	271.85	294.97	204.79
Equals: Cash conversion cycle		7.88	−79.77	−251.89	−275.54	−187.84

**Notes*: Calculated using Cost of goods sold as an approximation of purchases. Ending inventories 2008 and 2009 are reported as $0 million; therefore, inventory turnover for 2009 cannot be measured. However, given inventory and average sales per day, DOH in 2009 is 0.00.

Source: Raw data from Compustat. Ratios calculated.

The reason for the negative cash conversion cycle is that the company's accounts payable increased substantially over the period. An increase from approximately 66 days in 2005 to 295 days in 2008 to pay trade creditors is clearly a negative signal. In addition, the company's inventories disappeared, most likely because the company did not have enough cash to purchase new inventory and was unable to get additional credit from its suppliers.

Of course, an analyst would have immediately noted the negative trends in these data, as well as additional data throughout the company's financial statements. In its MD&A, the company clearly reports the risks as follows:

> Because we have historically had losses and only a limited amount of cash has been generated from operations, we have funded our operating activities to date primarily from the sale of securities and from the sale of a product line in 2009. In order to continue to fund our operations, we may need to raise additional capital, through the sale of securities. We cannot be certain that any such financing will be available on acceptable terms, or at all. Moreover, additional equity financing, if available, would likely be dilutive to the holders of our common stock, and debt financing, if available, would likely involve restrictive covenants and a security interest in all or substantially all of our assets. If we fail to obtain acceptable financing when needed, we may not have sufficient resources to fund our normal operations which would have a material adverse effect on our business.
>
> IF WE ARE UNABLE TO GENERATE ADEQUATE WORKING CAPITAL FROM OPERATIONS OR RAISE ADDITIONAL CAPITAL THERE IS SUBSTANTIAL DOUBT ABOUT THE COMPANY'S ABILITY TO CONTINUE AS A GOING CONCERN. (emphasis added by company)
>
> *Source*: National Datacomputer Inc., 2009 Form 10-K, page 7.

Subsequently, the company's 2010 Form 10K reported:

> "In January 2011, due to our inability to meet our financial obligations and the impending loss of a critical distribution agreement granting us the right to distribute certain products, our secured lenders ("Secured Parties") acting upon an event of default, sold certain of our assets (other than cash and accounts receivable) to Micronet, Ltd. ("Micronet"), an unaffiliated corporation pursuant to the terms of an asset purchase agreement between the Secured Parties and Micronet dated January 10, 2010 (the "Asset Purchase Agreement"). In order to induce Micronet to enter into the agreement, the Company also provided certain representations and warranties regarding certain business matters."

In summary, it is always necessary to consider ratios within bounds of reasonability and to understand the reasons underlying changes in ratios. Ratios must not only be calculated but must also be interpreted by an analyst.

4.4 Solvency Ratios

Solvency refers to a company's ability to fulfill its long-term debt obligations. Assessment of a company's ability to pay its long-term obligations (i.e., to make interest and principal payments) generally includes an in-depth analysis of the components of its financial structure. Solvency ratios provide information regarding the relative amount of debt in the company's capital structure and the adequacy of earnings and cash flow to cover interest expenses and other fixed charges (such as lease or rental payments) as they come due.

Analysts seek to understand a company's use of debt for several main reasons. One reason is that the amount of debt in a company's capital structure is important for assessing the company's risk and return characteristics, specifically its financial leverage. Leverage is a magnifying effect that results from the use of **fixed costs**—costs that stay the same within some range of activity—and can take two forms: operating leverage and financial leverage.

Operating leverage results from the use of fixed costs in conducting the company's business. Operating leverage magnifies the effect of changes in sales on operating income. Profitable companies may use operating leverage because when revenues increase, with operating leverage, their operating income increases at a faster rate. The explanation is that, although **variable costs** will rise proportionally with revenue, fixed costs will not.

When financing a company (i.e., raising capital for it), the use of debt constitutes **financial leverage** because interest payments are essentially fixed financing costs. As a result of interest payments, a given percent change in EBIT results in a larger percent change in earnings before taxes (EBT). Thus, financial leverage tends to magnify the effect of changes in EBIT on returns flowing to equity holders. Assuming that a company can earn more on funds than it pays in interest, the inclusion of some level of debt in a company's capital structure may lower a company's overall cost of capital and increase returns to equity holders. However, a higher level of debt in a company's capital structure increases the risk of default and results in higher borrowing costs for the company to compensate lenders for assuming greater credit risk. Starting with Modigliani and Miller (1958, 1963), a substantial amount of research has focused on determining a company's optimal capital structure and the subject remains an important one in corporate finance.

In analyzing financial statements, an analyst aims to understand levels and trends in a company's use of financial leverage in relation to past practices and the practices of peer companies. Analysts also need to be aware of the relationship between operating leverage (results from the use of non-current assets with fixed costs) and financial leverage (results from the use of long-term debt with fixed costs). The greater a company's operating leverage, the greater the risk of the operating income stream available to cover debt payments; operating leverage can thus limit a company's capacity to use financial leverage.

A company's relative solvency is fundamental to valuation of its debt securities and its creditworthiness. Finally, understanding a company's use of debt can provide analysts with insight into the company's future business prospects because management's decisions about financing may signal their beliefs about a company's future. For example, the issuance of long-term debt to repurchase common shares may indicate that management believes the market is underestimating the company's prospects and that the shares are undervalued.

4.4.1 *Calculation of Solvency Ratios*

Solvency ratios are primarily of two types. Debt ratios, the first type, focus on the balance sheet and measure the amount of debt capital relative to equity capital. Coverage ratios, the second type, focus on the income statement and measure the ability of a company to cover its debt payments. These ratios are useful in assessing a company's solvency and, therefore, in evaluating the quality of a company's bonds and other debt obligations.

Exhibit 14 describes commonly used solvency ratios. The first three of the debt ratios presented use total debt in the numerator. The definition of total debt used in these ratios varies among informed analysts and financial data vendors, with some using the total of interest-bearing short-term and long-term debt, excluding liabilities such as accrued expenses and accounts payable. (For calculations in this reading, we use this definition.) Other analysts use definitions that are more inclusive (e.g., all liabilities) or restrictive (e.g., long-term debt only, in which case the ratio is sometimes qualified as "long-term," as in "long-term debt-to-equity ratio"). If using different definitions of total debt materially changes conclusions about a company's solvency, the reasons for the discrepancies warrant further investigation.

Exhibit 14 Definitions of Commonly Used Solvency Ratios

Solvency Ratios	Numerator	Denominator
Debt Ratios		
Debt-to-assets ratio[a]	Total debt[b]	Total assets
Debt-to-capital ratio	Total debt[b]	Total debt[b] + Total shareholders' equity
Debt-to-equity ratio	Total debt[b]	Total shareholders' equity
Financial leverage ratio[c]	Average total assets	Average total equity
Debt-to-EBITDA	Total debt	EBITDA

Exhibit 14 (Continued)

Coverage Ratios		
Interest coverage	EBIT	Interest payments
Fixed charge coverage	EBIT + Lease payments	Interest payments + Lease payments

[a] "Total debt ratio" is another name sometimes used for this ratio.
[b] In this reading, total debt is the sum of interest-bearing short-term and long-term debt.
[c] *Average* total assets divided by *average* total equity is used for the purposes of this reading (in particular, Dupont analysis covered later). In practice, period-end total assets divided by period-end total equity is often used.

4.4.2 *Interpretation of Solvency Ratios*

In the following, we discuss the interpretation of the basic solvency ratios presented in Exhibit 14.

Debt-to-Assets Ratio This ratio measures the percentage of total assets financed with debt. For example, a **debt-to-assets ratio** of 0.40 or 40 percent indicates that 40 percent of the company's assets are financed with debt. Generally, higher debt means higher financial risk and thus weaker solvency.

Debt-to-Capital Ratio The **debt-to-capital ratio** measures the percentage of a company's capital (debt plus equity) represented by debt. As with the previous ratio, a higher ratio generally means higher financial risk and thus indicates weaker solvency.

Debt-to-Equity Ratio The **debt-to-equity ratio** measures the amount of debt capital relative to equity capital. Interpretation is similar to the preceding two ratios (i.e., a higher ratio indicates weaker solvency). A ratio of 1.0 would indicate equal amounts of debt and equity, which is equivalent to a debt-to-capital ratio of 50 percent. Alternative definitions of this ratio use the market value of stockholders' equity rather than its book value (or use the market values of both stockholders' equity and debt).

Financial Leverage Ratio This ratio (often called simply the "leverage ratio") measures the amount of total assets supported for each one money unit of equity. For example, a value of 3 for this ratio means that each €1 of equity supports €3 of total assets. The higher the **financial leverage ratio**, the more leveraged the company is in the sense of using debt and other liabilities to finance assets. This ratio is often defined in terms of average total assets and average total equity and plays an important role in the DuPont decomposition of return on equity that will be presented in Section 4.6.2.

Debt-to-EBITDA Ratio This ratio estimates how many years it would take to repay total debt based on earnings before income taxes, depreciation and amortization (an approximation of operating cash flow).

Interest Coverage This ratio measures the number of times a company's EBIT could cover its interest payments. Thus, it is sometimes referred to as "times interest earned." A higher **interest coverage** ratio indicates stronger solvency, offering greater assurance that the company can service its debt (i.e., bank debt, bonds, notes) from operating earnings.

Fixed Charge Coverage This ratio relates fixed charges, or obligations, to the cash flow generated by the company. It measures the number of times a company's earnings (before interest, taxes, and lease payments) can cover the company's interest and lease payments.[9] Similar to the interest coverage ratio, a higher **fixed charge coverage** ratio implies stronger solvency, offering greater assurance that the company can service its debt (i.e., bank debt, bonds, notes, and leases) from normal earnings. The ratio is sometimes used as an indication of the quality of the preferred dividend, with a higher ratio indicating a more secure preferred dividend.

Example 11 demonstrates the use of solvency ratios in evaluating the creditworthiness of a company.

EXAMPLE 11

Evaluation of Solvency Ratios

A credit analyst is evaluating the solvency of Eskom, a South African public utility based on financial statements for the year ended 31 March 2017. The following data are gathered from the company's 2017 annual report:

South African Rand, millions	**2017**	**2016**	**2015**
Total Assets	710,009	663,170	559,688
Short Term Debt	18,530	15,688	19,976
Long Term Debt	336,770	306,970	277,458
Total Liabilities	534,067	480,818	441,269
Total Equity	175,942	182,352	118,419

1 A Calculate the company's financial leverage ratio for 2016 and 2017.

B Interpret the financial leverage ratio calculated in Part A.

2 A What are the company's debt-to-assets, debt-to-capital, and debt-to-equity ratios for the three years?

B Is there any discernable trend over the three years?

Solutions to 1:

(Amounts are millions of Rand.)

A For 2017, average total assets were (710,009 + 663,170)/2 = 686,590, and average total equity was (175,942 + 182,352)/2 = 179,147. Thus, financial leverage was 686,590/179,942 = 3.83. For 2016, financial leverage was 4.07.

	2017	**2016**
Average Assets	686,590	611,429
Average Equity	179,147	150,386
Financial Leverage	3.83	4.07

B For 2017, every Rand in total equity supported R3.83 in total assets, on average. Financial leverage decreased from 2016 to 2017 on this measure.

9 For computing this ratio, an assumption sometimes made is that one-third of the lease payment amount represents interest on the lease obligation and that the rest is a repayment of principal on the obligation. For this variant of the fixed charge coverage ratio, the numerator is EBIT plus one-third of lease payments and the denominator is interest payments plus one-third of lease payments.

Solutions to 2:

(Amounts are millions of Rand other than ratios)

A

	2017	2016	2015
Total Debt	355,300	322,658	297,434
Total Capital	531,242	505,010	415,853
Debt/Assets	50.0%	48.7%	53.1%
Debt/Capital	66.9%	63.9%	71.5%
Debt/Equity	2.02	1.77	2.51

B On all three metrics, the company's leverage decreased from 2015 to 2016 and increased from 2016 to 2017. For 2016 the decrease in leverage resulted from a conversion of subordinated debt into equity as well as additional issuance of equity. However, in 2017 debt levels increased again relative to assets, capital and equity indicating that the company's solvency has weakened. From a creditor's perspective, lower solvency (higher debt) indicates higher risk of default on obligations.

As with all ratio analysis, it is important to consider leverage ratios in a broader context. In general, companies with lower business risk and operations that generate steady cash flows are better positioned to take on more leverage without a commensurate increase in the risk of insolvency. In other words, a higher proportion of debt financing poses less risk of non-payment of interest and debt principal to a company with steady cash flows than to a company with volatile cash flows.

4.5 Profitability Ratios

The ability to generate profit on capital invested is a key determinant of a company's overall value and the value of the securities it issues. Consequently, many equity analysts would consider profitability to be a key focus of their analytical efforts.

Profitability reflects a company's competitive position in the market, and by extension, the quality of its management. The income statement reveals the sources of earnings and the components of revenue and expenses. Earnings can be distributed to shareholders or reinvested in the company. Reinvested earnings enhance solvency and provide a cushion against short-term problems.

4.5.1 *Calculation of Profitability Ratios*

Profitability ratios measure the return earned by the company during a period. Exhibit 15 provides the definitions of a selection of commonly used profitability ratios. Return-on-sales profitability ratios express various subtotals on the income statement (e.g., gross profit, operating profit, net profit) as a percentage of revenue. Essentially, these ratios constitute part of a common-size income statement discussed earlier. Return on investment profitability ratios measure income relative to assets, equity, or total capital employed by the company. For operating ROA, returns are measured as operating income, i.e., prior to deducting interest on debt capital. For ROA and ROE, returns are measured as net income, i.e., after deducting interest paid on debt capital. For return on common equity, returns are measured as net income minus preferred dividends (because preferred dividends are a return to preferred equity).

Exhibit 15 Definitions of Commonly Used Profitability Ratios

Profitability Ratios	Numerator	Denominator
Return on Sales[a]		
Gross profit margin	Gross profit	Revenue
Operating profit margin	Operating income[b]	Revenue
Pretax margin	EBT (earnings before tax but after interest)	Revenue
Net profit margin	Net income	Revenue
Return on Investment		
Operating ROA	Operating income	Average total assets
ROA	Net income	Average total assets
Return on total capital	EBIT	Average short- and long-term debt and equity
ROE	Net income	Average total equity
Return on common equity	Net income – Preferred dividends	Average common equity

[a] "Sales" is being used as a synonym for "revenue."
[b] Some analysts use EBIT as a shortcut representation of operating income. Note that EBIT, strictly speaking, includes non-operating items such as dividends received and gains and losses on investment securities. Of utmost importance is that the analyst compute ratios consistently whether comparing different companies or analyzing one company over time.

4.5.2 *Interpretation of Profitability Ratios*

In the following, we discuss the interpretation of the profitability ratios presented in Exhibit 15. For each of the profitability ratios, a higher ratio indicates greater profitability.

Gross Profit Margin **Gross profit margin** indicates the percentage of revenue available to cover operating and other expenses and to generate profit. Higher gross profit margin indicates some combination of higher product pricing and lower product costs. The ability to charge a higher price is constrained by competition, so gross profits are affected by (and usually inversely related to) competition. If a product has a competitive advantage (e.g., superior branding, better quality, or exclusive technology), the company is better able to charge more for it. On the cost side, higher gross profit margin can also indicate that a company has a competitive advantage in product costs.

Operating Profit Margin Operating profit is calculated as gross profit minus operating costs. So, an **operating profit margin** increasing faster than the gross profit margin can indicate improvements in controlling operating costs, such as administrative overheads. In contrast, a declining operating profit margin could be an indicator of deteriorating control over operating costs.

Pretax Margin Pretax income (also called "earnings before tax" or "EBT") is calculated as operating profit minus interest, and the **pretax margin** is the ratio of pretax income to revenue. The pretax margin reflects the effects on profitability of leverage and other (non-operating) income and expenses. If a company's pretax margin is increasing primarily as a result of increasing amounts of non-operating income, the analyst should evaluate whether this increase reflects a deliberate change in a company's business focus and, therefore, the likelihood that the increase will continue.

Net Profit Margin Net profit, or net income, is calculated as revenue minus all expenses. Net income includes both recurring and non-recurring components. Generally, the net income used in calculating the net profit margin is adjusted for non-recurring items to offer a better view of a company's potential future profitability.

ROA ROA measures the return earned by a company on its assets. The higher the ratio, the more income is generated by a given level of assets. Most databases compute this ratio as:

$$\frac{\text{Net income}}{\text{Average total assets}}$$

An issue with this computation is that net income is the return to equity holders, whereas assets are financed by both equity holders and creditors. Interest expense (the return to creditors) has already been subtracted in the numerator. Some analysts, therefore, prefer to add back interest expense in the numerator. In such cases, interest must be adjusted for income taxes because net income is determined after taxes. With this adjustment, the ratio would be computed as:

$$\frac{\text{Net income} + \text{Interest expense}(1 - \text{Tax rate})}{\text{Average total assets}}$$

Alternatively, some analysts elect to compute ROA on a pre-interest and pre-tax basis (operating ROA in Exhibit 15) as:

$$\frac{\text{Operating income or EBIT}}{\text{Average total assets}}$$

In this ROA calculation, returns are measured prior to deducting interest on debt capital (i.e., as operating income or EBIT). This measure reflects the return on all assets invested in the company, whether financed with liabilities, debt, or equity. Whichever form of ROA is chosen, the analyst must use it consistently in comparisons to other companies or time periods.

Return on Total Capital **Return on total capital** measures the profits a company earns on all of the capital that it employs (short-term debt, long-term debt, and equity). As with operating ROA, returns are measured prior to deducting interest on debt capital (i.e., as operating income or EBIT).

ROE ROE measures the return earned by a company on its equity capital, including minority equity, preferred equity, and common equity. As noted, return is measured as net income (i.e., interest on debt capital is not included in the return on equity capital). A variation of ROE is return on common equity, which measures the return earned by a company only on its common equity.

Both ROA and ROE are important measures of profitability and will be explored in more detail in section 4.6.2. As with other ratios, profitability ratios should be evaluated individually and as a group to gain an understanding of what is driving profitability (operating versus non-operating activities). Example 12 demonstrates the evaluation of profitability ratios and the use of the management report (sometimes called management's discussion and analysis or management commentary) that accompanies financial statements to explain the trend in ratios.

EXAMPLE 12

Evaluation of Profitability Ratios

Recall from Example 1 that an analysis found that Apple's gross margin declined over the three-year period FY2015 to FY2017. An analyst would like to further explore Apple's profitability using a five-year period. He gathers the following revenue data and calculates the following profitability ratios from information in Apple's annual reports:

Dollars in millions	2017	2016	2015	2014	2013
Sales	229,234	215,639	233,715	182,795	170,910
Gross Profit	88,186	84,263	93,626	70,537	64,304
Operating Income	61,344	60,024	71,230	52,503	48,999
Pre-tax Income	64,089	61,372	72,515	53,483	50,155
Net Income	48,351	45,687	53,394	39,510	37,037
Gross profit margin	38.47%	39.08%	40.06%	38.59%	37.62%
Operating income margin	26.76%	27.84%	30.48%	28.72%	28.67%
Pre-tax income	27.96%	28.46%	31.03%	29.26%	29.35%
Net profit margin	21.09%	21.19%	22.85%	21.61%	21.67%

Evaluate the overall trend in Apple's profitability ratios for the five-year period.

Solution:

Sales had increased steadily through 2015, dropped in 2016, and rebounded somewhat in 2017. As noted in Example 1, the sales decline in 2016 was related to a decline in iPhone sales and weakness in foreign currencies. Margins also rose from 2013 to 2015 and declined in 2016. However, in spite of the increase in sales in 2017, all margins declined slightly indicating costs were rising faster than sales. In spite of the fluctuations, Apple's bottom line net profit margin was relatively stable over the five-year period.

4.6 Integrated Financial Ratio Analysis

In prior sections, the text presented separately activity, liquidity, solvency, and profitability ratios. Prior to discussing valuation ratios, the following sections demonstrate the importance of examining a variety of financial ratios—not a single ratio or category of ratios in isolation—to ascertain the overall position and performance of a company. Experience shows that the information from one ratio category can be helpful in answering questions raised by another category and that the most accurate overall picture comes from integrating information from all sources. Section 4.6.1 provides some introductory examples of such analysis and Section 4.6.2 shows how return on equity can be analyzed into components related to profit margin, asset utilization (activity), and financial leverage.

4.6.1 *The Overall Ratio Picture: Examples*

This section presents two simple illustrations to introduce the use of a variety of ratios to address an analytical task. Example 13 shows how the analysis of a pair of activity ratios resolves an issue concerning a company's liquidity. Example 14 shows that examining the overall ratios of multiple companies can assist an analyst in drawing conclusions about their relative performances.

EXAMPLE 13

A Variety of Ratios

An analyst is evaluating the liquidity of a Canadian manufacturing company and obtains the following liquidity ratios:

Fiscal Year	10	9	8
Current ratio	2.1	1.9	1.6
Quick ratio	0.8	0.9	1.0

The ratios present a contradictory picture of the company's liquidity. Based on the increase in its current ratio from 1.6 to 2.1, the company appears to have strong and improving liquidity; however, based on the decline of the quick ratio from 1.0 to 0.8, its liquidity appears to be deteriorating. Because both ratios have exactly the same denominator, current liabilities, the difference must be the result of changes in some asset that is included in the current ratio but not in the quick ratio (e.g., inventories). The analyst collects the following activity ratios:

DOH	55	45	30
DSO	24	28	30

The company's DOH has deteriorated from 30 days to 55 days, meaning that the company is holding increasingly larger amounts of inventory relative to sales. The decrease in DSO implies that the company is collecting receivables faster. If the proceeds from these collections were held as cash, there would be no effect on either the current ratio or the quick ratio. However, if the proceeds from the collections were used to purchase inventory, there would be no effect on the current ratio and a decline in the quick ratio (i.e., the pattern shown in this example). Collectively, the ratios suggest that liquidity is declining and that the company may have an inventory problem that needs to be addressed.

EXAMPLE 14

A Comparison of Two Companies (1)

An analyst collects the information[10] shown in Exhibit 16 for two hypothetical companies:

10 Note that ratios are expressed in terms of two decimal places and are rounded. Therefore, expected relationships may not hold perfectly.

Exhibit 16

	Fiscal Year			
Anson Industries	**5**	**4**	**3**	**2**
Inventory turnover	76.69	89.09	147.82	187.64
DOH	4.76	4.10	2.47	1.95
Receivables turnover	10.75	9.33	11.14	7.56
DSO	33.95	39.13	32.77	48.29
Accounts payable turnover	4.62	4.36	4.84	4.22
Days payable	78.97	83.77	75.49	86.56
Cash from operations/Total liabilities	31.41%	11.15%	4.04%	8.81%
ROE	5.92%	1.66%	1.62%	−0.62%
ROA	3.70%	1.05%	1.05%	−0.39%
Net profit margin (Net income/Revenue)	3.33%	1.11%	1.13%	−0.47%
Total asset turnover (Revenue/Average assets)	1.11	0.95	0.93	0.84
Leverage (Average assets/Average equity)	1.60	1.58	1.54	1.60

	Fiscal Year			
Clarence Corporation	**5**	**4**	**3**	**2**
Inventory turnover	9.19	9.08	7.52	14.84
DOH	39.73	40.20	48.51	24.59
Receivables turnover	8.35	7.01	6.09	5.16
DSO	43.73	52.03	59.92	70.79
Accounts payable turnover	6.47	6.61	7.66	6.52
Days payable	56.44	55.22	47.64	56.00
Cash from operations/Total liabilities	13.19%	16.39%	15.80%	11.79%
ROE	9.28%	6.82%	−3.63%	−6.75%
ROA	4.64%	3.48%	−1.76%	−3.23%
Net profit margin (Net income/Revenue)	4.38%	3.48%	−1.60%	−2.34%
Total asset turnover (Revenue/Average assets)	1.06	1.00	1.10	1.38
Leverage (Average assets/Average equity)	2.00	1.96	2.06	2.09

Which of the following choices best describes reasonable conclusions an analyst might make about the companies' efficiency?

A Over the past four years, Anson has shown greater improvement in efficiency than Clarence, as indicated by its total asset turnover ratio increasing from 0.84 to 1.11.

B In FY5, Anson's DOH of only 4.76 indicated that it was less efficient at inventory management than Clarence, which had DOH of 39.73.

C In FY5, Clarence's receivables turnover of 8.35 times indicated that it was more efficient at receivables management than Anson, which had receivables turnover of 10.75.

Solution:

A is correct. Over the past four years, Anson has shown greater improvement in efficiency than Clarence, as indicated by its total asset turnover ratio increasing from 0.84 to 1.11. Over the same period of time, Clarence's total asset turnover ratio has declined from 1.38 to 1.06. Choices B and C are incorrect because DOH and receivables turnover are misinterpreted.

4.6.2 *DuPont Analysis: The Decomposition of ROE*

As noted earlier, ROE measures the return a company generates on its equity capital. To understand what drives a company's ROE, a useful technique is to decompose ROE into its component parts. (Decomposition of ROE is sometimes referred to as **DuPont analysis** because it was developed originally at that company.) Decomposing ROE involves expressing the basic ratio (i.e., net income divided by average shareholders' equity) as the product of component ratios. Because each of these component ratios is an indicator of a distinct aspect of a company's performance that affects ROE, the decomposition allows us to evaluate how these different aspects of performance affected the company's profitability as measured by ROE.[11]

Decomposing ROE is useful in determining the reasons for changes in ROE over time for a given company and for differences in ROE for different companies in a given time period. The information gained can also be used by management to determine which areas they should focus on to improve ROE. This decomposition will also show why a company's overall profitability, measured by ROE, is a function of its efficiency, operating profitability, taxes, and use of financial leverage. DuPont analysis shows the relationship between the various categories of ratios discussed in this reading and how they all influence the return to the investment of the owners.

Analysts have developed several different methods of decomposing ROE. The decomposition presented here is one of the most commonly used and the one found in popular research databases, such as Bloomberg. Return on equity is calculated as:

ROE = Net income/Average shareholders' equity

The decomposition of ROE makes use of simple algebra and illustrates the relationship between ROE and ROA. Expressing ROE as a product of only two of its components, we can write:

$$\begin{aligned}\text{ROE} &= \frac{\text{Net income}}{\text{Average shareholders' equity}} \\ &= \frac{\text{Net income}}{\text{Average total assets}} \times \frac{\text{Average total assets}}{\text{Average shareholders' equity}}\end{aligned} \quad (1a)$$

which can be interpreted as:

ROE = ROA × Leverage

11 For purposes of analyzing ROE, this method usually uses average balance sheet factors; however, the math will work out if beginning or ending balances are used throughout. For certain purposes, these alternative methods may be appropriate.

In other words, ROE is a function of a company's ROA and its use of financial leverage ("leverage" for short, in this discussion). A company can improve its ROE by improving ROA or making more effective use of leverage. Consistent with the definition given earlier, leverage is measured as average total assets divided by average shareholders' equity. If a company had no leverage (no liabilities), its leverage ratio would equal 1.0 and ROE would exactly equal ROA. As a company takes on liabilities, its leverage increases. As long as a company is able to borrow at a rate lower than the marginal rate it can earn investing the borrowed money in its business, the company is making an effective use of leverage and ROE would increase as leverage increases. If a company's borrowing cost exceeds the marginal rate it can earn on investing in the business, ROE would decline as leverage increased because the effect of borrowing would be to depress ROA.

Using the data from Example 14 for Anson Industries, an analyst can examine the trend in ROE and determine whether the increase from an ROE of −0.625 percent in FY2 to 5.925 percent in FY5 is a function of ROA or the use of leverage:

	ROE	=	ROA	×	Leverage
FY5	5.92%		3.70%		1.60
FY4	1.66%		1.05%		1.58
FY3	1.62%		1.05%		1.54
FY2	−0.62%		−0.39%		1.60

Over the four-year period, the company's leverage factor was relatively stable. The primary reason for the increase in ROE is the increase in profitability measured by ROA.

Just as ROE can be decomposed, the individual components such as ROA can be decomposed. Further decomposing ROA, we can express ROE as a product of three component ratios:

$$\frac{\text{Net income}}{\text{Average shareholders' equity}} = \frac{\text{Net income}}{\text{Revenue}} \times \frac{\text{Revenue}}{\text{Average total assets}} \times \frac{\text{Average total assets}}{\text{Average shareholders' equity}} \tag{1b}$$

which can be interpreted as:

ROE = Net profit margin × Total asset turnover × Leverage

The first term on the right-hand side of this equation is the net profit margin, an indicator of profitability: how much income a company derives per one monetary unit (e.g., euro or dollar) of sales. The second term on the right is the asset turnover ratio, an indicator of efficiency: how much revenue a company generates per one money unit of assets. Note that ROA is decomposed into these two components: net profit margin and total asset turnover. A company's ROA is a function of profitability (net profit margin) and efficiency (total asset turnover). The third term on the right-hand side of Equation 1b is a measure of financial leverage, an indicator of solvency: the total amount of a company's assets relative to its equity capital. This decomposition illustrates that a company's ROE is a function of its net profit margin, its efficiency, and its leverage. Again, using the data from Example 14 for Anson Industries, the analyst can evaluate in more detail the reasons behind the trend in ROE:[12]

12 Ratios are expressed in terms of two decimal places and are rounded. Therefore, ROE may not be the exact product of the three ratios.

	ROE	=	Net profit margin	×	Total asset turnover	×	Leverage
FY5	5.92%		3.33%		1.11		1.60
FY4	1.66%		1.11%		0.95		1.58
FY3	1.62%		1.13%		0.93		1.54
FY2	−0.62%		−0.47%		0.84		1.60

This further decomposition confirms that increases in profitability (measured here as net profit margin) are indeed an important contributor to the increase in ROE over the four-year period. However, Anson's asset turnover has also increased steadily. The increase in ROE is, therefore, a function of improving profitability and improving efficiency. As noted above, ROE decomposition can also be used to compare the ROEs of peer companies, as demonstrated in Example 15.

EXAMPLE 15

A Comparison of Two Companies (2)

Referring to the data for Anson Industries and Clarence Corporation in Example 14, which of the following choices best describes reasonable conclusions an analyst might make about the companies' ROE?

A Anson's inventory turnover of 76.69 indicates it is more profitable than Clarence.

B The main driver of Clarence's superior ROE in FY5 is its more efficient use of assets.

C The main drivers of Clarence's superior ROE in FY5 are its greater use of debt financing and higher net profit margin.

Solution:

C is correct. The main driver of Clarence's superior ROE (9.28 percent compared with only 5.92 percent for Anson) in FY5 is its greater use of debt financing (leverage of 2.00 compared with Anson's leverage of 1.60) and higher net profit margin (4.38 percent compared with only 3.33 percent for Anson). A is incorrect because inventory turnover is not a direct indicator of profitability. An increase in inventory turnover may indicate more efficient use of inventory which in turn could affect profitability; however, an increase in inventory turnover would also be observed if a company was selling more goods even if it was not selling those goods at a profit. B is incorrect because Clarence has less efficient use of assets than Anson, indicated by turnover of 1.06 for Clarence compared with Anson's turnover of 1.11.

To separate the effects of taxes and interest, we can further decompose the net profit margin and write:

$$\frac{\text{Net income}}{\text{Average shareholders' equity}} = \frac{\text{Net income}}{\text{EBT}} \times \frac{\text{EBT}}{\text{EBIT}} \times \frac{\text{EBIT}}{\text{Revenue}} \times \frac{\text{Revenue}}{\text{Average total assets}} \times \frac{\text{Average total assets}}{\text{Average shareholders' equity}} \qquad \text{(1c)}$$

which can be interpreted as:

ROE = Tax burden × Interest burden × EBIT margin × Total asset turnover × Leverage

This five-way decomposition is the one found in financial databases such as Bloomberg. The first term on the right-hand side of this equation measures the effect of taxes on ROE. Essentially, it reflects one minus the average tax rate, or how much of a company's pretax profits it gets to keep. This can be expressed in decimal or percentage form. So, a 30 percent tax rate would yield a factor of 0.70 or 70 percent. A higher value for the tax burden implies that the company can keep a higher percentage of its pretax profits, indicating a lower tax rate. A decrease in the tax burden ratio implies the opposite (i.e., a higher tax rate leaving the company with less of its pretax profits).

The second term on the right-hand side captures the effect of interest on ROE. Higher borrowing costs reduce ROE. Some analysts prefer to use operating income instead of EBIT for this term and the following term. Either operating income or EBIT is acceptable as long as it is applied consistently. In such a case, the second term would measure both the effect of interest expense and non-operating income on ROE.

The third term on the right-hand side captures the effect of operating margin (if operating income is used in the numerator) or EBIT margin (if EBIT is used) on ROE. In either case, this term primarily measures the effect of operating profitability on ROE.

The fourth term on the right-hand side is again the total asset turnover ratio, an indicator of the overall efficiency of the company (i.e., how much revenue it generates per unit of total assets). The fifth term on the right-hand side is the financial leverage ratio described above—the total amount of a company's assets relative to its equity capital.

This decomposition expresses a company's ROE as a function of its tax rate, interest burden, operating profitability, efficiency, and leverage. An analyst can use this framework to determine what factors are driving a company's ROE. The decomposition of ROE can also be useful in forecasting ROE based upon expected efficiency, profitability, financing activities, and tax rates. The relationship of the individual factors, such as ROA to the overall ROE, can also be expressed in the form of an ROE tree to study the contribution of each of the five factors, as shown in Exhibit 17 for Anson Industries.[13]

Exhibit 17 shows that Anson's ROE of 5.92 percent in FY5 can be decomposed into ROA of 3.70 percent and leverage of 1.60. ROA can further be decomposed into a net profit margin of 3.33 percent and total asset turnover of 1.11. Net profit margin can be decomposed into a tax burden of 0.70 (an average tax rate of 30 percent), an interest burden of 0.90, and an EBIT margin of 5.29 percent. Overall ROE is decomposed into five components.

13 Note that a breakdown of net profit margin was not provided in Example 14, but is added here.

Exhibit 17 DuPont Analysis of Anson Industries' ROE: Fiscal Year 5

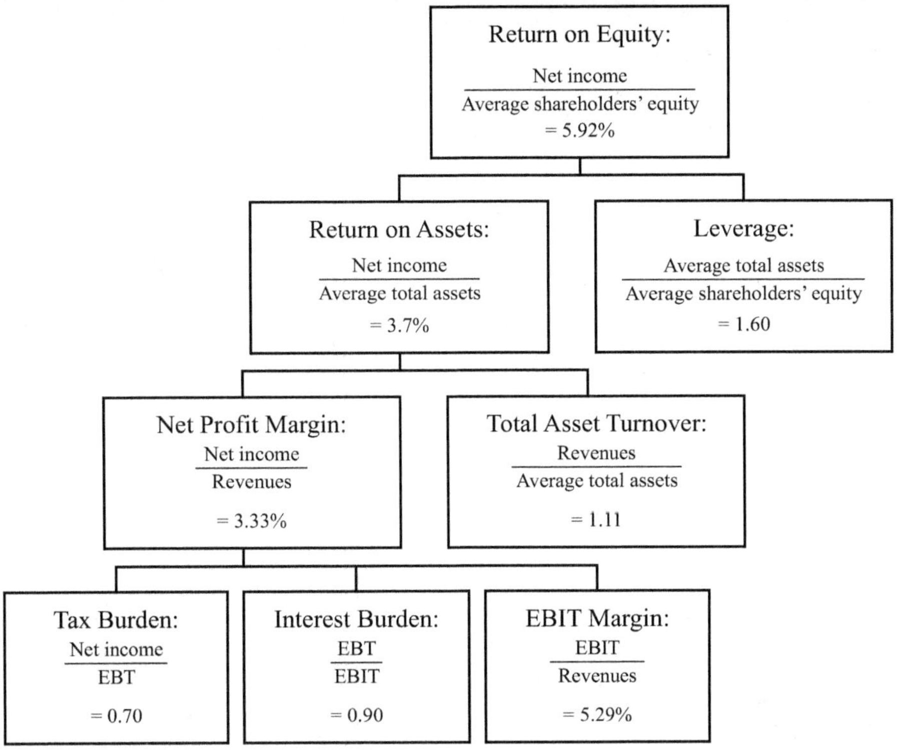

Example 16 demonstrates how the five-component decomposition can be used to determine reasons behind the trend in a company's ROE.

EXAMPLE 16

Five-Way Decomposition of ROE

An analyst examining Amsterdam PLC (a hypothetical company) wishes to understand the factors driving the trend in ROE over a four-year period. The analyst obtains and calculates the following data from Amsterdam's annual reports:

	2017	2016	2015	2014
ROE	9.53%	20.78%	26.50%	24.72%
Tax burden	60.50%	52.10%	63.12%	58.96%
Interest burden	97.49%	97.73%	97.86%	97.49%
EBIT margin	7.56%	11.04%	13.98%	13.98%
Asset turnover	0.99	1.71	1.47	1.44
Leverage	2.15	2.17	2.10	2.14

What might the analyst conclude?

Solution:

The tax burden measure has varied, with no obvious trend. In the most recent year, 2017, taxes declined as a percentage of pretax profit. (Because the tax burden reflects the relation of after-tax profits to pretax profits, the increase from 52.10 percent in 2016 to 60.50 percent in 2017 indicates that taxes declined as a percentage of pretax profits.) This decline in average tax rates could be a result of lower tax rates from new legislation or revenue in a lower tax jurisdiction. The interest burden has remained fairly constant over the four-year period indicating that the company maintains a fairly constant capital structure. Operating margin (EBIT margin) declined over the period, indicating the company's operations were less profitable. This decline is generally consistent with declines in oil prices in 2017 and declines in refining industry gross margins in 2016 and 2017. The company's efficiency (asset turnover) decreased in 2017. The company's leverage remained constant, consistent with the constant interest burden. Overall, the trend in ROE (declining substantially over the recent years) resulted from decreases in operating profits and a lower asset turnover. Additional research on the causes of these changes is required in order to develop expectations about the company's future performance.

The most detailed decomposition of ROE that we have presented is a five-way decomposition. Nevertheless, an analyst could further decompose individual components of a five-way analysis. For example, EBIT margin (EBIT/Revenue) could be further decomposed into a non-operating component (EBIT/Operating income) and an operating component (Operating income/Revenue). The analyst can also examine which other factors contributed to these five components. For example, an improvement in efficiency (total asset turnover) may have resulted from better management of inventory (DOH) or better collection of receivables (DSO).

5 EQUITY ANALYSIS

One application of financial analysis is to select securities as part of the equity portfolio management process. Analysts are interested in valuing a security to assess its merits for inclusion or retention in a portfolio. The valuation process has several steps, including:

1 understanding the business and the existing financial profile
2 forecasting company performance
3 selecting the appropriate valuation model
4 converting forecasts to a valuation
5 making the investment decision

Financial analysis assists in providing the core information to complete the first two steps of this valuation process: understanding the business and forecasting performance.

Fundamental equity analysis involves evaluating a company's performance and valuing its equity in order to assess its relative attractiveness as an investment. Analysts use a variety of methods to value a company's equity, including valuation ratios (e.g., the price-to-earnings or P/E ratio), discounted cash flow approaches, and residual income approaches (ROE compared with the cost of capital), among others. The following section addresses the first of these approaches—the use of valuation ratios.

5.1 Valuation Ratios

Valuation ratios have long been used in investment decision making. A well known example is the **price to earnings ratio** (P/E ratio)—probably the most widely cited indicator in discussing the value of equity securities—which relates share price to the earnings per share (EPS). Additionally, some analysts use other market multiples, such as price to book value (P/B) and price to cash flow (P/CF). The following sections explore valuation ratios and other quantities related to valuing equities.

5.1.1 *Calculation of Valuation Ratios and Related Quantities*

Exhibit 18 describes the calculation of some common valuation ratios and related quantities.

Exhibit 18 Definitions of Selected Valuation Ratios and Related Quantities

Valuation Ratios	Numerator	Denominator
P/E	Price per share	Earnings per share
P/CF	Price per share	Cash flow per share
P/S	Price per share	Sales per share
P/BV	Price per share	Book value per share

Per-Share Quantities	Numerator	Denominator
Basic EPS	Net income minus preferred dividends	Weighted average number of ordinary shares outstanding
Diluted EPS	Adjusted income available for ordinary shares, reflecting conversion of dilutive securities	Weighted average number of ordinary and potential ordinary shares outstanding
Cash flow per share	Cash flow from operations	Weighted average number of shares outstanding
EBITDA per share	EBITDA	Weighted average number of shares outstanding
Dividends per share	Common dividends declared	Weighted average number of ordinary shares outstanding

Dividend-Related Quantities	Numerator	Denominator
Dividend payout ratio	Common share dividends	Net income attributable to common shares
Retention rate (b)	Net income attributable to common shares – Common share dividends	Net income attributable to common shares
Sustainable growth rate	$b \times$ ROE	

The P/E ratio expresses the relationship between the price per share and the amount of earnings attributable to a single share. In other words, the P/E ratio tells us how much an investor in common stock pays per dollar of earnings.

Because P/E ratios are calculated using net income, the ratios can be sensitive to non-recurring earnings or one-time earnings events. In addition, because net income is generally considered to be more susceptible to manipulation than are cash flows, analysts may use **price to cash flow** as an alternative measure—particularly in situations where earnings quality may be an issue. EBITDA per share, because it is calculated using income before interest, taxes, and depreciation, can be used to eliminate the effect of different levels of fixed asset investment across companies. It facilitates comparison between companies in the same sector but at different stages of infrastructure maturity. **Price to sales** is calculated in a similar manner and is sometimes used as a comparative price metric when a company does not have positive net income.

Another price-based ratio that facilitates useful comparisons of companies' stock prices is **price to book value**, or P/B, which is the ratio of price to book value per share. This ratio is often interpreted as an indicator of market judgment about the relationship between a company's required rate of return and its actual rate of return. Assuming that book values reflect the fair values of the assets, a price to book ratio of one can be interpreted as an indicator that the company's future returns are expected to be exactly equal to the returns required by the market. A ratio greater than one would indicate that the future profitability of the company is expected to exceed the required rate of return, and values of this ratio less than one indicate that the company is not expected to earn excess returns.[14]

5.1.2 *Interpretation of Earnings per Share*

Exhibit 18 presented a number of per-share quantities that can be used in valuation ratios. In this section, we discuss the interpretation of one such critical quantity, earnings per share or EPS.[15]

EPS is simply the amount of earnings attributable to each share of common stock. In isolation, EPS does not provide adequate information for comparison of one company with another. For example, assume that two companies have only common stock outstanding and no dilutive securities outstanding. In addition, assume the two companies have identical net income of $10 million, identical book equity of $100 million and, therefore, identical profitability (10 percent, using ending equity in this case for simplicity). Furthermore, assume that Company A has 100 million weighted average common shares outstanding, whereas Company B has 10 million weighted average common shares outstanding. So, Company A will report EPS of $0.10 per share, and Company B will report EPS of $1 per share. The difference in EPS does not reflect a difference in profitability—the companies have identical profits and profitability. The difference reflects only a different number of common shares outstanding. Analysts should understand in detail the types of EPS information that companies report:

Basic EPS provides information regarding the earnings attributable to each share of common stock.[16] To calculate basic EPS, the weighted average number of shares outstanding during the period is first calculated. The weighted average number of shares consists of the number of ordinary shares outstanding at the beginning of the period, adjusted by those bought back or issued during the period, multiplied by a time-weighting factor.

Accounting standards generally require the disclosure of basic as well as **diluted EPS** (diluted EPS includes the effect of all the company's securities whose conversion or exercise would result in a reduction of basic EPS; dilutive securities include convertible debt, convertible preferred, warrants, and options). Basic EPS and diluted EPS must be shown with equal prominence on the face of the income statement for each class of ordinary share. Disclosure includes the amounts used as the numerators in calculating basic and diluted EPS, and a reconciliation of those amounts to the company's profit or loss for the period. Because both basic and diluted EPS are presented in a company's financial statements, an analyst does not need to calculate these measures for reported financial statements. Understanding the calculations is, however, helpful for situations requiring an analyst to calculate expected future EPS.

14 For more detail on valuation ratios as used in equity analysis, see the curriculum reading "Equity Valuation: Concepts and Basic Tools."
15 For more detail on EPS calculation, see the reading "Understanding Income Statements."
16 IAS 33, *Earnings per Share* and FASB ASC Topic 260 [Earnings per Share].

To calculate diluted EPS, earnings are adjusted for the after-tax effects assuming conversion, and the following adjustments are made to the weighted number of shares:

- The weighted average number of shares for basic EPS, *plus* those that would be issued on conversion of all potentially dilutive ordinary shares. Potential ordinary shares are treated as dilutive when their conversion would decrease net profit per share from continuing ordinary operations.
- These shares are deemed to have been converted into ordinary shares at the beginning of the period or, if later, at the date of the issue of the shares.
- Options, warrants (and their equivalents), convertible instruments, contingently issuable shares, contracts that can be settled in ordinary shares or cash, purchased options, and written put options should be considered.

5.1.3 *Dividend-Related Quantities*

In this section, we discuss the interpretation of the dividend-related quantities presented in Exhibit 18. These quantities play a role in some present value models for valuing equities.

Dividend Payout Ratio The **dividend payout ratio** measures the percentage of earnings that the company pays out as dividends to shareholders. The amount of dividends per share tends to be relatively fixed because any reduction in dividends has been shown to result in a disproportionately large reduction in share price. Because dividend amounts are relatively fixed, the dividend payout ratio tends to fluctuate with earnings. Therefore, conclusions about a company's dividend payout policies should be based on examination of payout over a number of periods. Optimal dividend policy, similar to optimal capital structure, has been examined in academic research and continues to be a topic of significant interest in corporate finance.

Retention Rate The retention rate, or earnings retention rate, is the complement of the payout ratio or dividend payout ratio (i.e., 1 – payout ratio). Whereas the payout ratio measures the percentage of earnings that a company pays out as dividends, the retention rate is the percentage of earnings that a company retains. (Note that both the payout ratio and retention rate are both percentages of earnings. The difference in terminology—"ratio" versus "rate" versus "percentage"—reflects common usage rather than any substantive differences.)

Sustainable Growth Rate A company's **sustainable growth rate** is viewed as a function of its profitability (measured as ROE) and its ability to finance itself from internally generated funds (measured as the retention rate). The sustainable growth rate is ROE times the retention rate. A higher ROE and a higher retention rate result in a higher sustainable growth rate. This calculation can be used to estimate a company's growth rate, a factor commonly used in equity valuation.

5.2 Industry-Specific Ratios

As stated earlier in this reading, a universally accepted definition and classification of ratios does not exist. The purpose of ratios is to serve as indicators of important aspects of a company's performance and value. Aspects of performance that are considered important in one industry may be irrelevant in another, and industry-specific ratios reflect these differences. For example, companies in the retail industry may report same-store sales changes because, in the retail industry, it is important to distinguish between growth that results from opening new stores and growth that results from generating more sales at existing stores. Industry-specific metrics can be especially important to the value of equity in early stage industries, where companies are not yet profitable.

In addition, regulated industries—especially in the financial sector—often are required to comply with specific regulatory ratios. For example, the banking sector's liquidity and cash reserve ratios provide an indication of banking liquidity and reflect monetary and regulatory requirements. Banking capital adequacy requirements attempt to relate banks' solvency requirements directly to their specific levels of risk exposure.

Exhibit 19 presents, for illustrative purposes only, some industry-specific and task-specific ratios.[17]

Exhibit 19 Definitions of Some Common Industry- and Task-Specific Ratios

Ratio	Numerator	Denominator
Business Risk		
Coefficient of variation of operating income	Standard deviation of operating income	Average operating income
Coefficient of variation of net income	Standard deviation of net income	Average net income
Coefficient of variation of revenues	Standard deviation of revenue	Average revenue
Financial Sector Ratios	**Numerator**	**Denominator**
Capital adequacy—banks	Various components of capital	Various measures such as risk-weighted assets, market risk exposure, or level of operational risk assumed
Monetary reserve requirement (Cash reserve ratio)	Reserves held at central bank	Specified deposit liabilities
Liquid asset requirement	Approved "readily marketable" securities	Specified deposit liabilities
Net interest margin	Net interest income	Total interest-earning assets
Retail Ratios	**Numerator**	**Denominator**
Same (or comparable) store sales	Average revenue growth year over year for stores open in both periods	Not applicable
Sales per square meter (or square foot)	Revenue	Total retail space in square meters (or square feet)

17 There are many other industry- and task-specific ratios that are outside the scope of this reading. Resources such as Standard and Poor's Industry Surveys present useful ratios for each industry. Industry organizations may present useful ratios for the industry or a task specific to the industry.

Exhibit 19 (Continued)

Service Companies	Numerator	Denominator
Revenue per employee	Revenue	Total number of employees
Net income per employee	Net income	Total number of employees

Hotel	Numerator	Denominator
Average daily rate	Room revenue	Number of rooms sold
Occupancy rate	Number of rooms sold	Number of rooms available

5.3 Historical Research on Ratios in Equity Analysis

Some ratios may be particularly useful in equity analysis. The end product of equity analysis is often a valuation and investment recommendation. Theoretical valuation models are useful in selecting ratios that would be useful in this process. For example, a company's P/B is theoretically linked to ROE, growth, and the required return. ROE is also a primary determinant of residual income in a residual income valuation model. In both cases, higher ROE relative to the required return denotes a higher valuation. Similarly, profit margin is related to justified price-to-sales (P/S) ratios. Another common valuation method involves forecasts of future cash flows that are discounted back to the present. Trends in ratios can be useful in forecasting future earnings and cash flows (e.g., trends in operating profit margin and collection of customer receivables). Future growth expectations are a key component of all of these valuation models. Trends may be useful in assessing growth prospects (when used in conjunction with overall economic and industry trends). The variability in ratios and common-size data can be useful in assessing risk, an important component of the required rate of return in valuation models. A great deal of academic research has focused on the use of these fundamental ratios in evaluating equity investments.

A classic study, Ou and Penman (1989a and 1989b), found that ratios and common-size metrics generated from accounting data were useful in forecasting earnings and stock returns. Ou and Penman examined 68 such metrics and found that these could be reduced to a more parsimonious list of relevant variables, including percentage changes in a variety of measures such as current ratio, inventory, and sales; gross and pretax margins; and returns on assets and equity. These variables were found to be useful in forecasting earnings and stock returns.

Subsequent studies have also demonstrated the usefulness of ratios in evaluation of equity investments and valuation. Lev and Thiagarajan (1993) examined fundamental financial variables used by analysts to assess whether they are useful in security valuation. They found that fundamental variables add about 70 percent to the explanatory power of earnings alone in predicting excess returns (stock returns in excess of those expected). The fundamental variables they found useful included percentage changes in inventory and receivables relative to sales, gross margin, sales per employee, and the change in bad debts relative to the change in accounts receivable, among others. Abarbanell and Bushee (1997) found some of the same variables useful in predicting future accounting earnings. Abarbanell and Bushee (1998) devised an investment strategy using these same variables and found that they can generate excess returns under this strategy.

Piotroski (2000) used financial ratios to supplement a value investing strategy and found that he can generate significant excess returns. Variables used by Piotroski include ROA, cash flow ROA, change in ROA, change in leverage, change in liquidity, change in gross margin, and change in inventory turnover.

This research shows that in addition to being useful in evaluating the past performance of a company, ratios can be useful in predicting future earnings and equity returns.

6 CREDIT ANALYSIS

Credit risk is the risk of loss caused by a counterparty's or debtor's failure to make a promised payment. For example, credit risk with respect to a bond is the risk that the obligor (the issuer of the bond) is not able to pay interest and principal according to the terms of the bond indenture (contract). **Credit analysis** is the evaluation of credit risk.

Approaches to credit analysis vary and, as with all financial analysis, depend on the purpose of the analysis and the context in which it is done. Credit analysis for specific types of debt (e.g., acquisition financing and other highly leveraged financing) often involves projections of period-by-period cash flows similar to projections made by equity analysts. Whereas the equity analyst may discount projected cash flows to determine the value of the company's equity, a credit analyst would use the projected cash flows to assess the likelihood of a company complying with its financial covenants in each period and paying interest and principal as due.[18] The analysis would also include expectations about asset sales and refinancing options open to the company.

Credit analysis may relate to the borrower's credit risk in a particular transaction or to its overall creditworthiness. In assessing overall creditworthiness, one general approach is credit scoring, a statistical analysis of the determinants of credit default.

Another general approach to credit analysis is the credit rating process that is used, for example, by credit rating agencies to assess and communicate the probability of default by an issuer on its debt obligations (e.g., commercial paper, notes, and bonds). A credit rating can be either long term or short term and is an indication of the rating agency's opinion of the creditworthiness of a debt issuer with respect to a specific debt security or other obligation. Where a company has no debt outstanding, a rating agency can also provide an issuer credit rating that expresses an opinion of the issuer's overall capacity and willingness to meet its financial obligations. The following sections review research on the use of ratios in credit analysis and the ratios commonly used in credit analysis.

6.1 The Credit Rating Process

The credit rating process involves both the analysis of a company's financial reports as well as a broad assessment of a company's operations. In assigning credit ratings, rating agencies emphasize the importance of the relationship between a company's business risk profile and its financial risk.

For corporate entities, credit ratings typically reflect a combination of qualitative and quantitative factors. Qualitative factors generally include an industry's growth prospects, volatility, technological change, and competitive environment. At the individual company level, qualitative factors may include operational effectiveness,

18 Financial covenants are clauses in bond indentures relating to the financial condition of the bond issuer.

strategy, governance, financial policies, risk management practices, and risk tolerance. In contrast, quantitative factors generally include profitability, leverage, cash flow adequacy, and liquidity.[19]

When analyzing financial ratios, rating agencies normally investigate deviations of ratios from the median ratios of the universe of companies for which such ratios have been calculated and also use the median ratings as an indicator for the ratings grade given to a specific debt issuer. This so-called universe of rated companies frequently changes, and any calculations are obviously affected by economic factors as well as by mergers and acquisitions. International ratings include the influence of country and economic risk factors. Exhibit 20 presents a few key financial ratios used by Standard & Poor's in evaluating industrial companies. Note that before calculating ratios, rating agencies make certain adjustments to reported financials such as adjusting debt to include off-balance sheet debt in a company's total debt.

Exhibit 20 Selected Credit Ratios

Credit Ratio	Numerator[a]	Denominator[a]
EBITDA interest coverage	EBITDA[b]	Interest expense, including non-cash interest on conventional debt instruments
FFO[c] (Funds from operations) to debt	FFO	Total debt
Free operating cash flow to debt	CFO[d] (adjusted) minus capital expenditures	Total debt
EBIT margin	EBIT[e]	Total revenues
EBITDA margin	EBITDA	Total revenues
Debt to EBITDA	Total debt	EBITDA
Return on capital	EBIT	Average beginning-of-year and end-of-year capital[f]

[a] Note that both the numerator and the denominator definitions are adjusted from ratio to ratio and may not correspond to the definitions used elsewhere in this reading.
[b] EBITDA = earnings before interest, taxes, depreciation, and amortization.
[c] FFO = funds from operations, defined as EBITDA minus net interest expense minus current tax expense (plus or minus all applicable adjustments).
[d] CFO = cash flow from operations.
[e] EBIT = earnings before interest and taxes.
[f] Capital = debt plus noncurrent deferred taxes plus equity (plus or minus all applicable adjustments).
Source: Based on data from Standard & Poor's *Corporate Methodology: Ratios And Adjustments* (2013). This represents the last updated version at the time of publication.

6.2 Historical Research on Ratios in Credit Analysis

A great deal of academic and practitioner research has focused on determining which ratios are useful in assessing the credit risk of a company, including the risk of bankruptcy.

One of the earliest studies examined individual ratios to assess their ability to predict failure of a company up to five years in advance. Beaver (1967) found that six ratios could correctly predict company failure one year in advance 90 percent of the

19 Concepts in this paragraph are based on Standard & Poor's *General Criteria: Principles of Credit Ratings* (2011). This represents the last updated version at the time of publication.

time and five years in advance at least 65 percent of the time. The ratios found effective by Beaver were cash flow to total debt, ROA, total debt to total assets, working capital to total assets, the current ratio, and the no-credit interval ratio (the length of time a company could go without borrowing). Altman (1968) and Altman, Haldeman, and Narayanan (1977) found that financial ratios could be combined in an effective model for predicting bankruptcy. Altman's initial work involved creation of a Z-score that was able to correctly predict financial distress. The Z-score was computed as

$$\begin{aligned} Z = {} & 1.2 \times (\text{Current assets} - \text{Current liabilities})/\text{Total assets} \\ & + 1.4 \times (\text{Retained earnings}/\text{Total assets}) \\ & + 3.3 \times (\text{EBIT}/\text{Total assets}) \\ & + 0.6 \times (\text{Market value of stock}/\text{Book value of liabilities}) \\ & + 1.0 \times (\text{Sales}/\text{Total assets}) \end{aligned}$$

In his initial study, a Z-score of lower than 1.81 predicted failure and the model was able to accurately classify 95 percent of companies studied into a failure group and a non-failure group. The original model was designed for manufacturing companies. Subsequent refinements to the models allow for other company types and time periods. Generally, the variables found to be useful in prediction include profitability ratios, coverage ratios, liquidity ratios, capitalization ratios, and earnings variability (Altman 2000).

Similar research has been performed on the ability of ratios to predict bond ratings and bond yields. For example, Ederington, Yawtiz, and Roberts (1987) found that a small number of variables (total assets, interest coverage, leverage, variability of coverage, and subordination status) were effective in explaining bond yields. Similarly, Ederington (1986) found that nine variables in combination could correctly classify more than 70 percent of bond ratings. These variables included ROA, long-term debt to assets, interest coverage, cash flow to debt, variability of coverage and cash flow, total assets, and subordination status. These studies have shown that ratios are effective in evaluating credit risk, bond yields, and bond ratings.

7 BUSINESS AND GEOGRAPHIC SEGMENTS

Analysts often need to evaluate the performance underlying business segments (subsidiary companies, operating units, or simply operations in different geographic areas) to understand in detail the company as a whole. Although companies are not required to provide full financial statements for segments, they are required to provide segment information under both IFRS and US GAAP.[20]

7.1 Segment Reporting Requirements

An operating segment is defined as a component of a company: a) that engages in activities that may generate revenue and create expenses, including a start-up segment that has yet to earn revenues, b) whose results are regularly reviewed by the company's senior management, and c) for which discrete financial information is available.[21] A company must disclose separate information about any operating segment which meets certain quantitative criteria—namely, the segment constitutes 10 percent or more of the combined operating segments' revenue, assets, or profit. (For purposes

20 IFRS 8, *Operating Segments* and FASB ASC Topic 280 [Segment Reporting].
21 IFRS 8, *Operating Segments,* paragraph 5.

of determining whether a segment constitutes 10 percent or more of combined profits or losses, the criteria is expressed in terms of the absolute value of the segment's profit or loss as a percentage of the greater of (i) the combined profits of all profitable segments and (ii) the absolute amount of the combined losses of all loss-making segments.) If, after applying these quantitative criteria, the combined revenue from external customers for all reportable segments combined is less than 75 percent of the total company revenue, the company must identify additional reportable segments until the 75 percent level is reached. Small segments might be combined as one if they share a substantial number of factors that define a business or geographical segment, or they might be combined with a similar significant reportable segment. Information about operating segments and businesses that are not reportable is combined in an "all other segments" category.

Companies may internally report business results in a variety of ways (e.g., product segments and geographical segments). Companies identify the segments for external reporting purposes considering the definition of an operating segment and using factors such as what information is reported to the board of directors and whether a manager is responsible for each segment. Companies must disclose the factors used to identify reportable segments and the types of products and services sold by each reportable segment.

For each reportable segment, the following should also be disclosed:

- a measure of profit or loss;
- a measure of total assets and liabilities[22] (if these amounts are regularly reviewed by the company's chief decision-making officer);
- segment revenue, distinguishing between revenue to external customers and revenue from other segments;
- interest revenue and interest expense;
- cost of property, plant, and equipment, and intangible assets acquired;
- depreciation and amortisation expense;
- other non-cash expenses;
- income tax expense or income; and
- share of the net profit or loss of an investment accounted for under the equity method.

Companies also must provide a reconciliation between the information of reportable segments and the consolidated financial statements in terms of segment revenue, profit or loss, assets, and liabilities.

Another disclosure required is the company's reliance on any single customer. If any single customer represents 10 percent or more of the company's total revenues, the company must disclose that fact. From an analysts' perspective, information about a concentrated customer base can be useful in assessing the risks faced by the company.

7.2 Segment Ratios

Based on the segment information that companies are required to present, a variety of useful ratios can be computed, as shown in Exhibit 21.

22 IFRS 8 and FASB ASC Topic 280 are largely converged. One notable difference is that US GAAP does not require disclosure of segment liabilities, while IFRS requires disclosure of segment liabilities if that information is regularly provided to the company's "chief operating decision maker."

Exhibit 21 Definitions of Segment Ratios

Segment Ratios	Numerator	Denominator
Segment margin	Segment profit (loss)	Segment revenue
Segment turnover	Segment revenue	Segment assets
Segment ROA	Segment profit (loss)	Segment assets
Segment debt ratio	Segment liabilities	Segment assets

The segment margin measures the operating profitability of the segment relative to revenues, whereas the segment ROA measures the operating profitability relative to assets. Segment turnover measures the overall efficiency of the segment: how much revenue is generated per unit of assets. The segment debt ratio examines the level of liabilities (hence solvency) of the segment. Example 17 demonstrates the evaluation of segment ratios.

EXAMPLE 17

The Evaluation of Segment Ratios

The information contained in Exhibit 22 relates to the business segments of Groupe Danone for 2016 and 2017 in millions of euro. According to the company's 2017 annual report the company operates in four business segments which are primarily evaluated on operating income and operating margin and in two geographic segments for which they also provide information on assets deployed.

Evaluate the performance of the segments using the relative proportion of sales of each segment, the segment margins, segment ROA where available, and segment turnover where available.

Exhibit 22 Group Danone Segment Disclosures (in € millions)

	2016		2017	
Business Segments	Sales	Recurring Operating Income	Sales	Recurring Operating Income
Fresh Dairy Products – International	8,229	731	8,424	760
Fresh Dairy Products – North America	2,506	351	4,530	556
Specialized Nutrition	6,634	1,419	7,102	1,685
Waters	4,574	521	4,621	541
Group Total	21,944	3,022	24,677	3,542

Exhibit 22 (Continued)

Geographic Segments	2016 Sales	2016 Recurring Operating Income	2016 Non-Current Assets	2017 Sales	2017 Recurring Operating Income	2017 Non-Current Assets
Europe and North America	10,933	1,842	11,532	13,193	2,048	22,517
Rest of World	11,011	1,180	9,307	11,484	1,495	8,433
Group Total	21,944	3,022	20,839	24,677	3,543	30,950

Source: Company's 2017 Annual Report.

Solution:

Business Segments	2016 Segment Revenue Percent	2016 Recurring Operating Margin	2017 Segment Revenue Percent	2017 Recurring Operating Margin
Fresh Dairy Products – International	37.5%	8.9%	34.1%	9.0%
Fresh Dairy Products – North America	11.4%	14.0%	18.4%	12.3%
Specialized Nutrition	30.2%	21.4%	28.8%	23.7%
Waters	20.8%	11.4%	18.7%	11.7%
Group Total	100.0%	13.8%	100.0%	14.4%

Business Segments	2017 % change in revenue
Fresh Dairy Products – International	2.4%
Fresh Dairy Products – North America	80.8%
Specialized Nutrition	7.1%
Waters	1.0%
Group Total	12.5%

The business segment analysis shows that the largest proportion of the company's revenues occurs in the Fresh Dairy Products – International segment: 37.5% and 34.1% of the total in 2016 and 2017, respectively. The greatest increase in relative revenue, however, came from the Fresh Dairy Products – North America segment which grew by 80.8% and increased from 11.4% of total revenues in 2016 to 18.4% of total revenues in 2017. Examination of the company's full annual report reveals that Danone Group acquired a large health-oriented North American food company, Whitewave, in 2017. This caused the shift in the relative proportion of sales. The highest segment operating margin in both years comes from the Specialized Nutrition segment with operating margins of 21.4% in 2016 increasing to 23.7% in 2017. Margins increased slightly in the Fresh Dairy Products – International and Waters segments, while margins declined in Fresh Dairy Products – North America. The latter is likely due to costs associated with the Whitewave acquisition.

Geographic Segments	2016 Segment Revenue Percent	2016 Recurring Operating Margin	2016 Segment ROA	2016 Segment Asset Turnover	2017 Segment Revenue Percent	2017 Recurring Operating Margin	2017 Segment ROA	2017 Segment Asset Turnover
Europe and North America	49.8%	16.8%	16.0%	0.9	53.5%	15.5%	9.1%	0.6
Rest of World	50.2%	10.7%	12.7%	1.2	46.5%	13.0%	17.7%	1.4
Group Total	100.0%	13.8%	14.5%	1.1	100.0%	14.4%	11.4%	0.8

As used in this table, ROA refers to operating income divided by ending assets, and Asset Turnover is defined as Revenue divided by non-current assets.

The geographic segment analysis shows that the company's sales are split roughly evenly between the two geographic segments. Operating margins were higher in the Europe and North America segment in both years but declined from 16.8% in 2016 to 15.5% in 2017, likely in connection with the North American acquisition of Whitewave. Operating margins in the rest of the world, however, increased in 2017. Segment return on assets and segment asset turnover declined significantly for the Europe and North America segment in 2017, again largely due to the acquisition of Whitewave. An examination of the annual report disclosures reveals that the large increase in segment assets came from intangible assets (mainly goodwill) recorded in the Whitewave acquisition. In contrast, segment return on assets and turnover improved significantly in the Rest of World segment.

8 MODEL BUILDING AND FORECASTING

Analysts often need to forecast future financial performance. For example, analysts' EPS forecasts and related equity valuations are widely followed by Wall Street. Analysts use data about the economy, industry, and company in arriving at a company's forecast. The results of an analyst's financial analysis, including common-size and ratio analyses, are integral to this process, along with the judgment of the analysts.

Based upon forecasts of growth and expected relationships among the financial statement data, the analyst can build a model (sometimes referred to as an "earnings model") to forecast future performance. In addition to budgets, pro forma financial statements are widely used in financial forecasting within companies, especially for use by senior executives and boards of directors. Last but not least, these budgets and forecasts are also used in presentations to credit analysts and others in obtaining external financing.

For example, based on a revenue forecast, an analyst may budget expenses based on expected common-size data. Forecasts of balance sheet and cash flow statements can be derived from expected ratio data, such as DSO. Forecasts are not limited to a single point estimate but should involve a range of possibilities. This can involve several techniques:

- **Sensitivity analysis**: Also known as "what if" analysis, sensitivity analysis shows the range of possible outcomes as specific assumptions are changed; this could, in turn, influence financing needs or investment in fixed assets.

- **Scenario analysis**: This type of analysis shows the changes in key financial quantities that result from given (economic) events, such as the loss of customers, the loss of a supply source, or a catastrophic event. If the list of events is mutually exclusive and exhaustive and the events can be assigned probabilities, the analyst can evaluate not only the range of outcomes but also standard statistical measures such as the mean and median value for various quantities of interest.
- **Simulation**: This is computer-generated sensitivity or scenario analysis based on probability models for the factors that drive outcomes. Each event or possible outcome is assigned a probability. Multiple scenarios are then run using the probability factors assigned to the possible values of a variable.

SUMMARY

Financial analysis techniques, including common-size financial statements and ratio analysis, are useful in summarizing financial reporting data and evaluating the performance and financial position of a company. The results of financial analysis techniques provide important inputs into security valuation. Key facets of financial analysis include the following:

- Common-size financial statements and financial ratios remove the effect of size, allowing comparisons of a company with peer companies (cross-sectional analysis) and comparison of a company's results over time (trend or time-series analysis).
- Activity ratios measure the efficiency of a company's operations, such as collection of receivables or management of inventory. Major activity ratios include inventory turnover, days of inventory on hand, receivables turnover, days of sales outstanding, payables turnover, number of days of payables, working capital turnover, fixed asset turnover, and total asset turnover.
- Liquidity ratios measure the ability of a company to meet short-term obligations. Major liquidity ratios include the current ratio, quick ratio, cash ratio, and defensive interval ratio.
- Solvency ratios measure the ability of a company to meet long-term obligations. Major solvency ratios include debt ratios (including the debt-to-assets ratio, debt-to-capital ratio, debt-to-equity ratio, and financial leverage ratio) and coverage ratios (including interest coverage and fixed charge coverage).
- Profitability ratios measure the ability of a company to generate profits from revenue and assets. Major profitability ratios include return on sales ratios (including gross profit margin, operating profit margin, pretax margin, and net profit margin) and return on investment ratios (including operating ROA, ROA, return on total capital, ROE, and return on common equity).
- Ratios can also be combined and evaluated as a group to better understand how they fit together and how efficiency and leverage are tied to profitability.
- ROE can be analyzed as the product of the net profit margin, asset turnover, and financial leverage. This decomposition is sometimes referred to as DuPont analysis.
- Valuation ratios express the relation between the market value of a company or its equity (for example, price per share) and some fundamental financial metric (for example, earnings per share).

- Ratio analysis is useful in the selection and valuation of debt and equity securities and is a part of the credit rating process.
- Ratios can also be computed for business segments to evaluate how units within a business are performing.
- The results of financial analysis provide valuable inputs into forecasts of future earnings and cash flow.

REFERENCES

Abarbanell, J.S., and B. J. Bushee. 1997. "Fundamental Analysis, Future Earnings, and Stock Prices." *Journal of Accounting Research*, vol. 35, no. 1:1–24.

Abarbanell, J.S., and B.J. Bushee. 1998. "Abnormal Returns to a Fundamental Analysis Strategy." *Accounting Review*, vol. 73, no. 1:19–46.

Altman, E. 1968. "Financial Ratios, Discriminant Analysis and the Prediction of Corporate Bankruptcy." *Journal of Finance*, vol. 23, no. 4:589–609.

Altman, E.I. 2013, "Predicting Financial Distress of Companies: Revisiting the Z-Score and Zeta Models," in Prokopczuk, Marcel; Brooks, Chris; Bell, Adrian R., *Handbook of Research Methods and Applications in Empirical Finance*: 428-456.

Altman, E., R. Haldeman, and P. Narayanan. 1977. "Zeta Analysis: A New Model to Identify Bankruptcy Risk of Corporations." *Journal of Banking & Finance*, vol. 1, no. 1.

Beaver, W. 1967. "Financial Ratios as Predictors of Failures." *Empirical Research in Accounting*, selected studies supplement to *Journal of Accounting Research*, 4 (1).

Benninga, Simon Z., and Oded H. Sarig. 1997. *Corporate Finance: A Valuation Approach*. New York: McGraw-Hill Publishing.

Ederington, L.H. 1986. "Why Split Ratings Occur." *Financial Management*, vol. 15, no. 1:37–47.

Ederington, L.H., J.B. Yawitz, and B.E. Robert. 1987. "The Information Content of Bond Ratings." *Journal of Financial Research*, vol. 10, no. 3:211–226.

Lev, B., and S.R. Thiagarajan. 1993. "Fundamental Information Analysis." *Journal of Accounting Research*, vol. 31, no. 2:190–215.

Modigliani, F., and M. Miller. 1958. "The Cost of Capital, Corporation Finance and the Theory of Investment." *American Economic Review*, vol. 48:261–298.

Modigliani, F., and M. Miller. 1963. "Corporate Income Taxes and the Cost of Capital: A Correction." *American Economic Review*, vol. 53:433–444.

Ou, J.A., and S.H. Penman. 1989a. "Financial Statement Analysis and the Prediction of Stock Returns." *Journal of Accounting and Economics*, vol. 11, no. 4:295–329.

Ou, J.A., and S.H. Penman. 1989b. "Accounting Measurement, Price-Earnings Ratio, and the Information Content of Security Prices." *Journal of Accounting Research*, vol. 27, no. Supplement:111–144.

Piotroski, J.D. 2000. "Value Investing: The Use of Historical Financial Statement Information to Separate Winners from Losers." *Journal of Accounting Research*, vol. 38, no. Supplement:1–41.

Robinson, T., and P. Munter. 2004. "Financial Reporting Quality: Red Flags and Accounting Warning Signs." *Commercial Lending Review*, vol. 19, no. 1:2–15.

van Greuning, H., and S. Brajovic Bratanovic. 2003. *Analyzing and Managing Banking Risk: A Framework for Assessing Corporate Governance and Financial Risk*. Washington, DC: World Bank.

PRACTICE PROBLEMS

1 Comparison of a company's financial results to other peer companies for the same time period is called:

A technical analysis.

B time-series analysis.

C cross-sectional analysis.

2 In order to assess a company's ability to fulfill its long-term obligations, an analyst would *most likely* examine:

A activity ratios.

B liquidity ratios.

C solvency ratios.

3 Which ratio would a company *most likely* use to measure its ability to meet short-term obligations?

A Current ratio.

B Payables turnover.

C Gross profit margin.

4 Which of the following ratios would be *most* useful in determining a company's ability to cover its lease and interest payments?

A ROA.

B Total asset turnover.

C Fixed charge coverage.

5 An analyst is interested in assessing both the efficiency and liquidity of Spherion PLC. The analyst has collected the following data for Spherion:

	FY3	FY2	FY1
Days of inventory on hand	32	34	40
Days sales outstanding	28	25	23
Number of days of payables	40	35	35

Based on this data, what is the analyst *least likely* to conclude?

A Inventory management has contributed to improved liquidity.

B Management of payables has contributed to improved liquidity.

C Management of receivables has contributed to improved liquidity.

6 An analyst is evaluating the solvency and liquidity of Apex Manufacturing and has collected the following data (in millions of euro):

	FY5 (€)	FY4 (€)	FY3 (€)
Total debt	2,000	1,900	1,750
Total equity	4,000	4,500	5,000

Which of the following would be the analyst's *most likely* conclusion?

A The company is becoming increasingly less solvent, as evidenced by the increase in its debt-to-equity ratio from 0.35 to 0.50 from FY3 to FY5.

© 2011 CFA Institute. All rights reserved.

B The company is becoming less liquid, as evidenced by the increase in its debt-to-equity ratio from 0.35 to 0.50 from FY3 to FY5.

C The company is becoming increasingly more liquid, as evidenced by the increase in its debt-to-equity ratio from 0.35 to 0.50 from FY3 to FY5.

7 With regard to the data in Problem 6, what would be the *most* reasonable explanation of the financial data?

A The decline in the company's equity results from a decline in the market value of this company's common shares.

B The €250 increase in the company's debt from FY3 to FY5 indicates that lenders are viewing the company as increasingly creditworthy.

C The decline in the company's equity indicates that the company may be incurring losses, paying dividends greater than income, and/or repurchasing shares.

8 An analyst observes a decrease in a company's inventory turnover. Which of the following would *most likely* explain this trend?

A The company installed a new inventory management system, allowing more efficient inventory management.

B Due to problems with obsolescent inventory last year, the company wrote off a large amount of its inventory at the beginning of the period.

C The company installed a new inventory management system but experienced some operational difficulties resulting in duplicate orders being placed with suppliers.

9 Which of the following would *best* explain an increase in receivables turnover?

A The company adopted new credit policies last year and began offering credit to customers with weak credit histories.

B Due to problems with an error in its old credit scoring system, the company had accumulated a substantial amount of uncollectible accounts and wrote off a large amount of its receivables.

C To match the terms offered by its closest competitor, the company adopted new payment terms now requiring net payment within 30 days rather than 15 days, which had been its previous requirement.

10 Brown Corporation had average days of sales outstanding of 19 days in the most recent fiscal year. Brown wants to improve its credit policies and collection practices and decrease its collection period in the next fiscal year to match the industry average of 15 days. Credit sales in the most recent fiscal year were \$300 million, and Brown expects credit sales to increase to \$390 million in the next fiscal year. To achieve Brown's goal of decreasing the collection period, the change in the average accounts receivable balance that must occur is *closest* to:

A +\$0.41 million.

B –\$0.41 million.

C –\$1.22 million.

11 An analyst observes the following data for two companies:

	Company A (\$)	Company B (\$)
Revenue	4,500	6,000
Net income	50	1,000
Current assets	40,000	60,000
Total assets	100,000	700,000

	Company A ($)	Company B ($)
Current liabilities	10,000	50,000
Total debt	60,000	150,000
Shareholders' equity	30,000	500,000

Which of the following choices *best* describes reasonable conclusions that the analyst might make about the two companies' ability to pay their current and long-term obligations?

A Company A's current ratio of 4.0 indicates it is more liquid than Company B, whose current ratio is only 1.2, but Company B is more solvent, as indicated by its lower debt-to-equity ratio.

B Company A's current ratio of 0.25 indicates it is less liquid than Company B, whose current ratio is 0.83, and Company A is also less solvent, as indicated by a debt-to-equity ratio of 200 percent compared with Company B's debt-to-equity ratio of only 30 percent.

C Company A's current ratio of 4.0 indicates it is more liquid than Company B, whose current ratio is only 1.2, and Company A is also more solvent, as indicated by a debt-to-equity ratio of 200 percent compared with Company B's debt-to-equity ratio of only 30 percent.

The following information relates to Questions 12–15

The data in Exhibit 1 appear in the five-year summary of a major international company. A business combination with another major manufacturer took place in FY13.

Exhibit 1

	FY10	FY11	FY12	FY13	FY14
Financial statements	GBP m	GBP m	GBP m	GBP m	GBP m
Income statements					
Revenue	4,390	3,624	3,717	8,167	11,366
Profit before interest and taxation (EBIT)	844	700	704	933	1,579
Net interest payable	−80	−54	−98	−163	−188
Taxation	−186	−195	−208	−349	−579
Minorities	−94	−99	−105	−125	−167
Profit for the year	484	352	293	296	645
Balance sheets					
Fixed assets	3,510	3,667	4,758	10,431	11,483
Current asset investments, cash at bank and in hand	316	218	290	561	682
Other current assets	558	514	643	1,258	1,634
Total assets	4,384	4,399	5,691	12,250	13,799
Interest bearing debt (long term)	−602	−1,053	−1,535	−3,523	−3,707

(continued)

Exhibit 1 (Continued)

	FY10	FY11	FY12	FY13	FY14
Other creditors and provisions (current)	−1,223	−1,054	−1,102	−2,377	−3,108
Total liabilities	−1,825	−2,107	−2,637	−5,900	−6,815
Net assets	2,559	2,292	3,054	6,350	6,984
Shareholders' funds	2,161	2,006	2,309	5,572	6,165
Equity minority interests	398	286	745	778	819
Capital employed	2,559	2,292	3,054	6,350	6,984
Cash flow					
Working capital movements	−53	5	71	85	107
Net cash inflow from operating activities	864	859	975	1,568	2,292

12 The company's total assets at year-end FY9 were GBP 3,500 million. Which of the following choices *best* describes reasonable conclusions an analyst might make about the company's efficiency?

A Comparing FY14 with FY10, the company's efficiency improved, as indicated by a total asset turnover ratio of 0.86 compared with 0.64.

B Comparing FY14 with FY10, the company's efficiency deteriorated, as indicated by its current ratio.

C Comparing FY14 with FY10, the company's efficiency deteriorated due to asset growth faster than turnover revenue growth.

13 Which of the following choices *best* describes reasonable conclusions an analyst might make about the company's solvency?

A Comparing FY14 with FY10, the company's solvency improved, as indicated by an increase in its debt-to-assets ratio from 0.14 to 0.27.

B Comparing FY14 with FY10, the company's solvency deteriorated, as indicated by a decrease in interest coverage from 10.6 to 8.4.

C Comparing FY14 with FY10, the company's solvency improved, as indicated by the growth in its profits to GBP 645 million.

14 Which of the following choices *best* describes reasonable conclusions an analyst might make about the company's liquidity?

A Comparing FY14 with FY10, the company's liquidity improved, as indicated by an increase in its debt-to-assets ratio from 0.14 to 0.27.

B Comparing FY14 with FY10, the company's liquidity deteriorated, as indicated by a decrease in interest coverage from 10.6 to 8.4.

C Comparing FY14 with FY10, the company's liquidity improved, as indicated by an increase in its current ratio from 0.71 to 0.75.

15 Which of the following choices *best* describes reasonable conclusions an analyst might make about the company's profitability?

A Comparing FY14 with FY10, the company's profitability improved, as indicated by an increase in its debt-to-assets ratio from 0.14 to 0.27.

B Comparing FY14 with FY10, the company's profitability deteriorated, as indicated by a decrease in its net profit margin from 11.0 percent to 5.7 percent.

C Comparing FY14 with FY10, the company's profitability improved, as indicated by the growth in its shareholders' equity to GBP 6,165 million.

---

16 Assuming no changes in other variables, which of the following would decrease ROA?

A A decrease in the effective tax rate.

B A decrease in interest expense.

C An increase in average assets.

17 An analyst compiles the following data for a company:

	FY13	FY14	FY15
ROE	19.8%	20.0%	22.0%
Return on total assets	8.1%	8.0%	7.9%
Total asset turnover	2.0	2.0	2.1

Based only on the information above, the *most* appropriate conclusion is that, over the period FY13 to FY15, the company's:

A net profit margin and financial leverage have decreased.

B net profit margin and financial leverage have increased.

C net profit margin has decreased but its financial leverage has increased.

18 A decomposition of ROE for Integra SA is as follows:

	FY12	FY11
ROE	18.90%	18.90%
Tax burden	0.70	0.75
Interest burden	0.90	0.90
EBIT margin	10.00%	10.00%
Asset turnover	1.50	1.40
Leverage	2.00	2.00

Which of the following choices *best* describes reasonable conclusions an analyst might make based on this ROE decomposition?

A Profitability and the liquidity position both improved in FY12.

B The higher average tax rate in FY12 offset the improvement in profitability, leaving ROE unchanged.

C The higher average tax rate in FY12 offset the improvement in efficiency, leaving ROE unchanged.

19 A decomposition of ROE for Company A and Company B is as follows:

	Company A		Company B	
	FY15	FY14	FY15	FY14
ROE	26.46%	18.90%	26.33%	18.90%
Tax burden	0.7	0.75	0.75	0.75
Interest burden	0.9	0.9	0.9	0.9

(continued)

	Company A		Company B	
	FY15	FY14	FY15	FY14
EBIT margin	7.00%	10.00%	13.00%	10.00%
Asset turnover	1.5	1.4	1.5	1.4
Leverage	4	2	2	2

An analyst is *most likely* to conclude that:

A Company A's ROE is higher than Company B's in FY15, and one explanation consistent with the data is that Company A may have purchased new, more efficient equipment.

B Company A's ROE is higher than Company B's in FY15, and one explanation consistent with the data is that Company A has made a strategic shift to a product mix with higher profit margins.

C The difference between the two companies' ROE in FY15 is very small and Company A's ROE remains similar to Company B's ROE mainly due to Company A increasing its financial leverage.

20 What does the P/E ratio measure?

A The "multiple" that the stock market places on a company's EPS.

B The relationship between dividends and market prices.

C The earnings for one common share of stock.

21 A creditor *most likely* would consider a decrease in which of the following ratios to be positive news?

A Interest coverage (times interest earned).

B Debt-to-total assets.

C Return on assets.

22 When developing forecasts, analysts should *most likely*:

A develop possibilities relying exclusively on the results of financial analysis.

B use the results of financial analysis, analysis of other information, and judgment.

C aim to develop extremely precise forecasts using the results of financial analysis.

SOLUTIONS

1 C is correct. Cross-sectional analysis involves the comparison of companies with each other for the same time period. Technical analysis uses price and volume data as the basis for investment decisions. Time-series or trend analysis is the comparison of financial data across different time periods.

2 C is correct. Solvency ratios are used to evaluate the ability of a company to meet its long-term obligations. An analyst is more likely to use activity ratios to evaluate how efficiently a company uses its assets. An analyst is more likely to use liquidity ratios to evaluate the ability of a company to meet its short-term obligations.

3 A is correct. The current ratio is a liquidity ratio. It compares the net amount of current assets expected to be converted into cash within the year with liabilities falling due in the same period. A current ratio of 1.0 would indicate that the company would have just enough current assets to pay current liabilities.

4 C is correct. The fixed charge coverage ratio is a coverage ratio that relates known fixed charges or obligations to a measure of operating profit or cash flow generated by the company. Coverage ratios, a category of solvency ratios, measure the ability of a company to cover its payments related to debt and leases.

5 C is correct. The analyst is *unlikely* to reach the conclusion given in Statement C because days of sales outstanding increased from 23 days in FY1 to 25 days in FY2 to 28 days in FY3, indicating that the time required to collect receivables has increased over the period. This is a negative factor for Spherion's liquidity. By contrast, days of inventory on hand dropped over the period FY1 to FY3, a positive for liquidity. The company's increase in days payable, from 35 days to 40 days, shortened its cash conversion cycle, thus also contributing to improved liquidity.

6 A is correct. The company is becoming increasingly less solvent, as evidenced by its debt-to-equity ratio increasing from 0.35 to 0.50 from FY3 to FY5. The amount of a company's debt and equity do not provide direct information about the company's liquidity position.

Debt to equity:

FY5: 2,000/4,000 = 0.5000

FY4: 1,900/4,500 = 0.4222

FY3: 1,750/5,000 = 0.3500

7 C is correct. The decline in the company's equity indicates that the company may be incurring losses, paying dividends greater than income, or repurchasing shares. Recall that Beginning equity + New shares issuance − Shares repurchased + Comprehensive income − Dividends = Ending equity. The book value of a company's equity is not affected by changes in the market value of its common stock. An increased amount of lending does not necessarily indicate that lenders view a company as increasingly creditworthy. Creditworthiness is not evaluated based on how much a company has increased its debt but rather on its willingness and ability to pay its obligations. (Its financial strength is indicated by its solvency, liquidity, profitability, efficiency, and other aspects of credit analysis.)

8 C is correct. The company's problems with its inventory management system causing duplicate orders would likely result in a higher amount of inventory and would, therefore, result in a decrease in inventory turnover. A more efficient inventory management system and a write off of inventory at the beginning of

the period would both likely decrease the average inventory for the period (the denominator of the inventory turnover ratio), thus increasing the ratio rather than decreasing it.

9 B is correct. A write off of receivables would decrease the average amount of accounts receivable (the denominator of the receivables turnover ratio), thus increasing this ratio. Customers with weaker credit are more likely to make payments more slowly or to pose collection difficulties, which would likely increase the average amount of accounts receivable and thus decrease receivables turnover. Longer payment terms would likely increase the average amount of accounts receivable and thus decrease receivables turnover.

10 A is correct. The average accounts receivable balances (actual and desired) must be calculated to determine the desired change. The average accounts receivable balance can be calculated as an average day's credit sales times the DSO. For the most recent fiscal year, the average accounts receivable balance is $15.62 million [= ($300,000,000/365) × 19]. The desired average accounts receivable balance for the next fiscal year is $16.03 million (= ($390,000,000/365) × 15). This is an increase of $0.41 million (= 16.03 million – 15.62 million). An alternative approach is to calculate the turnover and divide sales by turnover to determine the average accounts receivable balance. Turnover equals 365 divided by DSO. Turnover is 19.21 (= 365/19) for the most recent fiscal year and is targeted to be 24.33 (= 365/15) for the next fiscal year. The average accounts receivable balances are $15.62 million (= $300,000,000/19.21), and $16.03 million (= $390,000,000/24.33). The change is an increase in receivables of $0.41 million

11 A is correct. Company A's current ratio of 4.0 (= $40,000/$10,000) indicates it is more liquid than Company B, whose current ratio is only 1.2 (= $60,000/$50,000). Company B is more solvent, as indicated by its lower debt-to-equity ratio of 30 percent (= $150,000/$500,000) compared with Company A's debt-to-equity ratio of 200 percent (= $60,000/$30,000).

12 C is correct. The company's efficiency deteriorated, as indicated by the decline in its total asset turnover ratio from 1.11 {= 4,390/[(4,384 + 3,500)/2]} for FY10 to 0.87 {= 11,366/[(12,250 + 13,799)/2]} for FY14. The decline in the total asset turnover ratio resulted from an increase in average total assets from GBP3,942 [= (4,384 + 3,500)/2] for FY10 to GBP13,024.5 for FY14, an increase of 230 percent, compared with an increase in revenue from GBP4,390 in FY10 to GBP11,366 in FY14, an increase of only 159 percent. The current ratio is not an indicator of efficiency.

13 B is correct. Comparing FY14 with FY10, the company's solvency deteriorated, as indicated by a decrease in interest coverage from 10.6 (= 844/80) in FY10 to 8.4 (= 1,579/188) in FY14. The debt-to-asset ratio increased from 0.14 (= 602/4,384) in FY10 to 0.27 (= 3,707/13,799) in FY14. This is also indicative of deteriorating solvency. In isolation, the amount of profits does not provide enough information to assess solvency.

14 C is correct. Comparing FY14 with FY10, the company's liquidity improved, as indicated by an increase in its current ratio from 0.71 [= (316 + 558)/1,223] in FY10 to 0.75 [= (682 + 1,634)/3,108] in FY14. Note, however, comparing only current investments with the level of current liabilities shows a decline in liquidity from 0.26 (= 316/1,223) in FY10 to 0.22 (= 682/3,108) in FY14. Debt-to-assets ratio and interest coverage are measures of solvency not liquidity.

15 B is correct. Comparing FY14 with FY10, the company's profitability deteriorated, as indicated by a decrease in its net profit margin from 11.0 percent (= 484/4,390) to 5.7 percent (= 645/11,366). Debt-to-assets ratio is a measure of solvency not an indicator of profitability. Growth in shareholders' equity, in isolation, does not provide enough information to assess profitability.

16 C is correct. Assuming no changes in other variables, an increase in average assets (an increase in the denominator) would decrease ROA. A decrease in either the effective tax rate or interest expense, assuming no changes in other variables, would increase ROA.

17 C is correct. The company's net profit margin has decreased and its financial leverage has increased. ROA = Net profit margin × Total asset turnover. ROA decreased over the period despite the increase in total asset turnover; therefore, the net profit margin must have decreased.

ROE = Return on assets × Financial leverage. ROE increased over the period despite the drop in ROA; therefore, financial leverage must have increased.

18 C is correct. The increase in the average tax rate in FY12, as indicated by the decrease in the value of the tax burden (the tax burden equals one minus the average tax rate), offset the improvement in efficiency indicated by higher asset turnover) leaving ROE unchanged. The EBIT margin, measuring profitability, was unchanged in FY12 and no information is given on liquidity.

19 C is correct. The difference between the two companies' ROE in 2010 is very small and is mainly the result of Company A's increase in its financial leverage, indicated by the increase in its Assets/Equity ratio from 2 to 4. The impact of efficiency on ROE is identical for the two companies, as indicated by both companies' asset turnover ratios of 1.5. Furthermore, if Company A had purchased newer equipment to replace older, depreciated equipment, then the company's asset turnover ratio (computed as sales/assets) would have declined, assuming constant sales. Company A has experienced a significant decline in its operating margin, from 10 percent to 7 percent which, all else equal, would not suggest that it is selling more products with higher profit margins.

20 A is correct. The P/E ratio measures the "multiple" that the stock market places on a company's EPS.

21 B is correct. In general, a creditor would consider a decrease in debt to total assets as positive news. A higher level of debt in a company's capital structure increases the risk of default and will, in general, result in higher borrowing costs for the company to compensate lenders for assuming greater credit risk. A decrease in either interest coverage or return on assets is likely to be considered negative news.

22 B is correct. The results of an analyst's financial analysis are integral to the process of developing forecasts, along with the analysis of other information and judgment of the analysts. Forecasts are not limited to a single point estimate but should involve a range of possibilities.

FINANCIAL REPORTING AND ANALYSIS

STUDY SESSION

8

Financial Reporting and Analysis (3)

This study session examines financial reporting for specific categories of assets and liabilities. Inventories, long-lived assets, income taxes, and non-current liabilities are examined in greater detail because of their effect on financial statements and reported measures of profitability, liquidity, and solvency. For these items in particular, the analyst should be attentive to chosen accounting treatment, corresponding effect on reported performance, and the potential for financial statement manipulation.

READING ASSIGNMENTS

Reading 25	Inventories by Michael Broihahn, CPA, CIA, CFA
Reading 26	Long-lived Assets by Elaine Henry, PhD, CFA, and Elizabeth A. Gordon, PhD, MBA, CPA
Reading 27	Income Taxes By Elbie Louw, PhD, CFA, CIPM, and Michael A. Broihahn, CPA, CIA, CFA
Reading 28	Non-current (Long-term) Liabilities by Elizabeth A. Gordon, PhD, MBA, CPA, and Elaine Henry, PhD, CFA

Note: Changes in accounting standards as well as new rulings and/or pronouncements issued after the publication of the readings on financial reporting and analysis may cause some of the information in these readings to become dated. Candidates are *not* responsible for anything that occurs after the readings were published. In addition, candidates are expected to be familiar with the analytical frameworks contained in the readings, as well as the implications of alternative accounting methods for financial analysis and valuation discussed in the readings. Candidates are also responsible for the content of accounting standards, but not for the actual reference numbers. Finally, candidates should be aware that certain ratios may be defined and calculated differently. When alternative ratio definitions exist and no specific definition is given, candidates should use the ratio definitions emphasized in the readings.

© 2019 CFA Institute. All rights reserved.

READING

25

Inventories

by Michael A. Broihahn, CPA, CIA, CFA

Michael A. Broihahn, CPA, CIA, CFA, is at Barry University (USA).

LEARNING OUTCOMES

Mastery	The candidate should be able to:
☐	a. distinguish between costs included in inventories and costs recognised as expenses in the period in which they are incurred;
☐	b. describe different inventory valuation methods (cost formulas);
☐	c. calculate and compare cost of sales, gross profit, and ending inventory using different inventory valuation methods and using perpetual and periodic inventory systems;
☐	d. calculate and explain how inflation and deflation of inventory costs affect the financial statements and ratios of companies that use different inventory valuation methods;
☐	e. explain LIFO reserve and LIFO liquidation and their effects on financial statements and ratios;
☐	f. convert a company's reported financial statements from LIFO to FIFO for purposes of comparison;
☐	g. describe the measurement of inventory at the lower of cost and net realisable value;
☐	h. describe implications of valuing inventory at net realisable value for financial statements and ratios;
☐	i. describe the financial statement presentation of and disclosures relating to inventories;
☐	j. explain issues that analysts should consider when examining a company's inventory disclosures and other sources of information;
☐	k. calculate and compare ratios of companies, including companies that use different inventory methods;
☐	l. analyze and compare the financial statements of companies, including companies that use different inventory methods.

Note: Changes in accounting standards as well as new rulings and/or pronouncements issued after the publication of the readings on financial reporting and analysis may cause some of the information in these readings to become dated. Candidates are *not* responsible for anything that occurs after the readings were published. In addition, candidates are expected to be familiar with the analytical frameworks contained in the readings, as well as the implications of alternative accounting methods for financial analysis and valuation discussed in the readings. Candidates are also responsible for the content of accounting standards, but not for the actual reference numbers. Finally, candidates should be aware that certain ratios may be defined and calculated differently. When alternative ratio definitions exist and no specific definition is given, candidates should use the ratio definitions emphasized in the readings.

© 2019 CFA Institute. All rights reserved.

1 INTRODUCTION

Merchandising and manufacturing companies generate revenues and profits through the sale of inventory. Further, inventory may represent a significant asset on these companies' balance sheets. Merchandisers (wholesalers and retailers) purchase inventory, ready for sale, from manufacturers and thus account for only one type of inventory—finished goods inventory. Manufacturers, however, purchase raw materials from suppliers and then add value by transforming the raw materials into finished goods. They typically classify inventory into three different categories:[1] raw materials, work in progress,[2] and finished goods. Work-in-progress inventories have started the conversion process from raw materials but are not yet finished goods ready for sale. Manufacturers may report either the separate carrying amounts of their raw materials, work-in-progress, and finished goods inventories on the balance sheet or simply the total inventory amount. If the latter approach is used, the company must then disclose the carrying amounts of its raw materials, work-in-progress, and finished goods inventories in a footnote to the financial statements.

Inventories and cost of sales (cost of goods sold)[3] are significant items in the financial statements of many companies. Comparing the performance of these companies is challenging because of the allowable choices for valuing inventories: Differences in the choice of inventory valuation method can result in significantly different amounts being assigned to inventory and cost of sales. Financial statement analysis would be much easier if all companies used the same inventory valuation method or if inventory price levels remained constant over time. If there was no inflation or deflation with respect to inventory costs and thus unit costs were unchanged, the choice of inventory valuation method would be irrelevant. However, inventory price levels typically do change over time.

International Financial Reporting Standards (IFRS) permit the assignment of inventory costs (costs of goods available for sale) to inventories and cost of sales by three cost formulas: specific identification, first-in, first-out (FIFO), and weighted average cost.[4] US generally accepted accounting principles (US GAAP) allow the same three inventory valuation methods, referred to as cost flow assumptions in US GAAP, but also include a fourth method called last-in, first-out (LIFO).[5] The choice of inventory valuation method affects the allocation of the cost of goods available for sale to ending inventory and cost of sales. Analysts must understand the various inventory valuation methods and the related impact on financial statements and financial ratios in order to evaluate a company's performance over time and relative to industry peers. The company's financial statements and related notes provide important information that the analyst can use in assessing the impact of the choice of inventory valuation method on financial statements and financial ratios.

This reading is organized as follows: Section 2 discusses the costs that are included in inventory and the costs that are recognised as expenses in the period in which they are incurred. Section 3 describes inventory valuation methods and compares the measurement of ending inventory, cost of sales and gross profit under each method, and when using periodic versus perpetual inventory systems. Section 4 describes the LIFO method, LIFO reserve, and effects of LIFO liquidations, and demonstrates the adjustments required to compare a company that uses LIFO with one that uses FIFO.

1 Other classifications are possible. Inventory classifications should be appropriate to the entity.

2 This category is commonly referred to as *work in process* under US GAAP.

3 Typically, *cost of sales* is IFRS terminology and *cost of goods sold* is US GAAP terminology.

4 International Accounting Standard (IAS) 2 [Inventories].

5 Financial Accounting Standards Board *Accounting Standards Codification* (FASB ASC) Topic 330 [Inventory].

Section 5 describes the financial statement effects of a change in inventory valuation method. Section 6 discusses the measurement and reporting of inventory when its value changes. Section 7 describes the presentation of inventories on the financial statements and related disclosures, discusses inventory ratios and their interpretation, and shows examples of financial analysis with respect to inventories. A summary and practice problems conclude the reading.

COST OF INVENTORIES

2

Under IFRS, the costs to include in inventories are "all costs of purchase, costs of conversion, and other costs incurred in bringing the inventories to their present location and condition."[6] The costs of purchase include the purchase price, import and tax-related duties, transport, insurance during transport, handling, and other costs directly attributable to the acquisition of finished goods, materials, and services. Trade discounts, rebates, and similar items reduce the price paid and the costs of purchase. The costs of conversion include costs directly related to the units produced, such as direct labour, and fixed and variable overhead costs.[7] Including these product-related costs in inventory (i.e., as an asset) means that they will not be recognised as an expense (i.e., as cost of sales) on the income statement until the inventory is sold. US GAAP provide a similar description of the costs to be included in inventory.[8]

Both IFRS and US GAAP exclude the following costs from inventory: abnormal costs incurred as a result of waste of materials, labour or other production conversion inputs, any storage costs (unless required as part of the production process), and all administrative overhead and selling costs. These excluded costs are treated as expenses and recognised on the income statement in the period in which they are incurred. Including costs in inventory defers their recognition as an expense on the income statement until the inventory is sold. Therefore, including costs in inventory that should be expensed will overstate profitability on the income statement (because of the inappropriate deferral of cost recognition) and create an overstated inventory value on the balance sheet.

EXAMPLE 1

Treatment of Inventory-Related Costs

Acme Enterprises, a hypothetical company that prepares its financial statements in accordance with IFRS, manufactures tables. In 2018, the factory produced 900,000 finished tables and scrapped 1,000 tables. For the finished tables, raw material costs were €9 million, direct labour conversion costs were €18 million, and production overhead costs were €1.8 million. The 1,000 scrapped tables (attributable to abnormal waste) had a total production cost of €30,000 (€10,000 raw material costs and €20,000 conversion costs; these costs are not included in the €9 million raw material and €19.8 million total conversion costs of the finished

6 International Accounting Standard (IAS) 2 [Inventories].

7 Fixed production overhead costs (depreciation, factory maintenance, and factory management and administration) represent indirect costs of production that remain relatively constant regardless of the volume of production. Variable production overhead costs are indirect production costs (indirect labour and materials) that vary with the volume of production.

8 FASB Accounting Standards Codification™ (ASC) Topic 330 [Inventory].

tables). During the year, Acme spent €1 million for freight delivery charges on raw materials and €500,000 for storing finished goods inventory. Acme does not have any work-in-progress inventory at the end of the year.

1 What costs should be included in inventory in 2018?
2 What costs should be expensed in 2018?

Solution to 1:

Total inventory costs for 2018 are as follows:

Raw materials	€9,000,000
Direct labour	18,000,000
Production overhead	1,800,000
Transportation for raw materials	1,000,000
Total inventory costs	€29,800,000

Solution to 2:

Total costs that should be expensed (not included in inventory) are as follows:

Abnormal waste	€30,000
Storage of finished goods inventory	500,000
Total	€530,000

3 INVENTORY VALUATION METHODS

Generally, inventory purchase costs and manufacturing conversion costs change over time. As a result, the allocation of total inventory costs (i.e., cost of goods available for sale) between cost of sales on the income statement and inventory on the balance sheet will vary depending on the inventory valuation method used by the company. As mentioned in the introduction, inventory valuation methods are referred to as cost formulas and cost flow assumptions under IFRS and US GAAP, respectively. If the choice of method results in more cost being allocated to cost of sales and less cost being allocated to inventory than would be the case with other methods, the chosen method will cause, in the current year, reported gross profit, net income, and inventory carrying amount to be lower than if alternative methods had been used. Accounting for inventory, and consequently the allocation of costs, thus has a direct impact on financial statements and their comparability.

Both IFRS and US GAAP allow companies to use the following inventory valuation methods: specific identification; first-in, first-out (FIFO); and weighted average cost. US GAAP allow companies to use an additional method: last-in, first-out (LIFO). A company must use the same inventory valuation method for all items that have a similar nature and use. For items with a different nature or use, a different inventory valuation method can be used.[9] When items are sold, the carrying amount of the inventory is recognised as an expense (cost of sales) according to the cost formula (cost flow assumption) in use.

9 For example, if a clothing manufacturer produces both a retail line and one-of-a-kind designer garments, the retail line might be valued using FIFO and the designer garments using specific identification.

Specific identification is used for inventory items that are not ordinarily interchangeable, whereas FIFO, weighted average cost, and LIFO are typically used when there are large numbers of interchangeable items in inventory. Specific identification matches the actual historical costs of the specific inventory items to their physical flow; the costs remain in inventory until the actual identifiable inventory is sold. FIFO, weighted average cost, and LIFO are based on cost flow assumptions. Under these methods, companies must make certain assumptions about which goods are sold and which goods remain in ending inventory. As a result, the allocation of costs to the units sold and to the units in ending inventory can be different from the physical movement of the items.

The choice of inventory valuation method would be largely irrelevant if inventory costs remained constant or relatively constant over time. Given relatively constant prices, the allocation of costs between cost of goods sold and ending inventory would be very similar under each of the four methods. Given changing price levels, however, the choice of inventory valuation method can have a significant impact on the amount of reported cost of sales and inventory. And the reported cost of sales and inventory balances affect other items, such as gross profit, net income, current assets, and total assets.

3.1 Specific Identification

The specific identification method is used for inventory items that are not ordinarily interchangeable and for goods that have been produced and segregated for specific projects. This method is also commonly used for expensive goods that are uniquely identifiable, such as precious gemstones. Under this method, the cost of sales and the cost of ending inventory reflect the actual costs incurred to purchase (or manufacture) the items specifically identified as sold and the items specifically identified as remaining in inventory. Therefore, this method matches the physical flow of the specific items sold and remaining in inventory to their actual cost.

3.2 First-In, First-Out (FIFO)

FIFO assumes that the oldest goods purchased (or manufactured) are sold first and the newest goods purchased (or manufactured) remain in ending inventory. In other words, the first units included in inventory are assumed to be the first units sold from inventory. Therefore, cost of sales reflects the cost of goods in beginning inventory plus the cost of items purchased (or manufactured) earliest in the accounting period, and the value of ending inventory reflects the costs of goods purchased (or manufactured) more recently. In periods of rising prices, the costs assigned to the units in ending inventory are higher than the costs assigned to the units sold. Conversely, in periods of declining prices, the costs assigned to the units in ending inventory are lower than the costs assigned to the units sold.

3.3 Weighted Average Cost

Weighted average cost assigns the average cost of the goods available for sale (beginning inventory plus purchase, conversion, and other costs) during the accounting period to the units that are sold as well as to the units in ending inventory. In an accounting period, the weighted average cost per unit is calculated as the total cost of the units available for sale divided by the total number of units available for sale in the period (Total cost of goods available for sale/Total units available for sale).

3.4 Last-In, First-Out (LIFO)

LIFO is permitted only under US GAAP. This method assumes that the newest goods purchased (or manufactured) are sold first and the oldest goods purchased (or manufactured), including beginning inventory, remain in ending inventory. In other words, the last units included in inventory are assumed to be the first units sold from inventory. Therefore, cost of sales reflects the cost of goods purchased (or manufactured) more recently, and the value of ending inventory reflects the cost of older goods. In periods of rising prices, the costs assigned to the units in ending inventory are lower than the costs assigned to the units sold. Conversely, in periods of declining prices, the costs assigned to the units in ending inventory are higher than the costs assigned to the units sold.

3.5 Calculation of Cost of Sales, Gross Profit, and Ending Inventory

In periods of changing prices, the allocation of total inventory costs (i.e., cost of goods available for sale) between cost of sales on the income statement and inventory on the balance sheet will vary depending on the inventory valuation method used by the company. The following example illustrates how cost of sales, gross profit, and ending inventory differ based on the choice of inventory valuation method.

EXAMPLE 2

Inventory Cost Flow Illustration for the Specific Identification, Weighted Average Cost, FIFO, and LIFO Methods

Global Sales, Inc. (GSI) is a hypothetical Dubai-based distributor of consumer products, including bars of luxury soap. The soap is sold by the kilogram. GSI began operations in 2018, during which it purchased and received initially 100,000 kg of soap at 110 dirham (AED)/kg, then 200,000 kg of soap at 100 AED/kg, and finally 300,000 kg of soap at 90 AED/kg. GSI sold 520,000 kg of soap at 240 AED/kg. GSI stores its soap in its warehouse so that soap from each shipment received is readily identifiable. During 2018, the entire 100,000 kg from the first shipment received, 180,000 kg of the second shipment received, and 240,000 kg of the final shipment received was sent to customers. Answers to the following questions should be rounded to the nearest 1,000 AED.

1 What are the reported cost of sales, gross profit, and ending inventory balances for 2018 under the specific identification method?

2 What are the reported cost of sales, gross profit, and ending inventory balances for 2018 under the weighted average cost method?

3 What are the reported cost of sales, gross profit, and ending inventory balances for 2018 under the FIFO method?

4 What are the reported cost of sales, gross profit, and ending inventory balances for 2018 under the LIFO method?

Solution to 1:

Under the specific identification method, the physical flow of the specific inventory items sold is matched to their actual cost.

Sales = 520,000 × 240 = 124,800,000 AED

Cost of sales = (100,000 × 110) + (180,000 × 100) + (240,000 × 90) = 50,600,000 AED

Gross profit = 124,800,000 – 50,600,000 = 74,200,000 AED

Ending inventory = (20,000 × 100) + (60,000 × 90) = 7,400,000 AED

Note that in spite of the segregation of inventory within the warehouse, it would be inappropriate to use specific identification for this inventory of interchangeable items. The use of specific identification could potentially result in earnings manipulation through the shipment decision.

Solution to 2:

Under the weighted average cost method, costs are allocated to cost of sales and ending inventory by using a weighted average mix of the actual costs incurred for all inventory items. The weighted average cost per unit is determined by dividing the total cost of goods available for sale by the number of units available for sale.

Weighted average cost = [(100,000 × 110) + (200,000 × 100) + (300,000 × 90)]/600,000 = 96.667 AED/kg

Sales = 520,000 × 240 = 124,800,000 AED

Cost of sales = 520,000 × 96.667 = 50,267,000 AED

Gross profit = 124,800,000 – 50,267,000 = 74,533,000 AED

Ending inventory = 80,000 × 96.667 = 7,733,360 AED

Solution to 3:

Under the FIFO method, the oldest inventory units acquired are assumed to be the first units sold. Ending inventory, therefore, is assumed to consist of those inventory units most recently acquired.

Sales = 520,000 × 240 = 124,800,000 AED

Cost of sales = (100,000 × 110) + (200,000 × 100) + (220,000 × 90) = 50,800,000 AED

Gross profit = 124,800,000 – 50,800,000 = 74,000,000 AED

Ending inventory = 80,000 × 90 = 7,200,000 AED

Solution to 4:

Under the LIFO method, the newest inventory units acquired are assumed to be the first units sold. Ending inventory, therefore, is assumed to consist of the oldest inventory units.

Sales = 520,000 × 240 = 124,800,000 AED

Cost of sales = (20,000 × 110) + (200,000 × 100) + (300,000 × 90) = 49,200,000 AED

Gross profit = 124,800,000 – 49,200,000 = 75,600,000 AED

Ending inventory = 80,000 × 110 = 8,800,000 AED

The following table (in thousands of AED) summarizes the cost of sales, the ending inventory, and the cost of goods available for sale that were calculated for each of the four inventory valuation methods. Note that in the first year of operation, the total cost of goods available for sale is the same under all four methods. Subsequently, the cost of goods available for sale will typically differ because beginning inventories will differ. Also shown is the gross profit figure for each of the four methods. Because the cost of a kg of soap declined over the period, LIFO had the highest ending inventory amount, the lowest cost of sales, and the highest gross profit. FIFO had the lowest ending inventory amount, the highest cost of sales, and the lowest gross profit.

Inventory Valuation Method	Specific ID	Weighted Average Cost	FIFO	LIFO
Cost of sales	50,600	50,267	50,800	49,200
Ending inventory	7,400	7,733	7,200	8,800
Total cost of goods available for sale	58,000	58,000	58,000	58,000
Gross profit	74,200	74,533	74,000	75,600

3.6 Periodic versus Perpetual Inventory Systems

Companies typically record changes to inventory using either a periodic inventory system or a perpetual inventory system. Under a periodic inventory system, inventory values and costs of sales are determined at the end of an accounting period. Purchases are recorded in a purchases account. The total of purchases and beginning inventory is the amount of goods available for sale during the period. The ending inventory amount is subtracted from the goods available for sale to arrive at the cost of sales. The quantity of goods in ending inventory is usually obtained or verified through a physical count of the units in inventory. Under a perpetual inventory system, inventory values and cost of sales are continuously updated to reflect purchases and sales.

Under either system, the allocation of goods available for sale to cost of sales and ending inventory is the same if the inventory valuation method used is either specific identification or FIFO. This is not generally true for the weighted average cost method. Under a periodic inventory system, the amount of cost of goods available for sale allocated to cost of sales and ending inventory may be quite different using the FIFO method compared to the weighted average cost method. Under a perpetual inventory system, inventory values and cost of sales are continuously updated to reflect purchases and sales. As a result, the amount of cost of goods available for sale allocated to cost of sales and ending inventory is similar under the FIFO and weighted average cost methods. Because of lack of disclosure and the dominance of perpetual inventory systems, analysts typically do not make adjustments when comparing a company using the weighted average cost method with a company using the FIFO method.

Using the LIFO method, the periodic and perpetual inventory systems will generally result in different allocations to cost of sales and ending inventory. Under either a perpetual or periodic inventory system, the use of the LIFO method will generally result in significantly different allocations to cost of sales and ending inventory compared to other inventory valuation methods. When inventory costs are increasing and inventory unit levels are stable or increasing, using the LIFO method will result in higher cost of sales and lower inventory carrying amounts than using the FIFO method. The higher cost of sales under LIFO will result in lower gross profit, operating income, income before taxes, and net income. Income tax expense will be lower under LIFO, causing the company's net operating cash flow to be higher. On the balance sheet, the lower inventory carrying amount will result in lower reported current assets, working capital, and total assets. Analysts must carefully assess the financial statement implications of the choice of inventory valuation method when comparing companies that use the LIFO method with companies that use the FIFO method.

Example 3 illustrates the impact of the choice of system under LIFO.

EXAMPLE 3

Perpetual versus Periodic Inventory Systems

If GSI (the company in Example 2) had used a perpetual inventory system, the timing of purchases and sales would affect the amounts of cost of sales and inventory. Below is a record of the purchases, sales, and quantity of inventory on hand after the transaction in 2018.

Date	Purchased	Sold	Inventory on Hand
5 January	100,000 kg at 110 AED/kg		100,000 kg
1 February		80,000 kg at 240 AED/kg	20,000 kg
8 March	200,000 kg at 100 AED/kg		220,000 kg
6 April		100,000 kg at 240 AED/kg	120,000 kg
23 May		60,000 kg at 240 AED/kg	60,000 kg
7 July		40,000 kg at 240 AED/kg	20,000 kg
2 August	300,000 kg at 90 AED/kg		320,000 kg
5 September		70,000 kg at 240 AED/kg	250,000 kg
17 November		90,000 kg at 240 AED/kg	160,000 kg
8 December		80,000 kg at 240 AED/kg	80,000 kg
	Total goods available for sale = 58,000,000 AED	Total sales = 124,800,000 AED	

The amounts for total goods available for sale and sales are the same under either the perpetual or periodic system in this first year of operation. The carrying amount of the ending inventory, however, may differ because the perpetual system will apply LIFO continuously throughout the year. Under the periodic system, it was assumed that the ending inventory was composed of 80,000 units of the oldest inventory, which cost 110 AED/kg.

What are the ending inventory, cost of sales, and gross profit amounts using the perpetual system and the LIFO method? How do these compare with the amounts using the periodic system and the LIFO method, as in Example 2?

Solution:

The carrying amounts of the inventory at the different time points using the perpetual inventory system are as follows:

Date	Quantity on Hand	Quantities and Cost	Carrying Amount
5 January	100,000 kg	100,000 kg at 110 AED/kg	11,000,000 AED
1 February	20,000 kg	20,000 kg at 110 AED/kg	2,200,000 AED
8 March	220,000 kg	20,000 kg at 110 AED/kg + 200,000 kg at 100 AED/kg	22,200,000 AED
6 April	120,000 kg	20,000 kg at 110 AED/kg + 100,000 kg at 100 AED/kg	12,200,000 AED
23 May	60,000 kg	20,000 kg at 110 AED/kg + 40,000 kg at 100 AED/kg	6,200,000 AED
7 July	20,000 kg	20,000 kg at 110 AED/kg	2,200,000 AED
2 August	320,000 kg	20,000 kg at 110 AED/kg + 300,000 kg at 90 AED/kg	29,200,000 AED
5 September	250,000 kg	20,000 kg at 110 AED/kg + 230,000 kg at 90 AED/kg	22,900,000 AED

(continued)

Date	Quantity on Hand	Quantities and Cost	Carrying Amount
17 November	160,000 kg	20,000 kg at 110 AED/kg + 140,000 kg at 90 AED/kg	14,800,000 AED
8 December	80,000 kg	20,000 kg at 110 AED/kg + 60,000 kg at 90 AED/kg	7,600,000 AED

Perpetual system

Sales = 520,000 × 240 = 124,800,000 AED

Cost of sales = 58,000,000 – 7,600,000 = 50,400,000 AED

Gross profit = 124,800,000 – 50,400,000 = 74,400,000 AED

Ending inventory = 7,600,000 AED
Periodic system from Example 2

Sales = 520,000 × 240 = 124,800,000 AED

Cost of sales = (20,000 × 110) + (200,000 × 100) + (300,000 × 90) = 49,200,000 AED

Gross profit = 124,800,000 – 49,200,000 = 75,600,000 AED

Ending inventory = 80,000 × 110 = 8,800,000 AED

In this example, the ending inventory amount is lower under the perpetual system because only 20,000 kg of the oldest inventory with the highest cost is assumed to remain in inventory. The cost of sales is higher and the gross profit is lower under the perpetual system compared to the periodic system.

3.7 Comparison of Inventory Valuation Methods

As shown in Example 2, the allocation of the total cost of goods available for sale to cost of sales on the income statement and to ending inventory on the balance sheet varies under the different inventory valuation methods. In an environment of declining inventory unit costs and constant or increasing inventory quantities, FIFO (in comparison with weighted average cost or LIFO) will allocate a higher amount of the total cost of goods available for sale to cost of sales on the income statement and a lower amount to ending inventory on the balance sheet. Accordingly, because cost of sales will be higher under FIFO, a company's gross profit, operating profit, and income before taxes will be lower.

Conversely, in an environment of rising inventory unit costs and constant or increasing inventory quantities, FIFO (in comparison with weighted average cost or LIFO) will allocate a lower amount of the total cost of goods available for sale to cost of sales on the income statement and a higher amount to ending inventory on the balance sheet. Accordingly, because cost of sales will be lower under FIFO, a company's gross profit, operating profit, and income before taxes will be higher.

The carrying amount of inventories under FIFO will more closely reflect current replacement values because inventories are assumed to consist of the most recently purchased items. The cost of sales under LIFO will more closely reflect current replacement value. LIFO ending inventory amounts are typically not reflective of current replacement value because the ending inventory is assumed to be the oldest inventory and costs are allocated accordingly. Example 4 illustrates the different results obtained by using either the FIFO or LIFO methods to account for inventory.

EXAMPLE 4

Impact of Inflation Using LIFO Compared to FIFO

Company L and Company F are identical in all respects except that Company L uses the LIFO method and Company F uses the FIFO method. Each company has been in business for five years and maintains a base inventory of 2,000 units each year. Each year, except the first year, the number of units purchased equaled the number of units sold. Over the five year period, unit sales increased 10 percent each year and the unit purchase and selling prices increased at the beginning of each year to reflect inflation of 4 percent per year. In the first year, 20,000 units were sold at a price of $15.00 per unit and the unit purchase price was $8.00.

1 What was the end of year inventory, sales, cost of sales, and gross profit for each company for each of the five years?

2 Compare the inventory turnover ratios (based on ending inventory carrying amounts) and gross profit margins over the five year period and between companies.

Solution to 1:

Company L using LIFO	Year 1	Year 2	Year 3	Year 4	Year 5
Ending inventory[a]	$16,000	$16,000	$16,000	$16,000	$16,000
Sales[b]	$300,000	$343,200	$392,621	$449,158	$513,837
Cost of sales[c]	160,000	183,040	209,398	239,551	274,046
Gross profit	$140,000	$160,160	$183,223	$209,607	$239,791

[a] Inventory is unchanged at $16,000 each year (2,000 units × $8). 2,000 of the units acquired in the first year are assumed to remain in inventory.

[b] Sales Year X = $(20{,}000 \times \$15)(1.10)^{X-1}(1.04)^{X-1}$. The quantity sold increases by 10 percent each year and the selling price increases by 4 percent each year.

[c] Cost of sales Year X = $(20{,}000 \times \$8)(1.10)^{X-1}(1.04)^{X-1}$. In Year 1, 20,000 units are sold with a cost of $8. In subsequent years, the number of units purchased equals the number of units sold and the units sold are assumed to be those purchased in the year. The quantity purchased increases by 10 percent each year and the purchase price increases by 4 percent each year.

Note that if the company sold more units than it purchased in a year, inventory would decrease. This is referred to as LIFO liquidation. The cost of sales of the units sold in excess of those purchased would reflect the inventory carrying amount. In this example, each unit sold in excess of those purchased would have a cost of sales of $8 and a higher gross profit.

Company F using FIFO	Year 1	Year 2	Year 3	Year 4	Year 5
Ending inventory[a]	$16,000	$16,640	$17,306	$17,998	$18,718
Sales[b]	$300,000	$343,200	$392,621	$449,158	$513,837
Cost of sales[c]	160,000	182,400	208,732	238,859	273,326
Gross profit	$140,000	$160,800	$183,889	$210,299	$240,511

[a] Ending Inventory Year X = 2,000 units × Cost in Year X = 2,000 units [$8 × $(1.04)^{X-1}$]. 2,000 units of the units acquired in Year X are assumed to remain in inventory.

[b] Sales Year X = (20,000 × $15)$(1.10)^{X-1}(1.04)^{X-1}$

[c] Cost of sales Year 1 = $160,000 (= 20,000 units × $8). There was no beginning inventory.

Cost of sales Year X (where X ≠ 1) = Beginning inventory plus purchases less ending inventory

= (Inventory at Year X–1) + [(20,000 × $8)$(1.10)^{X-1}(1.04)^{X-1}$] – (Inventory at Year X)

= 2,000($8)$(1.04)^{X-2}$ + [(20,000 × $8)$(1.10)^{X-1}(1.04)^{X-1}$] – [2,000 ($8)$(1.04)^{X-1}$]

For example, cost of sales Year 2 = 2,000($8) + [(20,000 × $8)(1.10)(1.04)] – [2,000 ($8)(1.04)] = $16,000 + 183,040 – 16,640 = $182,400

Solution to 2:

	Company L					Company F				
Year	1	2	3	4	5	1	2	3	4	5
Inventory turnover	10.0	11.4	13.1	15.0	17.1	10.0	11.0	12.1	13.3	14.6
Gross profit margin (%)	46.7	46.7	46.7	46.7	46.7	46.7	46.9	46.8	46.8	46.8

Inventory turnover ratio = Cost of sales ÷ Ending inventory. The inventory turnover ratio increased each year for both companies because the units sold increased, whereas the units in ending inventory remained unchanged. The increase in the inventory turnover ratio is higher for Company L because Company L's cost of sales is increasing for inflation but the inventory carrying amount is unaffected by inflation. It might appear that a company using the LIFO method manages its inventory more effectively, but this is deceptive. Both companies have identical quantities and prices of purchases and sales and only differ in the inventory valuation method used.

Gross profit margin = Gross profit ÷ Sales. The gross profit margin is stable under LIFO because both sales and cost of sales increase at the same rate of inflation. The gross profit margin is slightly higher under the FIFO method after the first year because a proportion of the cost of sales reflects an older purchase price.

THE LIFO METHOD

4

The potential income tax savings are a benefit of using the LIFO method when inventory costs are increasing. The higher cash flows due to lower income taxes may make the company more valuable because the value of a company is based on the present value of its future cash flows. Under the LIFO method, ending inventory is assumed to consist of those units that have been held the longest. This generally results in ending inventories with carrying amounts lower than current replacement costs because inventory costs typically increase over time. Cost of sales will more closely reflect current replacement costs.

If the purchase prices (purchase costs) or production costs of inventory are increasing, the income statement consequences of using the LIFO method compared to other methods will include higher cost of sales, and lower gross profit, operating profit, income tax expense, and net income. The balance sheet consequences include lower ending inventory, working capital, total assets, retained earnings, and shareholders' equity. The lower income tax paid will result in higher net cash flow from operating activities. Some of the financial ratio effects are a lower current ratio, higher debt-to-equity ratios, and lower profitability ratios.

If the purchase prices or production costs of inventory are decreasing, it is unlikely that a company will use the LIFO method for tax purposes (and therefore for financial reporting purposes due to the LIFO conformity rule) because this will result in lower cost of sales, and higher taxable income and income taxes. However, if the company had elected to use the LIFO method and cannot justify changing the inventory valuation method for tax and financial reporting purposes when inventory costs begin to decrease, the income statement, balance sheet, and ratio effects will be opposite to the effects during a period of increasing costs.

4.1 LIFO Reserve

For companies using the LIFO method, US GAAP requires disclosure, in the notes to the financial statements or on the balance sheet, of the amount of the LIFO reserve. The **LIFO reserve** is the difference between the reported LIFO inventory carrying amount and the inventory amount that would have been reported if the FIFO method had been used (in other words, the FIFO inventory value less the LIFO inventory value). The disclosure provides the information that analysts need to adjust a company's cost of sales (cost of goods sold) and ending inventory balance based on the LIFO method, to the FIFO method.

To compare companies using LIFO with companies not using LIFO, inventory is adjusted by adding the disclosed LIFO reserve to the inventory balance that is reported on the balance sheet. The reported inventory balance, using LIFO, plus the LIFO reserve equals the inventory that would have been reported under FIFO. Cost of sales is adjusted by subtracting the increase in the LIFO reserve during the period from the cost of sales amount that is reported on the income statement. If the LIFO reserve has declined during the period,[10] the decrease in the reserve is added to the cost of sales amount that is reported on the income statement. The LIFO reserve disclosure can be used to adjust the financial statements of a US company using the LIFO method to make them comparable with a similar company using the FIFO method.

10 This typically results from a reduction in inventory units and is referred to as LIFO liquidation. LIFO liquidation is discussed in the next section.

4.2 LIFO Liquidations

In periods of rising inventory unit costs, the carrying amount of inventory under FIFO will always exceed the carrying amount of inventory under LIFO. The LIFO reserve may increase over time as the result of the increasing difference between the older costs used to value inventory under LIFO and the more recent costs used to value inventory under FIFO. Also, when the number of inventory units manufactured or purchased exceeds the number of units sold, the LIFO reserve may increase as the result of the addition of new LIFO layers (the quantity of inventory units is increasing and each increase in quantity creates a new LIFO layer).

When the number of units sold exceeds the number of units purchased or manufactured, the number of units in ending inventory is lower than the number of units in beginning inventory and a company using LIFO will experience a LIFO liquidation (some of the older units held in inventory are assumed to have been sold). If inventory unit costs have been rising from period to period and LIFO liquidation occurs, this will produce an inventory-related increase in gross profits. The increase in gross profits occurs because of the lower inventory carrying amounts of the liquidated units. The lower inventory carrying amounts are used for cost of sales and the sales are at the current prices. The gross profit on these units is higher than the gross profit that would be recognised using more current costs. These inventory profits caused by a LIFO liquidation, however, are one-time events and are not sustainable.

LIFO liquidations can occur for a variety of reasons. The reduction in inventory levels may be outside of management's control; for example, labour strikes at a supplier may force a company to reduce inventory levels to meet customer demands. In periods of economic recession or when customer demand is declining, a company may choose to reduce existing inventory levels rather than invest in new inventory. Analysts should be aware that management can potentially manipulate and inflate their company's reported gross profits and net income at critical times by intentionally reducing inventory quantities and liquidating older layers of LIFO inventory (selling some units of beginning inventory). During economic downturns, LIFO liquidation may result in higher gross profit than would otherwise be realised. If LIFO layers of inventory are temporarily depleted and not replaced by fiscal year-end, LIFO liquidation will occur resulting in unsustainable higher gross profits. Therefore, it is imperative to review the LIFO reserve footnote disclosures to determine if LIFO liquidation has occurred. A decline in the LIFO reserve from the prior period may be indicative of LIFO liquidation.

EXAMPLE 5

Inventory Conversion from LIFO to FIFO

Caterpillar Inc. (CAT), based in Peoria, Illinois, USA, is the largest maker of construction and mining equipment, diesel and natural gas engines, and industrial gas turbines in the world. Excerpts from CAT's consolidated financial statements are shown in Exhibits 1 and 2; notes pertaining to CAT's inventories are presented in Exhibit 3. CAT's Management Discussion and Analysis (MD&A) disclosure states that effective income tax rates were 28 percent for 2017 and 36 percent for 2016.

1 What inventory values would CAT report for 2017, 2016, and 2015 if it had used the FIFO method instead of the LIFO method?

2 What amount would CAT's cost of goods sold for 2017 and 2016 be if it had used the FIFO method instead of the LIFO method?

3 What net income (profit) would CAT report for 2017 and 2016 if it had used the FIFO method instead of the LIFO method?

4 By what amount would CAT's 2017 and 2016 net cash flow from operating activities decline if CAT used the FIFO method instead of the LIFO method?

5 What is the cumulative amount of income tax savings that CAT has generated through 2017 by using the LIFO method instead of the FIFO method?

6 What amount would be added to CAT's retained earnings (profit employed in the business) at 31 December 2017 if CAT had used the FIFO method instead of the LIFO method?

7 What would be the change in Cat's cash balance if CAT had used the FIFO method instead of the LIFO method?

8 Calculate and compare the following for 2017 under the LIFO method and the FIFO method: inventory turnover ratio, days of inventory on hand, gross profit margin, net profit margin, return on assets, current ratio, and total liabilities-to-equity ratio.

Exhibit 1 Caterpillar Inc. Consolidated Results of Operation (US$ millions)

For the years ended 31 December	2017	2016	2015
Sales and revenues:			
Sales of Machinery and Engines	42,676	35,773	44,147
Revenue of Financial Products	2,786	2,764	2,864
Total sales and revenues	45,462	38,537	47,011
Operating costs:			
Cost of goods sold	31,049	28,309	33,546
⋮	⋮	⋮	⋮
Interest expense of Financial Products	646	596	587
⋮	⋮	⋮	⋮
Total operating costs	41,056	38,039	43,226
Operating profit	4,406	498	3,785
Interest expense excluding Financial Products	531	505	507
Other income (expense)	207	146	161
Consolidated profit before taxes	4,082	139	4,439
Provision for income taxes	3,339	192	916
Profit (loss) of consolidated companies	743	(53)	2,523
Equity in profit (loss) of unconsolidated affiliated companies	16	(6)	—
Profit attributable to noncontrolling interests	5	8	11
Profit (loss)	754	(67)	2,512

Exhibit 2 Caterpillar Inc. Consolidated Financial Position (US$ millions)

31 December	2017	2016	2015
Assets			
Current assets:			
Cash and short-term investments	8,261	7,168	6,460
⋮	⋮	⋮	⋮
Inventories	10,018	8,614	9,700
Total current assets	36,244	31,967	33,508
⋮	⋮	⋮	⋮
Total assets	76,962	74,704	78,342
Liabilities			
Total current liabilities	26,931	26,132	26,242
⋮	⋮	⋮	⋮
Total liabilities	63,196	61,491	63,457
Stockholders' equity			
Common stock of $1.00 par value:			
Authorized shares: 2,000,000,000			
Issued shares (2017, 2016 and 2015 – 814,894,624) at paid-in amount	5,593	5,277	5,238
Treasury stock (2017 – 217,268,852 shares; 2016 – 228,408,600 shares and 2015 – 232,572,734 shares) at cost	(17,005)	(17,478)	(17,640)
Profit employed in the business	26,301	27,377	29,246
Accumulated other comprehensive income (loss)	(1,192)	(2,039)	(2,035)
Noncontrolling interests	69	76	76
Total stockholders' equity	13,766	13,213	14,885
Total liabilities and stockholders' equity	76,962	74,704	78,342

Exhibit 3 Caterpillar Inc. Selected Notes to Consolidated Financial Statements

Note 1. Operations and Summary of Significant Accounting Policies
D. Inventories

Inventories are stated at the lower of cost or net realizable value. Cost is principally determined using the last-in, first-out (LIFO) method. The value of inventories on the LIFO basis represented about 65% of total inventories at December 31, 2017 and about 60% of total inventories at December 31, 2016 and 2015.

If the FIFO (first-in, first-out) method had been in use, inventories would have been $1,924 million, $2,139 million and $2,498 million higher than reported at December 31, 2017, 2016 and 2015, respectively.

Note 7. Inventories

Exhibit 3 (Continued)

31 December (millions of dollars)	2017	2016	2015
Raw Materials	2,802	2,102	2,467
Work-in-process	2,254	1,719	1,857
Finished goods	4,761	4,576	5,122
Supplies	261	217	254
Total inventories	10,018	8,614	9,700

We had long-term material purchase obligations of approximately $813 million at December 31, 2017.

Solution to 1:

31 December (millions of dollars)	2017	2016	2015
Total inventories (LIFO method)	10,018	8,614	9,700
From Note 1.D (LIFO reserve)	1,934	2,139	2,498
Total inventories (FIFO method)	11,952	10,753	12,198

Note that the decrease in the LIFO reserve from 2015–2016 and again from 2016–2017 likely indicates a LIFO liquidation for both 2016 and 2017.

Solution to 2:

31 December (millions of dollars)	2017	2016
Cost of goods sold (LIFO method)	31,049	28,309
Plus: Decrease in LIFO reserve*	215	359
Cost of goods sold (FIFO method)	31,264	28,668

* From Note 1.D, the decrease in LIFO reserve for 2017 is 215 (1,924 – 2,139) and for 2016 is 359 (2,139 – 2,498).

Solution to 3:

31 December (millions of dollars)	2017	2016
Net income (loss) (LIFO method)	754	–67
Less: Increase in cost of goods sold (decrease in operating profit)	–215	–359
Tax reduction on decreased operating profit*	60	129
Net income (loss) (FIFO method)	599	–297

* The reduction in taxes on the decreased operating profit are 60 (215 × 28%) for 2017 and 129 (359 × 36%) for 2016.

Solution to 4:

The effect on a company's net cash flow from operating activities is limited to the impact of the change on income taxes paid; changes in allocating inventory costs to ending inventory and cost of goods sold does not change any cash flows except income taxes. Consequently, the effect of using FIFO on CAT's net operating cash flow from operating activities would be an increase of $60 million in 2017 and an increase of $129 million in 2016. These are the approximate incremental decreases in income taxes that CAT would have incurred if the FIFO method were used instead of the LIFO method (see solution to 3 above).

Solution to 5:

Using the previously mentioned effective tax rates of 28 percent for 2017 and 36 percent for 2016 (as well as for earlier years), the cumulative amount of income tax savings that CAT has generated by using the LIFO method instead of FIFO is approximately $710 million (–215 × 28% + 2,139 × 36%). Note 1.D indicates a LIFO reserve of $2,139 million at the end of 2016 and a decrease in the LIFO reserve of $215 million in 2017. Therefore, under the FIFO method, cumulative gross profits would have been $2,139 million higher as of the end of 2016 and $1,924 million higher as of the end of 2017. The estimated tax savings would be higher (lower) if income tax rates were assumed to be higher (lower).

Solution to 6:

The amount that would be added to CAT's retained earnings is $1,214 million (1,924 – 710) or (–215 × 72% + 2,139 × 64%). This represents the cumulative increase in operating profit due to the decrease in cost of goods sold (LIFO reserve of $1,924 million) less the assumed taxes on that profit ($710 million, see solution to 5 above). Some analysts advocate ignoring the tax consequences and suggest simply adjusting inventory and equity by the same amount. They argue that the reported equity of the firm is understated by the difference between the current value of its inventory (approximated by the value under FIFO) and its carrying value (value under LIFO).

Solution to 7:

Under the FIFO method, an additional $710 million is assumed to have been incurred for tax expenses. If CAT switched to FIFO, it would have an additional tax liability of $710 million as a consequence of the restatement of financial statements to the FIFO method. This illustrates the significant immediate income tax liabilities that may arise in the year of transition from the LIFO method to the FIFO method. If CAT switched to FIFO for tax purposes, there would be a cash outflow of $710 million for the additional taxes. However, because the company is not actually converting at this point for either tax or reporting purposes, it is appropriate to reflect a deferred tax liability rather than a reduction in cash. In this case for analysis purposes, under FIFO, inventory would increase by $1,924 million, equity by $1,214 million, and non-current liabilities by $710 million.

Solution to 8:

CAT's ratios for 2017 under the LIFO and FIFO methods are as follows:

	LIFO	FIFO
Inventory turnover	3.33	2.76
Days of inventory on hand	109.6 days	132.2 days
Gross profit margin	27.24%	26.74%
Net profit margin	1.66%	1.32%

	LIFO	FIFO
Return on assets	0.99%	0.77%
Current ratio	1.35	1.42
Total liabilities-to-equity ratio	4.59	4.27

Inventory turnover ratio = Cost of goods sold ÷ Average inventory

LIFO = 3.33 = 31,049 ÷ [(10,018 + 8,614) ÷ 2]

FIFO = 2.76 = 31,264 ÷ [(11,942 + 10,753) ÷ 2]

The ratio is higher under LIFO because, given rising inventory costs, cost of goods sold will be higher and inventory carrying amounts will be lower under LIFO. If an analyst made no adjustment for the difference in inventory methods, it might appear that a company using the LIFO method manages its inventory more effectively.

Days of inventory on hand = Number of days in period ÷ Inventory turnover ratio

LIFO = 109.6 days = (365 days ÷ 3.33)

FIFO = 132.2 days = (365 days ÷ 2.76)

Without adjustment, a company using the LIFO method might appear to manage its inventory more effectively. This is primarily the result of the lower inventory carrying amounts under LIFO.

Gross profit margin = Gross profit ÷ Total revenue

LIFO = 27.24 percent = [(42,676 – 31,049) ÷ 42,676]

FIFO = 26.74 percent = [(42,676 – 31,264) ÷ 42,676]

Revenue of financial products is excluded from the calculation of gross profit. Gross profit is sales of machinery and engines less cost of goods sold. The gross profit margin is lower under FIFO because the cost of goods sold is lower from the LIFO reserve reduction.

Net profit margin = Net income ÷ Total revenue

LIFO = 1.66 percent = (754 ÷ 45,462)

FIFO = 1.32 percent = (599 ÷ 45,462]

The net profit margin is higher under LIFO because the cost of goods sold is lower due to the LIFO liquidation. The absolute percentage difference is less than that of the gross profit margin because of lower income taxes on the decreased income reported under FIFO and because net income is divided by total revenue including sales of machinery and engines and revenue of financial products. The company appears to be more profitable under LIFO.

Return on assets = Net income ÷ Average total assets

LIFO = 0.99 percent = 754 ÷ [(76,962 + 74,704) ÷ 2]

FIFO = 0.77 percent = 599 ÷ [(76,962 + 1,924) + (74,704 + 2,139) ÷ 2]

The total assets under FIFO are the LIFO total assets increased by the LIFO reserve. The return on assets is lower under FIFO because the of the lower net income due to the higher cost of goods sold as well as higher total assets due to the LIFO reserve adjustment. The company appears to be less profitable under FIFO.

Current ratio = Current assets ÷ Current liabilities

LIFO = 1.35 = (36,244 ÷ 26,931)

FIFO = 1.42 = [(36,244 + 1,924) ÷ 26,931]

The current ratio is lower under LIFO primarily because of lower inventory carrying amount. The company appears to be less liquid under LIFO.

Total liabilities-to-equity ratio = Total liabilities ÷ Total shareholders' equity

LIFO = 4.59 = (63,196 ÷ 13,766)

FIFO = 4.27 = [(63,196 + 710) ÷ (13,766 + 1,214)]

The ratio is higher under LIFO because the addition to retained earnings under FIFO reduces the ratio. The company appears to be more highly leveraged under LIFO.

In summary, the company appears to be more profitable, less liquid, and more highly leveraged under LIFO. Yet, because a company's value is based on the present value of future cash flows, LIFO will increase the company's value because the cash flows are higher in earlier years due to lower taxes. LIFO is primarily used for the tax benefits it provides.

EXAMPLE 6

LIFO Liquidation Illustration

Reliable Fans, Inc. (RF), a hypothetical company, sells high quality fans and has been in business since 2015. Exhibit 4 provides relevant data and financial statement information about RF's inventory purchases and sales of fan inventory for the years 2015 through 2018. RF uses the LIFO method and a periodic inventory system. What amount of RF's 2018 gross profit is due to LIFO liquidation?

Exhibit 4 RF Financial Statement Information under LIFO

	2015	2016	2017	2018
Fans units purchased	12,000	12,000	12,000	12,000
Purchase cost per fan	$100	$105	$110	$115
Fans units sold	10,000	12,000	12,000	13,000
Sales price per fan	$200	$205	$210	$215
LIFO Method				
Beginning inventory	$0	$200,000	$200,000	$200,000
Purchases	1,200,000	1,260,000	1,320,000	1,380,000
Goods available for sale	1,200,000	1,460,000	1,520,000	1,580,000
Ending inventory*	(200,000)	(200,000)	(200,000)	(100,000)
Cost of goods sold	$1,000,000	1,260,000	$1,320,000	$1,480,000
Income Statement				
Sales	$2,000,000	$2,460,000	$2,520,000	$2,795,000
Cost of goods sold	1,000,000	1,260,000	1,320,000	1,480,000
Gross profit	$1,000,000	$1,200,000	$1,200,000	$1,315,000

Exhibit 4 (Continued)

	2015	2016	2017	2018
Balance Sheet				
Inventory	$200,000	$200,000	$200,000	$100,000

* Ending inventory 2015, 2016, and 2017 = (2,000 × $100); Ending inventory 2018 = (1,000 × $100).

Solution:

RF's reported gross profit for 2018 is $1,315,000. RF's 2018 gross profit due to LIFO liquidation is $15,000. If RF had purchased 13,000 fans in 2018 rather than 12,000 fans, the cost of goods sold under the LIFO method would have been $1,495,000 (13,000 fans sold at $115.00 purchase cost per fan), and the reported gross profit would have been $1,300,000 ($2,795,000 less $1,495,000). The gross profit due to LIFO liquidation is $15,000 ($1,315,000 reported gross profit less the $1,300,000 gross profit that would have been reported without the LIFO liquidation). The gross profit due to LIFO liquidation may also be determined by multiplying the number of units liquidated times the difference between the replacement cost of the units liquidated and their historical purchase cost. For RF, 1,000 units times $15 ($115 replacement cost per fan less the $100 historical cost per fan) equals the $15,000 gross profit due to LIFO liquidation.

INVENTORY METHOD CHANGES

5

Companies on rare occasion change inventory valuation methods. Under IFRS, a change in method is acceptable only if the change "results in the financial statements providing reliable and more relevant information about the effects of transactions, other events, or conditions on the business entity's financial position, financial performance, or cash flows."[11] If the change is justifiable, then it is applied retrospectively.

This means that the change is applied to comparative information for prior periods as far back as is practicable. The cumulative amount of the adjustments relating to periods prior to those presented in the current financial statements is made to the opening balance of each affected component of equity (i.e., retained earnings or comprehensive income) of the earliest period presented. For example, if a company changes its inventory method in 2018 and it presents three years of comparative financial statements (2016, 2017, and 2018) in its annual report, it would retrospectively reflect this change as far back as possible. The change would be reflected in the three years of financial statements presented; the financial statements for 2016 and 2017 would be restated as if the new method had been used in these periods, and the cumulative effect of the change on periods prior to 2016 would be reflected in the 2016 opening balance of each affected component of equity. An exemption to the restatement applies when it is impracticable to determine either the period-specific effects or the cumulative effect of the change.

11 IAS 8 [Accounting Policies, Changes in Accounting Estimates and Errors].

Under US GAAP, the conditions to make a change in accounting policy and the accounting for a change in inventory policy are similar to IFRS.[12] US GAAP, however, requires companies to thoroughly explain why the newly adopted inventory accounting method is superior and preferable to the old method. If a company decides to change from LIFO to another inventory method, US GAAP requires a retrospective restatement as described above. However, if a company decides to change to the LIFO method, it must do so on a prospective basis and retrospective adjustments are not made to the financial statements. The carrying amount of inventory under the old method becomes the initial LIFO layer in the year of LIFO adoption.

Analysts should carefully evaluate changes in inventory valuation methods. Although the stated reason for the inventory change may be to better match inventory costs with sales revenue (or some other plausible business explanation), the real underlying (and unstated) purpose may be to reduce income tax expense (if changing to LIFO from FIFO or average cost), or to increase reported profits (if changing from LIFO to FIFO or average cost). As always, the choice of inventory valuation method can have a significant impact on financial statements and the financial ratios that are derived from them. As a consequence, analysts must carefully consider the impact of the change in inventory valuation methods and the differences in inventory valuation methods when comparing a company's performance with that of its industry or its competitors.

6 INVENTORY ADJUSTMENTS

Significant financial risk can result from the holding of inventory. The cost of inventory may not be recoverable due to spoilage, obsolescence, or declines in selling prices. IFRS state that inventories shall be measured (and carried on the balance sheet) at the lower of cost and net realisable value.[13] **Net realisable value** is the estimated selling price in the ordinary course of business less the estimated costs necessary to make the sale and estimated costs to get the inventory in condition for sale. The assessment of net realisable value is typically done item by item or by groups of similar or related items. In the event that the value of inventory declines below the carrying amount on the balance sheet, the inventory carrying amount must be written down to its net realisable value[14] and the loss (reduction in value) recognised as an expense on the income statement. This expense may be included as part of cost of sales or reported separately.

In each subsequent period, a new assessment of net realisable value is made. Reversal (limited to the amount of the original write-down) is required for a subsequent increase in value of inventory previously written down. The reversal of any write-down of inventories is recognised as a reduction in cost of sales (reduction in the amount of inventories recognised as an expense).

US GAAP used to specify the lower of cost or market to value inventories.[15] For fiscal years beginning after December 15, 2016, inventories measured using other than LIFO and retail inventory methods are measured at the lower of cost or net realisable value. This is broadly consistent with IFRS with one major difference: US GAAP prohibit the reversal of write-downs. For inventories measured using LIFO and

12 FASB ASC Topic 250 [Accounting Changes and Error Corrections].
13 IAS 2 paragraphs 28–33 [Inventories – Net realisable value].
14 Frequently, rather than writing inventory down directly, an inventory valuation allowance account is used. The allowance account is netted with the inventory accounts to arrive at the carrying amount that appears on the balance sheet.
15 FASB ASC Section 330-10-35 [Inventory – Overall – Subsequent Measurement].

retail inventory methods, market value is defined as current replacement cost subject to upper and lower limits. Market value cannot exceed net realisable value (selling price less reasonably estimated costs of completion and disposal). The lower limit of market value is net realisable value less a normal profit margin. Any write-down to market value or net realisable value reduces the value of the inventory, and the loss in value (expense) is generally reflected in the income statement in cost of goods sold.

An inventory write-down reduces both profit and the carrying amount of inventory on the balance sheet and thus has a negative effect on profitability, liquidity, and solvency ratios. However, activity ratios (for example, inventory turnover and total asset turnover) will be positively affected by a write-down because the asset base (denominator) is reduced. The negative impact on some key ratios, due to the decrease in profit, may result in the reluctance by some companies to record inventory write-downs unless there is strong evidence that the decline in the value of inventory is permanent. This is especially true under US GAAP where reversal of a write-down is prohibited.

IAS 2 [Inventories] does not apply to the inventories of producers of agricultural and forest products and minerals and mineral products, nor to commodity broker–traders. These inventories may be measured at net realisable value (fair value less costs to sell and complete) according to well-established industry practices. If an active market exists for these products, the quoted market price in that market is the appropriate basis for determining the fair value of that asset. If an active market does not exist, a company may use market determined prices or values (such as the most recent market transaction price) when available for determining fair value. Changes in the value of inventory (increase or decrease) are recognised in profit or loss in the period of the change. US GAAP is similar to IFRS in its treatment of inventories of agricultural and forest products and mineral ores. Mark-to-market inventory accounting is allowed for bullion.

EXAMPLE 7

Accounting for Declines and Recoveries of Inventory Value

Hatsumei Enterprises, a hypothetical company, manufactures computers and prepares its financial statements in accordance with IFRS. In 2017, the cost of ending inventory was €5.2 million but its net realisable value was €4.9 million. The current replacement cost of the inventory is €4.7 million. This figure exceeds the net realisable value less a normal profit margin. In 2018, the net realisable value of Hatsumei's inventory was €0.5 million greater than the carrying amount.

1 What was the effect of the write-down on Hatsumei's 2017 financial statements? What was the effect of the recovery on Hatsumei's 2018 financial statements?

2 Under US GAAP, if Hatsumei used the LIFO method, what would be the effects of the write-down on Hatsumei's 2017 financial statements and of the recovery on Hatsumei's 2018 financial statements?

3 What would be the effect of the recovery on Hatsumei's 2018 financial statements if Hatsumei's inventory were agricultural products instead of computers?

Solution to 1:

For 2017, Hatsumei would write its inventory down to €4.9 million and record the change in value of €0.3 million as an expense on the income statement. For 2018, Hatsumei would increase the carrying amount of its inventory and reduce the cost of sales by €0.3 million (the recovery is limited to the amount of the original write-down).

Solution to 2:

Under US GAAP, for 2017, Hatsumei would write its inventory down to €4.7 million and typically include the change in value of €0.5 million in cost of goods sold on the income statement. For 2018, Hatsumei would not reverse the write-down.

Solution to 3:

If Hatsumei's inventory were agricultural products instead of computers, inventory would be measured at net realisable value and Hatsumei would, therefore, increase inventory by and record a gain of €0.5 million for 2018.

Analysts should consider the possibility of an inventory write-down because the impact on a company's financial ratios may be substantial. The potential for inventory write-downs can be high for companies in industries where technological obsolescence of inventories is a significant risk. Analysts should carefully evaluate prospective inventory impairments (as well as other potential asset impairments) and their potential effects on the financial ratios when debt covenants include financial ratio requirements. The breaching of debt covenants can have a significant impact on a company.

Companies that use specific identification, weighted average cost, or FIFO methods are more likely to incur inventory write-downs than companies that use the LIFO method. Under the LIFO method, the *oldest* costs are reflected in the inventory carrying amount on the balance sheet. Given increasing inventory costs, the inventory carrying amounts under the LIFO method are already conservatively presented at the oldest and lowest costs. Thus, it is far less likely that inventory write-downs will occur under LIFO—and if a write-down does occur, it is likely to be of a lesser magnitude.

EXAMPLE 8

Effect of Inventory Write-downs on Financial Ratios

The Volvo Group, based in Göteborg, Sweden, is a leading supplier of commercial transport products such as construction equipment, trucks, busses, and drive systems for marine and industrial applications as well as aircraft engine components.[16] Excerpts from Volvo's consolidated financial statements are shown in Exhibits 5 and 6. Notes pertaining to Volvo's inventories are presented in Exhibit 7.

1 What inventory values would Volvo have reported for 2017, 2016, and 2015 if it had no allowance for inventory obsolescence?

2 Assuming that any changes to the allowance for inventory obsolescence are reflected in the cost of sales, what amount would Volvo's cost of sales be for 2017 and 2016 if it had not recorded inventory write-downs in 2017 and 2016?

---

16 The Volvo line of automobiles has not been under the control and management of the Volvo Group since 1999.

3 What amount would Volvo's profit (net income) be for 2017 and 2016 if it had not recorded inventory write-downs in 2017 and 2016? Volvo's effective income tax rate was reported as 25 percent for 2017 and 31 percent for 2016.

4 What would Volvo's 2017 profit (net income) have been if it had reversed all past inventory write-downs in 2017? This question is independent of 1, 2, and 3. The effective income tax rate was 25 percent for 2017.

5 Compare the following for 2017 based on the numbers as reported and those assuming no allowance for inventory obsolescence as in questions 1, 2, and 3: inventory turnover ratio, days of inventory on hand, gross profit margin, and net profit margin.

6 CAT (Example 5) has no disclosures indicative of either inventory write-downs or a cumulative allowance for inventory obsolescence in its 2017 financial statements. Provide a conceptual explanation as to why Volvo incurred inventory write-downs for 2017 but CAT did not.

Exhibit 5 Volvo Group Consolidated Income Statements (Swedish Krona in millions, except per share data)

For the years ended 31 December	2017	2016	2015
Net sales	334,748	301,914	312,515
Cost of sales	(254,581)	(231,602)	(240,653)
Gross income	80,167	70,312	71,862
⋮	⋮	⋮	⋮
Operating income	30,327	20,826	23,318
Interest income and similar credits	164	240	257
Income expenses and similar charges	(1,852)	(1,847)	(2,366)
Other financial income and expenses	(386)	11	(792)
Income after financial items	28,254	19,230	20,418
Income taxes	(6,971)	(6,008)	(5,320)
Income for the period	21,283	13,223	15,099
Attributable to:			
Equity holders of the parent company	20,981	13,147	15,058
Minority interests	302	76	41
Profit	21,283	13,223	15,099

Exhibit 6 Volvo Group Consolidated Balance Sheets (Swedish Krona in millions)

31 December	2017	2016	2015
Assets			
Total non-current assets	213,455	218,465	203,478
Current assets:			
Inventories	52,701	48,287	44,390
⋮	⋮	⋮	⋮

(continued)

Exhibit 6 (Continued)

31 December	2017	2016	2015
Cash and cash equivalents	36,092	23,949	21,048
Total current assets	199,039	180,301	170,687
Total assets	412,494	398,916	374,165
Shareholders' equity and liabilities			
Equity attributable to equity holders of the parent company	107,069	96,061	83,810
Minority interests	1,941	1,703	1,801
Total shareholders' equity	109,011	97,764	85,610
Total non-current provisions	29,147	29,744	26,704
Total non-current liabilities	96,213	104,873	91,814
Total current provisions	10,806	11,333	14,176
Total current liabilities	167,317	155,202	155,860
Total shareholders' equity and liabilities	412,404	398,916	374,165

Exhibit 7 Volvo Group Selected Notes to Consolidated Financial Statements

Note 17. Inventories

Accounting Policy

Inventories are reported at the lower of cost and net realisable value. The cost is established using the first-in, first-out principle (FIFO) and is based on the standard cost method, including costs for all direct manufacturing expenses and the attributable share of capacity and other related manufacturing-related costs. The standard costs are tested regularly and adjustments are made based on current conditions. Costs for research and development, selling, administration and financial expenses are not included. Net realisable value is calculated as the selling price less costs attributable to the sale.

Sources of Estimation Uncertainty

Inventory obsolescence

If the net realisable value is lower than cost, a valuation allowance is established for inventory obsolescence. The total inventory value, net of inventory obsolescence allowance, was: SEK (in millions) 52,701 as of December 2017 and 48,287 as of 31 December 2016.

Inventory

31 December (millions of Krona)	2017	2016	2015
Finished products	32,304	31,012	27,496
Production materials, etc.	20,397	17,275	16,894
Total	**52,701**	**48,287**	**44,390**

Increase (decrease) in allowance for inventory obsolescence			
31 December (millions of Krona)	**2017**	**2016**	**2015**
Opening balance	3,683	3,624	3,394
Change in allowance for inventory obsolescence charged to income	304	480	675
Scrapping	(391)	(576)	(435)
Translation differences	(116)	177	(29)
Reclassifications, etc.	8	(23)	20
Allowance for inventory obsolescence as of 31 December	3,489	3,683	3,624

Solution to 1:

31 December (Swedish krona in millions)	2017	2016	2015
Total inventories, net	52,701	48,287	44,390
From Note 17. (Allowance for obsolescence)	3,489	3,683	3,624
Total inventories (without allowance)	56,190	51,970	48,014

Solution to 2:

31 December (Swedish krona in millions)	2017	2016
Cost of sales	254,581	231,602
(Increase) decrease in allowance for obsolescence*	194	(59)
Cost of sales without allowance	254,775	231,543

* From Note 17, the decrease in allowance for obsolescence for 2017 is 194 (3,489 – 3,683) and the increase for 2016 is 59 (3,683 – 3,624).

Solution to 3:

31 December (Swedish krona in millions)	2017	2016
Profit (Net income)	21,283	13,223
Increase (reduction) in cost of sales	(194)	59
Taxes (tax reduction) on operating profit*	49	(18)
Profit (without allowance)	21,138	13,264

* Taxes (tax reductions) on the operating profit are assumed to be 49 (194 × 25%) for 2017 and –18 (–59 × 31%) for 2016.

Solution to 4:

31 December (Swedish krona in millions)	2017
Profit (Net income)	21,283
Reduction in cost of sales (increase in operating profit)	3,489
Taxes on increased operating profit*	–872
Profit (after recovery of previous write-downs)	23,900

* Taxes on the increased operating profit are assumed to be 872 (3,489 × 25%) for 2017.

Solution to 5:

The Volvo Group's financial ratios for 2017 with the allowance for inventory obsolescence and without the allowance for inventory obsolescence are as follows:

	With Allowance (As Reported)	Without Allowance (Adjusted)
Inventory turnover ratio	5.04	4.71
Days of inventory on hand	72.4	77.5
Gross profit margin	23.95%	23.89%
Net profit margin	6.36%	6.31%

Inventory turnover ratio = Cost of sales ÷ Average inventory

With allowance (as reported) = 5.04 = 254,581 ÷ [(52,701 + 48,287) ÷ 2]

Without allowance (adjusted) = 4.71 = 254,775 ÷ [(56,190 + 51,970) ÷ 2]

Inventory turnover is higher based on the numbers as reported because inventory carrying amounts will be lower with an allowance for inventory obsolescence. The company might appear to manage its inventory more efficiently when it has inventory write-downs.

Days of inventory on hand = Number of days in period ÷ Inventory turnover ratio

With allowance (as reported) = 72.4 days = (365 days ÷ 5.04)

Without allowance (adjusted) = 77.5 days = (365 days ÷ 4.71)

Days of inventory on hand are lower based on the numbers as reported because the inventory turnover is higher. A company with inventory write-downs might appear to manage its inventory more effectively. This is primarily the result of the lower inventory carrying amounts.

Gross profit margin = Gross income ÷ Net sales

With allowance (as reported) = 23.95 percent = (80,167 ÷ 334,748)

Without allowance (adjusted) = 23.89 percent = [(80,167 – 194) ÷ 334,748]

In this instance, the gross profit margin is slightly higher with inventory write-downs because the cost of sales is lower (due to the reduction in the allowance for inventory obsolescence). This assumes that inventory write-downs (and inventory write-down recoveries) are reported as part of cost of sales.

Net profit margin = Profit ÷ Net sales

With allowance (as reported) = 6.36 percent = (21,283 ÷ 334,748)

Without allowance (adjusted) = 6.31 percent = (21,138 ÷ 334,748)

In this instance, the net profit margin is higher with inventory write-downs because the cost of sales is lower (due to the reduction in the allowance for inventory obsolescence). The absolute percentage difference is less than that of the gross profit margin because of the income tax reduction on the decreased income without write-downs.

The profitability ratios (gross profit margin and net profit margin) for Volvo Group would have been slightly lower for 2017 if the company had not recorded inventory write-downs. The activity ratio (inventory turnover ratio) would appear less attractive without the write-downs. The inventory turnover ratio is slightly better (higher) with inventory write-downs because inventory write-downs decrease the average inventory (denominator), making inventory management appear more efficient with write-downs.

Solution to 6:

CAT uses the LIFO method whereas Volvo uses the FIFO method. Given increasing inventory costs, companies that use the FIFO inventory method are far more likely to incur inventory write-downs than those companies that use the LIFO method. This is because under the LIFO method, the inventory carrying amounts reflect the *oldest* costs and therefore the *lowest* costs given increasing inventory costs. Because inventory carrying amounts under the LIFO method are already conservatively presented, it is less likely that inventory write-downs will occur.

EVALUATION OF INVENTORY MANAGEMENT 7

The choice of inventory valuation method impacts the financial statements. The financial statement items impacted include cost of sales, gross profit, net income, inventories, current assets, and total assets. Therefore, the choice of inventory valuation method also affects financial ratios that contain these items. Ratios such as current ratio, return on assets, gross profit margin, and inventory turnover are impacted. As a consequence, analysts must carefully consider inventory valuation method differences when evaluating a company's performance over time or when comparing its performance with the performance of the industry or industry competitors. Additionally, the financial statement items and ratios may be impacted by adjustments of inventory carrying amounts to net realisable value or current replacement cost.

7.1 Presentation and Disclosure

Disclosures are useful when analyzing a company. IFRS require the following financial statement disclosures concerning inventory:

a the accounting policies adopted in measuring inventories, including the cost formula (inventory valuation method) used;

b the total carrying amount of inventories and the carrying amount in classifications (for example, merchandise, raw materials, production supplies, work in progress, and finished goods) appropriate to the entity;

c the carrying amount of inventories carried at fair value less costs to sell;

d the amount of inventories recognised as an expense during the period (cost of sales);

e the amount of any write-down of inventories recognised as an expense in the period;

f the amount of any reversal of any write-down that is recognised as a reduction in cost of sales in the period;

g the circumstances or events that led to the reversal of a write-down of inventories; and

h the carrying amount of inventories pledged as security for liabilities.

Inventory-related disclosures under US GAAP are very similar to the disclosures above, except that requirements (f) and (g) are not relevant because US GAAP do not permit the reversal of prior-year inventory write-downs. US GAAP also require disclosure of significant estimates applicable to inventories and of any material amount of income resulting from the liquidation of LIFO inventory.

7.2 Inventory Ratios

Three ratios often used to evaluate the efficiency and effectiveness of inventory management are **inventory turnover**, **days of inventory on hand**, and **gross profit margin**.[17] These ratios are directly impacted by a company's choice of inventory valuation method. Analysts should be aware, however, that many other ratios are also affected by the choice of inventory valuation method, although less directly. These include the current ratio, because inventory is a component of current assets; the return-on-assets ratio, because cost of sales is a key component in deriving net income and inventory is a component of total assets; and even the debt-to-equity ratio, because the cumulative measured net income from the inception of a business is an aggregate component of retained earnings.

The inventory turnover ratio measures the number of times during the year a company sells (i.e., turns over) its inventory. The higher the turnover ratio, the more times that inventory is sold during the year and the lower the relative investment of resources in inventory. Days of inventory on hand can be calculated as days in the period divided by inventory turnover. Thus, inventory turnover and days of inventory on hand are inversely related. It may be that inventory turnover, however, is calculated using average inventory in the year whereas days of inventory on hand is based on the ending inventory amount. In general, inventory turnover and the number of days of inventory on hand should be benchmarked against industry norms and compared across years.

A high inventory turnover ratio and a low number of days of inventory on hand might indicate highly effective inventory management. Alternatively, a high inventory ratio and a low number of days of inventory on hand could indicate that the company does not carry an adequate amount of inventory or that the company has written down inventory values. Inventory shortages could potentially result in lost sales or production problems in the case of the raw materials inventory of a manufacturer. To assess which explanation is more likely, analysts can compare the company's inventory turnover and sales growth rate with those of the industry and review financial statement disclosures. Slower growth combined with higher inventory turnover could indicate inadequate inventory levels. Write-downs of inventory could reflect poor inventory management. Minimal write-downs and sales growth rates at or above the industry's growth rates would support the interpretation that the higher turnover reflects greater efficiency in managing inventory.

A low inventory turnover ratio and a high number of days of inventory on hand relative to industry norms could be an indicator of slow-moving or obsolete inventory. Again, comparing the company's sales growth across years and with the industry and reviewing financial statement disclosures can provide additional insight.

17 *Days of inventory on hand* is also referred to as *days in inventory* and *average inventory days outstanding*.

The gross profit margin, the ratio of gross profit to sales, indicates the percentage of sales being contributed to net income as opposed to covering the cost of sales. Firms in highly competitive industries generally have lower gross profit margins than firms in industries with fewer competitors. A company's gross profit margin may be a function of its type of product. A company selling luxury products will generally have higher gross profit margins than a company selling staple products. The inventory turnover of the company selling luxury products, however, is likely to be much lower than the inventory turnover of the company selling staple products.

7.3 Financial Analysis Illustrations

IFRS and US GAAP require companies to disclose, either on the balance sheet or in the notes to the financial statements, the carrying amounts of inventories in classifications suitable to the company. For manufacturing companies, these classifications might include production supplies, raw materials, work in progress, and finished goods. For a retailer, these classifications might include significant categories of merchandise or the grouping of inventories with similar attributes. These disclosures may provide signals about a company's future sales and profits.

For example, a significant increase (attributable to increases in unit volume rather than increases in unit cost) in raw materials and/or work-in-progress inventories may signal that the company expects an increase in demand for its products. This suggests an anticipated increase in sales and profit. However, a substantial increase in finished goods inventories while raw materials and work-in-progress inventories are declining may signal a decrease in demand for the company's products and hence lower future sales and profit. This may also signal a potential future write down of finished goods inventory. Irrespective of the signal, an analyst should thoroughly investigate the underlying reasons for any significant changes in a company's raw materials, work-in-progress, and finished goods inventories.

Analysts also should compare the growth rate of a company's sales to the growth rate of its finished goods inventories, because this could also provide a signal about future sales and profits. For example, if the growth of inventories is greater than the growth of sales, this could indicate a decline in demand and a decrease in future earnings. The company may have to lower (mark down) the selling price of its products to reduce its inventory balances, or it may have to write down the value of its inventory because of obsolescence, both of which would negatively affect profits. Besides the potential for mark-downs or write-downs, having too much inventory on hand or the wrong type of inventory can have a negative financial effect on a company because it increases inventory related expenses such as insurance, storage costs, and taxes. In addition, it means that the company has less cash and working capital available to use for other purposes.

Inventory write-downs may have a substantial impact on a company's activity, profitability, liquidity, and solvency ratios. It is critical for the analyst to be aware of industry trends toward product obsolescence and to analyze the financial ratios for their sensitivity to potential inventory impairment. Companies can minimise the impact of inventory write-downs by better matching their inventory composition and growth with prospective customer demand. To obtain additional information about a company's inventory and its future sales, a variety of sources of information are available. Analysts should consider the Management Discussion and Analysis (MD&A) or similar sections of the company's financial reports, industry related news and publications, and industry economic data.

When conducting comparisons, differences in the choice of inventory valuation method can significantly affect the comparability of financial ratios between companies. A restatement from the LIFO method to the FIFO method is critical to make a valid comparison with companies using a method other than the LIFO method such as those companies reporting under IFRS. Analysts should seek out as much information as feasible when analyzing the performance of companies.

EXAMPLE 9

Comparative Illustration

1 Using CAT's LIFO numbers as reported and FIFO adjusted numbers (Example 5) and Volvo's numbers as reported (Example 8), compare the following for 2017: inventory turnover ratio, days of inventory on hand, gross profit margin, net profit margin, return on assets, current ratio, total liabilities-to-equity ratio, and return on equity. For the current ratio, include current provisions as part of current liabilities. For the total liabilities-to-equity ratio, include provisions in total liabilities.

2 How much do inventories represent as a component of total assets for CAT using LIFO numbers as reported and FIFO adjusted numbers, and for Volvo using reported numbers in 2017 and 2016? Discuss any changes that would concern an analyst.

3 Using the reported numbers, compare the 2016 and 2017 growth rates of CAT and Volvo for sales, finished goods inventory, and inventories other than finished goods.

Solution to 1:

The comparisons between Caterpillar and Volvo for 2017 are as follows:

	CAT (LIFO)	CAT (FIFO)	Volvo
Inventory turnover ratio	3.33	2.76	5.04
Days of inventory on hand	109.6 days	132.2 days	72.4 days
Gross profit margin	27.24%	26.74%	23.95%
Net profit margin	1.66%	1.32%	6.36%
Return on assets[a]	0.99%	0.77%	5.25%
Current ratio[b]	1.35	1.42	1.12
Total liabilities-to-equity ratio[c]	4.59	4.27	2.78
Return on equity[d]	5.59%	4.05%	20.59%

Calculations for ratios previously calculated (see Examples 5 and 8) are not shown again.

[a] Return on assets = Net income ÷ Average total assets
Volvo = 5.25 percent = 21,283 ÷ [(412,494 + 398,916) ÷ 2]

[b] Current ratio = Current assets ÷ Current liabilities
Volvo = 1.12 = [199,039 ÷ (10,806 + 167,317)]
The question indicates to include current provisions in current liabilities.

[c] Total liabilities-to-equity ratio = Total liabilities ÷ Total shareholders' equity
Volvo = 2.78 = [(29,147 + 96,213 + 10,806 + 167,317) ÷ 109,011]
The question indicates to include provisions in total liabilities.

[d] Return on equity = Net income ÷ Average shareholders' equity
CAT (LIFO) = 5.59 percent = 754 ÷ [(13,766 + 13,213) ÷ 2]
CAT (FIFO) = 4.05 percent = 599 ÷ {[(13,766 + 1,924 – 710) + (13,213 + 2,139 – 770)] ÷ 2}
Volvo = 20.59 percent = 21,283 ÷ [(109,011 + 97,764) ÷ 2]

Comparing CAT (FIFO) and Volvo, it appears that Volvo manages its inventory more effectively. It has higher inventory turnover and fewer days of inventory on hand. Volvo appears to have superior profitability based on net profit margin. A primary reason for CAT's low profitability in 2017 was due to a substantial increase in the provision for income taxes. An analyst would likely further investigate CAT's increase in provision for income taxes, as well as other reported numbers, rather than reaching a conclusion based on ratios alone (in other words, try to identify the underlying causes of changes or differences in ratios).

Solution to 2:

The 2017 and 2016 inventory to total assets ratios for CAT using LIFO and adjusted to FIFO and for Volvo as reported, are as follows:

	CAT (LIFO)	CAT (FIFO)	Volvo
2017	13.02%	15.28%	12.78%
2016	11.53%	14.14%	12.10%

Inventory to total assets

CAT (LIFO) 2017 =13.02 percent = 10,018 ÷ 76,962
CAT (LIFO) 2016 = 11.53 percent = 8,614 ÷ 74,704
CAT (FIFO) 2017 = 15.28 percent = 11,942 ÷ (76,962 + 1,924 – 710)
CAT (FIFO) 2016 = 14.14 percent = 10,753 ÷ (74,704 + 2,139 – 770)
Volvo 2017 = 12.78 percent = 52,701 ÷ 412,494
Volvo 2016 = 12.10 percent = 48,287 ÷ 398,916

Based on the numbers as reported, CAT appears to have a similar percentage of assets tied up in inventory as Volvo. However, when CAT's inventory is adjusted to FIFO, it has a higher percentage of its assets tied up in inventory than Volvo.

The increase in inventory as a percentage of total assets is cause for some concern. Higher inventory typically results in higher maintenance costs (for example, storage and financing costs). A build-up of slow moving or obsolete inventories may result in future inventory write-downs. In Volvo's Note 17, the breakdown by inventory classification shows a significant increase in the inventory of production materials. Volvo may be planning on increasing production of more finished goods inventory (which has also increased). Looking at CAT's Note 7, all classifications of inventory seem to be increasing and because these are valued using the LIFO method, there is some cause for concern. The company must be increasing inventory quantities and adding new LIFO layers.

Solution to 3:

CAT's and Volvo's 2017 and 2016 growth rates for sales ("Sales of machinery and engines" for CAT and "Net sales" for Volvo), finished goods, and inventories other than finished goods" are as follows:

2017	CAT	Volvo
Sales	19.3%	10.9%
Finished goods	4.0%	4.2%
Inventories other than finished goods	30.2%	18.1%

2016	CAT	Volvo
Sales	−19.0%	−3.4%
Finished goods	−10.7%	12.8%
Inventories other than finished goods	−11.8%	2.3%

Growth rate = (Value for year – Value for previous year)/Value for previous year

2017 CAT

Sales = 19.3 percent = (42,676 – 35,773) ÷ 35,773

Finished goods = 4.0 percent = (4,761 – 4,576) ÷ 4,576

Inventories other than finished goods = 30.2 percent = [(2,802 + 2,254 + 201) – (2,102 + 1,719 + 217)] ÷ (2,102 + 1,719 + 217)

2017 Volvo

Sales = 10.9 percent = (334,748 – 301,914) ÷ 301,914

Finished products = 4.2 percent = (32,304 – 31,012) ÷ 31,012

Inventories other than finished products =18.1 percent = (20,397 – 17,275) ÷ 17,275

2016 CAT

Sales = −19.0 percent = (35,773 – 44,147) ÷ 44,147

Finished goods = −10.7 percent = (4,576 – 5,122) ÷ 5,122

Inventories other than finished goods = −11.8 percent = [(2,102+ 1,719 + 217) – (2,467 + 1,857 + 254)] ÷ (2,467 + 1,857 + 254)

2016 Volvo

Sales = – 3.4 percent = (301,914 – 312,515) ÷ 312,515

Finished products = 12.8 percent = (31,012 – 27,496) ÷ 27,496

Inventories other than finished products = 2.3 percent = (17,275 – 16,894) ÷ 16,894

For both companies, the growth rates in finished goods inventory exceeds the growth rate in sales; this could be indicative of accumulating excess inventory. Volvo's growth rate in finished goods compared to its growth rate in sales is significantly higher but the lower growth rates in finished goods inventory for CAT is potentially a result of using the LIFO method versus the FIFO method. It appears Volvo is aware that an issue exists and is planning on cutting back production given the relatively small increase in inventories other than finished products. Regardless, an analyst should do further investigation before reaching any conclusion about a company's future prospects for sales and profit.

EXAMPLE 10

Single Company Illustration

Selected excerpts from the consolidated financial statements and notes to consolidated financial statements for Jollof Inc., a hypothetical telecommunications company providing networking and communications solutions, are presented in Exhibits 8, 9, and 10. Exhibit 8 contains excerpts from the consolidated income statements, and Exhibit 9 contains excerpts from the consolidated balance sheets. Exhibit 10 contains excerpts from three of the notes to consolidated financial statements.

Note 1 (a) discloses that Jollof's finished goods inventories and work in progress are valued at the lower of cost or net realisable value. Note 2 (a) discloses that the impact of inventory and work in progress write-downs on Jollof's income before tax was a net reduction of €239 million in 2017, a net reduction of €156 million in 2016, and a net reduction of €65 million in 2015.[18] The inventory impairment loss amounts steadily increased from 2015 to 2017 and are included as a component, (additions)/reversals, of Jollof's change in valuation allowance as disclosed in Note 3 (b) from Exhibit 10. Observe also that Jollof discloses its valuation allowance at 31 December 2017, 2016, and 2015 in Note 3 (b) and details on the allocation of the allowance are included in Note 19 (a). The €549 million valuation allowance is the total of a €528 million allowance for inventories and a €21 million allowance for work in progress on construction contracts. Finally, observe that the €1,845 million net value for inventories (excluding construction contracts) at 31 December 2017 in Note 19 (a) reconciles with the balance sheet amount for inventories and work in progress, net, on 31 December 2017, as presented in Exhibit 9.

The inventory valuation allowance represents the total amount of inventory write-downs taken for the inventory reported on the balance sheet (which is measured at the lower of cost or net realisable value). Therefore, an analyst can determine the historical cost of the company's inventory by adding the inventory valuation allowance to the reported inventory carrying amount on the balance sheet. The valuation allowance increased in magnitude and as a percentage of gross inventory values from 2015 to 2017.

Exhibit 8 Alcatel-Lucent Consolidated Income Statements (€ millions)

For years ended 31 December	2017	2016	2015
Revenues	14,267	14,945	10,317
Cost of sales	(9,400)	(10,150)	(6,900)
Gross profit	4,867	4,795	3,417
Administrative and selling expenses	(2,598)	(2,908)	(1,605)
Research and development costs	(2,316	(2,481)	(1,235)
Income from operating activities before restructuring costs, impairment of assets, gain/(loss) on disposal of consolidated entities, and post-retirement benefit plan amendments	(47)	(594)	577
Restructuring costs	(472)	(719)	(594)
Impairment of assets	(3,969)	(2,473)	(118)
Gain/(loss) on disposal of consolidated entities	(6)	—	13
Post-retirement benefit plan amendments	39	217	—
Income (loss) from operating activities	(4,455)	(3,569)	(122)
⋮	⋮	⋮	⋮
Income (loss) from continuing operations	(4,373)	(3,433)	(184)
Income (loss) from discontinued operations	28	512	133
Net income (loss)	(4,345)	(2,921)	51

18 This reduction is often referred to as a *charge*. An accounting charge is the recognition of a loss or expense. In this case, the charge is attributable to the impairment of assets.

Exhibit 9 Alcatel-Lucent Consolidated Balance Sheets (€ millions)

31 December	2017	2016	2015
⋮	⋮	⋮	⋮
Total non-current assets	10,703	16,913	21,559
Inventories and work in progress, net	1,845	1,877	1,898
Amounts due from customers on construction contracts	416	591	517
Trade receivables and related accounts, net	3,637	3,497	3,257
Advances and progress payments	83	92	73
⋮	⋮	⋮	⋮
Total current assets	12,238	11,504	13,629
Total assets	22,941	28,417	35,188
⋮	⋮	⋮	⋮
Retained earnings, fair value, and other reserves	(7,409)	(3,210)	(2,890)
⋮	⋮	⋮	⋮
Total shareholders' equity	4,388	9,830	13,711
Pensions, retirement indemnities, and other post-retirement benefits	4,038	3,735	4,577
Bonds and notes issued, long-term	3,302	3,794	4,117
Other long-term debt	56	40	123
Deferred tax liabilities	968	1,593	2,170
Other non-current liabilities	372	307	232
Total non-current liabilities	8,736	9,471	11,219
Provisions	2,036	2,155	1,987
Current portion of long-term debt	921	406	975
Customers' deposits and advances	780	711	654
Amounts due to customers on construction contracts	158	342	229
Trade payables and related accounts	3,840	3,792	3,383
Liabilities related to disposal groups held for sale	—	—	1,349
Current income tax liabilities	155	59	55
Other current liabilities	1,926	1,651	1,625
Total current liabilities	9,817	9,117	10,257
Total liabilities and shareholders' equity	22,941	28,417	35,188

Exhibit 10 Jollof Inc. Selected Notes to Consolidated Financial Statements

Note 1. Summary of Significant Accounting Policies
(a) Inventories and work in progress

Exhibit 10 (Continued)

Inventories and work in progress are valued at the lower of cost (including indirect production costs where applicable) or net realizable value.[19] Net realizable value is the estimated sales revenue for a normal period of activity less expected completion and selling costs.

Note 2. Principal uncertainties regarding the use of estimates

(a) Valuation allowance for inventories and work in progress

Inventories and work in progress are measured at the lower of cost or net realizable value. Valuation allowances for inventories and work in progress are calculated based on an analysis of foreseeable changes in demand, technology, or the market, in order to determine obsolete or excess inventories and work in progress.

The valuation allowances are accounted for in cost of sales or in restructuring costs, depending on the nature of the amounts concerned.

	31 December		
(€ millions)	**2017**	**2016**	**2015**
Valuation allowance for inventories and work in progress on construction contracts	(549)	(432)	318
Impact of inventory and work in progress write-downs on income (loss) before income tax related reduction of goodwill and discounted operations	(239)	(156)	(65)

Note 3. Inventories and work in progress

(a) Analysis of net value

(€ millions)	**2017**	**2016**	**2015**
Raw materials and goods	545	474	455
Work in progress excluding construction contracts	816	805	632
Finished goods	1,011	995	1,109
Gross value (excluding construction contracts)	2,373	2,274	2,196
Valuation allowance	(528)	(396)	(298)
Net value (excluding construction contracts)	1,845	1,877	1,898
Work in progress on construction contracts, gross*	184	228	291
Valuation allowance	(21)	(35)	(19)
Work in progress on construction contracts, net	163	193	272
Total, net	2,008	2,071	2,170

* Included in the amounts due from/to construction contracts.

(b) Change in valuation allowance

19 *Cost* approximates cost on a first-in, first-out basis.

(€ millions)	2017	2016	2015
At 1 January	(432)	(318)	(355)
(Additions)/reversals	(239)	(156)	(65)
Utilization	58	32	45
Changes in consolidation group	—	—	45
Net effect of exchange rate changes and other changes	63	10	12
At 31 December	(549)	(432)	(318)

Rounding differences may result in totals that are slightly different from the sum and from corresponding numbers in the note.

1 Calculate Jollof's inventory turnover, number of days of inventory on hand, gross profit margin, current ratio, debt-to-equity ratio, and return on total assets for 2017 and 2016 based on the numbers reported. Use an average for inventory and total asset amounts and year-end numbers for other ratio items. For debt, include only bonds and notes issued, long-term; other long-term debt; and current portion of long-term debt.

2 Based on the answer to Question 1, comment on the changes from 2016 to 2017.

3 If Jollof had used the weighted average cost method instead of the FIFO method during 2017, 2016, and 2015, what would be the effect on Jollof's reported cost of sales and inventory carrying amounts? What would be the directional impact on the financial ratios that were calculated for Jollof in Question 1?

Solution to 1:

The financial ratios are as follows:

	2017	2016
Inventory turnover ratio	5.05	5.38
Number of days of inventory on hand	72.3 days	67.8 days
Gross profit margin	34.1%	32.1%
Current ratio	1.25	1.26
Debt-to-equity ratio	0.98	0.43
Return on total assets	−16.9%	−9.2%

Inventory turnover ratio = Cost of sales ÷ Average inventory

2017 inventory turnover ratio = 5.05 = 9,400 ÷ [(1,845 + 1,877) ÷ 2]

2016 inventory turnover ratio = 5.38 = 10,150 ÷ [(1,877 + 1,898) ÷ 2]

Number of days of inventory = 365 days ÷ Inventory turnover ratio

2017 number of days of inventory = 72.3 days = 365 days ÷ 5.05

2016 number of days of inventory = 67.8 days = 365 days ÷ 5.38

Gross profit margin = Gross profit ÷ Total revenue

2017 gross profit margin = 34.1% = 4,867 ÷ 14,267

2016 gross profit margin = 32.1% = 4,795 ÷ 14,945

Current ratio = Current assets ÷ Current liabilities

2017 current ratio = 1.25 = 12,238 ÷ 9,817

2016 current ratio = 1.26 = 11,504 ÷ 9,117

Debt-to-equity ratio = Total debt ÷ Total shareholders' equity

2017 debt-to-equity ratio = 0.98 = (3,302 + 56 + 921) ÷ 4,388

2016 debt-to-equity ratio = 0.43 = (3,794 + 40 + 406) ÷ 9,830

Return on assets = Net income ÷ Average total assets

2017 return on assets = −16.9% = −4,345 ÷ [(22,941 + 28,417) ÷ 2]

2016 return on assets = −9.2% = −2,921 ÷ [(28,417 + 35,188) ÷ 2]

Solution to 2:

From 2016 to 2017, the inventory turnover ratio declined and the number of days of inventory increased by 4.5 days. Jollof appears to be managing inventory less efficiently. The gross profit margin improved by 2.0 percent, from 32.1 percent in 2016 to 34.1 percent in 2017. The current ratio is relatively unchanged from 2016 to 2017. The debt-to-equity ratio has risen significantly in 2017 compared to 2016. Although Jollofn's total debt has been relatively stable during this time period, the company's equity has been declining rapidly because of the cumulative effect of its net losses on retained earnings.

The return on assets is negative and deteriorated in 2017 compared to 2016. A larger net loss and lower total assets in 2017 resulted in a higher negative return on assets. The analyst should investigate the underlying reasons for the sharp decline in Jollof's return on assets. From Exhibit 8, it is apparent that Jollof's gross profit margins were insufficient to cover the administrative and selling expenses and research and development costs in 2016 and 2017. Large restructuring costs and asset impairment losses contributed to the loss from operating activities in both 2016 and 2017.

Solution to 3:

If inventory replacement costs were increasing during 2015, 2016, and 2017 (and inventory quantity levels were stable or increasing), Jollof's cost of sales would have been higher and its gross profit margin would have been lower under the weighted average cost inventory method than what was reported under the FIFO method (assuming no inventory write-downs that would otherwise neutralize the differences between the inventory valuation methods). FIFO allocates the oldest inventory costs to cost of sales; the reported cost of sales would be lower under FIFO given increasing inventory costs. Inventory carrying amounts would be higher under the FIFO method than under the weighted average cost method because the more recently purchased inventory items would be included in inventory at their higher costs (again assuming no inventory write-downs that would otherwise neutralize the differences between the inventory valuation methods). Consequently, Jollof's reported gross profit, net income, and retained earnings would also be higher for those years under the FIFO method.

The effects on ratios are as follows:

- The inventory turnover ratios would all be higher under the weighted average cost method because the numerator (cost of sales) would be higher and the denominator (inventory) would be lower than what was reported by Jollof under the FIFO method.
- The number of days of inventory would be lower under the weighted average cost method because the inventory turnover ratios would be higher.
- The gross profit margin ratios would all be lower under the weighted average cost method because cost of sales would be higher under the weighted average cost method than under the FIFO method.
- The current ratios would all be lower under the weighted average cost method because inventory carrying values would be lower than under the FIFO method (current liabilities would be the same under both methods).
- The return-on-assets ratios would all be lower under the weighted average cost method because the incremental profit added to the numerator (net income) has a greater impact than the incremental increase to the denominator (total assets). By way of example, assume that a company has €3 million in net income and €100 million in total assets using the weighted average cost method. If the company reports another €1 million in net income by using FIFO instead of weighted average cost, it would then also report an additional €1 million in total assets (after tax). Based on this example, the return on assets is 3.00 percent (€3/€100) under the weighted average cost method and 3.96 percent (€4/€101) under the FIFO method.
- The debt-to-equity ratios would all be higher under the weighted average cost method because retained earnings would be lower than under the FIFO method (again assuming no inventory write-downs that would otherwise neutralize the differences between the inventory valuation methods).

Conversely, if inventory replacement costs were decreasing during 2015, 2016, and 2017 (and inventory quantity levels were stable or increasing), Jollof's cost of sales would have been lower and its gross profit and inventory would have been higher under the weighted average cost method than were reported under the FIFO method (assuming no inventory write-downs that would otherwise neutralize the differences between the inventory valuation methods). As a result, the ratio assessment that was performed above would result in directly opposite conclusions.

SUMMARY

The choice of inventory valuation method (cost formula or cost flow assumption) can have a potentially significant impact on inventory carrying amounts and cost of sales. These in turn impact other financial statement items, such as current assets, total assets, gross profit, and net income. The financial statements and accompanying notes provide important information about a company's inventory accounting policies that the analyst needs to correctly assess financial performance and compare it with that of other companies. Key concepts in this reading are as follows:

- Inventories are a major factor in the analysis of merchandising and manufacturing companies. Such companies generate their sales and profits through inventory transactions on a regular basis. An important consideration in determining profits for these companies is measuring the cost of sales when inventories are sold.
- The total cost of inventories comprises all costs of purchase, costs of conversion, and other costs incurred in bringing the inventories to their present location and condition. Storage costs of finished inventory and abnormal costs due to waste are typically treated as expenses in the period in which they occurred.
- The allowable inventory valuation methods implicitly involve different assumptions about cost flows. The choice of inventory valuation method determines how the cost of goods available for sale during the period is allocated between inventory and cost of sales.
- IFRS allow three inventory valuation methods (cost formulas): first-in, first-out (FIFO); weighted average cost; and specific identification. The specific identification method is used for inventories of items that are not ordinarily interchangeable and for goods or services produced and segregated for specific projects. US GAAP allow the three methods above plus the last-in, first-out (LIFO) method. The LIFO method is widely used in the United States for both tax and financial reporting purposes because of potential income tax savings.
- The choice of inventory method affects the financial statements and any financial ratios that are based on them. As a consequence, the analyst must carefully consider inventory valuation method differences when evaluating a company's performance over time or in comparison to industry data or industry competitors.
- A company must use the same cost formula for all inventories having a similar nature and use to the entity.
- The inventory accounting system (perpetual or periodic) may result in different values for cost of sales and ending inventory when the weighted average cost or LIFO inventory valuation method is used.
- Under US GAAP, companies that use the LIFO method must disclose in their financial notes the amount of the LIFO reserve or the amount that would have been reported in inventory if the FIFO method had been used. This information can be used to adjust reported LIFO inventory and cost of goods sold balances to the FIFO method for comparison purposes.
- LIFO liquidation occurs when the number of units in ending inventory declines from the number of units that were present at the beginning of the year. If inventory unit costs have generally risen from year to year, this will produce an inventory-related increase in gross profits.
- Consistency of inventory costing is required under both IFRS and US GAAP. If a company changes an accounting policy, the change must be justifiable and applied retrospectively to the financial statements. An exception to the retrospective restatement is when a company reporting under US GAAP changes to the LIFO method.
- Under IFRS, inventories are measured at the lower of cost and net realisable value. Net realisable value is the estimated selling price in the ordinary course of business less the estimated costs necessary to make the sale. Under US GAAP, inventories are measured at the lower of cost, market value, or net

realisable value depending upon the inventory method used. Market value is defined as current replacement cost subject to an upper limit of net realizable value and a lower limit of net realizable value less a normal profit margin. Reversals of previous write-downs are permissible under IFRS but not under US GAAP.

- Reversals of inventory write-downs may occur under IFRS but are not allowed under US GAAP.
- Changes in the carrying amounts within inventory classifications (such as raw materials, work-in-process, and finished goods) may provide signals about a company's future sales and profits. Relevant information with respect to inventory management and future sales may be found in the Management Discussion and Analysis or similar items within the annual or quarterly reports, industry news and publications, and industry economic data.
- The inventory turnover ratio, number of days of inventory ratio, and gross profit margin ratio are useful in evaluating the management of a company's inventory.
- Inventory management may have a substantial impact on a company's activity, profitability, liquidity, and solvency ratios. It is critical for the analyst to be aware of industry trends and management's intentions.
- Financial statement disclosures provide information regarding the accounting policies adopted in measuring inventories, the principal uncertainties regarding the use of estimates related to inventories, and details of the inventory carrying amounts and costs. This information can greatly assist analysts in their evaluation of a company's inventory management.

PRACTICE PROBLEMS

1 Inventory cost is *least likely* to include:

A production-related storage costs.

B costs incurred as a result of normal waste of materials.

C transportation costs of shipping inventory to customers.

2 Mustard Seed PLC adheres to IFRS. It recently purchased inventory for €100 million and spent €5 million for storage prior to selling the goods. The amount it charged to inventory expense (€ millions) was *closest* to:

A €95.

B €100.

C €105.

3 Carrying inventory at a value above its historical cost would *most likely* be permitted if:

A the inventory was held by a producer of agricultural products.

B financial statements were prepared using US GAAP.

C the change resulted from a reversal of a previous write-down.

The following information relates to Questions 4 and 5.

A retail company is comparing different approaches to valuing inventory. The company has one product that it sells for $50.

Table 1 Units Purchased and Sold (first quarter)

Date	Units Purchased	Purchase Price	Units Sold	Selling Price	Inventory Units on Hand
2 Jan	1,000	$20.00			1,000
17 Jan			500	$50.00	500
16 Feb	1,000	$18.00			1,500
3 Mar			1,200	$50.00	300
13 Mar	1,000	$17.00			1,300
23 Mar			500	$50.00	800
End of quarter totals:	3,000	$55,000	2,200	$110,000	

© 2019 CFA Institute. All rights reserved.

Table 2 Comparison of Inventory Methods and Models

End of Quarter Valuations 31 March	Perpetual LIFO	Periodic LIFO	Perpetual FIFO
Sales	$110,000	$110,000	$110,000
Ending inventory		$16,000	$13,600
Cost of goods sold		$39,000	$41,400
Gross profit		$71,000	$68,600
Inventory turnover ratio	279%		

Note: LIFO is last in, first out and FIFO is first in, first out.

4 What is the value of ending inventory for the first quarter if the company uses a perpetual LIFO inventory valuation method?

A $14,500

B $15,000

C $16,000

5 Which inventory accounting method results in the lowest inventory turnover ratio for the first quarter?

A Periodic LIFO

B Perpetual LIFO

C Perpetual FIFO

6 During periods of rising inventory unit costs, a company using the FIFO method rather than the LIFO method will report a lower:

A current ratio.

B inventory turnover.

C gross profit margin.

7 LIFO reserve is *most likely* to increase when inventory unit:

A costs are increasing.

B costs are decreasing.

C levels are decreasing.

8 If inventory unit costs are increasing from period-to-period, a LIFO liquidation is *most likely* to result in an increase in:

A gross profit.

B LIFO reserve.

C inventory carrying amounts.

9 A company using the LIFO method reports the following in £:

	2018	2017
Cost of goods sold (COGS)	50,800	48,500
Ending inventories	10,550	10,000
LIFO reserve	4,320	2,600

Cost of goods sold for 2018 under the FIFO method is *closest* to:

A £48,530.

B £49,080.

C £52,520.

10 Eric's Used Book Store prepares its financial statements in accordance with IFRS. Inventory was purchased for £1 million and later marked down to £550,000. One of the books, however, was later discovered to be a rare collectible item, and the inventory is now worth an estimated £3 million. The inventory is *most likely* reported on the balance sheet at:

A £550,000.

B £1,000,000.

C £3,000,000.

11 Fernando's Pasta purchased inventory and later wrote it down. The current net realisable value is higher than the value when written down. Fernando's inventory balance will *most likely* be:

A higher if it complies with IFRS.

B higher if it complies with US GAAP.

C the same under US GAAP and IFRS.

12 A write down of the value of inventory to its net realizable value will have a positive effect on the:

A balance sheet.

B income statement.

C inventory turnover ratio.

For questions 13–24, assume the companies use a periodic inventory system.

13 Cinnamon Corp. started business in 2017 and uses the weighted average cost method. During 2017, it purchased 45,000 units of inventory at €10 each and sold 40,000 units for €20 each. In 2018, it purchased another 50,000 units at €11 each and sold 45,000 units for €22 each. Its 2018 cost of sales (€ thousands) was *closest* to:

A €490.

B €491.

C €495.

14 Zimt AG started business in 2017 and uses the FIFO method. During 2017, it purchased 45,000 units of inventory at €10 each and sold 40,000 units for €20 each. In 2018, it purchased another 50,000 units at €11 each and sold 45,000 units for €22 each. Its 2018 ending inventory balance (€ thousands) was *closest* to:

A €105.

B €109.

C €110.

15 Zimt AG uses the FIFO method, and Nutmeg Inc. uses the LIFO method. Compared to the cost of replacing the inventory, during periods of rising prices, the cost of sales reported by:

A Zimt is too low.

B Nutmeg is too low.

C Nutmeg is too high.

16 Zimt AG uses the FIFO method, and Nutmeg Inc. uses the LIFO method. Compared to the cost of replacing the inventory, during periods of rising prices the ending inventory balance reported by:

A Zimt is too high.

B Nutmeg is too low.

C Nutmeg is too high.

17 Like many technology companies, TechnoTools operates in an environment of declining prices. Its reported profits will tend to be *highest* if it accounts for inventory using the:

A FIFO method.

B LIFO method.

C weighted average cost method.

18 Compared to using the weighted average cost method to account for inventory, during a period in which prices are generally rising, the current ratio of a company using the FIFO method would *most likely* be:

A lower.

B higher.

C dependent upon the interaction with accounts payable.

19 Zimt AG wrote down the value of its inventory in 2017 and reversed the write-down in 2018. Compared to the ratios that would have been calculated if the write-down had never occurred, Zimt's reported 2017:

A current ratio was too high.

B gross margin was too high.

C inventory turnover was too high.

20 Zimt AG wrote down the value of its inventory in 2017 and reversed the write-down in 2018. Compared to the results the company would have reported if the write-down had never occurred, Zimt's reported 2018:

A profit was overstated.

B cash flow from operations was overstated.

C year-end inventory balance was overstated.

21 Compared to a company that uses the FIFO method, during periods of rising prices a company that uses the LIFO method will *most likely* appear more:

A liquid.

B efficient.

C profitable.

22 Nutmeg, Inc. uses the LIFO method to account for inventory. During years in which inventory unit costs are generally rising and in which the company purchases more inventory than it sells to customers, its reported gross profit margin will *most likely* be:

A lower than it would be if the company used the FIFO method.

B higher than it would be if the company used the FIFO method.

C about the same as it would be if the company used the FIFO method.

23 Compared to using the FIFO method to account for inventory, during periods of rising prices, a company using the LIFO method is *most likely* to report higher:

A net income.

B cost of sales.

C income taxes.

24 Carey Company adheres to US GAAP, whereas Jonathan Company adheres to IFRS. It is *least likely* that:

A Carey has reversed an inventory write-down.

B Jonathan has reversed an inventory write-down.

C Jonathan and Carey both use the FIFO inventory accounting method.

---

25 Company A adheres to US GAAP and Company B adheres to IFRS. Which of the following is *most likely* to be disclosed on the financial statements of both companies?

A Any material income resulting from the liquidation of LIFO inventory

B The amount of inventories recognized as an expense during the period

C The circumstances that led to the reversal of a write down of inventories

26 Which of the following *most likely* signals that a manufacturing company expects demand for its product to increase?

A Finished goods inventory growth rate higher than the sales growth rate

B Higher unit volumes of work in progress and raw material inventories

C Substantially higher finished goods, with lower raw materials and work-in-process

27 Compared with a company that uses the FIFO method, during a period of rising unit inventory costs, a company using the LIFO method will *most likely* appear more:

A liquid.

B efficient.

C profitable.

28 In a period of declining inventory unit costs and constant or increasing inventory quantities, which inventory method is *most likely* to result in a higher debt-to-equity ratio?

A LIFO

B FIFO

C Weighted average cost

The following information relates to Questions 29–36

Hans Annan, CFA, a food and beverage analyst, is reviewing Century Chocolate's inventory policies as part of his evaluation of the company. Century Chocolate, based in Switzerland, manufactures chocolate products and purchases and resells other confectionery products to complement its chocolate line. Annan visited Century Chocolate's manufacturing facility last year. He learned that cacao beans, imported from Brazil, represent the most significant raw material and that the work-in-progress inventory consists primarily of three items: roasted cacao beans, a thick paste produced from the beans (called chocolate liquor), and a sweetened mixture that needs to be "conched" to produce chocolate. On the tour, Annan learned that the conching process ranges from a few hours for lower-quality products to six days for the highest-quality chocolates. While there, Annan saw the facility's climate-controlled area where manufactured finished products (cocoa and chocolate) and purchased finished goods are stored prior to shipment to customers. After touring the facility, Annan had a discussion with Century Chocolate's CFO regarding the types of costs that were included in each inventory category.

Annan has asked his assistant, Joanna Kern, to gather some preliminary information regarding Century Chocolate's financial statements and inventories. He also asked Kern to calculate the inventory turnover ratios for Century Chocolate and another chocolate manufacturer for the most recent five years. Annan does not know Century Chocolate's most direct competitor, so he asks Kern to do some research and select the most appropriate company for the ratio comparison.

Kern reports back that Century Chocolate prepares its financial statements in accordance with IFRS. She tells Annan that the policy footnote states that raw materials and purchased finished goods are valued at purchase cost whereas work in progress and manufactured finished goods are valued at production cost. Raw material inventories and purchased finished goods are accounted for using the FIFO (first-in, first-out) method, and the weighted average cost method is used for other inventories. An allowance is established when the net realisable value of any inventory item is lower than the value calculated above.

Kern provides Annan with the selected financial statements and inventory data for Century Chocolate shown in Exhibits 1 through 5. The ratio exhibit Kern prepared compares Century Chocolate's inventory turnover ratios to those of Gordon's Goodies, a US-based company. Annan returns the exhibit and tells Kern to select a different competitor that reports using IFRS rather than US GAAP. During this initial review, Annan asks Kern why she has not indicated whether Century Chocolate uses a perpetual or a periodic inventory system. Kern replies that she learned that Century Chocolate uses a perpetual system but did not include this information in her report because inventory values would be the same under either a perpetual or periodic inventory system. Annan tells Kern she is wrong and directs her to research the matter.

While Kern is revising her analysis, Annan reviews the most recent month's Cocoa Market Review from the International Cocoa Organization. He is drawn to the statement that "the ICCO daily price, averaging prices in both futures markets, reached a 29-year high in US$ terms and a 23-year high in SDRs terms (the SDR unit comprises a basket of major currencies used in international trade: US$, euro, pound sterling and yen)." Annan makes a note that he will need to factor the potential continuation of this trend into his analysis.

Exhibit 1 Century Chocolate Income Statements (CHF Millions)

For Years Ended 31 December	2018	2017
Sales	95,290	93,248
Cost of sales	−41,043	−39,047
Marketing, administration, and other expenses	−35,318	−42,481
Profit before taxes	**18,929**	**11,720**
Taxes	−3,283	−2,962
Profit for the period	**15,646**	**8,758**

Exhibit 2 Century Chocolate Balance Sheets (CHF Millions)

31 December	2018	2017
Cash, cash equivalents, and short-term investments	6,190	8,252
Trade receivables and related accounts, net	11,654	12,910
Inventories, net	8,100	7,039
Other current assets	2,709	2,812
Total current assets	**28,653**	**31,013**
Property, plant, and equipment, net	18,291	19,130
Other non-current assets	45,144	49,875
Total assets	**92,088**	**100,018**
Trade and other payables	10,931	12,299
Other current liabilities	17,873	25,265
Total current liabilities	**28,804**	**37,564**
Non-current liabilities	15,672	14,963
Total liabilities	**44,476**	**52,527**
Equity		
Share capital	332	341
Retained earnings and other reserves	47,280	47,150
Total equity	**47,612**	**47,491**
Total liabilities and shareholders' equity	**92,088**	**100,018**

Exhibit 3 Century Chocolate Supplementary Footnote Disclosures: Inventories (CHF Millions)

31 December	2018	2017
Raw Materials	2,154	1,585
Work in Progress	1,061	1,027
Finished Goods	5,116	4,665
Total inventories before allowance	8,331	7,277
Allowance for write-downs to net realisable value	–231	–238
Total inventories net of allowance	8,100	7,039

Exhibit 4 Century Chocolate Inventory Record for Purchased Lemon Drops

Date		Cartons	Per Unit Amount (CHF)
	Beginning inventory	100	22
4 Feb 09	Purchase	40	25

(continued)

Exhibit 4 (Continued)

Date		Cartons	Per Unit Amount (CHF)
3 Apr 09	Sale	50	32
23 Jul 09	Purchase	70	30
16 Aug 09	Sale	100	32
9 Sep 09	Sale	35	32
15 Nov 09	Purchase	100	28

Exhibit 5 Century Chocolate Net Realisable Value Information for Black Licorice Jelly Beans

	2018	2017
FIFO cost of inventory at 31 December (CHF)	314,890	374,870
Ending inventory at 31 December (Kilograms)	77,750	92,560
Cost per unit (CHF)	4.05	4.05
Net Realisable Value (CHF per Kilograms)	4.20	3.95

29 The costs *least likely* to be included by the CFO as inventory are:

A storage costs for the chocolate liquor.

B excise taxes paid to the government of Brazil for the cacao beans.

C storage costs for chocolate and purchased finished goods awaiting shipment to customers.

30 What is the *most likely* justification for Century Chocolate's choice of inventory valuation method for its purchased finished goods?

A It is the preferred method under IFRS.

B It allocates the same per unit cost to both cost of sales and inventory.

C Ending inventory reflects the cost of goods purchased most recently.

31 In Kern's comparative ratio analysis, the 2018 inventory turnover ratio for Century Chocolate is *closest* to:

A 5.07.

B 5.42.

C 5.55.

32 The *most accurate* statement regarding Annan's reasoning for requiring Kern to select a competitor that reports under IFRS for comparative purposes is that under US GAAP:

A fair values are used to value inventory.

B the LIFO method is permitted to value inventory.

C the specific identification method is permitted to value inventory.

33 Annan's statement regarding the perpetual and periodic inventory systems is most significant when which of the following costing systems is used?

A LIFO.

B FIFO.

C Specific identification.

34 Using the inventory record for purchased lemon drops shown in Exhibit 4, the cost of sales for 2018 will be *closest* to:

A CHF 3,550.

B CHF 4,550.

C CHF 4,850.

35 Ignoring any tax effect, the 2018 net realisable value reassessment for the black licorice jelly beans will *most likely* result in:

A an increase in gross profit of CHF 7,775.

B an increase in gross profit of CHF 11,670.

C no impact on cost of sales because under IFRS, write-downs cannot be reversed.

36 If the trend noted in the ICCO report continues and Century Chocolate plans to maintain constant or increasing inventory quantities, the *most likely* impact on Century Chocolate's financial statements related to its raw materials inventory will be:

A a cost of sales that more closely reflects current replacement values.

B a higher allocation of the total cost of goods available for sale to cost of sales.

C a higher allocation of the total cost of goods available for sale to ending inventory.

The following information relates to Questions 37–42

John Martinson, CFA, is an equity analyst with a large pension fund. His supervisor, Linda Packard, asks him to write a report on Karp Inc. Karp prepares its financial statements in accordance with US GAAP. Packard is particularly interested in the effects of the company's use of the LIFO method to account for its inventory. For this purpose, Martinson collects the financial data presented in Exhibits 1 and 2.

Exhibit 1 Balance Sheet Information (US$ Millions)

As of 31 December	2018	2017
Cash and cash equivalents	172	157
Accounts receivable	626	458
Inventories	620	539
Other current assets	125	65
Total current assets	1,543	1,219
Property and equipment, net	3,035	2,972
Total assets	4,578	4,191
Total current liabilities	1,495	1,395
Long-term debt	644	604

(continued)

Exhibit 1 (Continued)

As of 31 December	2018	2017
Total liabilities	2,139	1,999
Common stock and paid in capital	1,652	1,652
Retained earnings	787	540
Total shareholders' equity	2,439	2,192
Total liabilities and shareholders' equity	4,578	4,191

Exhibit 2 Income Statement Information (US$ Millions)

For the Year Ended 31 December	2018	2017
Sales	4,346	4,161
Cost of goods sold	2,211	2,147
Depreciation and amortisation expense	139	119
Selling, general, and administrative expense	1,656	1,637
Interest expense	31	18
Income tax expense	62	48
Net income	247	192

Martinson finds the following information in the notes to the financial statements:

- The LIFO reserves as of 31 December 2018 and 2017 are $155 million and $117 million respectively, and
- The effective income tax rate applicable to Karp for 2018 and earlier periods is 20 percent.

37 If Karp had used FIFO instead of LIFO, the amount of inventory reported as of 31 December 2018 would have been *closest* to:

A $465 million.

B $658 million.

C $775 million.

38 If Karp had used FIFO instead of LIFO, the amount of cost of goods sold reported by Karp for the year ended 31 December 2018 would have been *closest* to:

A $2,056 million.

B $2,173 million.

C $2,249 million.

39 If Karp had used FIFO instead of LIFO, its reported net income for the year ended 31 December 2018 would have been higher by an amount *closest to*:

A $30 million.

B $38 million.

C $155 million.

40 If Karp had used FIFO instead of LIFO, Karp's retained earnings as of 31 December 2018 would have been higher by an amount *closest to*:

A \$117 million.

B \$124 million.

C \$155 million.

41 If Karp had used FIFO instead of LIFO, which of the following ratios computed as of 31 December 2018 would *most likely* have been lower?

A Cash ratio.

B Current ratio.

C Gross profit margin.

42 If Karp had used FIFO instead of LIFO, its debt to equity ratio computed as of 31 December 2018 would have:

A increased.

B decreased.

C remained unchanged.

The following information relates to Questions 43–48

Robert Groff, an equity analyst, is preparing a report on Crux Corp. As part of his report, Groff makes a comparative financial analysis between Crux and its two main competitors, Rolby Corp. and Mikko Inc. Crux and Mikko report under US GAAP and Rolby reports under IFRS.

Groff gathers information on Crux, Rolby, and Mikko. The relevant financial information he compiles is in Exhibit 1. Some information on the industry is in Exhibit 2.

Exhibit 1 Selected Financial Information (US\$ Millions)

	Crux	Rolby	Mikko
Inventory valuation method	LIFO	FIFO	LIFO
From the Balance Sheets			
As of 31 December 2018			
Inventory, gross	480	620	510
Valuation allowance	20	25	14
Inventory, net	460	595	496
Total debt	1,122	850	732
Total shareholders' equity	2,543	2,403	2,091
As of 31 December 2017			
Inventory, gross	465	602	401
Valuation allowance	23	15	12
Inventory, net	442	587	389
From the Income Statements			
Year Ended 31 December 2018			

(continued)

Exhibit 1 (Continued)

	Crux	Rolby	Mikko
Revenues	4,609	5,442	3,503
Cost of goods sold[a]	3,120	3,782	2,550
Net income	229	327	205
[a]Charges included in cost of goods sold for inventory write-downs*	13	15	15

* This does not match the change in the inventory valuation allowance because the valuation allowance is reduced to reflect the valuation allowance attached to items sold and increased for additional necessary write-downs.

LIFO Reserve			
As of 31 December 2018	55	0	77
As of 31 December 2017	72	0	50
As of 31 December 2016	96	0	43
Tax Rate			
Effective tax rate	30%	30%	30%

Exhibit 2 Industry Information

	2018	2017	2016
Raw materials price index	112	105	100
Finished goods price index	114	106	100

To compare the financial performance of the three companies, Groff decides to convert LIFO figures into FIFO figures, and adjust figures to assume no valuation allowance is recognized by any company.

After reading Groff's draft report, his supervisor, Rachel Borghi, asks him the following questions:

Question 1 Which company's gross profit margin would best reflect current costs of the industry?

Question 2 Would Rolby's valuation method show a higher gross profit margin than Crux's under an inflationary, a deflationary, or a stable price scenario?

Question 3 Which group of ratios usually appears more favorable with an inventory write-down?

43 Crux's inventory turnover ratio computed as of 31 December 2018, after the adjustments suggested by Groff, is *closest* to:

A 5.67.

B 5.83.

C 6.13.

44 Rolby's net profit margin for the year ended 31 December 2018, after the adjustments suggested by Groff, is *closest* to:

A 6.01%.

B 6.20%.

C 6.28%.

45 Compared with its unadjusted debt-to-equity ratio, Mikko's debt-to-equity ratio as of 31 December 2018, after the adjustments suggested by Groff, is:

A lower.

B higher.

C the same.

46 The *best* answer to Borghi's Question 1 is:

A Crux's.

B Rolby's.

C Mikko's.

47 The *best* answer to Borghi's Question 2 is:

A Stable.

B Inflationary.

C Deflationary.

48 The *best* answer to Borghi's Question 3 is:

A Activity ratios.

B Solvency ratios.

C Profitability ratios.

The following information relates to Questions 49–55

ZP Corporation is a (hypothetical) multinational corporation headquartered in Japan that trades on numerous stock exchanges. ZP prepares its consolidated financial statements in accordance with US GAAP. Excerpts from ZP's 2018 annual report are shown in Exhibits 1–3.

Exhibit 1 Consolidated Balance Sheets (¥ Millions)

31 December	2017	2018
Current Assets		
Cash and cash equivalents	¥542,849	¥814,760
⋮	⋮	⋮
Inventories	608,572	486,465
⋮	⋮	⋮
Total current assets	4,028,742	3,766,309
⋮	⋮	⋮
Total assets	**¥10,819,440**	**¥9,687,346**

(continued)

Exhibit 1 (Continued)

31 December	2017	2018
⋮	⋮	⋮
Total current liabilities	¥3,980,247	¥3,529,765
⋮	⋮	⋮
Total long-term liabilities	2,663,795	2,624,002
Minority interest in consolidated subsidiaries	218,889	179,843
Total shareholders' equity	3,956,509	3,353,736
Total liabilities and shareholders' equity	**¥10,819,440**	**¥9,687,346**

Exhibit 2 Consolidated Statements of Income (¥ Millions)

For the years ended 31 December	2016	2017	2018
Net revenues			
Sales of products	¥7,556,699	¥8,273,503	¥6,391,240
Financing operations	425,998	489,577	451,950
	7,982,697	8,763,080	6,843,190
Cost and expenses			
Cost of products sold	6,118,742	6,817,446	5,822,805
Cost of financing operations	290,713	356,005	329,128
Selling, general and administrative	827,005	832,837	844,927
⋮	⋮	⋮	⋮
Operating income (loss)	746,237	756,792	–153,670
⋮	⋮	⋮	⋮
Net income	¥548,011	¥572,626	–¥145,646

Exhibit 3 Selected Disclosures in the 2018 Annual Report

Management's Discussion and Analysis of Financial Condition and Results of Operations

Cost reduction efforts were offset by increased prices of raw materials, other production materials and parts ... Inventories decreased during fiscal 2009 by ¥122.1 billion, or 20.1%, to ¥486.5 billion. This reflects the impacts of decreased sales volumes and fluctuations in foreign currency translation rates.

Management & Corporate Information

Risk Factors

Industry and Business Risks

Exhibit 3 (Continued)

The worldwide market for our products is highly competitive. ZP faces intense competition from other manufacturers in the respective markets in which it operates. Competition has intensified due to the worldwide deterioration in economic conditions. In addition, competition is likely to further intensify because of continuing globalization, possibly resulting in industry reorganization. Factors affecting competition include product quality and features, the amount of time required for innovation and development, pricing, reliability, safety, economy in use, customer service and financing terms. Increased competition may lead to lower unit sales and excess production capacity and excess inventory. This may result in a further downward price pressure.

ZP's ability to adequately respond to the recent rapid changes in the industry and to maintain its competitiveness will be fundamental to its future success in maintaining and expanding its market share in existing and new markets.

Notes to Consolidated Financial Statements

2. Summary of significant accounting policies:

Inventories. Inventories are valued at cost, not in excess of market. Cost is determined on the "average-cost" basis, except for the cost of finished products carried by certain subsidiary companies which is determined "last-in, first-out" ("LIFO") basis. Inventories valued on the LIFO basis totaled ¥94,578 million and ¥50,037 million at December 31, 2017 and 2018, respectively. Had the "first-in, first-out" basis been used for those companies using the LIFO basis, inventories would have been ¥10,120 million and ¥19,660 million higher than reported at December 31, 2017 and 2018, respectively.

9. Inventories:

Inventories consist of the following:

31 December (¥ Millions)	2017	2018
Finished goods	¥ 403,856	¥ 291,977
Raw materials	99,869	85,966
Work in process	79,979	83,890
Supplies and other	24,868	24,632
	¥ 608,572	**¥ 486,465**

49 The MD&A indicated that the prices of raw material, other production materials, and parts increased. Based on the inventory valuation methods described in Note 2, which inventory classification would *least accurately* reflect current prices?

A Raw materials.

B Finished goods.

C Work in process.

50 The 2017 inventory value as reported on the 2018 Annual Report if the company had used the FIFO inventory valuation method instead of the LIFO inventory valuation method for a portion of its inventory would be *closest* to:

A ¥104,698 million.

B ¥506,125 million.

C ¥618,692 million.

51 If ZP had prepared its financial statement in accordance with IFRS, the inventory turnover ratio (using average inventory) for 2018 would be:

A lower.

B higher.

C the same.

52 Inventory levels decreased from 2017 to 2018 for all of the following reasons *except*:

A LIFO liquidation.

B decreased sales volume.

C fluctuations in foreign currency translation rates.

53 Which observation is *most likely* a result of looking only at the information reported in Note 9?

A Increased competition has led to lower unit sales.

B There have been significant price increases in supplies.

C Management expects a further downturn in sales during 2010.

54 Note 2 indicates that, "Inventories valued on the LIFO basis totaled ¥94,578 million and ¥50,037 million at December 31, 2017 and 2018, respectively." Based on this, the LIFO reserve should *most likely*:

A increase.

B decrease.

C remain the same.

55 The Industry and Business Risk excerpt states that, "Increased competition may lead to lower unit sales and excess production capacity and excess inventory. This may result in a further downward price pressure." The downward price pressure could lead to inventory that is valued above current market prices or net realisable value. Any write-downs of inventory are *least likely* to have a significant effect on the inventory valued using:

A weighted average cost.

B first-in, first-out (FIFO).

C last-in, first-out (LIFO).

SOLUTIONS

1 C is correct. Transportation costs incurred to ship inventory to customers are an expense and may not be capitalized in inventory. (Transportation costs incurred to bring inventory to the business location can be capitalized in inventory.) Storage costs required as part of production, as well as costs incurred as a result of normal waste of materials, can be capitalized in inventory. (Costs incurred as a result of abnormal waste must be expensed.)

2 B is correct. Inventory expense includes costs of purchase, costs of conversion, and other costs incurred in bringing the inventories to their present location and condition. It does not include storage costs not required as part of production.

3 A is correct. IFRS allow the inventories of producers and dealers of agricultural and forest products, agricultural produce after harvest, and minerals and mineral products to be carried at net realisable value even if above historical cost. (US GAAP treatment is similar.)

4 A is correct. A perpetual inventory system updates inventory values and quantities and cost of goods sold continuously to reflect purchases and sales. The ending inventory of 800 units consists of 300 units at $20 and 500 units at $17.

$$(300 \times \$20) + (500 \times \$17) = \$14,500$$

5 A is correct. In an environment with falling inventory costs and declining inventory levels, periodic LIFO will result in a higher ending inventory value and lower cost of goods sold versus perpetual LIFO and perpetual FIFO methods. This results in a lower inventory turnover ratio, which is calculated as follows:

$$\text{Inventory turnover ratio} = \text{Cost of goods sold/Ending inventory}$$

The inventory turnover ratio using periodic LIFO is $39,000/$16,000 = 244% or 2.44 times.

The inventory turnover ratio using perpetual LIFO is 279% or 2.79 times, which is provided in Table 2 (= 40,500/14,500 from previous question).

The inventory turnover for perpetual FIFO is $41,400/$13,600 = 304% or 3.04 times.

6 B is correct. During a period of rising inventory costs, a company using the FIFO method will allocate a lower amount to cost of goods sold and a higher amount to ending inventory as compared with the LIFO method. The inventory turnover ratio is the ratio of cost of sales to ending inventory. A company using the FIFO method will produce a lower inventory turnover ratio as compared with the LIFO method. The current ratio (current assets/current liabilities) and the gross profit margin [gross profit/sales = (sales less cost of goods sold)/sales] will be higher under the FIFO method than under the LIFO method in periods of rising inventory unit costs.

7 A is correct. LIFO reserve is the FIFO inventory value less the LIFO inventory value. In periods of rising inventory unit costs, the carrying amount of inventory under FIFO will always exceed the carrying amount of inventory under LIFO. The LIFO reserve may increase over time as a result of the increasing difference between the older costs used to value inventory under LIFO and the

more recent costs used to value inventory under FIFO. When inventory unit levels are decreasing, the company will experience a LIFO liquidation, reducing the LIFO reserve.

8 A is correct. When the number of units sold exceeds the number of units purchased, a company using LIFO will experience a LIFO liquidation. If inventory unit costs have been rising from period-to-period and a LIFO liquidation occurs, it will produce an increase in gross profit as a result of the lower inventory carrying amounts of the liquidated units (lower cost per unit of the liquidated units).

9 B is correct. The adjusted COGS under the FIFO method is equal to COGS under the LIFO method less the increase in LIFO reserve:

COGS (FIFO) = COGS (LIFO) – Increase in LIFO reserve
COGS (FIFO) = £50,800 – (£4,320 – £2,600)
COGS (FIFO) = £49,080

10 B is correct. Under IFRS, the reversal of write-downs is required if net realisable value increases. The inventory will be reported on the balance sheet at £1,000,000. The inventory is reported at the lower of cost or net realisable value. Under US GAAP, inventory is carried at the lower of cost or market value. After a write-down, a new cost basis is determined and additional revisions may only reduce the value further. The reversal of write-downs is not permitted.

11 A is correct. IFRS require the reversal of inventory write-downs if net realisable values increase; US GAAP do not permit the reversal of write-downs.

12 C is correct. Activity ratios (for example, inventory turnover and total asset turnover) will be positively affected by a write down to net realizable value because the asset base (denominator) is reduced. On the balance sheet, the inventory carrying amount is written down to its net realizable value and the loss in value (expense) is generally reflected on the income statement in cost of goods sold, thus reducing gross profit, operating profit, and net income.

13 B is correct. Cinnamon uses the weighted average cost method, so in 2018, 5,000 units of inventory were 2017 units at €10 each and 50,000 were 2008 purchases at €11. The weighted average cost of inventory during 2008 was thus (5,000 × 10) + (50,000 × 11) = 50,000 + 550,000 = €600,000, and the weighted average cost was approximately €10.91 = €600,000/55,000. Cost of sales was €10.91 × 45,000, which is approximately €490,950.

14 C is correct. Zimt uses the FIFO method, and thus the first 5,000 units sold in 2018 depleted the 2017 inventory. Of the inventory purchased in 2018, 40,000 units were sold and 10,000 remain, valued at €11 each, for a total of €110,000.

15 A is correct. Zimt uses the FIFO method, so its cost of sales represents units purchased at a (no longer available) lower price. Nutmeg uses the LIFO method, so its cost of sales is approximately equal to the current replacement cost of inventory.

16 B is correct. Nutmeg uses the LIFO method, and thus some of the inventory on the balance sheet was purchased at a (no longer available) lower price. Zimt uses the FIFO method, so the carrying value on the balance sheet represents the most recently purchased units and thus approximates the current replacement cost.

17 B is correct. In a declining price environment, the newest inventory is the lowest-cost inventory. In such circumstances, using the LIFO method (selling the newer, cheaper inventory first) will result in lower cost of sales and higher profit.

18 B is correct. In a rising price environment, inventory balances will be higher for the company using the FIFO method. Accounts payable are based on amounts due to suppliers, not the amounts accrued based on inventory accounting.

19 C is correct. The write-down reduced the value of inventory and increased cost of sales in 2017. The higher numerator and lower denominator mean that the inventory turnover ratio as reported was too high. Gross margin and the current ratio were both too low.

20 A is correct. The reversal of the write-down shifted cost of sales from 2018 to 2017. The 2017 cost of sales was higher because of the write-down, and the 2018 cost of sales was lower because of the reversal of the write-down. As a result, the reported 2018 profits were overstated. Inventory balance in 2018 is the same because the write-down and reversal cancel each other out. Cash flow from operations is not affected by the non-cash write-down, but the higher profits in 2018 likely resulted in higher taxes and thus lower cash flow from operations.

21 B is correct. LIFO will result in lower inventory and higher cost of sales. Gross margin (a profitability ratio) will be lower, the current ratio (a liquidity ratio) will be lower, and inventory turnover (an efficiency ratio) will be higher.

22 A is correct. LIFO will result in lower inventory and higher cost of sales in periods of rising costs compared to FIFO. Consequently, LIFO results in a lower gross profit margin than FIFO.

23 B is correct. The LIFO method increases cost of sales, thus reducing profits and the taxes thereon.

24 A is correct. US GAAP do not permit inventory write-downs to be reversed.

25 B is correct. Both US GAAP and IFRS require disclosure of the amount of inventories recognized as an expense during the period. Only US GAAP allows the LIFO method and requires disclosure of any material amount of income resulting from the liquidation of LIFO inventory. US GAAP does not permit the reversal of prior-year inventory write downs.

26 B is correct. A significant increase (attributable to increases in unit volume rather than increases in unit cost) in raw materials and/or work-in-progress inventories may signal that the company expects an increase in demand for its products. If the growth of finished goods inventories is greater than the growth of sales, it could indicate a decrease in demand and a decrease in future earnings. A substantial increase in finished goods inventories while raw materials and work-in-progress inventories are declining may signal a decrease in demand for the company's products.

27 B is correct. During a period of rising inventory prices, a company using the LIFO method will have higher cost of cost of goods sold and lower inventory compared with a company using the FIFO method. The inventory turnover ratio will be higher for the company using the LIFO method, thus making it appear more efficient. Current assets and gross profit margin will be lower for the company using the LIFO method, thus making it appear less liquid and less profitable.

28 B is correct. In an environment of declining inventory unit costs and constant or increasing inventory quantities, FIFO (in comparison with weighted average cost or LIFO) will have higher cost of goods sold (and net income) and lower inventory. Because both inventory and net income are lower, total equity is lower, resulting in a higher debt-to-equity ratio.

29 C is correct. The storage costs for inventory awaiting shipment to customers are not costs of purchase, costs of conversion, or other costs incurred in bringing the inventories to their present location and condition and are not included in inventory. The storage costs for the chocolate liquor occur during the production process and are thus part of the conversion costs. Excise taxes are part of the purchase cost.

30 C is correct. The carrying amount of inventories under FIFO will more closely reflect current replacement values because inventories are assumed to consist of the most recently purchased items. FIFO is an acceptable, but not preferred, method under IFRS. Weighted average cost, not FIFO, is the cost formula that allocates the same per unit cost to both cost of sales and inventory.

31 B is correct. Inventory turnover = Cost of sales/Average inventory = 41,043/7,569.5 = 5.42. Average inventory is (8,100 + 7,039)/2 = 7,569.5.

32 B is correct. For comparative purposes, the choice of a competitor that reports under IFRS is requested because LIFO is permitted under US GAAP.

33 A is correct. The carrying amount of the ending inventory may differ because the perpetual system will apply LIFO continuously throughout the year, liquidating layers as sales are made. Under the periodic system, the sales will start from the last layer in the year. Under FIFO, the sales will occur from the same layers regardless of whether a perpetual or periodic system is used. Specific identification identifies the actual products sold and remaining in inventory, and there will be no difference under a perpetual or periodic system.

34 B is correct. The cost of sales is closest to CHF 4,550. Under FIFO, the inventory acquired first is sold first. Using Exhibit 4, a total of 310 cartons were available for sale (100 + 40 + 70 + 100) and 185 cartons were sold (50 + 100 + 35), leaving 125 in ending inventory. The FIFO cost would be as follows:

100 (beginning inventory) × 22 = 2,200

40 (4 February 2009) × 25 = 1,000

45 (23 July 2009) × 30 = 1,350

Cost of sales = 2,200 + 1,000 + 1,350 = CHF 4,550

35 A is correct. Gross profit will most likely increase by CHF 7,775. The net realisable value has increased and now exceeds the cost. The write-down from 2017 can be reversed. The write-down in 2017 was 9,256 [92,560 × (4.05 – 3.95)]. IFRS require the reversal of any write-downs for a subsequent increase in value of inventory previously written down. The reversal is limited to the lower of the subsequent increase or the original write-down. Only 77,750 kilograms remain in inventory; the reversal is 77,750 × (4.05 – 3.95) = 7,775. The amount of any reversal of a write-down is recognised as a reduction in cost of sales. This reduction results in an increase in gross profit.

36 C is correct. Using the FIFO method to value inventories when prices are rising will allocate more of the cost of goods available for sale to ending inventories (the most recent purchases, which are at higher costs, are assumed to remain in inventory) and less to cost of sales (the oldest purchases, which are at lower costs, are assumed to be sold first).

37 C is correct. Karp's inventory under FIFO equals Karp's inventory under LIFO plus the LIFO reserve. Therefore, as of 31 December 2018, Karp's inventory under FIFO equals:

$$\begin{aligned}\text{Inventory (FIFO method)} &= \text{Inventory (LIFO method)} + \text{LIFO reserve}\\ &= \$620 \text{ million} + 155 \text{ million}\\ &= \$775 \text{ million}\end{aligned}$$

38 B is correct. Karp's cost of goods sold (COGS) under FIFO equals Karp's cost of goods sold under LIFO minus the increase in the LIFO reserve. Therefore, for the year ended 31 December 2018, Karp's cost of goods sold under FIFO equals:

$$\begin{aligned}\text{COGS (FIFO method)} &= \text{COGS (LIFO method)} - \text{Increase in LIFO reserve}\\ &= \$2{,}211 \text{ million} - (155 \text{ million} - 117 \text{ million})\\ &= \$2{,}173 \text{ million}\end{aligned}$$

39 A is correct. Karp's net income (NI) under FIFO equals Karp's net income under LIFO plus the after-tax increase in the LIFO reserve. For the year ended 31 December 2018, Karp's net income under FIFO equals:

$$\begin{aligned}\text{NI (FIFO method)} &= \text{NI (LIFO method)} + \text{Increase in LIFO reserve} \times (1 - \text{Tax rate})\\ &= \$247 \text{ million} + 38 \text{ million} \times (1 - 20\%)\\ &= \$277.4 \text{ million}\end{aligned}$$

Therefore, the increase in net income is:

$$\begin{aligned}\text{Increase in NI} &= \text{NI (FIFO method)} - \text{NI (LIFO method)}\\ &= \$277 \text{ million} - 247 \text{ million}\\ &= \$30.4 \text{ million}\end{aligned}$$

40 B is correct. Karp's retained earnings (RE) under FIFO equals Karp's retained earnings under LIFO plus the after-tax LIFO reserve. Therefore, for the year ended 31 December 2018, Karp's retained earnings under FIFO equals:

$$\begin{aligned}\text{RE (FIFO method)} &= \text{RE (LIFO method)} + \text{LIFO reserve} \times (1 - \text{Tax rate})\\ &= \$787 \text{ million} + 155 \text{ million} \times (1 - 20\%)\\ &= \$911 \text{ million}\end{aligned}$$

Therefore, the increase in retained earnings is:

$$\begin{aligned}\text{Increase in RE} &= \text{RE (FIFO method)} - \text{RE (LIFO method)}\\ &= \$911 \text{ million} - 787 \text{ million}\\ &= \$124 \text{ million}\end{aligned}$$

41 A is correct. The cash ratio (cash and cash equivalents ÷ current liabilities) would be lower because cash would have been less under FIFO. Karp's income before taxes would have been higher under FIFO, and consequently taxes paid by Karp would have also been higher and cash would have been lower. There is no impact on current liabilities. Both Karp's current ratio and gross profit margin would have been higher if FIFO had been used. The current ratio would have been higher because inventory under FIFO increases by a larger amount than the cash decreases for taxes paid. Because the cost of goods sold under FIFO is lower than under LIFO, the gross profit margin would have been higher.

42 B is correct. If Karp had used FIFO instead of LIFO, the debt-to-equity ratio would have decreased. No change in debt would have occurred, but shareholders' equity would have increased as a result of higher retained earnings.

43 B is correct. Crux's adjusted inventory turnover ratio must be computed using cost of goods sold (COGS) under FIFO and excluding charges for increases in valuation allowances.

COGS (adjusted) = COGS (LIFO method) – Charges included in cost of goods sold for inventory write-downs – Change in LIFO reserve
= \$3,120 million – 13 million – (55 million – 72 million)
= \$3,124 million

Note: Minus the change in LIFO reserve is equivalent to plus the decrease in LIFO reserve. The adjusted inventory turnover ratio is computed using average inventory under FIFO.

Ending inventory (FIFO) = Ending inventory (LIFO) + LIFO reserve

Ending inventory 2018 (FIFO) = \$480 + 55 = \$535

Ending inventory 2017 (FIFO) = \$465 + 72 = \$537

Average inventory = (\$535 + 537)/2 = \$536

Therefore, adjusted inventory turnover ratio equals:

Inventory turnover ratio = COGS/Average inventory = \$3,124/\$536 = 5.83

44 B is correct. Rolby's adjusted net profit margin must be computed using net income (NI) under FIFO and excluding charges for increases in valuation allowances.

NI (adjusted) = NI (FIFO method) + Charges, included in cost of goods sold for inventory write-downs, after tax
= \$327 million + 15 million × (1 – 30%)
= \$337.5 million

Therefore, adjusted net profit margin equals:

Net profit margin = NI/Revenues = \$337.5/\$5,442 = 6.20%

45 A is correct. Mikko's adjusted debt-to-equity ratio is lower because the debt (numerator) is unchanged and the adjusted shareholders' equity (denominator) is higher. The adjusted shareholders' equity corresponds to shareholders' equity under FIFO, excluding charges for increases in valuation allowances. Therefore, adjusted shareholders' equity is higher than reported (unadjusted) shareholders' equity.

46 C is correct. Mikko's and Crux's gross margin ratios would better reflect the current gross margin of the industry than Rolby because both use LIFO. LIFO recognizes as cost of goods sold the cost of the most recently purchased units, therefore, it better reflects replacement cost. However, Mikko's gross margin ratio best reflects the current gross margin of the industry because Crux's LIFO reserve is decreasing. This could reflect a LIFO liquidation by Crux which would distort gross profit margin.

47 B is correct. The FIFO method shows a higher gross profit margin than the LIFO method in an inflationary scenario, because FIFO allocates to cost of goods sold the cost of the oldest units available for sale. In an inflationary environment, these units are the ones with the lowest cost.

48 A is correct. An inventory write-down increases cost of sales and reduces profit and reduces the carrying value of inventory and assets. This has a negative effect on profitability and solvency ratios. However, activity ratios appear positively affected by a write-down because the asset base, whether total assets or inventory (denominator), is reduced. The numerator, sales, in total asset turnover is unchanged, and the numerator, cost of sales, in inventory turnover is increased. Thus, turnover ratios are higher and appear more favorable as the result of the write-down.

49 B is correct. Finished goods least accurately reflect current prices because some of the finished goods are valued under the "last-in, first-out" ("LIFO") basis. The costs of the newest units available for sale are allocated to cost of goods sold, leaving the oldest units (at lower costs) in inventory. ZP values raw materials and work in process using the weighted average cost method. While not fully reflecting current prices, some inflationary effect will be included in the inventory values.

50 C is correct. FIFO inventory = Reported inventory + LIFO reserve = ¥608,572 + 10,120 = ¥618,692. The LIFO reserve is disclosed in Note 2 of the notes to consolidated financial statements.

51 A is correct. The inventory turnover ratio would be lower. The average inventory would be higher under FIFO and cost of products sold would be lower by the increase in LIFO reserve. LIFO is not permitted under IFRS.

Inventory turnover ratio = Cost of products sold ÷ Average inventory

2018 inventory turnover ratio as reported = 10.63 = ¥5,822,805/[(608,572 + 486,465)/2].

2018 inventory turnover ratio adjusted to FIFO as necessary = 10.34 = [¥5,822,805 – (19,660 – 10,120)]/[(608,572 + 10,120 + 486,465 + 19,660)/2].

52 A is correct. No LIFO liquidation occurred during 2018; the LIFO reserve increased from ¥10,120 million in 2008 to ¥19,660 million in 2018. Management stated in the MD&A that the decrease in inventories reflected the impacts of decreased sales volumes and fluctuations in foreign currency translation rates.

53 C is correct. Finished goods and raw materials inventories are lower in 2018 when compared to 2017. Reduced levels of inventory typically indicate an anticipated business contraction.

54 B is correct. The decrease in LIFO inventory in 2018 would typically indicate that more inventory units were sold than produced or purchased. Accordingly, one would expect a liquidation of some of the older LIFO layers and the LIFO reserve to decrease. In actuality, the LIFO reserve *increased* from ¥10,120 million in 2017 to ¥19,660 million in 2009. This is not to be expected and is likely caused by the increase in prices of raw materials, other production materials, and parts of foreign currencies as noted in the MD&A. An analyst should seek to confirm this explanation.

55 B is correct. If prices have been decreasing, write-downs under FIFO are least likely to have a significant effect because the inventory is valued at closer to the new, lower prices. Typically, inventories valued using LIFO are less likely to incur inventory write-downs than inventories valued using weighted average cost or FIFO. Under LIFO, the *oldest* costs are reflected in the inventory carrying value on the balance sheet. Given increasing inventory costs, the inventory carrying values under the LIFO method are already conservatively presented at the oldest and lowest costs. Thus, it is far less likely that inventory write-downs will occur under LIFO; and if a write-down does occur, it is likely to be of a lesser magnitude.

READING

26

Long-Lived Assets

by Elaine Henry, PhD, CFA, and Elizabeth A. Gordon, PhD, MBA, CPA

Elaine Henry, PhD, CFA, is at Stevens Institute of Technology (USA). Elizabeth A. Gordon, PhD, MBA, CPA, is at Temple University (USA).

LEARNING OUTCOMES

Mastery	*The candidate should be able to:*
□	**a.** distinguish between costs that are capitalised and costs that are expensed in the period in which they are incurred;
□	**b.** compare the financial reporting of the following types of intangible assets: purchased, internally developed, acquired in a business combination;
□	**c.** explain and evaluate how capitalising versus expensing costs in the period in which they are incurred affects financial statements and ratios;
□	**d.** describe the different depreciation methods for property, plant, and equipment and calculate depreciation expense;
□	**e.** describe how the choice of depreciation method and assumptions concerning useful life and residual value affect depreciation expense, financial statements, and ratios;
□	**f.** describe the different amortisation methods for intangible assets with finite lives and calculate amortisation expense;
□	**g.** describe how the choice of amortisation method and assumptions concerning useful life and residual value affect amortisation expense, financial statements, and ratios;
□	**h.** describe the revaluation model;
□	**i.** explain the impairment of property, plant, and equipment and intangible assets;
□	**j.** explain the derecognition of property, plant, and equipment and intangible assets;
□	**k.** explain and evaluate how impairment, revaluation, and derecognition of property, plant, and equipment and intangible assets affect financial statements and ratios;

(continued)

Note: Changes in accounting standards as well as new rulings and/or pronouncements issued after the publication of the readings on financial reporting and analysis may cause some of the information in these readings to become dated. Candidates are *not* responsible for anything that occurs after the readings were published. In addition, candidates are expected to be familiar with the analytical frameworks contained in the readings, as well as the implications of alternative accounting methods for financial analysis and valuation discussed in the readings. Candidates are also responsible for the content of accounting standards, but not for the actual reference numbers. Finally, candidates should be aware that certain ratios may be defined and calculated differently. When alternative ratio definitions exist and no specific definition is given, candidates should use the ratio definitions emphasized in the readings.

© 2019 CFA Institute. All rights reserved.

LEARNING OUTCOMES	
Mastery	***The candidate should be able to:***
☐	**l.** describe the financial statement presentation of and disclosures relating to property, plant, and equipment and intangible assets;
☐	**m.** analyze and interpret financial statement disclosures regarding property, plant, and equipment and intangible assets;
☐	**n.** compare the financial reporting of investment property with that of property, plant, and equipment.

1 INTRODUCTION

Long-lived assets, also referred to as non-current assets or long-term assets, are assets that are expected to provide economic benefits over a future period of time, typically greater than one year.[1] Long-lived assets may be tangible, intangible, or financial assets. Examples of long-lived tangible assets, typically referred to as **property, plant, and equipment** and sometimes as fixed assets, include land, buildings, furniture and fixtures, machinery and equipment, and vehicles; examples of long-lived **intangible assets** (assets lacking physical substance) include patents and trademarks; and examples of long-lived financial assets include investments in equity or debt securities issued by other entities. The scope of this reading is limited to long-lived tangible and intangible assets (hereafter, referred to for simplicity as long-lived assets).

The first issue in accounting for a long-lived asset is determining its cost at acquisition. The second issue is how to allocate the cost to expense over time. The costs of most long-lived assets are capitalised and then allocated as expenses in the profit or loss (income) statement over the period of time during which they are expected to provide economic benefits. The two main types of long-lived assets with costs that are typically *not* allocated over time are land, which is not depreciated, and those intangible assets with indefinite useful lives. Additional issues that arise are the treatment of subsequent costs incurred related to the asset, the use of the cost model versus the revaluation model, unexpected declines in the value of the asset, classification of the asset with respect to intent (for example, held for use or held for sale), and the derecognition of the asset.

This reading is organised as follows. Section 2 describes and illustrates accounting for the acquisition of long-lived assets, with particular attention to the impact of capitalizing versus expensing expenditures. Section 3 describes the allocation of the costs of long-lived assets over their useful lives. Section 4 discusses the revaluation model that is based on changes in the fair value of an asset. Section 5 covers the concepts of impairment (unexpected decline in the value of an asset). Section 6 describes accounting for the derecognition of long-lived assets. Section 7 describes financial statement presentation, disclosures, and analysis of long-lived assets. Section 8 discusses differences in financial reporting of investment property compared with property, plant, and equipment. A summary is followed by practice problems.

1 In some industries, inventory is held longer than one year but is nonetheless reported as a current asset.

ACQUISITION OF LONG-LIVED ASSETS

2

Upon acquisition, property, plant, and equipment (tangible assets with an economic life of longer than one year and intended to be held for the company's own use) are recorded on the balance sheet at cost, which is typically the same as their fair value.[2] Accounting for an intangible asset depends on how the asset is acquired. If several assets are acquired as part of a group, the purchase price is allocated to each asset on the basis of its fair value. An asset's cost potentially includes expenditures additional to the purchase price.

A key concept in accounting for expenditures related to long-lived assets is whether and when such expenditures are capitalised (i.e., included in the asset shown on the balance sheet) versus expensed (i.e., treated as an expense of the period on the income statement). After examining the specific treatment of certain expenditures, we will consider the general financial statement impact of capitalising versus expensing and two analytical issues related to the decision—namely, the effects on an individual company's trend analysis and on comparability across companies.

2.1 Property, Plant, and Equipment

This section primarily discusses the accounting treatment for the acquisition of long-lived tangible assets (property, plant, and equipment) through purchase. Assets can be acquired by methods other than purchase.[3] When an asset is exchanged for another asset, the asset acquired is recorded at fair value if reliable measures of fair value exist. Fair value is the fair value of the asset given up unless the fair value of the asset acquired is more clearly evident. If there is no reliable measure of fair value, the acquired asset is measured at the carrying amount of the asset given up. In this case, the carrying amount of the assets is unchanged, and no gain or loss is reported.

Typically, accounting for the exchange involves removing the carrying amount of the asset given up, adding a fair value for the asset acquired, and reporting any difference between the carrying amount and the fair value as a gain or loss. A gain would be reported when the fair value used for the newly acquired asset exceeds the carrying amount of the asset given up. A loss would be reported when the fair value used for the newly acquired asset is less than the carrying amount of the asset given up.

When property, plant, or equipment is purchased, the buyer records the asset at cost. In addition to the purchase price, the buyer also includes, as part of the cost of an asset, all the expenditures necessary to get the asset ready for its intended use. For example, freight costs borne by the purchaser to get the asset to the purchaser's place of business and special installation and testing costs required to make the asset usable are included in the total cost of the asset.

Subsequent expenditures related to long-lived assets are included as part of the recorded value of the assets on the balance sheet (i.e., capitalised) if they are expected to provide benefits beyond one year in the future and are expensed if they are not expected to provide benefits in future periods. Expenditures that extend the original life of the asset are typically capitalised. Example 1 illustrates the difference between costs that are capitalised and costs that are expensed in a period.

---

2 Fair value is defined in International Financial Reporting Standards (IFRS) and under US generally accepted accounting principles (US GAAP) in the Financial Accounting Standards Board (FASB) Accounting Standards Codification (ASC) as "the price that would be received to sell an asset or paid to transfer a liability in an orderly transaction between market participants at the measurement date." [IFRS 13 and FASB ASC Topic 820]

3 IAS 16 *Property, Plant and Equipment*, paragraphs 24–26 [Measurement of Cost]; IAS 38 *Intangible Assets*, paragraphs 45–47 [Exchange of Assets]; and FASB ASC Section 845-10-30 [Nonmonetary Transactions – Overall – Initial Measurement].

EXAMPLE 1

Acquisition of PPE

Assume a (hypothetical) company, Trofferini S.A., incurred the following expenditures to purchase a towel and tissue roll machine: €10,900 purchase price including taxes, €200 for delivery of the machine, €300 for installation and testing of the machine, and €100 to train staff on maintaining the machine. In addition, the company paid a construction team €350 to reinforce the factory floor and ceiling joists to accommodate the machine's weight. The company also paid €1,500 to repair the factory roof (a repair expected to extend the useful life of the factory by five years) and €1,000 to have the exterior of the factory and adjoining offices repainted for maintenance reasons. The repainting neither extends the life of factory and offices nor improves their usability.

1 Which of these expenditures will be capitalised and which will be expensed?

2 How will the treatment of these expenditures affect the company's financial statements?

Solution to 1:

The company will capitalise as part of the cost of the machine all costs that are necessary to get the new machine ready for its intended use: €10,900 purchase price, €200 for delivery, €300 for installation and testing, and €350 to reinforce the factory floor and ceiling joists to accommodate the machine's weight (which was necessary to use the machine and does not increase the value of the factory). The €100 to train staff is not necessary to get the asset ready for its intended use and will be expensed.

The company will capitalise the expenditure of €1,500 to repair the factory roof because the repair is expected to extend the useful life of the factory. The company will expense the €1,000 to have the exterior of the factory and adjoining offices repainted because the painting does not extend the life or alter the productive capacity of the buildings.

Solution to 2:

The costs related to the machine that are capitalised—€10,900 purchase price, €200 for delivery, €300 for installation and testing, and €350 to prepare the factory—will increase the carrying amount of the machine asset as shown on the balance sheet and will be included as investing cash outflows. The item related to the factory that is capitalised—the €1,500 roof repair—will increase the carrying amount of the factory asset as shown on the balance sheet and is an investing cash outflow. The expenditures of €100 to train staff and €1,000 to paint are expensed in the period and will reduce the amount of income reported on the company's income statement (and thus reduce retained earnings on the balance sheet) and the operating cash flow.

Example 1 describes capitalising versus expensing in the context of purchasing property, plant, and equipment. When a company constructs an asset (or acquires an asset that requires a long period of time to get ready for its intended use), borrowing costs incurred directly related to the construction are generally capitalised. Constructing a building, whether for sale (in which case, the building is classified as inventory) or for the company's own use (in which case, the building is classified as a long-lived asset), typically requires a substantial amount of time. To finance construction, any borrowing costs incurred prior to the asset being ready for its intended use are capitalised as part of the cost of the asset. The company determines the interest rate to use on the basis of its existing borrowings or, if applicable, on a borrowing specifically incurred for constructing the asset. If a company takes out a loan specifically to construct a building, the interest cost on that loan during the time of construction would be capitalised as part of the building's cost. Under IFRS, but not under US GAAP, income earned on temporarily investing the borrowed monies decreases the amount of borrowing costs eligible for capitalisation.

Thus, a company's interest costs for a period are included either on the balance sheet (to the extent they are capitalised as part of an asset) or on the income statement (to the extent they are expensed). If the interest expenditure is incurred in connection with constructing an asset for the company's own use, the capitalised interest appears on the balance sheet as a part of the relevant long-lived asset (i.e., property, plant, and equipment). The capitalised interest is expensed over time as the property is depreciated and is thus part of subsequent years' depreciation expense rather than interest expense of the current period. If the interest expenditure is incurred in connection with constructing an asset to sell (for example, by a home builder), the capitalised interest appears on the company's balance sheet as part of inventory. The capitalised interest is expensed as part of the cost of goods sold when the asset is sold. Interest payments made prior to completion of construction that are capitalised are classified as an investing cash outflow. Expensed interest may be classified as an operating or financing cash outflow under IFRS and is classified as an operating cash outflow under US GAAP.

EXAMPLE 2

Capitalised Borrowing Costs

BILDA S.A., a hypothetical company, borrows €1,000,000 at an interest rate of 10 percent per year on 1 January 2010 to finance the construction of a factory that will have a useful life of 40 years. Construction is completed after two years, during which time the company earns €20,000 by temporarily investing the loan proceeds.

1 What is the amount of interest that will be capitalised under IFRS, and how would that amount differ from the amount that would be capitalised under US GAAP?

2 Where will the capitalised borrowing cost appear on the company's financial statements?

Solution to 1:

The total amount of interest paid on the loan during construction is €200,000 (= €1,000,000 × 10% × 2 years). Under IFRS, the amount of borrowing cost eligible for capitalisation is reduced by the €20,000 interest income from temporarily investing the loan proceeds, so the amount to be capitalised is €180,000. Under US GAAP, the amount to be capitalised is €200,000.

Solution to 2:

The capitalised borrowing costs will appear on the company's balance sheet as a component of property, plant, and equipment. In the years prior to completion of construction, the interest paid will appear on the statement of cash flows as an investment activity. Over time, as the property is depreciated, the capitalised interest component is part of subsequent years' depreciation expense on the company's income statement.

2.2 Intangible Assets

Intangible assets are assets lacking physical substance. Intangible assets include items that involve exclusive rights, such as patents, copyrights, trademarks, and franchises. Under IFRS, identifiable intangible assets must meet three definitional criteria. They must be (1) identifiable (either capable of being separated from the entity or arising from contractual or legal rights), (2) under the control of the company, and (3) expected to generate future economic benefits. In addition, two recognition criteria must be met: (1) It is probable that the expected future economic benefits of the asset will flow to the company, and (2) the cost of the asset can be reliably measured. Goodwill, which is not considered an identifiable intangible asset,[4] arises when one company purchases another and the acquisition price exceeds the fair value of the net identifiable assets (both the tangible assets and the identifiable intangible assets, minus liabilities) acquired.

Accounting for an intangible asset depends on how it is acquired. The following sections describe accounting for intangible assets obtained in three ways: purchased in situations other than business combinations, developed internally, and acquired in business combinations.

2.2.1 *Intangible Assets Purchased in Situations Other Than Business Combinations*

Intangible assets purchased in situations other than business combinations, such as buying a patent, are treated at acquisition the same as long-lived tangible assets; they are recorded at their fair value when acquired, which is assumed to be equivalent to the purchase price. If several intangible assets are acquired as part of a group, the purchase price is allocated to each asset on the basis of its fair value.

In deciding how to treat individual intangible assets for analytical purposes, analysts are particularly aware that companies must use a substantial amount of judgment and numerous assumptions to determine the fair value of individual intangible assets. For analysis, therefore, understanding the types of intangible assets acquired can often be more useful than focusing on the values assigned to the individual assets. In other words, an analyst would typically be more interested in understanding what assets a company acquired (for example, franchise rights) than in the precise portion of the purchase price a company allocated to each asset. Understanding the types of assets a company acquires can offer insights into the company's strategic direction and future operating potential.

2.2.2 *Intangible Assets Developed Internally*

In contrast with the treatment of construction costs of tangible assets, the costs to internally develop intangible assets are generally expensed when incurred. There are some situations, however, in which the costs incurred to internally develop an intangible asset are capitalised. The general analytical issues related to the capitalising-versus-expensing decision apply here—namely, comparability across companies and the effect on an individual company's trend analysis.

The general requirement that costs to internally develop intangible assets be expensed should be compared with capitalising the cost of acquiring intangible assets in situations other than business combinations. Because costs associated with internally developing intangible assets are usually expensed, a company that has internally developed such intangible assets as patents, copyrights, or brands through expenditures on R&D or advertising will recognise a lower amount of assets than a company that has

4 The IFRS definition of an intangible asset as an "identifiable non-monetary asset without physical substance" applies to intangible assets not specifically dealt with in standards other than IAS 38. The definition of intangible assets under US GAAP—"assets (other than financial assets) that lack physical substance"—includes goodwill in the definition of an intangible asset.

obtained intangible assets through external purchase. In addition, on the statement of cash flows, costs of internally developing intangible assets are classified as operating cash outflows whereas costs of acquiring intangible assets are classified as investing cash outflows. Differences in strategy (developing versus acquiring intangible assets) can thus impact financial ratios.

IFRS require that expenditures on research (or during the research phase of an internal project) be expensed rather than capitalised as an intangible asset.[5] Research is defined as "original and planned investigation undertaken with the prospect of gaining new scientific or technical knowledge and understanding."[6] The "research phase of an internal project" refers to the period during which a company cannot demonstrate that an intangible asset is being created—for example, the search for alternative materials or systems to use in a production process. In contrast with the treatment of research-phase expenditures, IFRS allow companies to recognise an intangible asset arising from development expenditures (or the development phase of an internal project) if certain criteria are met, including a demonstration of the technical feasibility of completing the intangible asset and the intent to use or sell the asset. Development is defined as "the application of research findings or other knowledge to a plan or design for the production of new or substantially improved materials, devices, products, processes, systems or services before the start of commercial production or use."[7]

Generally, US GAAP require that both research and development costs be expensed as incurred but require capitalisation of certain costs related to software development.[8] Costs incurred to develop a software product for sale are expensed until the product's technological feasibility is established and are capitalised thereafter. Similarly, companies expense costs related to the development of software for internal use until it is probable that the project will be completed and that the software will be used as intended. Thereafter, development costs are capitalised. The probability that the project will be completed is easier to demonstrate than is technological feasibility. The capitalised costs, related directly to developing software for sale or internal use, include the costs of employees who help build and test the software. The treatment of software development costs under US GAAP is similar to the treatment of all costs of internally developed intangible assets under IFRS.

---

5 IAS 38 *Intangible Assets.*
6 IAS 38 *Intangible Assets*, paragraph 8 [Definitions].
7 IAS 38 *Intangible Assets*, paragraph 8 [Definitions].
8 FASB ASC Section 350-40-25 [Intangibles—Goodwill and Other – Internal-Use Software – Recognition] and FASB ASC Section 985-20-25 [Software – Costs of Software to be Sold, Leased, or Marketed – Recognition] specify US GAAP accounting for software development costs for software for internal use and for software to be sold, respectively.

EXAMPLE 3

Software Development Costs

Assume REH AG, a hypothetical company, incurs expenditures of €1,000 per month during the fiscal year ended 31 December 2019 to develop software for internal use. Under IFRS, the company must treat the expenditures as an expense until the software meets the criteria for recognition as an intangible asset, after which time the expenditures can be capitalised as an intangible asset.

1 What is the accounting impact of the company being able to demonstrate that the software met the criteria for recognition as an intangible asset on 1 February versus 1 December?

2 How would the treatment of expenditures differ if the company reported under US GAAP and it had established in 2018 that the project was likely to be completed and the software used to perform the function intended?

Solution to 1:

If the company is able to demonstrate that the software met the criteria for recognition as an intangible asset on 1 February, the company would recognise the €1,000 expended in January as an expense on the income statement for the fiscal year ended 31 December 2019. The other €11,000 of expenditures would be recognised as an intangible asset (on the balance sheet). Alternatively, if the company is not able to demonstrate that the software met the criteria for recognition as an intangible asset until 1 December, the company would recognise the €11,000 expended in January through November as an expense on the income statement for the fiscal year ended 31 December 2019, with the other €1,000 of expenditures recognised as an intangible asset.

Solution to 2:

Under US GAAP, the company would capitalise the entire €12,000 spent to develop software for internal use.

2.2.3 *Intangible Assets Acquired in a Business Combination*

When one company acquires another company, the transaction is accounted for using the **acquisition method** of accounting.[9] Under the acquisition method, the company identified as the acquirer allocates the purchase price to each asset acquired (and each liability assumed) on the basis of its fair value. If the purchase price exceeds the sum of the amounts that can be allocated to individual identifiable assets and liabilities, the excess is recorded as goodwill. Goodwill cannot be identified separately from the business as a whole.

Under IFRS, the acquired individual assets include identifiable intangible assets that meet the definitional and recognition criteria.[10] Otherwise, if the item is acquired in a business combination and cannot be recognised as a tangible or identifiable intangible asset, it is recognised as goodwill. Under US GAAP, there are two criteria to judge whether an intangible asset acquired in a business combination should be recognised separately from goodwill: The asset must be either an item arising from contractual or legal rights or an item that can be separated from the acquired company. Examples of

9 Both IFRS and US GAAP require the use of the acquisition method in accounting for business combinations (IFRS 3 and FASB ASC Section 805).

10 As previously described, the definitional criteria are identifiability, control by the company, and expected future benefits. The recognition criteria are probable flows of the expected economic benefits to the company and measurability.

intangible assets treated separately from goodwill include the intangible assets previously mentioned that involve exclusive rights (patents, copyrights, franchises, licenses), as well as such items as internet domain names and video and audiovisual materials.

Exhibit 1 describes how AB InBev allocated the $103 billion purchase consideration in its 2016 acquisition of SABMiller Group. The combined company was renamed Anheuser-Busch InBev SA/NV. The majority of the intangible asset valuation relates to brands with indefinite life ($19.9 billion of the $20.0 billion total). Of $63.0 billion total assets acquired, assets to be divested were valued at $24.8 billion and assets to be held for were valued at $38.2 billion. In total, intangible assets represent 52 percent of the total assets to be held for use. In addition, $74.1 billion of goodwill was recognized in the transaction.

Exhibit 1 Acquisition of Intangible Assets through a Business Combination

Excerpt from the 2016 annual report of AB InBev:

> "On 10 October 2016, AB InBev announced the ... successful completion of the business combination with the former SABMiller Group ("SAB").
>
> "The transaction resulted in 74.1 billion US dollar of goodwill provisionally allocated primarily to the businesses in Colombia, Ecuador, Peru, Australia, South Africa and other African, Asia Pacific and Latin American countries. The factors that contributed to the recognition of goodwill include the acquisition of an assembled workforce and the premiums paid for cost synergies expected to be achieved in SABMiller. Management's assessment of the future economic benefits supporting recognition of this goodwill is in part based on expected savings through the implementation of AB InBev best practices such as, among others, a zero based budgeting program and initiatives that are expected to bring greater efficiency and standardization, generate cost savings and maximize purchasing power. Goodwill also arises due to the recognition of deferred tax liabilities in relation to the preliminary fair value adjustments on acquired intangible assets for which the amortization does not qualify as a tax deductible expense. None of the goodwill recognized is deductible for tax purposes.
>
> "The majority of the intangible asset valuation relates to brands with indefinite life, valued for a total amount of 19.9 billion US dollar. The valuation of the brands with indefinite life is based on a series of factors, including the brand history, the operating plan and the countries in which the brands are sold. The fair value of brands was estimated by applying a combination of known valuation methodologies, such as the royalty relief and excess earnings valuation approaches.
>
> "The intangibles with an indefinite life mainly include the Castle and Carling brand families in Africa, the Aguila and Poker brand families in Colombia, the Cristal and Pilsner brand families in Ecuador, and the Carlton brand family in Australia.
>
> "Assets held for sale were recognized in relation to the divestiture of SABMiller's interests in the MillerCoors LLC joint venture and certain of SABMiller's portfolio of Miller brands outside of the U.S. to Molson Coors Brewing company; the divestiture of SABMiller's European premium brands to Asahi Group Holdings, Ltd and the divestiture of SABMiller's interest in China Resources Snow Breweries Ltd. to China Resources Beer (Holdings) Co. Ltd. ...." [Excerpt]

(continued)

Exhibit 1 (Continued)

The following is a summary of the provisional allocation of AB InBev's purchase price of SABMiller:

Assets	**$ million**
Property, plant and equipment	9,060
Intangible assets	20,040
Investment in associates	4,386
Inventories	977
Trade and other receivables	1,257
Cash and cash equivalents	1,410
Assets held for sale	24,805
All other assets	*1,087*
Total assets	*63,022*
Total liabilities	*−27,769*
Net identified assets and liabilities	**35,253**
Non-controlling interests	−6,200
Goodwill on acquisition	**74,083**
Purchase consideration	**103,136**

Table is excerpted from the company's 2016 Annual Report. Portions of detail are omitted, and subtotals are shown in italics.

Source: AB InBev 2016 Annual Report, pp. 82-85.

2.3 Capitalising versus Expensing: Impact on Financial Statements and Ratios

This section discusses the implications for financial statements and ratios of capitalising versus expensing costs in the period in which they are incurred. We first summarize the general financial statement impact of capitalising versus expensing and two analytical issues related to the decision—namely the effect on an individual company's trend analysis and on comparability across companies.

In the period of the expenditure, an expenditure that is capitalised increases the amount of assets on the balance sheet and appears as an investing cash outflow on the statement of cash flows. After initial recognition, a company allocates the capitalised amount over the asset's useful life as depreciation or amortisation expense (except assets that are not depreciated, i.e., land, or amortised, e.g., intangible assets with indefinite lives). This expense reduces net income on the income statement and reduces the value of the asset on the balance sheet. Depreciation and amortisation are non-cash expenses and therefore, apart from their effect on taxable income and taxes payable, have no impact on the cash flow statement. In the section of the statement of cash flows that reconciles net income to operating cash flow, depreciation and amortisation expenses are added back to net income.

Alternatively, an expenditure that is expensed reduces net income by the after-tax amount of the expenditure in the period it is made. No asset is recorded on the balance sheet and thus no depreciation or amortisation occurs in subsequent periods. The lower amount of net income is reflected in lower retained earnings on the balance sheet. An expenditure that is expensed appears as an operating cash outflow in the period it is made. There is no effect on the financial statements of subsequent periods.

Example 4 illustrates the impact on the financial statements of capitalising versus expensing an expenditure.

EXAMPLE 4

General Financial Statement Impact of Capitalising Versus Expensing

Assume two identical (hypothetical) companies, CAP Inc. (CAP) and NOW Inc. (NOW), start with €1,000 cash and €1,000 common stock. Each year the companies recognise total revenues of €1,500 cash and make cash expenditures, excluding an equipment purchase, of €500. At the beginning of operations, each company pays €900 to purchase equipment. CAP estimates the equipment will have a useful life of three years and an estimated salvage value of €0 at the end of the three years. NOW estimates a much shorter useful life and expenses the equipment immediately. The companies have no other assets and make no other asset purchases during the three-year period. Assume the companies pay no dividends, earn zero interest on cash balances, have a tax rate of 30 percent, and use the same accounting method for financial and tax purposes.

The left side of Exhibit 2 shows CAP's financial statements; i.e., with the expenditure capitalised and depreciated at €300 per year based on the straight-line method of depreciation (€900 cost minus €0 salvage value equals €900, divided by a three-year life equals €300 per year). The right side of the exhibit shows NOW's financial statements, with the entire €900 expenditure treated as an expense in the first year. All amounts are in euro.

Exhibit 2 Capitalising versus Expensing

CAP Inc.				NOW Inc.			
Capitalise €900 as asset and depreciate				Expense €900 immediately			
For Year	1	2	3	For Year	1	2	3
Revenue	1,500	1,500	1,500	Revenue	1,500	1,500	1,500
Cash expenses	500	500	500	Cash expenses	1,400	500	500
Depreciation	300	300	300	Depreciation	0	0	0
Income before tax	700	700	700	Income before tax	100	1,000	1,000
Tax at 30%	210	210	210	Tax at 30%	30	300	300
Net income	490	490	490	Net income	70	700	700
Cash from operations	790	790	790	Cash from operations	70	700	700
Cash used in investing	(900)	0	0	Cash used in investing	0	0	0
Total change in cash	(110)	790	790	Total change in cash	70	700	700

As of	Time 0	End of Year 1	End of Year2	End of Year 3	Time	Time 0	End of Year 1	End of Year 2	End of Year 3
Cash	1,000	890	1,680	2,470	Cash	1,000	1,070	1,770	2,470
PP & E (net)	—	600	300	—	PP & E (net)	—	—	—	—
Total Assets	1,000	1,490	1,980	2,470	Total Assets	1,000	1,070	1,770	2,470
Retained earnings	0	490	980	1,470	Retained earnings	0	70	770	1,470
Common stock	1,000	1,000	1,000	1,000	Common stock	1,000	1,000	1,000	1,000
Total shareholders' equity	1,000	1,490	1,980	2,470	Total shareholders' equity	1,000	1,070	1,770	2,470

1 Which company reports higher net income over the three years? Total cash flow? Cash from operations?

2 Based on ROE and net profit margin, how does the profitability of the two companies compare?

3 Why does NOW report change in cash of €70 in Year 1, while CAP reports total change in cash of (€110)?

Solution to 1:

Neither company reports higher total net income or cash flow over the three years. The sum of net income over the three years is identical (€1,470 total) whether the €900 is capitalised or expensed. Also, the sum of the change in cash (€1,470 total) is identical under either scenario. CAP reports higher cash from operations by an amount of €900 because, under the capitalisation scenario, the €900 purchase is treated as an investing cash flow.

Note: Because the companies use the same accounting method for both financial and taxable income, absent the assumption of zero interest on cash balances, expensing the €900 would have resulted in higher income and cash flow for NOW because the lower taxes paid in the first year (€30 versus €210) would have allowed NOW to earn interest income on the tax savings.

Solution to 2:

In general, Ending shareholders' equity = Beginning shareholders' equity + Net income + Other comprehensive income – Dividends + Net capital contributions from shareholders. Because the companies in this example do not have other comprehensive income, did not pay dividends, and reported no capital contributions from shareholders, Ending retained earnings = Beginning retained earnings + Net income, and Ending shareholders' equity = Beginning shareholders' equity + Net income.

ROE is calculated as Net income divided by Average shareholders' equity, and Net profit margin is calculated as Net income divided by Total revenue. For example, CAP had Year 1 ROE of 39 percent (€490/[(€1,000 + €1,490)/2]), and Year 1 net profit margin of 33 percent (€490/€1,500).

CAP Inc.				NOW Inc.			
Capitalise €900 as asset and depreciate				Expense €900 immediately			
For year	1	2	3	For year	1	2	3
ROE	39%	28%	22%	ROE	7%	49%	33%
Net profit margin	33%	33%	33%	Net profit margin	5%	47%	47%

As shown, compared to expensing, capitalising results in higher profitability ratios (ROE and net profit margin) in the first year, and lower profitability ratios in subsequent years. For example, CAP's Year 1 ROE of 39 percent was higher than NOW's Year 1 ROE of 7 percent, but in Years 2 and 3, NOW reports superior profitability.

Note also that NOW's superior growth in net income between Year 1 and Year 2 is not attributable to superior performance compared to CAP but rather to the accounting decision to recognise the expense sooner than CAP. In general, all else equal, accounting decisions that result in recognising expenses sooner will give the appearance of greater subsequent growth. Comparison of the growth of the two companies' net incomes without an awareness of the difference in accounting methods would be misleading. As a corollary, NOW's income and profitability exhibit greater volatility across the three years, not because of more volatile performance but rather because of the different accounting decision.

Solution to 3:

NOW reports an increase in cash of €70 in Year 1, while CAP reports a decrease in cash of €110 because NOW's taxes were €180 lower than CAP's taxes (€30 versus €210).

Note that this problem assumes the accounting method used by each company for its tax purposes is identical to the accounting method used by the company for its financial reporting. In many countries, companies are allowed to use different depreciation methods for financial reporting and taxes, which may give rise to deferred taxes.

As shown, discretion regarding whether to expense or capitalise expenditures can impede comparability across companies. Example 4 assumes the companies purchase a single asset in one year. Because the sum of net income over the three-year period is identical whether the asset is capitalised or expensed, it illustrates that although capitalising results in higher profitability compared to expensing in the first year, it results in lower profitability in the subsequent years. Conversely, expensing results in lower profitability in the first year but higher profitability in later years, indicating a favorable trend.

Similarly, shareholders' equity for a company that capitalises the expenditure will be higher in the early years because the initially higher profits result in initially higher retained earnings. Example 4 assumes the companies purchase a single asset in one year and report identical amounts of total net income over the three-year period, so shareholders' equity (and retained earnings) for the firm that expenses will be identical to shareholders' equity (and retained earnings) for the capitalising firm at the end of the three-year period.

Although Example 4 shows companies purchasing an asset only in the first year, if a company continues to purchase similar or increasing amounts of assets each year, the profitability-enhancing effect of capitalising continues if the amount of the expenditures in a period continues to be more than the depreciation expense. Example 5 illustrates this point.

EXAMPLE 5

Impact of Capitalising Versus Expensing for Ongoing Purchases

A company buys a £300 computer in Year 1 and capitalises the expenditure. The computer has a useful life of three years and an expected salvage value of £0, so the annual depreciation expense using the straight-line method is £100 per year. Compared to expensing the entire £300 immediately, the company's pre-tax profit in Year 1 is £200 greater.

1 Assume that the company continues to buy an identical computer each year at the same price. If the company uses the same accounting treatment for each of the computers, when does the profit-enhancing effect of capitalising versus expensing end?
2 If the company buys another identical computer in Year 4, using the same accounting treatment as the prior years, what is the effect on Year 4 profits of capitalising versus expensing these expenditures?

Solution to 1:

The profit-enhancing effect of capitalising versus expensing would end in Year 3. In Year 3, the depreciation expense on each of the three computers bought in Years 1, 2, and 3 would total £300 (£100 + £100 + £100). Therefore, the total depreciation expense for Year 3 will be exactly equal to the capital expenditure in Year 3. The expense in Year 3 would be £300, regardless of whether the company capitalised or expensed the annual computer purchases.

Solution to 2:

There is no impact on Year 4 profits. As in the previous year, the depreciation expense on each of the three computers bought in Years 2, 3, and 4 would total £300 (£100 + £100 + £100). Therefore, the total depreciation expense for Year 4 will be exactly equal to the capital expenditure in Year 4. Pre-tax profits would be reduced by £300, regardless of whether the company capitalised or expensed the annual computer purchases.

Compared to expensing an expenditure, capitalising the expenditure typically results in greater amounts reported as cash from operations. Capitalised expenditures are typically treated as an investment cash outflow whereas expenses reduce operating cash flows. Because cash flow from operating activities is an important consideration in some valuation models, companies may try to maximise reported cash flow from operations by capitalising expenditures that should be expensed. Valuation models that use free cash flow will consider not only operating cash flows but also investing cash flows. Analysts should be alert to evidence of companies manipulating reported cash flow from operations by capitalising expenditures that should be expensed.

In summary, holding all else constant, capitalising an expenditure enhances current profitability and increases reported cash flow from operations. The profitability-enhancing effect of capitalising continues so long as capital expenditures exceed the depreciation expense. Profitability-enhancing motivations for decisions to capitalise should be considered when analyzing performance. For example, a company may choose to capitalise more expenditures (within the allowable bounds of accounting standards) to achieve earnings targets for a given period. Expensing a cost in the period reduces current period profits but enhances future profitability and thus enhances the profit trend. Profit trend-enhancing motivations should also be considered when analyzing performance. If the company is in a reporting environment which requires identical accounting methods for financial reporting and taxes (unlike the United States, which permits companies to use depreciation methods for reporting purposes that differ from the depreciation method required by tax purposes), then expensing will have a more favorable cash flow impact because paying lower taxes in an earlier period creates an opportunity to earn interest income on the cash saved.

In contrast with the relatively simple examples above, it is generally neither possible nor desirable to identify individual instances involving discretion about whether to capitalise or expense expenditures. An analyst can, however, typically identify significant items of expenditure treated differently across companies. The items of expenditure giving rise to the most relevant differences across companies will vary by industry. This cross-industry variation is apparent in the following discussion of the capitalisation of expenditures.

2.4 Capitalisation of Interest Costs

As noted above, companies generally must capitalise interest costs associated with acquiring or constructing an asset that requires a long period of time to get ready for its intended use.[11]

As a consequence of this accounting treatment, a company's interest costs for a period can appear either on the balance sheet (to the extent they are capitalised) or on the income statement (to the extent they are expensed).

If the interest expenditure is incurred in connection with constructing an asset for the company's own use, the capitalised interest appears on the balance sheet as a part of the relevant long-lived asset. The capitalised interest is expensed over time as the property is depreciated—and is thus part of depreciation expense rather than interest expense. If the interest expenditure is incurred in connection with constructing an asset to sell, for example by a real estate construction company, the capitalised interest appears on the company's balance sheet as part of inventory. The capitalised interest is then expensed as part of the cost of sales when the asset is sold.

The treatment of capitalised interest poses certain issues that analysts should consider. First, capitalised interest appears as part of investing cash outflows, whereas expensed interest typically reduces operating cash flow. US GAAP reporting companies are required to categorize interest in operating cash flow, and IFRS reporting companies can categorize interest in operating, investing, or financing cash flows. Although the treatment is consistent with accounting standards, an analyst may want to examine the impact on reported cash flows. Second, interest coverage ratios are solvency indicators measuring the extent to which a company's earnings (or cash flow) in a period covered its interest costs. To provide a true picture of a company's interest coverage, the entire amount of interest expenditure, both the capitalised portion and the expensed portion, should be used in calculating interest coverage

11 IAS 23 [Borrowing Costs] and FASB ASC Subtopic 835-20 [Interest – Capitalization of Interest] specify respectively IFRS and US GAAP for capitalisation of interest costs. Although the standards are not completely converged, the standards are in general agreement.

ratios. Additionally, if a company is depreciating interest that it capitalised in a previous period, income should be adjusted to eliminate the effect of that depreciation. Example 6 illustrates the calculations.

EXAMPLE 6

Effect of Capitalised Interest Costs on Coverage Ratios and Cash Flow

Melco Resorts & Entertainment Limited (NASDAQ: MLCO), a Hong Kong SAR based casino company which is listed on the NASDAQ stock exchange and prepares financial reports under US GAAP, disclosed the following information in one of the footnotes to its 2017 financial statements: "Interest and amortization of deferred financing costs associated with major development and construction projects is capitalized and included in the cost of the project. .... Total interest expenses incurred amounted to $267,065, $252,600, and $253,168, of which $37,483, $29,033, and $134,838 were capitalized during the years ended December 31, 2017, 2016, and 2015, respectively. Amortization of deferred financing costs of $26,182, $48,345, and $38,511, net of amortization capitalized of nil, nil, and $5,458, were recorded during the years ended December 31, 2017, 2016, and 2015, respectively." (Form 20-F filed 12 April 2018). Cash payments for deferred financing costs were reported in cash flows from financing activities.

Exhibit 3 Melco Resorts & Entertainment Limited Selected Data, as Reported (Dollars in thousands)

	2017	2016	2015
EBIT (from income statement)	544,865	298,663	58,553
Interest expense (from income statement)	229,582	223,567	118,330
Capitalized interest (from footnote)	37,483	29,033	134,838
Amortization of deferred financing costs (from footnote)	26,182	48,345	38,511
Net cash provided by operating activities	1,162,500	1,158,128	522,026
Net cash from (used) in investing activities	(410,226)	280,604	(469,656)
Net cash from (used) in financing activities	(1,046,041)	(1,339,717)	(29,688)

Notes: EBIT represents "Income (Loss) Before Income Tax" plus "Interest expenses, net of capitalized interest" from the income statement.

1 Calculate and interpret Melco's interest coverage ratio with and without capitalised interest.

2 Calculate Melco's percentage change in operating cash flow from 2016 to 2017. Assuming the financial reporting does not affect reporting for income taxes, what were the effects of capitalised interest on operating and investing cash flows?

Solution to 1:

Interest coverage ratios with and without capitalised interest were as follows:

For 2017

2.37 ($544,865 ÷ $229,582) without adjusting for capitalised interest; and

2.14 [($544,865 + $26,182) ÷ ($229,582 + $37,483)] including an adjustment to EBIT for depreciation of previously capitalised interest and an adjustment to interest expense for the amount of interest capitalised in 2017.

For 2016

1.34 ($298,663÷ $223,567) without adjusting for capitalised interest; and

1.37 [($298,663 + $48,345) ÷ ($223,567 + $29,033)] including an adjustment to EBIT for depreciation of previously capitalised interest and an adjustment to interest expense for the amount of interest capitalised in 2016.

For 2015

0.49 ($58,533÷ $118,330) without adjusting for capitalised interest; and

0.36 [($58,533 + $33,053) ÷ ($118,330+ $134,838)] including an adjustment to EBIT for depreciation of previously capitalised interest and an adjustment to interest expense for the amount of interest capitalised in 2015.

The above calculations indicate that Melco's interest coverage improved in 2017 compared to the previous two years. In both 2017 and 2015, the coverage ratio is lower when adjusted for capitalised interest.

Solution to 2:

If the interest had been expensed rather than capitalised, operating cash flows would have been lower in all three years. On an adjusted basis, but not an unadjusted basis, the company's operating cash flow declined in 2017 compared to 2016. On an unadjusted basis, for 2017 compared with 2016, Melco's operating cash flow increased by 0.4 percent in 2017 [($1,162,500 ÷ $1,158,128) − 1]. Including adjustments to expense all interest costs, Melco's operating cash flow also decreased by 0.4 percent in 2017 {[$1,162,500 − $37,483) ÷ ($1,158,128 − $29,033)] − 1}.

If the interest had been expensed rather than capitalised, financing cash flows would have been higher in all three years.

The treatment of capitalised interest raises issues for consideration by an analyst. First, capitalised interest appears as part of investing cash outflows, whereas expensed interest reduces operating or financing cash flow under IFRS and operating cash flow under US GAAP. An analyst may want to examine the impact on reported cash flows of interest expenditures when comparing companies. Second, interest coverage ratios are solvency indicators measuring the extent to which a company's earnings (or cash flow) in a period covered its interest costs. To provide a true picture of a company's interest coverage, the entire amount of interest, both the capitalised portion and the expensed portion, should be used in calculating interest coverage ratios.

Generally, including capitalised interest in the calculation of interest coverage ratios provides a better assessment of a company's solvency. In assigning credit ratings, rating agencies include capitalised interest in coverage ratios. For example, Standard & Poor's calculates the EBIT interest coverage ratio as EBIT divided by gross interest (defined as interest prior to deductions for capitalised interest or interest income).

Maintaining a minimum interest coverage ratio is a financial covenant often included in lending agreements, e.g., bank loans and bond indentures. The definition of the coverage ratio can be found in the company's credit agreement. The definition is relevant because treatment of capitalised interest in calculating coverage ratios would affect an assessment of how close a company's actual ratios are to the levels specified by its financial covenants and thus the probability of breaching those covenants.

2.5 Capitalisation of Internal Development Costs

As noted above, accounting standards require companies to capitalise software development costs after a product's feasibility is established. Despite this requirement, judgment in determining feasibility means that companies' capitalisation practices may differ. For example, as illustrated in Exhibit 4, Microsoft judges product feasibility to be established very shortly before manufacturing begins and, therefore, effectively expenses—rather than capitalises—research and development costs.

Exhibit 4 Disclosure on Software Development Costs

Excerpt from Management's Discussion and Analysis (MD&A) of Microsoft Corporation, Application of Critical Accounting Policies, Research and Development Costs:

> "Costs incurred internally in researching and developing a computer software product are charged to expense until technological feasibility has been established for the product. Once technological feasibility is established, all software costs are capitalized until the product is available for general release to customers. Judgment is required in determining when technological feasibility of a product is established. We have determined that technological feasibility for our software products is reached after all high-risk development issues have been resolved through coding and testing. Generally, this occurs shortly before the products are released to production. The amortization of these costs is included in cost of revenue over the estimated life of the products."
>
> *Source*: Microsoft Corporation Annual Report on Form 10-K 2017, p. 45.

Expensing rather than capitalising development costs results in lower net income in the current period. Expensing rather than capitalising will continue to result in lower net income so long as the amount of the current-period development expenses is higher than the amortisation expense that would have resulted from amortising prior periods' capitalised development costs—the typical situation when a company's development costs are increasing. On the statement of cash flows, expensing rather than capitalising development costs results in lower net operating cash flows and higher net investing cash flows. This is because the development costs are reflected as operating cash outflows rather than investing cash outflows.

In comparing the financial performance of a company that expenses most or all software development costs, such as Microsoft, with another company that capitalises software development costs, adjustments can be made to make the two comparable. For the company that capitalises software development costs, an analyst can adjust (a) the income statement to include software development costs as an expense and to exclude amortisation of prior years' software development costs; (b) the balance sheet to exclude capitalised software (decrease assets and equity); and (c) the statement of cash flows to decrease operating cash flows and decrease cash used in investing by the amount of the current period development costs. Any ratios that include income, long-lived assets, or cash flow from operations—such as return on equity—will also be affected.

EXAMPLE 7

Software Development Costs

You are working on a project involving the analysis of JHH Software, a (hypothetical) software development company that established technical feasibility for its first product in 2017. Part of your analysis involves computing certain market-based ratios, which you will use to compare JHH to another company that expenses all of its software development expenditures. Relevant data and excerpts from the company's annual report are included in Exhibit 5.

Exhibit 5 JHH SOFTWARE (Dollars in Thousands, Except Per-Share Amounts)

CONSOLIDATED STATEMENT OF EARNINGS—abbreviated

For year ended 31 December:	2018	2017	2016
Total revenue	$91,424	$91,134	$96,293
Total operating expenses	78,107	78,908	85,624
Operating income	13,317	12,226	10,669
Provision for income taxes	3,825	4,232	3,172
Net income	$9,492	$7,994	$7,479
Earnings per share (EPS)	$1.40	$0.82	$0.68

STATEMENT OF CASH FLOWS—abbreviated

For year ended 31 December:	2018	2017	2016
Net cash provided by operating activities	$15,007	$14,874	$15,266
Net cash used in investing activities*	(11,549)	(4,423)	(5,346)
Net cash used in financing activities	(8,003)	(7,936)	(7,157)
Net change in cash and cash equivalents	($4,545)	$2,515	$2,763
**Includes software development expenses of and includes capital expenditures of*	*($6,000)* *($2,000)*	*($4,000)* *($1,600)*	*($2,000)* *($1,200)*

Additional information:

For year ended 31 December:	2018	2017	2016
Market value of outstanding debt	0	0	0
Amortisation of capitalised software development expenses	($2,000)	($667)	0
Depreciation expense	($2,200)	($1,440)	($1,320)

(continued)

Exhibit 5 (Continued)

CONSOLIDATED STATEMENT OF EARNINGS—abbreviated

For year ended 31 December:	2018	2017	2016
Market price per share of common stock	$42	$26	$17
Shares of common stock outstanding (thousands)	6,780	9,765	10,999

Footnote disclosure of accounting policy for software development:
Expenses that are related to the conceptual formulation and design of software products are expensed to research and development as incurred. The company capitalises expenses that are incurred to produce the finished product after technological feasibility has been established.

1 Compute the following ratios for JHH based on the reported financial statements for fiscal year ended 31 December 2018, with no adjustments. Next, determine the approximate impact on these ratios if the company had expensed rather than capitalised its investments in software. (Assume the financial reporting does not affect reporting for income taxes. There would be no change in the effective tax rate.)

   A P/E: Price/Earnings per share

   B P/CFO: Price/Operating cash flow per share

   C EV/EBITDA: Enterprise value/EBITDA, where enterprise value is defined as the total market value of all sources of a company's financing, including equity and debt, and EBITDA is earnings before interest, taxes, depreciation, and amortisation.

2 Interpret the changes in the ratios.

Solution to 1:

(Dollars are in thousands, except per-share amounts.) JHH's 2019 ratios are presented in the following table:

	Ratios	As reported	As adjusted
A.	P/E ratio	30.0	42.9
B.	P/CFO	19.0	31.6
C.	EV/EBITDA	16.3	24.7

A Based on the information as reported, the P/E ratio was 30.0 ($42 ÷ $1.40). Based on EPS adjusted to expense software development costs, the P/E ratio was 42.9 ($42 ÷ $0.98).

- Price: Assuming that the market value of the company's equity is based on its fundamentals, the price per share is $42, regardless of a difference in accounting.
- EPS: As reported, EPS was $1.40. Adjusted EPS was $0.98. Expensing software development costs would have reduced JHH's 2018 operating income by $6,000, but the company would have reported no amortisation of prior years' software costs, which would have increased operating income by $2,000. The net change of $4,000 would have reduced operating income from the reported $13,317 to $9,317. The effective tax rate for 2018 ($3,825 ÷ $13,317) is 28.72%, and using this effective tax rate would give an adjusted net income of $6,641 [$9,317 × (1

– 0.2872)], compared to \$9,492 before the adjustment. The EPS would therefore be reduced from the reported \$1.40 to \$0.98 (adjusted net income of \$6,641 divided by 6,780 shares).

B Based on information as reported, the P/CFO was 19.0 (\$42 ÷ \$2.21). Based on CFO adjusted to expense software development costs, the P/CFO was 31.6 (\$42 ÷ \$1.33).

- Price: Assuming that the market value of the company's equity is based on its fundamentals, the price per share is \$42, regardless of a difference in accounting.
- CFO per share, as reported, was \$2.21 (total operating cash flows \$15,007 ÷ 6,780 shares).
- CFO per share, as adjusted, was \$1.33. The company's \$6,000 expenditure on software development costs was reported as a cash outflow from investing activities, so expensing those costs would reduce cash from operating activities by \$6,000, from the reported \$15,007 to \$9,007. Dividing adjusted total operating cash flow of \$9,007 by 6,780 shares results in cash flow per share of \$1.33.

C Based on information as reported, the EV/EBITDA was 16.3 (\$284,760 ÷ \$17,517). Based on EBITDA adjusted to expense software development costs, the EV/EBITDA was 24.7 (\$284,760 ÷ \$11,517).

- Enterprise Value: Enterprise value is the sum of the market value of the company's equity and debt. JHH has no debt, and therefore the enterprise value is equal to the market value of its equity. The market value of its equity is \$284,760 (\$42 per share × 6,780 shares).
- EBITDA, as reported, was \$17,517 (earnings before interest and taxes of \$13,317 plus \$2,200 depreciation plus \$2,000 amortisation).
- EBITDA, adjusted for expensing software development costs by the inclusion of \$6,000 development expense and the exclusion of \$2,000 amortisation of prior expense, would be \$11,517 (earnings before interest and taxes of \$9,317 plus \$2,200 depreciation plus \$0 amortisation).

Solution to 2:

Expensing software development costs would decrease historical profits, operating cash flow, and EBITDA, and would thus increase all market multiples. So JHH's stock would appear more expensive if it expensed rather than capitalised the software development costs.

If the unadjusted market-based ratios were used in the comparison of JHH to its competitor that expenses all software development expenditures, then JHH might appear to be under-priced when the difference is solely related to accounting factors. JHH's adjusted market-based ratios provide a better basis for comparison.

For the company in Example 7, current period software development expenditures exceed the amortisation of prior periods' capitalised software development expenditures. As a result, expensing rather than capitalising software development costs would have the effect of lowering income. If, however, software development expenditures slowed such that current expenditures were lower than the amortisation of prior periods' capitalised software development expenditures, then expensing software development costs would have the effect of increasing income relative to capitalising it.

This section illustrated how decisions about capitalising versus expensing impact financial statements and ratios. Earlier expensing lowers current profits but enhances trends, whereas capitalising now and expensing later enhances current profits. Having described the accounting for acquisition of long-lived assets, we now turn to the topic of measuring long-lived assets in subsequent periods.

3 DEPRECIATION AND AMORTISATION OF LONG-LIVED ASSETS

Under the cost model of reporting long-lived assets, which is permitted under IFRS and required under US GAAP, the capitalised costs of long-lived tangible assets (other than land, which is not depreciated) and intangible assets with finite useful lives are allocated to subsequent periods as depreciation and amortisation expenses. Depreciation and amortisation are effectively the same concept, with the term depreciation referring to the process of allocating tangible assets' costs and the term amortisation referring to the process of allocating intangible assets' costs.[12] The alternative model of reporting long-lived assets is the **revaluation model**, which is permitted under IFRS but not under US GAAP. Under the revaluation model, a company reports the long-lived asset at fair value rather than at acquisition cost (historical cost) less accumulated depreciation or amortisation, as in the cost model.

An asset's carrying amount is the amount at which the asset is reported on the balance sheet. Under the cost model, at any point in time, the carrying amount (also called carrying value or net book value) of a long-lived asset is equal to its historical cost minus the amount of depreciation or amortisation that has been accumulated since the asset's purchase (assuming that the asset has not been impaired, a topic which will be addressed in Section 5). Companies may present on the balance sheet the total net amount of property, plant, and equipment and the total net amount of intangible assets. However, more detail is disclosed in the notes to financial statements. The details disclosed typically include the acquisition costs, the depreciation and amortisation expenses, the accumulated depreciation and amortisation amounts, the depreciation and amortisation methods used, and information on the assumptions used to depreciate and amortise long-lived assets.

3.1 Depreciation Methods and Calculation of Depreciation Expense

Depreciation methods include the **straight-line method**, in which the cost of an asset is allocated to expense evenly over its useful life; **accelerated methods**, in which the allocation of cost is greater in earlier years; and the **units-of-production method**, in which the allocation of cost corresponds to the actual use of an asset in a particular period. The choice of depreciation method affects the amounts reported on the financial statements, including the amounts for reported assets and operating and net income. This, in turn, affects a variety of financial ratios, including fixed asset turnover, total asset turnover, operating profit margin, operating return on assets, and return on assets.

12 Depletion is the term applied to a similar concept for natural resources; costs associated with those resources are allocated to a period on the basis of the usage or extraction of those resources.

Using the straight-line method, depreciation expense is calculated as depreciable cost divided by estimated useful life and is the same for each period. Depreciable cost is the historical cost of the tangible asset minus the estimated residual (salvage) value.[13] A commonly used accelerated method is the declining balance method, in which the amount of depreciation expense for a period is calculated as some percentage of the carrying amount (i.e., cost net of accumulated depreciation at the beginning of the period). When an accelerated method is used, depreciable cost is not used to calculate the depreciation expense but the carrying amount should not be reduced below the estimated residual value. In the units-of-production method, the amount of depreciation expense for a period is based on the proportion of the asset's production during the period compared with the total estimated productive capacity of the asset over its useful life. The depreciation expense is calculated as depreciable cost times production in the period divided by estimated productive capacity over the life of the asset. Equivalently, the company may estimate a depreciation cost per unit (depreciable cost divided by estimated productive capacity) and calculate depreciation expense as depreciation cost per unit times production in the period. Regardless of the depreciation method used, the carrying amount of the asset is not reduced below the estimated residual value. Example 8 provides an example of these depreciation methods.

EXAMPLE 8

Alternative Depreciation Methods

You are analyzing three hypothetical companies: EVEN-LI Co., SOONER Inc., and AZUSED Co. At the beginning of Year 1, each company buys an identical piece of box manufacturing equipment for $2,300 and has the same assumptions about useful life, estimated residual value, and productive capacity. The annual production of each company is the same, but each company uses a different method of depreciation. As disclosed in each company's notes to the financial statements, each company's depreciation method, assumptions, and production are as follows:

Depreciation method

- EVEN-LI Co.: straight-line method
- SOONER Inc.: double-declining balance method (the rate applied to the carrying amount is double the depreciation rate for the straight-line method)
- AZUSED Co.: units-of-production method

Assumptions and production

- Estimated residual value: $100
- Estimated useful life: 4 years

13 The residual value is the estimated amount that an entity will obtain from disposal of the asset at the end of its useful life.

- Total estimated productive capacity: 800 boxes
- Production in each of the four years: 200 boxes in the first year, 300 in the second year, 200 in the third year, and 100 in the fourth year

1 Using the following template for each company, record its beginning and ending net book value (carrying amount), end-of-year accumulated depreciation, and annual depreciation expense for the box manufacturing equipment.

Template:

	Beginning Net Book Value	Depreciation Expense	Accumulated Depreciation	Ending Net Book Value
Year 1				
Year 2				
Year 3				
Year 4				

2 Explain the significant differences in the timing of the recognition of the depreciation expense.

3 For each company, assume that sales, earnings before interest, taxes, depreciation, and amortization, and assets other than the box manufacturing equipment are as shown in the following table. Calculate the total asset turnover ratio, the operating profit margin, and the operating return on assets for each company for each of the four years. Discuss the ratios, comparing results within and across companies.

	Sales	Earnings before Interest, Taxes, Depreciation, and Amortization	Carrying Amount of Total Assets, Excluding the Box Manufacturing Equipment, at Year End*
Year 1	$300,000	$36,000	$30,000
Year 2	320,000	38,400	32,000
Year 3	340,000	40,800	34,000
Year 4	360,000	43,200	36,000

* Assume that total assets at the beginning of Year 1, *including* the box manufacturing equipment, had a value of $30,300. Assume that depreciation expense on assets other than the box manufacturing equipment totaled $1,000 per year.

Solution to 1:

For *each* company, the following information applies: Beginning net book value in Year 1 equals the purchase price of $2,300; accumulated year-end depreciation equals the balance from the previous year plus the current year's depreciation expense; ending net book value (carrying amount) equals original cost minus accumulated year-end depreciation (which is the same as beginning net book value minus depreciation expense); and beginning net book value in Years 2, 3, and 4 equals the ending net book value of the prior year. The following text and filled-in templates describe how depreciation *expense* is calculated for each company.

EVEN-LI Co. uses the straight-line method, so depreciation expense in each year equals $550, which is calculated as ($2,300 original cost – $100 residual value)/4 years. The net book value at the end of Year 4 is the estimated residual value of $100.

EVEN-LI Co.	Beginning Net Book Value	Depreciation Expense	Accumulated Year-End Depreciation	Ending Net Book Value
Year 1	$2,300	$550	$550	$1,750
Year 2	1,750	550	1,100	1,200
Year 3	1,200	550	1,650	650
Year 4	650	550	2,200	100

SOONER Inc. uses the double-declining balance method. The depreciation rate for the double-declining balance method is double the depreciation rate for the straight-line method. The depreciation rate under the straight-line method is 25 percent (100 percent divided by 4 years). Thus, the depreciation rate for the double-declining balance method is 50 percent (2 times 25 percent). The depreciation expense for the first year is $1,150 (50 percent of $2,300). Note that under this method, the depreciation rate of 50 percent is applied to the carrying amount (net book value) of the asset, without adjustment for expected residual value. Because the carrying amount of the asset is not depreciated below its estimated residual value, however, the depreciation expense in the final year of depreciation decreases the ending net book value (carrying amount) to the estimated residual value.

SOONER Inc.	Beginning Net Book Value	Depreciation Expense	Accumulated Year-End Depreciation	Ending Net Book Value
Year 1	$2,300	$1,150	$1,150	$1,150
Year 2	1,150	575	1,725	575
Year 3	575	288	2,013	287
Year 4	287	187	2,200	100

Another common approach (not required in this question) is to use an accelerated method, such as the double-declining method, for some period (a year or more) and then to change to the straight-line method for the remaining life of the asset. If SOONER had used the double-declining method for the first year and then switched to the straight-line method for Years 2, 3, and 4, the depreciation expense would be $350 [($1,150 – $100 estimated residual value)/3 years] a year for Years 2, 3, and 4. The results for SOONER under this alternative approach are shown below.

SOONER Inc.	Beginning Net Book Value	Depreciation Expense	Accumulated Year-End Depreciation	Ending Net Book Value
Year 1	$2,300	$1,150	$1,150	$1,150
Year 2	1,150	350	1,500	800
Year 3	800	350	1,850	450
Year 4	450	350	2,200	100

AZUSED Co. uses the units-of-production method. Dividing the equipment's total depreciable cost by its total productive capacity gives a cost per unit of $2.75, calculated as ($2,300 original cost – $100 residual value)/800. The depreciation expense recognised each year is the number of units produced times \$2.75. For Year 1, the amount of depreciation expense is \$550 (200 units times \$2.75). For Year 2, the amount is \$825 (300 units times \$2.75). For Year 3, the amount is \$550. For Year 4, the amount is \$275.

AZUSED Co.	Beginning Net Book Value	Depreciation Expense	Accumulated Year-End Depreciation	Ending Net Book Value
Year 1	\$2,300	\$550	\$550	\$1,750
Year 2	1,750	825	1,375	925
Year 3	925	550	1,925	375
Year 4	375	275	2,200	100

Solution to 2:

All three methods result in the same total amount of accumulated depreciation over the life of the equipment. The significant differences are simply in the timing of the recognition of the depreciation expense. The straight-line method recognises the expense evenly, the accelerated method recognises most of the expense in the first year, and the units-of-production method recognises the expense on the basis of production (or use of the asset). Under all three methods, the ending net book value is \$100.

Solution to 3:

Total asset turnover ratio = Total revenue ÷ Average total assets

Operating profit margin = Earnings before interest and taxes ÷ Total revenue

Operating return on assets = Earnings before interest and taxes ÷ Average total assets

Ratios are shown in the table below, and details of the calculations for Years 1 and 2 are described after discussion of the ratios.

	EVEN-LI Co.			SOONER Inc.			AZUSED Co.		
Ratio*	AT	PM (%)	ROA (%)	AT	PM (%)	ROA (%)	AT	PM (%)	ROA (%)
Year 1	9.67	11.48	111.04	9.76	11.28	110.17	9.67	11.48	111.04
Year 2	9.85	11.52	113.47	10.04	11.51	115.57	9.90	11.43	113.10
Year 3	10.02	11.54	115.70	10.17	11.62	118.21	10.10	11.54	116.64
Year 4	10.18	11.57	117.74	10.23	11.67	119.42	10.22	11.65	118.98

* AT = Total asset turnover ratio. PM = Operating profit margin. ROA = Operating return on assets.

For all companies, the asset turnover ratio increased over time because sales grew at a faster rate than that of the assets. SOONER had consistently higher asset turnover ratios than the other two companies, however, because higher depreciation expense in the earlier periods decreased its average total assets. In addition, the higher depreciation in earlier periods resulted in SOONER having lower operating profit margin and operating ROA in the first year and higher operating profit margin and operating ROA in the later periods. SOONER appears to be more efficiently run, on the basis of its higher asset turnover and greater increases in profit margin and ROA over time; however, these comparisons reflect differences in the companies' choice of depreciation method. In addition, an analyst might question the sustainability of the extremely high ROAs for all three companies because such high profitability levels would probably attract new competitors, which would likely put downward pressure on the ratios.

EVEN-LI Co.

Year 1:

$$\text{Total asset turnover ratio} = 300{,}000/[(30{,}300 + 30{,}000 + 1{,}750)/2] = 300{,}000/31{,}025 = 9.67$$

$$\text{Operating profit margin} = (36{,}000 - 1{,}000 - 550)/300{,}000 = 34{,}450/300{,}000 = 11.48\%$$

$$\text{Operating ROA} = 34{,}450/31{,}025 = 111.04\%$$

Year 2:

$$\text{Total asset turnover ratio} = 320{,}000/[(30{,}000 + 1{,}750 + 32{,}000 + 1{,}200)/2] = 320{,}000/32{,}475 = 9.85$$

$$\text{Operating profit margin} = (38{,}400 - 1{,}000 - 550)/320{,}000 = 36{,}850/320{,}000 = 11.52\%$$

$$\text{Operating ROA} = 36{,}850/32{,}475 = 113.47\%$$

SOONER Inc.

Year 1:

$$\text{Total asset turnover ratio} = 300{,}000/[(30{,}300 + 30{,}000 + 1{,}150)/2] = 300{,}000/30{,}725 = 9.76$$

$$\text{Operating profit margin} = (36{,}000 - 1{,}000 - 1{,}150)/300{,}000 = 33{,}850/300{,}000 = 11.28\%$$

$$\text{Operating ROA} = 33{,}850/30{,}725 = 110.17\%$$

Year 2:

$$\text{Total asset turnover ratio} = 320{,}000/[(30{,}000 + 1{,}150 + 32{,}000 + 575)/2] = 320{,}000/31{,}862.50 = 10.04$$

$$\text{Operating profit margin} = (38{,}400 - 1{,}000 - 575)/320{,}000 = 36{,}825/320{,}000 = 11.51\%$$

$$\text{Operating ROA} = 36{,}825/31{,}862.50 = 115.57\%$$

AZUSED Co.

Year 1:

$$\text{Total asset turnover ratio} = 300{,}000/[(30{,}300 + 30{,}000 + 1{,}750)/2] = 300{,}000/31{,}025 = 9.67$$

$$\text{Operating profit margin} = (36{,}000 - 1{,}000 - 550)/300{,}000 = 34{,}450/300{,}000 = 11.48\%$$

$$\text{Operating ROA} = 34{,}450/31{,}025 = 111.04\%$$

Year 2:

$$\text{Total asset turnover ratio} = 320{,}000/[(30{,}000 + 1{,}750 + 32{,}000 + 925)/2] = 320{,}000/32{,}337.50 = 9.90$$

$$\text{Operating profit margin} = (38{,}400 - 1{,}000 - 825)/320{,}000 = 36{,}575/320{,}000 = 11.43\%$$

$$\text{Operating ROA} = 36{,}575/32{,}337.50 = 113.10\%$$

In many countries, a company must use the same depreciation methods for both financial and tax reporting. In other countries, including the United States, a company need not use the same depreciation method for financial reporting and taxes. As a result of using different depreciation methods for financial and tax reporting, pre-tax income on the income statement and taxable income on the tax return may differ. Thus, the amount of tax expense computed on the basis of pre-tax income and the amount of taxes actually owed on the basis of taxable income may differ. Although these differences eventually reverse because the total depreciation is the same regardless of the timing of its recognition in financial statements versus on tax returns, during the period of the difference, the balance sheet will show what is known as deferred taxes. For instance, if a company uses straight-line depreciation for financial reporting and an accelerated depreciation method for tax purposes, the company's financial statements will report lower depreciation expense and higher pre-tax income in the first year, compared with the amount of depreciation expense and taxable income in its tax reporting. (Compare the depreciation expense in Year 1 for EVEN-LI Co. and SOONER Inc. in the previous example.) Tax expense calculated on the basis of the financial statements' pre-tax income will be higher than taxes payable on the basis of taxable income; the difference between the two amounts represents a deferred tax liability. The deferred tax liability will be reduced as the difference reverses (i.e., when depreciation for financial reporting is higher than the depreciation for tax purposes) and the income tax is paid.

Significant estimates required for calculating depreciation include the useful life of the asset (or its total lifetime productive capacity) and its expected residual value at the end of that useful life. A longer useful life and higher expected residual value decrease the amount of annual depreciation expense relative to a shorter useful life and lower expected residual value. Companies should review their estimates periodically to ensure they remain reasonable. IFRS require companies to review estimates annually.

Although no significant differences exist between IFRS and US GAAP with respect to the definition of depreciation and the acceptable depreciation methods, IFRS require companies to use a component method of depreciation.[14] Companies are required to separately depreciate the significant components of an asset (parts of an item with a cost that is significant in relation to the total cost and/or with different useful lives) and thus require additional estimates for the various components. For instance, it may be appropriate to depreciate separately the engine, frame, and interior furnishings of an aircraft. Under US GAAP, the component method of depreciation is allowed but is seldom used in practice.[15] The following example illustrates depreciating components of an asset.

EXAMPLE 9

Illustration of Depreciating Components of an Asset

CUTITUP Co., a hypothetical company, purchases a milling machine, a type of machine used for shaping metal, at a total cost of $10,000. $2,000 was estimated to represent the cost of the rotating cutter, a significant component of the machine. The company expects the machine to have a useful life of eight years and a residual value of $3,000 and that the rotating cutter will need to be

14 IAS 16 *Property, Plant and Equipment*, paragraphs 43–47 [Depreciation].

15 According to KPMG's *IFRS Compared to US GAAP*, December 2017, kpmg.com.

replaced every two years. Assume the entire residual value is attributable to the milling machine itself, and assume the company uses straight-line depreciation for all assets.

1 How much depreciation expense would the company report in Year 1 if it uses the component method of depreciation, and how much depreciation expense would the company report in Year 1 if it does not use the component method?

2 Assuming a new cutter with an estimated two-year useful life is purchased at the end of Year 2 for $2,000, what depreciation expenses would the company report in Year 3 if it uses the component method and if it does not use the component method?

3 Assuming replacement of the cutter every two years at a price of $2,000, what is the total depreciation expense over the eight years if the company uses the component method compared with the total depreciation expense if the company does not use the component method?

4 How many different items must the company estimate in the first year to compute depreciation expense for the milling machine if it uses the component method, and how does this compare with what would be required if it does not use the component method?

Solution to 1:

Depreciation expense in Year 1 under the component method would be $1,625. For the portion of the machine excluding the cutter, the depreciable base is total cost minus the cost attributable to the cutter minus the estimated residual value = $10,000 – $2,000 – $3,000 = $5,000. Depreciation expense for the machine excluding the cutter in the first year equals $625 (depreciable cost divided by the useful life of the machine = $5,000/8 years). For the cutter, the depreciation expense equals $1,000 (depreciable cost divided by the useful life of the cutter = $2,000/2 years). Thus, the total depreciation expense for Year 1 under the component method is $1,625 (the sum of the depreciation expenses of the two components = $625 + $1,000). Depreciation expense in Year 2 would also be $1,625.

If the company does not use the component method, depreciation expense in Year 1 is $875 (the depreciable cost of the total milling machine divided by its useful life = [$10,000 – $3,000]/8 years). Depreciation expense in Year 2 would also be $875.

Solution to 2:

Assuming that at the end of Year 2, the company purchases a new cutter for $2,000 with an estimated two-year life, under the component method, the depreciation expense in Year 3 will remain at $1,625. If the company does not use the component method and purchases a new cutter with an estimated two-year life for $2,000 at the end of Year 2, the depreciation expense in Year 3 will be $1,875 [$875 + ($2,000/2) = $875 + $1,000].

Solution to 3:

Over the eight years, assuming replacement of the cutters every two years at a price of $2,000, the total depreciation expense will be $13,000 [$1,625 × 8 years] when the component method is used. When the component method is not used, the total depreciation expense will also be $13,000 [$875 × 2 years + $1,875 × 6 years]. This amount equals the total expenditures of $16,000 [$10,000 + 3 cutters × $2,000] less the residual value of $3,000.

Solution to 4:

The following table summarizes the estimates required in the first year to compute depreciation expense if the company does or does not use the component method:

Estimate	Required using component method?	Required if not using component method?
Useful life of milling machine	Yes	Yes
Residual value of milling machine	Yes	Yes
Portion of machine cost attributable to cutter	Yes	No
Portion of residual value attributable to cutter	Yes	No
Useful life of cutter	Yes	No

Total depreciation expense may be allocated between the cost of sales and other expenses. Within the income statement, depreciation expense of assets used in production is usually allocated to the cost of sales, and the depreciation expense of assets not used in production may be allocated to some other expense category. For instance, depreciation expense may be allocated to selling, general, and administrative expenses if depreciable assets are used in those functional areas. Notes to the financial statements sometimes disclose information regarding which income statement line items include depreciation expense, although the exact amount of detail disclosed by individual companies varies.

3.2 Amortisation Methods and Calculation of Amortisation Expense

Amortisation is similar in concept to depreciation. The term amortisation applies to intangible assets, and the term depreciation applies to tangible assets. Both terms refer to the process of allocating the cost of an asset over the asset's useful life. Only those intangible assets assumed to have finite useful lives are amortised over their useful lives, following the pattern in which the benefits are used up. Acceptable amortisation methods are the same as the methods acceptable for depreciation. Assets assumed to have an indefinite useful life (in other words, without a finite useful life) are not amortised. An intangible asset is considered to have an indefinite useful life when there is "no foreseeable limit to the period over which the asset is expected to generate net cash inflows" for the company.[16]

Intangible assets with finite useful lives include an acquired customer list expected to provide benefits to a direct-mail marketing company for two to three years, an acquired patent or copyright with a specific expiration date, an acquired license with a specific expiration date and no right to renew the license, and an acquired trademark for a product that a company plans to phase out over a specific number of years. Examples of intangible assets with indefinite useful lives include an acquired license that, although it has a specific expiration date, can be renewed at little or no cost and an acquired trademark that, although it has a specific expiration, can be renewed at a minimal cost and relates to a product that a company plans to continue selling for the foreseeable future.

16 IAS 38 *Intangible Assets*, paragraph 88.

As with depreciation for a tangible asset, the calculation of amortisation for an intangible asset requires the original amount at which the intangible asset is recognised and estimates of the length of its useful life and its residual value at the end of its useful life. Useful lives are estimated on the basis of the expected use of the asset, considering any factors that may limit the life of the asset, such as legal, regulatory, contractual, competitive, or economic factors.

EXAMPLE 10

Amortisation Expense

IAS 38 *Intangible Assets* provides illustrative examples regarding the accounting for intangible assets, including the following:

> A direct-mail marketing company acquires a customer list and expects that it will be able to derive benefit from the information on the list for at least one year, but no more than three years. The customer list would be amortised over management's best estimate of its useful life, say 18 months. Although the direct-mail marketing company may intend to add customer names and other information to the list in the future, the expected benefits of the acquired customer list relate only to the customers on that list at the date it was acquired.

In this example, in what ways would management's decisions and estimates affect the company's financial statements?

Solution:

Because the acquired customer list is expected to generate future economic benefits for a period greater than one year, the cost of the list should be capitalised and not expensed. The acquired customer list is determined to not have an indefinite life and must be amortised. Management must estimate the useful life of the customer list and must select an amortisation method. In this example, the list appears to have no residual value. Both the amortisation method and the estimated useful life affect the amount of the amortisation expense in each period. A shorter estimated useful life, compared with a longer estimated useful life, results in a higher amortisation expense each year over a shorter period, but the *total* accumulated amortisation expense over the life of the intangible asset is unaffected by the estimate of the useful life. Similarly, the total accumulated amortisation expense over the life of the intangible asset is unaffected by the choice of amortisation method. The amortisation expense per period depends on the amortisation method. If the straight-line method is used, the amortisation expense is the same for each year of useful life. If an accelerated method is used, the amortisation expense will be higher in earlier years.

THE REVALUATION MODEL

4

The revaluation model is an alternative to the cost model for the periodic valuation and reporting of long-lived assets. IFRS permit the use of either the revaluation model or the cost model, but the revaluation model is not allowed under US GAAP. Revaluation changes the carrying amounts of classes of long-lived assets to fair value (the fair value must be measured reliably). Under the cost model, carrying amounts are historical costs less accumulated depreciation or amortisation. Under the revaluation model, carrying amounts are the fair values at the date of revaluation less any subsequent accumulated depreciation or amortisation.

IFRS allow companies to value long-lived assets either under a cost model at historical cost minus accumulated depreciation or amortisation or under a revaluation model at fair value. In contrast, US accounting standards require that the cost model be used. A key difference between the two models is that the cost model allows only decreases in the values of long-lived assets compared with historical costs but the revaluation model may result in increases in the values of long-lived assets to amounts greater than historical costs.

IFRS allow a company to use the cost model for some classes of assets and the revaluation model for others, but the company must apply the same model to all assets within a particular class of assets and must revalue all items within a class to avoid selective revaluation. Examples of different classes of assets include land, land and buildings, machinery, motor vehicles, furniture and fixtures, and office equipment. The revaluation model may be used for classes of intangible assets but only if an active market for the assets exists, because the revaluation model may only be used if the fair values of the assets can be measured reliably. For practical purposes, the revaluation model is rarely used for either tangible or intangible assets, but its use is especially rare for intangible assets.

Under the revaluation model, whether an asset revaluation affects earnings depends on whether the revaluation initially increases or decreases an asset class' carrying amount. If a revaluation initially decreases the carrying amount of the asset class, the decrease is recognised in profit or loss. Later, if the carrying amount of the asset class increases, the increase is recognised in profit or loss to the extent that it reverses a revaluation decrease of the same asset class previously recognised in profit or loss. Any increase in excess of the reversal amount will not be recognised in the income statement but will be recorded directly to equity in a revaluation surplus account. An upward revaluation is treated the same as the amount in excess of the reversal amount. In other words, if a revaluation initially increases the carrying amount of the asset class, the increase in the carrying amount of the asset class bypasses the income statement and goes directly to equity under the heading of revaluation surplus. Any subsequent decrease in the asset's value first decreases the revaluation surplus and then goes to income. When an asset is retired or disposed of, any related amount of revaluation surplus included in equity is transferred directly to retained earnings.

Asset revaluations offer several considerations for financial statement analyses. First, an increase in the carrying amount of depreciable long-lived assets increases total assets and shareholders' equity, so asset revaluations that increase the carrying amount of an asset can be used to reduce reported leverage. Defining leverage as average total assets divided by average shareholders' equity, increasing both the numerator (assets) and denominator (equity) by the same amount leads to a decline in the ratio. (Mathematically, when a ratio is greater than one, as in this case, an increase in both the numerator and the denominator by the same amount leads to a decline in the ratio.) Therefore, the leverage motivation for the revaluation should be considered in analysis. For example, a company may revalue assets up if it is seeking new capital or approaching leverage limitations set by financial covenants.

Second, assets revaluations that decrease the carrying amount of the assets reduce net income. In the year of the revaluation, profitability measures such as return on assets and return on equity decline. However, because total assets and shareholders' equity are also lower, the company may appear more profitable in future years. Additionally, reversals of downward revaluations also go through income, thus increasing earnings. Managers can then opportunistically time the reversals to manage earnings and increase income. Third, asset revaluations that increase the carrying amount of an asset initially increase depreciation expense, total assets, and shareholders' equity. Therefore, profitability measures, such as return on assets and return on equity, would decline. Although upward asset revaluations also generally decrease income (through higher depreciation expense), the increase in the value of the long-lived asset is presumably based on increases in the operating capacity of the asset, which will likely be evidenced in increased future revenues.

Finally, an analyst should consider who did the appraisal—i.e. an independent external appraiser or management—and how often revaluations are made. Appraisals of the fair value of long-lived assets involve considerable judgment and discretion. Presumably, appraisals of assets from independent external sources are more reliable. How often assets are revalued can provide an indicator of whether their reported value continues to be representative of their fair values.

The next two examples illustrate revaluation of long-lived assets under IFRS.

EXAMPLE 11

Revaluation Resulting in an Increase in Carrying Amount Followed by Subsequent Revaluation Resulting in a Decrease in Carrying Amount

UPFIRST, a hypothetical manufacturing company, has elected to use the revaluation model for its machinery. Assume for simplicity that the company owns a single machine, which it purchased for €10,000 on the first day of its fiscal period, and that the measurement date occurs simultaneously with the company's fiscal period end.

1 At the end of the first fiscal period after acquisition, assume the fair value of the machine is determined to be €11,000. How will the company's financial statements reflect the asset?

2 At the end of the second fiscal period after acquisition, assume the fair value of the machine is determined to be €7,500. How will the company's financial statements reflect the asset?

Solution to 1:

At the end of the first fiscal period, the company's balance sheet will show the asset at a value of €11,000. The €1,000 increase in the value of the asset will appear in other comprehensive income and be accumulated in equity under the heading of revaluation surplus.

Solution to 2:

At the end of the second fiscal period, the company's balance sheet will show the asset at a value of €7,500. The total decrease in the carrying amount of the asset is €3,500 (€11,000 – €7,500). Of the €3,500 decrease, the first €1,000 will reduce the amount previously accumulated in equity under the heading of revaluation surplus. The other €2,500 will be shown as a loss on the income statement.

EXAMPLE 12

Revaluation Resulting in a Decrease in Asset's Carrying Amount Followed by Subsequent Revaluation Resulting in an Increase in Asset's Carrying Amount

DOWNFIRST, a hypothetical manufacturing company, has elected to use the revaluation model for its machinery. Assume for simplicity that the company owns a single machine, which it purchased for €10,000 on the first day of its fiscal period, and that the measurement date occurs simultaneously with the company's fiscal period end.

1 At the end of the first fiscal period after acquisition, assume the fair value of the machine is determined to be €7,500. How will the company's financial statements reflect the asset?

2 At the end of the second fiscal period after acquisition, assume the fair value of the machine is determined to be €11,000. How will the company's financial statements reflect the asset?

Solution to 1:

At the end of the first fiscal period, the company's balance sheet will show the asset at a value of €7,500. The €2,500 decrease in the value of the asset will appear as a loss on the company's income statement.

Solution to 2:

At the end of the second fiscal period, the company's balance sheet will show the asset at a value of €11,000. The total increase in the carrying amount of the asset is an increase of €3,500 (€11,000 – €7,500). Of the €3,500 increase, the first €2,500 reverses a previously reported loss and will be reported as a gain on the income statement. The other €1,000 will bypass profit or loss and be reported as other comprehensive income and be accumulated in equity under the heading of revaluation surplus.

Exhibit 6 provides two examples of disclosures concerning the revaluation model. The first disclosure is an excerpt from the 2006 annual report of KPN, a Dutch telecommunications and multimedia company. The report was produced at a time during which any IFRS-reporting company with a US stock exchange listing was required to explain differences between its reporting under IFRS and its reporting if it had used US GAAP.[17] One of these differences, as previously noted, is that US GAAP do not allow revaluation of fixed assets held for use. KPN's disclosure states that the company elected to report a class of fixed assets (cables) at fair value and explained that under US GAAP, using the cost model, the value of the asset class would have been €350 million lower. The second disclosure is an excerpt from the 2017 annual report of Avianca Holdings S.A., a Latin American airline that reports under IFRS and uses the revaluation model for one component of its fixed assets.

17 On 15 November 2007, the SEC approved rule amendments under which financial statements from foreign private issuers in the United States will be accepted without reconciliation to US GAAP if the financial statements are prepared in accordance with IFRS as issued by the International Accounting Standards Board. The rule took effect for the 2007 fiscal year. As a result, companies such as KPN no longer need to provide reconciliations to US GAAP.

Exhibit 6 Impact of Revaluation

1 Excerpt from the annual report of Koninklijke KPN N.V. explaining certain differences between IFRS and US GAAP regarding "Deemed cost fixed assets":

> KPN elected the exemption to revalue certain of its fixed assets upon the transition to IFRS to fair value and to use this fair value as their deemed cost. KPN applied the depreciated replacement cost method to determine this fair value. The revalued assets pertain to certain cables, which form part of property, plant & equipment. Under US GAAP, this revaluation is not allowed and therefore results in a reconciling item. As a result, the value of these assets as of December 31, 2006 under US GAAP is EUR 350 million lower (2005: EUR 415 million; 2004: EUR 487 million) than under IFRS.
>
> *Source*: KPN's Form 20-F, p. 168, filed 1 March 2007.

2 The 2017 annual report of Avianca Holdings S.A. and Subsidiaries shows $58.4 million of "Revaluation and Other Reserves" as a component of Equity on its balance sheet and $31.0 million in Other Comprehensive Income for the current year's "Revaluation of Administrative Property". The relevant footnote disclosure explains:

> "Administrative property in Bogota, Medellín, El Salvador, and San Jose is recorded at fair value less accumulated depreciation on buildings and impairment losses recognized at the date of revaluation. Valuations are performed with sufficient frequency to ensure that the fair value of a revalued asset does not differ materially from its carrying amount. A revaluation reserve is recorded in other comprehensive income and credited to the asset revaluation reserve in equity. However, to the extent that it reverses a revaluation deficit of the same asset previously recognized in profit or loss, the increase is recognized in profit and loss. A revaluation deficit is recognized in the income statement, except to the extent that it offsets an existing surplus on the same asset recognized in the asset revaluation reserve. Upon disposal, any revaluation reserve relating to the particular asset being sold is transferred to retained earnings.
>
> *Source*: AVIANCA HOLDINGS S.A. Form 20-F filed 01 May 2018.

Clearly, the use of the revaluation model as opposed to the cost model can have a significant impact on the financial statements of companies. This has potential consequences for comparing financial performance using financial ratios of companies that use different models.

IMPAIRMENT OF ASSETS

5

In contrast with depreciation and amortisation charges, which serve to allocate the depreciable cost of a long-lived asset over its useful life, impairment charges reflect an unanticipated decline in the value of an asset. Both IFRS and US GAAP require companies to write down the carrying amount of impaired assets. Impairment reversals for identifiable, long-lived assets are permitted under IFRS but typically not under US GAAP.

An asset is considered to be impaired when its carrying amount exceeds its recoverable amount. Although IFRS and US GAAP define recoverability differently (as described below), in general, impairment losses are recognised when the asset's carrying amount is not recoverable. The following paragraphs describe accounting for impairment for different categories of assets.

5.1 Impairment of Property, Plant, and Equipment

Accounting standards do not require that property, plant, and equipment be tested annually for impairment. Rather, at the end of each reporting period (generally, a fiscal year), a company assesses whether there are indications of asset impairment. If there is no indication of impairment, the asset is not tested for impairment. If there is an indication of impairment, such as evidence of obsolescence, decline in demand for products, or technological advancements, the recoverable amount of the asset should be measured in order to test for impairment. For property, plant, and equipment, impairment losses are recognised when the asset's carrying amount is not recoverable; the carrying amount is more than the recoverable amount. The amount of the impairment loss will reduce the carrying amount of the asset on the balance sheet and will reduce net income on the income statement. The impairment loss is a non-cash item and will not affect cash from operations.

IFRS and US GAAP differ somewhat both in the guidelines for determining that impairment has occurred and in the measurement of an impairment loss. Under IAS 36, an impairment loss is measured as the excess of carrying amount over the recoverable amount of the asset. The recoverable amount of an asset is defined as "the higher of its fair value less costs to sell and its value in use." Value in use is based on the present value of expected future cash flows. Under US GAAP, assessing recoverability is separate from measuring the impairment loss. The carrying amount of an asset "group" is considered not recoverable when it exceeds the undiscounted expected future cash flows of the group. If the asset's carrying amount is considered not recoverable, the impairment loss is measured as the difference between the asset's fair value and carrying amount.

EXAMPLE 13

Impairment of Property, Plant, and Equipment

Sussex, a hypothetical manufacturing company in the United Kingdom, has a machine it uses to produce a single product. The demand for the product has declined substantially since the introduction of a competing product. The company has assembled the following information with respect to the machine:

Carrying amount	£18,000
Undiscounted expected future cash flows	£19,000
Present value of expected future cash flows	£16,000
Fair value if sold	£17,000
Costs to sell	£2,000

1 Under IFRS, what would the company report for the machine?

2 Under US GAAP, what would the company report for the machine?

Solution to 1:

Under IFRS, the company would compare the carrying amount (£18,000) with the higher of its fair value less costs to sell (£15,000) and its value in use (£16,000). The carrying amount exceeds the value in use, the higher of the two amounts, by £2,000. The machine would be written down to the recoverable amount of £16,000, and a loss of £2,000 would be reported in the income statement. The carrying amount of the machine is now £16,000. A new depreciation schedule based on the carrying amount of £16,000 would be developed.

Solution to 2:

Under US GAAP, the carrying amount (£18,000) is compared with the undiscounted expected future cash flows (£19,000). The carrying amount is less than the undiscounted expected future cash flows, so the carrying amount is considered recoverable. The machine would continue to be carried at £18,000, and no loss would be reported.

In Example 13, a write down in the value of a piece of property, plant, and equipment occurred under IFRS but not under US GAAP. In Example 14, a write down occurs under both IFRS and US GAAP.

EXAMPLE 14

Impairment of Property, Plant, and Equipment

Essex, a hypothetical manufacturing company, has a machine it uses to produce a single product. The demand for the product has declined substantially since the introduction of a competing product. The company has assembled the following information with respect to the machine:

Carrying amount	£18,000
Undiscounted expected future cash flows	£16,000
Present value of expected future cash flows	£14,000
Fair value if sold	£10,000
Costs to sell	£2,000

1 Under IFRS, what would the company report for the machine?
2 Under US GAAP, what would the company report for the machine?

Solution to 1:

Under IFRS, the company would compare the carrying amount (£18,000) with the higher of its fair value less costs to sell (£8,000) and its value in use (£14,000). The carrying amount exceeds the value in use, the higher of the two amounts, by £4,000. The machine would be written down to the recoverable amount of £14,000, and a loss of £4,000 would be reported in the income statement. The carrying amount of the machine is now £14,000. A new depreciation schedule based on the carrying amount of £14,000 would be developed.

Solution to 2:

Under US GAAP, the carrying amount (£18,000) is compared with the undiscounted expected future cash flows (£16,000). The carrying amount exceeds the undiscounted expected future cash flows, so the carrying amount is considered not recoverable. The machine would be written down to fair value of £10,000, and a loss of £8,000 would be reported in the income statement. The carrying amount of the machine is now £10,000. A new depreciation schedule based on the carrying amount of £10,000 would be developed.

Example 14 shows that the write down to value in use under IFRS can be less than the write down to fair value under US GAAP. The difference in recognition of impairment losses is ultimately reflected in difference in book value of equity.

5.2 Impairment of Intangible Assets with a Finite Life

Intangible assets with a finite life are amortised (carrying amount decreases over time) and may become impaired. As is the case with property, plant, and equipment, the assets are not tested annually for impairment. Instead, they are tested only when significant events suggest the need to test. The company assesses at the end of each reporting period whether a significant event suggesting the need to test for impairment has occurred. Examples of such events include a significant decrease in the market price or a significant adverse change in legal or economic factors. Impairment accounting for intangible assets with a finite life is essentially the same as for tangible assets; the amount of the impairment loss will reduce the carrying amount of the asset on the balance sheet and will reduce net income on the income statement.

5.3 Impairment of Intangibles with Indefinite Lives

Intangible assets with indefinite lives are not amortised. Instead, they are carried on the balance sheet at historical cost but are tested at least annually for impairment. Impairment exists when the carrying amount exceeds its fair value.

5.4 Impairment of Long-Lived Assets Held for Sale

A long-lived (non-current) asset is reclassified as held for sale rather than held for use when management's intent is to sell it and its sale is highly probable. (Additionally, accounting standards require that the asset must be available for immediate sale in its present condition.)[18] For instance, assume a building is no longer needed by a company and management's intent is to sell it, if the transaction meets the accounting criteria, the building is reclassified from property, plant, and equipment to non-current assets held for sale. At the time of reclassification, assets previously held for use are tested for impairment. If the carrying amount at the time of reclassification exceeds the fair value less costs to sell, an impairment loss is recognised and the asset is written down to fair value less costs to sell. Long-lived assets held for sale cease to be depreciated or amortised.

5.5 Reversals of Impairments of Long-Lived Assets

After an asset has been deemed impaired and an impairment loss has been reported, the asset's recoverable amount could potentially increase. For instance, a lawsuit appeal may successfully challenge a patent infringement by another company, with the result that a patent previously written down has a higher recoverable amount. IFRS permit impairment losses to be reversed if the recoverable amount of an asset increases regardless of whether the asset is classified as held for use or held for sale. Note that IFRS permit the reversal of impairment losses only. IFRS do not permit the

18 IFRS 5 *Non-current Assets Held for Sale and Discontinued Operations.*

revaluation to the recoverable amount if the recoverable amount exceeds the previous carrying amount. Under US GAAP, the accounting for reversals of impairments depends on whether the asset is classified as held for use or held for sale.[19] Under US GAAP, once an impairment loss has been recognised for assets held for use, it cannot be reversed. In other words, once the value of an asset held for use has been decreased by an impairment charge, it cannot be increased. For assets held for sale, if the fair value increases after an impairment loss, the loss can be reversed.

DERECOGNITION 6

A company derecognises an asset (i.e., removes it from the financial statements) when the asset is disposed of or is expected to provide no future benefits from either use or disposal. A company may dispose of a long-lived operating asset by selling it, exchanging it, abandoning it, or distributing it to existing shareholders. As previously described, non-current assets that management intends to sell or to distribute to existing shareholders and which meet the accounting criteria (immediately available for sale in current condition and the sale is highly probable) are reclassified as non-current assets held for sale.

6.1 Sale of Long-Lived Assets

The gain or loss on the sale of long-lived assets is computed as the sales proceeds minus the carrying amount of the asset at the time of sale. An asset's carrying amount is typically the net book value (i.e., the historical cost minus accumulated depreciation), unless the asset's carrying amount has been changed to reflect impairment and/or revaluation, as previously discussed.

EXAMPLE 15

Calculation of Gain or Loss on the Sale of Long-Lived Assets

Moussilauke Diners Inc., a hypothetical company, as a result of revamping its menus to focus on healthier food items, sells 450 used pizza ovens and reports a gain on the sale of $1.2 million. The ovens had a carrying amount of $1.9 million (original cost of $5.1 million less $3.2 million of accumulated depreciation). At what price did Moussilauke sell the ovens?

A $0.7 million

B $3.1 million

C $6.3 million

Solution:

B is correct. The ovens had a carrying amount of $1.9 million, and Moussilauke recognised a gain of $1.2 million. Therefore, Moussilauke sold the ovens at a price of $3.1 million. The gain on the sale of $1.2 million is the selling price of

19 FASB ASC Section 360-10-35 [Property, Plant, and Equipment – Overall – Subsequent Measurement].

$3.1 million minus the carrying amount of $1.9 million. Ignoring taxes, the cash flow from the sale is $3.1 million, which would appear as a cash inflow from investing.

A gain or loss on the sale of an asset is disclosed on the income statement, either as a component of other gains and losses or in a separate line item when the amount is material. A company typically discloses further detail about the sale in the management discussion and analysis and/or financial statement footnotes. In addition, a statement of cash flows prepared using the indirect method adjusts net income to remove any gain or loss on the sale from operating cash flow and to include the amount of proceeds from the sale in cash from investing activities. Recall that the indirect method of the statement of cash flows begins with net income and makes all adjustments to arrive at cash from operations, including removal of gains or losses from non-operating activities.

6.2 Long-Lived Assets Disposed of Other Than by a Sale

Long-lived assets to be disposed of other than by a sale (e.g., abandoned, exchanged for another asset, or distributed to owners in a spin-off) are classified as held for use until disposal or until they meet the criteria to be classified as held for sale or held for distribution.[20] Thus, the long-lived assets continue to be depreciated and tested for impairment, unless their carrying amount is zero, as required for other long-lived assets owned by the company.

When an asset is retired or abandoned, the accounting is similar to a sale, except that the company does not record cash proceeds. Assets are reduced by the carrying amount of the asset at the time of retirement or abandonment, and a loss equal to the asset's carrying amount is recorded.

When an asset is exchanged, accounting for the exchange typically involves removing the carrying amount of the asset given up, adding a fair value for the asset acquired, and reporting any difference between the carrying amount and the fair value as a gain or loss. The fair value used is the fair value of the asset given up unless the fair value of the asset acquired is more clearly evident. If no reliable measure of fair value exists, the acquired asset is measured at the carrying amount of the asset given up. A gain is reported when the fair value used for the newly acquired asset exceeds the carrying amount of the asset given up. A loss is reported when the fair value used for the newly acquired asset is less than the carrying amount of the asset given up. If the acquired asset is valued at the carrying amount of the asset given up because no reliable measure of fair value exists, no gain or loss is reported.

When a spin-off occurs, typically, an entire cash generating unit of a company with all its assets is spun off. As an illustration of a spin-off, Fiat Chrysler Automobiles (FCA) spun off its ownership of Ferrari in 2016. Prior to the spinoff, FCA had sold 10 percent of its ownership of Ferrari in an IPO and recognized an increase in Shareholders' equity of € 873 million (the difference between the consideration it received in the IPO of € 866 million and the carrying amount of the equity interest sold of € 7 million.) In contrast, the spin-off, in which FCA distributed its ownership in Ferrari to the existing FCA shareholders, did not result in any gain or loss.

FCA's spinoff was completed on 3 January 2016, with each FCA shareholder receiving one common share of Ferrari N.V. for every ten common shares of FCA. In its financial statements for the prior fiscal year, FCA shows the assets and liabilities of

20 In a spin-off, shareholders of the parent company receive a proportional number of shares in a new, separate entity.

Ferrari as held for distribution. Specifically, its balance sheet includes € 3,650 million Assets Held for Distribution as a component of current assets and € 3,584 million Liabilities Held for Distribution. Exhibit 7 includes excerpts from the company's 31 December 2015 annual report.

Exhibit 7 Fiat Chrysler Automobiles (FCA) Excerpts from Notes to the Consolidated Financial Statements - 2015 Annual Report

Ferrari Spin-off and Discontinued Operations

"As the spin-off of Ferrari N.V. became highly probable with the aforementioned shareholders' approval and since it was available for immediate distribution at that date, the Ferrari segment met the criteria to be classified as a disposal group held for distribution to owners and a discontinued operation pursuant to IFRS 5 - *Non-current Assets Held for Sale and Discontinued Operations*."

The following assets and liabilities of the Ferrari segment were classified as held for distribution at December 31, 2015:

	At December 31, 2015
Assets classified as held for distribution	(€ million)
Goodwill	786
Other intangible assets	297
Property, plant and equipment	627
Other non-current assets	134
Receivables from financing activities	1,176
Cash and cash equivalents	182
Other current assets	448
Total Assets held for distribution	**3,650**
Liabilities classified as held for distribution	
Provisions	224
Debt	2,256
Other current liabilities	624
Trade payables	480
Total Liabilities held for distribution	**3,584**

Source: Fiat Chrysler Automobiles (FCA)'s Form 20-F for the year ending 31 December 2015.

PRESENTATION AND DISCLOSURES

7

Under IFRS, for each class of property, plant, and equipment, a company must disclose the measurement bases, the depreciation method, the useful lives (or, equivalently, the depreciation rate) used, the gross carrying amount and the accumulated depreciation at the beginning and end of the period, and a reconciliation of the carrying amount at the beginning and end of the period.[21] In addition, disclosures of restrictions on title and pledges as security of property, plant, and equipment and contractual agreements to acquire property, plant, and equipment are required. If the revaluation model is used, the date of revaluation, details of how the fair value was obtained, the carrying amount under the cost model, and the revaluation surplus must be disclosed.

The disclosure requirements under US GAAP are less exhaustive.[22] A company must disclose the depreciation expense for the period, the balances of major classes of depreciable assets, accumulated depreciation by major classes or in total, and a general description of the depreciation method(s) used in computing depreciation expense with respect to the major classes of depreciable assets.

Under IFRS, for each class of intangible assets, a company must disclose whether the useful lives are indefinite or finite. If finite, for each class of intangible asset, a company must disclose the useful lives (or, equivalently, the amortisation rate) used, the amortisation methods used, the gross carrying amount and the accumulated amortisation at the beginning and end of the period, where amortisation is included on the income statement, and a reconciliation of the carrying amount at the beginning and end of the period.[23] If an asset has an indefinite life, the company must disclose the carrying amount of the asset and why it is considered to have an indefinite life. Similar to property, plant, and equipment, disclosures of restrictions on title and pledges as security of intangible assets and contractual agreements to acquire intangible assets are required. If the revaluation model is used, the date of revaluation, details of how the fair value was obtained, the carrying amount under the cost model, and the revaluation surplus must be disclosed.

Under US GAAP, companies are required to disclose the gross carrying amounts and accumulated amortisation in total and by major class of intangible assets, the aggregate amortisation expense for the period, and the estimated amortisation expense for the next five fiscal years.[24]

The disclosures related to impairment losses also differ under IFRS and US GAAP. Under IFRS, a company must disclose for each class of assets the amounts of impairment losses and reversals of impairment losses recognised in the period and where those are recognised on the financial statements.[25] The company must also disclose in aggregate the main classes of assets affected by impairment losses and reversals of impairment losses and the main events and circumstances leading to recognition of these impairment losses and reversals of impairment losses. Under US GAAP, there is no reversal of impairment losses for assets held for use. The company must disclose a description of the impaired asset, what led to the impairment, the method of determining fair value, the amount of the impairment loss, and where the loss is recognised on the financial statements.[26]

Disclosures about long-lived assets appear throughout the financial statements: in the balance sheet, the income statement, the statement of cash flows, and the notes. The balance sheet reports the carrying value of the asset. For the income statement, depreciation expense may or may not appear as a separate line item. Under IFRS, whether the income statement discloses depreciation expense separately depends on whether the company is using a 'nature of expense' method or a 'function of expense' method. Under the nature of expense method, a company aggregates expenses "according to their nature (for example, depreciation, purchases of materials, transport costs,

---

21 IAS 16 *Property, Plant and Equipment*, paragraphs 73–79 [Disclosure].
22 FASB ASC Section 360-10-50 [Property, Plant, and Equipment – Overall – Disclosure].
23 IAS 38 *Intangible Assets*, paragraphs 118–128 [Disclosure].
24 FASB ASC Section 350-30-50 [Intangibles – General – Disclosure].
25 IAS 36 *Impairment of Assets*, paragraphs 126–137 [Disclosure].
26 FASB ASC Section 360-10-50 [Property, Plant, and Equipment – Overall – Disclosure] and FASB ASC Section 350-30-50 [Intangibles – General – Disclosure].

employee benefits and advertising costs), and does not reallocate them among functions within the entity."[27] Under the function of expense method, a company classifies expenses according to the function, for example as part of cost of sales or of SG&A (selling, general, and administrative expenses). At a minimum, a company using the function of expense method must disclose cost of sales, but the other line items vary.

The statement of cash flows reflects acquisitions and disposals of fixed assets in the investing section. In addition, when prepared using the indirect method, the statement of cash flows typically shows depreciation expense (or depreciation plus amortisation) as a line item in the adjustments of net income to cash flow from operations. The notes to the financial statements describe the company's accounting method(s), the range of estimated useful lives, historical cost by main category of fixed asset, accumulated depreciation, and annual depreciation expense.

To illustrate financial statement presentation and disclosures, the following example provides excerpts relating to intangible assets and property, plant, and equipment from the annual report of Orange SA for the year ended 31 December 2017.

EXAMPLE 16

Financial Statement Presentation and Disclosures for Long-Lived Assets

The following exhibits include excerpts from the annual report for the year ended 31 December 2017 of Orange SA, an international telecommunications company based in France.

Exhibit 8 Orange SA
Excerpts from the 2017 Consolidated Financial Statements

(Note that only selected line items/data are shown for illustrative purposes)

Excerpt from Consolidated income statement
EUR (€) € in Millions

	12 Months Ended		
	Dec. 31, 2017	**Dec. 31, 2016**	**Dec. 31, 2015**
Revenues	€41,096	€40,918	€40,236
...	...	...	...
Depreciation and amortization	(6,846)	(6,728)	(6,465)
...	...	...	...
Impairment of goodwill	(20)	(772)	
Impairment of fixed assets	(190)	(207)	(38)
...	...	...	...
Operating income	4,917	4,077	4,742
...	...	...	...
Consolidated net income of continuing operations	2,114	1,010	2,510

(continued)

27 IAS 1 paragraph 102.

Exhibit 8 (Continued)

Excerpt from Consolidated income statement
EUR (€) € in Millions

	12 Months Ended		
	Dec. 31, 2017	**Dec. 31, 2016**	**Dec. 31, 2015**
Consolidated net income of discontinued operations (EE)	29	2,253	448
Consolidated net income	**2,143**	**3,263**	**2,958**
Net income attributable to owners of the parent company	1,906	2,935	2,652
Non-controlling interests	€237	€328	€306

Excerpt from the Consolidated statement of financial position
EUR (€) € in Millions

Assets	**Dec. 31, 2017**	**Dec. 31, 2016**	**Dec. 31, 2015**
Goodwill	€27,095	€27,156	€27,071
Other intangible assets	14,339	14,602	14,327
Property, plant and equipment	26,665	25,912	25,123
...	...	...	...
Total non-current assets	74,035	74,819	71,330
...	...	...	...
Total current assets	20,679	19,849	14,312
Assets held for sale			5,788
Total assets	**94,714**	**94,668**	**91,430**
Equity and liabilities			
...	...	...	...
Total equity	32,942	33,174	33,267
...	...	...	...
Total non-current liabilities	32,736	35,590	36,537
...	...	...	...
Total current liabilities	29,036	25,904	21,626
Total equity and liabilities	**94,714**	**94,668**	**91,430**

Exhibit 9 Orange
Excerpts from the 2017 Notes to the Consolidated Financial Statements

Excerpt from Note 7.2 Goodwill

[Excerpt] Reconciliation of Changes in Goodwill (€ in Millions)

	12 Months Ended		
	Dec. 31, 2017	**Dec. 31, 2016**	**Dec. 31, 2015**
Gross Value in the opening balance	€32,689	€32,606	€30,271
Acquisitions	38	904	2,333
Disposals	0	(6)	(69)
Translation adjustment	(40)	(815)	73
Reclassifications and other items	0	0	(2)
Reclassification to assets held for sale	0	0	0
Gross Value in Closing Balance	32,687	32,689	32,606
Accumulated Impairment losses in the opening balance	(5,533)	(5,535)	(5,487)
Impairment	(20)	(772)	0
Disposals	0	0	0
Translation adjustment	(39)	774	(48)
Reclassifications and other items	0	0	0
Reclassification to assets held for sale	0	0	0
Accumulated Impairment losses in the closing balance	€(5,592)	€(5,533)	€(5,535)
Net book value of goodwill	**27,095**	**27,156**	**27,071**

Excerpt* from Note 7.3 Key assumptions used to determine recoverable amounts as of 31 December 2017

The parameters used for the determination of recoverable amount of the main consolidated operations are set forth below:

	France	Spain	Poland	Belgium	Romania
Perpetuity growth rate	0.8%	1.5%	1.0%	0.5%	2.3%
Post-tax discount rate	5.5%	8.6%	8.3%	6.8%	8.8%

Excerpt* from Note 7.4 Sensitivity of recoverable amounts as of 31 December 2017

The level of sensitivity presented allows readers of the financial statements to estimate the impact in their own assessment.

(in billions of euros)	France	Spain	Poland	Belgium	Romania
Decrease by 1% in perpetuity growth rate	10.4	1.6	0.6	0.3	0.3
An increase by 1% in post-tax discount rate	11.4	2.0	0.6	0.3	0.3

* Table extracted presents only selected assumptions and selected countries. The company's annual report provides more detail.

Goodwill is not amortized. It is tested for impairment at least annually and more frequently when there is an indication that it may be impaired .... These tests are performed at the level of each Cash Generating Unit (CGU) (or group of CGUs)... To determine whether an impairment loss should be recognized, the carrying value of the assets and liabilities of the CGUs or groups of CGUs is compared to recoverable amount, for which Orange uses mostly the value in use.... Value in use is the present value of the future expected cash flows. Cash flow projections are based on economic and regulatory assumptions, license renewal assumptions and forecast trading and investment activity drawn up by the Group's management...

Excerpt from Note 8.3 Other intangible assets – Net book value

	December 31		
(in millions of euros)	**2017**	**2016**	**2015**
Telecommunications licenses	6,233	6,440	5,842
Orange brand	3,133	3,133	3,133
Other brands	88	102	137
Customer bases	555	703	729
Software	3,946	3,781	3,815
Other intangible assets	384	443	671
Total	€14,339	€14,602	€14,327

Excerpt from Note 8.4 Property, plant and equipment – Net book value

	December 31		
(in millions of euros)	**2017**	**2016**	**2015**
Land and buildings	2,535	2,661	2,733
Network and terminals	22,880	21,984	21,194
IT equipment	802	784	787
Other property, plant and equipment	448	483	409
Total	€26,665	€25,912	€25,123

Exhibit 10 Orange
Excerpt from the 2017 Analysis of the Group's financial position and earnings

"Orange group operating income stood at 4,077 million euros in 2016, compared with 4,742 million euros in 2015 on a historical basis, a drop of 14.0% or 665 million euros. This drop on a historical basis was largely attributable to:

- the recognition, in 2016, of 772 million euros in impairment loss of goodwill ... and 207 million euros in impairment loss of fixed assets ... primarily relating to:
  - Poland for 507 million euros. This impairment loss mainly reflects a decline in competitiveness in the ADSL market, a deterioration in revenue assumptions in the mobile market and an increase in the post-tax discount rate due to the downgrading of the country's sovereign rating by the rating agencies,
  - Egypt for 232 million euros. This impairment loss reflects the financial terms of the 4G license awarded in 2016, the sharp depreciation of the Egyptian pound and increased political and economic uncertainty,
  - in the Congo (DRC), for 109 million euros. This impairment loss reflects political and economic uncertainty, a decline in purchasing power with a knock-on effect on the consumption of telecommunications products and services and an increased regulatory burden (particularly connected with the implementation of customer identification),
  - Cameroon for 90 million euros. This impairment loss reflects a decline in voice revenues following the surge in messaging services and in VoIP of Over-The-Top (OTT) providers and heightened competition in the mobile market,
  - and Niger for 26 million euros;
- and the 263 million euro increase in depreciation and amortization ...

---

1 What proportion of Orange's total assets as of December 31, 2017, is represented by goodwill and other intangible assets?

2 What is the largest component of the company's impairment losses during the year ending December 2016?

3 The company discloses that it determines whether an impairment loss should be recognized by comparing the carrying value of a unit's assets and liabilities to the "recoverable amount" for which the company uses mostly the value in use. How does the company determine value in use?

4 By what amount would the estimated recoverable value of the company's operations in France, Spain, Poland, Belgium and Romania change if the company decreased its estimate of the perpetuity growth rate by 1%? By

what amount would the estimated recoverable value of these operations change if the company increased its estimate of the post-tax discount rate by 1%?

5 What are the largest components of other intangible assets as of December 31, 2017? What is the largest component of property, plant and equipment as of December 31, 2017?

Solution to 1:

As of 31 December 2017, goodwill represents 28% (= 27,095 ÷ 97,714) of Orange's total assets. Other intangible assets represent 15% (= 14,339 ÷ 97,714). Data are from the company's balance sheet in Exhibit 8.

Solution to 2:

The largest component of the € 772 impairment loss on goodwill and the € 207 million impairment loss of fixed assets related to a € 507 million loss in Poland. The company attributed the loss to a decline in the competitiveness of the market for its ADSL technology, a reduction in revenue assumptions, and an increase in the discount rate resulting from the downgrading of the country's debt rating. From Exhibit 10.

[The company's financial statements define ADSL (Asymmetrical Digital Subscriber Line) as a "broadband data transmission technology on the traditional telephone network. It enables broadband data transmission (first and foremost Internet access) via twisted paired copper cable (the most common type of telephone line found in buildings)."]

Solution to 3:

The company determines value in use – which it uses as a unit's assets and liabilities "recoverable amount" in impairment testing – as the present value of the future expected cash flows. The cash flow projections are based on management's assumptions. From Note 7.4 in Exhibit 9.

Solution to 4:

If the company decreased its estimate of the perpetuity growth rate by 1%, the estimated recoverable value of the company's operations in France, Spain, Poland, Belgium and Romania would change by €13.2 billion (=10.4 + 1.6 + 0.6 + 0.3 + 0.3). A decrease in estimated growth decreases the present value of the cash flows. If the company increased its estimate of the post-tax discount rate by 1%, the estimated recoverable value of these operations would change by €14.6 billion (=11.4 + 2.0 + 0.6 + 0.3 + 0.3). An increase in the discount rate decreases the present value of cash flows. Data are from Note 7.4 in Exhibit 9.

Solution to 5:

The largest components of other intangible assets as of December 31, 2017, are telecommunications licenses, software, and the Orange brand, reported at €6,233 million, €3,946 million, and €3,133 million, respectively. The largest component of property, plant and equipment as of December 31, 2017, is network and terminals (€22,880 million.) Data are from Note 8.3 and 8.4 in Exhibit 9.

Note that the exhibits in the previous example contain relatively brief excerpts from the company's disclosures. The complete text of the disclosures concerning the company's non-current assets spans numerous different footnotes, some of which are several pages long. Overall, an analyst can use the disclosures to understand a company's investments in tangible and intangible assets, how those investments changed during a reporting period, how those changes affected current performance, and what those changes might indicate about future performance.

Ratios used in analyzing fixed assets include the fixed asset turnover ratio and several asset age ratios. The fixed asset turnover ratio (total revenue divided by average net fixed assets) reflects the relationship between total revenues and investment in PPE. The higher this ratio, the higher the amount of sales a company is able to generate with a given amount of investment in fixed assets. A higher asset turnover ratio is often interpreted as an indicator of greater efficiency.

Asset age ratios generally rely on the relationship between historical cost and depreciation. Under the revaluation model (permitted under IFRS but not US GAAP), the relationship between carrying amount, accumulated depreciation, and depreciation expense will differ when the carrying amount differs significantly from the depreciated historical cost. Therefore, the following discussion of asset age ratios applies primarily to PPE reported under the cost model.

Asset age and remaining useful life, two asset age ratios, are important indicators of a company's need to reinvest in productive capacity. The older the assets and the shorter the remaining life, the more a company may need to reinvest to maintain productive capacity. The average age of a company's asset base can be estimated as accumulated depreciation divided by depreciation expense. The average remaining life of a company's asset base can be estimated as net PPE divided by depreciation expense. These estimates simply reflect the following relationships for assets accounted for on a historical cost basis: total historical cost minus accumulated depreciation equals net PPE; and, under straight-line depreciation, total historical cost less salvage value divided by estimated useful life equals annual depreciation expense. Equivalently, total historical cost less salvage value divided by annual depreciation expense equals estimated useful life. Assuming straight-line depreciation and no salvage value (for simplicity), we have the following:

Estimated total useful life	=	Time elapsed since purchase (Age)	+	Estimated remaining life
Historical cost ÷ annual depreciation expense	=	Estimated total useful life		
Historical cost	=	Accumulated depreciation	+	Net PPE

Equivalently,

Estimated total useful life	=	Estimated age of equipment	+	Estimated remaining life
Historical cost ÷ annual depreciation expense	=	Accumulated depreciation ÷ annual depreciation expense	+	Net PPE ÷ annual depreciation expense

The application of these estimates can be illustrated by a hypothetical example of a company with a single depreciable asset. Assume the asset initially cost \$100, had an estimated useful life of 10 years, and an estimated salvage value of \$0. Each year, the company records a depreciation expense of \$10, so accumulated depreciation will equal \$10 times the number of years since the asset was acquired (when the asset is 7 years old, accumulated depreciation will be \$70). Equivalently, the age of the asset will equal accumulated depreciation divided by the annual depreciation expense.

In practice, such estimates are difficult to make with great precision. Companies use depreciation methods other than the straight-line method and have numerous assets with varying useful lives and salvage values, including some assets that are fully depreciated, so this approach produces an estimate only. Moreover, fixed asset disclosures are often quite general. Consequently, these estimates may be primarily useful to identify areas for further investigation.

One further measure compares a company's current reinvestment in productive capacity. Comparing annual capital expenditures to annual depreciation expense provides an indication of whether productive capacity is being maintained. It is a very general indicator of the rate at which a company is replacing its PPE relative to the rate at which PPE is being depreciated.

EXAMPLE 17

Using Fixed Asset Disclosure to Compare Companies' Fixed Asset Turnover and Average Age of Depreciable Assets

You are analyzing the property, plant, and equipment of three international telecommunications companies:

- Orange SA, which we discussed previously, has been listed on Euronext Paris (symbol ORA) and on the New York Stock Exchange (symbol ORAN) since 1997. At December 31, 2017, the French government retained 22.95% of the share capital.
- BCE Inc., Canada's largest communications company, provides wireless, wireline, Internet, TV and business communications across Canada. BCE's shares are publicly traded on the Toronto Stock Exchange and on the New York Stock Exchange (TSX, NYSE: BCE).
- Verizon Communications Inc. is a US-based global provider of communications, information and entertainment products and services to consumers, businesses and governmental agencies. Verizon's shares are listed on the New York Stock Exchange and the NASDAQ Global Select Market (symbol VZ).

Exhibit 11 presents selected information from the companies' financial statements.

Exhibit 11

	Orange	BCE Inc	Verizon
Currency, Millions of:	**Euro €**	**Canadian $**	**US $**
Historical cost total PPE, end of year	€97,092	$69,230	$246,498
Accumulated depreciation, end of year	70,427	45,197	157,930
Net PPE, end of year	26,665	24,033	88,568
Net PPE, beginning of year	25,912	22,346	84,751
Revenues	41,096	22,719	126,034
Annual depreciation expense	4,708	3,037	14,741
Capital expenditure	5,677	4,149	17,247
Land included in PPE	Not separated	Not separated	806
Accounting standards	IFRS	IFRS	US GAAP

Exhibit 11 (Continued)

Currency, Millions of:	Orange Euro €	BCE Inc Canadian $	Verizon US $
PPE measurement	Historical cost	Historical cost	Historical cost
Depreciation method	Straight-line	Straight-line	Straight-line

Sources: Companies' 2017 Annual Financial Reports.

1 Based on the above data for each company, estimate the total useful life, age, and remaining useful life of PPE.

2 Interpret the estimates. What items might affect comparisons across these companies?

3 How does each company's 2017 depreciation expense compare to its capital expenditures for the year?

4 Calculate and compare fixed asset turnover for each company.

Solution to 1:

The following table presents the estimated total useful life, estimated age, and estimated remaining useful life of PPE for each of the companies.

Estimates	Orange	BCE Inc	Verizon
Estimated total useful life (years)	20.6	22.8	16.7
Estimated age (years)	15.0	14.9	10.7
Estimated remaining life (years)	5.7	7.9	6.0

The computations are demonstrated using Verizon's data ($ millions). The estimated total useful life of PPE is total historical cost of PPE of $246,498 divided by annual depreciation expense of $14,741, giving 16.7 years. Estimated age and estimated remaining life are obtained by dividing accumulated depreciation of $157,930 and net PPE of $88,568 by the annual depreciation expense of $14,741, giving 10.7 years and 6.0 years, respectively.

Ideally, the estimates of asset lives illustrated in this example should exclude land, which is not depreciable, when the information is available; however, both Orange and BCE report Land and Buildings as a combined amount. We will use Verizon, for which land appeared to be disclosed separately in the above table, to illustrate the estimates with adjusting for land. As an illustration of the calculations to exclude land, excluding Verizon's land would give an estimated total useful life for the non-land PPE of 16.7 years [(total cost €246,498 minus land cost of $806) divided by annual depreciation expense of €14,741 million]. The estimate is essentially unchanged from the estimate including land because land represents such a small component of Verizon's PPE.

Solution to 2:

The estimated total useful life suggests that Orange and BCE depreciate PPE over a much longer period than Verizon: 20.6 and 22.8 years for Orange and BCE, respectively, versus 16.7 years for Verizon.

The estimated age of the equipment suggests that Verizon has the newest PPE with an estimated age of 10.7 years. Additionally, the estimates suggest that around 73 percent of Orange's assets' useful lives have passed (15.0 years

÷ 20.6 years, or equivalently, €70,427 million ÷ €97,092 million). In comparison, around 65 and 64 percent of the useful lives of the PPE of BCE and Verizon, respectively, have passed.

Items that can affect comparisons across the companies include business differences, such as differences in composition of the companies' operations and differences in acquisition and divestiture activity. This result can be compared, to an extent, to the useful lives and asset mix disclosed in the companies' footnotes; however, differences in disclosures, e.g. in the categories of assets disclosed, can affect comparisons.

Solution to 3:

All three companies' capital expenditure exceeds its depreciation expense. Rounding to the nearest 10%, capital expenditure as a percentage of depreciation is 120 percent for Orange, 140 percent for BCE, and 120 percent for Verizon. All three companies are replacing PPE at a faster rate than the PPE is being depreciated, consistent with the companies' somewhat older asset base.

Solution to 4:

Fixed asset turnover is calculated as total revenues divided by average net PPE. Orange's fixed asset turnover is 1.6 (= 41,096/((26,665 + 25,912)/2). BCE's fixed asset turnover is 1.0, and Verizon's fixed asset turnover is 1.5.

Orange's and Verizon's higher levels of fixed asset turnover indicate these companies, compared to BCE, are able to generate more sales per unit of investment in fixed assets.

8 INVESTMENT PROPERTY

Investment property is defined under IFRS as property that is owned (or, in some cases, leased under a **finance lease**) for the purpose of earning rentals or capital appreciation or both.[28] An example of investment property is a building owned by a company and leased out to tenants. In contrast, other long-lived tangible assets (i.e., property considered to be property, plant, and equipment) are owner-occupied properties used for producing the company's goods and services or for housing the company's administrative activities. Investment properties do not include long-lived tangible assets held for sale in the ordinary course of business. For example, the houses and property owned by a housing construction company are considered to be its inventory.

Under IFRS, companies are allowed to value investment properties using either a cost model or a fair value model. The cost model is identical to the cost model used for property, plant, and equipment. If the cost model is used, the fair value of investment property must be disclosed.[29] The fair value model, however, differs from the revaluation model used for property, plant, and equipment. Under the revaluation model, whether an asset revaluation affects net income depends on whether the revaluation initially increases or decreases the carrying amount of the asset. In contrast, under the fair value model, all changes in the fair value of the asset affect net income. To use the fair value model, a company must be able to reliably determine the property's fair value on a continuing basis.

Example 18 presents an excerpt from the annual report of a property company reporting under IFRS.

---

28 IAS 40 *Investment Property* prescribes the accounting treatment for investment property.
29 Ibid., paragraph 32.

EXAMPLE 18

Financial Statement Presentation and Disclosures for Long-Lived Assets

The following exhibit presents information and excerpts from the annual report for the year ended 31 December 2017 of intu properties plc, a property company headquartered in London that owns, develops and manages shopping centres in the United Kingdom and Spain. Its common stock is listed in London and Johannesburg.

Exhibit 12 Information and excerpts from the Annual Report of intu properties plc (Currency in £ millions)

Financial Information

Financial Statement	Item Label	Amount 2017	Amount 2016
Balance Sheet	Investment and development property	9,179.4	9,212.1
Balance Sheet	Plant and equipment	12.2	7.6
Balance Sheet	Total assets	10,794.5	10,369.2
Income Statement	Net rental income	423.4	406.1
Income Statement	Revaluation of investment and development property	30.8	(78.0)

Excerpt from Note 2 Accounting policies

Investment and development property

Investment and development property is owned or leased by the Group and held for long-term rental income and capital appreciation.

The Group has elected to use the fair value model. Properties are initially recognised at cost and subsequently revalued at the balance sheet date to fair value as determined by professionally qualified external valuers on the basis of market value with the exception of certain development land where an assessment of fair value may be made internally. External valuations are received for significant development land once required planning permissions are obtained. The cost of investment and development property includes capitalised interest and other directly attributable outgoings incurred during development. Interest is capitalised on the basis of the average interest rate on the relevant debt outstanding. Interest ceases to be capitalised on the date of practical completion.

Gains or losses arising from changes in the fair value of investment and development property are recognised in the income statement. Depreciation is not provided in respect of investment and development property. Gains or losses arising on the sale of investment and development property are recognised when the significant risks and rewards of ownership have been transferred to the buyer. The gain or loss recognised is the proceeds received less the carrying value of the property and costs directly associated with the sale.

Plant and equipment

Plant and equipment consists of vehicles, fixtures, fittings and other equipment. Plant and equipment is stated at cost less accumulated depreciation and any accumulated impairment losses. Depreciation is charged to the income statement on a straight- line basis over an asset's estimated useful life up to a maximum of five years.

Excerpt from Note 14 Investment and development property

The market value of investment and development property at 31 December 2017 includes £8,831.9 million (31 December 2016: £9,088.6 million) in respect of investment property and £376.5 million (31 December 2016: £153.2 million) in respect of development property. ...All the Group's significant investment and development property relates to prime shopping centres which are of a similar nature and share characteristics and risks....

Valuation methodology

The fair value of the Group's investment and development property at 31 December 2017 was determined by independent external valuers ... Fair values for investment properties are calculated using the present value income approach. ...The key driver of the property valuations is the terms of the leases in place at the valuation date. These determine the majority of the cash flow profile of the property for a number of years and therefore form the base of the valuation...

1 How do the assets included in the balance sheet line item "Investment and development property" differ from the assets included in the balance sheet line item "Plant and equipment"?

2 How does the valuation model used by the company for its investment and development property differ from the valuation model used for its plant and equipment?

3 How does accounting for depreciation differ for investment and development property versus plant and equipment?

4 Do the revaluation gains and losses on investment and development properties indicate that the properties have been sold?

Solution to 1:

The assets included in the balance sheet line item "Investment and development property" are shopping centres which the company holds for long-term rental income and capital appreciation. In 2017, the company reported net rental income of £423.4 million. The balance sheet line item "Plant and equipment" includes vehicles, fixtures, fittings, and other equipment used by the company in its operations.

Solution to 2:

The valuation model used by the company for its investment and development property is the fair value model, in which properties are initially recognised at cost and subsequently revalued and shown on the balance sheet at fair value. All changes in the fair value of the asset affect net income. The company employs external valuation experts to determine the fair value, which is based on expected future cash flow from rental income.

The valuation model used for its plant and equipment is the historical cost model in which properties are shown on the balance sheet at cost minus accumulated depreciation and any impairment losses.

Solution to 3:

Depreciation in accounting refers to the allocation of the cost of a long-lived asset over its useful life. No depreciation is recorded for investment and development property. Depreciation expense for plant and equipment is calculated on a straight-line basis over the asset's estimated useful life.

Solution to 4:

No. The revaluation gains and losses on investment properties arise from changes in the fair value of properties that are owned by the company. The company reported a revaluation gain of £30.8 million in 2017 and a revaluation loss of £78.0 million in 2016.

Sales of property would have resulted in a gain or loss on disposal, calculated as the proceeds minus the carrying value of the property and related selling costs.

In general, a company must apply its chosen model (cost or fair value) to all of its investment property. If a company chooses the fair value model for its investment property, it must continue to use the fair value model until it disposes of the property or changes its use such that it is no longer considered investment property (e.g., it becomes owner-occupied property or part of inventory). The company must continue to use the fair value model for that property even if transactions on comparable properties, used to estimate fair value, become less frequent.

Certain valuation issues arise when a company changes the use of property such that it moves from being an investment property to owner-occupied property or part of inventory. If a company's chosen model for investment property is the cost model, such transfers do not change the carrying amount of the property transferred. If a company's chosen model is the fair value model, transfers from investment property to owner-occupied property or to inventory are made at fair value. In other words, the property's fair value at the time of transfer is considered to be its cost for ongoing accounting for the property. If a company's chosen model for investment property is the fair value model and it transfers a property from owner-occupied to investment property, the change in measurement of the property from depreciated cost to fair value is treated like a revaluation. If a company's chosen model is the fair value model and it transfers a property from inventory to investment property, any difference between the inventory carrying amount and the property's fair value at the time of transfer is recognised as profit or loss.

Investment property appears as a separate line item on the balance sheet. Companies are required to disclose whether they use the fair value model or the cost model for their investment property. If the company uses the fair value model, it must make additional disclosures about how it determines fair value and must provide reconciliation between the beginning and ending carrying amounts of investment property. If the company uses the cost model, it must make additional disclosures similar to those for property, plant, and equipment—for example, the depreciation method and useful lives must be disclosed. In addition, if the company uses the cost model, it must also disclose the fair value of investment property.

Under US GAAP, there is no specific definition of investment property. Most operating companies and real estate companies in the United States that hold investment-type property use the historical cost model.

SUMMARY

Understanding the reporting of long-lived assets at inception requires distinguishing between expenditures that are capitalised (i.e., reported as long-lived assets) and those that are expensed. Once a long-lived asset is recognised, it is reported under the cost model at its historical cost less accumulated depreciation (amortisation) and less any impairment or under the revaluation model at its fair value. IFRS permit the use of either the cost model or the revaluation model, whereas US GAAP require the use of the cost model. Most companies reporting under IFRS use the cost model. The choice of different methods to depreciate (amortise) long-lived assets can create challenges for analysts comparing companies.

Key points include the following:

- Expenditures related to long-lived assets are capitalised as part of the cost of assets if they are expected to provide future benefits, typically beyond one year. Otherwise, expenditures related to long-lived assets are expensed as incurred.
- Although capitalising expenditures, rather than expensing them, results in higher reported profitability in the initial year, it results in lower profitability in subsequent years; however, if a company continues to purchase similar or increasing amounts of assets each year, the profitability-enhancing effect of capitalisation continues.
- Capitalising an expenditure rather than expensing it results in a greater amount reported as cash from operations because capitalised expenditures are classified as an investing cash outflow rather than an operating cash outflow.
- Companies must capitalise interest costs associated with acquiring or constructing an asset that requires a long period of time to prepare for its intended use.
- Including capitalised interest in the calculation of interest coverage ratios provides a better assessment of a company's solvency.
- IFRS require research costs be expensed but allow all development costs (not only software development costs) to be capitalised under certain conditions. Generally, US accounting standards require that research and development costs be expensed; however, certain costs related to software development are required to be capitalised.
- When one company acquires another company, the transaction is accounted for using the acquisition method of accounting in which the company identified as the acquirer allocates the purchase price to each asset acquired (and each liability assumed) on the basis of its fair value. Under acquisition accounting, if the purchase price of an acquisition exceeds the sum of the amounts that can be allocated to individual identifiable assets and liabilities, the excess is recorded as goodwill.
- The capitalised costs of long-lived tangible assets and of intangible assets with finite useful lives are allocated to expense in subsequent periods over their useful lives. For tangible assets, this process is referred to as depreciation, and for intangible assets, it is referred to as amortisation.
- Long-lived tangible assets and intangible assets with finite useful lives are reviewed for impairment whenever changes in events or circumstances indicate that the carrying amount of an asset may not be recoverable.
- Intangible assets with an indefinite useful life are not amortised but are reviewed for impairment annually.

- Impairment disclosures can provide useful information about a company's expected cash flows.
- Methods of calculating depreciation or amortisation expense include the straight-line method, in which the cost of an asset is allocated to expense in equal amounts each year over its useful life; accelerated methods, in which the allocation of cost is greater in earlier years; and the units-of-production method, in which the allocation of cost corresponds to the actual use of an asset in a particular period.
- Estimates required for depreciation and amortisation calculations include the useful life of the equipment (or its total lifetime productive capacity) and its expected residual value at the end of that useful life. A longer useful life and higher expected residual value result in a smaller amount of annual depreciation relative to a shorter useful life and lower expected residual value.
- IFRS permit the use of either the cost model or the revaluation model for the valuation and reporting of long-lived assets, but the revaluation model is not allowed under US GAAP.
- Under the revaluation model, carrying amounts are the fair values at the date of revaluation less any subsequent accumulated depreciation or amortisation.
- In contrast with depreciation and amortisation charges, which serve to allocate the cost of a long-lived asset over its useful life, impairment charges reflect an unexpected decline in the fair value of an asset to an amount lower than its carrying amount.
- IFRS permit impairment losses to be reversed, with the reversal reported in profit. US GAAP do not permit the reversal of impairment losses.
- The gain or loss on the sale of long-lived assets is computed as the sales proceeds minus the carrying amount of the asset at the time of sale.
- Estimates of average age and remaining useful life of a company's assets reflect the relationship between assets accounted for on a historical cost basis and depreciation amounts.
- The average remaining useful life of a company's assets can be estimated as net PPE divided by depreciation expense, although the accounting useful life may not necessarily correspond to the economic useful life.
- Long-lived assets reclassified as held for sale cease to be depreciated or amortised. Long-lived assets to be disposed of other than by a sale (e.g., by abandonment, exchange for another asset, or distribution to owners in a spin-off) are classified as held for use until disposal. Thus, they continue to be depreciated and tested for impairment.
- Investment property is defined as property that is owned (or, in some cases, leased under a finance lease) for the purpose of earning rentals, capital appreciation, or both.
- Under IFRS, companies are allowed to value investment properties using either a cost model or a fair value model. The cost model is identical to the cost model used for property, plant, and equipment, but the fair value model differs from the revaluation model used for property, plant, and equipment. Unlike the revaluation model, under the fair value model, all changes in the fair value of investment property affect net income.
- Under US GAAP, investment properties are generally measured using the cost model.

PRACTICE PROBLEMS

1 JOOVI Inc. has recently purchased and installed a new machine for its manufacturing plant. The company incurred the following costs:

Purchase price	$12,980
Freight and insurance	$1,200
Installation	$700
Testing	$100
Maintenance staff training costs	$500

The total cost of the machine to be shown on JOOVI's balance sheet is *closest* to:

A $14,180.

B $14,980.

C $15,480.

2 Which costs incurred with the purchase of property and equipment are expensed?

A Delivery charges

B Installation and testing

C Training required to use the property and equipment

3 When constructing an asset for sale, directly related borrowing costs are *most likely*:

A expensed as incurred.

B capitalized as part of inventory.

C capitalized as part of property, plant, and equipment.

4 BAURU, S.A., a Brazilian corporation, borrows capital from a local bank to finance the construction of its manufacturing plant. The loan has the following conditions:

Borrowing date	1 January 2009
Amount borrowed	500 million Brazilian real (BRL)
Annual interest rate	14 percent
Term of the loan	3 years
Payment method	Annual payment of interest only. Principal amortization is due at the end of the loan term.

The construction of the plant takes two years, during which time BAURU earned BRL 10 million by temporarily investing the loan proceeds. Which of the following is the amount of interest related to the plant construction (in BRL million) that can be capitalized in BAURU's balance sheet?

A 130.

B 140.

C 210.

5 After reading the financial statements and footnotes of a company that follows IFRS, an analyst identified the following intangible assets:

- product patent expiring in 40 years;

© 2019 CFA Institute. All rights reserved.

- copyright with no expiration date; and
- goodwill acquired 2 years ago in a business combination.

Which of these assets is an intangible asset with a finite useful life?

	Product Patent	Copyright	Goodwill
A	Yes	Yes	No
B	Yes	No	No
C	No	Yes	Yes

6 Intangible assets with finite useful lives *mostly* differ from intangible assets with infinite useful lives with respect to accounting treatment of:

A revaluation.

B impairment.

C amortization.

7 Costs incurred for intangible assets are generally expensed when they are:

A internally developed.

B individually acquired.

C acquired in a business combination.

8 Under US GAAP, when assets are acquired in a business combination, goodwill *most likely* arises from:

A contractual or legal rights.

B assets that can be separated from the acquired company.

C assets that are neither tangible nor identifiable intangible assets.

9 All else equal, in the fiscal year when long-lived equipment is purchased:

A depreciation expense increases.

B cash from operations decreases.

C net income is reduced by the amount of the purchase.

10 Companies X and Z have the same beginning-of-the-year book value of equity and the same tax rate. The companies have identical transactions throughout the year and report all transactions similarly except for one. Both companies acquire a £300,000 printer with a three-year useful life and a salvage value of £0 on 1 January of the new year. Company X capitalizes the printer and depreciates it on a straight-line basis, and Company Z expenses the printer. The following year-end information is gathered for Company X.

	Company X As of 31 December
Ending shareholders' equity	£10,000,000
Tax rate	25%
Dividends	£0.00
Net income	£750,000

Based on the information given, Company Z's return on equity using year-end equity will be *closest* to:

A 5.4%.

B 6.1%.

C 7.5%.

11 A financial analyst is studying the income statement effect of two alternative depreciation methods for a recently acquired piece of equipment. She gathers the following information about the equipment's expected production life and use:

	Year 1	Year 2	Year 3	Year 4	Year 5	Total
Units of production	2,000	2,000	2,000	2,000	2,500	10,500

Compared with the units-of-production method of depreciation, if the company uses the straight-line method to depreciate the equipment, its net income in Year 1 will *most likely* be:

A lower.

B higher.

C the same.

12 A company purchases a piece of equipment for €1,500. The equipment is expected to have a useful life of five years and no residual value. In the first year of use, the units of production are expected to be 15% of the equipment's lifetime production capacity and the equipment is expected to generate €1,500 of revenue and incur €500 of cash expenses.

The depreciation method yielding the lowest operating profit on the equipment in the first year of use is:

A straight line.

B units of production.

C double-declining balance.

13 Juan Martinez, CFO of VIRMIN, S.A., is selecting the depreciation method to use for a new machine. The machine has an expected useful life of six years. Production is expected to be relatively low initially but to increase over time. The method chosen for tax reporting must be the same as the method used for financial reporting. If Martinez wants to minimize tax payments in the first year of the machine's life, which of the following depreciation methods is Martinez *most likely* to use?

A Straight-line method.

B Units-of-production method.

C Double-declining balance method.

The following information relates to Questions 14–15

Miguel Rodriguez of MARIO S.A., an Uruguayan corporation, is computing the depreciation expense of a piece of manufacturing equipment for the fiscal year ended 31 December 2009. The equipment was acquired on 1 January 2009. Rodriguez gathers the following information (currency in Uruguayan pesos, UYP):

Cost of the equipment	UYP 1,200,000
Estimated residual value	UYP 200,000
Expected useful life	8 years
Total productive capacity	800,000 units

Production in FY 2009	135,000 units
Expected production for the next 7 years	95,000 units each year

14 If MARIO uses the straight-line method, the amount of depreciation expense on MARIO's income statement related to the manufacturing equipment is *closest* to:

A 125,000.

B 150,000.

C 168,750.

15 If MARIO uses the units-of-production method, the amount of depreciation expense (in UYP) on MARIO's income statement related to the manufacturing equipment is *closest* to:

A 118,750.

B 168,750.

C 202,500.

---

16 Which of the following amortization methods is *most likely* to evenly distribute the cost of an intangible asset over its useful life?

A Straight-line method.

B Units-of-production method.

C Double-declining balance method.

17 Which of the following will cause a company to show a lower amount of amortization of intangible assets in the first year after acquisition?

A A higher residual value.

B A higher amortization rate.

C A shorter useful life.

18 A company purchases equipment for $200,000 with a five-year useful life and salvage value of zero. It uses the double-declining balance method of depreciation for two years, then shifts to straight-line depreciation at the beginning of Year 3. Compared with annual depreciation expense under the double-declining balance method, the resulting annual depreciation expense in Year 4 is:

A smaller.

B the same.

C greater.

19 An analyst in the finance department of BOOLDO S.A., a French corporation, is computing the amortization of a customer list, an intangible asset, for the fiscal year ended 31 December 2009. She gathers the following information about the asset:

Acquisition cost	€2,300,000
Acquisition date	1 January 2008
Expected residual value at time of acquisition	€500,000

The customer list is expected to result in extra sales for three years after acquisition. The present value of these expected extra sales exceeds the cost of the list.

If the analyst uses the straight-line method, the amount of accumulated amortization related to the customer list as of 31 December 2009 is *closest* to:

A €600,000.

B €1,200,000.

C €1,533,333.

20 A financial analyst is analyzing the amortization of a product patent acquired by MAKETTI S.p.A., an Italian corporation. He gathers the following information about the patent:

Acquisition cost	€5,800,000
Acquisition date	1 January 2009
Patent expiration date	31 December 2015
Total plant capacity of patented product	40,000 units per year
Production of patented product in fiscal year ended 31 December 2009	20,000 units
Expected production of patented product during life of the patent	175,000 units

If the analyst uses the units-of-production method, the amortization expense on the patent for fiscal year 2009 is *closest* to:

A €414,286.

B €662,857.

C €828,571.

21 A company acquires a patent with an expiration date in six years for ¥100 million. The company assumes that the patent will generate economic benefits that will decline over time and decides to amortize the patent using the double-declining balance method. The annual amortization expense in Year 4 is closest to:

A ¥6.6 million.

B ¥9.9 million.

C ¥19.8 million.

22 A company is comparing straight-line and double-declining balance amortization methods for a non-renewable six-year license, acquired for €600,000. The difference between the Year 4 ending net book values using the two methods is *closest to*:

A €81,400.

B €118,600.

C €200,000.

23 MARU S.A. de C.V., a Mexican corporation that follows IFRS, has elected to use the revaluation model for its property, plant, and equipment. One of MARU's machines was purchased for 2,500,000 Mexican pesos (MXN) at the beginning of the fiscal year ended 31 March 2010. As of 31 March 2010, the machine has a fair value of MXN 3,000,000. Should MARU show a profit for the revaluation of the machine?

A Yes.

B No, because this revaluation is recorded directly in equity.

C No, because value increases resulting from revaluation can never be recognized as a profit.

24 An analyst is studying the impairment of the manufacturing equipment of WLP Corp., a UK-based corporation that follows IFRS. He gathers the following information about the equipment:

Fair value	£16,800,000
Costs to sell	£800,000
Value in use	£14,500,000
Net carrying amount	£19,100,000

The amount of the impairment loss on WLP Corp.'s income statement related to its manufacturing equipment is *closest* to:

A £2,300,000.

B £3,100,000.

C £4,600,000.

25 Under IFRS, an impairment loss on a property, plant, and equipment asset is measured as the excess of the carrying amount over the asset's:

A fair value.

B recoverable amount.

C undiscounted expected future cash flows.

26 A financial analyst at BETTO S.A. is analyzing the result of the sale of a vehicle for 85,000 Argentine pesos (ARP) on 31 December 2009. The analyst compiles the following information about the vehicle:

Acquisition cost of the vehicle	ARP 100,000
Acquisition date	1 January 2007
Estimated residual value at acquisition date	ARP 10,000
Expected useful life	9 years
Depreciation method	Straight-line

The result of the sale of the vehicle is *most likely*:

A a loss of ARP 15,000.

B a gain of ARP 15,000.

C a gain of ARP 18,333.

27 CROCO S.p.A sells an intangible asset with a historical acquisition cost of €12 million and an accumulated depreciation of €2 million and reports a loss on the sale of €3.2 million. Which of the following amounts is *most likely* the sale price of the asset?

A €6.8 million

B €8.8 million

C €13.2 million

28 The impairment of intangible assets with finite lives affects:

A the balance sheet but not the income statement.

B the income statement but not the balance sheet.

C both the balance sheet and the income statement.

29 The gain or loss on a sale of a long-lived asset to which the revaluation model has been applied is *most likely* calculated using sales proceeds less:

A carrying amount.

B carrying amount adjusted for impairment.

C historical cost net of accumulated depreciation.

30 According to IFRS, all of the following pieces of information about property, plant, and equipment must be disclosed in a company's financial statements and footnotes *except for*:

A useful lives.

B acquisition dates.

C amount of disposals.

31 According to IFRS, all of the following pieces of information about intangible assets must be disclosed in a company's financial statements and footnotes *except for*:

A fair value.

B impairment loss.

C amortization rate.

32 Which of the following is a required financial statement disclosure for long-lived intangible assets under US GAAP?

A The useful lives of assets

B The reversal of impairment losses

C Estimated amortization expense for the next five fiscal years

33 Which of the following characteristics is *most likely* to differentiate investment property from property, plant, and equipment?

A It is tangible.

B It earns rent.

C It is long-lived.

34 If a company uses the fair value model to value investment property, changes in the fair value of the asset are *least likely* to affect:

A net income.

B net operating income.

C other comprehensive income.

35 Investment property is *most likely* to:

A earn rent.

B be held for resale.

C be used in the production of goods and services.

36 A company is *most likely* to:

A use a fair value model for some investment property and a cost model for other investment property.

B change from the fair value model when transactions on comparable properties become less frequent.

C change from the fair value model when the company transfers investment property to property, plant, and equipment.

37 Under the revaluation model for property, plant, and equipment and the fair model for investment property:

A fair value of the asset must be able to be measured reliably.

B net income is affected by all changes in the fair value of the asset.

C net income is never affected if the asset increases in value from its carrying amount.

38 Under IFRS, what must be disclosed under the cost model of valuation for investment properties?

A Useful lives

B The method for determining fair value

C Reconciliation between beginning and ending carrying amounts of investment property

The following information relates to Questions 39–42

Melanie Hart, CFA, is a transportation analyst. Hart has been asked to write a research report on Altai Mountain Rail Company (AMRC). Like other companies in the railroad industry, AMRC's operations are capital intensive, with significant investments in such long-lived tangible assets as property, plant, and equipment. In November of 2008, AMRC's board of directors hired a new team to manage the company. In reviewing the company's 2009 annual report, Hart is concerned about some of the accounting choices that the new management has made. These choices differ from those of the previous management and from common industry practice. Hart has highlighted the following statements from the company's annual report:

Statement 1 "In 2009, AMRC spent significant amounts on track replacement and similar improvements. AMRC expensed rather than capitalised a significant proportion of these expenditures."

Statement 2 "AMRC uses the straight-line method of depreciation for both financial and tax reporting purposes to account for plant and equipment."

Statement 3 "In 2009, AMRC recognized an impairment loss of €50 million on a fleet of locomotives. The impairment loss was reported as 'other income' in the income statement and reduced the carrying amount of the assets on the balance sheet."

Exhibits 1 and 2 contain AMRC's 2009 consolidated income statement and balance sheet. AMRC prepares its financial statements in accordance with International Financial Reporting Standards.

Exhibit 1 Consolidated Statement of Income

	2009		2008	
For the Years Ended 31 December	**€ Millions**	**% Revenues**	**€ Millions**	**% Revenues**
Operating revenues	2,600	100.0	2,300	100.0
Operating expenses				
Depreciation	(200)	(7.7)	(190)	(8.3)
Other operating expense	(1,590)	(61.1)	(1,515)	(65.9)
Total operating expenses	(1,790)	(68.8)	(1,705)	(74.2)
Operating income	810	31.2	595	25.8
Other income	(50)	(1.9)	—	0.0
Interest expense	(73)	(2.8)	(69)	(3.0)
Income before taxes	687	26.5	526	22.8

(continued)

Exhibit 1 (Continued)

	2009		2008	
For the Years Ended 31 December	**€ Millions**	**% Revenues**	**€ Millions**	**% Revenues**
Income taxes	(272)	(10.5)	(198)	(8.6)
Net income	415	16	328	14.2

Exhibit 2 Consolidated Balance Sheet

As of 31 December	2009		2008	
Assets	**€ Millions**	**% Assets**	**€ Millions**	**% Assets**
Current assets	500	9.4	450	8.5
Property & equipment:				
Land	700	13.1	700	13.2
Plant & equipment	6,000	112.1	5,800	109.4
Total property & equipment	6,700	125.2	6,500	122.6
Accumulated depreciation	(1,850)	(34.6)	(1,650)	(31.1)
Net property & equipment	4,850	90.6	4,850	91.5
Total assets	5,350	100.0	5,300	100.0
Liabilities and Shareholders' Equity				
Current liabilities	480	9.0	430	8.1
Long-term debt	1,030	19.3	1,080	20.4
Other long-term provisions and liabilities	1,240	23.1	1,440	27.2
Total liabilities	2,750	51.4	2,950	55.7
Shareholders' equity				
Common stock and paid-in-surplus	760	14.2	760	14.3
Retained earnings	1,888	35.5	1,600	30.2
Other comprehensive losses	(48)	(0.9)	(10)	(0.2)
Total shareholders' equity	2,600	48.6	2,350	44.3
Total liabilities & shareholders' equity	5,350	100.0	5,300	100.0

39 With respect to Statement 1, which of the following is the *most likely* effect of management's decision to expense rather than capitalise these expenditures?

A 2009 net profit margin is higher than if the expenditures had been capitalised.

B 2009 total asset turnover is lower than if the expenditures had been capitalised.

C Future profit growth will be higher than if the expenditures had been capitalised.

40 With respect to Statement 2, what would be the *most likely* effect in 2010 if AMRC were to switch to an accelerated depreciation method for both financial and tax reporting?

A Net profit margin would increase.

B Total asset turnover would decrease.

C Cash flow from operating activities would increase.

41 With respect to Statement 3, what is the *most likely* effect of the impairment loss?

A Net income in years prior to 2009 was likely understated.

B Net profit margins in years after 2009 will likely exceed the 2009 net profit margin.

C Cash flow from operating activities in 2009 was likely lower due to the impairment loss.

42 Based on Exhibits 1 and 2, the *best estimate* of the average remaining useful life of the company's plant and equipment at the end of 2009 is:

A 20.75 years.

B 24.25 years.

C 30.00 years.

The following information relates to Questions 43–48

Brian Jordan is interviewing for a junior equity analyst position at Orion Investment Advisors. As part of the interview process, Mary Benn, Orion's Director of Research, provides Jordan with information about two hypothetical companies, Alpha and Beta, and asks him to comment on the information on their financial statements and ratios. Both companies prepare their financial statements in accordance with International Financial Reporting Standards (IFRS) and are identical in all respects except for their accounting choices.

Jordan is told that at the beginning of the current fiscal year, both companies purchased a major new computer system and began building new manufacturing plants for their own use. Alpha capitalised and Beta expensed the cost of the computer system; Alpha capitalised and Beta expensed the interest costs associated with the construction of the manufacturing plants.

Benn asks Jordan, "What was the impact of these decisions on each company's current fiscal year financial statements and ratios?"

Jordan responds, "Alpha's decision to capitalise the cost of its new computer system instead of expensing it results in lower net income, lower total assets, and higher cash flow from operating activities in the current fiscal year. Alpha's decision to capitalise its interest costs instead of expensing them results in a lower fixed asset turnover ratio and a higher interest coverage ratio."

Jordan is told that Alpha uses the straight-line depreciation method and Beta uses an accelerated depreciation method; both companies estimate the same useful lives for long-lived assets. Many companies in their industry use the units-of-production method.

Benn asks Jordan, "What are the financial statement implications of each depreciation method, and how do you determine a company's need to reinvest in its productive capacity?"

Jordan replies, "All other things being equal, the straight-line depreciation method results in the least variability of net profit margin over time, while an accelerated depreciation method results in a declining trend in net profit margin over time. The units-of-production can result in a net profit margin trend that is quite variable. I use a three-step approach to estimate a company's need to reinvest in its productive capacity. First, I estimate the average age of the assets by dividing net property, plant, and equipment by annual depreciation expense. Second, I estimate the average remaining useful life of the assets by dividing accumulated depreciation by depreciation expense. Third, I add the estimates of the average remaining useful life and the average age of the assets in order to determine the total useful life."

Jordan is told that at the end of the current fiscal year, Alpha revalued a manufacturing plant; this increased its reported carrying amount by 15 percent. There was no previous downward revaluation of the plant. Beta recorded an impairment loss on a manufacturing plant; this reduced its carrying by 10 percent.

Benn asks Jordan "What was the impact of these decisions on each company's current fiscal year financial ratios?"

Jordan responds, "Beta's impairment loss increases its debt to total assets and fixed asset turnover ratios, and lowers its cash flow from operating activities. Alpha's revaluation increases its debt to capital and return on assets ratios, and reduces its return on equity."

At the end of the interview, Benn thanks Jordan for his time and states that a hiring decision will be made shortly.

43 Jordan's response about the financial statement impact of Alpha's decision to capitalise the cost of its new computer system is most likely *correct* with respect to:

A lower net income.

B lower total assets.

C higher cash flow from operating activities.

44 Jordan's response about the ratio impact of Alpha's decision to capitalise interest costs is most likely *correct* with respect to the:

A interest coverage ratio.

B fixed asset turnover ratio.

C interest coverage and fixed asset turnover ratios.

45 Jordan's response about the impact of the different depreciation methods on net profit margin is most likely *incorrect* with respect to:

A accelerated depreciation.

B straight-line depreciation.

C units-of-production depreciation.

46 Jordan's response about his approach to estimating a company's need to reinvest in its productive capacity is most likely *correct* regarding:

A estimating the average age of the asset base.

B estimating the total useful life of the asset base.

C estimating the average remaining useful life of the asset base.

47 Jordan's response about the effect of Beta's impairment loss is most likely *incorrect* with respect to the impact on its:

A debt to total assets.

B fixed asset turnover.

C cash flow from operating activities.

48 Jordan's response about the effect of Alpha's revaluation is most likely *correct* with respect to the impact on its:

A return on equity.

B return on assets.

C debt to capital ratio.

SOLUTIONS

1 B is correct. Only costs necessary for the machine to be ready to use can be capitalized. Therefore, Total capitalized costs = 12,980 + 1,200 + 700 + 100 = $14,980.

2 C is correct. When property and equipment are purchased, the assets are recorded on the balance sheet at cost. Costs for the assets include all expenditures required to prepare the assets for their intended use. Any other costs are expensed. Costs to train staff for using the machine are not required to prepare the property and equipment for their intended use, and these costs are expensed.

3 B is correct. When a company constructs an asset, borrowing costs incurred directly related to the construction are generally capitalized. If the asset is constructed for sale, the borrowing costs are classified as inventory.

4 A is correct. Borrowing costs can be capitalized under IFRS until the tangible asset is ready for use. Also, under IFRS, income earned on temporarily investing the borrowed monies decreases the amount of borrowing costs eligible for capitalization. Therefore, Total capitalized interest = (500 million × 14% × 2 years) – 10 million = 130 million.

5 B is correct. A product patent with a defined expiration date is an intangible asset with a finite useful life. A copyright with no expiration date is an intangible asset with an indefinite useful life. Goodwill is no longer considered an intangible asset under IFRS and is considered to have an indefinite useful life.

6 C is correct. An intangible asset with a finite useful life is amortized, whereas an intangible asset with an indefinite useful life is not.

7 A is correct. The costs to internally develop intangible assets are generally expensed when incurred.

8 C is correct. Under both International Financial Reporting Standards (IFRS) and US GAAP, if an item is acquired in a business combination and cannot be recognized as a tangible asset or identifiable intangible asset, it is recognized as goodwill. Under US GAAP, assets arising from contractual or legal rights and assets that can be separated from the acquired company are recognized separately from goodwill.

9 A is correct. In the fiscal year when long-lived equipment is purchased, the assets on the balance sheet increase and depreciation expense on the income statement increases because of the new long-lived asset.

10 B is correct. Company Z's return on equity based on year-end equity value will be 6.1%. Company Z will have an additional £200,000 of expenses compared with Company X. Company Z expensed the printer for £300,000 rather than capitalizing the printer and having a depreciation expense of £100,000 like Company X. Company Z's net income and shareholders' equity will be £150,000 lower (= £200,000 × 0.75) than that of Company X.

$$\begin{aligned}\text{ROE} &= \left(\frac{\text{Net income}}{\text{Shareholders' Equity}}\right)\\ &= £600{,}000/£9{,}850{,}000\\ &= 0.61 = 6.1\%\end{aligned}$$

11 A is correct. If the company uses the straight-line method, the depreciation expense will be one-fifth (20 percent) of the depreciable cost in Year 1. If it uses the units-of-production method, the depreciation expense will be 19 percent (2,000/10,500) of the depreciable cost in Year 1. Therefore, if the company uses the straight-line method, its depreciation expense will be higher and its net income will be lower.

12 C is correct. The operating income or earnings before interest and taxes will be lowest for the method that results in the highest depreciation expense. The double-declining balance method results in the highest depreciation expense in the first year of use.

Depreciation expense:

Straight line = €1,500/5 = €300.

Double-declining balance = €1,500 × 0.40 = €600.

Units of production = €1,500 × 0.15 = €225.

13 C is correct. If Martinez wants to minimize tax payments in the first year of the machine's life, he should use an accelerated method, such as the double-declining balance method.

14 A is correct. Using the straight-line method, depreciation expense amounts to

Depreciation expense = (1,200,000 – 200,000)/8 years = 125,000.

15 B is correct. Using the units-of-production method, depreciation expense amounts to

Depreciation expense = (1,200,000 – 200,000) × (135,000/800,000) = 168,750.

16 A is correct. The straight-line method is the method that evenly distributes the cost of an asset over its useful life because amortization is the same amount every year.

17 A is correct. A higher residual value results in a lower total depreciable cost and, therefore, a lower amount of amortization in the first year after acquisition (and every year after that).

18 C is correct. Shifting at the end of Year 2 from double-declining balance to straight-line depreciation methodology results in depreciation expense being the same in each of Years 3, 4, and 5. Shifting to the straight-line methodology at the beginning of Year 3 results in a greater depreciation expense in Year 4 than would have been calculated using the double-declining balance method.

Depreciation expense Year 4 (Using double-declining balance method all five years)

= 2 × Annual depreciation % using straight-line method × Carrying amount at end of Year 3
= 40% × $43,200

Depreciation expense Year 4 with switch to straight-line method in Year 3

= ⅓ × Remaining depreciable cost at start of Year 3
= ⅓ × $72,000
= $24,000

19 B is correct. Using the straight-line method, accumulated amortization amounts to

$$\text{Accumulated amortization} = [(2{,}300{,}000 - 500{,}000)/3 \text{ years}] \times 2 \text{ years} = 1{,}200{,}000$$

20 B is correct. Using the units-of-production method, depreciation expense amounts to

$$\text{Depreciation expense} = 5{,}800{,}000 \times (20{,}000/175{,}000) = 662{,}857$$

21 B is correct. As shown in the following calculations, under the double-declining balance method, the annual amortization expense in Year 4 is closest to ¥9.9 million.

Annual amortization expense = 2 × Straight-line amortization rate × Net book value.

Amortization expense Year 4 = 33.3% × ¥29.6 million = ¥9.9 million.

22 A is correct. As shown in the following calculations, at the end of Year 4, the difference between the net book values calculated using straight-line versus double-declining balance is closest to €81,400.

Net book value end of Year 4 using straight-line method = €600,000 – [4 × (€600,000/6)] = €200,000.

Net book value end of Year 4 using double-declining balance method = €600,000 $(1 - 33.33\%)^4 \approx$ €118,600.

23 B is correct. In this case, the value increase brought about by the revaluation should be recorded directly in equity. The reason is that under IFRS, an increase in value brought about by a revaluation can only be recognized as a profit to the extent that it reverses a revaluation decrease of the same asset previously recognized in the income statement.

24 B is correct. The impairment loss equals £3,100,000.

$$\begin{aligned}\text{Impairment} &= \max(\text{Fair value less costs to sell; Value in use}) - \text{Net carrying amount}\\ &= \max(16{,}800{,}000 - 800{,}000;\ 14{,}500{,}000) - 19{,}100{,}000\\ &= -3{,}100{,}000.\end{aligned}$$

25 B is correct. Under IFRS, an impairment loss is measured as the excess of the carrying amount over the asset's recoverable amount. The recoverable amount is the higher of the asset's fair value less costs to sell and its value in use. Value in use is a discounted measure of expected future cash flows. Under US GAAP, assessing recoverability is separate from measuring the impairment loss. If the asset's carrying amount exceeds its undiscounted expected future cash flows, the asset's carrying amount is considered unrecoverable and the impairment loss is measured as the excess of the carrying amount over the asset's fair value.

26 B is correct. The result on the sale of the vehicle equals

$$\begin{aligned}\text{Gain or loss on the sale} &= \text{Sale proceeds} - \text{Carrying amount}\\ &= \text{Sale proceeds} - (\text{Acquisition cost} - \text{Accumulated depreciation})\\ &= 85{,}000 - \{100{,}000 - [((100{,}000 - 10{,}000)/9 \text{ years}) \times 3 \text{ years}]\}\\ &= 15{,}000.\end{aligned}$$

27 A is correct. Gain or loss on the sale = Sale proceeds – Carrying amount. Rearranging this equation, Sale proceeds = Carrying amount + Gain or loss on sale. Thus, Sale price = (12 million – 2 million) + (–3.2 million) = 6.8 million.

28 C is correct. The carrying amount of the asset on the balance sheet is reduced by the amount of the impairment loss, and the impairment loss is reported on the income statement.

29 A is correct. The gain or loss on the sale of long-lived assets is computed as the sales proceeds minus the carrying amount of the asset at the time of sale. This is true under the cost and revaluation models of reporting long-lived assets. In the absence of impairment losses, under the cost model, the carrying amount will equal historical cost net of accumulated depreciation.

30 B is correct. IFRS do not require acquisition dates to be disclosed.

31 A is correct. IFRS do not require fair value of intangible assets to be disclosed.

32 C is correct. Under US GAAP, companies are required to disclose the estimated amortization expense for the next five fiscal years. Under US GAAP, there is no reversal of impairment losses. Disclosure of the useful lives—finite or indefinite and additional related details—is required under IFRS.

33 B is correct. Investment property earns rent. Investment property and property, plant, and equipment are tangible and long-lived.

34 C is correct. When a company uses the fair value model to value investment property, changes in the fair value of the property are reported in the income statement—not in other comprehensive income.

35 A is correct. Investment property earns rent. Inventory is held for resale, and property, plant, and equipment are used in the production of goods and services.

36 C is correct. A company will change from the fair value model to either the cost model or revaluation model when the company transfers investment property to property, plant, and equipment.

37 A is correct. Under both the revaluation model for property, plant, and equipment and the fair model for investment property, the asset's fair value must be able to be measured reliably. Under the fair value model, net income is affected by all changes in the asset's fair value. Under the revaluation model, any increase in an asset's value to the extent that it reverses a previous revaluation decrease will be recognized on the income statement and increase net income.

38 A is correct. Under IFRS, when using the cost model for its investment properties, a company must disclose useful lives. The method for determining fair value, as well as reconciliation between beginning and ending carrying amounts of investment property, is a required disclosure when the fair value model is used.

39 C is correct. Expensing rather than capitalising an investment in long-term assets will result in higher expenses and lower net income and net profit margin in the current year. Future years' incomes will not include depreciation expense related to these expenditures. Consequently, year-to-year growth in profitability will be higher. If the expenses had been capitalised, the carrying amount of the assets would have been higher and the 2009 total asset turnover would have been lower.

40 C is correct. In 2010, switching to an accelerated depreciation method would increase depreciation expense and decrease income before taxes, taxes payable, and net income. Cash flow from operating activities would increase because of the resulting tax savings.

41 B is correct. 2009 net income and net profit margin are lower because of the impairment loss. Consequently, net profit margins in subsequent years are likely to be higher. An impairment loss suggests that insufficient depreciation expense was recognized in prior years, and net income was overstated in prior years. The impairment loss is a non-cash item and will not affect operating cash flows.

42 A is correct. The estimated average remaining useful life is 20.75 years.

Estimate of remaining useful life = Net plant and equipment ÷ Annual depreciation expense
Net plant and equipment = Gross P & E – Accumulated depreciation
= €6000 – €1850 = €4150
Estimate of remaining useful life = Net P & E ÷ Depreciation expense
= €4150 ÷ €200 = 20.75

43 C is correct. The decision to capitalise the costs of the new computer system results in higher cash flow from operating activities; the expenditure is reported as an outflow of investing activities. The company allocates the capitalised amount over the asset's useful life as depreciation or amortisation expense rather than expensing it in the year of expenditure. Net income and total assets are higher in the current fiscal year.

44 B is correct. Alpha's fixed asset turnover will be lower because the capitalised interest will appear on the balance sheet as part of the asset being constructed. Therefore, fixed assets will be higher and the fixed asset turnover ratio (total revenue/average net fixed assets) will be lower than if it had expensed these costs. Capitalised interest appears on the balance sheet as part of the asset being constructed instead of being reported as interest expense in the period incurred. However, the interest coverage ratio should be based on interest payments, not interest expense (earnings before interest and taxes/interest payments), and should be unchanged. To provide a true picture of a company's interest coverage, the entire amount of interest expenditure, both the capitalised portion and the expensed portion, should be used in calculating interest coverage ratios.

45 A is correct. Accelerated depreciation will result in an improving, not declining, net profit margin over time, because the amount of depreciation expense declines each year. Under straight-line depreciation, the amount of depreciation expense will remain the same each year. Under the units-of-production method, the amount of depreciation expense reported each year varies with the number of units produced.

46 B is correct. The estimated average total useful life of a company's assets is calculated by adding the estimates of the average remaining useful life and the average age of the assets. The average age of the assets is estimated by dividing accumulated depreciation by depreciation expense. The average remaining useful life of the asset base is estimated by dividing net property, plant, and equipment by annual depreciation expense.

47 C is correct. The impairment loss is a non-cash charge and will not affect cash flow from operating activities. The debt to total assets and fixed asset turnover ratios will increase, because the impairment loss will reduce the carrying amount of fixed assets and therefore total assets.

48 A is correct. In an asset revaluation, the carrying amount of the assets increases. The increase in the asset's carrying amount bypasses the income statement and is reported as other comprehensive income and appears in equity under the heading of revaluation surplus. Therefore, shareholders' equity will increase but net income will not be affected, so return on equity will decline. Return on assets and debt to capital ratios will also decrease.

READING

27

Income Taxes

by Elbie Louw, PhD, CFA, CIPM, and Michael A. Broihahn, CPA, CIA, CFA

Elbie Louw, PhD, CFA, CIPM (South Africa). Michael A. Broihahn, CPA, CIA, CFA, is at Barry University (USA).

LEARNING OUTCOMES

Mastery	The candidate should be able to:
☐	a. describe the differences between accounting profit and taxable income and define key terms, including deferred tax assets, deferred tax liabilities, valuation allowance, taxes payable, and income tax expense;
☐	b. explain how deferred tax liabilities and assets are created and the factors that determine how a company's deferred tax liabilities and assets should be treated for the purposes of financial analysis;
☐	c. calculate the tax base of a company's assets and liabilities;
☐	d. calculate income tax expense, income taxes payable, deferred tax assets, and deferred tax liabilities, and calculate and interpret the adjustment to the financial statements related to a change in the income tax rate;
☐	e. evaluate the effect of tax rate changes on a company's financial statements and ratios;
☐	f. distinguish between temporary and permanent differences in pre-tax accounting income and taxable income;
☐	g. describe the valuation allowance for deferred tax assets—when it is required and what effect it has on financial statements;
☐	h. explain recognition and measurement of current and deferred tax items;
☐	i. analyze disclosures relating to deferred tax items and the effective tax rate reconciliation and explain how information included in these disclosures affects a company's financial statements and financial ratios;
☐	j. identify the key provisions of and differences between income tax accounting under International Financial Reporting Standards (IFRS) and US generally accepted accounting principles (GAAP).

Note: Changes in accounting standards as well as new rulings and/or pronouncements issued after the publication of the readings on financial reporting and analysis may cause some of the information in these readings to become dated. Candidates are *not* responsible for anything that occurs after the readings were published. In addition, candidates are expected to be familiar with the analytical frameworks contained in the readings, as well as the implications of alternative accounting methods for financial analysis and valuation discussed in the readings. Candidates are also responsible for the content of accounting standards, but not for the actual reference numbers. Finally, candidates should be aware that certain ratios may be defined and calculated differently. When alternative ratio definitions exist and no specific definition is given, candidates should use the ratio definitions emphasized in the readings.

© 2019 CFA Institute. All rights reserved.

1 INTRODUCTION

For those companies reporting under International Financial Reporting Standards (IFRS), IAS 12 [Income Taxes] covers accounting for a company's income taxes and the reporting of deferred taxes. For those companies reporting under United States generally accepted accounting principles (US GAAP), FASB ASC Topic 740 [Income Taxes] is the primary source for information on accounting for income taxes. Although IFRS and US GAAP follow similar conventions on many income tax issues, there are some key differences that will be discussed in the reading.

Differences between how and when transactions are recognized for financial reporting purposes relative to tax reporting can give rise to differences in tax expense and related tax assets and liabilities. To reconcile these differences, companies that report under either IFRS or US GAAP create a provision on the balance sheet called deferred tax assets or deferred tax liabilities, depending on the nature of the situation.

Deferred tax assets or liabilities usually arise when accounting standards and tax authorities recognize the timing of revenues and expenses at different times. Because timing differences such as these will eventually reverse over time, they are called "temporary differences." Deferred tax assets represent taxes that have been recognized for tax reporting purposes (or often the carrying forward of losses from previous periods) but have not yet been recognized on the income statement prepared for financial reporting purposes. Deferred tax liabilities represent tax expense that has appeared on the income statement for financial reporting purposes, but has not yet become payable under tax regulations.

This reading provides a primer on the basics of income tax accounting and reporting. The reading is organized as follows. Section 2 describes the differences between taxable income and accounting profit. Section 3 explains the determination of tax base, which relates to the valuation of assets and liabilities for tax purposes. Section 4 discusses several types of timing differences between the recognition of taxable and accounting profit. Section 5 examines unused tax losses and tax credits. Section 6 describes the recognition and measurement of current and deferred tax. Section 7 discusses the disclosure and presentation of income tax information on companies' financial statements and illustrates its practical implications for financial analysis. Section 8 provides an overview of the similarities and differences for income-tax reporting between IFRS and US GAAP. A summary of the key points and practice problems in the CFA Institute multiple-choice format conclude the reading.

2 DIFFERENCES BETWEEN ACCOUNTING PROFIT AND TAXABLE INCOME

A company's **accounting profit** is reported on its income statement in accordance with prevailing accounting standards. Accounting profit (also referred to as income before taxes or pretax income) does not include a provision for income tax expense.[1] A company's **taxable income** is the portion of its income that is subject to income taxes under the tax laws of its jurisdiction. Because of different guidelines for how income is reported on a company's financial statements and how it is measured for income tax purposes, accounting profit and taxable income may differ.

1 As defined under IAS 12, paragraph 5.

A company's taxable income is the basis for its **income tax payable** (a liability) or recoverable (an asset), which is calculated on the basis of the company's tax rate and appears on its balance sheet. A company's **tax expense**, or tax benefit in the case of a recovery, appears on its income statement and is an aggregate of its income tax payable (or recoverable in the case of a tax benefit) and any changes in deferred tax assets and liabilities.

When a company's taxable income is greater than its accounting profit, then its income taxes payable will be higher than what would have otherwise been the case had the income taxes been determined based on accounting profit. **Deferred tax assets**, which appear on the balance sheet, arise when an excess amount is paid for income taxes (taxable income higher than accounting profit) and the company expects to recover the difference during the course of future operations. Actual income taxes payable will thus exceed the financial accounting income tax expense (which is reported on the income statement and is determined based on accounting profit). Related to deferred tax assets is a **valuation allowance**, which is a reserve created against deferred tax assets. The valuation allowance is based on the likelihood of realizing the deferred tax assets in future accounting periods. **Deferred tax liabilities**, which also appear on the balance sheet, arise when a deficit amount is paid for income taxes and the company expects to eliminate the deficit over the course of future operations. In this case, financial accounting income tax expense exceeds income taxes payable.

Income tax paid in a period is the actual amount paid for income taxes (not a provision, but the actual cash outflow). The income tax paid may be less than the income tax expense because of payments in prior periods or refunds received in the current period. Income tax paid reduces the income tax payable, which is carried on the balance sheet as a liability.

The **tax base** of an asset or liability is the amount at which the asset or liability is valued for tax purposes, whereas the **carrying amount** is the amount at which the asset or liability is valued according to accounting principles.[2] Differences between the tax base and the carrying amount also result in differences between accounting profit and taxable income. These differences can carry through to future periods. For example, a **tax loss carry forward** occurs when a company experiences a loss in the current period that may be used to reduce future taxable income. The company's tax expense on its income statement must not only reflect the taxes payable based on taxable income, but also the effect of these differences.

2.1 Current Tax Assets and Liabilities

A company's current tax liability is the amount payable in taxes and is based on current taxable income. If the company expects to receive a refund for some portion previously paid in taxes, the amount recoverable is referred to as a current tax asset. The current tax liability or asset may, however, differ from what the liability would have been if it was based on accounting profit rather than taxable income for the period. Differences in accounting profit and taxable income are the result of the application of different rules. Such differences between accounting profit and taxable income can occur in several ways, including:

- Revenues and expenses may be recognized in one period for accounting purposes and a different period for tax purposes;

2 The terms "tax base" and "tax basis" are interchangeable. "Tax basis" is more commonly used in the United States. Similarly, "carrying amount" and "book value" refer to the same concept.

- Specific revenues and expenses may be either recognized for accounting purposes and not for tax purposes; or not recognized for accounting purposes but recognized for tax purposes;
- The carrying amount and tax base of assets and/or liabilities may differ;
- The deductibility of gains and losses of assets and liabilities may vary for accounting and income tax purposes;
- Subject to tax rules, tax losses of prior years might be used to reduce taxable income in later years, resulting in differences in accounting and taxable income (tax loss carryforward); and
- Adjustments of reported financial data from prior years might not be recognized equally for accounting and tax purposes or might be recognized in different periods.

2.2 Deferred Tax Assets and Liabilities

Deferred tax assets represent taxes that have been paid (or often the carrying forward of losses from previous periods) but have not yet been recognized on the income statement. Deferred tax liabilities occur when financial accounting income tax expense is greater than regulatory income tax expense. Deferred tax assets and liabilities usually arise when accounting standards and tax authorities recognize the timing of taxes due at different times; for example, when a company uses accelerated depreciation when reporting to the tax authority (to increase expense and lower tax payments in the early years) but uses the straight-line method on the financial statements. Although not similar in treatment on a year-to-year basis (e.g., depreciation of 5 percent on a straight-line basis may be permitted for accounting purposes whereas 10 percent is allowed for tax purposes) over the life of the asset, both approaches allow for the total cost of the asset to be depreciated (or amortized). Because these timing differences will eventually reverse or self-correct over the course of the asset's depreciable life, they are called "temporary differences."

Any deferred tax asset or liability is based on temporary differences that result in an excess or a deficit amount paid for taxes, which the company expects to recover from future operations. Because taxes will be recoverable or payable at a future date, it is only a temporary difference and a deferred tax asset or liability is created. Changes in the deferred tax asset or liability on the balance sheet reflect the difference between the amounts recognized in the previous period and the current period. The changes in deferred tax assets and liabilities are added to income tax payable to determine the company's income tax expense (or credit) as it is reported on the income statement.

At the end of each fiscal year, deferred tax assets and liabilities are recalculated by comparing the tax bases and carrying amounts of the balance sheet items. Identified temporary differences should be assessed on whether the difference will result in future economic benefits. For example, Pinto Construction (a hypothetical company) depreciates equipment on a straight-line basis of 10 percent per year. The tax authorities allow depreciation of 15 percent per year. At the end of the fiscal year, the carrying amount of the equipment for accounting purposes would be greater than the tax base of the equipment thus resulting in a temporary difference. A deferred tax item may only be created if it is not doubtful that the company will realize economic benefits in the future. In our example, the equipment is used in the core business of Pinto Construction. If the company is a going concern and stable, there should be no doubt that future economic benefits will result from the equipment and it would be appropriate to create the deferred tax item.

Should it be doubtful that future economic benefits will be realized from a temporary difference (such as Pinto Construction being under liquidation), the temporary difference will not lead to the creation of a deferred tax asset or liability. If a deferred tax asset or liability resulted in the past, but the criteria of economic benefits is not met on the current balance sheet date, then, under IFRS, an existing deferred tax asset or liability related to the item will be reversed. Under US GAAP, a valuation allowance is established. In assessing future economic benefits, much is left to the discretion of the auditor in assessing the temporary differences and the issue of future economic benefits.

EXAMPLE 1

The following information pertains to a hypothetical company, Reston Partners:

Reston Partners Consolidated Income Statement

Period Ending 31 March (£ Millions)	Year 3	Year 2	Year 1
Revenue	£40,000	£30,000	£25,000
Other net gains	2,000	0	0
Changes in inventories of finished goods and work in progress	400	180	200
Raw materials and consumables used	(5,700)	(4,000)	(8,000)
Depreciation expense	(2,000)	(2,000)	(2,000)
Other expenses	(6,000)	(5,900)	(4,500)
Interest expense	(2,000)	(3,000)	(6,000)
Profit before tax	£26,700	£15,280	£4,700

The financial performance and accounting profit of Reston Partners on this income statement is based on accounting principles appropriate for the jurisdiction in which Reston Partners operates. The principles used to calculate accounting profit (profit before tax in the example above) may differ from the principles applied for tax purposes (the calculation of taxable income). For illustrative purposes, however, assume that all income and expenses on the income statement are treated identically for tax and accounting purposes *except* depreciation.

The depreciation is related to equipment owned by Reston Partners. For simplicity, assume that the equipment was purchased at the beginning of the Year 1. Depreciation should thus be calculated and expensed for the full year. Assume that accounting standards permit equipment to be depreciated on a straight-line basis over a 10-year period, whereas the tax standards in the jurisdiction specify that equipment should be depreciated on a straight-line basis over a 7-year period. For simplicity, assume a salvage value of £0 at the end of the equipment's useful life. Both methods will result in the full depreciation of the asset over the respective tax or accounting life.

The equipment was originally purchased for £20,000. In accordance with accounting standards, over the next 10 years the company will recognize annual depreciation of £2,000 (£20,000 ÷ 10) as an expense on its income statement and for the determination of accounting profit. For tax purposes, however, the company will recognize £2,857 (£20,000 ÷ 7) in depreciation each year. Each fiscal year the depreciation expense related to the use of the equipment will, therefore, differ for tax and accounting purposes (tax base vs. carrying amount), resulting in a difference between accounting profit and taxable income.

The previous income statement reflects accounting profit (depreciation at £2,000 per year). The following table shows the taxable income for each fiscal year.

Taxable Income (£ Millions)	Year 3	Year 2	Year 1
Revenue	£40,000	£30,000	£25,000
Other net gains	2,000	0	0
Changes in inventories of finished goods and work in progress	400	180	200
Raw materials and consumables used	(5,700)	(4,000)	(8,000)
Depreciation expense	(2,857)	(2,857)	(2,857)
Other expenses	(6,000)	(5,900)	(4,500)
Interest expense	(2,000)	(3,000)	(6,000)
Taxable income	£25,843	£14,423	£3,843

The carrying amount and tax base for the equipment is as follows:

(£ Millions)	Year 3	Year 2	Year 1
Equipment value for accounting purposes (*carrying amount*) (depreciation of £2,000/year)	£14,000	£16,000	£18,000
Equipment value for tax purposes (*tax base*) (depreciation of £2,857/year)	£11,429	£14,286	£17,143
Difference	£2,571	£1,714	£857

At each balance sheet date, the tax base and carrying amount of all assets and liabilities must be determined. The income tax payable by Reston Partners will be based on the taxable income of each fiscal year. If a tax rate of 30 percent is assumed, then the income taxes payable for Year 1, Year 2, and Year 3 are £1,153 (30% × 3,843), £4,327 (30% × 14,423), and £7,753 (30% × 25,843).

Remember, though, that if the tax obligation is calculated based on accounting profits, it will differ because of the differences between the tax base and the carrying amount of equipment. The difference in each fiscal year is reflected in the table above. In each fiscal year the carrying amount of the equipment exceeds its tax base. For tax purposes, therefore, the asset tax base is less than its carrying value under financial accounting principles. The difference results in a deferred tax liability.

(£ Millions)	Year 3	Year 2	Year 1
Deferred tax liability	£771	£514	£257
(Difference between tax base and carrying amount) × tax rate			
Year 1: £(18,000 − 17,143) × 30% = 257			
Year 2: £(16,000 − 14,286) × 30% = 514			
Year 3: £(14,000 − 11,429) × 30% = 771			

The comparison of the tax base and carrying amount of equipment shows what the deferred tax liability should be on a particular balance sheet date. In each fiscal year, only the change in the deferred tax liability should be included in the calculation of the income tax expense reported on the income statement prepared for accounting purposes.

On the income statement, the company's income tax expense will be the sum of change in the deferred tax liability and the income tax payable.

(£ Millions)	Year 3	Year 2	Year 1
Income tax payable (based on tax accounting)	£7,753	£4,327	£1,153
Change in deferred tax liability	257	257	257
Income tax (based on financial accounting)	£8,010	£4,584	£1,410

Note that because the different treatment of depreciation is a temporary difference, the income tax on the income statement is 30 percent of the accounting profit, although only a part is income tax payable and the rest is a deferred tax liability.

The consolidated income statement of Reston Partners including income tax is presented as follows:

Reston Partners Consolidated Income Statement

Period Ending 31 March (£ Millions)	Year 3	Year 2	Year 1
Revenue	£40,000	£30,000	£25,000
Other net gains	2,000	0	0
Changes in inventories of finished goods and work in progress	400	180	200
Raw materials and consumables used	(5,700)	(4,000)	(8,000)
Depreciation expense	(2,000)	(2,000)	(2,000)
Other expenses	(6,000)	(5,900)	(4,500)
Interest expense	(2,000)	(3,000)	(6,000)
Profit before tax	£26,700	£15,280	£4,700
Income tax	(8,010)	(4,584)	(1,410)
Profit after tax	£18,690	£10,696	£3,290

Any amount paid to the tax authorities will reduce the liability for income tax payable and be reflected on the statement of cash flows of the company.

DETERMINING THE TAX BASE OF ASSETS AND LIABILITIES

3

As mentioned in Section 2, temporary differences arise from a difference in the tax base and carrying amount of assets and liabilities. The tax base of an asset or liability is the amount attributed to the asset or liability for tax purposes, whereas the carrying amount is based on accounting principles. Such a difference is considered temporary if it is expected that the taxes will be recovered or payable at a future date.

3.1 Determining the Tax Base of an Asset

The tax base of an asset is the amount that will be deductible for tax purposes in future periods as the economic benefits become realized and the company recovers the carrying amount of the asset.

For example, our previously mentioned Reston Partners (from Example 1) depreciates equipment on a straight-line basis at a rate of 10 percent per year. The tax authorities allow depreciation of approximately 15 percent per year. At the end of the fiscal year, the carrying amount of equipment for accounting purposes is greater than the asset tax base thus resulting in a temporary difference.

EXAMPLE 2

Determining the Tax Base of an Asset

The following information pertains to Entiguan Sports, a hypothetical developer of products used to treat sports-related injuries. (The treatment of items for accounting and tax purposes is based on hypothetical accounting and tax standards and is not specific to a particular jurisdiction.) Calculate the tax base and carrying amount for each item.

1 *Dividends receivable*: On its balance sheet, Entiguan Sports reports dividends of €1 million receivable from a subsidiary. Assume that dividends are not taxable.

2 *Development costs*: Entiguan Sports capitalized development costs of €3 million during the year. Entiguan amortized €500,000 of this amount during the year. For tax purposes amortization of 25 percent per year is allowed.

3 *Research costs*: Entiguan incurred €500,000 in research costs, which were all expensed in the current fiscal year for financial reporting purposes. Assume that applicable tax legislation requires research costs to be expensed over a four-year period rather than all in one year.

4 *Accounts receivable*: Included on the income statement of Entiguan Sports is a provision for doubtful debt of €125,000. The accounts receivable amount reflected on the balance sheet, after taking the provision into account, amounts to €1,500,000. The tax authorities allow a deduction of 25 percent of the gross amount for doubtful debt.

Solutions:

	Carrying Amount (€)	Tax Base (€)	Temporary Difference (€)
1. Dividends receivable	1,000,000	1,000,000	0
2. Development costs	2,500,000	2,250,000	250,000
3. Research costs	0	375,000	(375,000)
4. Accounts receivable	1,500,000	1,218,750	281,250

Comments:

1 *Dividends receivable*: Although the dividends received are economic benefits from the subsidiary, we are assuming that dividends are not taxable. Therefore, the carrying amount equals the tax base for dividends receivable.

2 *Development costs*: First, we assume that development costs will generate economic benefits for Entiguan Sports. Therefore, it may be included as an asset on the balance sheet for the purposes of this example. Second, the amortization allowed by the tax authorities exceeds the amortization accounted for based on accounting rules. Therefore, the carrying amount

of the asset exceeds its tax base. The carrying amount is (€3,000,000 – €500,000) = €2,500,000 whereas the tax base is [€3,000,000 – (25% × €3,000,000)] = €2,250,000.

3 *Research costs*: We assume that research costs will result in future economic benefits for the company. If this were not the case, creation of a deferred tax asset or liability would not be allowed. The tax base of research costs exceeds their carrying amount. The carrying amount is €0 because the full amount has been expensed for financial reporting purposes in the year in which it was incurred. Therefore, there would not have been a balance sheet item "Research costs" for tax purposes, and only a proportion may be deducted in the current fiscal year. The tax base of the asset is (€500,000 – €500,000/4) = €375,000.

4 *Accounts receivable*: The economic benefits that should have been received from accounts receivable have already been included in revenues included in the calculation of the taxable income when the sales occurred. Because the receipt of a portion of the accounts receivable is doubtful, the provision is allowed. The provision, based on tax legislation, results in a greater amount allowed in the current fiscal year than would be the case under accounting principles. This results in the tax base of accounts receivable being lower than its carrying amount. Note that the example specifically states that the balance sheet amount for accounts receivable after the provision for accounting purposes amounts to €1,500,000. Therefore, accounts receivable before any provision was €1,500,000 + €125,000 = €1,625,000. The tax base is calculated as (€1,500,000 + €125,000) – [25% × (€1,500,000 + €125,000)] = €1,218,750.

3.2 Determining the Tax Base of a Liability

The tax base of a liability is the carrying amount of the liability less any amounts that will be deductible for tax purposes in the future. With respect to payments from customers received in advance of providing the goods and services, the tax base of such a liability is the carrying amount less any amount of the revenue that will not be taxable in future. Keep in mind the following fundamental principle: In general, a company will recognize a deferred tax asset or liability when recovery/settlement of the carrying amount will affect future tax payments by either increasing or reducing the taxable profit. Remember, an analyst is not only evaluating the difference between the carrying amount and the tax base, but the relevance of that difference on future profits and losses and thus by implication future taxes.

IFRS offers specific guidelines with regard to revenue received in advance: IAS 12 states that the tax base is the carrying amount less any amount of the revenue that will not be taxed at a future date. Under US GAAP, an analysis of the tax base would result in a similar outcome. The tax legislation within the jurisdiction will determine the amount recognized on the income statement and whether the liability (revenue received in advance) will have a tax base greater than zero. This will depend on how tax legislation recognizes revenue received in advance.

EXAMPLE 3

Determining the Tax Base of a Liability

The following information pertains to the hypothetical company Entiguan Sports for the fiscal year -end. The treatment of items for accounting and tax purposes is based on fictitious accounting and tax standards and is not specific to a particular jurisdiction. Calculate the tax base and carrying amount for each item.

1 *Donations*: Entiguan Sports made donations of €100,000 in the current fiscal year. The donations were expensed for financial reporting purposes, but are not tax deductible based on applicable tax legislation.

2 *Interest received in advance*: Entiguan Sports received in advance interest of €300,000. The interest is taxed because tax authorities recognize the interest to accrue to the company (part of taxable income) on the date of receipt.

3 *Rent received in advance*: Entiguan recognized €10 million for rent received in advance from a lessee for an unused warehouse building. Rent received in advance is deferred for accounting purposes but taxed on a cash basis.

4 *Loan*: Entiguan Sports secured a long-term loan for €550,000 in the current fiscal year. Interest is charged at 13.5 percent per annum and is payable at the end of each fiscal year.

Solutions:

	Carrying Amount (€)	Tax Base (€)	Temporary Difference (€)
1. Donations	0	0	0
2. Interest received in advance	300,000	0	(300,000)
3. Rent received in advance	10,000,000	0	(10,000,000)
4. Loan (capital)	550,000	550,000	0
Interest paid	0	0	0

Comments:

1 *Donations*: The amount of €100,000 was immediately expensed on Entiguan's income statement; therefore, the carrying amount is €0. Tax legislation does not allow donations to be deducted for tax purposes, so the tax base of the donations equals the carrying amount. Note that while the carrying amount and tax base are the same, the difference in the treatment of donations for accounting and tax purposes (expensed for accounting purposes, but not deductible for tax purposes) represents a permanent difference (a difference that will not be reversed in future). Permanent and temporary differences are elaborated on in Section 4 and it will refer to this particular case with an expanded explanation.

2 *Interest received in advance*: Based on the information provided, for tax purposes, interest is deemed to accrue to the company on the date of receipt. For tax purposes, it is thus irrelevant whether it is for the current or a future accounting period; it must be included in taxable income in the financial year received. Interest received in advance is, for accounting purposes though, included in the financial period in which it is deemed to have been earned. For this reason, the interest income received in advance

is a balance sheet liability. It was not included on the income statement because the income relates to a future financial year. Because the full €300,000 is included in taxable income in the current fiscal year, the tax base is €300,000 – 300,000 = €0. Note that although interest received in advance and rent received in advance are both taxed, the timing depends on how the particular item is treated in tax legislation.

3 *Rent received in advance*: The result is similar to interest received in advance. The carrying amount of rent received in advance would be €10,000,000 while the tax base is €0.

4 *Loan*: Repayment of the loan has no tax implications. The repayment of the capital amount does not constitute an income or expense. The interest paid is included as an expense in the calculation of taxable income as well as accounting income. Therefore, the tax base and carrying amount is €0. For clarity, the interest paid that would be included on the income statement for the year amounts to 13.5% × €550,000 = €74,250 if the loan was acquired at the beginning of the current fiscal year.

3.3 Changes in Income Tax Rates

The measurement of deferred tax assets and liabilities is based on current tax law. But if there are subsequent changes in tax laws or new income tax rates, existing deferred tax assets and liabilities must be adjusted for the effects of these changes. The resulting effects of the changes are also included in determining accounting profit in the period of change.

When income tax rates change, the deferred tax assets and liabilities are adjusted to the new tax rate. If income tax rates increase, deferred taxes (that is, the deferred tax assets and liabilities) will also increase. Likewise, if income tax rates decrease, deferred taxes will decrease. A decrease in tax rates decreases deferred tax liabilities, which reduces future tax payments to the taxing authorities. A decrease in tax rates will also decrease deferred tax assets, which reduces their value toward the offset of future tax payments to the taxing authorities.

To illustrate the effect of a change in tax rate, consider Example 1 again. In that illustration, the timing difference that led to the recognition of a deferred tax liability for Reston Partners was attributable to differences in the method of depreciation and the related effects on the accounting carrying value and the asset tax base. The relevant information is restated below.

The carrying amount and tax base for the equipment is:

(£ Millions)	Year 3	Year 2	Year 1
Equipment value for accounting purposes (*carrying amount*) (depreciation of £2,000/year)	£14,000	£16,000	£18,000
Equipment value for tax purposes (*tax base*) (depreciation of £2,857/year)	£11,429	£14,286	£17,143
Difference	£2,571	£1,714	£857

At a 30 percent income tax rate, the deferred tax liability was then determined as follows:

(£ Millions)	Year 3	Year 2	Year 1
Deferred tax liability	£771	£514	£257
(Difference between tax base and carrying amount)			
Year 1: £(18,000 – 17,143) × 30% = £257			

(continued)

(£ Millions)	Year 3	Year 2	Year 1
Year 2: £(16,000 − 14,286) × 30% = £514			
Year 3: £(14,000 − 11,429) × 30% = £771			

For this illustration, assume that the taxing authority has changed the income tax rate to 25 percent for Year 3. Although the difference between the carrying amount and the tax base of the depreciable asset are the same, the deferred tax liability for 2017 will be £643 (instead of £771 or a reduction of £128 in the liability). 2017: £(14,000 − 11,429) × 25% = £643.

Reston Partners' provision for income tax expense is also affected by the change in tax rates. Taxable income for Year 3 will now be taxed at a rate of 25 percent. The benefit of the Year 3 accelerated depreciation tax shield is now only £214 (£857 × 25%) instead of the previous £257 (a reduction of £43). In addition, the reduction in the beginning carrying value of the deferred tax liability for Year 3 (the year of change) further reduces the income tax expense for Year 3. The reduction in income tax expense attributable to the change in tax rate is £86. Year 3: (30% − 25%) × £1,714 = £86. Note that these two components together account for the reduction in the deferred tax liability (£43 + £86 = £129).

As may be seen from this discussion, changes in the income tax rate have an effect on a company's deferred tax asset and liability carrying values as well as an effect on the measurement of income tax expense in the year of change. The analyst must thus note that proposed changes in tax law can have a quantifiable effect on these accounts (and any related financial ratios that are derived from them) if the proposed changes are subsequently enacted into law.

4 TEMPORARY AND PERMANENT DIFFERENCES BETWEEN TAXABLE AND ACCOUNTING PROFIT

Temporary differences arise from a difference between the tax base and the carrying amount of assets and liabilities. The creation of a deferred tax asset or liability from a temporary difference is only possible if the difference reverses itself at some future date and to such an extent that the balance sheet item is expected to create future economic benefits for the company. IFRS and US GAAP both prescribe the balance sheet liability method for recognition of deferred tax. This balance sheet method focuses on the recognition of a deferred tax asset or liability should there be a temporary difference between the carrying amount and tax base of balance sheet items.[3]

Permanent differences are differences between tax and financial reporting of revenue (expenses) that *will not* be reversed at some future date. Because they will not be reversed at a future date, these differences do not give rise to deferred tax. These items typically include

- Income or expense items not allowed by tax legislation, and
- Tax credits for some expenditures that directly reduce taxes.

3 Previously, IAS 12 required recognition of deferred tax based on the deferred method (also known as the income statement method), which focused on timing differences. Timing differences are differences in the recognition of income and expenses for accounting and tax purposes that originate in one period and will reverse in a future period. Given the definition of timing differences, all timing differences are temporary differences, such as the different treatment of depreciation for tax and accounting purposes (although the timing is different with regard to the allowed depreciation for tax and accounting purposes, the asset will eventually be fully depreciated).

Because no deferred tax item is created for permanent differences, all permanent differences result in a difference between the company's effective tax rate and statutory tax rate. The effective tax rate is also influenced by different statutory taxes should an entity conduct business in more than one tax jurisdiction. The formula for the reported effective tax rate is thus equal to:

Reported effective tax rate = Income tax expense ÷ Pretax income (accounting profit)

The net change in deferred tax during a reporting period is the difference between the balance of the deferred tax asset or liability for the current period and the balance of the previous period.

4.1 Taxable Temporary Differences

Temporary differences are further divided into two categories, namely taxable temporary differences and deductible temporary differences. **Taxable temporary differences** are temporary differences that result in a taxable amount in a future period when determining the taxable profit as the balance sheet item is recovered or settled. Taxable temporary differences result in a deferred tax liability when the carrying amount of an asset exceeds its tax base and, in the case of a liability, when the tax base of the liability exceeds its carrying amount.

Under US GAAP, a deferred tax asset or liability is not recognized for unamortizable goodwill. Under IFRS, a deferred tax account is not recognized for goodwill arising in a business combination. Since goodwill is a residual, the recognition of a deferred tax liability would increase the carrying amount of goodwill. Discounting deferred tax assets or liabilities is generally not allowed for temporary differences related to business combinations as it is for other temporary differences.

IFRS provides an exemption (that is, deferred tax is not provided on the temporary difference) for the initial recognition of an asset or liability in a transaction that: a) is not a business combination (e.g., joint ventures, branches and unconsolidated investments); and b) affects neither accounting profit nor taxable profit at the time of the transaction. US GAAP does not provide an exemption for these circumstances.

As a simple example of a temporary difference with no recognition of deferred tax liability, assume that a holding company of various leisure related businesses and holiday resorts buys an interest in a hotel in the current financial year. The goodwill related to the transaction will be recognized on the financial statements, but the related tax liability will not, as it relates to the initial recognition of goodwill.

4.2 Deductible Temporary Differences

Deductible temporary differences are temporary differences that result in a reduction or deduction of taxable income in a future period when the balance sheet item is recovered or settled. Deductible temporary differences result in a deferred tax asset when the tax base of an asset exceeds its carrying amount and, in the case of a liability, when the carrying amount of the liability exceeds its tax base. The recognition of a deferred tax asset is only allowed to the extent there is a reasonable expectation of future profits against which the asset or liability (that gave rise to the deferred tax asset) can be recovered or settled.

To determine the probability of sufficient future profits for utilization, one must consider the following: 1) Sufficient taxable temporary differences must exist that are related to the same tax authority and the same taxable entity; and 2) The taxable temporary differences that are expected to reverse in the same periods as expected for the reversal of the deductible temporary differences.

As with deferred tax liabilities, IFRS states that deferred tax assets should not be recognized in cases that would arise from the initial recognition of an asset or liability in transactions that are not a business combination and when, at the time of the transaction, there is no impact on either accounting or taxable profit. Subsequent to initial recognition under IFRS and US GAAP, any deferred tax assets that arise from investments in subsidiaries, branches, associates, and interests in joint ventures are recognized as a deferred tax asset.

IFRS and US GAAP allow the creation of a deferred tax asset in the case of tax losses and tax credits. These two unique situations will be further elaborated on in Section 6. IAS 12 *does not* allow the creation of a deferred tax asset arising from negative goodwill. Negative goodwill arises when the amount that an entity pays for an interest in a business is less than the net fair market value of the portion of assets and liabilities of the acquired company, based on the interest of the entity.

4.3 Examples of Taxable and Deductible Temporary Differences

Exhibit 1 summarizes how differences between the tax bases and carrying amounts of assets and liabilities give rise to deferred tax assets or deferred tax liabilities.

Exhibit 1 Treatment of Temporary Differences

Balance Sheet Item	Carrying Amount vs. Tax Base	Results in Deferred Tax Asset/Liability
Asset	Carrying amount > tax base	Deferred tax liability
Asset	Carrying amount < tax base	Deferred tax asset
Liability	Carrying amount > tax base	Deferred tax asset
Liability	Carrying amount < tax base	Deferred tax liability

EXAMPLE 4

Taxable and Deductible Temporary Differences

Examples 2 and 3 illustrated how to calculate the tax base of assets and liabilities, respectively. Based on the information provided in Examples 2 and 3, indicate whether the difference in the tax base and carrying amount of the assets and liabilities are temporary or permanent differences and whether a deferred tax asset or liability will be recognized based on the difference identified.

Solution to Example 2:

	Carrying Amount (€)	Tax Base (€)	Temporary Difference (€)	*Will Result in Deferred Tax Asset/Liability*
1. Dividends receivable	1,000,000	1,000,000	0	*N/A*
2. Development costs	2,500,000	2,250,000	250,000	*Deferred tax liability*
3. Research costs	0	375,000	(375,000)	*Deferred tax asset*
4. Accounts receivable	1,500,000	1,218,750	281,250	*Deferred tax liability*

Example 2 included comments on the calculation of the carrying amount and tax base of the assets.

1 *Dividends receivable*: As a result of non-taxability, the carrying amount equals the tax base of dividends receivable. This constitutes a permanent difference and will not result in the recognition of any deferred tax asset or liability. A temporary difference constitutes a difference that will, at some future date, be reversed. Although the timing of recognition is different for tax and accounting purposes, in the end the full carrying amount will be expensed/recognized as income. A permanent difference will never be reversed. Based on tax legislation, dividends from a subsidiary are not recognized as income. Therefore, no amount will be reflected as dividend income when calculating the taxable income, and the tax base of dividends receivable must be the total amount received, namely €1,000,000. The taxable income and accounting profit will permanently differ with the amount of dividends receivable, even on future financial statements as an effect on the retained earnings reflected on the balance sheet.

2 *Development costs*: The difference between the carrying amount and tax base is a temporary difference that, in the future, will reverse. In this fiscal year, it will result in a deferred tax liability.

3 *Research costs*: The difference between the carrying amount and tax base is a temporary difference that results in a deferred tax asset. Remember the explanation in Section 2 for deferred tax assets—a deferred tax asset arises because of an excess amount paid for taxes (when taxable income is greater than accounting profit), which is expected to be recovered from future operations. Based on accounting principles, the full amount was deducted resulting in a lower accounting profit, while the taxable income by implication, should be greater because of the lower amount expensed.

4 *Accounts receivable*: The difference between the carrying amount and tax base of the asset is a temporary difference that will result in a deferred tax liability.

Solution to Example 3:

	Carrying Amount (€)	Tax Base (€)	Temporary Difference (€)	*Will Result in Deferred Tax Asset/Liability*
1. Donations	0	0	0	*N/A*
2. Interest received in advance	300,000	0	(300,000)	*Deferred tax asset*
3. Rent received in advance	10,000,000	0	(10,000,000)	*Deferred tax asset*
4. Loan (capital)	550,000	550,000	0	*N/A*
Interest paid	0	0	0	*N/A*

Example 3 included extensive comments on the calculation of the carrying amount and tax base of the liabilities.

1 *Donations*: It was assumed that tax legislation does not allow donations to be deducted for tax purposes. No temporary difference results from donations, and thus a deferred tax asset or liability will not be recognized. This constitutes a permanent difference.

2 *Interest received in advance*: Interest received in advance results in a temporary difference that gives rise to a deferred tax asset. A deferred tax asset arises because of an excess amount paid for taxes (when taxable income is greater than accounting profit), which is expected to be recovered from future operations.

3 *Rent received in advance*: The difference between the carrying amount and tax base is a temporary difference that leads to the recognition of a deferred tax asset.

4 *Loan*: There are no temporary differences as a result of the loan or interest paid, and thus no deferred tax item is recognized.

4.4 Temporary Differences at Initial Recognition of Assets and Liabilities

In some situations the carrying amount and tax base of a balance sheet item may vary at initial recognition. For example, a company may deduct a government grant from the initial carrying amount of an asset or liability that appears on the balance sheet. For tax purposes, such grants may not be deducted when determining the tax base of the balance sheet item. In such circumstances, the carrying amount of the asset or liability will be lower than its tax base. Differences in the tax base of an asset or liability as a result of the circumstances described above may not be recognized as deferred tax assets or liabilities.

For example, a government may offer grants to Small, Medium, and Micro Enterprises (SMME) in an attempt to assist these entrepreneurs in their endeavors that contribute to the country's GDP and job creation. Assume that a particular grant is offered for infrastructure needs (office furniture, property, plant, and equipment, etc.). In these circumstances, although the carrying amount will be lower than the tax base of the asset, the related deferred tax may not be recognized. As mentioned earlier, deferred tax assets and liabilities should not be recognized in cases that would arise from the initial recognition of an asset or liability in transactions that are not a business combination and when, at the time of the transaction, there is no impact on either accounting or taxable profit.

A deferred tax liability will also not be recognized at the initial recognition of goodwill. Although goodwill may be treated differently across tax jurisdictions, which may lead to differences in the carrying amount and tax base of goodwill, IAS 12 does not allow the recognition of such a deferred tax liability. Any impairment that an entity should, for accounting purposes, impose on goodwill will again result in a temporary difference between its carrying amount and tax base. Any impairment that an entity should, for accounting purposes, impose on goodwill and if part of the goodwill is related to the initial recognition, that part of the difference in tax base and carrying amount should not result in any deferred taxation because the initial deferred tax liability was not recognized. Any future differences between the carrying amount and tax base as a result of amortization and the deductibility of a portion of goodwill constitute a temporary difference for which provision should be made.

4.5 Business Combinations and Deferred Taxes

The fair value of assets and liabilities acquired in a business combination is determined on the acquisition date and may differ from the previous carrying amount. It is highly probable that the values of acquired intangible assets, including goodwill, would differ from their carrying amounts. This temporary difference will affect deferred taxes as well as the amount of goodwill recognized as a result of the acquisition.

4.6 Investments in Subsidiaries, Branches, Associates and Interests in Joint Ventures

Investments in subsidiaries, branches, associates and interests in joint ventures may lead to temporary differences on the consolidated versus the parent's financial statements. The related deferred tax liabilities as a result of temporary differences will be recognized unless both of the following criterion are satisfied:

- The parent is in a position to control the timing of the future reversal of the temporary difference, and
- It is probable that the temporary difference will not reverse in the future.

With respect to deferred tax assets related to subsidiaries, branches, and associates and interests, deferred tax assets will only be recognized if the following criteria are satisfied:

- The temporary difference will reverse in the future, and
- Sufficient taxable profits exist against which the temporary difference can be used.

UNUSED TAX LOSSES AND TAX CREDITS 5

IAS 12 allows the recognition of unused tax losses and tax credits only to the extent that it is probable that in the future there will be taxable income against which the unused tax losses and credits can be applied. Under US GAAP, a deferred tax asset is recognized in full but is then reduced by a valuation allowance if it is more likely than not that some or all of the deferred tax asset will not be realized. The same requirements for creation of a deferred tax asset as a result of deductible temporary differences also apply to unused tax losses and tax credits. The existence of tax losses may indicate that the entity cannot reasonably be expected to generate sufficient future taxable income. All other things held constant, the greater the history of tax losses, the greater the concern regarding the company's ability to generate future taxable profits.

Should there be concerns about the company's future profitability, then the deferred tax asset may not be recognized until it is realized. When assessing the probability that sufficient taxable profit will be generated in the future, the following criteria can serve as a guide:

- If there is uncertainty as to the probability of future taxable profits, a deferred tax asset as a result of unused tax losses or tax credits is only recognized to the extent of the available taxable temporary differences;
- Assess the probability that the entity will in fact generate future taxable profits before the unused tax losses and/or credits expire pursuant to tax rules regarding the carry forward of the unused tax losses;
- Verify that the above is with the same tax authority and based on the same taxable entity;
- Determine whether the past tax losses were a result of specific circumstances that are unlikely to be repeated; and
- Discover if tax planning opportunities are available to the entity that will result in future profits. These may include changes in tax legislation that is phased in over more than one financial period to the benefit of the entity.

It is imperative that the timing of taxable and deductible temporary differences also be considered before creating a deferred tax asset based on unused tax credits.

6 RECOGNITION AND MEASUREMENT OF CURRENT AND DEFERRED TAX

Current taxes payable or recoverable from tax authorities are based on the applicable tax rates at the balance sheet date. Deferred taxes should be measured at the tax rate that is expected to apply when the asset is realized or the liability settled. With respect to the income tax for a current or prior period not yet paid, it is recognized as a tax liability until paid. Any amount paid in excess of any tax obligation is recognized as an asset. The income tax paid in excess or owed to tax authorities is separate from deferred taxes on the company's balance sheet.

When measuring deferred taxes in a jurisdiction, there are different forms of taxation such as income tax, capital gains tax (any capital gains made), or secondary tax on companies (tax payable on the dividends that a company declares) and possibly different tax bases for a balance sheet item (as in the case of government grants influencing the tax base of an asset such as property). In assessing which tax laws should apply, it is dependent on how the related asset or liability will be settled. It would be prudent to use the tax rate and tax base that is consistent with how it is expected the tax base will be recovered or settled.

Although deferred tax assets and liabilities are related to temporary differences expected to be recovered or settled at some future date, neither are discounted to present value in determining the amounts to be booked. Both must be adjusted for changes in tax rates.

Deferred taxes as well as income taxes should always be recognized on the income statement of an entity unless it pertains to:

- Taxes or deferred taxes charged directly to equity, or
- A possible provision for deferred taxes relates to a business combination.

The carrying amount of the deferred tax assets and liabilities should also be assessed. The carrying amounts may change even though there may have been no change in temporary differences during the period evaluated. This can result from:

- Changes in tax rates;
- Reassessments of the recoverability of deferred tax assets; or
- Changes in the expectations for how an asset will be recovered and what influences the deferred tax asset or liability.

All unrecognized deferred tax assets and liabilities must be reassessed at the balance sheet date and measured against the criteria of probable future economic benefits. If such a deferred asset is likely to be recovered, it may be appropriate to recognize the related deferred tax asset.

Different jurisdictions have different requirements for determining tax obligations that can range from different forms of taxation to different tax rates based on taxable income. When comparing financial statements of entities that conduct business in different jurisdictions subject to different tax legislation, the analyst should be cautious in reaching conclusions because of the potentially complex tax rules that may apply.

6.1 Recognition of a Valuation Allowance

Deferred tax assets must be assessed at each balance sheet date. If there is any doubt whether the deferral will be recovered, then the carrying amount should be reduced to the expected recoverable amount. Should circumstances subsequently change and suggest the future will lead to recovery of the deferral, the reduction may be reversed.

Under US GAAP, deferred tax assets are reduced by creating a valuation allowance. Establishing a valuation allowance reduces the deferred tax asset and income in the period in which the allowance is established. Should circumstances change to such an extent that a deferred tax asset valuation allowance may be reduced, the reversal will increase the deferred tax asset and operating income. Because of the subjective judgment involved, an analyst should carefully scrutinize any such changes.

6.2 Recognition of Current and Deferred Tax Charged Directly to Equity

In general, IFRS and US GAAP require that the recognition of deferred tax liabilities and current income tax should be treated similarly to the asset or liability that gave rise to the deferred tax liability or income tax based on accounting treatment. Should an item that gives rise to a deferred tax liability be taken directly to equity, the same should hold true for the resulting deferred tax.

The following are examples of such items:

- Revaluation of property, plant, and equipment (revaluations are not permissible under US GAAP);
- Long-term investments at fair value;
- Changes in accounting policies;
- Errors corrected against the opening balance of retained earnings;
- Initial recognition of an equity component related to complex financial instruments; and
- Exchange rate differences arising from the currency translation procedures for foreign operations.

Whenever it is determined that a deferred tax liability will not be reversed, an adjustment should be made to the liability. The deferred tax liability will be reduced and the amount by which it is reduced should be taken directly to equity. Any deferred taxes related to a business combination must also be recognized in equity.

Depending on the items that gave rise to the deferred tax liabilities, an analyst should exercise judgment regarding whether the taxes should be included with deferred tax liabilities or whether it should be taken directly to equity. It may be more appropriate simply to ignore deferred taxes.

EXAMPLE 5

Taxes Charged Directly to Equity

The following information pertains to Khaleej Company (a hypothetical company). A building owned by Khaleej Company was originally purchased for €1,000,000 on 1 January 20x1. For accounting purposes, buildings are depreciated at 5 percent a year on a straight-line basis, and depreciation for tax purposes is 10 percent a year on a straight-line basis. On the first day of 20x3, the building is revalued at €1,200,000. It is estimated that the remaining useful life of the building from the date of revaluation is 20 years. *Important*: For tax purposes the revaluation of the building is not recognized.

Based on the information provided, the following illustrates the difference in treatment of the building for accounting and tax purposes.

	Carrying Amount of Building	Tax Base of Building
Balance on 1 January 20x1	€1,000,000	€1,000,000
Depreciation 20x1	(50,000)	(100,000)
Balance on 31 December 20x1	€950,000	€900,000
Depreciation 20x2	(50,000)	(100,000)
Balance on 31 December 20x2	€900,000	€800,000
Revaluation on 1 January 20x3	300,000	n/a
Balance on 1 January 20x3	€1,200,000	€800,000
Depreciation 20x3	(60,000)	(100,000)
Balance on 31 December 20x3	€1,140,000	€700,000
Accumulated depreciation		
Balance on 1 January 20x1	€0	€0
Depreciation 20x1	50,000	100,000
Balance on 31 December 20x1	€50,000	€100,000
Depreciation 20x2	50,000	100,000
Balance on 31 December 20x2	€100,000	€200,000
Revaluation at 1 January 20x3	(100,000)	n/a
Balance on 1 January 20x3	€0	€200,000
Depreciation 20x3	60,000	100,000
Balance on 30 November 20x3	€60,000	€300,000

	Carrying Amount	Tax Base
On 31 December 20x1	€950,000	€900,000
On 31 December 20x2	€900,000	€800,000
On 31 December 20x3	€1,140,000	€700,000

31 December 20x1: On 31 December 20x1, different treatments for depreciation expense result in a temporary difference that gives rise to a deferred tax liability. The difference in the tax base and carrying amount of the building was a result of different depreciation amounts for tax and accounting purposes. Depreciation appears on the income statement. For this reason the deferred tax liability will also be reflected on the income statement. If we assume that the applicable tax rate in 20x1 was 40 percent, then the resulting deferred tax liability will be 40% × (€950,000 – €900,000) = €20,000.

31 December 20x2: As of 31 December 20x2, the carrying amount of the building remains greater than the tax base. The temporary difference again gives rise to a deferred tax liability. Again, assuming the applicable tax rate to be 40 percent, the deferred tax liability from the building is 40% × (€900,000 – €800,000) = €40,000.

31 December 20x3: On 31 December 20x3, the carrying amount of the building again exceeds the tax base. This is not the result of disposals or additions, but is a result of the revaluation at the beginning of the 20x3 fiscal year and the different rates of depreciation. The deferred tax liability would seem to be 40%

× (€1,140,000 – €700,000) = €176,000, *but* the treatment is different than it was for the 20x1 and 20x2. In 20x3, revaluation of the building gave rise to a balance sheet equity account, namely "Revaluation Surplus" in the amount of €300,000, which is not recognized for tax purposes.

The deferred tax liability would usually have been calculated as follows:

	20x3	20x2	20x1
Deferred tax liability (closing balance at end of fiscal year)	€176,000	€40,000	€20,000
(Difference between tax base and carrying amount)			
20x1: €(950,000 – 900,000) × 40% = 20,000			
20x2: €(900,000 – 800,000) × 40% = 40,000			
20x3: €(1,140,000 – 700,000) × 40% = 176,000			

The change in the deferred tax liability in 20x1 is €20,000, in 20x2: €20,000 (€40,000 – €20,000) and, it would seem, in 20x3: €136,000 (€176,000 – €40,000). In 20x3, although it would seem that the balance for deferred tax liability should be €176,000, the revaluation is not recognized for tax purposes. Only the portion of the difference between the tax base and carrying amount that is not a result of the revaluation is recognized as giving rise to a deferred tax liability.

The effect of the revaluation surplus and the associated tax effects are accounted for in a direct adjustment to equity. The revaluation surplus is reduced by the tax provision associated with the excess of the fair value over the carry value and it affects retained earnings (€300,000 × 40% = €120,000).

The deferred tax liability that should be reflected on the balance sheet is thus not €176,000 but only €56,000 (€176,000 – €120,000). Given the balance of deferred tax liability at the beginning of the 20x3 fiscal year in the amount of €40,000, the change in the deferred tax liability is only €56,000 – €40,000 = €16,000.

In the future, at the end of each year, an amount equal to the depreciation as a result of the revaluation minus the deferred tax effect will be transferred from the revaluation reserve to retained earnings. In 20x3 this will amount to a portion of depreciation resulting from the revaluation, €15,000 (€300,000 ÷ 20), minus the deferred tax effect of €6,000 (€15,000 × 40%), thus €9,000.

PRESENTATION AND DISCLOSURE

7

We will discuss the presentation and disclosure of income tax related information by way of example. The Consolidated Statements of Operations (Income Statements) and Consolidated Balance Sheets for Micron Technology (MU), a global technology company based in the US, are provided in Exhibits 2 and 3, respectively. Exhibit 4 provides the income tax note disclosures for MU for the 2015, 2016, and 2017 fiscal years.

MU's income tax provision (i.e., income tax expense) for fiscal year 2017 is $114 million (see Exhibit 2). The income tax note disclosure in Exhibit 4 reconciles how the income tax provision was determined beginning with MU's reported income before taxes (shown in Exhibit 4 as $5,196 million for fiscal year 2017). The note disclosure then denotes the income tax provision for 2017 that is current ($153 million), which is then offset by the deferred tax benefit for foreign taxes ($39 million), for a net income tax provision of $114 million. Exhibit 4 further shows a reconciliation of how the income tax provision was derived from the US federal statutory rate. Many public companies comply with this required disclosure by displaying the information in percentage terms, but MU has elected to provide the disclosure in absolute dollar amounts. From this knowledge, for 2017 we can see that the dollar amount shown for US federal income tax provision at the statutory rate ($1,819 million) was determined by multiplying MU's income before taxes by the 35 percent US federal statutory rate ($5,196 × 0.35 = $1,819).

In addition, the note disclosure in Exhibit 4 provides detailed information about the derivation of the deferred tax assets ($766 million for 2017) and deferred tax liabilities ($17 million for 2017). These deferred tax assets are shown separately on MU's consolidated balance sheet for fiscal year 2017 with noncurrent assets (see Exhibit 3), while the deferred tax liabilities are included in other noncurrent liabilities (also see Exhibit 3).

Exhibit 2 Micron Technology, Inc. Consolidated Statements of Operations (Amounts in US$ Millions except Per Share)

For the Year Ended	31 Aug. 2017	1 Sept. 2016	3 Sept. 2015
Net sales	20,322	$12,399	$16,192
Cost of goods sold	11,886	9,894	10,977
Gross margin	8,436	2,505	5,215
Selling, general and administrative	743	659	719
Research and development	1,824	1,617	1,540
Restructure and asset impairments	18	67	3
Other operating (income) expense, net	(17)	(6)	(45)
Operating income	5,868	168	2,998
Interest income (expense), net	(560)	(395)	(336)
Other non-operating income (expense), net	(112)	(54)	(53)
Income tax (provision) benefit	(114)	(19)	(157)
Equity in net income (loss) of equity method investees	8	25	447
Net income (loss) attributable to non-controlling interests	(1)	(1)	—
Net income (loss) attributable to Micron	$5,089	$(276)	$2,899
Earnings (loss) per share:			
Basic	$4.67	$(0.27)	$2.71
Diluted	$4.41	$(0.27)	$2.47
Number of shares used in per share calculations:			
Basic	1,089	1,036	1,070
Diluted	1,154	1,036	1,170

Exhibit 3 Micron Technology, Inc. Consolidated Balance Sheets (Amounts in US$ Millions)

As of	31 Aug. 2017	1 Sept. 2016
Assets		
Cash and equivalents	$5,109	$4,140
Short-term investments	319	258
Receivables	3,759	2,068
Inventories	3,123	2,889
Other current assets	147	140
Total current assets	12,457	9,495
Long-term marketable investments	617	414
Property, plant and equipment, net	19,431	14,686
Equity method investments	16	1,364
Intangible assets, net	387	464
Deferred tax assets	766	657
Other noncurrent assets	1,662	460
Total assets	$35,336	$27,540
Liabilities and shareholders' equity		
Accounts payable and accrued expenses	$3,664	$3,879
Deferred income	408	200
Current debt	1,262	756
Total current liabilities	5,334	4,835
Long-term debt	9,872	9,154
Other noncurrent liabilities	639	623
Total liabilities	15,845	14,612
Redeemable convertible notes	21	—
Micron shareholder's equity		
Common stock of $0.10 par value, 3,000 shares authorized, 1,116 shares issued and 1,112 shares outstanding (1,094 issued and 1,040 outstanding as of September 1, 2016)	112	109
Additional capital	8,287	7,736
Retained earnings	10,260	5,299
Treasury stock, 4 shares held (54 as of September 1, 2016)	(67)	(1,029)
Accumulated other comprehensive income (loss)	29	(35)
Total Micron shareholders' equity	18,621	12,080
Noncontrolling interests in subsidiaries	849	848
Total equity	19,470	12,928
Total liabilities and shareholders' equity	35,336	$27,540

Exhibit 4 Micron Technology, Inc. Income Taxes Note to the Consolidated Financial Statements

Income (loss) before taxes and the income tax (provision) benefit consisted of the following:

(in US$ Millions)	2017	2016	2015
Income (loss) before income taxes, net income (loss) attributable to noncontrolling interests, and equity in net income (loss) of equity method investees			
Foreign	$5,252	$(353)	$2,431
US	(56)	72	178
	$5,196	$(281)	$2,609
Income tax (provision) benefit:			
Current:			
Foreign	$(152)	$(27)	$(93)
State	(1)	(1)	(1)
US federal	—	—	6
	(153)	(28)	(88)
Deferred:			
US federal	—	39	15
State	—	2	1
Foreign	39	(32)	(85)
	39	9	(69)
Income tax (provision)	$(114)	$(19)	$(157)

The company's income tax (provision) computed using the US federal statutory rate and the company's income tax (provision) benefit is reconciled as follows:

(US$ Millions)	2017	2016	2015
US federal income tax (provision) benefit at statutory rate	$(1,819)	$98	$(913)
Foreign tax rate differential	1,571	(300)	515
Change in valuation allowance	64	63	260
Change in unrecognized tax benefits	12	52	(118)
Tax credits	66	48	53
Noncontrolling investment transactions	—	—	57
Other	(8)	20	(11)
Income tax (provision) benefit	(114)	$(19)	$(157)

State taxes reflect investment tax credits of $233 million as at 31 August 2017. Deferred income taxes reflect the net tax effects of temporary differences between the bases of assets and liabilities for financial reporting and income tax purposes. The company's deferred tax assets and liabilities consist of the following as of the end of the periods shown below:

(US$ Millions)	2017	2016
Deferred tax assets:		
Net operating loss and tax credit carryforwards	$3,426	$3,014

Exhibit 4 (Continued)

(US$ Millions)	2017	2016
Accrued salaries, wages, and benefits	211	142
Other accrued liabilities	59	76
Other	86	65
Gross deferred assets	3,782	3,297
Less valuation allowance	(2,321)	(2,107)
Deferred tax assets, net of valuation allowance	1,461	1,190
Deferred tax liabilities:		
Debt discount	(145)	(170)
Property, plant, and equipment	(300)	(135)
Unremitted earnings on certain subsidiaries	(123)	(121)
Product and process technology	(85)	(81)
Other	(59)	(28)
Deferred tax liabilities	(712)	(535)
Net deferred tax assets	$749	$655
Reported as:		
Current deferred tax assets (included in other current assets)	$—	$—
Deferred tax assets	766	657
Current deferred tax liabilities (included in accounts payable and accrued expenses)		—
Deferred tax liabilities (included in other noncurrent liabilities)	(17)	(2)
Net deferred tax assets	$749	$655

The company has a valuation allowance against substantially all of its US net deferred tax assets. As of 31 August 2017, the company had aggregate US tax net operating loss carryforwards of $3.88 billion and unused US tax credit carryforwards of $416 million. The company also has unused state tax net operating loss carryforwards of $1.95 billion and unused state tax credits of $233 million. The net operating loss carryforwards and the tax credit carryforwards expire between 2018 to 2037.

The changes in valuation allowance of $64 million and $63 million in 2017 and 2016, respectively, are primarily a result of uncertainties of realizing certain US and foreign net operating losses and certain tax credit carryforwards.

Provision has been made for deferred taxes on undistributed earnings of non-US subsidiaries to the extent that dividend payments from such companies are expected to result in additional tax liability. Remaining undistributed earnings of $12.91 billion as of 31 August 2017 have been indefinitely reinvested. Determination of the amount of unrecognized deferred tax liability on these unremitted earnings is not practicable.

EXAMPLE 6

Financial Analysis Example

Use the financial statement information and disclosures provided by MU in Exhibits 2, 3, and 4 to answer the following questions:

1 MU discloses a valuation allowance of $2,321 million (see Exhibit 4) against gross deferred assets of $3,782 million in 2017. Does the existence of this valuation allowance have any implications concerning MU's future earnings prospects?

2 How would MU's deferred tax assets and deferred tax liabilities be affected if the federal statutory tax rate was changed to 21 percent?

3 How would reported earnings have been affected if MU were not using a valuation allowance?

4 How would MU's $3.88 billion in net operating loss carryforwards in 2017 (see Exhibit 4) affect the valuation that an acquiring company would be willing to offer?

5 Under what circumstances should the analyst consider MU's deferred tax liability as debt or as equity? Under what circumstances should the analyst exclude MU's deferred tax liability from both debt and equity when calculating the debt-to-equity ratio?

Solution to 1:

According to Exhibit 4, MU's deferred tax assets expire gradually until 2037 (2018 to 2037 for the net operating loss carryforwards and the tax credit carryforwards).

Because the company is still relatively young, it is likely that most of these expirations occur toward the end of that period. Because cumulative US tax net operating loss carryforwards total $3.88 billion, the valuation allowance could imply that MU is not reasonably expected to earn $3.88 billion over the next 20 years. However, as we can see in Exhibit 2, MU earned a profit for 2017 and 2015, thereby showing that the allowance could be adjusted downward if the company continues to generate profits in the future, and making it more likely than not that the deferred tax asset would be recognized.

Solution to 2:

MU's total deferred tax assets exceed total deferred tax liabilities by $749 million. A change in the federal statutory tax rate to 21 percent from the current rate of 35 percent would make these net deferred assets less valuable. Also, because it is possible that the deferred tax asset valuation allowance could be adjusted downward in the future (see discussion to solution 1), the impact could be far greater in magnitude.

Solution to 3:

The disclosure in Exhibit 4 shows that the increase in the valuation allowance increased the income tax provision as reported on the income statement by $64 million in 2017. Additional potential reductions in the valuation allowance could similarly reduce reported income taxes (actual income taxes would not be affected by a valuation allowance established for financial reporting) in future years (see discussion to solution 1).

Solution to 4:

If an acquiring company is profitable, it may be able to use MU's tax loss carryforwards to offset its own tax liabilities. The value to an acquirer would be the present value of the carryforwards, based on the acquirer's tax rate and expected timing of realization. The higher the acquiring company's tax rate, and the more profitable the acquirer, the sooner it would be able to benefit. Therefore, an acquirer with a high current tax rate would theoretically be willing to pay more than an acquirer with a lower tax rate.

Solution to 5:

The analyst should classify the deferred tax liability as debt if the liability is expected to reverse with subsequent tax payment. If the liability is not expected to reverse, there is no expectation of a cash outflow and the liability should be treated as equity. By way of example, future company losses may preclude the payment of any income taxes, or changes in tax laws could result in taxes that are never paid. The deferred tax liability should be excluded from both debt and equity when both the amounts and timing of tax payments resulting from the reversals of temporary differences are uncertain.

COMPARISON OF IFRS AND US GAAP

8

As mentioned earlier, though IFRS and US GAAP follow similar conventions on many tax issues, there are some notable differences. Exhibit 5 summarizes many of the key similarities and differences between IFRS and US GAAP. Though both frameworks require a provision for deferred taxes, there are differences in the methodologies.

Exhibit 5 Deferred Income Tax Issues IFRS and US GAAP Methodology Similarities and Differences

IFRS	US GAAP
Introduction	
The objective in accounting for income taxes is to recognize the amount of taxes currently payable or refundable and deferred taxes. Income tax expense is the current tax expense (or recovery) plus the period change in deferred taxes (net of tax arising from a business combination or recorded outside profit or loss).	Similar to IFRS.
Unpaid taxes for current and prior periods are recognized as a liability, and an asset is recognised if the amount already paid exceeds the amount due. A prior tax loss benefit used to recover previous period current tax is also an asset.	The approach to calculating current taxes is similar to IFRS with some exceptions, such as the treatment of taxes on the elimination of intercompany profits.
In general, deferred taxes are recognized using an asset and liability approach which focuses on temporary differences arising between the tax base of an asset or liability and its carrying amount in the statement of financial position. Deferred taxes are recognized for the future tax consequences of events that have been recognized in an entity's financial statements or tax returns.	US GAAP also follows an asset and liability approach to calculating deferred taxes, although there are some differences in the application relative to IFRS.

(continued)

Exhibit 5 (Continued)

IFRS	US GAAP
Deferred taxes are not recognized for: ■ The initial recognition of goodwill ■ The initial recognition of an asset or liability in a non-business combination transaction and where accounting profit or taxable profit (tax loss) is not affected ■ Taxable temporary differences from investments in subsidiaries/branches/ associates, and interests in joint ventures in which the parent etc. is able to control the timing of the reversal of the temporary difference, and it is probable that the temporary difference will not reverse in the foreseeable future	Deferred taxes are not recognized for: ■ Goodwill for which amortization is not deductible for tax purposes ■ Unlike IFRS, US GAAP does not have a similar exception ■ An excess of the amount for the financial reporting over the tax basis of an investment in a foreign subsidiary or a foreign corporate joint venture that is essentially permanent in duration, unless it becomes apparent that those temporary differences will reverse in the foreseeable future. Unlike IFRS, this exception does not apply to domestic subsidiaries and corporate joint venture and investments in equity investees. Unlike IFRS, recognition of deferred taxes is prohibited for differences that are remeasured from the local currency into the functional currency using historical exchange rates and that result from changes in exchange rates or indexing for tax purposes.
Deferred taxes should be recognized for the difference between the carrying amount determined by using the historical exchange rate and the relevant tax base, which may have been affected by exchange rate changes or tax indexing.	
Recognition and measurement	
Current tax liabilities and assets for the current and prior periods are measured at amounts expected to be paid to (recovered from) the taxation authorities based on tax rates (and tax laws) that have been enacted or substantially enacted by the end of the reporting period. Deferred tax assets are measured at the tax rates that are expected to apply when the asset is realized or the liability is settled, based on tax rates (and tax laws) that have been enacted or substantively enacted by the end of the reporting period.	Similar to IFRS. Measurement of current and deferred tax assets and liabilities is based on enacted tax law. Deferred tax assets and liabilities are measured using enacted tax rate(s) expected to apply to taxable income in periods in which deferred tax is expected to be settled or realized. Unlike IFRS, use of substantially enacted tax rates is not permitted.
Deferred tax assets are recognized to the extent that it is probable (more likely than not) that taxable profit will be available to utilize the deductible temporary difference or carryforward of unused tax losses or tax credits. End of reporting period reviews may reduce the carrying amount if sufficient taxable profit is no longer probable such as to allow the utilization benefit of all or part of that deferred tax asset, and any such reduction is reversed if it subsequently becomes probable again.	Unlike IFRS, deferred tax assets are recognized in full and reduced by a valuation allowance if it is more likely than not that some portion or all of the deferred tax assets will not be realized.
Current and deferred taxes are recognized outside profit or loss if the tax relates to items that are recognized, in the same or a different period, in other comprehensive income (OCI), or directly to equity.	Similar to IFRS, the tax effects of certain items occurring during the year are charged or credited directly to OCI or to related components of shareholders' equity.
Deferred tax assets and liabilities are not discounted.	Similar to IFRS.
Presentation and disclosure	

Exhibit 5 (Continued)

IFRS	US GAAP
Deferred tax assets and liabilities are offset if the entity has a legally enforceable right to offset current tax assets against current tax liabilities and the deferred tax assets and deferred tax liabilities relate to income taxes levied by the same taxing authority on either the same taxable entity, or different taxable entities that intend either to settle current tax assets and liabilities on a net basis or to simultaneously realize/settle the asset/liability.	All deferred taxes are offset and presented as a single amount.
Deferred tax assets and liabilities are presented as separate line items in the statement of financial position. If a classified statement of financial position is used, deferred taxes are classified as noncurrent.	Deferred tax assets and deferred tax liabilities are presented as noncurrent in a classified statement of financial position, which aligns with IFRS.
All entities must disclose an explanation of the relationship between tax expense and accounting profit using either or both of the following formats: ■ A numerical reconciliation between tax expense (income) and the product of accounting profit multiplied by the applicable tax rate(s) including disclosure of the basis on which the applicable rate is computed. ■ A numerical reconciliation between the average effective tax rate and the applicable tax rate, including disclosure of the basis on which the applicable tax rate is computed.	Public companies must disclose a reconciliation using percentages or dollar amounts of the reported amount of income tax expense attributable to continuing operations for the year to that amount of income tax expense that would result from applying domestic federal statutory tax rates to pretax income from continuing operations. Nonpublic enterprises must disclose the nature of significant reconciling items but may omit a numerical reconciliation.

Sources: IFRS: IAS 12 and 32. US GAAP: ASC 740. "Comparison between US GAAP and IFRS Standards," Section 5.3 Taxation, Grant Thornton, April 2017. "IFRS and US GAAP: similarities and differences", PricewaterhouseCoopers LLC, 2018.

SUMMARY

Income taxes are a significant category of expense for profitable companies. Analyzing income tax expenses is often difficult for the analyst because there are many permanent and temporary timing differences between the accounting that is used for income tax reporting and the accounting that is used for financial reporting on company financial statements. The financial statements and notes to the financial statements of a company provide important information that the analyst needs to assess financial performance and to compare a company's financial performance with other companies. Key concepts in this reading are as follows:

- Differences between the recognition of revenue and expenses for tax and accounting purposes may result in taxable income differing from accounting profit. The discrepancy is a result of different treatments of certain income and expenditure items.
- The tax base of an asset is the amount that will be deductible for tax purposes as an expense in the calculation of taxable income as the company expenses the tax basis of the asset. If the economic benefit will not be taxable, the tax base of the asset will be equal to the carrying amount of the asset.

- The tax base of a liability is the carrying amount of the liability less any amounts that will be deductible for tax purposes in the future. With respect to revenue received in advance, the tax base of such a liability is the carrying amount less any amount of the revenue that will not be taxable in the future.
- Temporary differences arise from recognition of differences in the tax base and carrying amount of assets and liabilities. The creation of a deferred tax asset or liability as a result of a temporary difference will only be allowed if the difference reverses itself at some future date and to the extent that it is expected that the balance sheet item will create future economic benefits for the company.
- Permanent differences result in a difference in tax and financial reporting of revenue (expenses) that will not be reversed at some future date. Because it will not be reversed at a future date, these differences do not constitute temporary differences and do not give rise to a deferred tax asset or liability.
- Current taxes payable or recoverable are based on the applicable tax rates on the balance sheet date of an entity; in contrast, deferred taxes should be measured at the tax rate that is expected to apply when the asset is realized or the liability settled.
- All unrecognized deferred tax assets and liabilities must be reassessed on the appropriate balance sheet date and measured against their probable future economic benefit.
- Deferred tax assets must be assessed for their prospective recoverability. If it is probable that they will not be recovered at all or partly, the carrying amount should be reduced. Under US GAAP, this is done through the use of a valuation allowance.

PRACTICE PROBLEMS

1 Using the straight-line method of depreciation for reporting purposes and accelerated depreciation for tax purposes would *most likely* result in a:

A valuation allowance.

B deferred tax asset.

C temporary difference.

2 In early 2018 Sanborn Company must pay the tax authority €37,000 on the income it earned in 2017. This amount was recorded on the company's 31 December 2017 financial statements as:

A taxes payable.

B income tax expense.

C a deferred tax liability.

3 Income tax expense reported on a company's income statement equals taxes payable, plus the net increase in:

A deferred tax assets and deferred tax liabilities.

B deferred tax assets, less the net increase in deferred tax liabilities.

C deferred tax liabilities, less the net increase in deferred tax assets.

4 Analysts should treat deferred tax liabilities that are expected to reverse as:

A equity.

B liabilities.

C neither liabilities nor equity.

5 Deferred tax liabilities should be treated as equity when:

A they are not expected to reverse.

B the timing of tax payments is uncertain.

C the amount of tax payments is uncertain.

6 When both the timing and amount of tax payments are uncertain, analysts should treat deferred tax liabilities as:

A equity.

B liabilities.

C neither liabilities nor equity.

7 When accounting standards require recognition of an expense that is not permitted under tax laws, the result is a:

A deferred tax liability.

B temporary difference.

C permanent difference.

8 When certain expenditures result in tax credits that directly reduce taxes, the company will *most likely* record:

A a deferred tax asset.

B a deferred tax liability.

C no deferred tax asset or liability.

© 2019 CFA Institute. All rights reserved.

9 When accounting standards require an asset to be expensed immediately but tax rules require the item to be capitalized and amortized, the company will *most likely* record:

A a deferred tax asset.

B a deferred tax liability.

C no deferred tax asset or liability.

10 A company incurs a capital expenditure that may be amortized over five years for accounting purposes, but over four years for tax purposes. The company will *most likely* record:

A a deferred tax asset.

B a deferred tax liability.

C no deferred tax asset or liability.

11 A company receives advance payments from customers that are immediately taxable but will not be recognized for accounting purposes until the company fulfills its obligation. The company will *most likely* record:

A a deferred tax asset.

B a deferred tax liability.

C no deferred tax asset or liability.

The following information relates to Questions 12–14

Note I
Income Taxes

The components of earnings before income taxes are as follows ($ thousands):

	Year 3	Year 2	Year 1
Earnings before income taxes:			
United States	$88,157	$75,658	$59,973
Foreign	116,704	113,509	94,760
Total	$204,861	$189,167	$154,733

The components of the provision for income taxes are as follows ($ thousands):

	Year 3	Year 2	Year 1
Income taxes			
Current:			
Federal	$30,632	$22,031	$18,959
Foreign	28,140	27,961	22,263
	$58,772	$49,992	$41,222
Deferred:			
Federal	($4,752)	$5,138	$2,336
Foreign	124	1,730	621

	Year 3	Year 2	Year 1
	(4,628)	6,868	2,957
Total	$54,144	$56,860	$44,179

12 In Year 3, the company's US GAAP income statement recorded a provision for income taxes *closest* to:

A $30,632.

B $54,144.

C $58,772.

13 The company's effective tax rate was *highest* in:

A Year 1.

B Year 2.

C Year 3.

14 Compared to the company's effective tax rate on US income, its effective tax rate on foreign income was:

A lower in each year presented.

B higher in each year presented.

C higher in some periods and lower in others.

---

15 Zimt AG presents its financial statements in accordance with US GAAP. In Year 3, Zimt discloses a valuation allowance of $1,101 against total deferred tax assets of $19,201. In Year 2, Zimt disclosed a valuation allowance of $1,325 against total deferred tax assets of $17,325. The change in the valuation allowance *most likely* indicates that Zimt's:

A deferred tax liabilities were reduced in Year 3.

B expectations of future earning power has increased.

C expectations of future earning power has decreased.

16 Cinnamon, Inc. recorded a total deferred tax asset in Year 3 of $12,301, offset by a $12,301 valuation allowance. Cinnamon *most likely*:

A fully utilized the deferred tax asset in Year 3.

B has an equal amount of deferred tax assets and deferred tax liabilities.

C expects not to earn any taxable income before the deferred tax asset expires.

The following information relates to Questions 17–19

The tax effects of temporary differences that give rise to deferred tax assets and liabilities are as follows ($ thousands):

	Year 3	Year 2
Deferred tax assets:		
Accrued expenses	$8,613	$7,927
Tax credit and net operating loss carryforwards	2,288	2,554

(continued)

	Year 3	Year 2
LIFO and inventory reserves	5,286	4,327
Other	2,664	2,109
Deferred tax assets	18,851	16,917
Valuation allowance	(1,245)	(1,360)
Net deferred tax assets	$17,606	$15,557
Deferred tax liabilities:		
Depreciation and amortization	$(27,338)	$(29,313)
Compensation and retirement plans	(3,831)	(8,963)
Other	(1,470)	(764)
Deferred tax liabilities	(32,639)	(39,040)
Net deferred tax liability	($15,033)	($23,483)

17 A reduction in the statutory tax rate would *most likely* benefit the company's:

A income statement and balance sheet.

B income statement but not the balance sheet.

C balance sheet but not the income statement.

18 If the valuation allowance had been the same in Year 3 as it was in Year 2, the company would have reported $115 *higher*:

A net income.

B deferred tax assets.

C income tax expense.

19 Compared to the provision for income taxes in Year 3, the company's cash tax payments were:

A lower.

B higher.

C the same.

The following information relates to Questions 20–22

A company's provision for income taxes resulted in effective tax rates attributable to loss from continuing operations before cumulative effect of change in accounting principles that varied from the statutory federal income tax rate of 34 percent, as summarized in the table below.

Year Ended 30 June	Year 3	Year 2	Year 1
Expected federal income tax expense (benefit) from continuing operations at 34 percent	($112,000)	$768,000	$685,000
Expenses not deductible for income tax purposes	357,000	32,000	51,000
State income taxes, net of federal benefit	132,000	22,000	100,000

Year Ended 30 June	Year 3	Year 2	Year 1
Change in valuation allowance for deferred tax assets	(150,000)	(766,000)	(754,000)
Income tax expense	$227,000	$56,000	$82,000

20 In Year 3, the company's net income (loss) was *closest* to:

A ($217,000).

B ($329,000).

C ($556,000).

21 The $357,000 adjustment in Year 3 *most likely* resulted in:

A an increase in deferred tax assets.

B an increase in deferred tax liabilities.

C no change to deferred tax assets and liabilities.

22 Over the three years presented, changes in the valuation allowance for deferred tax assets were *most likely* indicative of:

A decreased prospect for future profitability.

B increased prospects for future profitability.

C assets being carried at a higher value than their tax base.

SOLUTIONS

1 C is correct. Because the differences between tax and financial accounting will correct over time, the resulting deferred tax liability, for which the expense was charged to the income statement but the tax authority has not yet been paid, will be a temporary difference. A valuation allowance would only arise if there was doubt over the company's ability to earn sufficient income in the future to require paying the tax.

2 A is correct. The taxes a company must pay in the immediate future are taxes payable.

3 C is correct. Higher reported tax expense relative to taxes paid will increase the deferred tax liability, whereas lower reported tax expense relative to taxes paid increases the deferred tax asset.

4 B is correct. If the liability is expected to reverse (and thus require a cash tax payment) the deferred tax represents a future liability.

5 A is correct. If the liability will not reverse, there will be no required tax payment in the future and the "liability" should be treated as equity.

6 C is correct. The deferred tax liability should be excluded from both debt and equity when both the amounts and timing of tax payments resulting from the reversals of temporary differences are uncertain.

7 C is correct. Accounting items that are not deductible for tax purposes will not be reversed and thus result in permanent differences.

8 C is correct. Tax credits that directly reduce taxes are a permanent difference, and permanent differences do not give rise to deferred tax.

9 A is correct. The capitalization will result in an asset with a positive tax base and zero carrying value. The amortization means the difference is temporary. Because there is a temporary difference on an asset resulting in a higher tax base than carrying value, a deferred tax asset is created.

10 B is correct. The difference is temporary, and the tax base will be lower (because of more rapid amortization) than the carrying value of the asset. The result will be a deferred tax liability.

11 A is correct. The advances represent a liability for the company. The carrying value of the liability exceeds the tax base (which is now zero). A deferred tax asset arises when the carrying value of a liability exceeds its tax base.

12 B is correct. The income tax provision in Year 3 was $54,144, consisting of $58,772 in current income taxes, of which $4,628 were deferred.

13 B is correct. The effective tax rate of 30.1 percent ($56,860/$189,167) was higher than the effective rates in Year 2 and Year 3.

14 A is correct. In Year 3 the effective tax rate on foreign operations was 24.2 percent [($28,140 + $124)/$116,704] and the effective US tax rate was [($30,632 – $4,752)/$88,157] = 29.4 percent. In Year 2 the effective tax rate on foreign operations was 26.2 percent and the US rate was 35.9 percent. In Year 1 the foreign rate was 24.1 percent and the US rate was 35.5 percent.

15 B is correct. The valuation allowance is taken against deferred tax assets to represent uncertainty that future taxable income will be sufficient to fully utilize the assets. By decreasing the allowance, Zimt is signaling greater likelihood that future earnings will be offset by the deferred tax asset.

16 C is correct. The valuation allowance is taken when the company will "more likely than not" fail to earn sufficient income to offset the deferred tax asset. Because the valuation allowance equals the asset, by extension the company expects *no* taxable income prior to the expiration of the deferred tax assets.

17 A is correct. A lower tax rate would increase net income on the income statement, and because the company has a net deferred tax liability, the net liability position on the balance sheet would also improve (be smaller).

18 C is correct. The reduction in the valuation allowance resulted in a corresponding reduction in the income tax provision.

19 B is correct. The net deferred tax liability was smaller in Year 3 than it was in Year 2, indicating that in addition to meeting the tax payments provided for in Year 3 the company also paid taxes that had been deferred in prior periods.

20 C is correct. The income tax provision at the statutory rate of 34 percent is a benefit of $112,000, suggesting that the pre-tax income was a loss of $112,000/0.34 = ($329,412). The income tax provision was $227,000. ($329,412) – $227,000 = ($556,412).

21 C is correct. Accounting expenses that are not deductible for tax purposes result in a permanent difference, and thus do not give rise to deferred taxes.

22 B is correct. Over the three-year period, changes in the valuation allowance reduced cumulative income taxes by $1,670,000. The reductions to the valuation allowance were a result of the company being "more likely than not" to earn sufficient taxable income to offset the deferred tax assets.

READING

28

Non-Current (Long-Term) Liabilities

by Elizabeth A. Gordon, PhD, MBA, CPA, and Elaine Henry, PhD, CFA

Elizabeth A. Gordon, PhD, MBA, CPA, is at Temple University (USA). Elaine Henry, PhD, CFA, is at Stevens Institute of Technology (USA).

LEARNING OUTCOMES

Mastery	*The candidate should be able to:*
☐	**a.** determine the initial recognition, initial measurement and subsequent measurement of bonds;
☐	**b.** describe the effective interest method and calculate interest expense, amortisation of bond discounts/premiums, and interest payments;
☐	**c.** explain the derecognition of debt;
☐	**d.** describe the role of debt covenants in protecting creditors;
☐	**e.** describe the financial statement presentation of and disclosures relating to debt;
☐	**f.** explain motivations for leasing assets instead of purchasing them;
☐	**g.** explain the financial reporting of leases from a lessee's perspective;
☐	**h.** explain the financial reporting of leases from a lessor's perspective;
☐	**i.** compare the presentation and disclosure of defined contribution and defined benefit pension plans;
☐	**j.** calculate and interpret leverage and coverage ratios.

Note: Changes in accounting standards as well as new rulings and/or pronouncements issued after the publication of the readings on financial reporting and analysis may cause some of the information in these readings to become dated. Candidates are *not* responsible for anything that occurs after the readings were published. In addition, candidates are expected to be familiar with the analytical frameworks contained in the readings, as well as the implications of alternative accounting methods for financial analysis and valuation discussed in the readings. Candidates are also responsible for the content of accounting standards, but not for the actual reference numbers. Finally, candidates should be aware that certain ratios may be defined and calculated differently. When alternative ratio definitions exist and no specific definition is given, candidates should use the ratio definitions emphasized in the readings.

© 2019 CFA Institute. All rights reserved.

1 INTRODUCTION

A non-current liability (long-term liability) broadly represents a probable sacrifice of economic benefits in periods generally greater than one year in the future. Common types of **non-current liabilities** reported in a company's financial statements include long-term debt (e.g., bonds payable, long-term notes payable), leases, pension liabilities, and deferred tax liabilities. This reading focuses on bonds payable, leases, and pension liabilities.

This reading is organised as follows. Section 2 describes and illustrates the accounting for long-term bonds, including the issuance of bonds, the recording of interest expense and interest payments, the amortisation of any discount or premium, the derecognition of debt, and the disclosure of information about debt financings. In discussing the financial statement effects and analyses of these issues, we focus on solvency and coverage ratios. Section 3 discusses leases, including benefits of leasing and accounting for leases by both lessees and lessors. Section 4 provides an introduction to pension accounting and the resulting non-current liabilities. Section 5 discusses the use of leverage and coverage ratios in evaluating solvency. Section 6 concludes and summarises the reading.

2 BONDS PAYABLE

This section discusses accounting for bonds payable—a common form of long-term debt. In some contexts (e.g., some government debt obligations), the word "bond" is used only for a debt security with a maturity of 10 years or longer; "note" refers to a debt security with a maturity between 2 and 10 years; and "bill" refers to a debt security with a maturity of less than 2 years. In this reading, we use the terms bond and note interchangeably because the accounting treatments of bonds payable and long-term notes payable are similar. In the following sections, we discuss bond issuance (initial recognition and measurement); bond amortisation, interest expense, and interest payments; market rates and fair value (subsequent measurement); repayment of bonds, including retirements and redemptions (derecognition); and other issues concerning disclosures related to debt. We also discuss debt covenants.

2.1 Accounting for Bond Issuance

Bonds are contractual promises made by a company (or other borrowing entity) to pay cash in the future to its lenders (i.e., bondholders) in exchange for receiving cash in the present. The terms of a bond contract are contained in a document called an indenture. The cash or sales proceeds received by a company when it issues bonds is based on the value (price) of the bonds at the time of issue; the price at the time of issue is determined as the present value of the future cash payments promised by the company in the bond agreement.

Ordinarily, bonds contain promises of two types of future cash payments: 1) the face value of the bonds, and 2) periodic interest payments. The **face value** of the bonds is the amount of cash payable by the company to the bondholders when the bonds mature. The face value is also referred to as the principal, par value, stated value, or maturity value. The date of maturity of the bonds (the date on which the face value is paid to bondholders) is stated in the bond contract and typically is a number of years in the future. Periodic interest payments are made based on the interest rate promised in the bond contract applied to the bonds' face value. The interest rate promised in the contract, which is the rate used to calculate the periodic interest payments, is referred to as the **coupon rate**, nominal rate, or stated rate. Similarly, the periodic interest payment is referred to as the coupon payment or simply the coupon. For fixed rate bonds (the primary focus of our discussion here), the coupon rate remains unchanged throughout the life of the bonds. The frequency with which interest payments are made is also stated in the bond contract. For example, bonds paying interest semi-annually will make two interest payments per year.[1]

The future cash payments are discounted to the present to arrive at the market value of the bonds. The **market rate of interest** is the rate demanded by purchasers of the bonds given the risks associated with future cash payment obligations of the particular bond issue. The market rate of interest at the time of issue often differs from the coupon rate because of interest rate fluctuations that occur between the time the issuer establishes the coupon rate and the day the bonds are actually available to investors. If the market rate of interest when the bonds are issued equals the coupon rate, the market value (price) of the bonds will equal the face value of the bonds. Thus, ignoring issuance costs, the issuing company will receive sales proceeds (cash) equal to the face value of the bonds. When a bond is issued at a price equal to its face value, the bond is said to have been issued at par.

If the coupon rate when the bonds are issued is higher than the market rate, the market value of the bonds—and thus the amount of cash the company receives—will be higher than the face value of the bonds. In other words, the bonds will sell at a premium to face value because they are offering an attractive coupon rate compared to current market rates. If the coupon rate is lower than the market rate, the market value and thus the sale proceeds from the bonds will be less than the face value of the bonds; the bond will sell at a discount to face value. The market rate at the time of issuance is the **effective interest rate** or borrowing rate that the company incurs on the debt. The effective interest rate is the discount rate that equates the present value of the two types of promised future cash payments to their selling price. For the issuing company, interest expense reported for the bonds in the financial statements is based on the effective interest rate.

On the issuing company's statement of cash flows, the cash received (sales proceeds) from issuing bonds is reported as a financing cash inflow. On the issuing company's balance sheet at the time of issue, bonds payable normally are measured and reported at the sales proceeds. In other words, the bonds payable are initially reported at the face value of the bonds minus any discount, or plus any premium.

Using a three-step approach, the following two examples illustrate accounting for bonds issued at face value and then accounting for bonds issued at a discount to face value. Accounting for bonds issued at a premium involves steps similar to the steps followed in the examples below. For simplicity, these examples assume a flat interest rate yield curve (i.e., that the market rate of interest is the same for each period). More-precise bond valuations use the interest rate applicable to each time period in which a payment of interest or principal occurs.

EXAMPLE 1

Bonds Issued at Face Value

Debond Corp. (a hypothetical company) issues £1,000,000 worth of five-year bonds, dated 1 January 2018, when the market interest rate on bonds of comparable risk and terms is 5 percent per annum. The bonds pay 5 percent interest annually on 31 December. What are the sales proceeds of the bonds when issued, and how is the issuance reflected in the financial statements?

1 Interest rates are stated on an annual basis regardless of the frequency of payment.

Solution:

Calculating the value of the bonds at issuance and thus the sales proceeds involves three steps: 1) identifying key features of the bonds and the market interest rate, 2) determining future cash outflows, and 3) discounting the future cash flows to the present.

First, identify key features of the bonds and the market interest rate necessary to determine sales proceeds:

Face value (principal):	£1,000,000	
Time to maturity:	5 years	
Coupon rate:	5%	
Market rate at issuance:	5%	
Frequency of interest payments:	annual	
Interest payment:	£50,000	Each annual interest payment is the face value times the coupon rate (£1,000,000 × 5%). If interest is paid other than annually, adjust the interest rate to match the interest payment period (e.g., divide the annual coupon rate by two for semi-annual interest payments).

Second, determine future cash outflows. Debond will pay bondholders £1,000,000 when the bonds mature in five years. On 31 December of each year until the bonds mature, Debond will make an interest payment of £50,000.

Third, sum the present value[2] of the future payments of interest and principal to obtain the value of the bonds and thus the sales proceeds from issuing the bonds. In this example, the sum is £1,000,000 = (£216,474 + £783,526).

Date	Interest Payment	Present Value at Market Rate (5%)	Face Value Payment	Present Value at Market Rate (5%)	Total Present Value
31 December 2018	£50,000	£47,619			
31 December 2019	50,000	45,352			
31 December 2020	50,000	43,192			
31 December 2021	50,000	41,135			
31 December 2022	50,000	39,176	£1,000,000	£783,526	
Total		£216,474		£783,526	£1,000,000
					Sales Proceeds

The sales proceeds of the bonds when issued are £1,000,000. There is no discount or premium because these bonds are issued at face value. The issuance is reflected on the balance sheet as an increase of cash and an increase in a long-term liability, bonds payable, of £1,000,000. The issuance is reflected in the statement of cash flows as a financing cash inflow of £1,000,000.

The price of bonds is often expressed as a percentage of face value. For example, the price of bonds issued at par, as in Example 1, is 100 (i.e., 100 percent of face value). In Example 2, in which bonds are issued at a discount, the price is 95.79 (i.e., 95.79 percent of face value).

2 Alternative ways to calculate the present value include 1) to treat the five annual interest payments as an annuity and use the formula for finding the present value of an annuity and then add the present value of the principal payment, or 2) to use a financial calculator to calculate the total present value.

EXAMPLE 2

Bonds Issued at a Discount

Debond Corp. issues £1,000,000 worth of five-year bonds, dated 1 January 2018, when the market interest rate on bonds of comparable risk and terms is 6 percent. The bonds pay 5 percent interest annually on 31 December. What are the sales proceeds of the bonds when issued, and how is the issuance reflected in the financial statements?

Solution:

The key features of the bonds and the market interest rate are:

Face value (principal):	£1,000,000	
Time to maturity:	5 years	
Coupon rate:	5%	
Market rate at issuance:	6%	
Frequency of interest payments:	annual	
Interest payment:	£50,000	Each annual interest payment is the face value times the coupon rate (£1,000,000 × 5%).

The future cash outflows (interest payments and face value payment), the present value of the future cash outflows, and the total present value are:

Date	Interest Payment	Present Value at Market Rate (6%)	Face Value Payment	Present Value at Market Rate (6%)	Total Present Value
31 December 2018	£50,000	£47,170			
31 December 2019	50,000	44,500			
31 December 2020	50,000	41,981			
31 December 2021	50,000	39,605			
31 December 2022	50,000	37,363	£1,000,000	£747,258	
Total		£210,618		£747,258	£957,876
					Sales Proceeds

The sales proceeds of the bonds when issued are £957,876. The bonds sell at a discount of £42,124 = (£1,000,000 – £957,876) because the market rate when the bonds are issued (6 percent) is greater than the bonds' coupon rate (5 percent). The issuance is reflected on the balance sheet as an increase of cash and an increase in a long-term liability, bonds payable, of £957,876. The bonds payable is composed of the face value of £1,000,000 minus a discount of £42,124. The issuance is reflected in the statement of cash flows as a financing cash inflow of £957,876.

In Example 2, the bonds were issued at a discount to face value because the bonds' coupon rate of 5 percent was less than the market rate. Bonds are issued at a premium to face value when the bonds' coupon rate exceeds the market rate.

Bonds issued with a coupon rate of zero (zero-coupon bonds) are always issued at a discount to face value. The value of zero-coupon bonds is based on the present value of the principal payment only because there are no periodic interest payments.

Such issuance costs as printing, legal fees, commissions, and other types of charges are costs incurred when bonds are issued. Under International Financial Reporting Standards (IFRS), all debt issuance costs are included in the measurement of the liability, bonds payable. Under US generally accepted accounting principles (US GAAP), companies generally used to show these debt issuance costs as an asset (a deferred charge), which was amortised on a straight-line basis to the relevant expense (e.g., legal fees) over the life of the bonds. Under US GAAP, debt issuance costs are deducted from the related debt liability. Companies reporting under US GAAP may still report debt issuance costs for lines of credit as an asset because the SEC indicated that it would not object to this treatment. Under IFRS and US GAAP, cash outflows related to bond issuance costs are included in the financing section of the statement of cash flows, usually netted against bond proceeds.

2.2 Accounting for Bond Amortisation, Interest Expense, and Interest Payments

In this section, we discuss accounting and reporting for bonds after they are issued. Most companies maintain the historical cost (sales proceeds) of the bonds after issuance, and they amortise any discount or premium over the life of the bond. The amount reported on the balance sheet for bonds is thus the historical cost plus or minus the cumulative amortisation, which is referred to as amortised cost. Companies also have the option to report the bonds at their current fair values.

The rationale for reporting the bonds at amortised historical cost is the company's intention to retain the debt until it matures. Therefore, changes in the underlying economic value of the debt are not relevant from the issuing company's perspective. From an investor's perspective, however, analysis of a company's underlying economic liabilities and solvency is more difficult when debt is reported at amortised historical cost. The rest of this section illustrates accounting and reporting of bonds at amortised historical cost. Section 2.3 discusses the alternative of reporting bonds at fair value.

Companies initially report bonds as a liability on their balance sheet at the amount of the sales proceeds net of issuance costs under both IFRS and US GAAP, ignoring any bond issuance costs. The amount at which bonds are reported on the company's balance sheet is referred to as the carrying amount, carrying value, book value, or net book value. If the bonds are issued at par, the initial carrying amount will be identical to the face value, and usually the carrying amount will not change over the life of the bonds.[3] For bonds issued at face value, the amount of periodic interest *expense* will be the same as the amount of periodic interest *payment* to bondholders.

If, however, the market rate differs from the bonds' coupon rate at issuance such that the bonds are issued at a premium or discount, the premium or discount is amortised systematically over the life of the bonds as a component of interest expense. For bonds issued at a premium to face value, the carrying amount of the bonds is initially greater than the face value. As the premium is amortised, the carrying amount (amortised cost) of the bonds will decrease to the face value. The reported interest expense will be less than the coupon payment. For bonds issued at a discount to face value, the carrying amount of the bonds is initially less than the face value. As the discount is amortised, the carrying amount (amortised cost) of the bonds will increase to the face value. The reported interest expense will be higher than the coupon payment.

The accounting treatment for bonds issued at a discount reflects the fact that the company essentially paid some of its borrowing costs at issuance by selling its bonds at a discount. Rather than there being an actual cash transfer in the future, this "payment" was made in the form of accepting less than the face value for the bonds at the

3 If a company reports debt at fair value, rather than amortised cost, the carrying value may change.

date of issuance. The remaining borrowing cost occurs as a cash interest payment to investors each period. The total interest expense reflects both components of the borrowing cost: the periodic interest payments plus the amortisation of the discount. The accounting treatment for bonds issued at a premium reflects the fact that the company essentially received a reduction on its borrowing costs at issuance by selling its bonds at a premium. Rather than there being an actual reduced cash transfer in the future, this "reduction" was made in the form of receiving more than face value for the bonds at the date of issuance. The total interest expense reflects both components of the borrowing cost: the periodic interest payments less the amortisation of the premium. When the bonds mature, the carrying amount will be equal to the face value regardless of whether the bonds were issued at face value, a discount, or a premium.

Two methods for amortising the premium or discount of bonds that were issued at a price other than par are the effective interest rate method and the straight-line method. The effective interest rate method is required under IFRS and preferred under US GAAP because it better reflects the economic substance of the transaction. The effective interest rate method applies the market rate in effect when the bonds were issued (historical market rate or effective interest rate) to the current amortised cost (carrying amount) of the bonds to obtain interest expense for the period. The difference between the interest expense (based on the effective interest rate and amortised cost) and the interest payment (based on the coupon rate and face value) is the **amortisation** of the discount or premium. The straight-line method of amortisation evenly amortises the premium or discount over the life of the bond, similar to straight-line depreciation on long-lived assets. Under either method, as the bond approaches maturity, the amortised cost approaches face value.

Example 3 illustrates both methods of amortisation for bonds issued at a discount. Example 4 shows amortisation for bonds issued at a premium.

EXAMPLE 3

Amortising a Bond Discount

Debond Corp. issues £1,000,000 face value of five-year bonds, dated 1 January 2017, when the market interest rate is 6 percent. The sales proceeds are £957,876. The bonds pay 5 percent interest annually on 31 December.

1 What is the interest *payment* on the bonds each year?

2 What amount of interest *expense* on the bonds would be reported in 2017 and 2018 using the effective interest rate method?

3 Determine the reported value of the bonds (i.e., the carrying amount) at 31 December 2017 and 2018, assuming the effective interest rate method is used to amortise the discount.

4 What amount of interest expense on the bonds would be reported under the straight-line method of amortising the discount?

Solution to 1:

The interest payment equals £50,000 annually (£1,000,000 × 5%).

Solution to 2:

The sales proceeds of £957,876 are less than the face value of £1,000,000; the bonds were issued at a discount of £42,124. The bonds are initially reported as a long-term liability, bonds payable, of £957,876, which comprises the face value of £1,000,000 minus a discount of £42,124. The discount is amortised over time, ultimately, increasing the carrying amount (amortised cost) to face value.

Under the effective interest rate method, interest expense on the bonds is calculated as the bonds' carrying amount times the market rate in effect when the bonds are issued (effective interest rate). For 2017, interest expense is £57,473 = (£957,876 × 6%). The amount of the discount amortised in 2017 is the difference between the interest expense of £57,473 and the interest payment of £50,000 (i.e., £7,473). The bonds' carrying amount increases by the discount amortisation; at 31 December 2017, the bonds' carrying amount is £965,349 (beginning balance of £957,876 plus £7,473 discount amortisation). At this point, the carrying amount reflects a remaining unamortised discount of £34,651 (£42,124 discount at issuance minus £7,473 amortised).

For 2018, interest expense is £57,921 = (£965,349 × 6%), the carrying amount of the bonds on 1 January 2018 times the effective interest rate. The amount of the discount amortised in 2018 is the difference between the interest expense of £57,921 and the interest payment of £50,000 (i.e., £7,921). At 31 December 2018, the bonds' carrying amount is £973,270 (beginning balance of £965,349 plus £7,921 discount amortisation).

The following table illustrates interest expense, discount amortisation, and carrying amount (amortised cost) over the life of the bonds.

Year	Carrying Amount (beginning of year)	Interest Expense (at effective interest rate of 6%)	Interest Payment (at coupon rate of 5%)	Amortisation of Discount	Carrying Amount (end of year)
	(a)	(b)	(c)	(d)	(e)
2017	£957,876	£57,473	£50,000	£7,473	£965,349
2018	965,349	57,921	50,000	7,921	973,270
2019	973,270	58,396	50,000	8,396	981,666
2020	981,666	58,900	50,000	8,900	990,566
2021	990,566	59,434	50,000	9,434	1,000,000
Total		£292,124	£250,000	£42,124	

Solution to 3:

The carrying amounts of the bonds at 31 December 2017 and 2018 are £965,349 and £973,270, respectively. Observe that the carrying amount of the bonds issued at a discount increases over the life of the bonds. At maturity, 31 December 2021, the carrying amount of the bonds equals the face value of the bonds. The carrying amount of the bonds will be reduced to zero when the principal payment is made.

Solution to 4:

Under the straight-line method, the discount (or premium) is evenly amortised over the life of the bonds. In this example, the £42,124 discount would be amortised by £8,424.80 (£42,124 divided by 5 years) each year under the straight-line method. So, the annual interest expense under the straight-line method would be £58,424.80 (£50,000 plus £8,424.80).

The accounting and reporting for zero-coupon bonds is similar to the example above except that no interest payments are made; thus, the amount of interest expense each year is the same as the amount of the discount amortisation for the year.

EXAMPLE 4

Amortising a Bond Premium

Prembond Corp. issues £1,000,000 face value of five-year bonds, dated 1 January 2017, when the market interest rate is 4 percent. The sales proceeds are £1,044,518. The bonds pay 5 percent interest annually on 31 December.

1 What is the interest *payment* on the bonds each year?
2 What amount of interest *expense* on the bonds would be reported in 2017 and 2018 using the effective interest rate method?
3 Determine the reported value of the bonds (i.e., the carrying amount) at 31 December 2017 and 2018, assuming the effective interest rate method is used to amortise the premium.
4 What amount of interest expense on the bonds would be reported under the straight-line method of amortising the premium?

Solution to 1:

The interest payment equals £50,000 annually (£1,000,000 × 5%).

Solution to 2:

The sales proceeds of £1,044,518 are more than the face value of £1,000,000; the bonds were issued at a premium of £44,518. The bonds are initially reported as a long-term liability, bonds payable, of £1,044,518, which comprises the face value of £1,000,000 plus a premium of £44,518. The premium is amortised over time, ultimately decreasing the carrying amount (amortised cost) to face value.

Under the effective interest rate method, interest expense on the bonds is calculated as the bonds' carrying amount times the market rate in effect when the bonds are issued (effective interest rate). For 2017, interest expense is £41,781 = (£1,044,518 × 4%). The amount of the premium amortised in 2017 is the difference between the interest expense of £41,781 and the interest payment of £50,000 (i.e., £8,219). The bonds' carrying amount decreases by the premium amortisation; at 31 December 2017, the bonds' carrying amount is £1,036,299 (beginning balance of £1,044,518 less £8,219 premium amortisation). At this point, the carrying amount reflects a remaining unamortised premium of £36,299 (£44,518 premium at issuance minus £8,219 amortised).

For 2018, interest expense is £41,452 = (£1,036,299 × 4%). The amount of the premium amortised in 2011 is the difference between the interest expense of £41,452 and the interest payment of £50,000 (i.e., £8,548). At 31 December 2018, the bonds' carrying amount is £1,027,751 (beginning balance of £1,036,299 less £8,548 premium amortisation).

The following table illustrates interest expense, premium amortisation, and carrying amount (amortised cost) over the life of the bonds.

Year	Carrying Amount (beginning of year)	Interest Expense (at effective interest rate of 4%)	Interest Payment (at coupon rate of 5%)	Amortisation of Premium	Carrying Amount (end of year)
	(a)	(b)	(c)	(d)	(e)
2017	£1,044,518	£41,781	£50,000	£8,219	£1,036,299
2018	1,036,299	41,452	50,000	8,548	1,027,751
2019	1,027,751	41,110	50,000	8,890	1,018,861
2020	1,018,861	40,754	50,000	9,246	1,009,615

(continued)

Year	Carrying Amount (beginning of year)	Interest Expense (at effective interest rate of 4%)	Interest Payment (at coupon rate of 5%)	Amortisation of Premium	Carrying Amount (end of year)
2021	1,009,615	40,385	50,000	9,615	1,000,000
Total				£44,518	

Solution to 3:

The carrying amounts of the bonds at 31 December 2017 and 2018 are £1,036,299 and £1,027,751, respectively. Observe that the carrying amount of the bonds issued at a premium decreases over the life of the bonds. At maturity, 31 December 2021, the carrying amount of the bonds equals the face value of the bonds. The carrying amount of the bonds will be reduced to zero when the principal payment is made.

Solution to 4:

Under the straight-line method, the premium is evenly amortised over the life of the bonds. In this example, the £44,518 premium would be amortised by £8,903.64 (£44,518 divided by 5 years) each year under the straight-line method. So, the annual interest expense under the straight-line method would be £41,096.36 (£50,000 less £8,903.64).

The reporting of interest payments on the statement of cash flows can differ under IFRS and US GAAP. Under IFRS, interest payments on bonds can be included as an outflow in either the operating section or the financing section of the statement of cash flows. US GAAP requires interest payments on bonds to be included as an operating cash outflow. (Some financial statement users consider the placement of interest payments in the operating section to be inconsistent with the placement of bond issue proceeds in the financing section of the statement of cash flows.) Typically, cash interest paid is not shown directly on the statement of cash flows, but companies are required to disclose interest paid separately.

Amortisation of a discount (premium) is a non-cash item and thus, apart from its effect on pretax income, has no effect on cash flow. In the section of the statement of cash flows that reconciles net income to operating cash flow, amortisation of a discount (premium) is added back to (subtracted from) net income.

2.3 Current Market Rates and Fair Value Reporting Option

Reporting bonds at amortised historical costs (historical cost plus or minus the cumulative amortisation) reflects the market rate at the time the bonds were *issued* (i.e., historical market rate or effective interest rate). As market interest rates change, the bonds' carrying amount diverges from the bonds' fair market value. When market interest rates decline, the fair value of a bond with a fixed coupon rate increases. As a result, a company's economic liabilities may be higher than its reported debt based on amortised historical cost. Conversely, when market interest rates increase, the fair value of a bond with a fixed coupon rate decreases and the company's economic liability may be lower than its reported debt. Using financial statement amounts based on amortised cost may underestimate (or overestimate) a company's debt-to-total-capital ratio and similar leverage ratios.

Companies have the option to report financial liabilities at fair value. Financial liabilities reported at fair value are designated as financial liabilities at fair value through profit or loss under IFRS, or, equivalently under US GAAP, as liabilities under the fair value option. Even if a company does not opt to report financial liabilities at fair value, the availability of fair value information in the financial statements has increased. IFRS and US GAAP require fair value disclosures in the financial statements unless the carrying amount approximates fair value or the fair value cannot be reliably measured.[4]

A company electing to measure a liability at fair value will report decreases in the liability's fair value as income and increases in the liability's fair value as losses. Because changes in a liability's fair value can result from changes in market rates and/or changes in the credit quality of the issuing company, accounting standards require companies to present separately the portion of the change resulting from changes in their own credit risk. Specifically, the company will report the portion of the change in value attributable to changes in their credit risk in other comprehensive income. Only the portion of the change in value not attributable to changes in their credit risk will be recognised in profit or loss.[5]

As of the end of 2018, few companies have selected the option to report financial liabilities at fair value. Those that have are primarily companies in the financial sector. Reporting standards for financial investments and derivatives already required these companies to report a significant portion of their assets at fair values. Measuring financial liabilities at other than fair value, when financial assets are measured at fair value, results in earnings volatility. This volatility is the result of using different bases of measurement for financial assets and financial liabilities. Furthermore, when a liability is related to a specific asset, using different measurement bases creates an accounting mismatch. Goldman Sachs elected to account for some financial liabilities at fair value under the fair value option. In its fiscal year 2017 10-K filing (page 136), Goldman explains this choice:

> "The primary reasons for electing the fair value option are to:
>
> - Reflect economic events in earnings on a timely basis;
> - Mitigate volatility in earnings from using different measurement attributes (e.g., transfers of financial instruments owned accounted for as financings are recorded at fair value, whereas the related secured financing would be recorded on an accrual basis absent electing the fair value option); and
> - Address simplification and cost-benefit considerations (e.g., accounting for hybrid financial instruments at fair value in their entirety versus bifurcation of embedded derivatives and hedge accounting for debt hosts)."

Most companies, as required under IFRS and US GAAP, disclose the fair values of financial liabilities. The primary exception to the disclosure occurs when fair value cannot be reliably measured. Example 5 illustrates ING Group's fair value disclosures, including the fair values of long-term debt.

---

4 IFRS (IAS 32, IFRS 7, IFRS 9) and US GAAP (FASB ASC 820 and 825).

5 IFRS 9, US GAAP (FASB ASC 825 and ASU 2016-01).

EXAMPLE 5

Fair Value Disclosures of Debt and Financial Instruments

ING Group 2017 Form 20-F

ING Group [Condensed] Balance Sheet as of 31 December 2017 and 2016 [Liabilities Only]

Amounts in billions of euros	2017	2016
Deposits from banks	36.8	32.0
Customer deposits	539.8	522.9
Financial liabilities at fair value through profit or loss	87.2	99.0
Other liabilities	18.9	20.1
Debt securities in issue/subordinated loans	112.1	120.4
Total liabilities	**794.8**	**794.4**

The following are excerpts from the footnotes to ING Group's financial statements.

Excerpt from Note 1 Accounting Policies

Financial assets and liabilities at fair value through profit or loss

... Financial liabilities at fair value through profit or loss comprise the following sub-categories: trading liabilities, non-trading derivatives, and other financial liabilities designated at fair value through profit or loss by management. Trading liabilities include equity securities, debt securities, funds on deposit, and derivatives.

A financial asset or financial liability is classified at fair value through profit or loss if acquired principally for the purpose of selling in the short term or if designated by management as such. Management will designate a financial asset or a financial liability as such only if this eliminates a measurement inconsistency or if the related assets and liabilities are managed on a fair value basis....

Financial liabilities at amortised cost

Financial liabilities at amortised cost include the following sub-categories: preference shares classified as debt, debt securities in issue, subordinated loans, and deposits from banks and customer deposits.

Financial liabilities at amortised cost are recognised initially at their issue proceeds (fair value of consideration received) net of transaction costs incurred. Liabilities in this category are subsequently stated at amortised cost; any difference between proceeds, net of transaction costs, and the redemption value is recognised in the statement of profit or loss over the period of the liability using the effective interest method....

Excerpt from Note 16 Debt securities in issue

Debt securities in issue relate to debentures and other issued debt securities with either fixed interest rates or interest rates based on floating interest rate levels, such as certificates of deposit and accepted bills issued by ING Group, except for subordinated items. Debt securities in issue do not include debt securities presented as Financial liabilities at fair value through profit or loss.

Excerpt from Note 37 Fair value of assets and liabilities

Fair Value of Financial Liabilities as of 31 December 2017 and 2016

	Estimated Fair Value		Statement of Financial Position Value	
Amounts in millions of euros	**2017**	**2016**	**2017**	**2016**
Financial liabilities				
Deposits from banks	36,868	32,352	36,821	31,964
Customer deposits	540,547	523,850	539,828	522,908
Financial liabilities at fair value through profit or loss				
• trading liabilities	73,596	83,167	73,596	83,167
• non-trading derivatives	2,331	3,541	2,331	3,541
• designated as at fair value through profit or loss	11,215	12,266	11,215	12,266
Other liabilities	14,488	15,247	14,488	15,247
Debt securities in issue	96,736	103,559	96,086	103,234
Subordinated loans	16,457	17,253	15,968	17,223
	792,238	**791,235**	**790,333**	**789,550**

Use the condensed balance sheet and excerpts from the notes to ING Group's financial statements shown above to address the following questions:

1 As of 31 December 2017, what proportion of the amount of liabilities on ING Group's balance sheet is reported at fair value through profit or loss?

2 As of 31 December 2017 and 2016, what is the percent difference between the carrying amount and fair value of the debt securities that are shown on ING Group's balance sheet at amortised cost?

Solution to 1:

Of ING Group's total €794.8 billion liabilities, 11 percent (=€87.2 billion/€794.8 billion) are reported at fair value through profit or loss.

Solution to 2:

ING's debt securities that are shown on the balance sheet at amortised cost appear in the line labeled "Debt securities in issue". Note 1 states that "Debt securities in issue" are reported at amortised cost. Note 16 indicates that this line item relates to debentures and other issued debt securities, and thus we exclude subordinated loans and deposits from banks and customer deposits in this case (there are no preference shares classified as debt listed in the Note 37 excerpt).

According to the above excerpt from Note 37, in each year the fair value of ING's debt securities is slightly higher than its carrying amount. The difference is 0.7% [= (96,736/96,086) – 1] on 31 December 2017 and 0.3% [= (103,559/103,234) – 1] on 31 December 2016.

2.4 Derecognition of Debt

Once bonds are issued, a company may leave the bonds outstanding until maturity or redeem the bonds before maturity either by calling the bonds (if the bond issue includes a call provision) or by purchasing the bonds in the open market. If the bonds remain outstanding until the maturity date, the company pays bondholders the face value of the bonds at maturity. The discount or premium on the bonds would be fully amortised at maturity; the carrying amount would equal face value. Upon repayment, the bonds payable account is reduced by the carrying amount at maturity (face value) of the bonds, and cash is reduced by an equal amount. Repayment of the bonds appears in the statement of cash flows as a financing cash outflow.

If a company decides to redeem bonds before maturity and thus extinguish the liability early, the bonds payable account is reduced by the carrying amount of the redeemed bonds. The difference between the cash required to redeem the bonds and the carrying amount of the bonds is a gain or loss on the extinguishment of debt. Under IFRS, debt issuance costs are included in the measurement of the liability and are thus part of its carrying amount. Under US GAAP, debt issuance costs are accounted for separately from bonds payable and are amortised over the life of the bonds. Any unamortised debt issuance costs must be written off at the time of redemption and included in the gain or loss on debt extinguishment.

For example, a company reporting under IFRS has a £10 million bond issuance with a carrying amount equal to its face value and five years remaining until maturity. The company redeems the bonds at a call price of 103. The redemption cost is £10.3 million (= £10 million × 103%). The company's loss on redemption would be £300 thousand (£10 million carrying amount minus £10.3 million cash paid to redeem the callable bonds).

A gain or loss on the extinguishment of debt is reported on the income statement, in a separate line item, when the amount is material. A company typically discloses further detail about the extinguishment in the management discussion and analysis (MD&A) and/or notes to the financial statements.[6] In addition, in a statement of cash flows prepared using the indirect method, net income is adjusted to remove any gain or loss on the extinguishment of debt from operating cash flows and the cash paid to redeem the bonds is classified as cash used for financing activities. (Recall that the indirect method of the statement of cash flows begins with net income and makes necessary adjustments to arrive at cash from operations, including removal of gains or losses from non-operating activities.)

To illustrate the financial statement impact of the extinguishment of debt, consider the notes payable repurchase in Example 6 below.

6 We use the term MD&A generally to refer to any management commentary provided on a company's financial condition, changes in financial condition, and results of operations. In the United States, the Securities and Exchange Commission (SEC) requires a management discussion and analysis for companies listed on US public markets. Reporting requirements for such a commentary as the SEC-required MD&A vary across exchanges, but some are similar to the SEC requirements. The IASB issued an IFRS Practice Statement, "Management Commentary," in December 2010 to guide all companies reporting under IFRS.

EXAMPLE 6

Debt Extinguishment Disclosure

The following excerpts are from the 2018 annual report of Monte Rock Inc. (a hypothetical company). In its statement of cash flows, the company uses the indirect method to reconcile net income with net cash (used in) provided by operations.

Excerpt from **Consolidated Statements of Income**
For the years ended 31 December 2018, 2017, and 2016

	2018	2017	2016
Revenues:			
⋮	⋮	⋮	⋮
Total revenues	104,908,900	112,416,800	96,879,000
⋮	⋮	⋮	⋮
Total operating expenses	100,279,900	96,140,600	71,018,900
Income from operations	4,629,000	16,276,200	25,860,100
Other income (expense):			
⋮	⋮	⋮	⋮
Gain on debt extinguishment	2,345,000	—	—
⋮	⋮	⋮	⋮
Total other income (expense), net	11,236,100	(14,257,000)	(7,085,800)
Net income	$15,865,100	$2,019,200	$18,774,300

Excerpt from **Consolidated Statements of Cash Flows**
For the years ended 31 December 2018, 2017, and 2016

	2018	2017	2016
CASH FLOWS FROM OPERATING ACTIVITIES:			
Net Income	$15,865,100	$2,019,200	$18,774,300
Adjustments to reconcile net income to net cash (used in) provided by operating activities:			
⋮	⋮	⋮	⋮
Gain on debt extinguishment	(2,345,000)	—	—
⋮	⋮	⋮	⋮
Total adjustments	(16,636,000)	38,842,400	19,815,800
Net cash (used in) provided by operating activities	(770,900)	40,861,600	38,590,100
⋮	⋮	⋮	⋮
CASH FLOWS FROM FINANCING ACTIVITIES:			
Payments for debt financing costs	(294,000)	(1,526,500)	(1,481,500)

(continued)

(Continued)

	2018	2017	2016
⋮	⋮	⋮	⋮
Purchase of debt securities	(2,155,000)	—	(5,000,000)
⋮	⋮	⋮	⋮
Payments of unsecured debt	—	(31,402,960)	(1,356,000)

***Excerpt from* NOTE 8: BONDS PAYABLE**

On December 12, 2014, the Company issued $25 million of unsecured bonds... Interest on the bonds is equal to Libor plus 4%, payable quarterly in arrears. ... During the 4th quarter of 2018, the Company repurchased the unsecured bonds with a face value of $4.5 million and realized a $2.3 million gain.

1 The balance in bonds payable was reduced at redemption by:

A $2,155,000.

B $2,345,000.

C $4,500,000.

2 How much cash did the Company pay to redeem the bonds?

A $2,155,000

B $2,345,000

C $4,500,000

Solution to 1:

C is correct. The bonds payable is reduced at redemption by the carrying amount of the bonds redeemed. The cash paid to extinguish the bonds plus the gain on redemption equals the carrying amount of the bonds. The carrying amount of the bonds was $4,500,000. In this case, the carrying amount equals the face value. The company recognised a gain of $2,345,000 when it extinguished the debt of $4,500,000 by paying only $2,155,000.

Solution to 2:

A is correct. As shown in the Statement of Cash flow, the company paid $2,155,000 to redeem the bonds. The company recognised a gain of $2,345,000 when it extinguished the debt of $4,500,000 by paying only $2,155,000.

2.5 Debt Covenants

Borrowing agreements (the bond indenture) often include restrictions called covenants that protect creditors by restricting activities of the borrower. Debt covenants benefit borrowers to the extent that they lower the risk to the creditors and thus reduce the cost of borrowing. Affirmative covenants restrict the borrower's activities by requiring certain actions. For instance, covenants may require that the borrower maintain certain ratios above a specified amount or perform regular maintenance on real assets used as collateral. Negative covenants require that the borrower not take certain actions.

These covenants may restrict the borrower's ability to invest, pay dividends, or make other operating and strategic decisions that might adversely affect the company's ability to pay interest and principal.

Common covenants include limitations on how borrowed monies can be used, maintenance of collateral pledged as security (if any), restrictions on future borrowings, and requirements that limit dividends. Covenants may also specify minimum acceptable levels of financial ratios, such as debt-to-equity ratio, current ratio, or interest coverage.

When a company violates a debt covenant, it is a breach of contract. Depending on the severity of the breach and the terms of the contract, lenders may choose to waive the covenant, be entitled to a penalty payment or higher interest rate, renegotiate, or call for payment of the debt. Bond contracts typically require that the decision to call for immediate repayment be made, on behalf of all the bondholders, by holders of some minimum percentage of the principal amount of the bond issue.

Example 7 illustrates common disclosures related to debt covenants included in financial statement disclosures (notes to the financial statements).

EXAMPLE 7

The following excerpts are from the 2017 Form 20-F filing of TORM plc, a tanker company which describes itself as one of the world's largest carriers of refined oil products. TORM plc was established in 2016 following the restructuring of TORM A/S.

Illustration of Debt Covenant Disclosures

The following excerpt is from the Risk Factors section of TORM's fiscal year 2017 Form 20-F.

> "Our current debt facilities impose restrictions on our financial and operational flexibility. Our debt facilities impose, and any future debt facility may impose, covenants and other operating and financial restrictions on our ability to, among other things, pay dividends, charter-in vessels, incur additional debt, sell vessels or refrain from procuring the timely release of arrested vessels. Our debt facilities require us to maintain various financial ratios, including a specified minimum liquidity requirement, a minimum equity requirement and a collateral maintenance requirement. Our ability to comply with these restrictions and covenants is dependent on our future performance and our ability to operate our fleet and may be affected by events beyond our control, including fluctuating vessel values. We may therefore need to seek permission from our lenders in order to engage in certain corporate actions.
>
> ... As of December 31, 2017, we were in compliance with the financial covenants contained in our debt facilities.

The following excerpt is from the Liquidity and Capital Resources section in TORM's fiscal year 2017 Form 20-F.

> The DSF [Danish Ship Finance] Facility contains, among others, the following financial and other covenants:
>
> • Loan-to-value. If at any time the aggregate market value of the vessels and the value of any additional security is less than 133% of the loan amount less amounts on credit in the deposit accounts and

reserve account and the value of any additional security, the borrower and guarantors shall, within 30 days of a written request, post additional security or prepay the loan to reduce the excess to zero.

- Free Liquidity. Minimum unencumbered cash and cash equivalents ... of the higher of $75 million and 5% of our total debt, of which $40 million is required to be unencumbered cash and cash equivalents.
- Equity Ratio. The ratio of market value adjusted shareholders' equity to total market value adjusted assets shall be at least 25%.
- Dividends. We are restricted from making any distributions, including payment of dividends and repayments of shareholders loans, except ....

1 Which of the covenants described in the above excerpts are affirmative covenants?

2 Based on the excerpt above, what are the potential consequences of breaching the loan covenants?

Solution to 1:

Examples of affirmative covenants in the above excerpts are from TORM's disclosure about the DSF Facility and include: the requirement for TORM to maintain a loan-to-value relationship such that the assets securing the loan (the vessels) are 133% of the loan amount; the requirement for TORM to maintain "free liquidity" (i.e., a minimum level of cash and cash equivalents); and the requirement that the equity ratio be at least 25%. These covenants require the issuer to do something. The dividend covenant requiring that TORM not take certain actions (i.e., not pay dividends unless certain conditions are met) is a negative covenant. In addition, the excerpt from Risk Factors describes other negative covenants in TORM's debt facilities including restrictions on chartering-in vessels, incurring additional debt, or selling vessels.

Solution to 2:

A breach of a loan covenant by TORM—an event of default—may result in the entire amount of its debt becoming due.

2.6 Presentation and Disclosure of Long-Term Debt

The non-current (long-term) liabilities section of the balance sheet usually includes a single line item of the total amount of a company's long-term debt due after one year, with the portion of long-term debt due in the next twelve months shown as a current liability. Notes to the financial statements provide more information on the types and nature of a company's debt. These note disclosures can be used to determine the amount and timing of future cash outflows. The notes generally include stated and effective interest rates, maturity dates, restrictions imposed by creditors (covenants), and collateral pledged (if any). The amount of scheduled debt repayments for the next five years also is shown in the notes.

Example 8 contains an excerpt from the 2017 Form 10-K of Johnson & Johnson (J&J), a US manufacturer of health care products.

EXAMPLE 8

Illustration of Long-Term Debt Disclosures

Exhibit 1 is an excerpt from Note 7 of Johnson & Johnson's 2017 annual report that illustrates financial statement disclosures for long-term debt, including type and nature of long-term debt, carrying amounts, effective interest rates, and required payments over the next five years. Johnson & Johnson reports its debt at amortised cost.

Exhibit 1 Johnson & Johnson Borrowings

The components of long-term debt are as follows:

(Dollars in Millions)	2017	Effective Rate %	2016	Effective Rate %
5.55% Debentures due 2017	$—	—	$1,000	5.55
1.125% Notes due 2017	—	—	699	1.15
5.15% Debentures due 2018	900	5.18	899	5.18
1.65% Notes due 2018	597	1.70	600	1.70
4.75% Notes due 2019 (1B Euro 1.1947)[2]/(1B Euro 1.0449)[3]	1,192	5.83	1,041	5.83
1.875% Notes due 2019	496	1.93	499	1.93
0.89% Notes due 2019	300	1.75	299	1.20
1.125% Notes due 2019	699	1.13	699	1.13
3% Zero Coupon Convertible Subordinated Debentures due 2020	60	3.00	84	3.00
2.95% Debentures due 2020	547	3.15	546	3.15
[PORTIONS OMITTED]				
Subtotal	**32,174**	**3.19**[1]	**24,146**	**3.33**[1]
Less current portion	1,499		1,704	
Total long-term debt	**$30,675**		**$22,442**	

(1) Weighted average effective rate.
(2) Translation rate at December 31, 2017.
(3) Translation rate at January 1, 2017.

"Fair value of the long-term debt was estimated using market prices, which were corroborated by quoted broker prices and significant other observable inputs.

"The Company has access to substantial sources of funds at numerous banks worldwide. In September 2017, the Company secured a new 364-day Credit Facility. Total credit available to the Company approximates $10 billion, which expires on September 13, 2018. Interest charged on borrowings under the credit line agreements is based on either bids provided by banks, the prime rate or London Interbank Offered Rates (Libor), plus applicable margins. Commitment fees under the agreements are not material… Throughout 2017, the Company continued to have access to liquidity through the commercial paper market. Short-term borrowings and the current portion of long-term debt amounted to approximately $3.9 billion at the end of 2017, of which $2.3 billion was borrowed under the Commercial Paper Program, $1.5 billion is the current portion of the long term debt, and the remainder principally represents local borrowing by international subsidiaries. …"

Aggregate maturities of long-term obligations commencing in 2018 are (dollars in millions):

2018	2019	2020	2021	2022	After 2022
$1,499	2,752	1,105	1,797	2,189	22,832

Use the information in Exhibit 1 to answer the following questions:

1 Why are the effective interest rates unchanged from 2016 to 2017 for most of the borrowings listed?

2 Why does the carrying amount of the "1.125% Notes due 2019" remain the same in 2016 and 2017?

3 Why is the carrying amount of the "4.75% Notes due 2019" higher in 2017 than in 2016?

Solution to 1:

The effective rate typically refers to the market rate at which the bonds are issued and typically does not change from year to year.

Solution to 2:

The carrying amount of the "1.125% Notes due 2019" remains the same because the effective interest rate at which the debentures were issued (1.13%) is approximately the same as the coupon rate indicating that the notes were issued approximately at par. Thus, there would be no amortization of a premium or discount to affect the carrying amount of the notes, and assuming no repurchases, the carrying amount would not change.

Solution to 3:

The notes are denominated in Euros, with a face value of €1 billion. The dollar/euro translation exchange rate at the end of 2017 was higher than the exchange rate at the end of 2016 (1.1947 versus 1.0449). That increase explains part of the increase in carrying value. In addition, the effective interest rate of 5.83 % is higher than the 4.75 % coupon rate – implying that the notes were issued at a discount. Thus, the increase in the carrying amount of the notes also reflects the amortisation of the issuance discount.

In this reading, we focus on accounting for simple debt contracts. Debt contracts can take on additional features, which lead to more complexity. For instance, convertible debt and debt with warrants are more complex instruments that have both debt and equity features. Convertible debt gives the debt holder the option to exchange the debt for equity. Bonds issued with warrants give holders the right to purchase shares of the issuer's common stock at a specific price, similar to stock options. Issuance of bonds with warrants is more common by non-US companies. Example 9 provides an example of a financial statement disclosure of bonds with warrants.

EXAMPLE 9

Financial Statement Disclosure of Bonds with Warrants

The following describes a company's issuance of convertible bonds with warrants.

> On 1 February 2018, the Company issued convertible bonds with stock warrants due 2024 with an aggregate principal amount of RMB 30 billion (the "Bonds with Warrants"). The Bonds with Warrants with fixed interest rate of 0.8% per annum and interest payable annually, were issued at par value of RMB 100. Each lot of the Bonds with Warrants, comprising ten Bonds with Warrants are entitled to warrants (the "Warrants") to subscribe 50.5 shares of the Company during the 5 trading days prior to 3 March 2020 at an initial exercise price of RMB 19.68 per share, subject to adjustment for, amongst other things, cash dividends, subdivision or consolidation of shares, bonus issues, rights issues, capital distribution, change of control and other events which have a dilutive effect on the issued share capital of the Company.

If all warrants were exercised, how many shares would be subscribed for?

Solution:

1,515,000,000 shares would be subscribed for [aggregate principal amount divided by par value of a lot times shares subscribed per lot = (RMB 30,000,000,000/RMB 1,000) × 50.5 shares].

In addition to disclosures in the notes to the financial statements, an MD&A commonly provides other information about a company's capital resources, including debt financing and off-balance-sheet financing. In the MD&A, management often provides a qualitative discussion on any material trends, favorable or unfavorable, in capital resources and indicates any expected material changes in their mix and relative cost. Additional quantitative information is typically provided, including schedules summarising a company's contractual obligations (e.g., bond payables) and other commitments (e.g., lines of credit and guarantees) in total and over the next five years.

LEASES

3

A lease is a contract between the owner of an asset (the **lessor)** and another party seeking use of the asset (the **lessee)**. As part of the lease, the lessor grants the right to use the asset to the lessee. The right to use the asset can be for a long period, such as 20 years, or a much shorter period such as a month. In exchange for the right to use the asset, the lessee makes periodic lease payments to the lessor. A lease, then, is a form of financing that enables the lessee to purchase the *use* of the leased asset.

There are several advantages to leasing an asset compared to purchasing it. Leases can provide a lessee with less costly financing, usually require little, if any, down payment, and are often at fixed interest rates. The negotiated lease contract may contain less restrictive provisions than other forms of borrowing. A lease can also reduce the lessee's exposure to risks of obsolescence, residual value, and disposition to the lessee because the lessee does not own the asset.

3.1 Lessee accounting

Accounting for leases changed significantly under both IFRS and US GAAP.[7] Prior to the introduction of these standards, many lessees used then-acceptable "off-balance sheet" leasing structures. Under the previous rules, if leases were classified as operating leases, companies were not required to report the asset and liability related to the lease; instead, for this type of lease, companies were only required to report the periodic lease payment as an expense. Analysts typically adjusted the amount of companies' reported debt, either by taking the present value of future lease payments or, as a short cut, multiplying the annual lease payment by 8.

Under the revised reporting standards under IFRS and US GAAP, a lessee must recognize an asset and a lease liability at inception of each of its leases (with an exception for short-term leases). The lessee reports a "right-of-use" ("ROU") asset and a lease liability, calculated essentially as the present value of fixed lease payments, on its balance sheet.

After the lease inception, a lessee's treatment of leases differs for IFRS and US GAAP. Under IFRS, after inception, the lessee records depreciation expense on the right-of-use asset, recognizes interest expense on the lease liability, and reduces the balance of the lease liability for the portion of the lease payment that represents repayment of the lease liability. In effect, the lease treatment is similar to having purchased a long-term asset, financed by a long-term interest-bearing liability.

Under US GAAP, lessee accounting after inception depends whether the lessee categorizes a lease as a finance lease or an operating lease. A **finance lease** is similar to purchasing an asset while an **operating lease** is similar to renting an asset. Criteria for categorizing a lease as a finance lease include indicators that the benefits and risks of owning the leased asset have been transferred to the lessee.[8] (Note that this categorization does not affect the requirement for recognition of the asset and lease liability at inception.) A lessee's accounting for a finance lease under US GAAP is the same as described above for leases under IFRS: after inception, the lessee records depreciation expense on the right-of-use asset, recognizes interest expense on the lease liability, and reduces the balance of the lease liability for the portion of the lease payment that represents repayment of the lease liability. For an operating lease after inception, under US GAAP, the lessee recognizes a single lease expense which is a straight-line allocation of the cost of the lease over its term.

Exceptions exist for short-term leases (those with a lease term less than one year) and, under IFRS, for leases where the leased asset is low in value. When these exceptions apply, the lessee is not required to recognize an asset and liability and instead records lease payments as an expense when paid.

When comparing an IFRS-reporting company to a US GAAP-reporting company, an analyst should be aware that the effects of a lease on the companies' income statements and statement of cash flows—even if the terms of the leases are identical—will differ. The most important difference between lessee accounting under IFRS and US GAAP is that IFRS has a single category of leases. On the income statement, every lease that an IFRS-reporting company records as a right-of-use asset and a lease liability at inception will result in a subsequent division of lease payments between depreciation expense and interest expense. Conversely, under US GAAP, a lessee reports

7 IFRS 16 [Leases] was issued in January 2016 and is effective beginning 1 January 2019. FASB ASC Topic 842 [Leases] was issued February 2016 as ASU 2016 – 02 and is effective for fiscal years beginning after 15 December 2018. Previous accounting standards did not require a lessee to report an asset and liability for Operating Leases.

8 A lessee classifies a lease as a finance lease if any of the following criteria are met: 1) transfers ownership of the asset to the lessee, 2) includes a bargain purchase option, 3) covers a period of time that is a major part of the asset's useful life, 4) involves lease payments that equal or exceed the asset's fair value, or 5) involves an asset that is so specialized that it will have no alternative use to the lessor after the lease ends.

depreciation expense and interest expense separately only in the case of finance leases. For operating leases, the lessee reports a single lease expense. On the statement of cash flows, IFRS allows companies to classify interest paid within operating, investing, or financing activities. Unlike IFRS, US GAAP requires companies to classify interest paid as an operating activity.

EXAMPLE 10

Lessee Accounting

An analyst is comparing the financial performance of two companies - one of which reports under IFRS and the other under US GAAP. Both companies extensively lease buildings and equipment in their operations. Assuming the companies enter into an identical long-term contract to lease an identical asset, which of the following metrics is *most* likely to differ because of differences in the companies' accounting standards? *(Assume that the leased asset would not qualify for the "low value" reporting exception under IFRS.)*

A Total assets

B Total liabilities

C Operating cash flows

Solution:

The answer is C. C is correct because IFRS requires interest to be reported separately for all leases and further permits companies to classify interest paid within operating, investing, or financing activities on the statement of cash flows. A and B are incorrect because at inception, both total assets and total liabilities are unlikely to differ because both IFRS and US GAAP require lessees to record a right-of-use asset and a lease liability for leases with a term longer than one year.

3.2 Lessor accounting

Under IFRS, a lessor classifies each lease as either a finance lease or an operating lease. For a finance lease, at inception, the lessor derecognizes the underlying leased asset and recognizes a lease asset comprising the lease receivable and relevant residual value. In addition, if the lessor is a manufacturer or dealer, the lessor recognizes revenue equal to the value of the leased asset, cost of goods sold equal to the carrying value of the leased asset, and selling profit or loss equal to the revenue minus the cost of goods sold. Subsequently for a finance lease, the lessor recognizes finance income over the lease term. For an operating lease, the lessor recognizes lease receipts as income and recognizes related costs, including deprecation of the leased asset, as expenses.

Under US GAAP, a lessor classifies a lease in one of three categories: sales-type, operating, or direct financing. The lessor's classification uses the same criteria that a lessee uses in determining whether the benefits and risks of owning the leased asset have been transferred to the lessee. If any of these criteria are met, the lessor will categorize the lease as a sales-type lease, assuming that collection of the future lease payments is probable.

If none of the criteria indicating that the benefits and risks of owning the leased asset have been transferred to the lessee or if collection of the future lease payments is not reasonably assured, the lessor is viewed as effectively continuing to own the leased asset and therefore does not recognize any selling profit at lease inception. In this case, the lessor will classify a lease as either an operating lease or a direct financing lease. Lessor accounting for an operating lease under US GAAP is similar to IFRS: over the lease term, the lessor recognizes lease receipts as income and recognizes related costs, including deprecation of the leased asset, as expenses.

A direct financing lease applies when a lease doesn't meet the ownership-transfer criteria to be considered a sale-type lease but yet results in the lessor relying on future lease receipts to recover the asset's cost. A financing lease is a type of lease transaction that "effectively converts the lessor's risk arising from ownership of the underlying asset (that is, asset risk) into credit risk.[9] A lease is considered a direct financing lease under US GAAP if the lease contract provides for a third-party guaranteed residual value, which, combined with the future lease payments by the lessee will equal or exceed the fair value of the leased asset.

Although the differences between IFRS and US GAAP for lessor accounting are not as significant as the differences for lessee accounting, it is nonetheless useful for an analyst to be aware of how the categorization differences can affect companies' financial statements. Because IFRS does not include a distinction between sales-type leases and direct financing leases, an IFRS-reporting lessor will recognize selling profit at the beginning of all leases that are not classified as operating leases. In contrast, a US-GAAP reporting lessor will recognize selling profit only on sales-type leases at the beginning of the lease term.

Exhibit 2 Summary of Financial Statement Impact of Leases on the Lessee and Lessor

	Balance Sheet	Income Statement	Statement of Cash Flows
Lessee			
All IFRS leases, and US GAAP finance leases	Recognise "right-of-use" (ROU) asset and lease liability	Report depreciation expense on ROU asset	Reduction of lease liability is a financing cash outflow
		Report interest expense on lease liability	Interest portion of lease payment is either an operating or financing cash outflow under IFRS and an operating cash outflow under US GAAP
US GAAP operating leases	Recognise "right-of-use" (ROU) asset and lease liability	Report single lease expense (a straight-line allocation of lease cost)	Entire cash payment is an operating cash outflow
Exceptions: short-term leases and, under IFRS, leases where leased asset is low value	No effect	Report rent expense	Rent payment is operating cash outflow
Lessor			
IFRS and US GAAP operating leases	Retain asset on balance sheet	Report lease income	Lease payments received are an operating cash inflow
		Report depreciation expense on leased asset	

9 FASB Accounting Standard Update ASU 2016-02 Leases (Topic 842) Section C – Background Information and Basis for Conclusions.

Exhibit 2 (Continued)

	Balance Sheet	Income Statement	Statement of Cash Flows
IFRS finance leases and US GAAP sales-type leases	Remove leased asset from balance sheet Recognise lease asset (lease receivable and residual)	Report interest revenue on lease receivable If applicable, report revenue, cost of goods sold, and selling profit.	Interest portion of lease payment received is either an operating or investing cash inflow under IFRS and an operating cash inflow under US GAAP. Receipt of lease principal is an investing cash inflow[a]
US GAAP direct financing leases	Remove leased asset from balance sheet Recognise lease receivable	Report interest revenue on lease receivable	Interest portion of lease payment received is an operating cash inflow under US GAAP Receipt of lease principal is an investing cash inflow[a]

[a] If providing leases is part of a company's normal business activity, the cash flows related to the leases are classified as operating cash.

INTRODUCTION TO PENSIONS AND OTHER POST-EMPLOYMENT BENEFITS

4

Pensions and other post-employment benefits give rise to non-current liabilities reported by many companies. Companies may offer various types of benefits to their employees following retirement, such as pension plans, health care plans, medical insurance, and life insurance. Pension plans often are the most significant post-employment benefits provided to retired employees.

The accounting and reporting for pension plans depends on the type of pension plan offered. Two common types of pension plans are **defined contribution pension plans** and **defined benefit pension plans**. Under a defined-contribution plan, a company contributes an agreed-upon (defined) amount into the plan. The agreed-upon amount is the pension expense. The amount the company contributes to the plan is treated as an operating cash outflow. The only impact on assets and liabilities is a decrease in cash, although if some portion of the agreed-upon amount has not been paid by fiscal year-end, a liability would be recognised on the balance sheet. Because the amount of the contribution is defined and the company has no further obligation once the contribution has been made, accounting for a defined-contribution plan is fairly straightforward.

Accounting for a defined-benefit plan is more complicated. Under a defined-benefit plan, a company makes promises of future benefits to be paid to the employee during retirement. For example, a company could promise an employee annual pension payments equal to 70 percent of his final salary at retirement until death. Estimating the eventual amount of the obligation arising from that promise requires the company to make many assumptions, such as the employee's expected salary at retirement and the number of years the employee is expected to live beyond retirement. The company estimates the future amounts to be paid and discounts the future estimated amounts to a present value (using a rate reflective of a high-quality corporate bond yield) to determine the pension obligation. The discount rate used to determine the pension obligation significantly affects the amount of the pension obligation. The pension obligation is allocated over the employee's employment as part of pension expense.

Most defined-benefit pension plans are funded through a separate legal entity, typically a pension trust fund. A company makes payments into the pension fund, and retirees are paid from the fund. The payments that a company makes into the fund are invested until they are needed to pay the retirees. If the fair value of the fund's assets is higher than the present value of the estimated pension obligation, the plan has a surplus and the company's balance sheet will reflect a net pension asset.[10] Conversely, if the present value of the estimated pension obligation exceeds the fund's assets, the plan has a deficit and the company's balance sheet will reflect a net pension liability.[11] Thus, a company reports either a net pension asset or a net pension liability. Each period, the change in the net pension asset or liability is recognised either in profit or loss or in other comprehensive income.

Under IFRS, the change in the net pension asset or liability each period is viewed as having three general components. Two of the components of this change are recognised as pension expense in profit and loss: (1) employees' service costs, and (2) the net interest expense or income accrued on the beginning net pension asset or liability. The service cost during the period for an employee is the present value of the increase in the pension benefit earned by the employee as a result of providing one more year of service. The service cost also includes past service costs, which are changes in the present value of the estimated pension obligation related to employees' service in prior periods, such as might arise from changes in the plan. The net interest expense or income represents the change in value of the net defined benefit pension asset or liability and is calculated as the net pension asset or liability multiplied by the discount rate used in estimating the present value of the pension obligation. The third component of the change in the net pension asset or liability during a period —"remeasurements"— is recognised in other comprehensive income. Remeasurements are not amortised into profit or loss over time.

Remeasurements include (a) actuarial gains and losses and (b) the actual return on plan assets less any return included in the net interest expense or income. Actuarial gains and losses can occur when changes are made to the assumptions on which a company bases its estimated pension obligation (e.g., employee turnover, mortality rates, retirement ages, compensation increases). The actual return on plan assets includes interest, dividends and other income derived from the plan assets, including realized and unrealized gains or losses. The actual return typically differs from the amount included in the net interest expense or income, which is calculated using a rate reflective of a high-quality corporate bond yield; plan assets are typically allocated across various asset classes, including equity as well as bonds.

Under US GAAP, the change in net pension asset or liability each period is viewed as having five components, some of which are recognised in profit and loss in the period incurred and some of which are recognised in other comprehensive income and amortised into profit and loss over time. The three components recognised in profit and loss in the period incurred are (1) employees' service costs for the period, (2) interest expense accrued on the beginning pension obligation, and (3) expected return on plan assets, which is a reduction in the amount of expense recognised. The other two components are past service costs and actuarial gains and losses. Past service costs are recognised in other comprehensive income in the period in which they arise and then subsequently amortised into pension expense over the future service period of the employees covered by the plan. Actuarial gains and losses are typically also recognised in other comprehensive income in the period in which they occur

10 The amount of any reported net pension asset is capped at the amount of any expected future economic benefits to the company from the plan; this cap is referred to as the asset ceiling.

11 The description of accounting for pensions presented in this reading corresponds to the June 2011 version of IAS 19 *Employee Benefits*, which took effect on 1 January 2013. Both IFRS and US GAAP require companies to present the amount of net pension liability or asset on the balance sheet.

and then amortised into pension expense over time. In effect, this treatment allows companies to "smooth" the effects on pension expense over time for these latter two components. US GAAP does permit companies to immediately recognize actuarial gains and losses in profit and loss.

Similar to other forms of employee compensation for a manufacturing company, the pension expense related to production employees is added to inventory and expensed through cost of sales (cost of goods sold). For employees not involved directly in the production process, the pension expense is included with salaries and other administrative expenses. Therefore, pension expense is not directly reported on the income statement. Rather, extensive disclosures are included in the notes to the financial statements.

Example 11 presents excerpts from the balance sheet and pension-related disclosures in BT Group plc's Annual Report for the year ended 31 March 2018.

EXAMPLE 11

BT Group plc: Excerpt from Balance Sheets

Below is an excerpt of BT Group plc's balance sheet from the annual report for the year ended 31 March 2018. BT reports under IFRS.

Non-current liabilities, GBP million	Mar. 31, 2018	Mar. 31, 2017	Mar. 31, 2016
Loans and other borrowings	11,994	10,081	11,025
Derivative financial instruments	787	869	863
Retirement benefit obligations	6,371	9,088	6,382
Other payables	1,326	1,298	1,106
Deferred tax liabilities	1,340	1,240	1,262
Provisions	452	536	565
Non-current liabilities	22,270	23,112	21,203

Pension-Related Disclosures

The following are excerpts of pension-related disclosures from BT Group plc's 2018 Annual Report.

Extract from Note 3 "Summary of Significant Accounting Policies"

> **Retirement benefits**
>
> The group's net obligation in respect of defined benefit pension plans is the present value of the defined benefit obligation less the fair value of the plan assets.
>
> The calculation of the obligation is performed by a qualified actuary using the projected unit credit method and key actuarial assumptions at the balance sheet date.
>
> The income statement expense is allocated between an operating charge and net finance income or expense. The operating charge reflects the increase in the defined benefit obligation resulting from the pension benefit earned by active employees in the current period, the costs of administering the plans and any past service costs/credits such as those arising from curtailments or settlements. The net finance income or expense reflects the interest on the net retirement benefit obligations recognised in the group balance sheet, based on

the discount rate at the start of the year. Actuarial gains and losses are recognised in full in the period in which they occur and are presented in the group statement of comprehensive income.

The group also operates defined contribution pension plans and the income statement expense represents the contributions payable for the year.

Extract from Note 20 "Retirement Benefit Plans" Information on Defined Benefit Pension Plans

£m	2018	2017	2016
Present value of liabilities	**57,327**	60,200	50,350
Fair value of plan assets	**50,956**	51,112	43,968

Use information in the excerpts to answer the following questions:

1 What type(s) of pension plans does BT have?

2 What proportion of BT's total non-current liabilities are related to its retirement benefit obligations?

3 Describe how BT's retirement benefit obligation is calculated.

Solution to 1:

Note 3 "Summary of Significant Accounting Policies" indicates that the company has both defined contribution and defined benefit pension plans.

Solution to 2:

Retirement benefit obligations represent 29%, 39%, and 30% of BT's total non-current liabilities for the years 2018, 2017, and 2016. Using 2018 to illustrate, £6,371/£22,270 = 29%. (£ million)

Solution to 3:

Note 3 "Summary of Significant Accounting Policies" indicates that BT's Retirement benefit obligation is calculated as the present value of the defined benefit obligation minus the fair value of the plan assets.

Using data from Note 20 "Retirement Benefit Plans" the retirement benefit obligation for each year can be calculated. Using 2018 to illustrate, £57,327 - £50,956 = £6,371 (£ million).

5 EVALUATING SOLVENCY: LEVERAGE AND COVERAGE RATIOS

Solvency refers to a company's ability to meet its long-term debt obligations, including both principal and interest payments. In evaluating a company's solvency, ratio analyses can provide information about the relative amount of debt in the company's capital structure and the adequacy of earnings and cash flow to cover interest expense and other fixed charges (such as lease or rental payments) as they come due. Ratios are useful to evaluate a company's performance over time compared to the performance of other companies and industry norms. Ratio analysis has the advantage of allowing the comparison of companies regardless of their size and reporting currency.

The two primary types of solvency ratios are leverage ratios and coverage ratios. Leverage ratios focus on the balance sheet and measure the extent to which a company uses liabilities rather than equity to finance its assets. Coverage ratios focus on the income statement and cash flows and measure the ability of a company to cover its debt-related payments.

Exhibit 3 describes the two types of commonly used solvency ratios. The first three leverage ratios use total debt in the numerator.[12] The *debt-to-assets ratio* expresses the percentage of total assets financed with debt. Generally, the higher the ratio, the higher the financial risk and thus the weaker the solvency. The *debt-to-capital ratio* measures the percentage of a company's total capital (debt plus equity) financed through debt. The *debt-to-equity ratio* measures the amount of debt financing relative to equity financing. A *debt-to-equity ratio* of 1.0 indicates equal amounts of debt and equity, which is the same as a debt-to-capital ratio of 50 percent. Interpretations of these ratios are similar. Higher debt-to-capital or debt-to-equity ratios imply weaker solvency. A caveat must be made when comparing debt ratios of companies in different countries. Within certain countries, companies historically have obtained more capital from debt than equity financing, so debt ratios tend to be higher for companies in these countries.

Exhibit 3 Definitions of Commonly Used Solvency Ratios

Solvency Ratios	Numerator	Denominator
Leverage ratios		
Debt-to-assets ratio	Total debt[a]	Total assets
Debt-to-capital ratio	Total debt[a]	Total debt[a] + Total shareholders' equity
Debt-to-equity ratio	Total debt[a]	Total shareholders' equity
Financial leverage ratio	Average total assets	Average shareholders' equity
Coverage ratios		
Interest coverage ratio	EBIT[b]	Interest payments
Fixed charge coverage ratio	EBIT[b] + lease payments	Interest payments + lease payments

[a] In this reading, debt is defined as the sum of interest-bearing short-term and long-term debt.
[b] EBIT is earnings before interest and taxes.

The *financial leverage ratio* (also called the 'leverage ratio' or 'equity multiplier') measures the amount of total assets supported by one money unit of equity. For example, a value of 4 for this ratio means that each €1 of equity supports €4 of total assets. The higher the financial leverage ratio, the more leveraged the company in the

12 For calculations in this reading, total debt is the sum of interest-bearing short-term and long-term debt, excluding non-interest-bearing liabilities, such as accrued expenses, accounts payable, and deferred income taxes. This definition of total debt differs from other definitions that are more inclusive (e.g., all liabilities) or more restrictive (e.g., long-term debt only). If the use of different definitions of total debt materially changes conclusions about a company's solvency, the reasons for the discrepancies should be further investigated.

sense of using debt and other liabilities to finance assets. This ratio often is defined in terms of average total assets and average total equity and plays an important role in the DuPont decomposition of return on equity.[13]

The *interest coverage ratio* measures the number of times a company's EBIT could cover its interest payments. A higher interest coverage ratio indicates stronger solvency, offering greater assurance that the company can service its debt from operating earnings. The *fixed charge coverage ratio* relates fixed financing charges, or obligations, to the cash flow generated by the company. It measures the number of times a company's earnings (before interest, taxes, and lease payments) can cover the company's interest and lease payments.

Example 12 demonstrates the use of solvency ratios in evaluating the creditworthiness of a company.

EXAMPLE 12

Evaluating Solvency Ratios

A credit analyst is evaluating and comparing the solvency of two companies—BT Group plc (BT) and Telefonica S A (Telefonica). The following data are gathered from the companies' fiscal 2017 annual reports (line item titles may vary between the two companies):

	BT Group plc (£ millions)		Telefonica S A (€ millions)	
	31-Mar-18	**31-Mar-17**	**31-Dec-17**	**31-Dec-16**
Short-term borrowings	2,281	2,632	9,414	14,749
Long-term debt	11,994	10,081	46,332	45,612
Total shareholders' equity	10,304	8,335	26,618	28,385
Total assets	42,759	42,372	115,066	123,641
EBIT*	3,381	3,167	6,791	5,469
Interest expense	776	817	3,363	4,476

* Operating profit (or operating income) is used as a proxy for EBIT for both companies.

Use the above information to answer the following questions:

1 With regard to leverage ratios of BT and Telefonica:

A What are each company's debt-to-assets, debt-to-capital, and debt-to-equity ratios for 2017 and 2016?

B Comment on any changes in the calculated leverage ratios from year-to-year for each company.

C Comment on the calculated leverage ratios of BT Group plc compared to Telefonica SA.

2 With regard to coverage ratios of BT and Telefonica:

A What is each company's interest coverage ratio for 2017 and 2016?

13 The basic DuPont decomposition is: Return on Equity = Net income/Average shareholders' equity = (Sales/Average total assets) × (Net income/Sales) × (Average total assets/Average shareholders' equity).

B Comment on any changes in the interest coverage ratio from year to year for each company.

C Comment on the interest coverage ratio of BT Group plc compared to Telefonica SA.

Solution to 1:

A The debt-to-assets, debt-to-capital, and debt-to-equity ratios are as follows, with supporting calculations from each company's most recent year demonstrated below.

	BT Group plc		Telefonica S A	
	31-Mar-18	**31-Mar-17**	**31-Dec-17**	**31-Dec-16**
Debt-to-assets	33.4%	30.0%	48.4%	48.8%
Debt-to-capital	58.1%	60.4%	67.7%	68.0%
Debt-to-equity	1.39	1.53	2.09	2.13

	BT Group plc	Telefonica S A
	31-Mar-18	***31-Dec-17***
Debt-to-assets	*33.4% = (2,281 + 11,994)/42,759*	*48.4% = (9,414 + 46,332)/115,066*
Debt-to-capital	*58.1% = (2,281 + 11,994)/(2,281 + 11,994 + 10,304)*	*67.7% = (9,414 + 46,332)/(9,414 + 46,332 + 26,618)*
Debt-to-equity	*1.39 = (2,281 + 11,994)/10,304*	*2.09 = (9,414 + 46,332)/26,618*

B BT's debt-to-assets ratio increased, while its debt-to-capital and debt-to-equity ratios both decreased. The decrease in BT's debt-to-capital and debt-to-equity ratios resulted primarily from the company's increase in total equity and indicate stronger solvency. In addition, we observe that BT decreased its short-term borrowings and increased its long-term debt.

Telefonica's leverage ratios appear fairly similar, albeit slightly lower, for 2017 compared to 2016. Similar to BT, it appears that Telefonica shifted away from short borrowings to long-term debt in 2017.

C In both years, all three of BT's leverage ratios were lower than Telefonica's. Based on these ratios, this may imply higher solvency of BT relative to Telefonica.

Solution to 2:

A The interest coverage ratios are as follows, with supporting calculations from each company's most recent year demonstrated below.

	BT Group plc		Telefonica S A	
	31-Mar-18	**31-Mar-17**	**31-Dec-17**	**31-Dec-16**
Interest coverage ratio	4.36	3.88	2.02	1.22

	BT Group plc	Telefonica S A
	31-Mar-18	*31-Dec-17*
Interest coverage ratio	*4.36 = 3,381/776*	*2.02 = 6,791/3,363*

B Both companies' interest coverage ratios increased from 2017 to 2018, indicating an improvement in solvency, consistent with the conclusions drawn from the companies' ratios in question 1. Both companies have sufficient operating earnings to cover interest payments.

C BT's ability to cover interest payments is greater than Telefonica's, although both companies have sufficient operating earnings to service its interest payments. This comparison indicates that BT has greater financial strength than Telefonica, which is also consistent with the conclusions drawn from a comparison of the companies' ratios in question 1.

SUMMARY

Non-current liabilities arise from different sources of financing and different types of creditors. Bonds are a common source of financing from debt markets. Key points in accounting and reporting of non-current liabilities include the following:

- The sales proceeds of a bond issue are determined by discounting future cash payments using the market rate of interest at the time of issuance (effective interest rate). The reported interest expense on bonds is based on the effective interest rate.
- Future cash payments on bonds usually include periodic interest payments (made at the stated interest rate or coupon rate) and the principal amount at maturity.
- When the market rate of interest equals the coupon rate for the bonds, the bonds will sell at par (i.e., at a price equal to the face value). When the market rate of interest is higher than the bonds' coupon rate, the bonds will sell at a discount. When the market rate of interest is lower than the bonds' coupon rate, the bonds will sell at a premium.
- An issuer amortises any issuance discount or premium on bonds over the life of the bonds.
- If a company redeems bonds before maturity, it reports a gain or loss on debt extinguishment computed as the net carrying amount of the bonds (including bond issuance costs under IFRS) less the amount required to redeem the bonds.
- Debt covenants impose restrictions on borrowers, such as limitations on future borrowing or requirements to maintain a minimum debt-to-equity ratio.
- The carrying amount of bonds is typically the amortised historical cost, which can differ from their fair value.
- Companies are required to disclose the fair value of financial liabilities, including debt. Although permitted to do so, few companies opt to report debt at fair values on the balance sheet.

- Beginning with fiscal year 2019, lessees report a right-of-use asset and a lease liability for all leases longer than one year. An exception under IFRS exists for leases when the underlying asset is of low value.
    - Subsequent to lease inception, the lessee's income statement will include both a depreciation expense on the right-of-use asset and an interest expense on the lease liability for all leases under IFRS and, under US GAAP for finance leases.
    - For lessee accounting, the distinction between finance leases and operating leases exists in US GAAP but not in IFRS. For operating leases under US GAAP, the lessee's income statement will show a single lease expense.
    - Under IFRS, a lessor classifies each lease as either a finance lease or an operating lease. A lease is classified as a finance lease if it "transfers substantially all the risks and rewards incidental to ownership of an underlying asset" and otherwise as an operating lease. For finance leases, but not for operating leases, the lessor derecognizes the underlying leased asset, and recognizes a lease receivable, and recognizes selling profit where applicable. For operating leases, the lessor does not derecognize the underlying asset and recognizes lease receipts as income.
    - Under US GAAP, a lessor classifies a lease in one of three categories: sales-type, direct financing, or operating. The lessor's classification and accounting for operating leases under US GAAP is similar to that under IFRS. For both sales-type and direct financing leases, the lessor derecognizes the underlying asset and recognizes a lease receivable; however, the lessor recognizes selling profit only if the lease is considered a sales-type lease.
- Two types of pension plans are defined contribution plans and defined benefits plans. In a defined contribution plan, the amount of contribution into the plan is specified (i.e., defined) and the amount of pension that is ultimately paid by the plan (received by the retiree) depends on the performance of the plan's assets. In a defined benefit plan, the amount of pension that is ultimately paid by the plan (received by the retiree) is defined, usually according to a benefit formula.
- Under a defined contribution pension plan, the cash payment made into the plan is recognised as pension expense.
- Under both IFRS and US GAAP, companies must report the difference between the defined benefit pension obligation and the pension assets as an asset or liability on the balance sheet. An underfunded defined benefit pension plan is shown as a non-current liability.
- Under IFRS, the change in the defined benefit plan net asset or liability is recognised as a cost of the period, with two components of the change (service cost and net interest expense or income) recognised in profit and loss and one component (remeasurements) of the change recognised in other comprehensive income.
- Under US GAAP, the change in the defined benefit plan net asset or liability is also recognised as a cost of the period with three components of the change (current service costs, interest expense on the beginning pension obligation, and expected return on plan assets) recognised in profit and loss and two components (past service costs and actuarial gains and losses) typically recognised in other comprehensive income.
- Solvency refers to a company's ability to meet its long-term debt obligations.

- In evaluating solvency, leverage ratios focus on the balance sheet and measure the amount of debt financing relative to equity financing.
- In evaluating solvency, coverage ratios focus on the income statement and cash flows and measure the ability of a company to cover its interest payments.

PRACTICE PROBLEMS

1 A company issues €1 million of bonds at face value. When the bonds are issued, the company will record a:

A cash inflow from investing activities.

B cash inflow from financing activities.

C cash inflow from operating activities.

2 At the time of issue of 4.50% coupon bonds, the effective interest rate was 5.00%. The bonds were *most likely* issued at:

A par.

B a discount.

C a premium.

3 Oil Exploration LLC paid $45,000 in printing, legal fees, commissions, and other costs associated with its recent bond issue. It is *most likely* to record these costs on its financial statements as:

A an asset under US GAAP and reduction of the carrying value of the debt under IFRS.

B a liability under US GAAP and reduction of the carrying value of the debt under IFRS.

C a cash outflow from investing activities under both US GAAP and IFRS.

4 A company issues $1,000,000 face value of 10-year bonds on 1 January 2015 when the market interest rate on bonds of comparable risk and terms is 5%. The bonds pay 6% interest annually on 31 December. At the time of issue, the bonds payable reflected on the balance sheet is *closest* to:

A $926,399.

B $1,000,000.

C $1,077,217.

5 Midland Brands issues three-year bonds dated 1 January 2015 with a face value of $5,000,000. The market interest rate on bonds of comparable risk and term is 3%. If the bonds pay 2.5% annually on 31 December, bonds payable when issued are most likely reported as *closest* to:

A $4,929,285.

B $5,000,000.

C $5,071,401.

6 A firm issues a bond with a coupon rate of 5.00% when the market interest rate is 5.50% on bonds of comparable risk and terms. One year later, the market interest rate increases to 6.00%. Based on this information, the effective interest rate is:

A 5.00%.

B 5.50%.

C 6.00%.

7 On 1 January 2010, Elegant Fragrances Company issues £1,000,000 face value, five-year bonds with annual interest payments of £55,000 to be paid each 31 December. The market interest rate is 6.0 percent. Using the effective interest rate method of amortisation, Elegant Fragrances is *most likely* to record:

© 2017 CFA Institute. All rights reserved.

- **A** an interest expense of £55,000 on its 2010 income statement.
- **B** a liability of £982,674 on the 31 December 2010 balance sheet.
- **C** a £58,736 cash outflow from operating activity on the 2010 statement of cash flows.

8 Consolidated Enterprises issues €10 million face value, five-year bonds with a coupon rate of 6.5 percent. At the time of issuance, the market interest rate is 6.0 percent. Using the effective interest rate method of amortisation, the carrying value after one year will be *closest* to:

- **A** €10.17 million.
- **B** €10.21 million.
- **C** €10.28 million.

9 A company issues €10,000,000 face value of 10-year bonds dated 1 January 2015 when the market interest rate on bonds of comparable risk and terms is 6%. The bonds pay 7% interest annually on 31 December. Based on the effective interest rate method, the interest expense on 31 December 2015 is *closest* to:

- **A** €644,161.
- **B** €700,000.
- **C** €751,521.

10 A company issues $30,000,000 face value of five-year bonds dated 1 January 2015 when the market interest rate on bonds of comparable risk and terms is 5%. The bonds pay 4% interest annually on 31 December. Based on the effective interest rate method, the carrying amount of the bonds on 31 December 2015 is *closest* to:

- **A** $28,466,099.
- **B** $28,800,000.
- **C** $28,936,215.

11 Lesp Industries issues five-year bonds dated 1 January 2015 with a face value of $2,000, 000 and 3% coupon rate paid annually on 31 December. The market interest rate on bonds of comparable risk and term is 4%. The sales proceeds of the bonds are $1,910,964. Under the effective interest rate method, the interest expense in 2017 is *closest* to:

- **A** $77,096.
- **B** $77,780.
- **C** $77,807.

12 For a bond issued at a premium, using the effective interest rate method, the:

- **A** carrying amount increases each year.
- **B** amortization of the premium increases each year.
- **C** premium is evenly amortized over the life of the bond.

13 Comte Industries issues $3,000,000 worth of three-year bonds dated 1 January 2015. The bonds pay interest of 5.5% annually on 31 December. The market interest rate on bonds of comparable risk and term is 5%. The sales proceeds of the bonds are $3,040,849. Under the straight-line method, the interest expense in the first year is *closest* to:

- **A** $150,000.
- **B** $151,384.
- **C** $152,042.

14 The management of Bank EZ repurchases its own bonds in the open market. They pay €6.5 million for bonds with a face value of €10.0 million and a carrying value of €9.8 million. The bank will *most likely* report:

A other comprehensive income of €3.3 million.

B other comprehensive income of €3.5 million.

C a gain of €3.3 million on the income statement.

15 A company redeems $1,000,000 face value bonds with a carrying value of $990,000. If the call price is 104 the company will:

A reduce bonds payable by $1,000,000.

B recognize a loss on the extinguishment of debt of $50,000.

C recognize a gain on the extinguishment of debt of $10,000.

16 Innovative Inventions, Inc. needs to raise €10 million. If the company chooses to issue zero-coupon bonds, its debt-to-equity ratio will *most likely*:

A rise as the maturity date approaches.

B decline as the maturity date approaches.

C remain constant throughout the life of the bond.

17 Fairmont Golf issued fixed rate debt when interest rates were 6 percent. Rates have since risen to 7 percent. Using only the carrying amount (based on historical cost) reported on the balance sheet to analyze the company's financial position would *most likely* cause an analyst to:

A overestimate Fairmont's economic liabilities.

B underestimate Fairmont's economic liabilities.

C underestimate Fairmont's interest coverage ratio.

18 Which of the following is an example of an affirmative debt covenant? The borrower is:

A prohibited from entering into mergers.

B prevented from issuing excessive additional debt.

C required to perform regular maintenance on equipment pledged as collateral.

19 Debt covenants are *least likely* to place restrictions on the issuer's ability to:

A pay dividends.

B issue additional debt.

C issue additional equity.

20 Regarding a company's debt obligations, which of the following is *most likely* presented on the balance sheet?

A Effective interest rate

B Maturity dates for debt obligations

C The portion of long-term debt due in the next 12 months

21 Compared to using a finance lease, a lessee that makes use of an operating lease will *most likely* report higher:

A debt.

B rent expense.

C cash flow from operating activity.

22 Which of the following is *most likely* a lessee's disclosure about operating leases?

A Lease liabilities.

B Future obligations by maturity.

C Net carrying amounts of leased assets.

23 For a lessor, the leased asset appears on the balance sheet and continues to be depreciated when the lease is classified as:

A a sales-type lease.

B an operating lease.

C a financing lease.

24 Under US GAAP, a lessor's reported revenues at lease inception will be *highest* if the lease is classified as:

A a sales-type lease.

B an operating lease.

C a direct financing lease.

25 A lessor will record interest income if a lease is classified as:

A a capital lease.

B an operating lease.

C either a capital or an operating lease.

26 Compared with a finance lease, an operating lease:

A is similar to renting an asset.

B is equivalent to the purchase of an asset.

C term is for the majority of the economic life of the asset.

27 Under US GAAP, which of the following would require the lessee to classify a lease as a capital lease?

A The term is 60% of the useful life of the asset.

B The lease contains an option to purchase the asset at fair value.

C The present value of the lease payments is 95% of the fair value.

28 A lessee that enters into a finance lease will report the:

A lease payable on its balance sheet.

B full lease payment on its income statement.

C full lease payment as an operating cash flow.

29 A company enters into a finance lease agreement to acquire the use of an asset for three years with lease payments of €19,000,000 starting next year. The leased asset has a fair market value of €49,000,000 and the present value of the lease payments is €47,250,188. Based on this information, the value of the lease payable reported on the company's balance sheet is *closest* to:

A €47,250,188.

B €49,000,000.

C €57,000,000.

30 Which of the following *best* describes reporting and disclosure requirements for a company that enters into an operating lease as the lessee? The operating lease obligation is:

A reported as a receivable on the balance sheet.

B disclosed in notes to the financial statements.

C reported as a component of debt on the balance sheet.

31 Cavalier Copper Mines has $840 million in total liabilities and $520 million in shareholders' equity. It discloses operating lease commitments over the next five years with a present value of $100 million. If the lease commitments are treated as debt, the debt-to-total-capital ratio is *closest* to:

A 0.58.

B 0.62.

C 0.64.

32 The following presents selected financial information for a company:

	$ Millions
Short-term borrowing	4,231
Current portion of long-term interest-bearing debt	29
Long-term interest-bearing debt	925
Average shareholders' equity	18,752
Average total assets	45,981

The financial leverage ratio is *closest* to:

A 0.113

B 0.277

C 2.452

33 An analyst evaluating three industrial companies calculates the following ratios:

	Company A	Company B	Company C
Debt-to-Equity	23.5%	22.5%	52.5%
Interest Coverage	15.6	49.5	45.5

The company with both the lowest financial leverage and the greatest ability to meet interest payments is:

A Company A.

B Company B.

C Company C.

34 An analyst evaluating a company's solvency gathers the following information:

	$ Millions
Short-term interest-bearing debt	1,258
Long-term interest-bearing debt	321
Total shareholder's equity	4,285
Total assets	8,750
EBIT	2,504
Interest payments	52

The company's debt-to-assets ratio is *closest* to:

A 0.18.

B 0.27.

C 0.37.

35 Penben Corporation has a defined benefit pension plan. At 31 December, its pension obligation is €10 million and pension assets are €9 million. Under either IFRS or US GAAP, the reporting on the balance sheet would be *closest* to which of the following?

A €10 million is shown as a liability, and €9 million appears as an asset.

B €1 million is shown as a net pension obligation.

C Pension assets and obligations are not required to be shown on the balance sheet but only disclosed in footnotes.

36 The following information is associated with a company that offers its employees a defined benefit plan:

Fair value of fund's assets	$1,500,000,000
Estimated pension obligations	$2,600,000,000
Present value of estimated pension obligations	$1,200,000,000

Based on this information, the company's balance sheet will present a net pension:

A asset of $300,000,000.

B asset of $1,400,000,000.

C liability of $1,100,000,000.

SOLUTIONS

1 B is correct. The company receives €1 million in cash from investors at the time the bonds are issued, which is recorded as a financing activity.

2 B is correct. The effective interest rate is greater than the coupon rate and the bonds will be issued at a discount.

3 A is correct. Under US GAAP, expenses incurred when issuing bonds are generally recorded as an asset and amortised to the related expense (legal, etc.) over the life of the bonds. Under IFRS, they are included in the measurement of the liability. The related cash flows are financing activities.

4 C is correct. The bonds will be issued at a premium because the coupon rate is higher than the market interest rate. The future cash outflows, the present value of the cash outflows, and the total present value are as follows:

Date	Interest Payment ($)	Present Value at Market Rate 5% ($)		Present Value at Market Rate 5% ($)	Total Present Value ($)
31 December 2015	60,000.00	57,142.86			
31 December 2016	60,000.00	54,421.77			
31 December 2017	60,000.00	51,830.26			
31 December 2018	60,000.00	49,362.15			
31 December 2019	60,000.00	47,011.57			
31 December 2020	60,000.00	44,772.92			
31 December 2021	60,000.00	42,640.88			
31 December 2022	60,000.00	40,610.36			
31 December 2023	60,000.00	38,676.53			
31 December 2024	60,000.00	36,834.80	1,000,000.00	613,913.25	
		463,304.10		613,913.25	1,077,217.35
					Sales Proceeds

The following illustrates the keystrokes for many financial calculators to calculate sales proceeds of $1,077,217.35:

Calculator Notation	Numerical Value for This Problem
N	10
% *i* or I/Y	5
FV	$1,000,000.00
PMT	$60,000.00
PV compute	X

Thus, the sales proceeds are reported on the balance sheet as an increase in long-term liability, bonds payable of $1,077,217.

5 A is correct. The bonds payable reported at issue is equal to the sales proceeds. The interest payments and future value of the bond must be discounted at the market interest rate of 3% to determine the sales proceeds.

Date	Interest Payment	Present Value at Market Rate (3%)	Face Value Payment	Present Value at Market Rate (3%)	Total Present Value
31 December 2015	$125,000.00	$121,359.22			
31 December 2016	$125,000.00	$117,824.49			
31 December 2017	$125,000.00	$114,392.71	$5,000,000.00	$4,575,708.30	
Total		$353,576.42		$4,575,708.30	$4,929,284.72

The following illustrates the keystrokes for many financial calculators to calculate sales proceeds of $4,929,284.72:

Calculator Notation	Numerical Value for This Problem
N	3
% *i* or I/Y	3.0
FV	$5,000,000.00
PMT	$125,000.00
PV compute	X

6 B is correct. The market interest rate at the time of issuance is the effective interest rate that the company incurs on the debt. The effective interest rate is the discount rate that equates the present value of the coupon payments and face value to their selling price. Consequently, the effective interest rate is 5.50%.

7 B is correct. The bonds will be issued at a discount because the market interest rate is higher than the stated rate. Discounting the future payments to their present value indicates that at the time of issue, the company will record £978,938 as both a liability and a cash inflow from financing activities. Interest expense in 2010 is £58,736 (£978,938 times 6.0 percent). During the year, the company will pay cash of £55,000 related to the interest payment, but interest expense on the income statement will also reflect £3,736 related to amortisation of the initial discount (£58,736 interest expense less the £55,000 interest payment). Thus, the value of the liability at 31 December 2010 will reflect the initial value (£978,938) plus the amortised discount (£3,736), for a total of £982,674. The cash outflow of £55,000 may be presented as either an operating or financing activity under IFRS.

8 A is correct. The coupon rate on the bonds is higher than the market rate, which indicates that the bonds will be issued at a premium. Taking the present value of each payment indicates an issue date value of €10,210,618. The interest expense is determined by multiplying the carrying amount at the beginning of the period (€10,210,618) by the market interest rate at the time of issue (6.0 percent) for an interest expense of €612,637. The value after one year will equal the beginning value less the amount of the premium amortised to date, which is the difference between the amount paid (€650,000) and the expense accrued (€612,637) or €37,363. €10,210,618 – €37,363 = €10,173,255 or €10.17 million.

9 A is correct. The future cash outflows, the present value of the cash outflows, and the total present value are as follows:

Date	Interest Payment (€)	Present Value at Market Rate 6% (€)		Present Value at Market Rate 6% (€)	Total Present Value (€)
31 December 2015	700,000.00	660,377.36			
31 December 2016	700,000.00	622,997.51			
31 December 2017	700,000.00	587,733.50			
31 December 2018	700,000.00	554,465.56			
31 December 2019	700,000.00	523,080.72			
31 December 2020	700,000.00	493,472.38			
31 December 2021	700,000.00	465,539.98			
31 December 2022	700,000.00	439,188.66			
31 December 2023	700,000.00	414,328.92			
31 December 2024	700,000.00	390,876.34	10,000,000.00	5,583,947.77	
		5,152,060.94		5,583,947.77	10,736,008.71
					Sales Proceeds

The following illustrates the keystrokes for many financial calculators to calculate sales proceeds of €10,736,008.71:

Calculator Notation	Numerical Value for This Problem
N	10
% *i* or I/Y	6
FV	$10,000,000.00
PMT	$700,000.00
PV compute	X

The interest expense is calculated by multiplying the carrying amount at the beginning of the year by the effective interest rate at issuance. As a result, the interest expense at 31 December 2015 is €644,161 (€10,736,008.71 × 6%).

10 C is correct. The future cash outflows, the present value of the cash outflows, and the total present value are as follows:

Date	Interest Payment ($)	Present Value at Market Rate 5% ($)		Present Value at Market Rate 5% ($)	Total Present Value ($)
31 December 2015	1,200,000	1,142,857.14			
31 December 2016	1,200,000	1,088,435.37			
31 December 2017	1,200,000	1,036,605.12			
31 December 2018	1,200,000	987,242.97			
31 December 2019	1,200,000	940,231.40	30,000,000	23,505,785.00	
		5,195,372.00		23,505,785.00	28,701,157.00
					Sales Proceeds

The following illustrates the keystrokes for many financial calculators to calculate sales proceeds of $28,701,157.00:

Calculator Notation	Numerical Value for This Problem
N	5
% *i* or I/Y	5
FV	$30,000,000.00
PMT	$1,200,000.00
PV compute	X

The following table illustrates interest expense, premium amortization, and carrying amount (amortized cost) for 2015.

Year	Carrying Amount (beginning of year)	Interest Expense (at effective interest rate of 5%)	Interest Payment (at coupon rate of 4%)	Amortization of Discount	Carrying Amount (end of year)
2015	$28,701,157.00	$1,435,057.85	$1,200,000.00	$235,057.85	$28,936,214.85

The carrying amount at the end of the year is found by adding the amortization of the discount to the carrying amount at the beginning of the year. As a result, the carrying amount on 31 December 2015 is $28,936,215.

Alternatively, the following illustrates the keystrokes for many financial calculators to calculate the carrying value at the end of first year of $28,936, 215:

Calculator Notation	Numerical Value for This Problem
N	4
% *i* or I/Y	5
FV	$30,000,000.00
PMT	$1,200,000.00
PV compute	X

11 B is correct. The interest expense for a given year is equal to the carrying amount at the beginning of the year times the effective interest of 4%. Under the effective interest rate method, the difference between the interest expense and the interest payment (based on the coupon rate and face value) is the discount amortized in the period, which increases the carrying amount annually. For 2017, the interest expense is the beginning carrying amount ($1,944,499) times the effective interest of 4%.

Year	Carrying Amount (beginning)	Interest Expense (at effective interest of 4%)	Interest Payment (at coupon rate of 3%)	Amortization of Discount	Carrying Amount (end of year)
2015	$1,910,964	$76,439	$60,000.00	$16,439	$1,927,403
2016	$1,927,403	$77,096	$60,000.00	$17,096	$1,944,499
2017	$1,944,499	$77,780	$60,000.00	$17,780	$1,962,279

12 B is correct. The amortization of the premium equals the interest payment minus the interest expense. The interest payment is constant and the interest expense decreases as the carrying amount decreases. As a result, the amortization of the premium increases each year.

13 B is correct. Under the straight-line method, the bond premium is amortized equally over the life of the bond. The annual interest payment is $165,000 ($3,000,000 × 5.5%) and annual amortization of the premium under the straight-line method is $13,616 [($3,040,849 – $3,000,000)/3)]. The interest expense is the interest payment less the amortization of the premium ($165,000 – $13,616 = $151,384).

14 C is correct. A gain of €3.3 million (carrying amount less amount paid) will be reported on the income statement.

15 B is correct. If a company decides to redeem a bond before maturity, bonds payable is reduced by the carrying amount of the debt. The difference between the cash required to redeem the bonds and the carrying amount of the bonds is a gain or loss on the extinguishment of debt. Because the call price is 104 and the face value is $1,000,000, the redemption cost is 104% of $1,000,000 or $1,040,000. The company's loss on redemption would be $50,000 ($990,000 carrying amount of debt minus $1,040,000 cash paid to redeem the callable bonds).

16 A is correct. The value of the liability for zero-coupon bonds increases as the discount is amortised over time. Furthermore, the amortised interest will reduce earnings at an increasing rate over time as the value of the liability increases. Higher relative debt and lower relative equity (through retained earnings) will cause the debt-to-equity ratio to increase as the zero-coupon bonds approach maturity.

17 A is correct. When interest rates rise, bonds decline in value. Thus, the carrying amount of the bonds being carried on the balance sheet is higher than the market value. The company could repurchase the bonds for less than the carrying amount, so the economic liabilities are overestimated. Because the bonds are issued at a fixed rate, there is no effect on interest coverage.

18 C is correct. Affirmative covenants require certain actions of the borrower. Requiring the company to perform regular maintenance on equipment pledged as collateral is an example of an affirmative covenant because it requires the company to do something. Negative covenants require that the borrower not take certain actions. Prohibiting the borrower from entering into mergers and preventing the borrower from issuing excessive additional debt are examples of negative covenants.

19 C is correct. Covenants protect debtholders from excessive risk taking, typically by limiting the issuer's ability to use cash or by limiting the overall levels of debt relative to income and equity. Issuing additional equity would increase the company's ability to meet its obligations, so debtholders would not restrict that ability.

20 C is correct. The non-current liabilities section of the balance sheet usually includes a single line item of the total amount of a company's long-term debt due after 1 year, and the current liabilities section shows the portion of a company's long-term debt due in the next 12 months. Notes to the financial statements generally present the stated and effective interest rates and maturity dates for a company's debt obligations

21 B is correct. An operating lease is not recorded on the balance sheet (debt is lower), and lease payments are entirely categorised as rent (interest expense is lower.) Because the rent expense is an operating outflow but principal repayments are financing cash flows, the operating lease will result in lower cash flow from operating activity.

22 B is correct. The lessee will disclose the future obligation by maturity of its operating leases. The future obligations by maturity, leased assets, and lease liabilities will all be shown for finance leases.

23 B is correct. When a lease is classified as an operating lease, the underlying asset remains on the lessor's balance sheet. The lessor will record a depreciation expense that reduces the asset's value over time.

24 A is correct. A sales-type lease treats the lease as a sale of the asset, and revenue is recorded at the time of sale equal to the present value of future lease payments. Under a direct financing lease, only interest income is reported as earned. Under an operating lease, revenue from rent is reported when collected.

25 A is correct. A portion of the payments for capital leases, either direct financing or sales-type, is reported as interest income. With an operating lease, all revenue is recorded as rental revenue.

26 A is correct. An operating lease is an agreement that allows the lessee to use an asset for a period of time. Thus, an operating lease is similar to renting an asset, whereas a finance lease is equivalent to the purchase of an asset by the lessee that is directly financed by the lessor.

27 C is correct. If the present value of the lease payments is greater than 90% of the fair value of the asset, the lease is considered a capital lease. A lease with a term that is 75% or more of the useful life of the asset is deemed to be a capital lease. The option to purchase the asset must be deemed to be cheap (bargain purchase option), not just include the option to purchase the asset.

28 A is correct. A finance lease is similar to borrowing money and buying an asset; a company that enters into a finance lease as the lessee reports an asset (leased asset) and related debt (lease payable) on its balance sheet. A company that enters into a finance lease as the lessee will report interest expense and depreciation expense on its income statement. A company that enters into an operating lease will report the lease payment on its income statement. For a finance lease, only the portion of the lease payment relating to interest expense reduces operating cash flow; the portion of the lease payment that reduces the lease liability appears as a cash outflow in the financing section. A company that enters into an operating lease as the lessee will report the full lease payment as an operating cash outflow.

29 A is correct. A company that enters into a finance lease reports the value of both the leased asset and lease payable as the lower of the present value of future lease payments and the fair value of the leased asset. The present value of the future lease payments, €47,250,188, is lower than the fair market value of the leased asset, €49,000,000. The company will record a lease payable on the balance sheet of €47,250,188.

30 B is correct. An operating lease is economically similar to renting an asset. A company that enters into an operating lease as a lessee reports a lease expense on its income statement during the period it uses the asset and reports no asset or liability on its balance sheet. The operating lease is disclosed in notes to the financial statements.

31 C is correct. The current debt-to-total-capital ratio is \$840/(\$840 + \$520) = 0.62. To adjust for the lease commitments, an analyst should add \$100 to both the numerator and denominator: \$940/(\$940 + \$520) = 0.64.

32 C is correct. The financial leverage ratio is calculated as follows:

$$\frac{\text{Average total assets}}{\text{Average shareholder's equity}} = \frac{\$45{,}981 \text{ million}}{\$18{,}752 \text{ million}} = \$2.452 \text{ million}$$

33 B is correct. Company B has the lowest debt-to-equity ratio, indicating the lowest financial leverage, and the highest interest coverage ratio, indicating the greatest number of times that EBIT covers interest payments.

34 A is correct because the debt-to-assets (total debt)/(total assets) ratio is (1,258 + 321)/(8,750) = 1,579/8,750 = 0.18

35 B is correct. The company will report a net pension obligation of €1 million equal to the pension obligation (€10 million) less the plan assets (€9 million).

36 A is correct. A company that offers a defined benefit plan makes payments into a pension fund and the retirees are paid from the fund. The payments that a company makes into the fund are invested until they are needed to pay retirees. If the fair value of the fund's assets is higher than the present value of the estimated pension obligation, the plan has a surplus and the company's balance sheet will reflect a net pension asset. Because the fair value of the fund's assets is $1,500,000,000 and the present value of estimated pension obligations is $1,200,000,000, the company will present a net pension asset of $300,000,000 on its balance sheet.

FINANCIAL REPORTING AND ANALYSIS
STUDY SESSION 9

Financial Reporting and Analysis (4)

This study session introduces the concept of financial reporting quality. The session examines the financial reporting quality differences that may exist between companies and the means for identifying them. Warning signs of poor or low quality reporting are covered. The application of financial analysis techniques to evaluate a company's past and projected performance, assess credit risk, and screen for potential equity investments follows. Common adjustments to reported financials to facilitate cross-company comparisons conclude the session.

READING ASSIGNMENTS

Reading 29	Financial Reporting Quality by Jack T. Ciesielski, CPA, CFA, Elaine Henry, PhD, CFA, and Thomas I. Selling, PhD, CPA
Reading 30	Financial Statement Analysis: Applications by Thomas R. Robinson, PhD, CFA, Jan Hendrik van Greuning, DCom, CFA, Elaine Henry, PhD, CFA, and Michael A. Broihahn, CPA, CIA, CFA

Note: Changes in accounting standards as well as new rulings and/or pronouncements issued after the publication of the readings on financial reporting and analysis may cause some of the information in these readings to become dated. Candidates are *not* responsible for anything that occurs after the readings were published. In addition, candidates are expected to be familiar with the analytical frameworks contained in the readings, as well as the implications of alternative accounting methods for financial analysis and valuation discussed in the readings. Candidates are also responsible for the content of accounting standards, but not for the actual reference numbers. Finally, candidates should be aware that certain ratios may be defined and calculated differently. When alternative ratio definitions exist and no specific definition is given, candidates should use the ratio definitions emphasized in the readings.

© 2019 CFA Institute. All rights reserved.

READING

29

Financial Reporting Quality

by Jack T. Ciesielski, CPA, CFA, Elaine Henry, PhD, CFA, and Thomas I. Selling, PhD, CPA

Jack T. Ciesielski, CPA, CFA, is at R.G. Associates, Inc., former publisher of The Analyst's Accounting Observer (USA). Elaine Henry, PhD, CFA, is at Stevens Institute of Technology (USA). Thomas I. Selling, PhD, CPA, is at the Cox School of Business, Southern Methodist University (USA).

LEARNING OUTCOMES

Mastery	*The candidate should be able to:*
☐	a. distinguish between financial reporting quality and quality of reported results (including quality of earnings, cash flow, and balance sheet items);
☐	b. describe a spectrum for assessing financial reporting quality;
☐	c. distinguish between conservative and aggressive accounting;
☐	d. describe motivations that might cause management to issue financial reports that are not high quality;
☐	e. describe conditions that are conducive to issuing low-quality, or even fraudulent, financial reports;
☐	f. describe mechanisms that discipline financial reporting quality and the potential limitations of those mechanisms;
☐	g. describe presentation choices, including non-GAAP measures, that could be used to influence an analyst's opinion;
☐	h. describe accounting methods (choices and estimates) that could be used to manage earnings, cash flow, and balance sheet items;
☐	i. describe accounting warning signs and methods for detecting manipulation of information in financial reports.

Note: Changes in accounting standards as well as new rulings and/or pronouncements issued after the publication of the readings on financial reporting and analysis may cause some of the information in these readings to become dated. Candidates are *not* responsible for anything that occurs after the readings were published. In addition, candidates are expected to be familiar with the analytical frameworks contained in the readings, as well as the implications of alternative accounting methods for financial analysis and valuation discussed in the readings. Candidates are also responsible for the content of accounting standards, but not for the actual reference numbers. Finally, candidates should be aware that certain ratios may be defined and calculated differently. When alternative ratio definitions exist and no specific definition is given, candidates should use the ratio definitions emphasized in the readings.

© 2019 CFA Institute. All rights reserved.

1 INTRODUCTION

Ideally, analysts would always have access to financial reports that are based on sound financial reporting standards, such as those from the International Accounting Standards Board (IASB) and the Financial Accounting Standards Board (FASB), and are free from manipulation. But, in practice, the quality of financial reports can vary greatly. High-quality financial reporting provides information that is useful to analysts in assessing a company's performance and prospects. Low-quality financial reporting contains inaccurate, misleading, or incomplete information.

Extreme lapses in financial reporting quality have given rise to high-profile scandals that resulted not only in investor losses but also in reduced confidence in the financial system. Financial statement users who were able to accurately assess financial reporting quality were better positioned to avoid losses. These lapses illustrate the challenges analysts face as well as the potential costs of failing to recognize practices that result in misleading or inaccurate financial reports.[1] Examples of misreporting can provide an analyst with insight into various signals that may indicate poor-quality financial reports.

This reading addresses *financial reporting quality*, which pertains to the quality of information in financial reports, including disclosures in notes. High-quality reporting provides decision-useful information, which is relevant and faithfully represents the economic reality of the company's activities during the reporting period as well as the company's financial condition at the end of the period. A separate but interrelated attribute of quality is *quality of reported results* or *earnings quality*, which pertains to the earnings and cash generated by the company's actual economic activities and the resulting financial condition. The term "earnings quality" is commonly used in practice and will be used broadly to encompass the quality of earnings, cash flow, and/or balance sheet items. High-quality earnings result from activities that a company will likely be able to sustain in the future and provide a sufficient return on the company's investment. The concepts of earnings quality and financial reporting quality are interrelated because a correct assessment of earnings quality is possible only when there is some basic level of financial reporting quality. Beyond this basic level, as the quality of reporting increases, the ability of financial statement users to correctly assess earnings quality and to develop expectations for future performance arguably also increases.

Section 2 provides a conceptual overview of reporting quality. Section 3 discusses motivations that might cause, and conditions that might enable, management to issue financial reports that are not high quality and mechanisms that aim to provide discipline to financial reporting quality. Section 4 describes choices made by management that can affect financial reporting quality—presentation choices, accounting methods, and estimates—as well as warning signs of poor-quality financial reporting.

2 CONCEPTUAL OVERVIEW

As indicated in the introduction, financial reporting quality and results or earnings quality are interrelated attributes of quality. Exhibit 1 illustrates this interrelationship and its implications.

1 In this reading, the examples of misleading or inaccurate financial reports occurred in prior years—*not* because there are no current examples of questionable financial reporting, but rather because it has been conclusively resolved that misreporting occurred in the historical examples.

Exhibit 1 Relationships between Financial Reporting Quality and Earnings Quality

		Financial Reporting Quality: Low	Financial Reporting Quality: High
Earnings (Results) Quality	High	LOW financial reporting quality impedes assessment of earnings quality and impedes valuation.	HIGH financial reporting quality enables assessment. HIGH earnings quality increases company value.
	Low		HIGH financial reporting quality enables assessment. LOW earnings quality decreases company value.

As can be seen in Exhibit 1, if financial reporting quality is low, the information provided is of little use in assessing the company's performance, and thus in making investment and other decisions.

Financial reporting quality varies across companies. High-quality reports contain information that is relevant, complete, neutral, and free from error. The lowest-quality reports contain information that is pure fabrication. Earnings (results) quality can range from high and sustainable to low and unsustainable. Providers of resources prefer high and sustainable earnings. Combining the two measures of quality—financial reporting and earnings—the overall quality of financial reports from a user perspective can be thought of as spanning a continuum from the highest to the lowest. Exhibit 2 presents a quality spectrum that provides a basis for evaluating better versus poorer quality reports. This spectrum ranges from reports that are of high financial reporting quality and reflect high and sustainable earnings quality to reports that are not useful because of poor financial reporting quality.

Exhibit 2 Quality Spectrum of Financial Reports

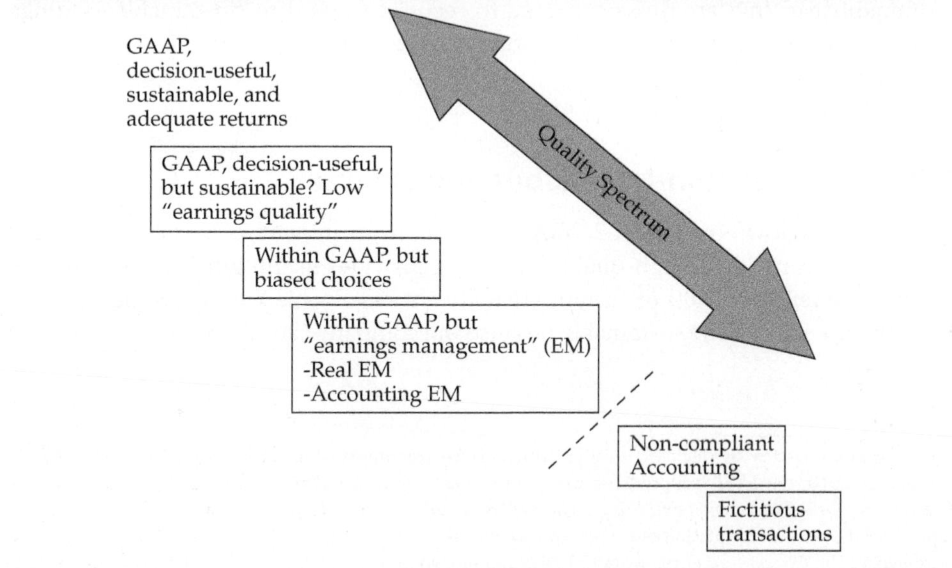

2.1 GAAP, Decision-Useful, Sustainable, and Adequate Returns

At the top of the spectrum, labeled in Exhibit 2 as "GAAP, decision-useful, sustainable, and adequate returns," are high-quality reports that provide useful information about high-quality earnings.

- High-quality financial reports conform to the generally accepted accounting principles (GAAP) of the jurisdiction, such as International Financial Reporting Standards (IFRS), US GAAP, or other home-country GAAP. The exhibit uses the term GAAP to refer generically to the accounting standards accepted in a company's jurisdiction.
- In addition to conforming to GAAP, high-quality financial reports also embody the characteristics of decision-useful information such as those defined in the *Conceptual Framework*.[2] Recall that the fundamental characteristics of useful information are relevance and faithful representation. Relevant information is defined as information that can affect a decision and encompasses the notion of materiality. (Information is considered material if "omitting it or misstating it could influence decisions that users make on the basis of the financial information of a specific reporting entity."[3]) Faithful representation of economic events is complete, neutral, and free from error.

  The *Conceptual Framework* also enumerates enhancing characteristics of useful information: comparability, verifiability, timeliness, and understandability. Of course, the desirable characteristics for financial information require trade-offs. For example, financial reports must balance the aim of providing information that is produced quickly enough to be timely and thus relevant, and yet not so quickly that errors occur. Financial reports must balance the aim of providing information that is complete but not so exhaustive that immaterial information is included. High-quality information results when these and other tradeoffs are made in an unbiased, skillful manner.
- High-quality earnings indicate an adequate level of return on investment and derive from activities that a company will likely be able to sustain in the future. An adequate level of return on investment exceeds the cost of the investment and also equals or exceeds the expected return. Sustainable activities and sustainable earnings are those expected to recur in the future. Sustainable earnings that provide a high return on investment contribute to higher valuation of a company and its securities.

2.2 GAAP, Decision-Useful, but Sustainable?

The next level down in Exhibit 2, "GAAP, decision-useful, but sustainable?" refers to circumstances in which high-quality reporting provides useful information, but that information reflects results or earnings that are not sustainable (lower earnings quality). The earnings may not be sustainable because the company cannot expect earnings that

2 The characteristics of decision-useful information are identical under IFRS and US GAAP. In September 2010, the IASB adopted the *Conceptual Framework for Financial Reporting* in place of the *Framework for the Preparation and Presentation of Financial Statements* (1989). The *Conceptual Framework* represents the partial completion of a joint convergence project between the IASB and FASB on an updated framework. The *Conceptual Framework* (2010) contains two updated chapters: "The Objective of Financial Reporting" and "Qualitative Characteristics of Useful Financial Information." The remainder of the material in the *Conceptual Framework* is from the *Framework* (1989) and will be updated as the project is completed. Also in September 2010, the FASB issued Concepts Statement 8, "Conceptual Framework for Financial Reporting," to replace Concepts Statements 1 and 2.

3 Text from conceptual frameworks referenced in Note 4.

generate the same level of return on investment in the future or because the earnings, although replicable, will not generate sufficient return on investment to sustain the company. Earnings quality is low in both cases. Reporting can be high quality even when the economic reality being depicted is not of high quality. For example, consider a company that generates a loss, or earnings that do not provide an adequate return on investment, or earnings that resulted from non-recurring activities. The relatively undesirable economic reality could nonetheless be depicted in financial reporting that provides high-quality, decision-useful information.

Exhibit 3 presents an excerpt from the fiscal year 2014 first-quarter results of Toyota Motor Corporation, a Japanese automobile company. As highlighted by a *Wall Street Journal* article,[4] the company sold fewer cars but reported an 88% increase in operating profits compared with the prior year, primarily because of the change in exchange rates. The weaker yen benefited Toyota both because the company manufactures more cars in Japan (compared with its competitors) and because the company sells a significant number of cars outside of Japan. Exchange rate weakening is a less sustainable source of profits than manufacturing and selling cars. In summary, this example is a case of high-quality financial reporting coupled with lower earnings quality.

Exhibit 3 Excerpt from Toyota Motor Corporation's Consolidated Financial Results for FY2014 First Quarter Ending 30 June 2013

Consolidated vehicle unit sales in Japan and overseas decreased by 37 thousand units, or 1.6%, to 2,232 thousand units in FY2014 first quarter (the three months ended June 30, 2013) compared with FY2013 first quarter (the three months ended June 30, 2012). Vehicle unit sales in Japan decreased by 51 thousand units, or 8.8%, to 526 thousand units in FY2014 first quarter compared with FY2013 first quarter. Meanwhile, overseas vehicle unit sales increased by 14 thousand units, or 0.8%, to 1,706 thousand units in FY2014 first quarter compared with FY2013 first quarter.

As for the results of operations, net revenues increased by 753.7 billion yen, or 13.7%, to 6,255.3 billion yen in FY2014 first quarter compared with FY2013 first quarter, and operating income increased by 310.2 billion yen, or 87.9%, to 663.3 billion yen in FY2014 first quarter compared with FY2013 first quarter. The factors contributing to an increase in operating income were the effects of changes in exchange rates of 260.0 billion yen, cost reduction efforts of 70.0 billion yen, marketing efforts of 30.0 billion yen and other factors of 10.2 billion yen. On the other hand, the factors contributing to a decrease in operating income were the increase in expenses and others of 60.0 billion yen.

2.3 Biased Accounting Choices

The next level down in the spectrum in Exhibit 2 is "Within GAAP, but biased choices." Biased choices result in financial reports that do not faithfully represent the economic substance of what is being reported. The problem with bias in financial reporting, as with other deficiencies in reporting quality, is that it impedes an investor's ability to correctly assess a company's past performance, to accurately forecast future performance, and thus to appropriately value the company.

Choices are deemed to be "aggressive" if they increase a company's reported performance and financial position in the period under review. The choice can increase the amount of revenues, earnings, and/or operating cash flow reported for the period,

4 Back (2013).

or decrease expenses, and/or reduce the level of debt reported on the balance sheet. Aggressive choices may lead to a reduction in the company's reported performance and in its financial position in later periods. In contrast, choices are deemed "conservative" if they decrease a company's performance and financial position in the reporting period. This can include lowering the reported revenues, earnings, and/or operating cash flow reported or increasing expenses, or recording a higher level of debt on the balance sheet. Conservative choices may lead to a rise in the company's reported performance and financial position in later periods.

Another type of bias is understatement of earnings volatility, so-called earnings "smoothing". Earnings smoothing can result from conservative choices to understate earnings in periods when a company's operations are performing well, building up (often hidden) reserves that allow aggressive choices in periods when its operations are struggling.

Biased choices can be made not only in the context of reported amounts but also in the context of how information is presented. For example, companies can disclose information transparently, which facilitates analysis, or they can disclose it in a manner that aims to obscure unfavorable and/or emphasize favorable information.

EXAMPLE 1

Quality of Financial Reports

PACCAR Inc. designs, manufactures, and distributes trucks and related aftermarket parts that are sold worldwide under the Kenworth, Peterbilt, and DAF nameplates. In 2013, the US SEC charged PACCAR for various accounting deficiencies that "clouded their financial reporting to investors in the midst of the financial crisis." The SEC complaint cites the company's 2009 segment reporting. Exhibit 4A presents an excerpt from the notes to PACCAR's financial statements, and Exhibit 4B presents an excerpt from the management's discussion and analysis (MD&A) of PACCAR's annual report.

Exhibit 4A Excerpt from Notes to PACCAR's 2009 Financial Statements

S. SEGMENT AND RELATED INFORMATION

PACCAR operates in two principal segments, Truck and Financial Services. The Truck segment includes the manufacture of trucks and the distribution of related aftermarket parts, both of which are sold through a network of independent dealers... The Financial Services segment is composed of finance and leasing products and services provided to truck customers and dealers ... Included in All Other is PACCAR's industrial winch manufacturing business. Also within this category are other sales, income and expenses not attributable to a reportable segment, including a portion of corporate expense.

Business Segment Data ($ millions)

	2009	2008	2007
Income before Income Taxes			
Truck	$25.9	$1,156.5	$1,352.8
All other	42.2	6.0	32.0
	68.1	1,162.5	1,384.8

Exhibit 4A (Continued)

	2009	2008	2007
Financial services	84.6	216.9	284.1
Investment income	22.3	84.6	95.4
	$175.0	$1,464.0	$1,764.3

Exhibit 4B Excerpt from MD&A of PACCAR's 2009 Annual Report

Net sales and revenues and gross margins for truck units and aftermarket parts are provided below. The aftermarket parts gross margin includes direct revenues and costs, but excludes certain truck segment costs.

	2009	2008	% Change
Net Sales and Revenues			
Trucks	$5,103.30	$11,281.30	−55
Aftermarket parts	1,890.70	2,266.10	−17
	$6,994.00	$13,547.40	−48
Gross Margin			
Trucks	−$46.6	$1,141.70	−104
Aftermarket parts	625.7	795.20	−21
	$579.1	$1,936.90	−70

1 Based on the segment data excerpted from the notes to the financial statements, was PACCAR's truck segment profitable in 2009?

2 Based on the data about the truck's gross margin presented in the MD&A, was PACCAR's truck segment profitable in 2009?

3 What is the main difference between the note presentation and the MD&A presentation?

4 The SEC complaint stated that "PACCAR failed to report the operating results of its aftermarket parts business separately from its truck sales business as required under segment reporting requirements, which are in place to ensure that investors gain the same insight into a company as its executives." Is the PACCAR situation an example of issues with financial reporting quality, earnings quality, or both?

Solution to 1:

Yes, the segment data presented in the note to the financial statements indicates that the Truck segment earned $25.9 million in 2009.

Solution to 2:

No, the segment data presented in the MD&A indicates that the Truck segment had a negative gross margin.

Solution to 3:

The main difference between the note presentation and the MD&A presentation is that the aftermarket parts business is combined with the trucks business in the notes but separated in the MD&A. Although the data are not exactly comparable in the two disclosures (because the note shows income before taxes and the MD&A shows gross profit), the two disclosures present a different picture of PACCAR's profits from truck sales.

Solution to 4:

The PACCAR situation appears to be an example of issues with both financial reporting quality and earnings quality. The substantial decrease in truck sales and the negative gross margin reflect poor earnings quality. The failure to disclose clear segment information is an instance of poor financial reporting quality.

While choices exist within GAAP for the presentation of a desired economic picture, non-GAAP reporting adds yet another dimension of management discretion. Non-GAAP reporting of financial metrics not in compliance with generally accepted accounting principles such as US GAAP and IFRS includes both financial metrics and operating metrics.[5] Non-GAAP financial metrics relate directly to the financial statements. A common non-GAAP financial metric is "non-GAAP earnings," which are created by companies "that adjust standards-compliant earnings to *exclude items required* by accounting standards or to *include items not permitted* by accounting standards" (Ciesielski and Henry, 2017). In contrast, non-GAAP operating metrics do not relate directly to the financial statements and include metrics that are typically industry-driven, such as subscriber numbers, active users, and occupancy rates.

Non-GAAP financial reporting has become increasingly common, presenting challenges to analysts. An important challenge is that non-GAAP financial reporting diminishes comparability across financial statements. The adjustments that companies make to create non-GAAP earnings, for example, are generally ad hoc and thus differ significantly. When evaluating non-GAAP metrics, investors must decide the extent to which specific adjustments should be incorporated into their analyses and forecasts.[6]

Another challenge arises from differences in terminology. Non-GAAP earnings are sometimes referred to as underlying earnings, adjusted earnings, recurring earnings, core earnings, or similar. Exhibit 5 provides an example from Jaguar Land Rover Automotive plc (JLR), a subsidiary of Tata Motors Ltd. The company prepares its financial reports under IFRS. The exhibit is an excerpt from JLR's 2016/17 annual report and uses the term "alternative performance measures". Exhibit 6 is from Tata Motors Ltd's Form 6-K filed with the US SEC, containing supplemental information regarding JLR and using the term "non-IFRS Financial Measures". The information in the two exhibits is essentially identical, but the terminology and formatting differ.

5 The term "non-GAAP" refers generally to all metrics that are non-compliant with generally accepted accounting principles and thus includes "non-IFRS" metrics.

6 A survey of non-GAAP earnings in the S&P 500 is presented in Ciesielski and Henry (2017). Some observers even recommend that investors shift their focus from a company's earnings to a company's "strategic assets" and the contribution of these assets to its competitive edge (Gu and Lev, 2017).

Exhibit 5

JLR's 2016/17 Annual Report: Footnote 3 [Excerpt]

3) ALTERNATIVE PERFORMANCE MEASURES

Many companies use alternative performance measures (APMs) to provide helpful additional information for users of their financial statements, telling a clearer story of how the business has performed over the period... These measures exclude certain items that are included in comparable statutory measures....

Reconciliations between these alternative performance measures and statutory reported measures are shown below.

EBIT AND EBITDA (£m)

Year ended 31 March	2017
EBITDA	**2,955**
Depreciation and amortisation	–1,656
Share of profit/(loss) of equity accounted investments	159
EBIT	**1,458**
Foreign exchange (loss)/gain on derivatives	–11
Unrealised gain/(loss) on commodities	148
Foreign exchange loss on loans	–101
Finance income	33
Finance expense (net)	–68
Exceptional item	151
Profit before tax	**1,610**

Exhibit 6

Tata Motors Ltd. SEC Form 6-K [Excerpt]

Non-IFRS Financial Measures

This Report includes references to certain non-IFRS measures, including EBITDA, EBIT ... [These measures] and related ratios should not be considered in isolation and are not measures of JLR's financial performance or liquidity under IFRS and should not be considered as an alternative to profit or loss for the period or any other performance measures derived in accordance with IFRS or as an alternative to cash flow from operating, investing or financing activities or any other measure of JLR's liquidity derived in accordance with IFRS. ... In addition, EBITDA, EBIT... as defined, may not be comparable to other similarly titled measures used by other companies.

Exhibit 1 to Form 6-K Supplemental Information Regarding the Jaguar and Land Rover Business of Tata Motors Limited [Excerpt]

The reconciliation of JLR's EBIT and EBITDA to profit for the period line item is:

Fiscal year ended March 31, 2017	£m
Profit for the period	1,272
Add back taxation	338
Add/(less) back exceptional charge/(credit)	−151
Add back/(less) foreign exchange (gains)/loss – financing	101
Add back/(less) foreign exchange (gains)/loss – derivatives	11
Add back/(less) unrealized commodity losses/(gains) – unrealized derivatives	−148
Less finance income	−33
Add back finance expense (net)	68
EBIT	**1,458**
Add back depreciation and amortization	1,656
Add/(less) back share of loss/(profit) from equity accounted investees	−159
EBITDA	**2,955**

Management emphasis on non-GAAP financial measures to deflect attention from less-than-desirable GAAP financial results is an example of an aggressive presentation choice. Since 2003, if a company uses a non-GAAP financial measure[7] in an SEC filing, it is required to display the most directly comparable GAAP measure with equal prominence and to provide a reconciliation between the non-GAAP measure and the equivalent GAAP measure. In other words, a company is not allowed to give more prominence to a non-GAAP financial measure in an SEC filing.

Similarly, the IFRS Practice Statement "Management Commentary," issued December 2010, requires disclosures when non-IFRS measures are included in financial reports:

> If information from the financial statements has been adjusted for inclusion in management commentary, that fact should be disclosed. If financial performance measures that are not required or defined by IFRSs are included within management commentary, those measures should be defined and explained, including an explanation of the relevance of the measure to users. When financial performance measures are derived or drawn from the financial statements, those measures should be reconciled to measures presented in the financial statements that have been prepared in accordance with IFRSs. (Page 17)

The reconciliation between as-reported measures (GAAP financial measures presented in the financial statements) and as-adjusted measures (non-GAAP financial measures presented in places other than the financial statements) can provide important information.

7 Non-domestic private issuers can file financial statements prepared in accordance with IFRS without reconciliation to US GAAP. The SEC recognizes US GAAP and IFRS as GAAP.

The European Securities and Markets Authority (ESMA) published guidelines in October 2015 *(ESMA Guidelines on Alternative Performance Measures)* covering such points as the definition of APMs, reconciliation to GAAP, explanation of the metrics' relevance, and consistency over time. We discuss ESMA in more detail later in this reading.

EXAMPLE 2

Presentation of Non-GAAP Financial Measures

Convatec Group PLC (Convatec), a global medical products manufacturer, raised $1.8 billion via an initial public offering (IPO) on the London Stock Exchange in 2016. The company had been purchased by private equity firms from Bristol-Myers Squibb in 2008 for $4.1 billion. Exhibit 7 presents excerpts from the company's regulatory filing at the London Stock Exchange announcing its full year 2016 results.

Exhibit 7 Excerpt from ConvaTec's Press Release for Full Year 2016 Results

Headline: "Strong results, delivering on strategy"

CEO Review [Excerpt]

At constant currency, revenue grew 4% to $1,688 million and adjusted EBITDA was $508 million, up 6.5% at constant currency...

[Footnote] Constant currency growth 'CER' is calculated by restating 2016 results using 2015 foreign exchange rates for the relevant period.

Consolidated Statement of Profit or Loss for the year ended 31 December 2016 ($ m)

	2016	2015
Revenue	1,688.3	1,650.4
Cost of goods sold	−821.0	−799.9
Gross profit	867.3	850.5
Selling and distribution expenses	−357.0	−346.7
General and administrative expenses	−318.2	−233.1
Research and development expenses	−38.1	−40.3
Operating profit	154.0	230.4
Finance costs	−271.4	−303.6
Other expense, net	−8.4	−37.1
Loss before income taxes	−125.8	−110.3
Income tax (expense) benefit	−77.0	16.9
Net loss	−202.8	−93.4

Non-IFRS Financial Information [Excerpt]

This release contains certain financial measures that are not defined or recognised under IFRS. These measures are referred to as "Adjusted" measures... These measures are not measurements of financial performance or liquidity under IFRS and should not replace measures of liquidity or operating profit that are derived in accordance with IFRS.

Reconciliation to adjusted earnings [Excerpt]

2016	Reported	(a)	(b)	(c)	(d)	(e)	(f)	(g)	Adjusted
Revenue	1,688.3	—	—	—	—	—	—	—	1,688.3
...									
Operating profit	**154.0**	**155.1**	**30.9**	**11.7**	**0.8**	—	**90.2**	**29.5**	**472.2**
...									
(Loss) profit before income taxes	−125.8	155.1	30.9	11.7	0.8	37.6	90.2	29.5	230.0
Income tax expense(h)	−77.0								−51.2
Net (loss) profit	−202.8								178.8

(a) Represents an adjustment to exclude (i) acquisition-related amortisation expense ... (ii) accelerated depreciation ...related to the closure of certain manufacturing facilities, and (iii) impairment charges and assets write offs related to property, plant and equipment and intangible assets ....
(b) Represents restructuring costs and other related costs ...
(c) Represents remediation costs which include regulatory compliance costs related to FDA activities, IT enhancement costs, and professional service fees associated with activities that were undertaken in respect of the Group's compliance function and to strengthen its control environment within finance.
(d) Represents costs primarily related to (i) corporate development activities and (ii) a settlement of ordinary course multi-year patent-related litigations in 2015 ....
(e) Represents adjustments to exclude (i) loss on extinguishment of debt and write off of deferred financing fees ... and (ii) foreign exchange related transactions.
(f) Represents an adjustment to exclude (i) share-based compensation expense ... arising from pre-IPO employee equity grants and (ii) pre-IPO ownership structure related costs, including management fees to Nordic Capital and Avista (refer to Note 6 Related Party Transactions for further information).
(g) Represents IPO related costs, primary advisory fees.
(h) Adjusted income tax expense/benefit is income tax (expense) benefit net of tax adjustments.

Adjusted EBITDA [Excerpt]

Adjusted EBITDA is defined as Adjusted EBIT...further adjusted to exclude (i) software and R&D amortisation, (ii) depreciation and (iii) post-IPO share-based compensation.

The following table reconciles the Group's Adjusted EBIT to Adjusted EBITDA.

	2016 ($m)
Adjusted EBIT	472.2
Software and R&D amortization	6.7
Depreciation	27.9

	2016 ($m)
Post-IPO share-based compensation	0.8
Adjusted EBITDA	507.6

1 Based on the information provided, explain the differences between the following two disclosures contained in Convatec's press release:

A The CEO Review of 2016 results, at the beginning of the release, states that "revenue grew 4% to $1,688 million."

B Convatec's Consolidated Statement of Profit or Loss shows 2016 revenues of $1,688.3 million and 2015 revenues of $1,650.4 million.

2 Based on the information provided, explain the differences between the following two disclosures contained in Convatecs's earnings release:

A The CEO Review of 2016 results states that "adjusted EBITDA was $508 million, up 6.5% at constant currency."

B Convatec's Consolidated Statement of Profit or Loss shows 2016 net loss of $202.8 million and 2015 net loss of $93.4 million.

Solution to 1:

The amount of revenue reported on the company's income statement conforms to International Financial Reporting Standards (IFRS). Using the amounts from the income statement, the company's total revenue increased by 2.3 % (= $1,688.3/$1,650.4 – 1). The revenue growth rate of 4% in the CEO review is a non-IFRS measure, calculated on a "constant currency" basis, which the footnote describes as a comparison using 2016 revenues restated at 2015 foreign exchange rates.

Solution to 2:

The amounts reported on the company's income statement conform to IFRS. Using amounts from the income statement, the company reported a loss in 2016 of $202.8 million, which was more than twice as large a loss as the $93.4 million loss reported in 2015. Also referring to the income statement, the company reported 2016 operating profit (referred to elsewhere as EBIT) of $154.0 million, a decline of 33.2% from the $230.4 million operating profit reported in 2016.

In contrast, the "Adjusted EBITDA" amount highlighted in the CEO Review is neither defined nor recognized under IFRS. It is a non-IFRS measure. To create the Adjusted EBITDA, the company first begins with EBIT (called Operating profit in excerpts II and III) of $154.0 and creates Adjusted EBIT ($472.2 million) by adding back 8 different expenses that IFRS requires the company to recognize. These adjustments are listed beneath the first tabular reconciliation in Items a through g. After developing Adjusted EBIT, the company creates Adjusted EBITDA ($507.6 million) by adding back a further 3 different expenses that IFRS requires the company to recognize.

Overall, there are three key differences between Disclosures A and B: (1) Most importantly, disclosure A refers to a non-IFRS metric rather than an IFRS-compliant metric; (2) Disclosure A refers to operating profit, which was positive, rather than to net income, which was negative; and (3) Disclosure A highlights a positive economic outcome—i.e., an increase, on a currency adjusted basis. An analyst should be aware of the alternative means by which earnings announcements can paint a positive picture of companies' results.

Often, poor reporting quality occurs simultaneously with poor earnings quality; for example, aggressive accounting choices are made to obscure poor performance. It is also possible, of course, for poor reporting quality to occur with high-quality earnings. Although a company with good performance would not require aggressive accounting choices to obscure poor performance, it might nonetheless produce poor-quality reports for other reasons. A company with good performance might be unable to produce high-quality reports because of inadequate internal systems.

Another scenario in which poor reporting quality might occur simultaneously with high quality earnings is that a company with good performance might deliberately produce reports based on "conservative" rather than aggressive accounting choices—that is, choices that make current performance look worse. One motivation might be to avoid unwanted political attention. Another motivation could arise in a period in which management had already exceeded targets before the end of the period and thus made conservative accounting choices that would delay reporting profits until the following period (so-called "hidden reserves"). Similar motivations might also contribute to accounting choices that create the appearance that the trajectory of future results would appear more attractive. For example, a company might make choices to accelerate losses in the first year of an acquisition or the first year of a new CEO's tenure so that the trajectory of future results would appear more attractive.

Overall, *unbiased* financial reporting is the ideal. Some investors may prefer conservative choices rather than aggressive ones, however, because a positive surprise is easier to tolerate than a negative surprise. Biased reporting, whether conservative or aggressive, adversely affects a user's ability to assess a company.

The quality spectrum considers the more intuitive situation in which less-than-desired underlying economics are the central motivation for poor reporting quality. In addition, it is necessary to have some degree of reporting quality in order to evaluate earnings quality. Proceeding down the spectrum, therefore, the concepts of reporting quality and earnings quality become progressively less distinguishable.

2.3.1 *Within GAAP, but "Earnings Management"*

The next level down on the spectrum in Exhibit 2 is labeled "Within GAAP, but 'earnings management.'" The term "earnings management" is defined here as making intentional choices that create biased financial reports.[8] The distinction between earnings management and biased choices is subtle and, primarily, a matter of intent. Earnings management represents "deliberate actions to influence reported earnings and their interpretation" (Ronen and Yaari, 2008). Earnings can be "managed" upward (increased) by taking *real* actions, such as deferring research and development (R&D) expenses into the next reporting period. Alternatively, earnings can be increased by *accounting* choices, such as changing accounting estimates. For example, the amount of estimated product returns, bad debt expense, or asset impairment could be decreased to create higher earnings. Because it is difficult to determine intent, we include earnings management under the biased choices discussion.

2.4 Departures from GAAP

The next levels down on the spectrum in Exhibit 2 mark departures from GAAP. Financial reporting that departs from GAAP can generally be considered low quality. In such situations, earnings quality is likely difficult or impossible to assess because

8 Various definitions have appeared in academic research. Closest to the discussion here is Schipper (1989), which uses the term "earnings management" to mean "'disclosure management' in the sense of a purposeful intervention in the external financial reporting process, with the intent of obtaining some private gain (as opposed to, say, merely facilitating the neutral operation of the process)."

comparisons with earlier periods and/or other entities cannot be made. An example of improper accounting was Enron (accounting issues revealed in 2001), whose inappropriate use of off-balance-sheet structures and other complex transactions resulted in vastly understated indebtedness as well as overstated profits and operating cash flow. Another notorious example of improper accounting was WorldCom (accounting issues discovered in 2002), a company that by improperly capitalizing certain expenditures dramatically understated its expenses and thus overstated its profits. More recently, New Century Financial (accounting issues revealed in 2007) issued billions of dollars of subprime mortgages and improperly reserved only minimal amounts for loan repurchase losses. Each of these companies subsequently filed for bankruptcy.

In the 1980s, Polly Peck International (PPI) reported currency losses, incurred in the normal course of operations, directly through equity rather than in its profit and loss statements. In the 1990s, Sunbeam improperly reported revenues from "bill-and-hold" sales and also manipulated the timing of expenses in an effort to falsely portray outstanding performance of its then-new chief executive.

At the bottom of the quality spectrum, fabricated reports portray fictitious events, either to fraudulently obtain investments by misrepresenting the company's performance and/or to obscure fraudulent misappropriation of the company's assets. Examples of fraudulent reporting are unfortunately easy to find, although they were not necessarily easy to identify at the time. In the 1970s, Equity Funding Corp. created fictitious revenues and even fictitious policyholders. In the 1980s, Crazy Eddie's reported fictitious inventory as well as fictitious revenues supported by fake invoices. In 2004, Parmalat reported fictitious bank balances.

EXAMPLE 3

Spectrum for Assessing Quality of Financial Reports

Jake Lake, a financial analyst, has identified several items in the financial reports of several (hypothetical) companies. Describe each of these items in the context of the financial reporting quality spectrum.

1 ABC Co.'s 2018 earnings totaled $233 million, including a $100 million gain from selling one of its less profitable divisions. ABC's earnings for the prior three years totaled $120 million, $107 million, and $111 million. The company's financial reports are extremely clear and detailed, and the company's earnings announcement highlights the one-time nature of the $100 million gain.

2 DEF Co. discloses that in 2018, it changed the depreciable life of its equipment from 3 years to 15 years. Equipment represents a substantial component of the company's assets. The company's disclosures indicate that the change is permissible under the accounting standards of its jurisdiction but provide only limited explanation of the change.

3 GHI Co.'s R&D expenditures for the past five years have been approximately 3% of sales. In 2018, the company significantly reduced its R&D expenditures. Without the reduction in R&D expenditures, the company would have reported a loss. No explanation is disclosed.

Solution to 1:

ABC's 2018 total earnings quality can be viewed as low because nearly half of the earnings are derived from a non-sustainable activity, namely the sale of a division. ABC's 2018 quality of earnings from continuing operations may be high because the amounts are fairly consistent from year to year, although an analyst would undertake further analysis to confirm earnings quality. In general, a user of financial reports should look beyond the bottom-line net income. The description provided suggests that the company's reporting quality is high; the reports are clear and detailed, and the one-time nature of the $100 million gain is highlighted.

Solution to 2:

DEF's accounting choice appears to be within permissible accounting standards, but its effect is to substantially lower depreciation expense and thus to increase earnings for the year. The quality of reported earnings is questionable. Although the new level of earnings may be sustainable, similar increases in earnings for future periods might not be achievable, because increasing earnings solely by changing accounting estimates is likely not sustainable. In addition, the description provided suggests that the company's reporting quality is low because it offers only a limited explanation for the change.

Solution to 3:

GHI's operational choice to reduce its R&D may reflect real earnings management because the change enabled the company to avoid reporting a loss. In addition, the description provided suggests that the company's reporting quality is low because it does not offer an explanation for the change.

2.5 Differentiate between Conservative and Aggressive Accounting

This section returns to the implications of conservative and aggressive accounting choices. As mentioned earlier, *unbiased* financial reporting is the ideal. But some investors may prefer or be perceived to prefer conservative rather than aggressive accounting choices because a positive surprise is acceptable. In contrast, management may make, or be perceived to make, aggressive accounting choices because they increase the company's reported performance and financial position.

Aggressive accounting choices in the period under review may decrease the company's reported performance and financial position in later periods, which creates a sustainability issue. Conservative choices do not typically create a sustainability issue because they decrease the company's reported performance and financial position, and may increase them in later periods. In terms of establishing expectations for the future, however, financial reporting that is relevant and faithfully representative is the most useful.

A common presumption is that financial reports are typically biased upward, but that is not always the case. Although accounting standards ideally promote unbiased financial reporting, some accounting standards may specifically require a conservative treatment of a transaction or an event. Also, managers may choose to take a conservative approach when applying standards. It is important that an analyst consider the possibility of conservative choices and their effects.

At its most extreme, conservatism follows accounting practices that "anticipate no profit, but anticipate all losses" (Bliss, 1924). But in general, conservatism means that revenues may be recognized once a verifiable and legally enforceable receivable has been generated and that losses need not be recognized until it becomes "probable" that an actual loss will be incurred. Conservatism is not an absolute but is characterized by degrees, such as "the accountant's tendency to require a higher degree of verification to recognize good news as gains than to recognize bad news as losses" (Basu, 1997). From this perspective, "verification" (e.g., physical existence of inventories, evidence of costs incurred or to be incurred, or establishment of rights and obligations on legal grounds) drives the degree of conservatism. For recognition of revenues, a higher degree of verification would be required than for expenses.

2.5.1 *Conservatism in Accounting Standards*

The *Conceptual Framework* supports neutrality of information: "A neutral depiction is without bias in the selection or presentation of financial information."[9] Neutrality—lack of upward or downward bias—is considered a desirable characteristic of financial reporting. Conservatism directly conflicts with the characteristic of neutrality because the asymmetric nature of conservatism leads to bias in measuring assets and liabilities—and ultimately, earnings.

Despite efforts to support neutrality in financial reporting, many conservatively biased standards remain. Standards across jurisdictions may differ on the extent of conservatism embedded within them. An analyst should be aware of the implications of accounting standards for the financial reports.

An example is the different treatment by IFRS and US GAAP of the impairment of long-lived assets.[10] Both IFRS and US GAAP specify an impairment analysis protocol that begins with an assessment of whether recent events indicate that the economic benefit from an individual or group of long-lived assets may be less than its carrying amount(s). From that point on, however, the two regimes diverge:

- Under IFRS, if the "recoverable amount" (the higher of fair value less costs to sell and value in use) is less than the carrying amount, then an impairment charge will be recorded.
- Under US GAAP, an impairment charge will be recorded only when the sum of the undiscounted future cash flows expected to be derived from the asset(s) is less than the carrying amount(s). If the undiscounted future cash flows are less than the carrying amount, the asset is written down to fair value.

To illustrate the difference in application, assume that a factory is the unit of account eligible for impairment testing. Its carrying amount is $10,000,000; "fair value" and "recoverable amount" are both $6,000,000; and the undiscounted future net cash flows associated with the factory total $10,000,000. Under IFRS, an impairment charge of $4,000,000 would be recorded; but under US GAAP, no impairment charge would be recognized.

Thus, on its face, IFRS would be regarded as more conservative than US GAAP because impairment losses would normally be recognized earlier under IFRS than under US GAAP. But, taking the analysis one step further, such a broad generalization may not hold up. For example, if an asset is impaired under both IFRS and US GAAP and the asset's value in use exceeds its fair value, the impairment loss under US GAAP will be greater. Also, IFRS permits the recognition of recoveries of the recoverable amount in subsequent periods if evidence indicates that the recoverable amount has subsequently increased. In contrast, US GAAP prohibits the subsequent write-up of an asset after an impairment charge has been taken; it would recognize the asset's increased value only when the asset is ultimately sold.

Common examples of conservatism in accounting standards include the following:

- *Research costs.* Because the future benefit of research costs is uncertain at the time the costs are incurred, both US GAAP and IFRS require immediate expensing instead of capitalization.

---

9 IASB and FASB, *The Conceptual Framework for Financial Reporting* (2010): QC 14.
10 See IAS 36 and FASB ASC Section 360-10-35.

- *Litigation losses.* When it becomes "probable" that a cost will be incurred, both US GAAP and IFRS require expense recognition, even though a legal liability may not be incurred until a future date.
- *Insurance recoverables.* Generally, a company that receives payment on an insurance claim may not recognize a receivable until the insurance company acknowledges the validity of the claimed amount.

Watts (2003) reviews empirical studies of conservatism, and identifies four potential benefits of conservatism:

- Given asymmetrical information, conservatism may protect the contracting parties with less information and greater risk. This protection is necessary because the contracting party may be at a disadvantage. For example, corporations that access debt markets have limited liability, and lenders thus have limited recourse to recover their losses from shareholders. As another example, executives who receive earnings-based bonuses might not be subject to having those bonuses "clawed back" if earnings are subsequently discovered to be overstated.
- Conservatism reduces the possibility of litigation and, by extension, litigation costs. Rarely, if ever, is a company sued because it understated good news or overstated bad news.
- Conservative rules may protect the interests of regulators and politicians by reducing the possibility that fault will be found with them if companies overstate earnings or assets.
- In many tax jurisdictions, financial and tax reporting rules are linked. For example, in Germany and Japan, only deductions taken against reported income can be deducted against taxable income. Hence, companies can reduce the present value of their tax payments by electing conservative accounting policies for certain types of events.

Analysts should consider possible conservative and aggressive biases and their consequences when examining financial reports. Current-period financial reports may be unbiased, upward biased through aggressive accounting choices, downward biased through conservative accounting choices, or biased through a combination of conservative and aggressive accounting choices.

2.5.2 *Bias in the Application of Accounting Standards*

Any application of accounting standards, whether the standard itself is neutral or not, often requires significant amounts of judgment. Characterizing the application of an accounting standard as conservative or aggressive is more a matter of intent rather than definition.

Careful analysis of disclosures, facts, and circumstances contributes to making an accurate inference of intent. Management seeking to manipulate earnings may take a longer view by sacrificing short-term profitability in order to ensure higher profits in later periods. One example of biased accounting in the guise of conservatism is the so-called "big bath" restructuring charges. Both US GAAP and IFRS provide for accrual of future costs associated with restructurings, and these costs are often associated with and presented along with asset impairments. But in some instances, companies use the accounting provisions to estimate "big" losses in the period under review so that performance in future periods will appear better. Having observed numerous instances of manipulative practices in the late 1990s, in which US companies set up opportunities to report higher profits in future periods that were not connected with performance in those periods, the SEC staff issued rules that narrowed the circumstances under which costs can be categorized as part of a "non-recurring" restructuring event and enhanced the transparency surrounding restructuring charges and asset impairments.[11]

A similar manifestation of "big bath" accounting is often referred to as "cookie jar reserve accounting." Both US GAAP and IFRS require accruals of estimates of future non-payments of loans. In his 1998 speech "The 'Numbers Game,'" SEC chair Arthur Levitt expressed the general concern that corporations were overstating loans and other forms of loss allowances for the purpose of smoothing income over time.[12] In 2003, the SEC issued interpretive guidance that essentially requires a company to provide a separate section in management's discussion and analysis (MD&A) titled "Critical Accounting Estimates."[13] If the effects of subjective estimates and judgments of highly uncertain matters are material to stakeholders (investors, customers, suppliers, and other users of the financial statements), disclosures of their nature and exposure to uncertainty should be made in the MD&A. This requirement is in addition to required disclosures in the notes to the financial statements.

CONTEXT FOR ASSESSING FINANCIAL REPORTING QUALITY

3

In assessing financial reporting quality, it is useful to consider whether a company's managers may be motivated to issue financial reports that are not high quality. If motivation exists, an analyst should consider whether the reporting environment is conducive to managers' misreporting. It is important to consider mechanisms within the reporting environment that discipline financial reporting quality, such as the regulatory regime.

3.1 Motivations

Managers may be motivated to issue financial reports that are not high quality to mask poor performance, such as loss of market share or lower profitability than competitors. Lewis (2012) stated, "A firm experiencing performance problems, particularly those it considers transient, may induce a response that inflates current earnings numbers in exchange for lower future earnings."

- Even when there is no need to mask poor performance, managers frequently have incentives to meet or beat market expectations as reflected in analysts' forecasts and/or management's own forecasts. Exceeding forecasts typically increases the stock price, if only temporarily. Additionally, exceeding forecasts can increase management compensation that is linked to increases in stock price or to reported earnings. Graham, Harvey, and Rajgopal (2005) found that the CFOs they surveyed view earnings as the most important financial metric to financial markets. Achieving (or exceeding) particular benchmarks, including prior-year earnings and analysts' forecasts, is very important. The authors examined a variety of motivations for why managers might "exercise accounting

11 SEC, "Restructuring and Impairment Charges," Staff Accounting Bulletin (SAB) No. 100 (1999): www.sec.gov/interps/account/sab100.htm.

12 Arthur Levitt, "The 'Numbers Game,'" Remarks given at NYU Center for Law and Business (28 September 1998): www.sec.gov/news/speech/speecharchive/1998/spch220.txt.

13 SEC, "Commission Guidance Regarding Management's Discussion and Analysis of Financial Condition and Results of Operations," Financial Reporting Release (FRR) No. 72 (2003): www.sec.gov/rules/interp/33-8350.htm.

discretion to achieve some desirable earnings goal." Motivations to meet earnings benchmarks include equity market effects (for example, building credibility with market participants and positively affecting stock price) and trade effects (for example, enhancing reputation with customers and suppliers). Equity market effects are the most powerful incentives, but trade effects are important, particularly for smaller companies.

- Career concerns and incentive compensation may motivate accounting choices. For example, managers might be concerned that working for a company that performs poorly will limit their future career opportunities or that they will not receive a bonus based on exceeding a particular earnings target. In both cases, management might be motivated to make accounting choices to increase earnings. In a period of marginally poor performance, a manager might accelerate or inflate revenues and/or delay or under report expenses. Conversely, in a period of strong performance, a manager might delay revenue recognition or accelerate expense recognition to increase the probability of exceeding the next period's targets (i.e., to "bank" some earnings for the next period.) The surveyed managers indicated a greater concern with career implications of reported results than with incentive compensation implications.

Avoiding debt covenant violations can motivate managers to inflate earnings. Graham, Harvey, and Rajgopal's survey indicates that avoidance of bond covenant violation is important to highly leveraged and unprofitable companies but relatively unimportant overall.

3.2 Conditions Conducive to Issuing Low-Quality Financial Reports

As discussed, deviations from a neutral presentation of financial results could be driven by management choices or by a jurisdiction's financial reporting standards. Ultimately, a decision to issue low-quality, or even fraudulent, financial reports is made by an individual or individuals. Why individuals make such choices is not always immediately apparent. For example, why would the newly appointed CEO of Sunbeam, who already had a net worth of more than $100 million, commit accounting fraud by improperly reporting revenues from "bill-and-hold" sales and manipulating the timing of expenses, rather than admit to lower-than-expected financial results?

Typically, three conditions exist when low-quality financial reports are issued: opportunity, motivation, and rationalization. Opportunity can be the result of internal conditions, such as poor internal controls or an ineffective board of directors, or external conditions, such as accounting standards that provide scope for divergent choices or minimal consequences for an inappropriate choice. Motivation can result from pressure to meet some criteria for personal reasons, such as a bonus, or corporate reasons, such as concern about financing in the future. Rationalization is important because if an individual is concerned about a choice, he or she needs to be able to justify it to him- or herself.

Former Enron CFO Andrew Fastow, speaking at the 2013 Association of Certified Fraud Examiners Annual Fraud Conference, indicated that he knew at the time he was doing something wrong but followed procedure to justify his decision (Pavlo, 2013). He made sure to get management and board approval, as well as legal and accounting opinions, and to include appropriate disclosures. The incentive and corporate culture was to create earnings rather than focus on long-term value. Clearly, as reflected in his prison sentence, he did something that was not only wrong but illegal.

3.3 Mechanisms That Discipline Financial Reporting Quality

Markets potentially discipline financial reporting quality. Companies and nations compete for capital, and the cost of capital is a function of perceived risk—including the risk that a company's financial statements will skew investors' expectations. Thus, in the absence of other conflicting economic incentives, a company seeking to minimize its long-term cost of capital should aim to provide high-quality financial reports. In addition to markets, other mechanisms that discipline financial reporting quality include market regulatory authorities, auditors, and private contracts.

3.3.1 *Market Regulatory Authorities*

Companies seeking to minimize the cost of capital should maximize reporting quality, but as discussed earlier, conflicting incentives often exist. For this reason, national regulations, and the regulators that establish and enforce rules, can play a significant role in financial reporting quality. Many of the world's securities regulators are members of the International Organization of Securities Commissions (IOSCO). IOSCO is recognized as the "global standard setter for the securities sector" although it does not actually set standards but rather establishes objectives and principles to guide securities and capital market regulation. IOSCO's membership includes more than 120 securities regulators and 80 other securities market participants, such as stock exchanges.[14]

One member of IOSCO is ESMA , an independent EU authority with a mission to "enhance the protection of investors and reinforce stable and well-functioning financial markets in the European Union."[15] ESMA organizes financial reporting enforcement activities through a forum consisting of European enforcers from European Economic Area countries. Direct supervision and enforcement activities are performed at the national level. For example, the Financial Conduct Authority (FCA) is the IOSCO member with primary responsibility for securities regulation in the United Kingdom. ESMA reported that European enforcers examined the interim and/or annual financial statements of 1,141 issuers in 2017, which in turn led to enforcement actions for 328 issuers with the following outcomes: 12 required reissuances of financial statements, 71 public corrective notes, and 245 required corrections in future financial statements.[16]

Another member of IOSCO is the US regulatory authority, the Securities and Exchange Commission. The SEC is responsible for overseeing approximately 9,100 US public companies (along with investment advisers, broker/dealers, securities exchanges, and other entities) and reviews the disclosures of these companies at least once every three years with the aim of improving information available to investors and potentially uncovering possible violations of securities laws.[17] In 2017, the SEC reported that it had filed 754 total and 446 standalone enforcement actions, about 20% of which concerned issuer reporting/accounting and auditing.[18]

Examples of regulatory bodies in Asia include the Financial Services Agency in Japan, the China Securities Regulatory Commission, and the Securities and Exchange Board of India. Examples of regulatory bodies in South America include the Comisión Nacional de Valores in Argentina, Comissão de Valores Mobiliários in Brazil, and Superintendencia de Valores y Seguros in Chile. A full list of IOSCO members can be found on the organization's website.

---

14 Visit www.iosco.org for more information.

15 Text from ESMA's mission statement on their website: www.esma.europa.eu.

16 ESMA, "Enforcement and Regulatory Activities of Accounting Enforcers in 2017," ESMA32-63-424, European Securities and Markets Authority (03 April 2018): www.esma.europa.eu.

17 SEC, "FY2013 Congressional Justification," Securities and Exchange Commission (February 2012): www.sec.gov/about/secfy13congbudgjust.pdf.

18 SEC, Securities and Exchange Commission Division of Enforcement Annual Report, "A Look Back at Fiscal Year 2017" www.sec.gov/report.

Typical features of a regulatory regime that most directly affect financial reporting quality include the following:

- *Registration requirements.* Market regulators typically require publicly traded companies to register securities before offering the securities for sale to the public. A registration document typically contains current financial statements, other relevant information about the risks and prospects of the company issuing the securities, and information about the securities being offered.
- *Disclosure requirements.* Market regulators typically require publicly traded companies to make public periodic reports, including financial reports and management comments. Standard-setting bodies, such as the IASB and FASB, are typically private sector, self-regulated organizations with board members who are experienced accountants, auditors, users of financial statements, and academics. Regulatory authorities, such as the Accounting and Corporate Regulatory Authority in Singapore, the Securities and Exchange Commission in the United States, the Securities and Exchange Commission in Brazil, and the Financial Reporting Council in the United Kingdom, have the legal authority to enforce financial reporting requirements and exert other controls over entities that participate in the capital markets within their jurisdiction. In other words, *generally*, standard-setting bodies set the standards, and regulatory authorities recognize and enforce those standards. Without the recognition of standards by regulatory authorities, the private-sector standard-setting bodies would have no authority. Regulators often retain the legal authority to establish financial reporting standards in their jurisdiction and can overrule the private-sector standard-setting bodies.
- *Auditing requirements.* Market regulators typically require companies' financial statements to be accompanied by an audit opinion attesting that the financial statements conform to the relevant set of accounting standards. Some regulators, such as the SEC in the United States, require an additional audit opinion attesting to the effectiveness of the company's internal controls over financial reporting.
- *Management commentaries.* Regulations typically require publicly traded companies' financial reports to include statements by management. For example, the FCA in the United Kingdom requires a management report containing "(1) a fair review of the issuer's business; and (2) a description of the principal risks and uncertainties facing the issuer" (Disclosure Guidance and Transparency Rules sourcebook.)
- *Responsibility statements.* Regulations typically require a statement from the person or persons responsible for the company's filings. Such statements require the responsible individuals to explicitly acknowledge responsibility and to attest to the correctness of the financial reports. Some regulators, such as the SEC in the United States, require formal certifications that carry specific legal penalties for false certifications.
- *Regulatory review of filings.* Regulators typically undertake a review process to ensure that the rules have been followed. The review process typically covers all initial registrations and a sample of subsequent periodic financial reports.
- *Enforcement mechanisms.* Regulators are granted various powers to enforce the securities market rules. Such powers can include assessing fines, suspending or permanently barring market participants, and bringing criminal prosecutions. Public announcements of disciplinary actions are also a type of enforcement mechanism.

In summary, market regulatory authorities play a central role in encouraging high-quality financial reporting.

3.3.2 *Auditors*

As noted, regulatory authorities typically require that publicly traded companies' financial statements be audited by an independent auditor. Private companies also obtain audit opinions for their financial statements, either voluntarily or because audit reports are required by an outside party, such as providers of debt or equity capital.

Audit opinions provide financial statement users with some assurance that the information complies with the relevant set of accounting standards and presents the company's information fairly. Exhibits 8, 9, 10, and 11 provide excerpts from the independent auditors' reports for GlaxoSmithKline plc, Alibaba Group Holding Limited, Apple Inc., and Tata Motors Limited, respectively. For each company, the auditor issued an unqualified opinion on the financial statements, indicating that the financial statements present fairly the company's performance in accordance with relevant standards. (Note: The term "unqualified opinion" means that the opinion did not include any qualifications or exceptions; the term is synonymous with the less formal term "clean opinion." Unqualified opinions are the most common.) Other items in the audit reports reflect the specific requirements of the company's regulatory regime. For example, the audit report for GlaxoSmithKline spans nine pages and includes opinions on the company's financial statements as well as the Strategic Report and the Directors' Report. This audit report also includes disclosures about "Key audit matters," in accordance with International Standards on Auditing (ISAs) issued by the International Auditing and Assurance Standards Board (IAASB) in 2015 and effective for periods ending on or after December 15, 2016.

The excerpts for Alibaba, Apple, and Tata Motors show the auditors' opinions on the companies' financial statements and additionally the SEC-required opinions on the effectiveness of the companies' internal controls because these companies are listed in the United States. For Alibaba, a single report includes both unqualified opinions: (i) the financial statements present fairly the financial position, results of operations, and cash flows... in conformity with US GAAP; and (ii) the company maintained effective control over financial reporting. For Apple, the first report includes the unqualified opinion on the financial statements, and the second report includes the unqualified opinion on the company's effective internal controls. For Tata Motors, the first report includes the unqualified opinion that the financial statements present the company's position and results fairly in accordance with IFRS. (The SEC permits non-US companies to report using US GAAP, IFRS as issued by the IASB, or home-country GAAP.) However, the second report includes an *adverse* opinion on the effectiveness of the company's internal controls: "In our opinion, because of the effect of the material weakness ... the company has not maintained effective internal control." The report explains that the material weakness involved a third party's inappropriate access to the company's systems. The report further states that although the material weakness resulted in ineffective internal controls, it did not affect the audit opinion on the financial statements. Elsewhere in Tata Motors' annual report (not shown in the excerpt), the company discloses that the weakness did not result in a financial misstatement and that it has undertaken remedial measures.

Exhibit 8 Excerpts from Audit Opinion of PricewaterhouseCoopers LLP from the 2017 Annual Report *(pages 149–157)* of GlaxoSmithKline plc

In our opinion, GlaxoSmithKline plc's Group financial statements (the "financial statements"):

- give a true and fair view of the state of the Group's affairs as at 31 December 2017 and of its profit and cash flows for the year then ended;

(continued)

Exhibit 8 (Continued)

- have been properly prepared in accordance with International Financial Reporting Standards ("IFRSs") as adopted by the European Union; and
- have been prepared in accordance with the requirements of the Companies Act 2006 and Article 4 of the IAS Regulation.

...

In our opinion, the Group financial statements have been properly prepared in accordance with IFRSs as issued by the IASB.

...

Key audit matters

Key audit matters are those matters that, in the auditors' professional judgement, were of most significance in the audit of the financial statements of the current period and include the most significant assessed risks of material misstatement (whether or not due to fraud) identified by the auditors, including those which had the greatest effect on: the overall audit strategy; the allocation of resources in the audit; and directing the efforts of the engagement team. These matters, and any comments we make on the results of our procedures thereon, were addressed in the context of our audit of the financial statements as a whole, and in forming our opinion thereon, and we do not provide a separate opinion on these matters. This is not a complete list of all risks identified by our audit.

...

In our opinion, based on the work undertaken in the course of the audit, the information given in the Strategic Report and Directors' Report for the year ended 31 December 2017 is consistent with the financial statements and has been prepared in accordance with applicable legal requirements.

Exhibit 9 Excerpts from Audit Opinion of PricewaterhouseCoopers Hong Kong, SAR from the Annual Report *(SEC Form 20-F, Pages F-2 and F-3)* of Alibaba Group Holding Limited for the year ended March 31, 2018

In our opinion, the consolidated financial statements referred to above present fairly, in all material respects, the financial position of the Company as of March 31, 2017 and 2018, and the results of their operations and their cash flows for each of the three years in the period ended March 31, 2018 in conformity with accounting principles generally accepted in the United States of America. Also in our opinion, the Company maintained, in all material respects, effective internal control over financial reporting as of March 31, 2018, based on criteria established in Internal Control — Integrated Framework (2013) issued by the COSO.

Exhibit 10 Excerpt from Audit Opinion of Ernst & Young from the Annual Report (*SEC Form 10-K, pages 70 and 71*) of Apple Inc. for the year ended September 30, 2017

[From the Financial Statement Opinion]

Exhibit 10 (Continued)

We have audited the accompanying consolidated balance sheets of Apple Inc. as of September 30, 2017 and September 24, 2016, and the related consolidated statements of operations, comprehensive income, shareholders' equity and cash flows for each of the three years in the period ended September 30, 2017.

....

In our opinion, the financial statements referred to above present fairly, in all material respects, the consolidated financial position of Apple Inc. at September 30, 2017 and September 24, 2016, and the consolidated results of its operations and its cash flows for each of the three years in the period ended September 30, 2017, in conformity with U.S. generally accepted accounting principles.

...

We also have audited, in accordance with the standards of the Public Company Accounting Oversight Board (United States), Apple Inc.'s internal control over financial reporting as of September 30, 2017, based on criteria established in Internal Control – Integrated Framework issued by the Committee of Sponsoring Organizations of the Treadway Commission (2013 framework) and our report dated November 3, 2017 expressed an unqualified opinion thereon.

[From the Internal Controls Opinion]

We have audited Apple Inc.'s internal control over financial reporting as of September 30, 2017, based on criteria established in Internal Control – Integrated Framework issued by the Committee of Sponsoring Organizations of the Treadway Commission (2013 framework) ("the COSO criteria").

...

In our opinion, Apple Inc. maintained, in all material respects, effective internal control over financial reporting as of September 30, 2017, based on the COSO criteria.

We also have audited, in accordance with the standards of the Public Company Accounting Oversight Board (United States), the 2017 consolidated financial statements of Apple Inc. and our report dated November 3, 2017 expressed an unqualified opinion thereon.

Exhibit 11 Excerpt from Audit Opinion of KPMG Mumbai, India from the Annual Report (*SEC Form 20-F, pages F2 to F4*) of Tata Motors Limited for the year ended March 31, 2018

Opinion on the Consolidated Financial Statements

We have audited the accompanying consolidated balance sheet of Tata Motors Limited and its subsidiaries (the "Company") as of March 31, 2018, the related consolidated income statement, statement of comprehensive income, statement of cash flows, and statement of changes in equity for the year ended March 31, 2018, and the related notes and financial statement schedule 1 (collectively, the consolidated financial statements).

In our opinion, the consolidated financial statements present fairly, in all material respects, the financial position of the Company as of March 31, 2018, and the results of its operations and its cash flows for the year ended March 31, 2018, in conformity with the International Financial Reporting Standards as issued by the International Accounting Standards Board ("IFRS").

(continued)

Exhibit 11 (Continued)

We also have audited, in accordance with the standards of the Public Company Accounting Oversight Board (United States) (PCAOB), the Company's internal control over financial reporting as of March 31, 2018, based on criteria established in *Internal Control – Integrated Framework (2013)* issued by the Committee of Sponsoring Organizations of the Treadway Commission, and our report dated July, 31, 2018 expressed an adverse opinion on the effectiveness of the Company's internal control over financial reporting.

...

Opinion on Internal Control Over Financial Reporting

We have audited Tata Motors Limited's and subsidiaries' (the Company) internal control over financial reporting as of March 31, 2018, based on criteria established in Internal Control – Integrated Framework (2013) issued by the Committee of Sponsoring Organizations of the Treadway Commission. In our opinion, because of the effect of the material weakness described below, on the achievement of the objectives of the control criteria, the Company has not maintained effective internal control over financial reporting as of March 31, 2018, based on criteria established in *Internal Control – Integrated Framework (2013)* issued by the Committee of Sponsoring Organizations of the Treadway Commission.

...

A material weakness is a deficiency, or a combination of deficiencies, in internal control over financial reporting, such that there is a reasonable possibility that a material misstatement of the company's annual or interim financial statements will not be prevented or detected on a timely basis. A material weakness related to inappropriate system access restrictions at a third party logistics provider has been identified and included in management's assessment. The material weakness was considered in determining the nature, timing, and extent of audit tests applied in our audit of the 2018 consolidated financial statements, and this report does not affect our report on those consolidated financial statements.

Although audit opinions provide discipline for financial reporting quality, inherent limitations exist. First, an audit opinion is based on a review of information prepared by the company. If a company deliberately intends to deceive its auditor, a review of information might not uncover misstatements. Second, an audit is based on sampling, and the sample might not reveal misstatements. Third, an "expectations gap" may exist between the auditor's role and the public's expectation of auditors. An audit is not typically intended to detect fraud; it is intended to provide assurance that the financial reports are fairly presented. Finally, the company being audited pays the audit fees, often established through a competitive process. This situation could provide an auditor with an incentive to show leniency to the company being audited, particularly if the auditor's firm provides additional services to the company.

3.3.3 *Private Contracting*

Aspects of private contracts, such as loan agreements or investment contracts, can serve as mechanisms to discipline financial reporting quality. Many parties that have a contractual arrangement with a company have an incentive to monitor that company's performance and to ensure that the company's financial reports are high quality. For example, loan agreements often contain loan covenants, which create specifically tailored financial reporting requirements that are legally binding for the issuer. As noted earlier, avoidance of debt covenant violation is a potential motivation for managers to inflate earnings. As another example, an investment contract could contain provisions giving investors the option to recover all or part of their investment if certain financial triggers occur. Such provisions could motivate the investee's managers to manipulate reported results to avoid the financial triggers.

Because the financial reports prepared by the investees or borrowers directly affect the contractual outcomes—potentially creating a motivation for misreporting—investors and lenders are motivated to monitor financial reports and to ensure that they are high quality.

EXAMPLE 4

Financial Reporting Manipulation: Motivations and Disciplining Mechanisms

For each of the following two scenarios, identify (1) factors that might motivate the company's managers to manipulate reported financial amounts and (2) applicable mechanisms that could discipline financial reporting quality.

1 ABC Co. is a private company. Bank NTBig has made a loan to ABC Co. ABC is required to maintain a minimum 2.0 interest coverage ratio. In its most recent financial reports, ABC reported earnings before interest and taxes of $1,200 and interest expense of $600. In the report's notes, the company discloses that it changed the estimated useful life of its property, plant, and equipment during the year. Depreciation was approximately $150 lower as a result of this change in estimate.

2 DEF Co. is a publicly traded company. For the most recent quarter, the average of analysts' forecasts for earnings per share was $2.50. In its quarterly earnings announcement, DEF reported net income of $3,458,780. The number of common shares outstanding was 1,378,000. DEF's main product is a hardware device that includes a free two-year service contract in the selling price. Based on management estimates, the company allocates a portion of revenues to the hardware device, which it recognizes immediately, and a portion to the service contract, which it defers and recognizes over the two years of the contract. Based on the disclosures, a higher percentage of revenue was allocated to hardware than in the past, with an estimated after-tax impact on net income of $27,000.

Solution to 1:

The need to maintain a minimum interest coverage ratio of 2.0 might motivate ABC's managers to manipulate reported financial amounts. The company's coverage ratio based on the reported amounts is exactly equal to 2.0. If ABC's managers had not changed the estimated useful life of the property, plant, and equipment, the coverage ratio would have fallen below the required level.

EBIT, as reported	$1,200
Impact on depreciation expense of changed assumptions about useful life	150
EBIT, as adjusted	$1,050
Interest expense	$600
Coverage ratio, as reported	2.00
Coverage ratio, as adjusted	1.75

The potential disciplining mechanisms include the auditors, who will assess the reasonableness of the depreciable lives estimates. In addition, the lenders will carefully scrutinize the change in estimate because the company only barely achieved the minimum coverage ratio and would not have achieved the minimum without the change in accounting estimate.

Solution to 2:

The desire to meet or exceed the average of analysts' forecasts for earnings per share might motivate DEF Co.'s managers to manipulate reported financial amounts. As illustrated in the following calculations, the impact of allocating a greater portion of revenue to hardware enabled the company to exceed analysts' earnings per share forecasts by $0.01.

Net income, as reported	$3,458,780
Impact on gross profit of changed revenue recognition, net of tax	27,000
Net income, as adjusted	$3,431,780
Weighted average number of shares	1,378,000
Earnings per share, as reported	$2.51
Earnings per share, as adjusted	$2.49

The potential disciplining mechanisms include the auditors, market regulators, financial analysts, and financial journalists.

4 DETECTION OF FINANCIAL REPORTING QUALITY ISSUES

Choices in the application of accounting standards abound, which is perhaps one reason why accounting literature and texts are so voluminous. Compounding the complexity, measurement often depends on estimates of economic phenomena. Two estimates might be justifiable, but they may have significantly different effects on the company's financial statements. As discussed earlier, the choice of a particular estimate may depend on the motivations of the reporting company's managers. With many choices available, and the inherent flexibility of estimates in the accounting process, managers have many tools for managing and meeting analysts' expectations through financial reporting.

An understanding of the choices that companies make in financial reporting is fundamental to evaluating the overall quality—both financial reporting and earnings quality—of the reports produced. Choices exist both in how information is presented (financial reporting quality) and in how financial results are calculated (earnings quality). Choices in presentation (financial reporting quality) may be fairly transparent to investors. Choices in the calculation of financial results (earnings quality), however, are more difficult to discern because they can be deeply embedded in the construction of reported financial results.

The availability of accounting choices enables managers to affect the reporting of financial results. Some choices increase performance and financial position in the reporting period (aggressive choices), and others increase them in later periods (conservative choices). A manager that wants to increase performance and financial position in the reporting period could:

- Recognize revenue prematurely;
- Use non-recurring transactions to increase profits;
- Defer expenses to later periods;
- Measure and report assets at higher values; and/or
- Measure and report liabilities at lower values.

A manager that wants to increase performance and financial position in a later period could:

- Defer current income to a later period (save income for a "rainy day"); and/or
- Recognize future expenses in a current period, setting the table for improving future performance.

The following sections describe some of the potential choices for how information is presented and how accounting elements [assets, liabilities, owners' equity, revenue and gains (income), and expenses and losses] are recognized, measured, and reported. In addition to choices within GAAP, companies may prepare fraudulent reports. For example, these reports may include non-existent revenue or assets. Section 4 concludes with some of the warning signs that can indicate poor-quality financial reports.

4.1 Presentation Choices

The technology boom of the 1990s and the internet bubble of the early 2000s featured companies, popular with investors, that often shared the same characteristic: They could not generate enough current earnings to justify their stock prices using the traditional price-to-earnings ratio (P/E) approaches to valuation. Many investors chose to explain these apparent anomalies by rationalizing that the old focus on profits and traditional valuation approaches no longer applied to such companies. Strange new metrics for determining operating performance emerged. Website operators spoke of the "eyeballs" they had captured in a quarter, or the "stickiness" of their websites for web surfers' visits. Various versions of "pro forma earnings"—that is, "non-GAAP earnings measures"—became a financial reporting staple of the era.

Many technology companies were accomplished practitioners of pro forma reporting, but they were not the first to use it. In the early 1990s, downsizing of large companies was a commonplace event, and massive restructuring charges obscured the operating performance at many established companies. For example, as it learned to cope in a world that embraced the personal computer rather than mainframe computing, International Business Machines (IBM) reported massive restructuring charges in 1991, 1992, and 1993: \$3.7 billion, \$11.6 billion, and \$8.9 billion, respectively. IBM was not alone. Sears incurred \$2.7 billion of restructuring charges in 1993, and AT&T reported restructuring charges of \$7.7 billion in 1995. These events were not isolated; restructuring charges were a standard quarterly reporting event. To counter perceptions that their operations were floundering, and supposedly to assist investors in evaluating operating performance, companies often sanitized earnings releases by excluding restructuring charges in pro forma measures of financial performance.

Accounting principles for reporting business combinations also played a role in boosting the popularity of pro forma earnings. Before 2001, acquisitions of one company by another often resulted in goodwill amortization charges that made subsequent earnings reports look weak. Complicating matters, there were two accounting methods for recording acquisitions: pooling-of-interests and purchase methods. The now-extinct pooling-of-interests treatment was difficult for companies to achieve because of the many restrictive criteria for its use, but it was greatly desired because it did not result in goodwill amortization charges. In the technology boom period, acquisitions were common and many were reported as purchases, with consequential goodwill amortization dragging down earnings for as long as 40 years under the then-existing rules. Acquisitive companies reporting under purchase accounting standards perceived themselves to be at a reporting disadvantage compared with companies able to apply pooling-of-interests. They responded by presenting earnings adjusted for the exclusion of amortization of intangible assets and goodwill.

Because investors try to make intercompany comparisons on a consistent basis, earnings before interest, taxes, depreciation, and amortization has become an extremely popular performance measure. EBITDA is widely viewed as eliminating noisy reporting signals. That noise may be introduced by different accounting methods among companies for depreciation, amortization of intangible assets, and restructuring charges. Companies may construct and report their own version of EBITDA, sometimes referring to it as "adjusted EBITDA," by adding to the list of items to exclude from net income. Items that analysts might encounter include the following:

- Rental payments for operating leases, resulting in EBITDAR (earnings before interest, taxes, depreciation, amortization, and rentals);
- Equity-based compensation, usually justified on the grounds that it is a non-cash expense;
- Acquisition-related charges;
- Impairment charges for goodwill or other intangible assets;
- Impairment charges for long-lived assets;
- Litigation costs; and
- Loss/gain on debt extinguishments.

Among other incentives for the spread of non-GAAP earnings measures are loan covenants. Lenders may make demands on a borrowing company that require achieving and maintaining performance criteria that use GAAP net income as a starting point but arrive at a measure suitable to the lender. The company may use this measure as its preferred non-GAAP metric in earnings releases, and also when describing its liquidity or solvency situation in the management commentary (called management discussion and analysis in the United States).

As mentioned earlier, if a company uses a non-GAAP financial measure in an SEC filing, it must display the most directly comparable GAAP measure with equal prominence and provide a reconciliation between the two. Management must explain why it believes that the non-GAAP financial measure provides useful information regarding the company's financial condition and operations. Management must also disclose additional purposes, if material, for which it uses the non-GAAP financial measures.

Similarly, IFRS requires a definition and explanation of any non-IFRS measures included in financial reports, including why the measure is potentially relevant to users. Management must provide reconciliations of non-IFRS measures with IFRS measures. There is a concern that management may use non-GAAP measures to distract attention from GAAP measures.

The SEC intended that the definition of non-GAAP financial measures would capture all measures with the effect of depicting either:

- a measure of performance that differs from that presented in the financial statements, such as income or loss before taxes or net income or loss, as calculated in accordance with GAAP; or
- a measure of liquidity that differs from cash flow or cash flow from operations computed in accordance with GAAP.[19]

The SEC prohibits the exclusion of charges or liabilities requiring cash settlement from any non-GAAP liquidity measures, other than EBIT and EBITDA. Also prohibited is the calculation of a non-GAAP performance measure intended to eliminate or smooth items tagged as non-recurring, infrequent, or unusual when such items are very likely to occur again. The SEC views the period within two years of either before or after the reporting date as the relevant time frame for considering whether a charge or gain is a recurring item. Example 5 describes a case of misuse and misreporting of non-GAAP measures.

EXAMPLE 5

Misuse and Misreporting of Non-GAAP Measures

Groupon is an online discount merchant. In the company's initial S-1 registration statement in 2011, then-CEO Andrew Mason gave prospective investors an up-front warning in a section entitled "We don't measure ourselves in conventional ways", which described Groupon's adjusted consolidated segment operating income (adjusted CSOI) measure. Exhibit 12 provides excerpts from a section entitled "Non-GAAP Financial Measures," which offered a more detailed explanation. Exhibit 13, also from the initial registration statement, shows a reconciliation of CSOI to the most comparable US GAAP measure. In its review, the SEC took the position that online marketing expenses were a recurring cost of business. Groupon responded that the marketing costs were similar to acquisition costs, not recurring costs, and that "we'll ramp down marketing just as fast as we ramped it up, reducing the customer acquisition part of our marketing expenses" as time passes.[20]

Eventually, and after much negative publicity, Groupon changed its non-GAAP measure. Exhibit 14 shows an excerpt from the final prospectus filed in November, after the SEC's review. Use the three exhibits to answer the questions that follow.

Exhibit 12 Groupon's "Non-GAAP Financial Measures"

Disclosures from June S-1 Filing

Adjusted CSOI is operating income of our two segments, North America and International, adjusted for online marketing expense, acquisition-related costs and stock-based compensation expense. Online marketing expense primarily represents the cost to acquire new subscribers and is dictated by the amount of growth we wish to pursue. Acquisition-related costs are non-recurring non-cash items related to certain of our acquisitions. Stock-based compensation expense is a non-cash item. We consider

(continued)

19 SEC, "Final Rule: Conditions for Use of Non-GAAP Financial Measures," Securities and Exchange Commission (www.sec.gov/rules/final/33-8176.htm).

20 Correspondence between Groupon and SEC, filed in EDGAR on 16 September 2011.

Exhibit 12 (Continued)

Adjusted CSOI to be an important measure of the performance of our business as it excludes expenses that are non-cash or otherwise not indicative of future operating expenses. We believe it is important to view Adjusted CSOI as a complement to our entire consolidated statements of operations.

Our use of Adjusted CSOI has limitations as an analytical tool, and you should not consider this measure in isolation or as a substitute for analysis of our results as reported under GAAP. Some of these limitations are:

- Adjusted CSOI does not reflect the significant cash investments that we currently are making to acquire new subscribers;
- Adjusted CSOI does not reflect the potentially dilutive impact of issuing equity-based compensation to our management team and employees or in connection with acquisitions;
- Adjusted CSOI does not reflect any interest expense or the cash requirements necessary to service interest or principal payments on any indebtedness that we may incur;
- Adjusted CSOI does not reflect any foreign exchange gains and losses;
- Adjusted CSOI does not reflect any tax payments that we might make, which would represent a reduction in cash available to us;
- Adjusted CSOI does not reflect changes in, or cash requirements for, our working capital needs; and
- Other companies, including companies in our industry, may calculate Adjusted CSOI differently or may use other financial measures to evaluate their profitability, which reduces the usefulness of it as a comparative measure.

Because of these limitations, Adjusted CSOI should not be considered as a measure of discretionary cash available to us to invest in the growth of our business. When evaluating our performance, you should consider Adjusted CSOI alongside other financial performance measures, including various cash flow metrics, net loss and our other GAAP results.

Exhibit 13 Groupon's "Adjusted CSOI"

Excerpt from June S-1 Filing

The following is a reconciliation of CSOI to the most comparable US GAAP measure, "loss from operations," for the years ended December 31, 2008, 2009, and 2010 and the three months ended March 31, 2010 and 2011:

	Year Ended December 31,			Three Months Ended March 31,	
(in $ thousands)	**2008**	**2009**	**2010**	**2010**	**2011**
(Loss) Income from operations	(1,632)	(1,077)	(420,344)	8,571	(117,148)
Adjustments:					
Online marketing	162	4,446	241,546	3,904	179,903

Exhibit 13 (Continued)

(in $ thousands)	Year Ended December 31, 2008	2009	2010	Three Months Ended March 31, 2010	2011
Stock-based compensation	24	115	36,168	116	18,864
Acquisition-related	—	—	203,183	—	—
Total adjustments	186	4,561	480,897	4,020	198,767
Adjusted CSOI	(1,446)	3,484	60,553	12,591	81,619

Exhibit 14 Groupon's "CSOI"

Excerpt from Revised S-1 Filing

The following is a reconciliation of CSOI to the most comparable US GAAP measure, "loss from operations," for the years ended December 31, 2008, 2009, and 2010 and the nine months ended September 30, 2010 and 2011:

(in $ thousands)	Year Ended December 31, 2008	2009	2010	Nine Months Ended September 30, 2010	2011
Loss from operations	(1,632)	(1,077)	(420,344)	(84,215)	(218,414)
Adjustments:					
Stock-based compensation	24	115	36,168	8,739	60,922
Acquisition-related	—	—	203,183	37,844	(4,793)
Total adjustments	24	115	239,351	46,583	56,129
CSOI	(1,608)	(962)	(180,993)	(37,632)	(162,285)

1 What cautions did Groupon include along with its description of the "Adjusted CSOI" metric?

2 Groupon excludes "online marketing" from "Adjusted CSOI." How does the exclusion of this expense compare with the SEC's limits on non-GAAP performance measures?

3 In the first quarter of 2011, what was the effect of excluding online marketing expenses on the calculation of "Adjusted CSOI"?

4 For 2010, how did results under the revised non-GAAP metric compare with the originally reported metric?

Solution to 1:

Groupon cautioned that the "Adjusted CSOI" metric should not be considered in isolation, should not be considered as a substitute for analysis using GAAP results, and "should not be considered a measure of discretionary cash flow." The company lists numerous limitations, primarily citing items that adjusted CSOI did not reflect.

Solution to 2:

The SEC specifies that non-GAAP measures should not eliminate items tagged as non-recurring, infrequent, or unusual when such items may be very likely to occur again. Because the online marketing expense occurred in every period reported and is likely to occur again, exclusion of this item appears contrary to SEC requirements.

Solution to 3:

As shown in Exhibit 13, in the first quarter of 2011, the exclusion of the online marketing expense was enough to swing the company from a net loss under US GAAP reporting to a profit—at least, a profit as defined by adjusted CSOI. Using adjusted CSOI as a performance measure, the company showed results that were 35% higher for the first *quarter* of 2011 compared with the entire previous *year*.

Solution to 4:

As shown in Exhibit 14, the revised metric is now called "CSOI" and no longer refers to "Adjusted CSOI." For 2010, results under the revised non-GAAP metric, which includes online marketing costs, shows a loss of $180,993,000 instead of a profit of $60,553,000.

In the case described in Example 5, Groupon changed its reporting and corrected the non-GAAP metric that the SEC had identified as misleading. In other cases, the SEC has pursued enforcement actions against companies for reporting misleading non-GAAP information. One such action was brought in 2009 against SafeNet Inc., where the SEC charged the company with improperly classifying ordinary operating expenses as non-recurring. This related to the integration of an acquired company and exclusion of the expenses from non-GAAP earnings in order to exceed earnings targets. A second action was brought by the SEC in 2017 against MDC Partners Inc. ("MDCA") for improper reconciliation of a non-GAAP measure and for improperly displaying the non-GAAP measure with greater prominence in its earnings releases. The case was brought after the company agreed to follow the rules but then failed to do so, as evidenced by the remark in the SEC's action: "Despite agreeing to comply with non-GAAP financial measure disclosure rules in December 2012 correspondence with the [SEC's] Division of Corporation Finance, MDCA continued to violate those rules for six quarters ..." Exhibit 15 presents the headline and sub-headings for one of MDC Partners' earnings announcements that was the subject of the enforcement action.

Exhibit 15 MDC Partners Inc. Press Release [Excerpt]

SEC Form 8-K filed 24 April 2014

This excerpt shows the headline, sub-heads, and lead sentence of the company's press release announcing periodic earnings.

MDC PARTNERS INC. REPORTS RECORD RESULTS FOR THE THREE MONTHS ENDED MARCH 31, 2014

Exhibit 15 (Continued)

ORGANIC REVENUE GROWTH OF 8.3%, EBITDA GROWTH OF 18.1% AND 90 BASIS POINTS OF MARGIN IMPROVEMENT
FREE CASH FLOW GROWTH OF 34.0%
INCREASED 2014 GUIDANCE IMPLIES YEAR-OVER-YEAR EBITDA GROWTH OF +13.5% TO +16.1%, MARGIN IMPROVEMENT OF 60 TO 70 BASIS POINTS, AND FREE CASH FLOW GROWTH OF +15.8% TO +20.2%

FIRST QUARTER HIGHLIGHTS:

- Revenue increased to $292.6 million from $265.6 million, an increase of 10.1%
- Organic revenue increased 8.3%
- EBITDA increased to $36.4 million from $30.8 million, an increase of 18.1%
- EBITDA margin increased 90 basis points to 12.5% from 11.6%
- Free Cash Flow increased to $20.6 million from $15.4 million, an increase of 34.0%
- Net New Business wins totaled $24.4 million

NEW YORK, NY (April 24, 2014) – MDC Partners Inc. (NASDAQ: MDCA; TSX: MDZ.A) today announced financial results for the three months ended March 31, 2014.

...

In general, management may choose to construct non-GAAP financial measures not only to help investors better understand the company's performance but also to paint a more flattering picture of its performance. In some cases, management may attempt to present non-GAAP measures in a way that diverts attention from the standards-compliant financial information that it is required to present.

4.2 Accounting Choices and Estimates

Choices do not necessarily involve complex accounting standards. Something as simple as the shipping terms for goods delivered to customers can have a profound effect on the timing of revenue. On the last day of the first quarter, suppose a company ships $10,000 of goods to a customer on the terms "free on board (FOB) shipping point," arriving the next day. This shipping term means that the customer takes title to the goods, and bears the risk of loss, at the time the goods leave the seller's loading dock. Barring any issues with collectability of the receivable, or a likelihood of a return, the seller would be able to recognize revenue on the sale along with the associated profit. That revenue and profit would be recognized in the first quarter of the year. Change the point at which the goods' title transfers to the customer to "FOB destination" and the revenue pattern will be completely different. Under these terms, the title—and risk of loss—transfers to the customer when the goods arrive at their destination, which is the customer's address. The seller cannot recognize the sale and profit until the shipment arrives the following day, which is the start of a new accounting period.

A simple change in shipping terms can make the difference between revenue and profits in the reporting period or postponing them until the next period. Shipping terms can also influence management behavior. To "make the numbers," managers might push product out the door prematurely under FOB shipping point arrangements in order to reflect as much revenue as possible in the reporting period. Alternatively, in the case of an over-abundance of orders, the company could run the risk of exceeding analysts' consensus estimates by a large margin. Management might be uncomfortable with this situation because investors might extrapolate too much from one reporting period in which expectations were exceeded. Management might want to prevent investors from becoming too optimistic and, if possible, delay revenue recognition until the next quarter. This result could be accomplished by fulfilling customer orders by initiating delivery on the last day of the quarter, with shipping terms set as FOB destination. By doing so, title would transfer in the next accounting period. Another possibility in this scenario is that if the customers insisted on FOB shipping point terms, the selling company could simply delay shipment until after the close of the quarter.

This illustration also highlights a difficult distinction for investors to make. A company may use accounting as a tool to aggressively promote earnings growth—as in the example with the premature shipment of goods with FOB shipping point terms—but it may be aggressively managing the business flow by slacking off on shipping goods when business is "too good," as in the second example. In either case, a desired management outcome is obtained by a simple change in shipping terms. Yet, many investors might be inclined to say that the second example is a conservative kind of earnings management and accept it, even though it artificially masks the actual economic activity that occurred at the time.

4.2.1 *How Accounting Choices and Estimates Affect Earnings and Balance Sheets*

Assumptions about inventory cost flows provide another example of how accounting choices can affect financial reporting. Companies may assume that their purchases of inventory items are sold to customers on a first-in-first-out (FIFO) basis, with the result that the remaining inventory reflects the most recent costs. Alternatively, they may assume that their purchases of inventory items are sold to customers on a weighted-average cost basis. Example 6 makes the point that merely choosing a cost flow assumption can affect profitability.

EXAMPLE 6

Effect of Cost Flow Assumption

A company starts operations with no inventory at the beginning of a fiscal year and makes purchases of a good for resale five times during the period at increasing prices. Each purchase is for the same number of units of the good. The purchases, and the cost of goods available for sale, appear in the following table. Notice that the price per unit has increased by 140% by the end of the period.

	Units	Price	Cost
Purchase 1	5	$100	$500
Purchase 2	5	150	750
Purchase 3	5	180	900
Purchase 4	5	200	1,000
Purchase 5	5	240	1,200
Cost of goods available for sale			$4,350

During the period, the company sells, at $250 each, all of the goods purchased except for five of them. Although the ending inventory consists of five units, the cost attached to those units can vary greatly.

1 What are the ending inventory and cost of goods sold if the company uses the FIFO method of inventory costing?

2 What are the ending inventory and cost of goods sold if the company uses the weighted-average method of inventory costing?

3 Compare cost of goods sold and gross profit calculated under the two methods.

Solution to 1:

The ending inventory and cost of goods sold if the company uses the FIFO method of inventory costing are $1,200 and $3,150.

Solution to 2:

The ending inventory and cost of goods sold if the company uses the weighted-average method of inventory costing are $870 and $3,480.

Solution to 3:

The following table shows how the choice of inventory costing methods—FIFO versus weighted average—affects the cost of goods sold and gross profit.

Cost Flow Assumption	FIFO	Weighted Average
Cost of goods available for sale	$4,350	$4,350
Ending inventory (5 units)	(1,200)	(870)
Cost of goods sold	$3,150	$3,480
Sales	$5,000	$5,000
Cost of goods sold	3,150	3,480
Gross profit	$1,850	$1,520
Gross profit margin	37.0%	30.4%

Note: Average inventory cost is calculated as Cost of goods available for sale/Units purchased = $4,350/25 = $174. There are five units in ending inventory, yielding an inventory value of $870.

Depending on which cost flow assumption the company uses, the end-of-period inventory is either $870 (under the weighted-average method) or $1,200 (under FIFO). The choice of method results in a difference of $330 in gross profit and 6.6% in gross profit margin.

The previous example is simplified and extreme for purposes of illustration clarity, but the point is important: Management's choice among acceptable inventory assumptions and methods affects profit. The selection of an inventory costing method is a policy decision, and companies cannot arbitrarily switch from one method to another. The selection does matter to profitability, however, and it also matters to the balance sheet.

In periods of changing prices, the FIFO cost assumption will provide a more current picture of ending inventory value, because the most recent purchases will remain in inventory. The balance sheet will be more relevant to investors. Under the weighted-average cost assumption, however, the balance sheet will display a blend of old and new costs. During inflationary periods, the value of the inventory will be understated: The company will not be able to replenish its inventory at the value shown. At the same time, the weighted-average inventory cost method ensures that the more current costs are shown in cost of sales, making the income statement more relevant than under the FIFO assumption. Trade-offs exist, and investors should be aware of how accounting choices affect financial reports. High-quality financial reporting provides users with sufficient information to assess the effects of accounting choices.

Estimates abound in financial reporting because of the use of accrual accounting, which attempts to show the effects of all economic events on a company during a particular period. Accrual accounting stands in contrast to cash basis accounting, which shows only the cash transactions conducted by a company. Although a high degree of certainty exists with reporting only cash transactions, much information is hidden. For instance, a company with growing revenues that makes the majority of its sales on credit would be understating its revenues for each period if it reported only cash transactions. On an accrual basis, revenues reflect all transactions that occurred, whether they transacted on a cash basis or credit-extended basis. Estimates enter the process because some facts related to events occurring in a particular period might not yet be known. Estimates can be well grounded in reality and applied to present a complete picture of the events affecting a company, or they can be management tools for achieving a desired financial picture.

To illustrate how estimates can affect financial reporting, consider sales made on credit. A company sells $1,000,000 of merchandise on credit and records the sale just before year end. Under accrual accounting, that amount is included in revenues and accounts receivable. The company's managers know from experience that they will never collect every dollar of the accounts receivable. Past experience is that, on average, only 97% of accounts receivable is collected. The company would estimate an amount of the uncollectible accounts at the time the sales occur and record an uncollectible accounts expense of $30,000, lowering earnings. The other side of the entry would be to establish an allowance for uncollectible accounts of $30,000. This allowance would be a contra asset account, presented as an offset to accounts receivable. The accounts receivable, net of the allowance for uncollectible accounts, would be stated at $970,000, which is the amount of cash the company ultimately expects to receive. If cash-basis accounting had been used, no revenues or accounts receivable would have been reported even though sales of merchandise had occurred. Accrual accounting, which contains estimates about future events, provides a much fuller picture of what transpired in the period than pure cash-basis accounting.

Yet, accrual accounting poses temptations to managers to manage the numbers, rather than to manage the business. Suppose a company's managers realize that the company will not meet analysts' consensus estimates in a particular quarter, and further, their bonus pay is dependent on reaching specified earnings targets. By offering special payment terms, or discounts, the managers may induce customers to take delivery of products that they would normally not order, so they could ship the products on FOB shipping point terms and recognize the revenues in the current quarter. They could even be so bold as to ship the goods under those terms even if the customer did not order them, in the hope that the customer would keep them or, at worst, return them in the next accounting period. Their aim would be to move the product off the company's property with FOB shipping point terms.

To further improve earnings in order to meet the consensus estimates, the company's managers might revise their estimate of the uncollectible accounts. The company's collection history shows a typical non-collection rate of 3% of sales, but the managers might rationalize the use of a 2% non-collection rate. This change will reduce the allowance for uncollectible accounts and the expense reported for the period. The managers might be able to justify the reduction on the grounds that the sales occurred in a part of the country that was experiencing an improved economic outlook, or that the company's collection history had been biased by the inclusion of a prolonged period of economic downturn. Whatever the justification, it would be hard to prove that the new estimate was completely right or wrong until time had passed. Because proof of the reliability of estimates is rarely available at the time the estimate is recorded, managers have a readily available means for manipulating earnings at their discretion.

ConAgra Foods Inc. provides an example of how the allowance for uncollectible accounts may be manipulated to manage earnings.[21] A subsidiary, called United Agri-Products (UAP), engaged in several improper accounting practices, one of them being the understatement of uncollectible accounts expense for several years. Exhibit 16 presents an excerpt from the SEC's Accounting and Auditing Enforcement Release.

Exhibit 16 SEC's Accounting and Auditing Enforcement Release Regarding United Agri-Products

... Generally, UAP's policy required that accounts which were past due between 90 days and one year should be reserved at 50%, and accounts over one year past due were to be reserved at 100%.

... In FY 1999 and continuing through FY 2000, UAP had substantial bad debt problems. In FY 2000, certain former UAP senior executives were informed that UAP needed to record an additional $50 million of bad debt expense. Certain former UAP senior executives were aware that in FY 1999 the size of the bad debt at certain IOCs had been substantial enough that it could have negatively impacted those IOC's ability to achieve PBT (profits before taxes) targets. In addition, just prior to the end of UAP's FY 2000, the former UAP COO (chief operating officer), in the presence of other UAP employees, ordered that UAP's bad debt reserve be reduced by $7 million in order to assist the Company in meeting its PBT target for the fiscal year.

... At the end of FY 2000, former UAP senior executives reported financial results to ConAgra which they knew, or were reckless in not knowing, overstated UAP's income before income taxes because UAP had failed to record sufficient bad debt expense. The misconduct with respect to bad debt expense caused ConAgra to overstate its reported income before income taxes by $7 million, or 1.13%, in FY 2000. At the Agricultural Products' segment level, the misconduct caused that segment's reported operating profit to be overstated by 5.05%.

Deferred-tax assets provide a similar example of choices in estimates affecting the earnings outcome. Deferred-tax assets may arise when a company reports a net operating loss under tax accounting rules. A company may record a deferred-tax asset based on the expectation that losses in the reporting period will offset expected future profits and reduce the company's future income tax liability. Accounting standards require that the deferred tax asset be reduced by a "valuation allowance" to account for the possibility that the company will be unable to generate enough profit to use all of the available tax benefits.[22]

Assume a company loses €1 billion in 2012, generating a net operating loss of the same amount for tax purposes. The company's income tax rate is 25%, and it will be able to apply the net operating loss to its taxable income for the next 10 years. The net operating loss results in a deferred tax asset with a nominal value of €250 million (25% × €1,000,000,000). Initial recognition would result in a deferred tax asset of €250 million and a credit to deferred tax expense of €250 million. The company must address the question of whether or not the €250 million will ever be completely applied to future income. It may be experiencing increased competition and other circumstances that resulted in the €1 billion loss, and it may be unreasonable to

21 Accounting and Auditing Enforcement Release No. 2542, "SEC v. James Charles Blue, Randy Cook, and Victor Campbell,) United States District Court for the District of Colorado, Civ. Action No. 07-CV-00095 REB-MEH (17 January 2007).

22 See Accounting Standards Codification 740-10-30-16 to 25, "Establishment of a Valuation Allowance for Deferred Tax Assets."

assume it will have taxable income against which to apply the loss. In fact, the company's managers might believe it is reasonable to assume only that it will survive for five years, and with marginal profitability. The €250 million deferred tax asset is thus overstated if no valuation allowance is recorded to offset it.

The managers believe that only €100 million of the net operating losses will actually be applied to the company's taxable income. That belief implies that only €25 million of the tax benefits will ever be realized. The deferred tax assets reported on the balance sheet should not exceed this amount. The company should record a valuation allowance of €225 million, which would offset the deferred tax asset balance of €250 million, resulting in a net deferred tax asset balance of €25 million. There would also be a €225 million credit to the deferred tax provision. It is important to understand that the valuation allowance should be revised whenever facts and circumstances change.

The ultimate value of the deferred tax asset is driven by management's outlook for the future—and that outlook may be influenced by other factors. If the company needs to stay in compliance with debt covenants and needs every euro of value that can be justified by the outlook, its managers may take a more optimistic view of the future and keep the valuation allowance artificially low (in other words, the net deferred tax asset high).

PowerLinx Inc. provides an example of how over-optimism about the realizability of a deferred tax asset can lead to misstated financial reports. PowerLinx was a maker of security video cameras, underwater cameras, and accessories. Aside from fraudulently reporting 90% of its fiscal year 2000 revenue, PowerLinx had problems with valuation of its deferred tax assets. Exhibit 17 provides an excerpt from the SEC's Accounting and Auditing Enforcement Release with emphasis added.[23]

Exhibit 17 SEC's Accounting and Auditing Enforcement Release Regarding PowerLinx

PowerLinx improperly recorded on its fiscal year 2000 balance sheet a deferred tax asset of $1,439,322 without any valuation allowance. The tax asset was material, representing *almost forty percent of PowerLinx's total assets* of $3,841,944. PowerLinx also recorded deferred tax assets of $180,613, $72,907, and $44,921, respectively, in its financial statements for the first three quarters of 2000.

PowerLinx did not have a proper basis for recording the deferred tax assets. The company had accumulated significant losses in 2000 and had no historical operating basis from which to conclude that it would be profitable in future years. Underwater camera sales had declined significantly and the company had devoted most of its resources to developing its SecureView product. The sole basis for PowerLinx's "expectation" of future profitability was the purported $9 million backlog of SecureView orders, which management assumed would generate taxable income; however, this purported backlog, which predated Bauer's hiring, did not reflect actual demand for SecureView cameras and, consequently, was not a reasonable or reliable indicator of future profitability.

Another example of misstated financial results caused by improper reflection of the realizability of a deferred tax asset occurred with Hampton Roads Bankshares Inc. ("HRBS"), a commercial bank with deteriorating loan portfolio quality and commensurate losses in the years following the financial crisis. The company reported a deferred tax asset related to its loan losses; however, it did not establish a valuation allowance against its deferred tax asset. This decision was based on dubious projections indicating that the company would earn the

23 Accounting and Auditing Enforcement Release No. 2448, "In the Matter of Douglas R. Bauer, Respondent," SEC (27 June 2006): www.sec.gov/litigation/admin/2006/34-54049.pdf.

Exhibit 17 (Continued)

necessary future taxable income "to fully utilize the [deferred tax asset] DTA over the applicable carry-forward period."[24] Over time, it became clear that the earnings projections were not realistic, and ultimately the company restated its financial results to include a valuation allowance against almost the entire deferred tax asset. Exhibit 18 presents an excerpt from the company's amended Form 10-Q/A containing the restatement.

EXHIBIT 18 Hampton Roads Bankshares, Inc. Form 10-Q/A filed August 13, 2010 [Excerpt from footnotes]

NOTE B – RESTATEMENT OF CONSOLIDATED FINANCIAL STATEMENTS

Subsequent to filing the Company's annual report on Form 10-K for the year ended December 31, 2009 and its Form 10-Q for the three months ended March 31, 2010 the Company determined that a valuation allowance on its deferred tax assets should be recognized as of December 31, 2009. The Company decided to establish a valuation allowance against the deferred tax asset because it is uncertain when it will realize this asset.

Accordingly, the December 31, 2009 consolidated balance sheet and the March 31, 2010 consolidated financial statements have been restated to account for this determination. The effect of this change in the consolidated financial statements was as follows (in thousands, except per share amounts).

Consolidated Balance Sheet at March 31, 2010

	As Reported	Adjustment	As Restated
Deferred tax assets, net	$70,323	$(70,323)	—
Total assets	3,016,470	(70,323)	$2,946,147
Retained earnings deficit	(158,621)	(70,323)	(228,944)
Total shareholder's equity	156,509	(70,323)	86,186
Total Liabilities and shareholders' equity	3,016,470	(70,323)	2,946,147

Consolidated Balance Sheet at December 31, 2009

	As Reported	Adjustment	As Restated
Deferred tax assets, net	$56,380	$(55,983)	$397
Total assets	2,975,559	(55,983)	2,919,576
Retained earnings deficit	(132,465)	(55,983)	(188,488)

(continued)

24 Accounting and Auditing Enforcement Release No. 3600, "In the Matter of Hampton Roads Bankshares Inc., Respondent," SEC (5 December 2014) https://www.sec.gov/litigation/admin/2014/34-73750.pdf.

(Continued)

	As Reported	Adjustment	As Restated
Total shareholder's equity	180,996	(55,983)	125,013
Total Liabilities and shareholders' equity	2,975,559	(55,983)	2,919,576

Another example of how choices and estimates can affect reported results lies in the selection of a depreciation method for allocating the cost of long-lived assets to accounting periods subsequent to their acquisition. A company's managers may choose to depreciate long-lived assets (1) on a straight-line basis, with each year bearing the same amount of depreciation expense; (2) using an accelerated method, with greater depreciation expense recognition in the earlier part of an asset's life; or (3) using an activity-based depreciation method, which allocates depreciation expense based on units of use or production. Depreciation expense is affected by another set of choices and estimates regarding the salvage value of the assets being depreciated. A salvage value of zero will always increase depreciation expense under any method compared with the choice of a non-zero salvage value.

Assume a company invests $1,000,000 in manufacturing equipment and expects it to have a useful economic life of 10 years. During its expected life, the equipment will produce 400,000 units of product, or $2.50 depreciation expense per unit produced. When it is disposed of at the end of its expected life, the company's managers expect to realize no value for the equipment. The following table shows the differences in the three alternative methods of depreciation: straight-line, accelerated on a double-declining balance basis, and units-of-production method, with no salvage value assumed at the end of the equipment's life.

	Straight-Line Method	Double-Declining Balance Method			Units-of-Production Method		
Year	Depreciation Expense	Balance	Declining Balance Rate[1]	Depreciation Expense	Units Produced	Depreciation Rate/Unit	Depreciation Expense
1	$100,000	$1,000,000	20%	$200,000	90,000	$2.50	$225,000
2	100,000	800,000	20%	160,000	80,000	$2.50	200,000
3	100,000	640,000	20%	128,000	70,000	$2.50	175,000
4	100,000	512,000	20%	102,400	60,000	$2.50	150,000
5	100,000	409,600	20%	81,920	50,000	$2.50	125,000
6	100,000	327,680	20%	65,536	10,000	$2.50	25,000
7	100,000	262,144	20%	52,429	10,000	$2.50	25,000
8	100,000	209,715	20%	41,943	10,000	$2.50	25,000
9	100,000	167,772	20%	33,554	10,000	$2.50	25,000
10	100,000	134,218	20%	26,844	10,000	$2.50	25,000
Total	$1,000,000			$892,626	400,000		$1,000,000

[1] Declining balance rate of 20% calculated as 10-year life being equivalent to 10% annual depreciation rate, multiplied by 2 = 20%.

The straight-line method allocates the cost of the equipment evenly to all 10 years of the equipment's life. The double-declining balance method will have a higher allocation of cost to the earlier years of the equipment's life. As its name implies, the depreciation expense will decline in each succeeding year because it is based on a fixed rate applied to a declining balance. The rate used was double the straight-line rate, but it could have been any other rate that the company's managers believed was representative of the way the actual equipment depreciation occurred. Notice that the double-declining balance method also results in an incomplete depreciation of the machine at the end of 10 years; a balance of $107,374 (= $1,000,000 – $892,626) remains at the end of the expected life, which will result in a loss upon the retirement of the equipment if the company's expectation of zero salvage value turns out to be correct. Some companies may choose to depreciate the equipment to its expected salvage, zero in this case, in its final year of use. Some companies may use a policy of switching to straight-line depreciation after the mid-life of its depreciable assets in order to fully depreciate them. That particular pattern is coincidentally displayed in the units-of-production example, in which the equipment is used most heavily in the earliest part of its useful life, and then levels off to much less utilization in the second half of the expected life.

Exhibit 19 shows the different expense allocation patterns of the methods over the same life. Each will affect earnings differently.

Exhibit 19 Expense Allocation Patterns of Different Depreciation Methods

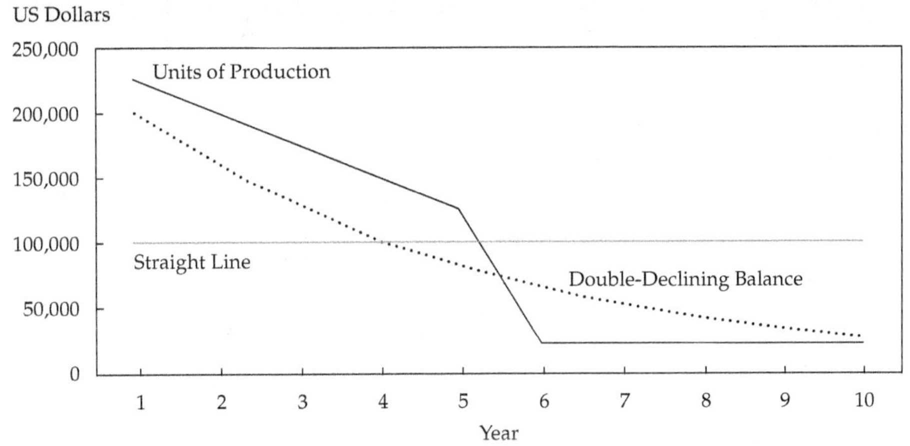

The company's managers could justify any of these methods. Each might fairly represent the way the equipment will be consumed over its expected economic life, which is a subjective estimate itself. The choices of methods and lives can profoundly affect reported income. These choices are not proven right or wrong until far into the future—but managers must estimate their effects in the present.

Exhibit 20 shows the effects of the three different methods on operating profit and operating profit margins, assuming that the production output of the equipment generates revenues of $500,000 each year and $200,000 of cash operating expenses are incurred, leaving $300,000 of operating profit before depreciation expense.

Exhibit 20 Effects of Depreciation Methods on Operating Profit

	Straight Line		
Year	**Depreciation**	**Operating Profit**	**Operating Profit Margin**
1	$100,000	$200,000	40.0%
2	100,000	200,000	40.0%

(continued)

Exhibit 20 (Continued)

Year	Straight Line Depreciation	Straight Line Operating Profit	Straight Line Operating Profit Margin
3	100,000	200,000	40.0%
4	100,000	200,000	40.0%
5	100,000	200,000	40.0%
6	100,000	200,000	40.0%
7	100,000	200,000	40.0%
8	100,000	200,000	40.0%
9	100,000	200,000	40.0%
10	100,000	200,000	40.0%

Year	Double Declining Balance Depreciation	Double Declining Balance Operating Profit	Double Declining Balance Operating Profit Margin
1	$200,000	$100,000	20.0%
2	160,000	140,000	28.0%
3	128,000	172,000	34.4%
4	102,400	197,600	39.5%
5	81,920	218,080	43.6%
6	65,536	234,464	46.9%
7	52,429	247,571	49.5%
8	41,943	258,057	51.6%
9	33,554	266,446	53.3%
10	134,218*	165,782	33.2%

Year	Units of Production Depreciation	Units of Production Operating Profit	Units of Production Operating Profit Margin
1	$225,000	$75,000	15.0%
2	200,000	100,000	20.0%
3	175,000	125,000	25.0%
4	150,000	150,000	30.0%
5	125,000	175,000	35.0%
6	25,000	275,000	55.0%
7	25,000	275,000	55.0%
8	25,000	275,000	55.0%
9	25,000	275,000	55.0%
10	25,000	275,000	55.0%

* Includes $107,374 of undepreciated basis, treated as depreciation expense in final year of service.

The straight-line method shows consistent operating profit margins, and the other two methods show varying degrees of increasing operating profit margins as the depreciation expense decreases over time.

The example above shows the differences among alternative methods, but even more depreciation expense variation is possible by changing estimated lives and assumptions about salvage value. For instance, change the expected life assumption to 5 years from 10 and add an expectation that the equipment will have a 10% salvage value at the end of its expected life. Exhibit 21 shows the revised depreciation calculations. Notice that under the double-declining balance method, the depreciation rate is applied to the gross cost, unlike the other two methods. The straight-line method and the units-of-production method subtract the salvage value from the cost before depreciation expense is calculated. Also note that the assumption about the usage of the equipment is revised so that it is depreciated only to its salvage value of $100,000 by the end of its estimated life. The total depreciation under each method is $900,000.

Exhibit 21 Depreciation Calculations for Each Method in Changed Scenario

	Straight-Line Method	Double-Declining Balance Method			Units-of-Production Method		
Year	Depreciation Expense	Balance	Declining Balance Rate[1]	Depreciation Expense	Units Produced	Depreciation Rate/Unit	Depreciation Expense
1	**$180,000**	$1,000,000	40%	**$400,000**	100,000	$2.25	**$225,000**
2	**180,000**	600,000	40%	**240,000**	90,000	$2.25	**202,500**
3	**180,000**	360,000	40%	**144,000**	80,000	$2.25	**180,000**
4	**180,000**	216,000	40%	**86,400**	70,000	$2.25	**157,500**
5	**180,000**	129,600	40%	**29,600[2]**	60,000	$2.25	**135,000**
Total	**$900,000**			**$900,000**	400,000		**$900,000**

[1] Declining balance rate of 40% calculated as 5-year life being equivalent to 20% annual depreciation rate, multiplied by 2 = 40%.
[2] Depreciation calculated as $29,600 instead of 40% × $129,600. Rote application of the declining-balance rate would have resulted in $51,840 of expense, which would have depreciated the asset below salvage value.

Exhibit 22 shows the different expense allocation patterns of the methods over the five-year expected life, and assuming a 10% salvage value. Although each method is distinctly different in the timing of the cost allocation over time, the variation is less pronounced than over the longer life used in the previous example.

Exhibit 22 Expense Allocation Patterns of Depreciation Methods in Changed Scenario

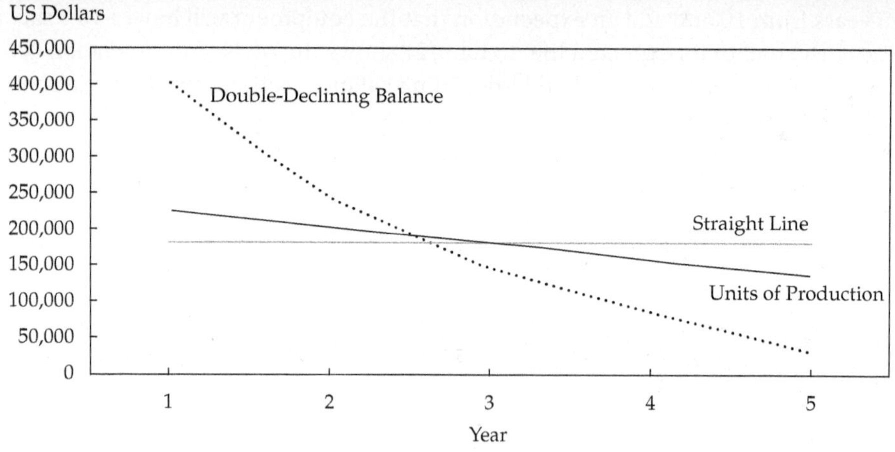

One of the clearest examples of how choices affect both the balance sheet and income statement can be found in capitalization practices. In classifying a payment made, management must determine whether the payment will benefit only the current period—making it an expense—or whether it will benefit future periods, leading to classification as a cost to be capitalized as an asset. This management judgment embodies an implicit forecast of how the item acquired by the payment will be used, or not used, in the future.

That judgment can be biased by the powerful effect a capitalization policy can have on earnings. Every amount capitalized on the balance sheet as a building, an item of inventory, a deferred cost, or any "other asset" is an amount that does not get recognized as an expense in the reporting period.

A real-life example can be found in the case of WorldCom Inc., a telecom concern that grew rapidly in the late 1990s. Much of WorldCom's financial reporting was eventually found to be fraudulent. An important part of the misreporting centered on its treatment of what is known in the telecom industry as "line costs". These are the costs of carrying a voice call or data transmission from its starting point to its ending point, and they represented WorldCom's largest expense. WorldCom's chief financial officer decided to capitalize such costs instead of treating them as an operating expense. As a consequence, from the second quarter of 1999 through the first quarter of 2002, WorldCom increased its operating income by $7 billion. In three of the five quarters in which the improper line cost capitalization took place, WorldCom would have recognized pre-tax losses instead of profits.[25]

Similarly, acquisitions are an area in which managers must exercise judgment. An allocation of the purchase price must be made to all of the different assets acquired based on their fair values, and those fair values are not always objectively verifiable. Management may have to make its own estimate of fair values for assets acquired, and it may be biased towards a low estimate for the values of depreciable assets in order to depress future depreciation expense. Another benefit to keeping depreciable asset values low is that the amount of the purchase price that cannot be allocated to specific assets is classified as goodwill, which is neither depreciated nor amortized in future reporting periods.

25 See Report of Investigation by the Special Investigative Committee of the Board of Directors of WorldCom, Inc., by Dennis R. Beresford, Nicholas deB. Katzenbach, & C.B. Rogers, Jr.PP 9-11: www.sec.gov/Archives/edgar/data/723527/000093176303001862/dex991.htm.

Goodwill reporting has choices of its own. Although goodwill has no effect on future earnings when unimpaired, annual testing of its fair value may reveal that the excess of price paid over the fair value of assets may not be recoverable, which should lead to a write-down of goodwill. The estimation process for the fair value of goodwill may depend heavily on projections of future performance. Those projections may be biased upward in order to avoid a goodwill write-down.

4.2.2 *How Choices Affect the Cash Flow Statement*

The cash flow statement consists of three sections: the operating section, which shows the cash generated or used by operations; the investing section, which shows cash used for investments or provided by their disposal; and the financing section, which shows transactions attributable to financing activities.

The operating section is closely scrutinized by investors. Many of them consider it a reality check on reported earnings, on the grounds that earnings attributable to accrual accounting only and unsupported by actual cash flows may indicate earnings manipulation. Such investors believe that amounts shown for cash generated by operations is more insulated from managerial manipulation than the income statement. Cash generated by operations can be managed to an extent, however.

The operating section of the cash flow statement can be shown either under the direct method or the indirect method. Under the direct method, "entities are encouraged to report major classes of gross cash receipts and gross cash payments and their arithmetic sum—the net cash flow from operating activities."[26] In practice, companies rarely use the direct method. Instead, they use the indirect method, which shows a reconciliation of net income to cash provided by operations. The reconciliation shows the non-cash items affecting net income along with changes in working capital accounts affecting cash from operations. Exhibit 23 provides an example of the indirect presentation method.

Exhibit 23 Indirect Presentation Method

Cash Flows from Operating Activities ($ millions)	2018
Net income	$3,000
Adjustments to reconcile net income to net cash provided by operating activities:	
Provision for doubtful receivables	10
Provision for depreciation and amortization	1,000
Goodwill impairment charges	35
Share-based compensation expense	100
Provision for deferred income taxes	200
Changes in assets and liabilities:	
Trade, notes and financing receivables related to sales	(2,000)
Inventories	(1,500)
Accounts payable	1,200
Accrued income taxes payable/receivable	(80)
Retirement benefits	90

(continued)

26 Accounting Standards Codification Section 230-10-45-25, "Reporting Operating, Investing, and Financing Activities." The direct method and indirect method are similar in IFRS, as addressed in IAS 7, Paragraph 18.

Exhibit 23 (Continued)

Cash Flows from Operating Activities ($ millions)	2018
Other	(250)
Net cash provided by operating activities	$1,805

Whether the indirect method or direct method is used, simple choices exist for managers to improve the *appearance* of cash flow provided by operations without actually improving it. One such choice is in the area of accounts payable management, shaded in Exhibit 23. Assume that the accounts payable balance is $5,200 million at the end of the period, an increase of $1,200 million from its previous year-end balance of $4,000 million. The $1,200 million increase in accounts payable matched increased expenses and/or assets but did not require cash. If the company's managers had further delayed paying creditors $500 million until the day *after* the balance sheet date, they could have increased the cash provided by operating activities by $500 million. If the managers believe that cash generated from operations is a metric of focus for investors, they can impress them with artificially strong cash flow by simply stretching the accounts payable credit period.

What might alert investors to such machinations? They need to examine the composition of the operations section of the cash flow statement—if they do not, then *nothing* will ever alert them. Studying changes in the working capital can reveal unusual patterns that may indicate manipulation of the cash provided by operations.

Another practice that might lead an investor to question the quality of cash provided by operations is to compare a company's cash generation with an industry-wide level or with the cash operating performance of one or more similar competitors. Cash generation performance can be measured several ways. One way is to compare the relationship between cash generated by operations and net income. Cash generated by operations in excess of net income signifies better quality of earnings, whereas a chronic excess of net income over cash generated by operations should be a cause for concern; it may signal the use of accounting methods to simply raise net income instead of depicting financial reality. Another way to measure cash generation performance is to compare cash generated by operations with debt service, capital expenditures, and dividends (if any). When there is a wide variance between the company's cash generation performance and that of its benchmarks, investors should seek an explanation and carefully examine the changes in working capital accounts.

Because investors may focus on cash from operations as an important metric, managers may resort to managing the working capital accounts as described in order to present the most favorable picture. But there are other ways to do this. A company may misclassify operating uses of cash into either the investing or financing sections of the cash flow statement, which enhances the appearance of cash generated by operating activities.

Dynegy Inc. provides an example of manipulation of cash from operations through clever construction of contracts and assistance from an unconsolidated special purpose entity named ABG Gas Supply LLC (ABG). In April 2001, Dynegy entered into a contract for the purchase of natural gas from ABG. According to the contract, Dynegy would purchase gas at *below-market* rates from ABG for nine months and sell it at the current market rate. The nine-month term coincided with Dynegy's 2001 year-end and would result in gains backed by cash flows. Dynegy also agreed to buy gas at *above-market* rates from ABG for the following 51 months and sell it at the current market rate. The contract was reported at its fair value at the end of fiscal year 2001. It had no effect on net income for the year. The earlier portion of the contract resulted in a gain, supported by $300 million of cash flow, but the latter portion of the contract resulted in non-cash losses that offset the profit. The mark-to-market rules required the recognition of both gains and losses from all parts of the contract, and hence the net effect on earnings was zero.

In April 2002, a *Wall Street Journal* article exposed the chicanery, thanks to leaked documents. The SEC required Dynegy to restate the cash flow statement by reclassifying $300 million from the operating section of the cash flow statement to the financing section, on the grounds that Dynegy had used ABG as a conduit to effectively borrow $300 million from Citigroup. The bank had extended credit to ABG, which it used to finance its losses on the contract (Lee, 2012).

Another area of flexibility in cash flow reporting is found in the area of interest capitalization, which creates differences between total interest payments and total interest costs.[27] Assume a company incurs total interest cost of $30,000, composed of $3,000 of discount amortization and $27,000 of interest payments. Of the $30,000, two-thirds of it ($20,000) is expensed; the remaining third ($10,000) is capitalized as plant assets. If the company uses the same interest expense/capitalization proportions to allocate the interest payments between operating and investing activities, then it will report $18,000 (2/3 × $27,000) as an operating outflow and $9,000 (1/3 × $27,000) as an investing outflow. The company might also choose to offset the entire $3,000 of non-cash discount amortization against the $20,000 treated as expense, resulting in an operating outflow as low as $17,000, or as much as $20,000 if it allocated all of the non-cash discount amortization to interest capitalized as investing activities. Similarly, the investing outflow could be as much as $10,000 or as little as $7,000, depending on the treatment of the non-cash discount amortization. There are choices within the choices, all in areas where investors believe choices do not even exist. Nurnberg and Largay (1998) note that companies apparently favor the method that reports the lowest operating outflow, presumably to maximize reported cash from operations.

Investors and analysts need to be aware that presentation choices permitted in IAS 7, "Statement of Cash Flows," offer flexibility in classification of certain items in the cash flow statement. This flexibility can drastically change the results in the operating section of the cash flow statement. An excerpt from IAS 7, Paragraphs 33 and 34, provides the background:

> 33. Interest paid and interest and dividends received are usually classified as operating cash flows for a financial institution. However, there is no consensus on the classification of these cash flows for other entities. Interest paid and interest and dividends received may be classified as operating cash flows because they enter into the determination of profit or loss. *Alternatively, interest paid and interest and dividends received may be classified as financing cash flows and investing cash flows respectively, because they are costs of obtaining financial resources or returns on investments.*
>
> 34. Dividends paid may be classified as a financing cash flow because they are a cost of obtaining financial resources. *Alternatively, dividends paid may be classified as a component of cash flows from operating activities in order to assist users to determine the ability of an entity to pay dividends out of operating cash flows.* [Emphasis added.]

By allowing a choice of operating or financing for the placement of interest and dividends received or paid, IAS 7 gives a company's managers the opportunities to select the presentation that gives the best-looking picture of operating performance. An example is Norse Energy Corp. ASA, a Norwegian gas explorer and producer, which changed its classifications of interest paid and interest received in 2007 (Gordon,

27 See Nurnberg and Largay (1998) and Nurnberg (2006).

Henry, Jorgensen, and Linthicum, 2017). Interest paid was switched to financing instead of decreasing cash generated from operations. Norse Energy also switched its classification of interest received to investing from operating cash flow. The net effect of these changes was to report positive, rather than negative, operating cash flows in both 2007 and 2008. With these simple changes, the company could also change the perception of its operations. The cash flow statement formerly presented the appearance of a company with operations that used more cash than it generated, and it possibly raised questions about the sustainability of operations. After the revision, the operating section of the cash flow statement depicted a much more viable operation.

Exhibit 24 shows the net effect of the reclassifications on Norse Energy's cash flows.

Exhibit 24 Reclassification of Cash Flows (amounts in $ millions)

	As Reported (following 2007 reclassification)		Adjustments, If No Reclassification*		Pro-forma (if no reclassification)	
	2008	2007	2008	2007	2008	2007
Operating	**$5.30**	**$2.80**	**($13.70)**	**($14.40)**	**($8.40)**	**($11.60)**
Investing	$0.90	($56.80)	($9.00)	($3.50)	($8.10)	($60.30)
Financing	($16.60)	$34.50	$22.70	$17.90	$6.10	$52.40
Total	($10.40)	($19.50)	$0	$0	($10.40)	($19.50)

* The adjustments reverse the addition of interest received to investing and instead add it to operating. The adjustments also reverse the deduction of interest paid from financing and instead subtract it from operating.

4.2.3 *Choices That Affect Financial Reporting*

Exhibit 25 summarizes some of the areas where choices can be made that affect financial reports.

Exhibit 25 Areas Where Choices and Estimates Affect Financial Reporting

Area of Choice/ Estimate	Analyst Concerns
Revenue recognition	■ How is revenue recognized: upon shipment or upon delivery of goods? ■ Is the company engaging in "channel stuffing"—the practice of overloading a distribution channel with more product than it is normally capable of selling? This can be accomplished by inducing customers to buy more through unusual discounts, the threat of near-term price increases, or both—or simply by shipping goods that were not ordered. These transactions may be corrected in a subsequent period and may result in restated results. Are accounts receivable relative to revenues abnormally high for relative to the company's history or to its peers? If so, channel stuffing may have occurred. ■ Is there unusual activity in the allowance for sales returns relative to past history?

Exhibit 25 (Continued)

Area of Choice/ Estimate	Analyst Concerns
	■ Does the company's days sales outstanding show any collection issues that might indicate shipment of unneeded or unwanted goods to customers? ■ Does the company engage in "bill-and-hold" transactions? This is when a customer purchases goods but requests that they remain with the seller until a later date. This kind of transaction makes it possible for a seller to manufacture fictitious sales by declaring end-of-period inventory as "sold but held," with a minimum of effort and phony documentation. ■ Does the company use rebates as part of its marketing approach? If so, how significantly do the estimates of rebate fulfillment affect net revenues, and have any unusual breaks with history occurred? ■ Does the company separate its revenue arrangements into multiple deliverables of goods or services? This area is one of great revenue recognition flexibility, and also one that provides little visibility to investors. They simply cannot examine a company's arrangements and decide for themselves whether revenue has been properly allocated to different components of a contract. If a company uses multiple deliverable arrangements with its customers as a routine matter, investors might be more sensitive to revenue reporting risks. In seeking a comfort level, they might ask the following questions: Does the company explain adequately how it determines the different allocations of deliverables and how revenue is recognized on each one? Do deferred revenues result? If not, does it seem reasonable that there are no deferred revenues for this kind of arrangement? Are there unusual trends in revenues and receivables, particularly with regard to cash conversion? If an investor is not satisfied with the answers to these questions, he or she might be more comfortable with other investment choices.
Long-lived assets: Depreciation policies	■ Do the estimated life spans of the associated assets make sense, or are they unusually low compared with others in the same industry? ■ Have there been changes in depreciable lives that have a positive effect on current earnings? ■ Do recent asset write-downs indicate that company policy on asset lives might need to be reconsidered?
Intangibles: Capitalization policies	■ Does the company capitalize expenditures related to intangibles, such as software? Does its balance sheet show any R&D capitalized as a result of acquisitions? Or, if the company is an IFRS filer, has it capitalized any internally generated development costs? ■ How do the company's capitalization policies compare with the competition? ■ Are amortization policies reasonable?

(continued)

Exhibit 25 (Continued)

Area of Choice/ Estimate	Analyst Concerns
Allowance for doubtful accounts/ loan loss reserves	■ Are additions to such allowances lower or higher than in the past? ■ Does the collection experience justify any difference from historical provisioning? ■ Is there a possibility that any lowering of the allowance may be the result of industry difficulties along with the difficulty of meeting earnings expectations?
Inventory cost methods	■ Does the company use a costing method that produces fair reporting results in view of its environment? How do its inventory methods compare with others in its industry? Are there differences that will make comparisons uneven if there are unusual changes in inflation? ■ Does the company use reserves for obsolescence in its inventory valuation? If so, are they subject to unusual fluctuations that might indicate adjusting them to arrive at a specified earnings result? ■ If a company reports under US GAAP and uses last-in-first-out (LIFO) inventory accounting, does LIFO liquidation (the assumed sale of old, lower-cost layers of inventory) occur through inventory reduction programs? This inventory reduction may generate earnings without supporting cash flow, and management may intentionally reduce the layers to produce specific earnings benefits.
Tax asset valuation accounts	■ Tax assets, if present, must be stated at the value at which management expects to realize them, and an allowance must be set up to restate tax assets to the level expected to eventually be converted into cash. Determining the allowance involves an estimate of future operations and tax payments. Does the amount of the valuation allowance seem reasonable, overly optimistic, or overly pessimistic? ■ Are there contradictions between the management commentary and the allowance level, or the tax note and the allowance level? There cannot be an optimistic management commentary and a fully reserved tax asset, or vice versa. One of them has to be wrong. ■ Look for changes in the tax asset valuation account. It may be 100% reserved at first, and then "optimism" increases whenever an earnings boost is needed. Lowering the reserve decreases tax expense and increases net income.
Goodwill	■ Companies must annually assess goodwill balances for impairment on a qualitative basis. If further testing appears necessary, it is based on estimates of the fair value of the reporting units (US GAAP issuers), or cash-generating units (IFRS issuers), associated with goodwill balances. The tests are based on subjective estimates, including future cash flows and the employment of discount rates. ■ Do the disclosures on goodwill testing suggest that the exercise was skewed to avoid impairment charges?

Exhibit 25 (Continued)

Area of Choice/ Estimate	Analyst Concerns
Warranty reserves	■ Have additions to the reserves been reduced, perhaps to make earnings targets? Examine the trend in the charges of actual costs against the reserves: Do they support or contradict the warranty provisioning activity? Do the actual costs charged against the reserve give the analyst any indication about the quality of the products sold?
Related-party transactions	■ Is the company engaged in transactions that disproportionately benefit members of management? Does one company have control over another's destiny through supply contracts or other dealings? ■ Do extensive dealings take place with *non-public* companies that are under management control? If so, those companies could absorb losses (through supply arrangements that are unfavorable to them, for example) in order to make the public company's performance look good. This scenario may provide opportunities for an owner to cash out.

The most important lesson is that choices exist among accounting methods and estimates, and an analyst needs a working knowledge of them in order to understand whether management may have made choices to achieve a desired result.

4.3 Warning Signs

The choices management makes to achieve desired results leave a trail, like tracks in sand or snow. The evidence, or warning signs, of information manipulation in financial reports is directly linked to the basic means of manipulation: biased revenue recognition and biased expense recognition. The bias may relate to timing and/or location of recognition. An example of the timing issue is that a company may choose to defer expenses by capitalizing them. Regarding location, it may recognize a loss in other comprehensive income or directly through equity, rather than through the profit and loss statement. The alert investor or analyst should do the following to find warning signs.

1) Pay attention to revenue. The single largest number on the income statement is revenue, and revenue recognition is a recurring source of accounting manipulation and even outright fraud. Answering the question, "Is revenue higher or lower than the previous comparable period?" is not sufficient. Many analytical procedures can be routinely performed to identify warning signals of malfeasance:

- *Examine the accounting policies note for a company's revenue recognition policies.*
  - Consider whether the policies make it easier to prematurely recognize revenue, such as recognizing revenue immediately upon shipment of goods, or if the company uses bill-and-hold arrangements whereby a sale is recognized before goods are actually shipped to the customer.
  - Barter transactions may exist, which can be difficult to value properly.

- Rebate programs involve many estimates, including forecasts of the amount of rebates that will ultimately be incurred, which can have significant effects on revenue recognition.
- Multiple-deliverable arrangements of goods and services are common, but clarity about the timing of revenue recognition for each item or service delivered is necessary for the investor to be comfortable with the reporting of revenues.

Although none of these decisions necessarily violates accounting standards, each involves significant judgement and warrants close attention if other warning signs are present.

- *Look at revenue relationships.* Compare a company's revenue growth with its primary competitors or its industry peer group.
  - If a company's revenue growth is out of line with its competitors, its industry, or the economy, the investor or analyst needs to understand the reasons for the outperformance. It may be a result of superior management or products and services, but not all management is superior, nor are the products and services of their companies. Revenue quality might be suspect, and the investor should take additional analytical steps.
  - Compare accounts receivable with revenues over several years.
    - Examine the trend to determine whether receivables are increasing as a percentage of total revenues. If so, a company might be engaging in channel-stuffing activities, or worse, recording fictitious sales transactions.
    - Calculate receivables turnover for several years:
      - Examine the trend for unusual changes and seek an explanation if they exist.
      - Compare a company's days sales outstanding (DSO) or receivables turnover with that of relevant competitors or an industry peer group and determine whether the company is an outlier.

    An increase in DSO or decrease in receivables turnover could suggest that some revenues are recorded prematurely or are even fictitious, or that the allowance for doubtful accounts is insufficient.
  - Examine asset turnover. If a company's managers make poor asset allocation choices, revenues may not be sufficient to justify the investment. Be particularly alert when asset allocation choices involve acquisitions of entire companies. If post-acquisition revenue generation is weak, managers might reach for revenue growth anywhere it can be found. That reach for growth might result in accounting abuses.

    Revenues, divided by total assets, indicate the productivity of assets in generating revenues. If the company's asset turnover is continually declining, or lagging the asset turnover of competitors or the industry, it may portend future asset write-downs, particularly in the goodwill balances of acquisitive companies.

2) Pay attention to signals from inventories. Although inventory is not a component of every company's asset base, its presence creates an opportunity for accounting manipulation.

- *Look at inventory relationships.* Because revenues involve items sold from inventory, the kind of examination an investor should perform on inventory is similar to that for revenues.

- Compare growth in inventories with competitors and industry benchmarks. If a company's inventory growth is out of line with its peers, without any concurrent sales growth, then it may be simply the result of poor inventory management—an operational inefficiency that might affect an investor's view of a company. It may also signal obsolescence problems in the company's inventory that have not yet been recognized through markdowns to the inventory's net realizable value. Reported gross and net profits could be overstated because of overstated inventory.
- Calculate the inventory turnover ratio. This ratio is the cost of sales divided by the average ending inventory. Declining inventory turnover could also suggest obsolescence problems that should be recognized.
- Companies reporting under US GAAP may use LIFO inventory cost flow assumptions. When this assumption is part of the accounting policies, and a company operates in an inflationary environment, investors should note whether old, low-cost inventory costs have been passed through current earnings and artificially improved gross, operating, and net profits.

3) Pay attention to capitalization policies and deferred costs. In a study of enforcement actions over a five-year period, the SEC found that improper revenue recognition was the most prevalent accounting issue.[28] Suppression of expenses was the next most prevalent problem noted. As the earlier discussion of WorldCom showed, improper capitalization practices can result in a significant misstatement of financial results.

- *Examine the company's accounting policy note for its capitalization policy for long-term assets, including interest costs, and for its handling of other deferred costs.* Compare the company's policy with the industry practice. If the company is the only one capitalizing certain costs while other industry participants treat them as expenses, a red flag is raised. If an outlier company of this type is encountered, it would be useful to cross-check such a company's asset turnover and profitability margins with others in its industry. An investor might expect such a company to be more profitable than its competitors, but the investor might also have lower confidence in the quality of the reported numbers.

4) Pay attention to the relationship of cash flow and net income. Net income propels stock prices, but cash flow pays bills. Management can manipulate either one, but sooner or later, net income must be realized in cash if a company is to remain viable. When net income is higher than cash provided by operations, one possibility is that aggressive accrual accounting policies have shifted current expenses to later periods. Increasing earnings in the presence of declining cash generated by operations might signal accounting irregularities.

- *Construct a time series of cash generated by operations divided by net income.* If the ratio is consistently below 1.0 or has declined repeatedly, there may be problems in the company's accrual accounts.

5) Other potential warnings signs. Other areas that might suggest the need for further analysis include the following:

- *Depreciation methods and useful lives.* As discussed earlier, selection of depreciation methods and useful lives can greatly influence profitability. An investor should compare a company's policies with those of its peers to determine

28 SEC, "Report Pursuant to Section 704 of the Sarbanes–Oxley Act of 2002" (www.sec.gov/news/studies/sox704report.pdf): 5–6.

whether it is particularly lenient in its effects on earnings. Investors should likewise compare the length of depreciable lives used by a company with those used by its peers.

- *Fourth-quarter surprises.* An investor should be suspicious of possible earnings management if a company routinely disappoints investors with poor earnings or overachieves in the fourth quarter of the year when no seasonality exists in the business. The company may be over- or under-reporting profits in the first three quarters of the year.
- *Presence of related-party transactions.* Related-party transactions often arise when a company's founders are still very active in managing the company, with much of their wealth tied to the company's fortunes. They may be more biased in their view of a company's performance because it relates directly to their own wealth and reputations, and they may be able to transact business with the company in ways that may not be detected. For instance, they may purchase unsellable inventory from the company for disposal in another company of their own in order to avoid markdowns.
- *Non-operating income or one-time sales included in revenue.* To disguise weakening revenue growth, or just to enhance revenue growth, a company might classify non-operating income items into revenues or fail to clarify the nature of revenues. In the first quarter of 1997, Sunbeam Corporation included one-time disposal of product lines in sales without indicating that such non-recurring sales were included in revenues. This inclusion gave investors a false impression of the company's sustainable revenue-generating capability.
- *Classification of expenses as "non-recurring."* To make operating performance look more attractive, managers might carve out "special items" in the income statement. Particularly when these items appear period after period, equity investors might find their interests best served by not accepting the carve-out of serial "special items" and instead focusing on the net income line in evaluating performance over long periods.
- *Gross/operating margins out of line with competitors or industry.* This disparity is an ambivalent warning sign. It might signal superior management ability. But it might also signal the presence of accounting manipulations to add a veneer of superior management ability to the company's reputation. Only the compilation and examination of other warning signals will enable an investor or analyst to decide which signal is being given.

Warning signals are just that: signals, not indisputable declarations of accounting manipulation guilt. Investors and analysts need to evaluate them cohesively, not on an isolated basis. When an investor finds a number of these signals, the investee company should be viewed with caution or even discarded in favor of alternatives.

Furthermore, as discussed earlier, context is important in judging the value of warning signals. A few examples of facts and circumstances to be aware of are as follows.

- *Younger companies with an unblemished record of meeting growth projections.* It is plausible, especially for a younger company with new and popular product offerings, to generate above-average returns for a period of time. But, as demand dissipates, products mature, and competitors challenge for market share, management may seek to extend its recent record of rapid growth in sales and profitability by unconventional means. At this point, the "earnings games" begin: aggressive estimates, drawing down "cookie jar" reserves, selling assets for accounting gains, taking on excess leverage, or entering into financial transactions with no apparent business purpose other than financial statement "window dressing."

- *Management has adopted a minimalist approach to disclosure.* Confidence in accounting quality depends on disclosure. If management does not seem to take seriously its obligation to provide information, one needs to be concerned. For example, for a large company, management might claim that it has only one reportable segment, or its commentary might be similar from period to period. A plausible explanation for minimalist disclosure policies could be that management is protecting investors' interests by withholding valuable information from competitors. But, this is not necessarily the case. For example, after Sony Corporation acquired CBS Records and Columbia Pictures, it incurred substantial losses for a number of years. Yet, Sony chose to hide its negative trends and doubtful future prospects by aggregating the results within a much larger "Entertainment Division." In 1998, after Sony ultimately wrote off much of the goodwill associated with these ill-fated acquisitions, the SEC sanctioned Sony and its CFO for failing to separately discuss them in MD&A in a balanced manner.[29]
- *Management fixation on earnings reports.* Beware of companies whose management appears to be fixated on reported earnings, sometimes to the detriment of attending to real drivers of value. Indicators of excessive earnings fixation include the aggressive use of non-GAAP measures of performance, special items, or non-recurring charges. Another indicator of earnings fixation is highly decentralized operations in which division managers' compensation packages are heavily weighted toward the attainment of reported earnings or non-GAAP measures of performance.

Company Culture A company's culture is an intangible that investors should bear in mind when they are evaluating financial statements for the possibility of accounting manipulation. A management's highly competitive mentality may serve investors well when the company conducts business (assuming that actions taken are not unethical, illegal, or harmfully myopic), but that kind of thinking should not extend to communications with the owners of the company: the shareholders. That mentality can lead to the kind of accounting gamesmanship seen in the early part of the century. In examining financial statements for warning signs of manipulation, the investor should consider whether that mindset exists in the preparation of the financial statements.

One notable example of the mindset comes from one of the most recognized corporate names in the world, General Electric. In the mid-1980s, GE acquired Kidder Peabody, and it was ultimately determined that much of the earnings that Kidder had reported were bogus. As a consequence, GE would announce within two days that it would take a non-cash write-off of $350 million. Here is how former CEO/Chair Jack Welsh described the ensuing meeting with senior management in his memoir, *Straight from the Gut*:

> "The response of our business leaders to the crisis was typical of the GE *culture* [emphasis added]. Even though the books had closed on the quarter, many immediately offered to pitch in to cover the Kidder gap. Some said they could find an extra $10 million, $20 million, and even $30 million from their businesses to offset the surprise. Though it was too late, their willingness to help was a dramatic contrast to the excuses I had been hearing from the Kidder people." (p. 225)

29 Accounting and Auditing Enforcement Release No. 1061, "In the Matter of Sony Corporation and Sumio Sano, Respondents," SEC (5 August 1998).

It appears that the corporate governance apparatus fostered a GE culture that extended the concept of teamwork to the point of "sharing" profits to win one for the team as a whole, which is incompatible with the concept of neutral financial reporting. Although research is not conclusive on this question, it may also be worth considering that predisposition to earnings manipulation is more likely to be present when the CEO and board chair are one and the same, or when the audit committee of the board essentially serves at the pleasure of the CEO and lacks financial reporting sophistication. Finally, one could discuss whether the financial reporting environment today would reward or penalize a CEO who openly endorsed a view that he could legitimately exercise financial reporting discretion—albeit within limits—for the purpose of artificially smoothing earnings.

Restructuring and/or impairment charges. At times, a company's stock price has been observed to rise after it recognized a "big bath" charge to reported earnings. The conventional wisdom explaining the stock price rise is that accounting recognition signals something positive: that management is now ready to part with the lagging portion of a company, so as to redirect its attention and talents to more-profitable activities. Consequently, the earnings charge should be disregarded for being solely related to past events.

The analyst should also consider, however, that the events leading ultimately to the big bath on the financial statements did not happen overnight, even though the accounting for those events occurs at a subsequent point. Management may want to communicate that the accounting adjustments reflect the company's new path, but the restructuring charge also indicates that the old path of reported earnings was not real. In particular, expenses reported in prior years were very likely understated—even assuming that no improper financial statement manipulation had occurred. To extrapolate historical earnings trends, an analyst should consider making pro forma analytical adjustments to prior years' earnings to reflect a reasonable division of the latest period's restructuring and impairment charges.

Management has a merger and acquisition orientation. Tyco International Ltd. acquired more than 700 companies from 1996 to 2002. Even assuming the best of intentions regarding financial reporting, a growth-at-any-cost corporate culture poses a severe challenge to operational and financial reporting controls. In Tyco's case, the SEC found that it consistently and fraudulently understated assets acquired (lowering future depreciation and amortization charges) and overstated liabilities assumed (avoiding expense recognition and potentially increasing earnings in future periods).[30]

SUMMARY

Financial reporting quality varies across companies. The ability to assess the quality of a company's financial reporting is an important skill for analysts. Indications of low-quality financial reporting can prompt an analyst to maintain heightened skepticism

30 Accounting and Auditing Enforcement Release No. 2414, "SEC Brings Settled Charges Against Tyco International Ltd. Alleging Billion Dollar Accounting Fraud," SEC (17 April 2006): www.sec.gov/litigation/litreleases/2006/lr19657.htm.

when reading a company's reports, to review disclosures critically when undertaking financial statement analysis, and to incorporate appropriate adjustments in assessments of past performance and forecasts of future performance.

- Financial reporting quality can be thought of as spanning a continuum from the highest (containing information that is relevant, correct, complete, and unbiased) to the lowest (containing information that is not just biased or incomplete but possibly pure fabrication).
- *Reporting quality*, the focus of this reading, pertains to the information disclosed. High-quality reporting represents the economic reality of the company's activities during the reporting period and the company's financial condition at the end of the period.
- *Results quality* (commonly referred to as earnings quality) pertains to the earnings and cash generated by the company's actual economic activities and the resulting financial condition, relative to expectations of current and future financial performance. Quality earnings are regarded as being sustainable, providing a sound platform for forecasts.
- An aspect of financial reporting quality is the degree to which accounting choices are conservative or aggressive. "Aggressive" typically refers to choices that aim to enhance the company's reported performance and financial position by inflating the amount of revenues, earnings, and/or operating cash flow reported in the period; or by decreasing expenses for the period and/or the amount of debt reported on the balance sheet.
- Conservatism in financial reports can result from either (1) accounting standards that specifically require a conservative treatment of a transaction or an event or (2) judgments made by managers when applying accounting standards that result in conservative results.
- Managers may be motivated to issue less-than-high-quality financial reports in order to mask poor performance, to boost the stock price, to increase personal compensation, and/or to avoid violation of debt covenants.
- Conditions that are conducive to the issuance of low-quality financial reports include a cultural environment that result in fewer or less transparent financial disclosures, book/tax conformity that shifts emphasis toward legal compliance and away from fair presentation, and limited capital markets regulation.
- Mechanisms that discipline financial reporting quality include the free market and incentives for companies to minimize cost of capital, auditors, contract provisions specifically tailored to penalize misreporting, and enforcement by regulatory entities.
- Pro forma earnings (also commonly referred to as non-GAAP or non-IFRS earnings) adjust earnings as reported on the income statement. Pro forma earnings that exclude negative items are a hallmark of aggressive presentation choices.
- Companies are required to make additional disclosures when presenting any non-GAAP or non-IFRS metric.
- Managers' considerable flexibility in choosing their companies' accounting policies and in formulating estimates provides opportunities for aggressive accounting.

- Examples of accounting choices that affect earnings and balance sheets include inventory cost flow assumptions, estimates of uncollectible accounts receivable, estimated realizability of deferred tax assets, depreciation method, estimated salvage value of depreciable assets, and estimated useful life of depreciable assets.
- Cash from operations is a metric of interest to investors that can be enhanced by operating choices, such as stretching accounts payable, and potentially by classification choices.

REFERENCES

Back, Aaron. 2013. "Toyota, What a Difference the Yen Makes." *Wall Street Journal* (4 August 2013).

Basu, Sudipta. 1997. "The Conservatism Principle and the Asymmetric Timeliness of Earnings." *Journal of Accounting and Economics*, vol. 24, no. 1 (December):3–37.

Bliss, James Harris. 1924. *Management through Accounts*. New York: Ronald Press Company.

Ciesielski, Jack T, and Elaine Henry. 2017. "Accounting's Tower of Babel: Key Considerations in Assessing Non-GAAP Earnings." *Financial Analysts Journal*, vol. 73, no. 2:34–50.

Dichev, Ilia, John Graham, Campbell Harvey, and Shivaram Rajgopal. 2013. "Earnings Quality: Evidence from the Field." *Journal of Accounting and Economics*, vol. 56, issues 2–3:1–33.

Dichev, Ilia, John Graham, Campbell Harvey, and Shiva Rajgopal. 2016. "The Misrepresentation of Earnings." *Financial Analysts Journal*, vol. 72, issue 1:22–35.

Ernst & Young. 2013. *Navigating Today's Complex Business Risks*. Europe, Middle East, India and Africa Fraud Survey 2013 (May): www.ey.com/Publication/vwLUAssets/Navigating_todays_complex_business_risks/$FILE/Navigating_todays_complex_business_risks.pdf.

Ernst & Young Global Limited. 2016. *Corporate misconduct—individual consequences*. 14th Global Fraud Survey. www.ey.com/gl/en/services/assurance/fraud-investigation---dispute-services/ey-global-fraud-survey-2016.

Gordon, Elizabeth, Elaine Henry, Bjorn Jorgensen, and Cheryl Linthicum. 2017. "Flexibility in Cash-Flow Classification under IFRS: Determinants and Consequences." *Review of Accounting Studies*, vol. 22, no. 2:839–872.

Graham, John, Campbell Harvey, and Shiva Rajgopal. 2005. "The Economic Implications of Corporate Financial Reporting." *Journal of Accounting and Economics*, vol. 40, no. 1 (December):3–73.

Lewis, Craig M. 2012. "Risk Modeling at the SEC: The Accounting Quality Model" Speech, the Financial Executives International Committee on Finance and Information Technology (13 December): www.sec.gov/news/speech/2012/spch121312cml.htm.

Nurnberg, H. 2006. "Perspectives on the Cash Flow Statement under FASB Statement No. 95." Center for Excellence in Accounting and Security Analysis Occasional Paper Series. Columbia Business School.

Nurnberg, H., and J. Largay. 1998. "Interest Payments in the Cash Flow Statement." *Accounting Horizons*, vol. 12, no. 4 (December):407–418.

Pavlo, Walter. 2013. "Fmr Enron CFO Andrew Fastow Speaks At ACFE Annual Conference," *Forbes* (26 June): www.forbes.com/sites/walterpavlo/2013/06/26/fmr-enron-cfo-andrew-fastow-speaks-at-acfe-annual-conference/.

Ronen, Joshua, and Varda Yaari. 2008. *Earnings Management: Emerging Insights in Theory, Practice, and Research*. New York: Springer.

Schipper, Katherine. 1989. "Commentary on Earnings Management." *Accounting Horizons*, vol. 3, no. 4 (December):91–102.

Watts, Ross. 2003. "Conservatism in Accounting Part I: Explanations and Implications." *Accounting Horizons*, vol. 17, no. 3 (September):207–221.

PRACTICE PROBLEMS

1 In contrast to earnings quality, financial reporting quality *most likely* pertains to:

   A sustainable earnings.

   B relevant information.

   C adequate return on investment.

2 The information provided by a low-quality financial report will *most likely*:

   A decrease company value.

   B indicate earnings are not sustainable.

   C impede the assessment of earnings quality.

3 To properly assess a company's past performance, an analyst requires:

   A high earnings quality.

   B high financial reporting quality.

   C both high earnings quality and high financial reporting quality.

4 Low quality earnings *most likely* reflect:

   A low-quality financial reporting.

   B company activities which are unsustainable.

   C information that does not faithfully represent company activities.

5 Earnings that result from non-recurring activities *most likely* indicate:

   A lower-quality earnings.

   B biased accounting choices.

   C lower-quality financial reporting.

6 Which attribute of financial reports would *most likely* be evaluated as optimal in the financial reporting spectrum?

   A Conservative accounting choices

   B Sustainable and adequate returns

   C Emphasized pro forma earnings measures

7 Financial reports of the lowest level of quality reflect:

   A fictitious events.

   B biased accounting choices.

   C accounting that is non-compliant with GAAP.

8 When earnings are increased by deferring research and development (R&D) investments until the next reporting period, this choice is considered:

   A non-compliant accounting.

   B earnings management as a result of a real action.

   C earnings management as a result of an accounting choice.

9 A high-quality financial report may reflect:

   A earnings smoothing.

   B low earnings quality.

   C understatement of asset impairment.

© 2019 CFA Institute. All rights reserved.

10 If a particular accounting choice is considered aggressive in nature, then the financial performance for the reporting period would *most likely*:

A be neutral.

B exhibit an upward bias.

C exhibit a downward bias.

11 Which of the following is *most likely* to reflect conservative accounting choices?

A Decreased reported earnings in later periods

B Increased reported earnings in the period under review

C Increased debt reported on the balance sheet at the end of the current period

12 Which of the following is *most likely* to be considered a potential benefit of accounting conservatism?

A A reduction in litigation costs

B Less biased financial reporting

C An increase in current period reported performance

13 Which of the following statements *most likely* describes a situation that would motivate a manager to issue low-quality financial reports?

A The manager's compensation is tied to stock price performance.

B The manager has increased the market share of products significantly.

C The manager has brought the company's profitability to a level higher than competitors.

14 Which of the following concerns would *most likely* motivate a manager to make conservative accounting choices?

A Attention to future career opportunities

B Expected weakening in the business environment

C Debt covenant violation risk in the current period

15 Which of the following conditions *best* explains why a company's manager would obtain legal, accounting, and board level approval prior to issuing low-quality financial reports?

A Motivation

B Opportunity

C Rationalization

16 A company is experiencing a period of strong financial performance. In order to increase the likelihood of exceeding analysts' earnings forecasts in the next reporting period, the company would *most likely* undertake accounting choices for the period under review that:

A inflate reported revenue.

B delay expense recognition.

C accelerate expense recognition.

17 Which of the following situations represents a motivation, rather than an opportunity, to issue low-quality financial reports?

A Poor internal controls

B Search for a personal bonus

C Inattentive board of directors

18 Which of the following situations will *most likely* motivate managers to inflate reported earnings?

A Possibility of bond covenant violation

B Earnings in excess of analysts' forecasts

C Earnings that are greater than the previous year

19 Which of the following *best* describes an opportunity for management to issue low-quality financial reports?

A Ineffective board of directors

B Pressure to achieve some performance level

C Corporate concerns about financing in the future

20 An audit opinion of a company's financial reports is *most likely* intended to:

A detect fraud.

B reveal misstatements.

C assure that financial information is presented fairly.

21 If a company uses a non-GAAP financial measure in an SEC filing, then the company must:

A give more prominence to the non-GAAP measure if it is used in earnings releases.

B provide a reconciliation of the non-GAAP measure and equivalent GAAP measure.

C exclude charges requiring cash settlement from any non-GAAP liquidity measures.

22 A company wishing to increase earnings in the reporting period may choose to:

A decrease the useful life of depreciable assets.

B lower estimates of uncollectible accounts receivables.

C classify a purchase as an expense rather than a capital expenditure.

23 Bias in revenue recognition would *least likely* be suspected if:

A the firm engages in barter transactions.

B reported revenue is higher than the previous quarter.

C revenue is recognized before goods are shipped to customers.

24 Which technique *most likely* increases the cash flow provided by operations?

A Stretching the accounts payable credit period

B Applying all non-cash discount amortization against interest capitalized

C Shifting classification of interest paid from financing to operating cash flows

25 Which of the following is an indication that a company may be recognizing revenue prematurely? Relative to its competitors, the company's:

A asset turnover is decreasing.

B receivables turnover is increasing.

C days sales outstanding is increasing.

26 Which of the following would *most likely* signal that a company may be using aggressive accrual accounting policies to shift current expenses to later periods? Over the last five-year period, the ratio of cash flow to net income has:

A increased each year.

B decreased each year.

C fluctuated from year to year.

27 An analyst reviewing a firm with a large reported restructuring charge to earnings should:

A view expenses reported in prior years as overstated.
B disregard it because it is solely related to past events.
C consider making pro forma adjustments to prior years' earnings.

SOLUTIONS

1 B is correct. Financial reporting quality pertains to the quality of information in financial reports. High-quality financial reporting provides decision-useful information, which is relevant and faithfully represents the economic reality of the company's activities. Earnings of high quality are sustainable and provide an adequate level of return. Highest-quality financial reports reflect both high financial reporting quality and high earnings quality.

2 C is correct. Financial reporting quality pertains to the quality of the information contained in financial reports. High-quality financial reports provide decision-useful information that faithfully represents the economic reality of the company. Low-quality financial reports impede assessment of earnings quality. Financial reporting quality is distinguishable from earnings quality, which pertains to the earnings and cash generated by the company's actual economic activities and the resulting financial condition. Low-quality earnings are not sustainable and decrease company value.

3 B is correct. Financial reporting quality pertains to the quality of the information contained in financial reports. If financial reporting quality is low, the information provided is of little use in assessing the company's performance. Financial reporting quality is distinguishable from earnings quality, which pertains to the earnings and cash generated by the company's actual economic activities and the resulting financial condition.

4 B is correct. Earnings quality pertains to the earnings and cash generated by the company's actual economic activities and the resulting financial condition. Low-quality earnings are likely not sustainable over time because the company does not expect to generate the same level of earnings in the future or because earnings will not generate sufficient return on investment to sustain the company. Earnings that are not sustainable decrease company value. Earnings quality is distinguishable from financial reporting quality, which pertains to the quality of the information contained in financial reports.

5 A is correct. Earnings that result from non-recurring activities are unsustainable. Unsustainable earnings are an example of lower-quality earnings. Recognizing earnings that result from non-recurring activities is neither a biased accounting choice nor indicative of lower quality financial reporting because it faithfully represents economic events.

6 B is correct. At the top of the quality spectrum of financial reports are reports that conform to GAAP, are decision useful, and have earnings that are sustainable and offer adequate returns. In other words, these reports have both high financial reporting quality and high earnings quality.

7 A is correct. Financial reports span a quality continuum from high to low based on decision-usefulness and earnings quality (see Exhibit 2 of the reading). The lowest-quality reports portray fictitious events, which may misrepresent the company's performance and/or obscure fraudulent misappropriation of the company's assets.

8 B is correct. Deferring research and development (R&D) investments into the next reporting period is an example of earnings management by taking a *real* action.

9 B is correct. High-quality financial reports offer useful information, meaning information that is relevant and faithfully represents actual performance. Although low earnings quality may not be desirable, if the reported earnings

are representative of actual performance, they are consistent with high-quality financial reporting. Highest-quality financial reports reflect both high financial reporting quality and high earnings quality.

10 B is correct. Aggressive accounting choices aim to enhance the company's reported performance by inflating the amount of revenues, earnings, and/or operating cash flow reported in the period. Consequently, the financial performance for that period would most likely exhibit an upward bias.

11 C is correct. Accounting choices are considered conservative if they decrease the company's reported performance and financial position in the period under review. Conservative choices may increase the amount of debt reported on the balance sheet. They may decrease the revenues, earnings, and/or operating cash flow reported for the period and increase those amounts in later periods.

12 A is correct. Conservatism reduces the possibility of litigation and, by extension, litigation costs. Rarely, if ever, is a company sued because it understated good news or overstated bad news. Accounting conservatism is a type of bias in financial reporting that decreases a company's reported performance. Conservatism directly conflicts with the characteristic of neutrality.

13 A is correct. Managers often have incentives to meet or beat market expectations, particularly if management compensation is linked to increases in stock prices or to reported earnings.

14 B is correct. Managers may be motivated to understate earnings in the reporting period and increase the probability of meeting or exceeding the next period's earnings target.

15 C is correct. Typically, conditions of opportunity, motivation, and rationalization exist when individuals issue low-quality financial reports. Rationalization occurs when an individual is concerned about a choice and needs to be able to justify it to herself or himself. If the manager is concerned about a choice in a financial report, she or he may ask for other opinions to convince herself or himself that it is okay.

16 C is correct. In a period of strong financial performance, managers may pursue accounting choices that increase the probability of exceeding earnings forecasts for the next period. By accelerating expense recognition or delaying revenue recognition, managers may inflate earnings in the next period and increase the likelihood of exceeding targets.

17 B is correct. Motivation can result from pressure to meet some criteria for personal reasons, such as a bonus, or corporate reasons, such as concern about future financing. Poor internal controls and an inattentive board of directors offer opportunities to issue low-quality financial reports.

18 A is correct. The possibility of bond covenant violations may motivate managers to inflate earnings in the reporting period. In so doing, the company may be able to avoid the consequences associated with violating bond covenants.

19 A is correct. Opportunities to issue low-quality financial reports include internal conditions, such as an ineffective board of directors, and external conditions, such as accounting standards that provide scope for divergent choices. Pressure to achieve a certain level of performance and corporate concerns about future financing are examples of motivations to issue low-quality financial reports. Typically, three conditions exist when low-quality financial reports are issued: opportunity, motivation, and rationalization.

20 C is correct. An audit is intended to provide assurance that the company's financial reports are presented fairly, thus providing discipline regarding financial reporting quality. Regulatory agencies usually require that the financial

statements of publicly traded companies be audited by an independent auditor to provide assurance that the financial statements conform to accounting standards. Privately held companies may also choose to obtain audit opinions either voluntarily or because an outside party requires it. An audit is not typically intended to detect fraud. An audit is based on sampling and it is possible that the sample might not reveal misstatements.

21 B is correct. If a company uses a non-GAAP financial measure in an SEC filing, it is required to provide the most directly comparable GAAP measure with equivalent prominence in the filing. In addition, the company is required to provide a reconciliation between the non-GAAP measure and the equivalent GAAP measure. Similarly, IFRS require that any non-IFRS measures included in financial reports must be defined and their potential relevance explained. The non-IFRS measures must be reconciled with IFRS measures.

22 B is correct. If a company wants to increase reported earnings, the company's managers may reduce the allowance for uncollected accounts and the related expense reported for the period. Decreasing the useful life of depreciable assets would increase depreciation expense and decrease earnings in the reporting period. Classifying a purchase as an expense, rather than capital expenditure, would decrease earnings in the reporting period. The use of accrual accounting may result in estimates in financial reports, because all facts associated with events may not be known at the time of recognition. These estimates can be grounded in reality or managed by the company to present a desired financial picture.

23 B is correct. Bias in revenue recognition can lead to manipulation of information presented in financial reports. Addressing the question as to whether revenue is higher or lower than the previous period is not sufficient to determine if there is bias in revenue recognition. Additional analytical procedures must be performed to identify warning signals of accounting malfeasance. Barter transactions are difficult to value properly and may result in bias in revenue recognition. Policies that make it easier to prematurely recognize revenue, such as before goods are shipped to customers, may be a warning sign of accounting malfeasance.

24 A is correct. Managers can temporarily show a higher cash flow from operations by stretching the accounts payable credit period. In other words, the managers delay payments until the next accounting period. Applying all non-cash discount amortization against interest capitalized causes reported interest expenses and operating cash outflow to be higher, resulting in a lower cash flow provided by operations. Shifting the classification of interest paid from financing to operating cash flows lowers the cash flow provided by operations.

25 C is correct. If a company's days sales outstanding (DSO) is increasing relative to competitors, this may be a signal that revenues are being recorded prematurely or are even fictitious. There are numerous analytical procedures that can be performed to provide evidence of manipulation of information in financial reporting. These warning signs are often linked to bias associated with revenue recognition and expense recognition policies.

26 B is correct. If the ratio of cash flow to net income for a company is consistently below 1 or has declined repeatedly over time, this may be a signal of manipulation of information in financial reports through aggressive accrual accounting policies. When net income is consistently higher than cash provided by operations, one possible explanation is that the company may be using aggressive accrual accounting policies to shift current expenses to later periods.

27 C is correct. To extrapolate historical earnings trends, an analyst should consider making pro forma analytical adjustments of prior years' earnings to reflect in those prior years a reasonable share of the current period's restructuring and impairment charges.

READING

30

Applications of Financial Statement Analysis

by Thomas R. Robinson, PhD, CFA, Jan Hendrik van Greuning, DCom, CFA, Elaine Henry, PhD, CFA, and Michael A. Broihahn, CPA, CIA, CFA

Thomas R. Robinson, PhD, CFA, is at AACSB International (USA). Jan Hendrik van Greuning, DCom, CFA, is at BIBD (Brunei). Elaine Henry, PhD, CFA, is at Stevens Institute of Technology (USA). Michael A. Broihahn, CPA, CIA, CFA, is at Barry University (USA).

LEARNING OUTCOMES

Mastery	*The candidate should be able to:*
☐	a. evaluate a company's past financial performance and explain how a company's strategy is reflected in past financial performance;
☐	b. forecast a company's future net income and cash flow;
☐	c. describe the role of financial statement analysis in assessing the credit quality of a potential debt investment;
☐	d. describe the use of financial statement analysis in screening for potential equity investments;
☐	e. explain appropriate analyst adjustments to a company's financial statements to facilitate comparison with another company.

Note: Changes in accounting standards as well as new rulings and/or pronouncements issued after the publication of the readings on financial reporting and analysis may cause some of the information in these readings to become dated. Candidates are *not* responsible for anything that occurs after the readings were published. In addition, candidates are expected to be familiar with the analytical frameworks contained in the readings, as well as the implications of alternative accounting methods for financial analysis and valuation discussed in the readings. Candidates are also responsible for the content of accounting standards, but not for the actual reference numbers. Finally, candidates should be aware that certain ratios may be defined and calculated differently. When alternative ratio definitions exist and no specific definition is given, candidates should use the ratio definitions emphasized in the readings.

© 2019 CFA Institute. All rights reserved.

1 INTRODUCTION

This reading presents several important applications of financial statement analysis. Among the issues we will address are the following:

- What are the key questions to address in evaluating a company's past financial performance?
- How can an analyst approach forecasting a company's future net income and cash flow?
- How can financial statement analysis be used to evaluate the credit quality of a potential fixed-income investment?
- How can financial statement analysis be used to screen for potential equity investments?
- How can differences in accounting methods affect financial ratio comparisons between companies, and what are some adjustments analysts make to reported financials to facilitate comparability among companies.

The reading "Financial Statement Analysis: An Introduction" described a framework for conducting financial statement analysis. Consistent with that framework, prior to undertaking any analysis, an analyst should explore the purpose and context of the analysis. The purpose and context guide further decisions about the approach, the tools, the data sources, and the format in which to report results of the analysis, and also suggest which aspects of the analysis are most important. Having identified the purpose and context, the analyst should then be able to formulate the key questions that the analysis must address. The questions will suggest the data the analyst needs to collect to objectively address the questions. The analyst then processes and analyzes the data to answer these questions. Conclusions and decisions based on the analysis are communicated in a format appropriate to the context, and follow-up is undertaken as required. Although this reading will not formally present applications as a series of steps, the process just described is generally applicable.

Section 2 of this reading describes the use of financial statement analysis to evaluate a company's past financial performance, and Section 3 describes basic approaches to projecting a company's future financial performance. Section 4 presents the use of financial statement analysis in assessing the credit quality of a potential debt investment. Section 5 concludes the survey of applications by describing the use of financial statement analysis in screening for potential equity investments. Analysts often encounter situations in which they must make adjustments to a company's reported financial results to increase their accuracy or comparability with the financials of other companies. Section 6 illustrates several common types of analyst adjustments. Section 7 presents a summary, and practice problems in the CFA Institute multiple-choice format conclude the reading.

APPLICATION: EVALUATING PAST FINANCIAL PERFORMANCE

2

Analysts examine a company's past financial performance for a number of reasons. Cross-sectional analysis of financial performance facilitates understanding of the comparability of companies for a market-based valuation.[1] Analysis of a company's historical performance over time can provide a basis for a forward-looking analysis of the company. Both cross-sectional and trend analysis can provide information for evaluating the quality and performance of a company's management.

An evaluation of a company's past performance addresses not only *what* happened (i.e., how the company performed) but also *why* it happened—the causes behind the performance and how the performance reflects the company's strategy. Evaluative judgments assess whether the performance is better or worse than a relevant benchmark, such as the company's own historical performance, a competitor's performance, or market expectations. Some key analytical questions include the following:

- How and why have corporate measures of profitability, efficiency, liquidity, and solvency changed over the periods being analyzed?
- How do the level and trend in a company's profitability, efficiency, liquidity, and solvency compare with the corresponding results of other companies in the same industry? What factors explain any differences?
- What aspects of performance are critical for a company to successfully compete in its industry, and how did the company perform relative to those critical performance aspects?
- What are the company's business model and strategy, and how did they influence the company's performance as reflected in, for example, its sales growth, efficiency, and profitability?

Data available to answer these questions include the company's (and its competitors') financial statements, materials from the company's investor relations department, corporate press releases, and non-financial-statement regulatory filings, such as proxies. Useful data also include industry information (e.g., from industry surveys, trade publications, and government sources), consumer information (e.g., from consumer satisfaction surveys), and information that is gathered by the analyst firsthand (e.g., through on-site visits). Processing the data typically involves creating common-size financial statements, calculating financial ratios, and reviewing or calculating industry-specific metrics. Example 1 illustrates the effects of strategy on performance and the use of basic economic reasoning in interpreting results.

EXAMPLE 1

A Change in Products Reflected in Financial Performance

Apple Inc. is a company that has evolved and adapted over time. In its 1994 Prospectus filed with the US SEC, Apple identified itself as "one of the world's leading personal computer technology companies." At that time, most of its revenue was generated by computer sales. In the prospectus, however, Apple stated, "The Company's strategy is to expand its market share in the personal

1 Pinto et al. (2010) describe market-based valuation as using price multiples—ratios of a stock's market price to some measure of value per share (e.g., price-to-earnings ratios). Although the valuation method may be used independently of an analysis of a company's past financial performance, such an analysis may provide reasons for differences in companies' price multiples.

computing industry while developing and expanding into new related business such as Personal Interactive Electronics and Apple Business Systems." Over time, products other than computers became significant generators of revenue and profit.

In 2005, an article in *Barron's* said, "In the last year, the iPod has become Apple's best-selling product, bringing in a third of revenues for the Cupertino, Calif. firm . . . Little noticed by these iPod zealots, however is a looming threat . . . Wireless phone companies are teaming up with the music industry to make most mobile phones into music players" (*Barron's* 27 June 2005, p. 19). The threat noted by *Barron's* was not unnoticed or ignored by Apple.

In June 2007, Apple itself entered the mobile phone market with the launch of the original iPhone, followed in June 2008 by the second-generation iPhone 3G (a handheld device combining the features of a mobile phone, an iPod, and an internet connection device). Soon after, the company launched the iTunes App Store, which allows users to download third-party applications onto their iPhones. As noted in a 2009 *Business Week* article, Apple "is the world's largest music distributor, having passed Wal-Mart Stores in early 2008. Apple sells around 90% of song downloads and 75% of digital music players in the United States" (*Business Week*, 28 September 2009, p. 34). Product innovations continue as evidenced by the introduction of the iPad in January 2010.

In analyzing the historical performance of Apple in 2018, an analyst might refer to the information presented in Exhibit 1, which shows sales, profitability, sales by product line and product mix.

Exhibit 1 (dollars in millions)

Sales and Profitability	**2017**	**2016**	**2015**	**2014**	**2013**	**2012**	**2011**	**2010**
Sales	229,234	215,639	233,715	182,795	170,910	156,608	108,249	65,225
Cost of goods sold	141,048	131,376	140,089	112,258	106,606	87,846	64,431	39,541
Gross profit	88,186	84,263	93,626	70,537	64,304	68,762	43,818	25,684
Gross margin	38.5%	39.1%	40.1%	38.6%	37.6%	43.9%	40.5%	39.4%
Net sales by product								
Mac	25,850	22,831	25,471	24,079	21,483	23,221	21,783	25,850
iPhone and related	141,319	136,700	155,041	101,991	91,279	78,692	45,998	141,319
iPad and related	19,222	20,628	23,227	30,283	31,980	30,945	19,168	19,222
Services	29,980	24,348	19,909	18,063	16,051	12,890	9,373	29,980
Other (includes iPod)	12,863	11,132	10,067	8,379	10,117	10,760	11,927	12,863
Total	229,234	215,639	233,715	182,795	170,910	156,508	108,249	65,225
Net sales % by product								
Mac	11.3%	10.6%	10.9%	13.2%	12.6%	14.8%	20.1%	26.8%
iPhone and related	61.6%	63.4%	66.3%	55.8%	53.4%	50.3%	42.5%	38.6%
iPad and related	8.4%	9.6%	9.9%	16.6%	18.7%	19.8%	17.7%	7.6%
Services	13.1%	11.3%	8.5%	9.9%	9.4%	8.2%	8.7%	15.5%

Exhibit 1 (Continued)

Sales and Profitability	2017	2016	2015	2014	2013	2012	2011	2010
Other (includes iPod)	5.6%	5.2%	4.3%	4.6%	5.9%	6.9%	11.0%	11.5%
Total	100.0%	100.0%	100.0%	100.0%	100.0%	100.0%	100.0%	100.0%

Source: Apple 10-K filings.

Using the information provided, address the following:

1 How have sales and gross margin changed over time?

2 How has the company's product mix changed since the introduction of the iPad in 2010, and what might this change suggest for an analyst in evaluating Apple's profitability over time and its ability to maintain that profitability?

Solution to 1:

Since 2010 total sales have increased from $65 billion to $229 billion. This represents an annualized growth rate of almost 20%. There was only one year that did not have sales growth in dollars (2016). Gross margin has ranged from 37.6% to 43.9%. Gross margin increased from 2010, when the iPad was introduced, through 2012, when it reached its peak. Gross margin then declined in 2013 and trended upward through 2015. There were modest declines in gross margin after 2015.

Solution to 2:

When the iPad was introduced in 2010 it received a significant share of the product mix, rising to 17.7% in 2011, the first full year after introduction. The iPad's product mix share approached 20% share in 2012 and then declined slightly for two years before a larger decline down to a relatively stable product mix share of around 9%. This could be explained by reaching fairly widespread adoption. The iPhone also gained significant product mix share, rising steadily from 38.6% in 2010 to 66.3% in 2015. Share declined slightly since 2015 but still remains the largest of Apple's product segments at more than 60%. Sales of their original product, the Mac, have declined from more than 25% of sales to around 10%. Services have changed significantly but have shown a steady increase in recent years, most likely due to Apple's music and other media subscription plans. Initially a blockbuster product, the iPod is now included in "other," and this is the largest driver of the decline in that category over time.

Apple had a history of introducing new products every few years, but in recent years the company has not created new product categories. Instead the company has periodically introduced new models of iPads and iPhones. The recent decline in margins is attributable in part to the lack of new products and services and highlights the importance of product innovation to Apple in maintaining historically healthy margins.

In calculating and interpreting financial statement ratios, an analyst needs to be aware of the potential impact on the financial statements and related ratios of companies reporting under different accounting standards, such as international financial reporting standards (IFRS), US generally accepted accounting principles (US GAAP), or other home-country GAAP. Furthermore, even within a given set of accounting standards, companies still have discretion to choose among acceptable methods. A company also may make different assumptions and estimates even when applying the same method as another company. Therefore, making selected adjustments to a company's financial statement data may be useful to facilitate comparisons with other companies or with the industry overall. Examples of such analyst adjustments will be discussed in Section 6.

Non-US companies that use any acceptable body of accounting standards (other than IFRS or US GAAP) and file with the US SEC (because their shares or depositary receipts based on their shares trade in the United States) are required to reconcile their net income and shareholders' equity accounts to US GAAP. Note that in 2007, the SEC eliminated the reconciliation requirement for non-US companies using IFRS and filing with the SEC, however companies may still voluntarily provide this information for comparison purposes.

In general, because the reconciliation data are no longer required by the SEC, we cannot always determine whether differences in net income, equity, and thus ROE also exist between IFRS and the companies' home-country GAAP (including US GAAP).

Comparison of the levels and trends in a company's performance provide information about *how* the company performed. The company's management presents its view about causes underlying its performance in the management commentary or management discussion and analysis (MD&A) section of its annual report and during periodic conference calls with analysts and investors. To gain additional understanding of the causes underlying a company's performance, an analyst can review industry information or seek information from additional sources, such as consumer surveys.

The results of an analysis of past performance provide a basis for reaching conclusions and making recommendations. For example, an analysis undertaken as the basis for a forward-looking study might conclude that a company's future performance is or is not likely to reflect continuation of recent historical trends. As another example, an analysis to support a market-based valuation of a company might focus on whether the company's profitability and growth outlook, which is better (worse) than the peer group median, justifies its relatively high (low) valuation. This analysis would consider market multiples, such as price-to-earnings ratio (P/E), price-to-book ratio, and total invested capital to EBITDA (earnings before interest, taxes, depreciation, and amortization).[2] As another example, an analysis undertaken as part of an evaluation of the management of two companies might result in conclusions about whether one company has grown as fast as another company, or as fast as the industry overall, and whether each company has maintained profitability while growing.

3 APPLICATION: PROJECTING FUTURE FINANCIAL PERFORMANCE

Projections of future financial performance are used in determining the value of a company or its equity component. Projections of future financial performance are also used in credit analysis—particularly in project finance or acquisition finance—to determine whether a company's cash flows will be adequate to pay the interest and principal on its debt and to evaluate whether a company will likely remain in compliance with its financial covenants.

2 **Total invested capital** is the sum of market value of common equity, book value of preferred equity, and face value of debt.

Sources of data for analysts' projections include some or all of the following: the company's projections, the company's previous financial statements, industry structure and outlook, and macroeconomic forecasts.

Evaluating a company's past performance may provide a basis for forward-looking analyses. An evaluation of a company's business and economic environment and its history may persuade the analyst that historical information constitutes a valid basis for such analyses and that the analyst's projections may be based on the continuance of past trends, perhaps with some adjustments. Alternatively, in the case of a major acquisition or divestiture, for a start-up company, or for a company operating in a volatile industry, past performance may be less relevant to future performance.

Projections of a company's near-term performance may be used as an input to market-based valuation or relative valuation (i.e., valuation based on price multiples). Such projections may involve projecting next year's sales and using the common-size income statement to project major expense items or particular margins on sales (e.g., gross profit margin or operating profit margin). These calculations will then lead to the development of an income measure for a valuation calculation, such as net income, earnings per share (EPS) or EBITDA. More complex projections of a company's future performance involve developing a more detailed analysis of the components of performance for multiple periods—for example, projections of sales and gross margin by product line, projection of operating expenses based on historical patterns, and projection of interest expense based on requisite debt funding, interest rates, and applicable taxes. Furthermore, a projection should include sensitivity analyses applied to the major assumptions.

3.1 Projecting Performance: An Input to Market-Based Valuation

One application of financial statement analysis involves projecting a company's near-term performance as an input to market-based valuation. For example, an analyst might project a company's sales and profit margin to estimate EPS and then apply a projected P/E to establish a target price for the company's stock.

Analysts often take a top-down approach to projecting a company's sales.[3] First, industry sales are projected on the basis of their historical relationship with some macroeconomic indicator, such as growth in real gross domestic product (GDP). In researching the automobile industry, for example, the analyst may find that the industry's annual domestic unit car sales (number of cars sold in domestic markets) bears a relationship to annual changes in real GDP. Regression analysis is often used to establish the parameters of such relationships. Other factors in projecting sales may include consumer income or tastes, technological developments, and the availability of substitute products or services. After industry sales are projected, a company's market share is projected. Company-level market share projections may be based on historical market share and a forward-looking assessment of the company's competitive position. The company's sales are then estimated as its projected market share multiplied by projected total industry sales.

After developing a sales forecast for a company, an analyst can choose among various methods for forecasting income and cash flow. An analyst must decide on the level of detail to consider in developing forecasts. For example, separate forecasts may be made for individual expense items or for more aggregated expense items, such as total operating expenses. Rather than stating a forecast in terms of expenses, the forecast might be stated in terms of a forecasted profit margin (gross, operating, or net). The net profit margin, in contrast to the gross or operating profit margins, is affected by

3 The discussion in this paragraph is indebted to Benninga and Sarig (1997).

financial leverage and tax rates, which are subject to managerial and legal/regulatory revisions; therefore, historical data may sometimes be more relevant for projecting gross or operating profit margins than for projecting net profit margins. Whatever the margin used, the forecasted amount of profit for a given period is the product of the forecasted amount of sales and the forecast of the selected profit margin.

As Example 2 illustrates, for relatively mature companies operating in non-volatile product markets, historical information on operating profit margins can provide a useful starting point for forecasting future operating profits (at least over short forecasting horizons). Historical operating profit margins are typically less reliable for projecting future margins for a new or relatively volatile business or one with significant fixed costs (which can magnify the volatility of operating margins).

EXAMPLE 2

Using Historical Operating Profit Margins to Forecast Operating Profit

One approach to projecting operating profit is to determine a company's average operating profit margin over the previous several years and apply that margin to a forecast of the company's sales. Use the following information on three companies to answer Questions 1 and 2 below:

- Johnson & Johnson (JNJ). This US health care conglomerate, founded in 1887, had 2017 sales of around \$76.5 billion from its three main businesses: pharmaceuticals, medical devices and diagnostics, and consumer products.
- BHP Billiton (BHP). This company, with group headquarters in Australia and secondary headquarters in London, is the world's largest natural resources company, reporting revenue of approximately US\$38.3 billion for the fiscal year ended June 2017. The company mines, processes, and markets coal, copper, nickel, iron, bauxite, and silver and also has substantial petroleum operations.
- Baidu. This Chinese company, which was established in 2000 and went public on NASDAQ in 2005, is the leading Chinese language search engine. The company's revenues for 2017 were 84.8 billion renminbi (RMB), an increase of 20 percent from 2016 and almost 4 times revenue in 2012.

1 For each of the three companies, state and justify whether the suggested forecasting method (applying the average operating profit over the previous several years to a forecast of sales) would be a reasonable starting point for projecting future operating profit.

2 Assume that the 2017 forecast of sales was perfect and, therefore, equal to the realized sales by the company in 2017. Compare the forecast of 2017 operating profit, using an average of the previous five years' operating profit margins, with the actual 2017 operating profit reported by the company given the following additional information:

- JNJ: For the five years prior to 2017, JNJ's average operating profit margin was approximately 25.6 percent. The company's actual operating profit for 2017 was \$18.2 billion.

- BHP: For the four years prior to the year ending June 2017, BHP's average operating profit margin was approximately 24.0 percent. The company's actual operating profit for the year ended June 2017 was US$11.8 billion.
- Baidu: Over the four years prior to 2017, Baidu's average operating profit margin was approximately 28.5 percent. The company's actual operating profit for 2017 was RMB15.7 billion.

Using the additional information given, state and justify whether actual results support the usefulness of the stable operating margin assumption.

Solution to 1:

JNJ. Because JNJ is an established company with diversified operations in relatively stable businesses, the suggested approach to projecting the company's operating profit would be a reasonable starting point.

BHP. Because commodity prices tend to be volatile and the mining industry is relatively capital intensive, the suggested approach to projecting BHP's operating profit would probably not be a useful starting point.

Baidu. Compared to the other two companies, Baidu has a more limited operating history and remains in a period of rapid growth. These aspects about the company suggests that the broad approach to projecting operating profit would not be a useful starting point for Baidu.

Solution to 2:

JNJ. JNJ's actual operating profit margin for 2017 was 23.8 percent ($18.2 billion divided by sales of $76.5 billion), which is a little less than company's five-year average operating profit margin of approximately 25.6 percent.

BHP. BHP's actual operating profit margin for the year ended June 2017 was 30.8 percent ($11.8 billion divided by sales of $38.3 billion). If the company's average profit margin of 24.0 percent had been applied to perfectly forecasted sales, the forecasted operating profit would have been approximately US$9.2 billion, around 22 percent lower than actual operating profit.

Baidu. Baidu's actual operating profit margin for 2017 was 18.5 percent (RMB15.7 billion divided by sales of RMB84.8 billion). If the average profit margin of 28.5 percent had been applied to perfectly forecasted sales, the forecasted operating profit would have been approximately RMB24.2 billion, or around 54 percent higher than Baidu's actual operating profit.

Although prior years' profit margins can provide a useful starting point in projections for companies with relatively stable business, the underlying data should, nonetheless, be examined to identify items that are not likely to occur again in the following year(s). Such non-recurring (i.e., transitory) items should be removed from computations of any profit amount or profit margin that will be used in projections. Example 3 illustrates this principle.

EXAMPLE 3

Issues in Forecasting

Following are excerpts from the 2017 annual report of Textron, a global aircraft, defense and industrial company.

Textron Consolidated Statements of Operations for each of the years in the three-year period ended December 31

(In millions, except per share data)	2017	2016	2015
Revenues			
	$	$	$
Manufacturing revenues	14,129	13,710	13,340
Finance revenues	69	78	83
Total revenues	14,198	13,788	13,423
Costs, expenses and other			
Cost of sales	11,795	11,311	10,979
Selling and administrative expense	1,337	1,304	1,304
Interest expense	174	174	169
Special charges	130	123	—
Total costs, expenses and other	13,436	12,912	12,452
Income from continuing operations before income taxes	762	876	971
Income tax expense	456	33	273
Income from continuing operations	306	843	698
Income (loss) from discontinued operations, net of income taxes*	1	119	(1)
Net income	307	962	697

Footnotes:
2017 Note 12 Special Charges

(Continued)

In 2016, we initiated a plan to restructure and realign our businesses by implementing headcount reductions, facility consolidations and other actions in order to improve overall operating efficiency across Textron. Under this plan, Textron Systems discontinued production of its sensor-fuzed weapon product within its Weapons and Sensors operating unit, we combined our Jacobsen business with the Textron Specialized Vehicles business by consolidating facilities and general and administrative functions, and we reduced headcount at Textron Aviation, as well as other businesses and corporate functions. In December 2017, we decided to take additional restructuring actions to further consolidate operating facilities and streamline product lines, primarily within the Bell, Textron Systems and Industrial segments, which resulted in additional special charges of $45 million in the fourth quarter of 2017. We recorded total special charges of $213 million since the inception of the 2016 plan, which included $97 million of severance costs, $84 million of asset impairments and $32 million in contract terminations and other costs. Of these amounts, $83 million was incurred at Textron Systems, $63 million at Textron Aviation, $38 million at Industrial, $28 million at Bell and $1 million at Corporate. The total headcount reduction under this plan is expected to be approximately 2,100 positions, representing 5% of our workforce. In connection with the acquisition of Arctic Cat, as discussed in Note 2, we initiated a restructuring plan in the first quarter of 2017 to integrate this business into our Textron Specialized Vehicles business within the Industrial segment and reduce operating redundancies and maximize efficiencies. Under the Arctic Cat plan, we recorded restructuring charges of $28 million in 2017, which included $19 million of severance costs, largely related to change-of-control provisions, and $9 million of contract termination and other costs. In addition, we recorded $12 million of acquisition-related integration and transaction costs in 2017.

2016 Financial Statement General Footnote

*Income from discontinued operations, net of income taxes for the year ended December 31, 2016 primarily includes the settlement of a U.S. federal income tax audit. See Note 13 to the Consolidated Financial Statements for additional information.

2016 Note 13 Income Taxes

The provision for income taxes for 2016 included a benefit of $319 million to reflect the settlement with the U.S. Internal Revenue Service Office of Appeals for our 1998 to 2008 tax years, which resulted in a $206 million benefit attributable to continuing operations and $113 million attributable to discontinued operations.

Source: Textron annual reports.

Discussion:

Results of discontinued operations and restructuring charges should generally not be included when assessing past performance or when forecasting future net income. For purposes of evaluating the company's ongoing operating and net profit margins the special charges related to restructuring and the special tax benefit related to discontinued operations should be removed. For example, the company's operating margin for 2017 including special charges would be 5.4% ($762 million/$14,198 million). Excluding special charges, the operating margin would be 6.3% ($762 million + $130 million)/$14,198 million. Similarly, the net profit margin would be determined by eliminating the income from discontinued operations, particularly for 2016.

In general, when earnings projections are used as a foundation for market-based valuations, an analyst will make appropriate allowance for transitory components of past earnings. Occasionally, an analyst will observe that a company takes special charges virtually every year. In such cases, they are not transitory and should not be removed in evaluating past and future margins.

3.2 Projecting Multiple-Period Performance

Projections of future financial performance over multiple periods are needed in valuation models that estimate the value of a company or its equity by discounting future cash flows. The value of a company or its equity developed in this way can then be compared with its current market price as a basis for investment decisions.

Projections of future performance are also used for credit analysis. These projections are important in assessing a borrower's ability to repay interest and principal of debt obligations. Investment recommendations depend on the needs and objectives of the client and on an evaluation of the risk of the investment relative to its expected return—both of which are a function of the terms of the debt obligation itself as well as financial market conditions. Terms of the debt obligation include amount, interest rate, maturity, financial covenants, and collateral.

Example 4 presents an elementary illustration of net income and cash flow forecasting to illustrate a format for analysis and some basic principles. In Example 4, assumptions are shown first; then, the period-by-period abbreviated financial statement resulting from the assumptions is shown.

Depending on the use of the forecast, an analyst may choose to compute further, more specific cash flow metrics. For example, free cash flow to equity, which is used in discounted cash flow approaches to equity valuation, can be estimated as net income adjusted for noncash items, minus investment in net working capital and in net fixed assets, plus net borrowing.

EXAMPLE 4

Basic Example of Financial Forecasting

Assume a company is formed with $100 of equity capital, all of which is immediately invested in working capital. Assumptions are as follows:

Dividends	Non-dividend-paying
First-year sales	$100
Sales growth	10% per year
Cost of goods sold/Sales	20%

Dividends	Non-dividend-paying
Operating expense/Sales	70%
Interest income rate	5%
Tax rate	30%
Working capital as percent of sales	90%

Based on this information, forecast the company's net income and cash flow for five years.

Solution:

Exhibit 2 shows the net income forecasts in Line 7 and cash flow forecasts ("Change in cash") in Line 18.

Exhibit 2 Basic Financial Forecasting

	Time Period					
	0	1	2	3	4	5
(1) Sales		100.0	110.0	121.0	133.1	146.4
(2) Cost of goods sold		(20.0)	(22.0)	(24.2)	(26.6)	(29.3)
(3) Operating expenses		(70.0)	(77.0)	(84.7)	(93.2)	(102.5)
(4) Interest income		0.0	0.9	0.8	0.8	0.7
(5) Income before tax		10.0	11.9	12.9	14.1	15.3
(6) Taxes		(3.0)	(3.6)	(3.9)	(4.2)	(4.6)
(7) Net income		7.0	8.3	9.0	9.9	10.7
(8) Cash/Borrowing	0.0	17.0	16.3	15.4	14.4	13.1
(9) Working capital (non-cash)	100.0	90.0	99.0	108.9	119.8	131.8
(10) Total assets	100.0	107.0	115.3	124.3	134.2	144.9
(11) Liabilities	0.0	0.0	0.0	0.0	0.0	0.0
(12) Equity	100.0	107.0	115.3	124.3	134.2	144.9
(13) Total liabilities + Equity	100.0	107.0	115.3	124.3	134.2	144.9
(14) Net income		7.0	8.3	9.0	9.9	10.7
(15) Plus: Non-cash items		0.0	0.0	0.0	0.0	0.0
(16) Less: Investment in working capital		−10.0	9.0	9.9	10.9	12.0
(17) Less: Investment in fixed capital		0.0	0.0	0.0	0.0	0.0
(18) Change in cash		17.0	−0.7	−0.9	−1.0	−1.3
(19) Beginning cash		0.0	17.0	16.3	15.4	14.4
(20) Ending cash		17.0	16.3	15.4	14.4	13.1

Exhibit 2 indicates that at time 0, the company is formed with $100 of equity capital (Line 12). All of the company's capital is assumed to be immediately invested in working capital (Line 9). In future periods, because it is assumed that no dividends are paid, book equity increases each year by the amount of net income (Line 14). Future periods' required working capital (Line 9) is assumed to be 90 percent of annual sales (Line 1). Sales are assumed to be $100 in the first period and to grow at a constant rate of 10 percent per year (Line 1). The cost of goods sold is assumed to be constant at 20 percent of sales (Line 2), so the gross profit margin is 80 percent. Operating expenses are assumed to be 70 percent of sales each year (Line 3). Interest income (Line 4) is calculated as 5 percent of the beginning balance of cash/borrowing or the ending balance of the previous period (Line 8) and is an income item when there is a cash balance, as in this example. (If available cash is inadequate to cover required cash outflows, the shortfall is presumed to be covered by borrowing. This borrowing would be shown as a negative balance on Line 8 and an associated interest expense on Line 4. Alternatively, a forecast can be presented with separate lines for cash and borrowing.) Taxes of 30 percent are deducted to obtain net income (Line 7).

To calculate each period's cash flow, begin with net income (Line 7 = Line 14), add back any noncash items, such as depreciation (Line 15), deduct investment in working capital in the period or change in working capital over the period (Line 16), and deduct investment in fixed capital in the period (Line 17).[4] In this simple example, we are assuming that the company does not invest in any fixed capital (long-term assets) but, rather, rents furnished office space. Therefore, there is no depreciation and noncash items are zero. Each period's change in cash (Line 18) is added to the beginning cash balance (Line 19) to obtain the ending cash balance (Line 20 = Line 8).

Example 4 is simplified to demonstrate some principles of forecasting. In practice, each aspect of a forecast presents a range of challenges. Sales forecasts may be very detailed, with separate forecasts for each year of each product line, each geographical, and/or each business segment. Sales forecasts may be based on past results (for relatively stable businesses), management forecasts, industry studies, and/or macroeconomic forecasts. Similarly, gross profit margins may be based on past results or forecasted relationships and may be detailed. Expenses other than cost of goods sold may be broken down into more detailed line items, each of which may be forecasted on the basis of its relationship with sales (if variable) or on the basis of its historical levels. Working capital requirements may be estimated as a proportion of the amount of sales (as in Example 4) or the change in sales or as a compilation of specific forecasts for inventory, receivables, and payables. Most forecasts will involve some investment in fixed assets, in which case, depreciation amounts affect taxable income and net income but not cash flow. Example 4 makes the simplifying assumption that interest is paid on the beginning-of-year cash balance.

Example 4 develops a series of point estimates for future net income and cash flow. In practice, forecasting generally includes an analysis of the risk in forecasts—in this case, an assessment of the impact on income and cash flow if the realized values of variables differ significantly from the assumptions used in the base case or if actual sales are much different from forecasts. Quantifying the risk in forecasts requires an analysis of the economics of the company's businesses and expense structure and the potential impact of events affecting the company, the industry, and the economy in general. When that investigation is completed, the analyst can use scenario analysis or Monte Carlo simulation to assess risk. Scenario analysis involves specifying assumptions that differ from those used as the base-case assumptions. In Example 4, the projections of net income and cash flow could be recast in a more pessimistic scenario, with assumptions changed to reflect slower sales growth and higher costs. A Monte Carlo simulation involves specifying probability distributions of values for

4 Working capital represents funds that must be invested in the daily operations of a business to, for example, carry inventory and accounts receivable. The term "investment" in this context means "addition to" or "increase in." The "investment in fixed capital" is also referred to as "capital expenditure" ("capex").

variables and random sampling from those distributions. In the analysis in Example 4, the projections would be repeatedly recast with the selected values for the drivers of net income and cash flow, thus permitting the analyst to evaluate a range of possible results and the probability of simulating the possible actual outcomes.

An understanding of financial statements and ratios can enable an analyst to make more detailed projections of income statement, balance sheet, and cash flow statement items. For example, an analyst may collect information on normal inventory and receivables turnover and use this information to forecast accounts receivable, inventory, and cash flows based on sales projections rather than use a composite working capital investment assumption, as in Example 4.

As the analyst makes detailed forecasts, he or she must ensure that the forecasts are consistent with each other. For instance, in Example 5, the analyst's forecast concerning days of sales outstanding (which is an estimate of the average time to collect payment from sales made on credit) should flow from a model of the company that yields a forecast of the change in the average accounts receivable balance. Otherwise, predicted days of sales outstanding and accounts receivable will not be mutually consistent.

EXAMPLE 5

Consistency of Forecasts

Brown Corporation, a hypothetical company, had an average days-of-sales-outstanding (DSO) period of 19 days in 2017. An analyst thinks that Brown's DSO will decline in 2018 (because of expected improvements in the company's collections department) to match the industry average of 15 days. Total sales (all on credit) in 2017 were $300 million, and Brown expects total sales (all on credit) to increase to $320 million in 2018. To achieve the lower DSO, the change in the average accounts receivable balance from 2017 to 2018 that must occur is *closest* to:

A −$3.51 million.

B −$2.46 million.

C $2.46 million.

D $3.51 million.

Solution:

B is correct. The first step is to calculate accounts receivable turnover from the DSO collection period. Receivable turnover equals 365/19 (DSO) = 19.2 for 2017 and 365/15 = 24.3 in 2018. Next, the analyst uses the fact that the average accounts receivable balance equals sales/receivable turnover to conclude that for 2017, average accounts receivable was $300,000,000/19.2 = $15,625,000 and for 2018, it must equal $320,000,000/24.3 = $13,168,724. The difference is a reduction in receivables of $2,456,276.

The next section illustrates the application of financial statement analysis to credit risk analysis.

4 APPLICATION: ASSESSING CREDIT RISK

Credit risk is the risk of loss caused by a counterparty's or debtor's failure to make a promised payment. For example, credit risk with respect to a bond is the risk that the obligor (the issuer of the bond) will not be able to pay interest and/or principal according to the terms of the bond indenture (contract). **Credit analysis** is the evaluation of credit risk. Credit analysis may relate to the credit risk of an obligor in a particular transaction or to an obligor's overall creditworthiness.

In assessing an obligor's overall creditworthiness, one general approach is credit scoring, a statistical analysis of the determinants of credit default. Credit analysis for specific types of debt (e.g., acquisition financing and other highly leveraged financing) typically involves projections of period-by-period cash flows.

Whatever the techniques adopted, the analytical focus of credit analysis is on debt-paying ability. Unlike payments to equity investors, payments to debt investors are limited by the agreed contractual interest. If a company experiences financial success, its debt becomes less risky but its success does not increase the amount of payments to its debtholders. In contrast, if a company experiences financial distress, it may be unable to pay interest and principal on its debt obligations. Thus, credit analysis has a special concern with the sensitivity of debt-paying ability to adverse events and economic conditions—cases in which the creditor's promised returns may be most at risk. Because those returns are generally paid in cash, credit analysis usually focuses on cash flow rather than accrual income. Typically, credit analysts use return measures related to operating cash flow because it represents cash generated internally, which is available to pay creditors.

These themes are reflected in Example 6, which illustrates Moody's application of four quantitative factors in the credit analysis of the aerospace and defense industry.[5] These factors include

1 scale,
2 business profile,
3 leverage and coverage, and
4 financial policy.

"Scale" relates to a company's sensitivity to adverse events, adverse economic conditions, and other factors—such as market leadership, purchasing power with suppliers, and access to capital markets—that may affect debt-paying ability. "Business profile" represents a company's competitive position, stability of revenues, product and geographic diversity, growth prospects, and the stability and volatility of cash flows. "Leverage and coverage" reflects a company's "financial flexibility" and viability. Finally, "financial policy" relates to a company's financial risk tolerance and its capital structure.

5 The information in this paragraph and in Example 7 are based upon the "Rating Methodology: Aerospace and Defense Industry" (Moody's, 2018).

EXAMPLE 6

Moody's Evaluation of Quantifiable Rating Factors for the Aerospace and Defense Industry

Moody's considers four broad rating factors for the aerospace and defense industry: scale; business profile, leverage and coverage; and financial policy. A company's ratings for each of these factors are weighted and aggregated in determining the overall credit rating assigned. The broad factors, the sub-factors, and weightings are as follows:

Broad Factor	Sub-factors	Sub-factor Weighting (%)	Broad Factor Weighting (%)
Scale	Total revenue	10	25
	Operating profit	15	
Business profile	Competitive position	10	20
	Expected revenue stability	10	
Leverage and coverage	Debt/EBITDA	10	35
	Retained cash flow[a]/Net debt	15	
	EBIT/Interest	10	
Financial policy	Financial policy	20	20
Total		100	100

[a] Retained cash flow is defined by Moody's as cash flow before working capital and after dividends.

Why might the leverage and coverage factor be weighted higher compared to the other rating factors?

Solution:

The level of debt relative to earnings and cash flow is a critical factor in assessing creditworthiness. Higher levels of debt for a company typically result in a higher risk in meeting interest and principal payments on its debt obligations.

A point to note regarding Example 6 is that the rating factors and the metrics used to represent each can vary by industry group.

Analyses of a company's historical and projected financial statements are an integral part of the credit evaluation process. Moody's and other rating agencies compute a variety of ratios in assessing creditworthiness. A comparison of a company's ratios with the ratios of its peers is informative in evaluating relative creditworthiness, as demonstrated in Example 7.

EXAMPLE 7

Peer Comparison of Ratios

A credit analyst is assessing the efficiency and leverage of two aerospace and defense companies based on certain sub-factors identified by Moody's in Example 7. The analyst collects the information from the companies' annual reports and calculates the following ratios:

	Company 1	Company 2
Debt/EBITDA	9.3	4.1
Retained cash flow/Net debt	2.6%	9.6%
EBIT/Interest	5.7	8.2

Based solely on the data given, which company is more likely to be assigned a higher credit rating, and why?

Solution:

The ratio comparisons are all in favor of Company 2, which has a lower level of debt relative to EBITDA, higher retained cash flow to net debt, and higher interest coverage. Based only on the data given, Company 2 is likely to be assigned a higher credit rating.

In calculating credit ratios, such as those presented in Example 8, analysts typically make certain adjustments to reported financial statements. We describe some common adjustments later in the reading.

Financial statement analysis, especially financial ratio analysis, can also be an important tool in selecting equity investments, as discussed in the next section.

5 APPLICATION: SCREENING FOR POTENTIAL EQUITY INVESTMENTS

Ratios constructed from financial statement data and market data are often used to screen for potential equity investments. **Screening** is the application of a set of criteria to reduce a set of potential investments to a smaller set having certain desired characteristics. Criteria involving financial ratios generally involve comparing one or more ratios with some pre-specified target or cutoff values.

A security selection approach incorporating financial ratios may be applied whether the investor uses top-down analysis or bottom-up analysis. **Top-down analysis** involves identifying attractive geographical segments and/or industry segments, from which the investor chooses the most attractive investments. **Bottom-up analysis** involves selection of specific investments from all companies within a specified investment universe. Regardless of the direction, screening for potential equity investments aims to identify companies that meet specific criteria. An analysis of this type may be used as the basis for directly forming a portfolio, or it may be undertaken as a preliminary part of a more thorough analysis of potential investment targets.

Fundamental to this type of analysis are decisions about which metrics to use as screens, how many metrics to include, what values of those metrics to use as cutoff points, and what weighting to give each metric. Metrics may include not only financial ratios but also characteristics such as market capitalization or membership as a component security in a specified index. Exhibit 3 presents a hypothetical example of a simple stock screen based on the following criteria: a valuation ratio (P/E) less than a specified value, a solvency ratio measuring financial leverage (total liabilities/ total assets) not exceeding a specified value, positive operating margin, and dividend yield (dividends per share divided by price per share) greater than a specified value. Exhibit 3 shows the results of applying the screen in August 2018 to a set of 6,406 US companies with market capitalization greater than $100 million, which compose a hypothetical equity manager's investment universe.

Exhibit 3 Example of a Stock Screen

	Stocks Meeting Criterion	
Criterion	**Number**	**Percent of Total**
Market Capitalization > $100 million	4,357	68.01%
P/E < 15	1,104	17.23%
Total liabilities/Total Assets ≤ 0.9	61	0.95%
Operating Income/Sales > 0	3,509	54.78%
Dividend yield > 0.5%	2,391	37.32%
Meeting all five criteria simultaneously	17	0.27%

Source for data: http://google.com/finance/.

Several points about the screen in Exhibit 3 are consistent with many screens used in practice:

- Some criteria serve as checks on the results from applying other criteria. In this hypothetical example, the second criterion selects stocks that appear relatively cheaply valued. The stocks might be cheap for a good reason, however, such as poor profitability or excessive financial leverage. So, the requirement for net income to be positive serves as a check on profitability, and the limitation on financial leverage serves as a check on financial risk. Of course, financial ratios or other statistics cannot generally control for exposure to certain other types of risk (e.g., risk related to regulatory developments or technological innovation).
- If all the criteria were completely independent of each other, the set of stocks meeting all four criteria would be 2, equal to 6,406 times 0.023 percent—the product of the fraction of stocks satisfying the four criteria individually (i.e., $0.6801 \times 0.1723 \times 0.0095 \times 0.5478 = 0.2723$, or 0.023 percent). As the screen illustrates, criteria are often not independent, and the result is that more securities pass the screening than if criteria were independent. In this example, 17 of the securities pass all five screens simultaneously. For an example of the lack of independence, we note that dividend-paying status is probably positively correlated with the ability to generate positive operating margin. If stocks that pass one test tend to also pass another, few are eliminated after the application of the second test.
- The results of screens can sometimes be relatively concentrated in a subset of the sectors represented in the benchmark. The financial leverage criterion in Exhibit 3 would exclude banking stocks, for example. What constitutes a high or low value of a measure of a financial characteristic can be sensitive to the industry in which a company operates.

Screens can be used by both **growth investors** (focused on investing in high-earnings-growth companies), **value investors** (focused on paying a relatively low share price in relation to earnings or assets per share), and **market-oriented investors** (an intermediate grouping of investors whose investment disciplines cannot be clearly categorized as value or growth). Growth screens would typically feature criteria related to earnings growth and/or momentum. Value screens, as a rule, feature criteria setting upper limits for the value of one or more valuation ratios. Market-oriented screens would not strongly emphasize valuation or growth criteria. The use of screens involving financial ratios may be most common among value investors.

An analyst may want to evaluate how a portfolio based on a particular screen would have performed historically. For this purpose, the analyst uses a process known as "back-testing." **Back-testing** applies the portfolio selection rules to historical data and calculates what returns would have been earned if a particular strategy had been used. The relevance of back-testing to investment success in practice, however, may be limited. Haugen and Baker (1996) described some of these limitations:

- Survivorship bias: If the database used in back-testing eliminates companies that cease to exist because of a bankruptcy or merger, then the remaining companies collectively will appear to have performed better.
- Look-ahead bias: If a database includes financial data updated for restatements (where companies have restated previously issued financial statements to correct errors or reflect changes in accounting principles), then there is a mismatch between what investors would have actually known at the time of the investment decision and the information used in the back-testing.
- Data-snooping bias: If researchers build a model on the basis of previous researchers' findings, then use the same database to test that model, they are not actually testing the model's predictive ability. When each step is backward looking, the same rules may or may not produce similar results in the future. The predictive ability of the model's rules can validly be tested only by using future data. One academic study has argued that the apparent ability of value strategies to generate excess returns is largely explainable as the result of collective data snooping (Conrad, Cooper, and Kaul, 2003).

EXAMPLE 8

Ratio-Based Screening for Potential Equity Investments

Below are two alternative strategies under consideration by an investment firm:

Strategy A: Invest in stocks that are components of a global equity index, have a ROE above the median ROE of all stocks in the index, and have a P/E less than the median P/E.

Strategy B: Invest in stocks that are components of a broad-based US equity index, have a ratio of price to operating cash flow in the lowest quartile of companies in the index, and have shown increases in sales for at least the past three years.

Both strategies were developed with the use of back-testing.

1 How would you characterize the two strategies?

2 What concerns might you have about using such strategies?

Solution to 1:

Strategy A appears to aim for global diversification and combines a requirement for high relative profitability with a traditional measure of value (low P/E). Strategy B focuses on both large and small companies in a single market and apparently aims to identify companies that are growing and have a lower price multiple based on cash flow from operations.

Solution to 2:

The use of *any* approach to investment decisions depends on the objectives and risk profile of the investor. With that crucial consideration in mind, we note that ratio-based benchmarks may be an efficient way to screen for potential equity investments. In screening, however, many questions arise.

First, unintentional selections can be made if criteria are not specified carefully. For example, Strategy A might unintentionally select a loss-making company with negative shareholders' equity because negative net income divided by negative shareholders' equity arithmetically results in a positive ROE. Strategy B might unintentionally select a company with negative operating cash flow because price to operating cash flow will be negative and thus very low in the ranking. In both cases, the analyst can add additional screening criteria to avoid unintentional selections; these additional criteria could include requiring positive shareholders' equity in Strategy A and requiring positive operating cash flow in Strategy B.

Second, the inputs to ratio analysis are derived from financial statements, and companies may differ in the financial standards they apply (e.g., IFRS versus US GAAP), the specific accounting method(s) they choose within those allowed by the reporting standards, and/or the estimates made in applying an accounting method.

Third, back-testing may not provide a reliable indication of future performance because of survivorship bias, look-ahead bias, or data-snooping bias. Also, as suggested by finance theory and by common sense, the past is not necessarily indicative of the future.

Fourth, implementation decisions can dramatically affect returns. For example, decisions about frequency and timing of portfolio re-evaluation and changes affect transaction costs and taxes paid out of the portfolio.

ANALYST ADJUSTMENTS TO REPORTED FINANCIALS 6

When comparing companies that use different accounting methods or estimate key accounting inputs in different ways, analysts frequently adjust a company's financials. In this section, we first provide a framework for considering potential analyst adjustments to facilitate such comparisons and then provide examples of such adjustments. In practice, required adjustments vary widely. The examples presented here are not intended to be comprehensive but, rather, to illustrate the use of adjustments to facilitate a meaningful comparison.

6.1 A Framework for Analyst Adjustments

In this discussion of potential analyst adjustments to a company's financial statements, we use a framework focused on the *balance sheet*. Because the financial statements are interrelated, however, adjustments to items reported on one statement may also be reflected in adjustments to items on another financial statement. For example, an analyst adjustment to inventory on the balance sheet affects cost of goods sold on the income statement (and thus also affects net income and, subsequently, the retained earnings account on the balance sheet).

Regardless of the particular order in which an analyst considers the items that may require adjustment for comparability, the following aspects are appropriate:

- *Importance (materiality).* Is an adjustment to this item likely to affect the conclusions? In other words, does it matter? For example, in an industry where companies require minimal inventory, does it matter that two companies use different inventory accounting methods?
- *Body of standards.* Is there a difference in the body of standards being used (US GAAP versus IFRS)? If so, in which areas is the difference likely to affect a comparison?
- *Methods.* Is there a difference in accounting methods used by the companies being compared?
- *Estimates.* Is there a difference in important estimates used by the companies being compared?

The following sections illustrate analyst adjustments—first, those relating to the asset side of the balance sheet and then those relating to the liability side.

6.2 Analyst Adjustments Related to Investments

Accounting for investments in the debt and equity securities of other companies (other than investments accounted for under the equity method and investments in consolidated subsidiaries) depends on management's intention (i.e., whether to actively trade the securities, make them available for sale, or in the case of debt securities, hold them to maturity). When securities are classified as "financial assets measured at fair value through profit or loss" (similar to "trading" securities in US GAAP), unrealized gains and losses are reported in the income statement. When securities are classified as "financial assets measured at fair value through other comprehensive income" (similar to "available-for-sale" securities in US GAAP), unrealized gains and losses are not reported in the income statement and, instead, are recognized in equity. If two otherwise comparable companies have significant differences in the classification of investments, analyst adjustments may be useful to facilitate comparison.

6.3 Analyst Adjustments Related to Inventory

With inventory, adjustments may be required for different accounting methods. As described in previous readings, a company's decision about inventory method will affect the value of inventory shown on the balance sheet as well as the value of inventory that is sold (cost of goods sold). If a company not reporting under IFRS[6] uses LIFO (last-in, first-out) and another uses FIFO (first-in, first-out), comparability of the financial results of the two companies will suffer. Companies that use the LIFO method, must also, however, disclose the value of their inventory under the FIFO method. To recast inventory values for a company using LIFO reporting on a FIFO basis, the analyst adds the ending balance of the LIFO reserve to the ending value of inventory under LIFO accounting. To adjust cost of goods sold to a FIFO basis, the analyst subtracts the change in the LIFO reserve from the reported cost of goods

6 IAS No. 2 does not permit the use of LIFO.

sold under LIFO accounting. Example 9 illustrates the use of a disclosure of the value of inventory under the FIFO method to make a more consistent comparison of the current ratios of two companies reporting in different methods.

EXAMPLE 9

Adjustment for a Company Using LIFO Accounting for Inventories

An analyst is comparing the financial performance of LP Technology Corporation (LP Tech), a hypothetical company, with the financial performance of a similar company that uses IFRS for reporting. The company reporting under IFRS uses the FIFO method of inventory accounting. Therefore, the analyst converts LP Tech's results to a comparable basis. Exhibit 4 provides balance sheet information on LP Tech.

Exhibit 4 Data for LP Technology Corporation

	30 June	
	2018	**2017**
Total current assets	820.2	749.7
Total current liabilities	218.1	198.5

NOTE 6. INVENTORIES

Inventories consist of the following ($ millions):

	30 June	
	2018	**2017**
Raw materials	$30.7	$29.5
Work in process	109.1	90.8
Finished goods	63.8	65.1
	$203.6	$185.4

If the first-in, first-out method of inventory had been used instead of the LIFO method, inventories would have been $331.8 and $305.8 million higher as of June 30, 2018 and 2017, respectively.

1 Based on the information in Exhibit 4, calculate LP Tech's current ratio under FIFO and LIFO for 2017 and 2018.

2 LP Tech makes the following disclosure in the risk section of its MD&A. Assuming an effective tax rate of 35 percent, estimate the impact on LPTC's tax liability.

> **"We value most of our inventory using the LIFO method, which could be repealed resulting in adverse effects on our cash flows and financial condition.**

The cost of our inventories is primarily determined using the Last-In First-Out ("LIFO") method. Under the LIFO inventory valuation method, changes in the cost of raw materials and production activities are recognized in cost of sales in the current period even though these materials and other costs may have been incurred at significantly different values due to the length of time of our production cycle. Generally in a period of rising prices, LIFO recognizes higher costs of goods sold, which both reduces current income and assigns a lower value to the year-end inventory. Recent proposals have been initiated aimed at repealing the election to use the LIFO method for income tax purposes. According to these proposals, generally taxpayers that currently use the LIFO method would be required to revalue their LIFO inventory to its first-in, first-out ("FIFO") value. As of June 30, 2018, if the FIFO method of inventory had been used instead of the LIFO method, our inventories would have been about $332 million higher. This increase in inventory would result in a one time increase in taxable income which would be taken into account ratably over the first taxable year and the following several taxable years. The repeal of LIFO could result in a substantial tax liability which could adversely impact our cash flows and financial condition."

3 LP Tech reported cash flow from operations of $115.2 million for the year ended 30 June 2018. In comparison with the company's operating cash flow, how significant is the additional potential tax liability?

Solution to 1:

The calculations of LP Tech's current ratio (current assets divided by current liabilities) are as follows:

	2018	2017
I. Current ratio (unadjusted)		
Total current assets	$820.2	$749.7
Total current liabilities	$218.1	$198.5
Current ratio (unadjusted)	3.8	3.8
II. Current ratio (adjusted)		
Total current assets	$820.2	$749.7
Adjust inventory to FIFO, add:	331.8	305.8
Total current assets (adjusted)	$1,152	$1,056
Total current liabilities	218.1	198.5
Current ratio (adjusted)	5.3	5.3

To adjust the LIFO inventory to FIFO, add the excess amounts of FIFO cost over LIFO cost to LIFO inventory and increase current assets by an equal amount. The effect of adjusting inventory on the current ratio is to increase the current ratio from 3.8 to 5.3 in both 2017 and 2018. LP Tech has greater liquidity according to the adjusted current ratio.

Solution to 2:

Assuming an effective tax rate of 35 percent, we find the total increase in LP Tech's tax liability to be $116.1 million (0.35 × $331.8 million).

Solution to 3:

The additional tax liability would be greater than the entire amount of the company's cash flow from operations of $115.2 million; the additional tax liability would be apportioned, however, over several years.

In summary, the information disclosed by companies that use LIFO allows an analyst to calculate the value of the company's inventory as if the company were using the FIFO method. If the LIFO method is used for a substantial part of a company's inventory and the LIFO reserve is large relative to reported inventory, however, the adjustment to a FIFO basis can be important for comparison of the LIFO-reporting company with a company that uses the FIFO method of inventory valuation. Example 10 illustrates a case in which such an adjustment would have a major impact on an analyst's conclusions.

EXAMPLE 10

Analyst Adjustment to Inventory Value for Comparability in a Current Ratio Comparison

Company A reports under IFRS and uses the FIFO method of inventory accounting. Company B reports under US GAAP and uses the LIFO method. Exhibit 5 gives data pertaining to current assets, LIFO reserves, and current liabilities of these companies.

Exhibit 5 Data for Companies Accounting for Inventory on Different Bases

	Company A (FIFO)	Company B (LIFO)
Current assets (includes inventory)	$ 300,000	$ 80,000
LIFO reserve	NA	$ 20,000
Current liabilities	$ 150,000	$ 45,000

NA = not applicable.

Based on the data given in Exhibit 5, compare the liquidity of the two companies as measured by the current ratio.

Solution:

Company A's current ratio is 2.0. Based on unadjusted balance sheet data, Company B's current ratio is 1.78. Company A's higher current ratio indicates that Company A appears to be more liquid than Company B; however, the use of unadjusted data for Company B is not appropriate for making comparisons with Company A.

After adjusting Company B's inventory to a comparable basis (i.e., to a FIFO basis), the conclusion changes. The following table summarizes the results when Company B's inventory is left on a LIFO basis and when it is placed on a FIFO basis for comparability with Company A.

		Company B	
	Company A (FIFO)	Unadjusted (LIFO basis)	Adjusted (FIFO basis)
Current assets (includes inventory)	$ 300,000	$ 80,000	$ 100,000
Current liabilities	$ 150,000	$ 45,000	$ 45,000
Current ratio	2.00	1.78	2.22

When both companies' inventories are stated on a FIFO basis, Company B appears to be the more liquid, as indicated by its current ratio of 2.22 versus Company A's ratio of 2.00.

The adjustment to place Company B's inventory on a FIFO basis was significant because Company B was assumed to use LIFO for its entire inventory and its inventory reserve was $20,000/$80,000 = 0.25, or 25 percent of its reported inventory.

As mentioned earlier, an analyst can also adjust the cost of goods sold for a company using LIFO to a FIFO basis by subtracting the change in the amount of the LIFO reserve from cost of goods sold. Such an adjustment would be appropriate for making profitability comparisons with a company reporting on a FIFO basis and is important to make when the impact of the adjustment would be material.

6.4 Analyst Adjustments Related to Property, Plant, and Equipment

Management generally has considerable discretion in determination of depreciation expense. Depreciation expense affects the values of reported net income and reported net fixed assets. Analysts often consider management's choices related to depreciation as a qualitative factor in evaluating the quality of a company's financial reporting, and in some cases, analysts may adjust reported depreciation expense for a specific analytical purpose.

The amount of depreciation expense depends on both the accounting method and the estimates used in the calculations. Companies can use the straight-line method, an accelerated method, or a usage method to depreciate fixed assets (other than land). The straight-line method reports an equal amount of depreciation expense each period, and the expense is computed as the depreciable cost divided by the estimated useful life of the asset (when acquired, an asset's depreciable cost is calculated as its total cost minus its estimated salvage value). Accelerated methods depreciate the asset more quickly; they apportion a greater amount of the depreciable cost to depreciation expense in the earlier periods. Usage-based methods depreciate an asset in proportion to its usage. In addition to selecting a depreciation method, companies must estimate an asset's salvage value and useful life to compute depreciation.

Disclosures required for depreciation often do not facilitate specific adjustments, so comparisons of companies concerning their decisions in depreciating assets are often qualitative and general. The accounts that are associated with depreciation include the balance sheet accounts for gross property, plant, and equipment (PPE) and accumulated depreciation; the income statement amount for depreciation expense; and the statement of cash flows disclosure of capital expenditure (capex) and asset disposals. The relationships among these items can reveal various pieces of information. Note, however, that PPE typically includes a mix of assets with different depreciable lives and salvage values, so the items in the following list reflect general relationships in the total pool of assets.

- Accumulated depreciation divided by gross PPE, from the balance sheet, suggests how much of the useful life of the company's overall asset base has passed.
- Accumulated depreciation divided by depreciation expense suggests how many years' worth of depreciation expense have already been recognized (i.e., the average age of the asset base).
- Net PPE (net of accumulated depreciation) divided by depreciation expense is an approximate indicator of how many years of useful life remain for the company's overall asset base.
- Gross PPE divided by depreciation expense suggests the average life of the assets at installation.
- Capex divided by the sum of gross PPE plus capex can suggest what percentage of the asset base is being renewed through new capital investment.
- Capex in relation to asset disposal provides information on growth of the asset base.

As Example 11 shows, these relationships can be evaluated for companies in an industry to suggest differences in their strategies for asset utilization or areas for further investigation.

EXAMPLE 11

Differences in Depreciation

An analyst is evaluating the financial statements of two companies in the same industry. The companies have similar strategies with respect to the use of equipment in manufacturing their products. The following information is provided (amounts in millions):

	Company A	Company B
Net PPE	$1,200	$750
Depreciation expense	$120	$50

1 Based on the information given, estimate the average remaining useful lives of the asset bases of Company A and Company B.

2 Suppose that, based on a physical inspection of the companies' plants and other industry information, the analyst believes that the actual remaining useful lives of Company A's and Company B's assets are roughly equal at 10 years. Based only on the facts given, what might the analyst conclude about Company B's reported net income?

Solution to 1:

The estimated average remaining useful life of Company A's asset base is 10 years (calculated as net PPE divided by depreciation expense, or $1,200/$120 = 10 years). For Company B, the average remaining useful life of the asset base appears to be far longer, 15 years ($750/$50).

Solution to 2:

If 10 years were used to calculate Company B's depreciation expense, the expense would be $75 million (i.e., $25 million higher than reported) and higher depreciation expense would decrease net income. The analyst might conclude that Company B's reported net income reflects relatively more aggressive accounting estimates than estimates reflected in Company A's reported net income.

6.5 Analyst Adjustments Related to Goodwill

Goodwill arises when one company purchases another for a price that exceeds the fair value of the net identifiable assets acquired. Net identifiable assets include current assets, fixed assets, and certain intangible assets that have value and meet recognition criteria under accounting standards. A broad range of intangible assets might require valuation in the context of a business combination—for example, brands, technology, and customer lists. Goodwill is recorded as an asset and essentially represents the difference between the purchase price and the net identifiable assets. For example, assume ParentCo purchases TargetCo for a purchase price of $400 million and the fair value of TargetCo's identifiable assets is $300 million (which includes the fair values of current assets, fixed assets, and a recognized brand). ParentCo will record total assets of $400 million consisting of $300 million in identifiable assets (including the fair value of the brand) and $100 million of goodwill. The goodwill is tested annually for impairment and if the value of the goodwill is determined to be impaired, ParentCo will then reduce the amount of the asset and report a write-off resulting from impairment.

One of the conceptual difficulties with goodwill arises in comparative financial statement analysis. Consider, for example, two hypothetical US companies, one of which has grown by making an acquisition and the other of which has grown internally. Assume that the economic value of the two companies is identical: Each has an identically valuable branded product, well-trained workforce, and proprietary technology. The company that has grown by acquisition will have recorded the transaction to acquire the target company and its underlying net assets on the basis of the total consideration paid for the acquisition. The company that has grown internally will have done so by incurring expenditures for advertising, staff training, and research, all of which are expensed as incurred under US GAAP. Given the immediate expensing, the value of the internally generated assets is not capitalized onto the balance sheet and is thus not directly reflected on the company's balance sheet (revenues, income, and cash flows should reflect the benefits derived from the investment in the intangible assets). Ratios based on asset values and/or income, including profitability ratios (such as ROA) and market value to book value (MV/BV),[7] will generally differ for the two companies because of differences in the accounting values of assets and income related to acquired intangibles and goodwill, although, by assumption, the economic value of the companies is identical.

7 MV/BV equals the total market value of the stock (the market capitalization) divided by total stockholders' equity. It is also referred to as the price-to-book ratio because it can also be calculated as price per share divided by stockholders' equity per share.

EXAMPLE 12

Ratio Comparisons for Goodwill

Miano Marseglia is an analyst who is evaluating the relative valuation of two securities brokerage companies: TD Ameritrade Holding Corporation (AMTD) and the Charles Schwab Corporation (SCHW). As one part of an overall analysis, Marseglia would like to see how the two companies compare with each other and with the industry based on market value to book value. Because both companies are large players in the industry, Marseglia expects them to sell at a higher MV/BV than the financial services sector median of 2.2. He collects the following data on the two companies.

	SCHW	AMTD
Market capitalization on 30 August 2018 (market price per share times the number of shares outstanding)	$68,620	$33,247
Total shareholders' equity (as of 30 June 2018 for both companies)	$20,097	$7,936
Goodwill	$1,227	$4,198
Other intangible assets	$93	$1,363

Marseglia computes the MV/BV for the companies as follows:

SCHW $68,620/$20,097 = 3.4

AMTD $33,247/$7,936 = 4.2

As expected, each company appears to be selling at a premium to the sector median MV/BV of 2.2. The companies have similar MV/BVs (i.e., they are somewhat equally valued relative to the book value of shareholders' equity). Marseglia is concerned, however, because he notes that AMTD has significant amounts of goodwill and acquired intangible assets. He wonders what the relative value would be if the MV/BV were computed after adjusting book value, first, to remove goodwill and, second, to remove all intangible assets. Book value reduced by all intangible assets (including goodwill) is known as "tangible book value."

1 Compute the MV/BV adjusted for goodwill and the price/tangible book value for each company.

2 Which company appears to be a better value based *solely* on this data? (Note that the MV/BV is only one part of a broader analysis. Much more evidence related to the valuations and the comparability of the companies would be required to reach a conclusion about whether one company is a better value.)

Solution to 1:

	($ millions)	
	SCHW	AMTD
Total stockholders' equity	$20,097	$7,936
Less: Goodwill	$1,227	$4,198
Book value, adjusted	$18,870	$3,738
Adjusted MV/BV	**3.6**	**8.9**

	($ millions)	
	SCHW	AMTD
Total stockholders' equity	$20,097	$7,936
Less: Goodwill	$1,227	$4,198
Less: Other intangible assets	$93	$1,363
Tangible book value	$18,777	$2,375
MV/tangible book value	**3.7**	**14.0**

Solution to 2:

After adjusting for goodwill, SCHW appears to be selling for a much lower price relative to book value than does AMTD (3.6 versus 8.9) after adjusting for goodwill. The difference is more extreme after adjusting for other intangibles.

SUMMARY

This reading described selected applications of financial statement analysis, including the evaluation of past financial performance, the projection of future financial performance, the assessment of credit risk, and the screening of potential equity investments. In addition, the reading introduced analyst adjustments to reported financials. In all cases, the analyst needs to have a good understanding of the financial reporting standards under which the financial statements were prepared. Because standards evolve over time, analysts must stay current in order to make good investment decisions.

The main points in the reading are as follows:

- Evaluating a company's historical performance addresses not only what happened but also the causes behind the company's performance and how the performance reflects the company's strategy.
- The projection of a company's future net income and cash flow often begins with a top-down sales forecast in which the analyst forecasts industry sales and the company's market share. By projecting profit margins or expenses and the level of investment in working and fixed capital needed to support projected sales, the analyst can forecast net income and cash flow.
- Projections of future performance are needed for discounted cash flow valuation of equity and are often needed in credit analysis to assess a borrower's ability to repay interest and principal of a debt obligation.
- Credit analysis uses financial statement analysis to evaluate credit-relevant factors, including tolerance for leverage, operational stability, and margin stability.
- When ratios constructed from financial statement data and market data are used to screen for potential equity investments, fundamental decisions include which metrics to use as screens, how many metrics to include, what values of those metrics to use as cutoff points, and what weighting to give each metric.
- Analyst adjustments to a company's reported financial statements are sometimes necessary (e.g., when comparing companies that use different accounting methods or assumptions). Adjustments can include those related to investments; inventory; property, plant, and equipment; and goodwill.

REFERENCES

Benninga, Simon Z., and Oded H. Sarig. 1997. *Corporate Finance: A Valuation Approach*. New York: McGraw-Hill Publishing.

Conrad, J., M. Cooper, and G. Kaul. 2003. "Value versus Glamour." *Journal of Finance*, vol. 58, no. 5:1969–1996.

Haugen, R.A., and N.L. Baker. 1996. "Commonality in the Determinants of Expected Stock Returns." *Journal of Financial Economics*, vol. 41, no. 3:401–439.

PRACTICE PROBLEMS

1 Projecting profit margins into the future on the basis of past results would be *most* reliable when the company:

A is in the commodities business.

B operates in a single business segment.

C is a large, diversified company operating in mature industries.

2 Galambos Corporation had an average receivables collection period of 19 days in 2003. Galambos has stated that it wants to decrease its collection period in 2004 to match the industry average of 15 days. Credit sales in 2003 were \$300 million, and analysts expect credit sales to increase to \$400 million in 2004. To achieve the company's goal of decreasing the collection period, the change in the average accounts receivable balance from 2003 to 2004 that must occur is *closest* to:

A –\$420,000.

B \$420,000.

C \$836,000.

3 Credit analysts are likely to consider which of the following in making a rating recommendation?

A Business risk but not financial risk

B Financial risk but not business risk

C Both business risk and financial risk

4 When screening for potential equity investments based on return on equity, to control risk, an analyst would be *most likely* to include a criterion that requires:

A positive net income.

B negative net income.

C negative shareholders' equity.

5 One concern when screening for stocks with low price-to-earnings ratios is that companies with low P/Es may be financially weak. What criterion might an analyst include to avoid inadvertently selecting weak companies?

A Net income less than zero

B Debt-to-total assets ratio below a certain cutoff point

C Current-year sales growth lower than prior-year sales growth

6 When a database eliminates companies that cease to exist because of a merger or bankruptcy, this can result in:

A look-ahead bias.

B back-testing bias.

C survivorship bias.

7 In a comprehensive financial analysis, financial statements should be:

A used as reported without adjustment.

B adjusted after completing ratio analysis.

C adjusted for differences in accounting standards, such as international financial reporting standards and US generally accepted accounting principles.

© 2019 CFA Institute. All rights reserved.

8 When comparing a US company that uses the last in, first out (LIFO) method of inventory with companies that prepare their financial statements under international financial reporting standards (IFRS), analysts should be aware that according to IFRS, the LIFO method of inventory:

A is never acceptable.

B is always acceptable.

C is acceptable when applied to finished goods inventory only.

9 An analyst is evaluating the balance sheet of a US company that uses last in, first out (LIFO) accounting for inventory. The analyst collects the following data:

	31 Dec 05	31 Dec 06
Inventory reported on balance sheet	$500,000	$600,000
LIFO reserve	$ 50,000	$70,000
Average tax rate	30%	30%

After adjusting the amounts to convert to the first in, first out (FIFO) method, inventory at 31 December 2006 would be closest to:

A $600,000.

B $620,000.

C $670,000.

10 An analyst gathered the following data for a company ($ millions):

	31 Dec 2000	31 Dec 2001
Gross investment in fixed assets	$2.8	$2.8
Accumulated depreciation	$1.2	$1.6

The average age and average depreciable life of the company's fixed assets at the end of 2001 are *closest* to:

	Average Age	Average Depreciable Life
A	1.75 years	7 years
B	1.75 years	14 years
C	4.00 years	7 years

11 To compute tangible book value, an analyst would:

A add goodwill to stockholders' equity.

B add all intangible assets to stockholders' equity.

C subtract all intangible assets from stockholders' equity.

12 Which of the following is an off-balance-sheet financing technique? The use of:

A capital leases.

B operating leases.

C the last in, first out inventory method.

13 To better evaluate the solvency of a company, an analyst would most likely add to total liabilities:

A the present value of future capital lease payments.

B the total amount of future operating lease payments.

C the present value of future operating lease payments.

SOLUTIONS

1 C is correct. For a large, diversified company, margin changes in different business segments may offset each other. Furthermore, margins are most likely to be stable in mature industries.

2 C is correct. Accounts receivable turnover is equal to 365/19 (collection period in days) = 19.2 for 2003 and needs to equal 365/15 = 24.3 in 2004 for Galambos to meet its goal. Sales/turnover equals the accounts receivable balance. For 2003, \$300,000,000/19.2 = \$15,625,000, and for 2004, \$400,000,000/24.3 = \$16,460,905. The difference of \$835,905 is the increase in receivables needed for Galambos to achieve its goal.

3 C is correct. Credit analysts consider both business risk and financial risk.

4 A is correct. Requiring that net income be positive would eliminate companies that report a positive return on equity only because both net income and shareholders' equity are negative.

5 B is correct. A lower value of debt/total assets indicates greater financial strength. Requiring that a company's debt/total assets be below a certain cutoff point would allow the analyst to screen out highly leveraged and, therefore, potentially financially weak companies.

6 C is correct. Survivorship bias exists when companies that merge or go bankrupt are dropped from the database and only surviving companies remain. Look-ahead bias involves using updated financial information in back-testing that would not have been available at the time the decision was made. Back-testing involves testing models in prior periods and is not, itself, a bias.

7 C is correct. Financial statements should be adjusted for differences in accounting standards (as well as accounting and operating choices). These adjustments should be made prior to common-size and ratio analysis.

8 A is correct. LIFO is not permitted under IFRS.

9 C is correct. To convert LIFO inventory to FIFO inventory, the entire LIFO reserve must be added back: \$600,000 + \$70,000 = \$670,000.

10 C is correct. The company made no additions to or deletions from the fixed asset account during the year, so depreciation expense is equal to the difference in accumulated depreciation at the beginning of the year and the end of the year, or \$0.4 million. Average age is equal to accumulated depreciation/depreciation expense, or \$1.6/\$0.4 = 4 years. Average depreciable life is equal to ending gross investment/depreciation expense = \$2.8/\$0.4 = 7 years.

11 C is correct. Tangible book value removes all intangible assets, including goodwill, from the balance sheet.

12 B is correct. Operating leases can be used as an off-balance-sheet financing technique because neither the asset nor liability appears on the balance sheet. Inventory and capital leases are reported on the balance sheet.

13 C is correct. The present value of future operating lease payments would be added to total assets and total liabilities.

Glossary

A priori probability A probability based on logical analysis rather than on observation or personal judgment.

Abnormal return The amount by which a security's actual return differs from its expected return, given the security's risk and the market's return.

Absolute advantage A country's ability to produce a good or service at a lower absolute cost than its trading partner.

Absolute dispersion The amount of variability present without comparison to any reference point or benchmark.

Absolute frequency The number of observations in a given interval (for grouped data).

Accelerated book build An offering of securities by an investment bank acting as principal that is accomplished in only one or two days.

Accelerated methods Depreciation methods that allocate a relatively large proportion of the cost of an asset to the early years of the asset's useful life.

Accounting costs Monetary value of economic resources used in performing an activity. These can be explicit, out-of-pocket, current payments, or an allocation of historical payments (depreciation) for resources. They do not include implicit opportunity costs.

Accounting profit Income as reported on the income statement, in accordance with prevailing accounting standards, before the provisions for income tax expense. Also called *income before taxes* or *pretax income*.

Accounts payable Amounts that a business owes to its vendors for goods and services that were purchased from them but which have not yet been paid.

Accounts receivable turnover Ratio of sales on credit to the average balance in accounts receivable.

Accrued expenses Liabilities related to expenses that have been incurred but not yet paid as of the end of an accounting period—an example of an accrued expense is rent that has been incurred but not yet paid, resulting in a liability "rent payable." Also called *accrued liabilities*.

Accrued interest Interest earned but not yet paid.

Acid-test ratio A stringent measure of liquidity that indicates a company's ability to satisfy current liabilities with its most liquid assets, calculated as (cash + short-term marketable investments + receivables) divided by current liabilities.

Acquisition method A method of accounting for a business combination where the acquirer is required to measure each identifiable asset and liability at fair value. This method was the result of a joint project of the IASB and FASB aiming at convergence in standards for the accounting of business combinations.

Action lag Delay from policy decisions to implementation.

Active investment An approach to investing in which the investor seeks to outperform a given benchmark.

Active return The return on a portfolio minus the return on the portfolio's benchmark.

Active strategy In reference to short-term cash management, an investment strategy characterized by monitoring and attempting to capitalize on market conditions to optimize the risk and return relationship of short-term investments.

Activity ratios Ratios that measure how efficiently a company performs day-to-day tasks, such as the collection of receivables and management of inventory. Also called *asset utilization ratios* or *operating efficiency ratios*.

Add-on rates Bank certificates of deposit, repos, and indexes such as Libor and Euribor are quoted on an add-on rate basis (bond equivalent yield basis).

Addition rule for probabilities A principle stating that the probability that *A* or *B* occurs (both occur) equals the probability that *A* occurs, plus the probability that *B* occurs, minus the probability that both *A* and *B* occur.

Agency bonds See *quasi-government bond*.

Agency RMBS In the United States, securities backed by residential mortgage loans and guaranteed by a federal agency or guaranteed by either of the two GSEs (Fannie Mae and Freddie Mac).

Aggregate demand The quantity of goods and services that households, businesses, government, and foreign customers want to buy at any given level of prices.

Aggregate demand curve Inverse relationship between the price level and real output.

Aggregate income The value of all the payments earned by the suppliers of factors used in the production of goods and services.

Aggregate output The value of all the goods and services produced in a specified period of time.

Aggregate supply The quantity of goods and services producers are willing to supply at any given level of price.

Aggregate supply curve The level of domestic output that companies will produce at each price level.

Aging schedule A breakdown of accounts into categories of days outstanding.

All-or-nothing (AON) orders An order that includes the instruction to trade only if the trade fills the entire quantity (size) specified.

Allocationally efficient A characteristic of a market, a financial system, or an economy that promotes the allocation of resources to their highest value uses.

Alternative data Non-traditional data types generated by the use of electronic devices, social media, satellite and sensor networks, and company exhaust.

Alternative investment markets Market for investments other than traditional securities investments (i.e., traditional common and preferred shares and traditional fixed income instruments). The term usually encompasses direct and indirect investment in real estate (including timberland and farmland) and commodities (including precious metals); hedge funds, private equity, and other investments requiring specialized due diligence.

Alternative trading systems Trading venues that function like exchanges but that do not exercise regulatory authority over their subscribers except with respect to the conduct of the subscribers' trading in their trading systems. Also called *electronic communications networks* or *multilateral trading facilities*.

American depository receipt A US dollar-denominated security that trades like a common share on US exchanges.

American depository share The underlying shares on which American depository receipts are based. They trade in the issuing company's domestic market.

American-style Type of option contract that can be exercised at any time up to the option's expiration date.

Amortisation The process of allocating the cost of intangible long-term assets having a finite useful life to accounting periods; the allocation of the amount of a bond premium or discount to the periods remaining until bond maturity.

Amortised cost The historical cost (initially recognised cost) of an asset, adjusted for amortisation and impairment.

Amortizing bond Bond with a payment schedule that calls for periodic payments of interest and repayments of principal.

Amortizing loan Loan with a payment schedule that calls for periodic payments of interest and repayments of principal.

Annual percentage rate The cost of borrowing expressed as a yearly rate.

Annuity A finite set of level sequential cash flows.

Annuity due An annuity having a first cash flow that is paid immediately.

Anticipation stock Excess inventory that is held in anticipation of increased demand, often because of seasonal patterns of demand.

Antidilutive With reference to a transaction or a security, one that would increase earnings per share (EPS) or result in EPS higher than the company's basic EPS—antidilutive securities are not included in the calculation of diluted EPS.

Arbitrage 1) The simultaneous purchase of an undervalued asset or portfolio and sale of an overvalued but equivalent asset or portfolio, in order to obtain a riskless profit on the price differential. Taking advantage of a market inefficiency in a risk-free manner. 2) The condition in a financial market in which equivalent assets or combinations of assets sell for two different prices, creating an opportunity to profit at no risk with no commitment of money. In a well-functioning financial market, few arbitrage opportunities are possible. 3) A risk-free operation that earns an expected positive net profit but requires no net investment of money.

Arbitrage-free pricing The overall process of pricing derivatives by arbitrage and risk neutrality. Also called the *principle of no arbitrage.*

Arbitrageurs Traders who engage in arbitrage. See *arbitrage.*

Arithmetic mean The sum of the observations divided by the number of observations.

Arms index A flow of funds indicator applied to a broad stock market index to measure the relative extent to which money is moving into or out of rising and declining stocks.

Artificial intelligence Computer systems that exhibit cognitive and decision-making ability comparable (or superior) to that of humans.

Asian call option A European-style option with a value at maturity equal to the difference between the stock price at maturity and the average stock price during the life of the option, or $0, whichever is greater.

Ask The price at which a dealer or trader is willing to sell an asset, typically qualified by a maximum quantity (ask size). See *offer.*

Ask size The maximum quantity of an asset that pertains to a specific ask price from a trader. For example, if the ask for a share issue is $30 for a size of 1,000 shares, the trader is offering to sell at $30 up to 1,000 shares.

Asset allocation The process of determining how investment funds should be distributed among asset classes.

Asset-backed securities A type of bond issued by a legal entity called a *special purpose entity* (SPE) on a collection of assets that the SPE owns. Also, securities backed by receivables and loans other than mortgages.

Asset-based loan A loan that is secured with company assets.

Asset-based valuation models Valuation based on estimates of the market value of a company's assets.

Asset beta The unlevered beta; reflects the business risk of the assets; the asset's systematic risk.

Asset class A group of assets that have similar characteristics, attributes, and risk/return relationships.

Asset swap Converts the periodic fixed coupon of a specific bond to a Libor plus or minus a spread.

Asset utilization ratios Ratios that measure how efficiently a company performs day-to-day tasks, such as the collection of receivables and management of inventory.

Assets Resources controlled by an enterprise as a result of past events and from which future economic benefits to the enterprise are expected to flow.

Assignment of accounts receivable The use of accounts receivable as collateral for a loan.

At the money An option in which the underlying's price equals the exercise price.

Auction A type of bond issuing mechanism often used for sovereign bonds that involves bidding.

Autarkic price The price of a good or service in an autarkic economy.

Autarky A state in which a country does not trade with other countries.

Automated Clearing House (ACH) An electronic payment network available to businesses, individuals, and financial institutions in the United States, US Territories, and Canada.

Automatic stabilizer A countercyclical factor that automatically comes into play as an economy slows and unemployment rises.

Available-for-sale Under US GAAP, debt securities not classified as either held-to-maturity or held-for-trading securities. The investor is willing to sell but not actively planning to sell. In general, available-for-sale debt securities are reported at fair value on the balance sheet, with unrealized gains included as a component of other comprehensive income.

Average accounting rate of return (ARR) Over the life of a project, the AAR can be defined as the average net income divided by the average book value.

Average fixed cost Total fixed cost divided by quantity produced.

Average life See *weighted average life.*

Average product Measures the productivity of inputs on average and is calculated by dividing total product by the total number of units for a given input that is used to generate that output.

Average revenue Total revenue divided by quantity sold.

Average total cost Total cost divided by quantity produced.

Average variable cost Total variable cost divided by quantity produced.

Back simulation Another term for the historical method of estimating VaR. This term is somewhat misleading in that the method involves not a *simulation* of the past but rather what *actually happened* in the past, sometimes adjusted to reflect the fact that a different portfolio may have existed in the past than is planned for the future.

Back-testing With reference to portfolio strategies, the application of a strategy's portfolio selection rules to historical data to assess what would have been the strategy's historical performance.

Backup lines of credit A type of credit enhancement provided by a bank to an issuer of commercial paper to ensure that the issuer will have access to sufficient liquidity to repay maturing commercial paper if issuing new paper is not a viable option.

Balance of payments A double-entry bookkeeping system that summarizes a country's economic transactions with the rest of the world for a particular period of time, typically a calendar quarter or year.

Balance of trade deficit When the domestic economy is spending more on foreign goods and services than foreign economies are spending on domestic goods and services.

Balance sheet The financial statement that presents an entity's current financial position by disclosing resources the entity controls (its assets) and the claims on those resources (its liabilities and equity claims), as of a particular point in time (the date of the balance sheet). Also called *statement of financial position* or *statement of financial condition*.

Balance sheet ratios Financial ratios involving balance sheet items only.

Balanced With respect to a government budget, one in which spending and revenues (taxes) are equal.

Balloon payment Large payment required at maturity to retire a bond's outstanding principal amount.

Bar chart A price chart with four bits of data for each time interval—the high, low, opening, and closing prices. A vertical line connects the high and low. A cross-hatch left indicates the opening price and a cross-hatch right indicates the close.

Barter economy An economy where economic agents as house-holds, corporations, and governments "pay" for goods and services with another good or service.

Base rates The reference rate on which a bank bases lending rates to all other customers.

Basic EPS Net earnings available to common shareholders (i.e., net income minus preferred dividends) divided by the weighted average number of common shares outstanding.

Basis point Used in stating yield spreads, one basis point equals one-hundredth of a percentage point, or 0.01%.

Basket of listed depository receipts An exchange-traded fund (ETF) that represents a portfolio of depository receipts.

Bearer bonds Bonds for which ownership is not recorded; only the clearing system knows who the bond owner is.

Behavioral finance A field of finance that examines the psychological variables that affect and often distort the investment decision making of investors, analysts, and portfolio managers.

Behind the market Said of prices specified in orders that are worse than the best current price; e.g., for a limit buy order, a limit price below the best bid.

Benchmark A comparison portfolio; a point of reference or comparison.

Benchmark issue The latest sovereign bond issue for a given maturity. It serves as a benchmark against which to compare bonds that have the same features but that are issued by another type of issuer.

Benchmark rate Typically the yield-to-maturity on a government bond having the same, or close to the same, time-to-maturity.

Benchmark spread The yield spread over a specific benchmark, usually measured in basis points.

Bernoulli random variable A random variable having the outcomes 0 and 1.

Bernoulli trial An experiment that can produce one of two outcomes.

Best bid The highest bid in the market.

Best effort offering An offering of a security using an investment bank in which the investment bank, as agent for the issuer, promises to use its best efforts to sell the offering but does not guarantee that a specific amount will be sold.

Best-in-class An ESG implementation approach that seeks to identify the most favorable companies in an industry based on ESG considerations.

Best offer The lowest offer (ask price) in the market.

Beta A measure of the sensitivity of a given investment or portfolio to movements in the overall market.

Bid The price at which a dealer or trader is willing to buy an asset, typically qualified by a maximum quantity.

Bid–ask spread The difference between the prices at which dealers will buy from a customer (bid) and sell to a customer (offer or ask). It is often used as an indicator of liquidity.

Bid–offer spread The difference between the prices at which dealers will buy from a customer (bid) and sell to a customer (offer or ask). It is often used as an indicator of liquidity.

Bid size The maximum quantity of an asset that pertains to a specific bid price from a trader.

Big Data The vast amount of data being generated by industry, governments, individuals, and electronic devices that arises from both traditional and non-traditional data sources.

Bilateral loan A loan from a single lender to a single borrower.

Binomial model A model for pricing options in which the underlying price can move to only one of two possible new prices.

Binomial random variable The number of successes in n Bernoulli trials for which the probability of success is constant for all trials and the trials are independent.

Binomial tree The graphical representation of a model of asset price dynamics in which, at each period, the asset moves up with probability p or down with probability $(1 - p)$.

Bitcoin A cryptocurrency using blockchain technology that was created in 2009.

Block brokers A broker (agent) that provides brokerage services for large-size trades.

Blockchain A type of digital ledger in which information is recorded sequentially and then linked together and secured using cryptographic methods.

Blue chip Widely held large market capitalization companies that are considered financially sound and are leaders in their respective industry or local stock market.

Bollinger Bands A price-based technical analysis indicator consisting of a moving average plus a higher line representing the moving average plus a set number of standard deviations from average price (for the same number of periods as used to calculate the moving average) and a lower line that is a moving average minus the same number of standard deviations.

Bond Contractual agreement between the issuer and the bondholders.

Bond equivalent yield A calculation of yield that is annualized using the ratio of 365 to the number of days to maturity. Bond equivalent yield allows for the restatement and comparison of securities with different compounding periods.

Bond indenture The governing legal credit agreement, typically incorporated by reference in the prospectus. Also called *trust deed.*

Bond market vigilantes Bond market participants who might reduce their demand for long-term bonds, thus pushing up their yields.

Bond yield plus risk premium approach An estimate of the cost of common equity that is produced by summing the before-tax cost of debt and a risk premium that captures the additional yield on a company's stock relative to its bonds. The additional yield is often estimated using historical spreads between bond yields and stock yields.

Bonus issue of shares A type of dividend in which a company distributes additional shares of its common stock to shareholders instead of cash.

Book building Investment bankers' process of compiling a "book" or list of indications of interest to buy part of an offering.

Book value The net amount shown for an asset or liability on the balance sheet; book value may also refer to the company's excess of total assets over total liabilities. Also called *carrying value.*

Boom An expansionary phase characterized by economic growth "testing the limits" of the economy.

Bottom-up analysis An investment selection approach that focuses on company-specific circumstances rather than emphasizing economic cycles or industry analysis.

Break point In the context of the weighted average cost of capital (WACC), a break point is the amount of capital at which the cost of one or more of the sources of capital changes, leading to a change in the WACC.

Breakeven point The number of units produced and sold at which the company's net income is zero (Revenues = Total cost); in the case of perfect competition, the quantity at which price, average revenue, and marginal revenue equal average total cost.

Bridge financing Interim financing that provides funds until permanent financing can be arranged.

Broad money Encompasses narrow money plus the entire range of liquid assets that can be used to make purchases.

Broker 1) An agent who executes orders to buy or sell securities on behalf of a client in exchange for a commission. 2) See *futures commission merchants.*

Broker–dealer A financial intermediary (often a company) that may function as a principal (dealer) or as an agent (broker) depending on the type of trade.

Brokered market A market in which brokers arrange trades among their clients.

Budget surplus/deficit The difference between government revenue and expenditure for a stated fixed period of time.

Bullet bond Bond in which the principal repayment is made entirely at maturity.

Business risk The risk associated with operating earnings. Operating earnings are uncertain because total revenues and many of the expenditures contributed to produce those revenues are uncertain.

Buy-side firm An investment management company or other investor that uses the services of brokers or dealers (i.e., the client of the sell side firms).

Buyback A transaction in which a company buys back its own shares. Unlike stock dividends and stock splits, share repurchases use corporate cash.

Call An option that gives the holder the right to buy an underlying asset from another party at a fixed price over a specific period of time.

Call market A market in which trades occur only at a particular time and place (i.e., when the market is called).

Call money rate The interest rate that buyers pay for their margin loan.

Call option An option that gives the holder the right to buy an underlying asset from another party at a fixed price over a specific period of time.

Call protection The time during which the issuer of the bond is not allowed to exercise the call option.

Callable bond A bond containing an embedded call option that gives the issuer the right to buy the bond back from the investor at specified prices on pre-determined dates.

Candlestick chart A price chart with four bits of data for each time interval. A candle indicates the opening and closing price for the interval. The body of the candle is shaded if the opening price was higher than the closing price, and the body is clear if the opening price was lower than the closing price. Vertical lines known as wicks or shadows extend from the top and bottom of the candle to indicate the high and the low prices for the interval.

Cannibalization Cannibalization occurs when an investment takes customers and sales away from another part of the company.

Capacity The ability of the borrower to make its debt payments on time.

Capital account A component of the balance of payments account that measures transfers of capital.

Capital allocation line (CAL) A graph line that describes the combinations of expected return and standard deviation of return available to an investor from combining the optimal portfolio of risky assets with the risk-free asset.

Capital asset pricing model (CAPM) An equation describing the expected return on any asset (or portfolio) as a linear function of its beta relative to the market portfolio.

Capital budgeting The process that companies use for decision making on capital projects—those projects with a life of one year or more.

Capital consumption allowance A measure of the wear and tear (depreciation) of the capital stock that occurs in the production of goods and services.

Capital deepening investment Increases the stock of capital relative to labor.

Capital expenditure Expenditure on physical capital (fixed assets).

Capital lease See *finance lease.*

Capital market expectations An investor's expectations concerning the risk and return prospects of asset classes.

Capital market line (CML) The line with an intercept point equal to the risk-free rate that is tangent to the efficient frontier of risky assets; represents the efficient frontier when a risk-free asset is available for investment.

Capital market securities Securities with maturities at issuance longer than one year.

Capital markets Financial markets that trade securities of longer duration, such as bonds and equities.

Capital rationing A capital rationing environment assumes that the company has a fixed amount of funds to invest.

Capital restrictions Controls placed on foreigners' ability to own domestic assets and/or domestic residents' ability to own foreign assets.

Capital stock The accumulated amount of buildings, machinery, and equipment used to produce goods and services.

Capital structure The mix of debt and equity that a company uses to finance its business; a company's specific mixture of long-term financing.

Captive finance subsidiary A wholly-owned subsidiary of a company that is established to provide financing of the sales of the parent company.

Carry The net of the costs and benefits of holding, storing, or "carrying" an asset.

Carrying amount The amount at which an asset or liability is valued according to accounting principles.

Carrying value The net amount shown for an asset or liability on the balance sheet; book value may also refer to the company's excess of total assets over total liabilities. For a bond, the purchase price plus (or minus) the amortized amount of the discount (or premium).

Cartel Participants in collusive agreements that are made openly and formally.

Cash collateral account Form of external credit enhancement whereby the issuer immediately borrows the credit-enhancement amount and then invests that amount, usually in highly rated short-term commercial paper.

Cash conversion cycle A financial metric that measures the length of time required for a company to convert cash invested in its operations to cash received as a result of its operations; equal to days of inventory on hand + days of sales outstanding – number of days of payables. Also called *net operating cycle.*

Cash flow additivity principle The principle that dollar amounts indexed at the same point in time are additive.

Cash flow from operating activities The net amount of cash provided from operating activities.

Cash flow from operations The net amount of cash provided from operating activities.

Cash flow yield The internal rate of return on a series of cash flows.

Cash market securities Money market securities settled on a "same day" or "cash settlement" basis.

Cash markets See *spot markets.*

Cash prices See *spot prices.*

Cash-settled forwards See *non-deliverable forwards.*

CBOE Volatility Index A measure of near-term market volatility as conveyed by S&P 500 stock index option prices.

Central bank funds market The market in which deposit-taking banks that have an excess reserve with their national central bank can loan money to banks that need funds for maturities ranging from overnight to one year. Called the Federal or Fed funds market in the United States.

Central bank funds rates Interest rates at which central bank funds are bought (borrowed) and sold (lent) for maturities ranging from overnight to one year. Called Federal or Fed funds rates in the United States.

Central banks The dominant bank in a country, usually with official or semi-official governmental status.

Certificate of deposit An instrument that represents a specified amount of funds on deposit with a bank for a specified maturity and interest rate. CDs are issued in various denominations and can be negotiable or non-negotiable.

Change in polarity principle A tenet of technical analysis that once a support level is breached, it becomes a resistance level. The same holds true for resistance levels; once breached, they become support levels.

Change of control put A covenant giving bondholders the right to require the issuer to buy back their debt, often at par or at some small premium to par value, in the event that the borrower is acquired.

Character The quality of a debt issuer's management.

Classified balance sheet A balance sheet organized so as to group together the various assets and liabilities into subcategories (e.g., current and noncurrent).

Clawback A requirement that the general partner return any funds distributed as incentive fees until the limited partners have received back their initial investment and a percentage of the total profit.

Clearing The process by which the exchange verifies the execution of a transaction and records the participants' identities.

Clearing instructions Instructions that indicate how to arrange the final settlement ("clearing") of a trade.

Clearinghouse An entity associated with a futures market that acts as middleman between the contracting parties and guarantees to each party the performance of the other.

Closed economy An economy that does not trade with other countries; an *autarkic economy.*

Closed-end fund A mutual fund in which no new investment money is accepted. New investors invest by buying existing shares, and investors in the fund liquidate by selling their shares to other investors.

Code of ethics An established guide that communicates an organization's values and overall expectations regarding member behavior. A code of ethics serves as a general guide for how community members should act.

Coefficient of variation (CV) The ratio of a set of observations' standard deviation to the observations' mean value.

Coincident economic indicators Turning points that are usually close to those of the overall economy; they are believed to have value for identifying the economy's present state.

Collateral manager Buys and sells debt obligations for and from the CDO's portfolio of assets (i.e., the collateral) to generate sufficient cash flows to meet the obligations to the CDO bondholders.

Collateral trust bonds Bonds secured by securities such as common shares, other bonds, or other financial assets.

Collateralized bond obligations A structured asset-backed security that is collateralized by a pool of bonds.

Collateralized debt obligation Generic term used to describe a security backed by a diversified pool of one or more debt obligations.

Collateralized loan obligations A structured asset-backed security that is collateralized by a pool of loans.

Collateralized mortgage obligation A security created through the securitization of a pool of mortgage-related products (mortgage pass-through securities or pools of loans).

Collaterals Assets or financial guarantees underlying a debt obligation that are above and beyond the issuer's promise to pay.

Combination A listing in which the order of the listed items does not matter.

Commercial paper A short-term, negotiable, unsecured promissory note that represents a debt obligation of the issuer.

Committed capital The amount that the limited partners have agreed to provide to the private equity fund.

Committed lines of credit A bank commitment to extend credit up to a pre-specified amount; the commitment is considered a short-term liability and is usually in effect for 364 days (one day short of a full year).

Commodity swap A swap in which the underlying is a commodity such as oil, gold, or an agricultural product.

Common market Level of economic integration that incorporates all aspects of the customs union and extends it by allowing free movement of factors of production among members.

Common shares A type of security that represent an ownership interest in a company.

Common-size analysis The restatement of financial statement items using a common denominator or reference item that allows one to identify trends and major differences; an example is an income statement in which all items are expressed as a percent of revenue.

Common stock See *common shares.*

Company analysis Analysis of an individual company.

Comparable company A company that has similar business risk; usually in the same industry and preferably with a single line of business.

Comparative advantage A country's ability to produce a good or service at a lower relative cost, or opportunity cost, than its trading partner.

Competitive strategy A company's plans for responding to the threats and opportunities presented by the external environment.

Complements Goods that tend to be used together; technically, two goods whose cross-price elasticity of demand is negative.

Complete markets Informally, markets in which the variety of distinct securities traded is so broad that any desired payoff in a future state-of-the-world is achievable.

Component cost of capital The rate of return required by suppliers of capital for an individual source of a company's funding, such as debt or equity.

Compounding The process of accumulating interest on interest.

Comprehensive income The change in equity of a business enterprise during a period from nonowner sources; includes all changes in equity during a period except those resulting from investments by owners and distributions to owners; comprehensive income equals net income plus other comprehensive income.

Conditional expected value The expected value of a stated event given that another event has occurred.

Conditional probability The probability of an event given (conditioned on) another event.

Conditional variances The variance of one variable, given the outcome of another.

Consistent With reference to estimators, describes an estimator for which the probability of estimates close to the value of the population parameter increases as sample size increases.

Constant-yield price trajectory A graph that illustrates the change in the price of a fixed-income bond over time assuming no change in yield-to-maturity. The trajectory shows the "pull to par" effect on the price of a bond trading at a premium or a discount to par value.

Constituent securities With respect to an index, the individual securities within an index.

Consumer surplus The difference between the value that a consumer places on units purchased and the amount of money that was required to pay for them.

Contingency provision Clause in a legal document that allows for some action if a specific event or circumstance occurs.

Contingent claims Derivatives in which the payoffs occur if a specific event occurs; generally referred to as options.

Contingent convertible bonds Bonds that automatically convert into equity if a specific event or circumstance occurs, such as the issuer's equity capital falling below the minimum requirement set by the regulators. Also called *CoCos.*

Continuation patterns A type of pattern used in technical analysis to predict the resumption of a market trend that was in place prior to the formation of a pattern.

Continuous random variable A random variable for which the range of possible outcomes is the real line (all real numbers between $-\infty$ and $+\infty$ or some subset of the real line).

Continuous time Time thought of as advancing in extremely small increments.

Continuous trading market A market in which trades can be arranged and executed any time the market is open.

Continuously compounded return The natural logarithm of 1 plus the holding period return, or equivalently, the natural logarithm of the ending price over the beginning price.

Contra account An account that offsets another account.

Contract rate See *mortgage rate.*

Contraction The period of a business cycle after the peak and before the trough; often called a *recession* or, if exceptionally severe, called a *depression.*

Contraction risk The risk that when interest rates decline, the security will have a shorter maturity than was anticipated at the time of purchase because borrowers refinance at the new, lower interest rates.

Contractionary Tending to cause the real economy to contract.

Contractionary fiscal policy A fiscal policy that has the objective to make the real economy contract.

Contracts for differences See *non-deliverable forwards.*

Contribution margin The amount available for fixed costs and profit after paying variable costs; revenue minus variable costs.

Controlling shareholders A particular shareholder or block of shareholders holding a percentage of shares that gives them significant voting power.

Convenience yield A non-monetary advantage of holding an asset.

Conventional bond See *plain vanilla bond.*

Conventional cash flow A conventional cash flow pattern is one with an initial outflow followed by a series of inflows.

Convergence The tendency for differences in output per capita across countries to diminish over time; in technical analysis, a term that describes the case when an indicator moves in the same manner as the security being analyzed.

Conversion price For a convertible bond, the price per share at which the bond can be converted into shares.

Conversion ratio For a convertible bond, the number of common shares that each bond can be converted into.

Conversion value For a convertible bond, the current share price multiplied by the conversion ratio.

Convertible bond Bond that gives the bondholder the right to exchange the bond for a specified number of common shares in the issuing company.

Convertible preference shares A type of equity security that entitles shareholders to convert their shares into a specified number of common shares.

Convexity adjustment For a bond, one half of the annual or approximate convexity statistic multiplied by the change in the yield-to-maturity squared.

Core inflation The inflation rate calculated based on a price index of goods and services except food and energy.

Corporate governance The system of internal controls and procedures by which individual companies are managed.

Correlation A number between −1 and +1 that measures the comovement (linear association) between two random variables.

Correlation coefficient A number between −1 and +1 that measures the consistency or tendency for two investments to act in a similar way. It is used to determine the effect on portfolio risk when two assets are combined.

Cost averaging The periodic investment of a fixed amount of money.

Cost of capital The rate of return that suppliers of capital require as compensation for their contribution of capital.

Cost of carry See *carry*.

Cost of debt The cost of debt financing to a company, such as when it issues a bond or takes out a bank loan.

Cost of preferred stock The cost to a company of issuing preferred stock; the dividend yield that a company must commit to pay preferred stockholders.

Cost-push Type of inflation in which rising costs, usually wages, compel businesses to raise prices generally.

Cost structure The mix of a company's variable costs and fixed costs.

Counterparty risk The risk that the other party to a contract will fail to honor the terms of the contract.

Coupon rate The interest rate promised in a contract; this is the rate used to calculate the periodic interest payments.

Cournot assumption Assumption in which each firm determines its profit-maximizing production level assuming that the other firms' output will not change.

Covariance A measure of the co-movement (linear association) between two random variables.

Covariance matrix A matrix or square array whose entries are covariances; also known as a variance–covariance matrix.

Covenants The terms and conditions of lending agreements that the issuer must comply with; they specify the actions that an issuer is obligated to perform (affirmative covenant) or prohibited from performing (negative covenant).

Covered bond Debt obligation secured by a segregated pool of assets called the cover pool. The issuer must maintain the value of the cover pool. In the event of default, bondholders have recourse against both the issuer and the cover pool.

Credit analysis The evaluation of credit risk; the evaluation of the creditworthiness of a borrower or counterparty.

Credit curve A curve showing the relationship between time to maturity and yield spread for an issuer with comparable bonds of various maturities outstanding, usually upward sloping.

Credit default swap (CDS) A type of credit derivative in which one party, the credit protection buyer who is seeking credit protection against a third party, makes a series of regularly scheduled payments to the other party, the credit protection seller. The seller makes no payments until a credit event occurs.

Credit derivatives A contract in which one party has the right to claim a payment from another party in the event that a specific credit event occurs over the life of the contract.

Credit enhancements Provisions that may be used to reduce the credit risk of a bond issue.

Credit-linked coupon bond Bond for which the coupon changes when the bond's credit rating changes.

Credit-linked note (CLN) Fixed-income security in which the holder of the security has the right to withhold payment of the full amount due at maturity if a credit event occurs.

Credit migration risk The risk that a bond issuer's creditworthiness deteriorates, or migrates lower, leading investors to believe the risk of default is higher. Also called *downgrade risk*.

Credit risk The risk of loss caused by a counterparty's or debtor's failure to make a promised payment. Also called *default risk*.

Credit scoring model A statistical model used to classify borrowers according to creditworthiness.

Credit spread option An option on the yield spread on a bond.

Credit tranching A structure used to redistribute the credit risk associated with the collateral; a set of bond classes created to allow investors a choice in the amount of credit risk that they prefer to bear.

Credit-worthiness The perceived ability of the borrower to pay what is owed on the borrowing in a timely manner; it represents the ability of a company to withstand adverse impacts on its cash flows.

Cross-default provisions Provisions whereby events of default such as non-payment of interest on one bond trigger default on all outstanding debt; implies the same default probability for all issues.

Cross-price elasticity of demand The percentage change in quantity demanded for a given percentage change in the price of another good; the responsiveness of the demand for Product A that is associated with the change in price of Product B.

Cross-sectional analysis Analysis that involves comparisons across individuals in a group over a given time period or at a given point in time.

Cross-sectional data Observations over individual units at a point in time, as opposed to time-series data.

Crossing networks Trading systems that match buyers and sellers who are willing to trade at prices obtained from other markets.

Crowding out The thesis that government borrowing may divert private sector investment from taking place.

Cryptocurrency An electronic medium of exchange that lacks physical form.

Cryptography An algorithmic process to encrypt data, making the data unusable if received by unauthorized parties.

Cumulative distribution function A function giving the probability that a random variable is less than or equal to a specified value.

Cumulative preference shares Preference shares for which any dividends that are not paid accrue and must be paid in full before dividends on common shares can be paid.

Cumulative relative frequency For data grouped into intervals, the fraction of total observations that are less than the value of the upper limit of a stated interval.

Cumulative voting A voting process whereby each shareholder can accumulate and vote all his or her shares for a single candidate in an election, as opposed to having to allocate their voting rights evenly among all candidates.

Currencies Monies issued by national monetary authorities.

Currency option bonds Bonds that give the bondholder the right to choose the currency in which he or she wants to receive interest payments and principal repayments.

Currency swap A swap in which each party makes interest payments to the other in different currencies.

Current account A component of the balance of payments account that measures the flow of goods and services.

Current assets Assets that are expected to be consumed or converted into cash in the near future, typically one year or less. *Also called liquid assets.*

Current cost With reference to assets, the amount of cash or cash equivalents that would have to be paid to buy the same or an equivalent asset today; with reference to liabilities, the undiscounted amount of cash or cash equivalents that would be required to settle the obligation today.

Current government spending With respect to government expenditures, spending on goods and services that are provided on a regular, recurring basis including health, education, and defense.

Current liabilities Short-term obligations, such as accounts payable, wages payable, or accrued liabilities, that are expected to be settled in the near future, typically one year or less.

Current ratio A liquidity ratio calculated as current assets divided by current liabilities.

Current yield The sum of the coupon payments received over the year divided by the flat price; also called the *income* or *interest yield* or *running yield*.

Curve duration The sensitivity of the bond price (or the market value of a financial asset or liability) with respect to a benchmark yield curve.

Customs union Extends the free trade area (FTA) by not only allowing free movement of goods and services among members, but also creating a common trade policy against nonmembers.

CVaR Conditional VaR, a tail loss measure. The weighted average of all loss outcomes in the statistical distribution that exceed the VaR loss.

Cyclical See *cyclical companies.*

Cyclical companies Companies with sales and profits that regularly expand and contract with the business cycle or state of economy.

Daily settlement See *mark to market* and *marking to market.*

Dark pools Alternative trading systems that do not display the orders that their clients send to them.

Data mining The practice of determining a model by extensive searching through a dataset for statistically significant patterns. Also called *data snooping.*

Data science An interdisciplinary field that brings computer science, statistics, and other disciplines together to analyze and produce insights from Big Data.

Data snooping See *data mining.*

Day order An order that is good for the day on which it is submitted. If it has not been filled by the close of business, the order expires unfilled.

Day's sales outstanding Estimate of the average number of days it takes to collect on credit accounts.

Days in receivables Estimate of the average number of days it takes to collect on credit accounts.

Days of inventory on hand An activity ratio equal to the number of days in the period divided by inventory turnover over the period.

Dealers A financial intermediary that acts as a principal in trades.

Dealing securities Securities held by banks or other financial intermediaries for trading purposes.

Death cross A technical analysis term that describes a situation where a short-term moving average crosses from above a longer-term moving average to below it; this movement is considered bearish.

Debentures Type of bond that can be secured or unsecured.

Debt incurrence test A financial covenant made in conjunction with existing debt that restricts a company's ability to incur additional debt at the same seniority based on one or more financial tests or conditions.

Debt-rating approach A method for estimating a company's before-tax cost of debt based upon the yield on comparably rated bonds for maturities that closely match that of the company's existing debt.

Debt-to-assets ratio A solvency ratio calculated as total debt divided by total assets.

Debt-to-capital ratio A solvency ratio calculated as total debt divided by total debt plus total shareholders' equity.

Debt-to-equity ratio A solvency ratio calculated as total debt divided by total shareholders' equity.

Declaration date The day that the corporation issues a statement declaring a specific dividend.

Decreasing returns to scale When a production process leads to increases in output that are proportionately smaller than the increase in inputs.

Deductible temporary differences Temporary differences that result in a reduction of or deduction from taxable income in a future period when the balance sheet item is recovered or settled.

Deep learning Machine learning using neural networks with many hidden layers.

Deep learning nets Machine learning using neural networks with many hidden layers.

Default probability The probability that a borrower defaults or fails to meet its obligation to make full and timely payments of principal and interest, according to the terms of the debt security. Also called *default risk.*

Default risk The probability that a borrower defaults or fails to meet its obligation to make full and timely payments of principal and interest, according to the terms of the debt security. Also called *default probability.*

Default risk premium An extra return that compensates investors for the possibility that the borrower will fail to make a promised payment at the contracted time and in the contracted amount.

Defensive companies Companies with sales and profits that have little sensitivity to the business cycle or state of the economy.

Defensive interval ratio A liquidity ratio that estimates the number of days that an entity could meet cash needs from liquid assets; calculated as (cash + short-term marketable investments + receivables) divided by daily cash expenditures.

Deferred coupon bond Bond that pays no coupons for its first few years but then pays a higher coupon than it otherwise normally would for the remainder of its life. Also called *split coupon bond.*

Deferred income A liability account for money that has been collected for goods or services that have not yet been delivered; payment received in advance of providing a good or service.

Deferred revenue A liability account for money that has been collected for goods or services that have not yet been delivered; payment received in advance of providing a good or service.

Deferred tax assets A balance sheet asset that arises when an excess amount is paid for income taxes relative to accounting profit. The taxable income is higher than accounting profit and income tax payable exceeds tax expense. The company expects to recover the difference during the course of future operations when tax expense exceeds income tax payable.

Deferred tax liabilities A balance sheet liability that arises when a deficit amount is paid for income taxes relative to accounting profit. The taxable income is less than the accounting profit and income tax payable is less than tax expense. The company expects to eliminate the liability over the course of future operations when income tax payable exceeds tax expense.

Defined benefit pension plans Plans in which the company promises to pay a certain annual amount (defined benefit) to the employee after retirement. The company bears the investment risk of the plan assets.

Defined contribution pension plans Individual accounts to which an employee and typically the employer makes contributions during their working years and expect to draw on the accumulated funds at retirement. The employee bears the investment and inflation risk of the plan assets.

Deflation Negative inflation.

Degree of confidence The probability that a confidence interval includes the unknown population parameter.

Degree of financial leverage (DFL) The ratio of the percentage change in net income to the percentage change in operating income; the sensitivity of the cash flows available to owners when operating income changes.

Degree of operating leverage (DOL) The ratio of the percentage change in operating income to the percentage change in units sold; the sensitivity of operating income to changes in units sold.

Degree of total leverage The ratio of the percentage change in net income to the percentage change in units sold; the sensitivity of the cash flows to owners to changes in the number of units produced and sold.

Degrees of freedom (df) The number of independent observations used.

Delta The sensitivity of the derivative price to a small change in the value of the underlying asset.

Demand curve Graph of the inverse demand function. A graph showing the demand relation, either the highest quantity willingly purchased at each price or the highest price willingly paid for each quantity.

Demand function A relationship that expresses the quantity demanded of a good or service as a function of own-price and possibly other variables.

Demand-pull Type of inflation in which increasing demand raises prices generally, which then are reflected in a business's costs as workers demand wage hikes to catch up with the rising cost of living.

Demand shock A typically unexpected disturbance to demand, such as an unexpected interruption in trade or transportation.

Dependent With reference to events, the property that the probability of one event occurring depends on (is related to) the occurrence of another event.

Depository bank A bank that raises funds from depositors and other investors and lends it to borrowers.

Depository institutions Commercial banks, savings and loan banks, credit unions, and similar institutions that raise funds from depositors and other investors and lend it to borrowers.

Depository receipt A security that trades like an ordinary share on a local exchange and represents an economic interest in a foreign company.

Depreciation The process of systematically allocating the cost of long-lived (tangible) assets to the periods during which the assets are expected to provide economic benefits.

Depression See *contraction.*

Derivative pricing rule A pricing rule used by crossing networks in which a price is taken (derived) from the price that is current in the asset's primary market.

Derivatives A financial instrument whose value depends on the value of some underlying asset or factor (e.g., a stock price, an interest rate, or exchange rate).

Descriptive statistics The study of how data can be summarized effectively.

Development capital Minority equity investments in more mature companies that are seeking capital to expand or restructure operations, enter new markets, or finance major acquisitions.

Diffuse prior The assumption of equal prior probabilities.

Diffusion index Reflects the proportion of the index's components that are moving in a pattern consistent with the overall index.

Diluted EPS The EPS that would result if all dilutive securities were converted into common shares.

Diluted shares The number of shares that would be outstanding if all potentially dilutive claims on common shares (e.g., convertible debt, convertible preferred stock, and employee stock options) were exercised.

Diminishing balance method An accelerated depreciation method, i.e., one that allocates a relatively large proportion of the cost of an asset to the early years of the asset's useful life.

Diminishing marginal productivity Describes a state in which each additional unit of input produces less output than previously.

Direct debit program An arrangement whereby a customer authorizes a debit to a demand account; typically used by companies to collect routine payments for services.

Direct financing leases Under US GAAP, a type of finance lease, from a lessor perspective, where the present value of the lease payments (lease receivable) equals the carrying value of the leased asset. No selling profit is recognized at lease inception. The revenues earned by the lessor are financing in nature.

Direct format With reference to the cash flow statement, a format for the presentation of the statement in which cash flow from operating activities is shown as operating cash receipts less operating cash disbursements. Also called *direct method.*

Direct method See *direct format.*

Direct taxes Taxes levied directly on income, wealth, and corporate profits.

Direct write-off method An approach to recognizing credit losses on customer receivables in which the company waits until such time as a customer has defaulted and only then recognizes the loss.

Disbursement float The amount of time between check issuance and a check's clearing back against the company's account.

Discount To reduce the value of a future payment in allowance for how far away it is in time; to calculate the present value of some future amount. Also, the amount by which an instrument is priced below its face (par) value.

Discount interest A procedure for determining the interest on a loan or bond in which the interest is deducted from the face value in advance.

Discount margin See *required margin.*

Discount rates In general, the interest rate used to calculate a present value. In the money market, however, discount rate is a specific type of quoted rate.

Discounted cash flow models Valuation models that estimate the intrinsic value of a security as the present value of the future benefits expected to be received from the security.

Discounted payback period the number of years it takes for the cumulative discounted cash flows from a project to equal the original investment.

Discouraged worker A person who has stopped looking for a job or has given up seeking employment.

Discrete random variable A random variable that can take on at most a countable number of possible values.

Discriminatory pricing rule A pricing rule used in continuous markets in which the limit price of the order or quote that first arrived determines the trade price.

Diseconomies of scale Increase in cost per unit resulting from increased production.

Dispersion The variability around the central tendency.

Display size The size of an order displayed to public view.

Distressed investing Investing in securities of companies in financial difficulty. Private equity funds that specialize in distressed investing typically buy the debt of mature companies in financial difficulty.

Distributed ledger A type of database that may be shared among entities in a network.

Distributed ledger technology Technology based on a distributed ledger.

Divergence In technical analysis, a term that describes the case when an indicator moves differently from the security being analyzed.

Diversification ratio The ratio of the standard deviation of an equally weighted portfolio to the standard deviation of a randomly selected security.

Dividend A distribution paid to shareholders based on the number of shares owned.

Dividend discount model (DDM) A present value model that estimates the intrinsic value of an equity share based on the present value of its expected future dividends.

Dividend discount model based approach An approach for estimating a country's equity risk premium. The market rate of return is estimated as the sum of the dividend yield and the growth rate in dividends for a market index. Subtracting the risk-free rate of return from the estimated market return produces an estimate for the equity risk premium.

Dividend payout ratio The ratio of cash dividends paid to earnings for a period.

Divisor A number (denominator) used to determine the value of a price return index. It is initially chosen at the inception of an index and subsequently adjusted by the index provider, as necessary, to avoid changes in the index value that are unrelated to changes in the prices of its constituent securities.

Domestic content provisions Stipulate that some percentage of the value added or components used in production should be of domestic origin.

Double bottoms In technical analysis, a reversal pattern that is formed when the price reaches a low, rebounds, and then sells off back to the first low level; used to predict a change from a downtrend to an uptrend.

Double coincidence of wants A prerequisite to barter trades, in particular that both economic agents in the transaction want what the other is selling.

Double declining balance depreciation An accelerated depreciation method that involves depreciating the asset at double the straight-line rate. This rate is multiplied by the book value of the asset at the beginning of the period (a declining balance) to calculate depreciation expense.

Double top In technical analysis, a reversal pattern that is formed when an uptrend reverses twice at roughly the same high price level; used to predict a change from an uptrend to a downtrend.

Down transition probability The probability that an asset's value moves down in a model of asset price dynamics.

Downgrade risk The risk that a bond issuer's creditworthiness deteriorates, or migrates lower, leading investors to believe the risk of default is higher. Also called *credit migration risk.*

Drag on liquidity When receipts lag, creating pressure from the decreased available funds.

Drawdown A percentage peak-to-trough reduction in net asset value.

Dual-currency bonds Bonds that make coupon payments in one currency and pay the par value at maturity in another currency.

DuPont analysis An approach to decomposing return on investment, e.g., return on equity, as the product of other financial ratios.

Duration A measure of the approximate sensitivity of a security to a change in interest rates (i.e., a measure of interest rate risk).

Duration gap A bond's Macaulay duration minus the investment horizon.

Dutch Book theorem A result in probability theory stating that inconsistent probabilities create profit opportunities.

Early repayment option See *prepayment option.*

Earnings per share The amount of income earned during a period per share of common stock.

Earnings surprise The portion of a company's earnings that is unanticipated by investors and, according to the efficient market hypothesis, merits a price adjustment.

Economic costs All the remuneration needed to keep a productive resource in its current employment or to acquire the resource for productive use; the sum of total accounting costs and implicit opportunity costs.

Economic indicator A variable that provides information on the state of the overall economy.

Economic loss The amount by which accounting profit is less than normal profit.

Economic order quantity–reorder point (EOQ–ROP) An approach to managing inventory based on expected demand and the predictability of demand; the ordering point for new inventory is determined based on the costs of ordering and carrying inventory, such that the total cost associated with inventory is minimized.

Economic profit Equal to accounting profit less the implicit opportunity costs not included in total accounting costs; the difference between total revenue (TR) and total cost (TC). Also called *abnormal profit* or *supernormal profit*.

Economic stabilization Reduction of the magnitude of economic fluctuations.

Economic union Incorporates all aspects of a common market and in addition requires common economic institutions and coordination of economic policies among members.

Economies of scale Reduction in cost per unit resulting from increased production.

Effective annual rate The amount by which a unit of currency will grow in a year with interest on interest included.

Effective convexity A *curve convexity* statistic that measures the secondary effect of a change in a benchmark yield curve on a bond's price.

Effective duration The sensitivity of a bond's price to a change in a benchmark yield curve.

Effective interest rate The borrowing rate or market rate that a company incurs at the time of issuance of a bond.

Efficient market A market in which asset prices reflect new information quickly and rationally.

Elastic Said of a good or service when the magnitude of elasticity is greater than one.

Elasticity The percentage change in one variable for a percentage change in another variable; a general measure of how sensitive one variable is to a change in the value of another variable.

Elasticity of demand A measure of the sensitivity of quantity demanded to a change in a product's own price: $\%\Delta Q^D/\%\Delta P$.

Elasticity of supply A measure of the sensitivity of quantity supplied to a change in price: $\%\Delta Q^S/\%\Delta P$.

Electronic communications networks See *alternative trading systems*.

Electronic funds transfer (EFT) The use of computer networks to conduct financial transactions electronically.

Elliott wave theory A technical analysis theory that claims that the market follows regular, repeated waves or cycles.

Embedded option Contingency provisions that provide the issuer or the bondholders the right, but not the obligation, to take action. These options are not part of the security and cannot be traded separately.

Empirical probability The probability of an event estimated as a relative frequency of occurrence.

Employed The number of people with a job.

Engagement/active ownership An ESG investment style that uses shareholder power to influence corporate behavior through direct corporate engagement (i.e., communicating with senior management and/or boards of companies), filing or co-filing shareholder proposals, and proxy voting that is directed by ESG guidelines.

Enterprise risk management An overall assessment of a company's risk position. A centralized approach to risk management sometimes called firmwide risk management.

Enterprise value A measure of a company's total market value from which the value of cash and short-term investments have been subtracted.

Equal weighting An index weighting method in which an equal weight is assigned to each constituent security at inception.

Equipment trust certificates Bonds secured by specific types of equipment or physical assets.

Equity Assets less liabilities; the residual interest in the assets after subtracting the liabilities.

Equity risk premium The expected return on equities minus the risk-free rate; the premium that investors demand for investing in equities.

Equity swap A swap transaction in which at least one cash flow is tied to the return to an equity portfolio position, often an equity index.

ESG An acronym that encompasses environmental, social and governance.

ESG integration The integration of qualitative and quantitative environmental, social, and governance factors into traditional security and industry analysis; also known as *ESG incorporation*.

ESG investing The consideration of environmental, social, and governance factors in the investment process.

Estimate The particular value calculated from sample observations using an estimator.

Estimation With reference to statistical inference, the subdivision dealing with estimating the value of a population parameter.

Estimator An estimation formula; the formula used to compute the sample mean and other sample statistics are examples of estimators.

Ethical principles Beliefs regarding what is good, acceptable, or obligatory behavior and what is bad, unacceptable, or forbidden behavior.

Ethics The study of moral principles or of making good choices. Ethics encompasses a set of moral principles and rules of conduct that provide guidance for our behavior.

Eurobonds Type of bond issued internationally, outside the jurisdiction of the country in whose currency the bond is denominated.

European option An option that can only be exercised on its expiration date.

European-style Said of an option contract that can only be exercised on the option's expiration date.

Event Any outcome or specified set of outcomes of a random variable.

Ex-dividend date The first date that a share trades without (i.e., "ex") the dividend.

Excess kurtosis Degree of kurtosis (fatness of tails) in excess of the kurtosis of the normal distribution.

Exchanges Places where traders can meet to arrange their trades.

Exclusionary screening An ESG implementation approach that excludes certain sectors or companies that deviate from an investor's accepted standards. Also called *negative screening* or *norms-based screening*.

Execution instructions Instructions that indicate how to fill an order.

Exercise The process of using an option to buy or sell the underlying.

Exercise price The fixed price at which an option holder can buy or sell the underlying. Also called *strike price, striking price,* or *strike*.

Exercise value The value obtained if an option is exercised based on current conditions. Also known as *intrinsic value*.

Exhaustive Covering or containing all possible outcomes.

Expansion The period of a business cycle after its lowest point and before its highest point.

Expansionary Tending to cause the real economy to grow.

Expansionary fiscal policy Fiscal policy aimed at achieving real economic growth.

Expected inflation The level of inflation that economic agents expect in the future.

Expected loss Default probability times Loss severity given default.

Expected value The probability-weighted average of the possible outcomes of a random variable.

Expenses Outflows of economic resources or increases in liabilities that result in decreases in equity (other than decreases because of distributions to owners); reductions in net assets associated with the creation of revenues.

Experience curve A curve that shows the direct cost per unit of good or service produced or delivered as a typically declining function of cumulative output.

Export subsidy Paid by the government to the firm when it exports a unit of a good that is being subsidized.

Exports Goods and services that an economy sells to other countries.

Extension risk The risk that when interest rates rise, fewer prepayments will occur because homeowners are reluctant to give up the benefits of a contractual interest rate that now looks low. As a result, the security becomes longer in maturity than anticipated at the time of purchase.

Externality An effect of a market transaction that is borne by parties other than those who transacted.

Extra dividend A dividend paid by a company that does not pay dividends on a regular schedule, or a dividend that supplements regular cash dividends with an extra payment.

Extreme value theory A branch of statistics that focuses primarily on extreme outcomes.

Face value The amount of cash payable by a company to the bondholders when the bonds mature; the promised payment at maturity separate from any coupon payment.

Factor A common or underlying element with which several variables are correlated.

Fair value The amount at which an asset could be exchanged, or a liability settled, between knowledgeable, willing parties in an arm's-length transaction; the price that would be received to sell an asset or paid to transfer a liability in an orderly transaction between market participants.

Fed funds rate The US interbank lending rate on overnight borrowings of reserves.

Federal funds rate The US interbank lending rate on overnight borrowings of reserves.

Fiat money Money that is not convertible into any other commodity.

Fibonacci sequence A sequence of numbers starting with 0 and 1, and then each subsequent number in the sequence is the sum of the two preceding numbers. In Elliott Wave Theory, it is believed that market waves follow patterns that are the ratios of the numbers in the Fibonacci sequence.

Fiduciary call A combination of a European call and a risk-free bond that matures on the option expiration day and has a face value equal to the exercise price of the call.

FIFO method The first in, first out, method of accounting for inventory, which matches sales against the costs of items of inventory in the order in which they were placed in inventory.

Fill or kill See *immediate or cancel order.*

Finance lease From the lessee perspective, under US GAAP, a type of lease which is more akin to the purchase of an asset by the lessee. From the lessor perspective, under IFRS, a lease which "transfers substantially all the risks and rewards incidental to ownership of an underlying asset."

Financial account A component of the balance of payments account that records investment flows.

Financial flexibility The ability to react and adapt to financial adversity and opportunities.

Financial leverage The extent to which a company can effect, through the use of debt, a proportional change in the return on common equity that is greater than a given proportional change in operating income; also, short for the financial leverage ratio.

Financial leverage ratio A measure of financial leverage calculated as average total assets divided by average total equity.

Financial risk The risk that environmental, social, or governance risk factors will result in significant costs or other losses to a company and its shareholders; the risk arising from a company's obligation to meet required payments under its financing agreements.

Financing activities Activities related to obtaining or repaying capital to be used in the business (e.g., equity and long-term debt).

Fintech Technological innovation in the design and delivery of financial services and products in the financial industry.

Firm commitment offering See *underwritten offering.*

First-degree price discrimination Where a monopolist is able to charge each customer the highest price the customer is willing to pay.

First lien debt Debt secured by a pledge of certain assets that could include buildings, but may also include property and equipment, licenses, patents, brands, etc.

First mortgage debt Debt secured by a pledge of a specific property.

Fiscal multiplier The ratio of a change in national income to a change in government spending.

Fiscal policy The use of taxes and government spending to affect the level of aggregate expenditures.

Fisher effect The thesis that the real rate of interest in an economy is stable over time so that changes in nominal interest rates are the result of changes in expected inflation.

Fisher index The geometric mean of the Laspeyres index.

Fixed charge coverage A solvency ratio measuring the number of times interest and lease payments are covered by operating income, calculated as (EBIT + lease payments) divided by (interest payments + lease payments).

Fixed costs Costs that remain at the same level regardless of a company's level of production and sales.

Fixed-for-floating interest rate swap An interest rate swap in which one party pays a fixed rate and the other pays a floating rate, with both sets of payments in the same currency. Also called *plain vanilla swap* or *vanilla swap.*

Fixed rate perpetual preferred stock Nonconvertible, noncallable preferred stock that has a fixed dividend rate and no maturity date.

Flags A technical analysis continuation pattern formed by parallel trendlines, typically over a short period.

Flat price The full price of a bond minus the accrued interest; also called the *quoted* or *clean* price.

Float In the context of customer receipts, the amount of money that is in transit between payments made by customers and the funds that are usable by the company.

Float-adjusted market-capitalization weighting An index weighting method in which the weight assigned to each constituent security is determined by adjusting its market capitalization for its market float.

Float factor An estimate of the average number of days it takes deposited checks to clear; average daily float divided by average daily deposit.

Floaters See *floating-rate notes*.

Floating-rate notes A note on which interest payments are not fixed, but instead vary from period to period depending on the current level of a reference interest rate.

Flotation cost Fees charged to companies by investment bankers and other costs associated with raising new capital.

Foreclosure Allows the lender to take possession of a mortgaged property if the borrower defaults and then sell it to recover funds.

Foreign currency reserves Holding by the central bank of non-domestic currency deposits and non-domestic bonds.

Foreign direct investment Direct investment by a firm in one country (the source country) in productive assets in a foreign country (the host country).

Foreign exchange gains (or losses) Gains (or losses) that occur when the exchange rate changes between the investor's currency and the currency that foreign securities are denominated in.

Foreign portfolio investment Shorter-term investment by individuals, firms, and institutional investors (e.g., pension funds) in foreign financial instruments such as foreign stocks and foreign government bonds.

Forward commitments Class of derivatives that provides the ability to lock in a price to transact in the future at a previously agreed-upon price.

Forward contract An agreement between two parties in which one party, the buyer, agrees to buy from the other party, the seller, an underlying asset at a later date for a price established at the start of the contract.

Forward curve A series of forward rates, each having the same timeframe.

Forward market For future delivery, beyond the usual settlement time period in the cash market.

Forward price The fixed price or rate at which the transaction scheduled to occur at the expiration of a forward contract will take place. This price is agreed on at the initiation date of the contract.

Forward rate The interest rate on a bond or money market instrument traded in a forward market. A forward rate can be interpreted as an incremental, or marginal, return for extending the time-to-maturity for an additional time period.

Forward rate agreements A forward contract calling for one party to make a fixed interest payment and the other to make an interest payment at a rate to be determined at the contract expiration.

Fractile A value at or below which a stated fraction of the data lies.

Fractional reserve banking Banking in which reserves constitute a fraction of deposits.

Free cash flow The actual cash that would be available to the company's investors after making all investments necessary to maintain the company as an ongoing enterprise (also referred to as free cash flow to the firm); the internally generated funds that can be distributed to the company's investors (e.g., shareholders and bondholders) without impairing the value of the company.

Free cash flow to equity (FCFE) The cash flow available to a company's common shareholders after all operating expenses, interest, and principal payments have been made, and necessary investments in working and fixed capital have been made.

Free-cash-flow-to-equity models Valuation models based on discounting expected future free cash flow to equity.

Free cash flow to the firm (FCFF) The cash flow available to the company's suppliers of capital after all operating expenses have been paid and necessary investments in working capital and fixed capital have been made.

Free float The number of shares that are readily and freely tradable in the secondary market.

Free trade When there are no government restrictions on a country's ability to trade.

Free trade areas One of the most prevalent forms of regional integration, in which all barriers to the flow of goods and services among members have been eliminated.

Frequency distribution A tabular display of data summarized into a relatively small number of intervals.

Frequency polygon A graph of a frequency distribution obtained by drawing straight lines joining successive points representing the class frequencies.

Full integration An ESG investment style that focuses on the explicit inclusion of ESG factors into the traditional financial analysis of individual stocks for the purpose of valuation (e.g., as inputs into cash flow forecasts and/or cost-of-capital estimates).

Full price The price of a security with accrued interest; also called the *invoice* or *dirty* price.

Fundamental analysis The examination of publicly available information and the formulation of forecasts to estimate the intrinsic value of assets.

Fundamental value The underlying or true value of an asset based on an analysis of its qualitative and quantitative characteristics. Also called *intrinsic value*.

Fundamental weighting An index weighting method in which the weight assigned to each constituent security is based on its underlying company's size. It attempts to address the disadvantages of market-capitalization weighting by using measures that are independent of the constituent security's price.

Funds of hedge funds Funds that hold a portfolio of hedge funds, more commonly shortened to *funds of funds*.

Future value (FV) The amount to which a payment or series of payments will grow by a stated future date.

Futures contract A variation of a forward contract that has essentially the same basic definition but with some additional features, such as a clearinghouse guarantee against credit losses, a daily settlement of gains and losses, and an organized electronic or floor trading facility.

Futures price The agreed-upon price of a futures contract.

FX swap The combination of a spot and a forward FX transaction.

G-spread The yield spread in basis points over an actual or interpolated government bond.

Gains Asset inflows not directly related to the ordinary activities of the business.

Game theory The set of tools decision makers use to incorporate responses by rival decision makers into their strategies.

Gamma A numerical measure of how sensitive an option's delta (the sensitivity of the derivative's price) is to a change in the value of the underlying.

GDP deflator A gauge of prices and inflation that measures the aggregate changes in prices across the overall economy.

General partner The partner that runs the business and ultimately bears unlimited liability for the business's debts and obligations.

Geometric mean A measure of central tendency computed by taking the nth root of the product of n non-negative values.

Giffen goods Goods that are consumed more as the price of the good rises because it is a very inferior good whose income effect overwhelms its substitution effect when price changes.

Gilts Bonds issued by the UK government.

Giro system An electronic payment system used widely in Europe and Japan.

Global depository receipt A depository receipt that is issued outside of the company's home country and outside of the United States.

Global minimum-variance portfolio The portfolio on the minimum-variance frontier with the smallest variance of return.

Global registered share A common share that is traded on different stock exchanges around the world in different currencies.

Gold standard With respect to a currency, if a currency is on the gold standard a given amount can be converted into a prespecified amount of gold.

Golden cross A technical analysis term that describes a situation where a short-term moving average crosses from below a longer-term moving average to above it; this movement is considered bullish.

Good-on-close An execution instruction specifying that an order can only be filled at the close of trading. Also called *market on close.*

Good-on-open An execution instruction specifying that an order can only be filled at the opening of trading.

Good-till-cancelled order An order specifying that it is valid until the entity placing the order has cancelled it (or, commonly, until some specified amount of time such as 60 days has elapsed, whichever comes sooner).

Goodwill An intangible asset that represents the excess of the purchase price of an acquired company over the value of the net assets acquired.

Government equivalent yield A yield that restates a yield-to-maturity based on 30/360 day-count to one based on actual/actual.

Green bonds A bond used in green finance whereby the proceeds are earmarked towards environmental-related products.

Green finance A type of finance that addresses environmental concerns while achieving economic growth.

Grey market The forward market for bonds about to be issued. Also called "when issued" market.

Gross domestic product The market value of all final goods and services produced within the economy in a given period of time (output definition) or, equivalently, the aggregate income earned by all households, all companies, and the government within the economy in a given period of time (income definition).

Gross margin Sales minus the cost of sales (i.e., the cost of goods sold for a manufacturing company).

Gross profit Sales minus the cost of sales (i.e., the cost of goods sold for a manufacturing company).

Gross profit margin The ratio of gross profit to revenues.

Grouping by function With reference to the presentation of expenses in an income statement, the grouping together of expenses serving the same function, e.g. all items that are costs of goods sold.

Grouping by nature With reference to the presentation of expenses in an income statement, the grouping together of expenses by similar nature, e.g., all depreciation expenses.

Growth cyclical A term sometimes used to describe companies that are growing rapidly on a long-term basis but that still experience above-average fluctuation in their revenues and profits over the course of a business cycle.

Growth investors With reference to equity investors, investors who seek to invest in high-earnings-growth companies.

Guarantee certificate A type of structured financial instrument that provides investors capital protection. It combines a zero-coupon bond and a call option on some underlying asset.

Haircut See *repo margin.*

Harmonic mean A type of weighted mean computed by averaging the reciprocals of the observations, then taking the reciprocal of that average.

Head and shoulders pattern In technical analysis, a reversal pattern that is formed in three parts: a left shoulder, head, and right shoulder; used to predict a change from an uptrend to a downtrend.

Headline inflation The inflation rate calculated based on the price index that includes all goods and services in an economy.

Hedge funds Private investment vehicles that typically use leverage, derivatives, and long and short investment strategies.

Hedge portfolio A hypothetical combination of the derivative and its underlying that eliminates risk.

Held-to-maturity Debt (fixed-income) securities that a company intends to hold to maturity; these are presented at their original cost, updated for any amortisation of discounts or premiums.

Herding Clustered trading that may or may not be based on information.

Hidden order An order that is exposed not to the public but only to the brokers or exchanges that receive it.

High-frequency trading A form of algorithmic trading that makes use of vast quantities of data to execute trades on ultra-high-speed networks in fractions of a second.

High-water mark The highest value, net of fees, that a fund has reached in history. It reflects the highest cumulative return used to calculate an incentive fee.

Histogram A bar chart of data that have been grouped into a frequency distribution.

Historical cost In reference to assets, the amount paid to purchase an asset, including any costs of acquisition and/or preparation; with reference to liabilities, the amount of proceeds received in exchange in issuing the liability.

Historical equity risk premium approach An estimate of a country's equity risk premium that is based upon the historical averages of the risk-free rate and the rate of return on the market portfolio.

Historical simulation Another term for the historical method of estimating VaR. This term is somewhat misleading in that the method involves not a *simulation* of the past but rather what *actually happened* in the past, sometimes adjusted to reflect the fact that a different portfolio may have existed in the past than is planned for the future.

Holder-of-record date The date that a shareholder listed on the corporation's books will be deemed to have ownership of the shares for purposes of receiving an upcoming dividend.

Holding period return The return that an investor earns during a specified holding period; a synonym for total return.

Homogeneity of expectations The assumption that all investors have the same economic expectations and thus have the same expectations of prices, cash flows, and other investment characteristics.

Horizon yield The internal rate of return between the total return (the sum of reinvested coupon payments and the sale price or redemption amount) and the purchase price of the bond.

Horizontal analysis Common-size analysis that involves comparing a specific financial statement with that statement in prior or future time periods; also, cross-sectional analysis of one company with another.

Horizontal demand schedule Implies that at a given price, the response in the quantity demanded is infinite.

Hostile takeover An attempt by one entity to acquire a company without the consent of the company's management.

Household A person or a group of people living in the same residence, taken as a basic unit in economic analysis.

Human capital The accumulated knowledge and skill that workers acquire from education, training, or life experience and the corresponding present value of future earnings to be generated by said skilled individual.

Hurdle rate The rate of return that must be met for a project to be accepted.

Hypothesis With reference to statistical inference, a statement about one or more populations.

Hypothesis testing With reference to statistical inference, the subdivision dealing with the testing of hypotheses about one or more populations.

I-spread The yield spread of a specific bond over the standard swap rate in that currency of the same tenor.

Iceberg order An order in which the display size is less than the order's full size.

If-converted method A method for accounting for the effect of convertible securities on earnings per share (EPS) that specifies what EPS would have been if the convertible securities had been converted at the beginning of the period, taking account of the effects of conversion on net income and the weighted average number of shares outstanding.

Immediate or cancel order An order that is valid only upon receipt by the broker or exchange. If such an order cannot be filled in part or in whole upon receipt, it cancels immediately. Also called *fill or kill*.

Impact lag The lag associated with the result of actions affecting the economy with delay.

Implicit price deflator for GDP A gauge of prices and inflation that measures the aggregate changes in prices across the overall economy.

Implied forward rates Calculated from spot rates, an implied forward rate is a break-even reinvestment rate that links the return on an investment in a shorter-term zero-coupon bond to the return on an investment in a longer-term zero-coupon bond.

Implied volatility The volatility that option traders use to price an option, implied by the price of the option and a particular option-pricing model.

Import license Specifies the quantity of a good that can be imported into a country.

Imports Goods and services that a domestic economy (i.e., house-holds, firms, and government) purchases from other countries.

In the money Options that, if exercised, would result in the value received being worth more than the payment required to exercise.

Incentive fee Fees paid to the general partner from the limited partner(s) based on realized net profits.

Income Increases in economic benefits in the form of inflows or enhancements of assets, or decreases of liabilities that result in an increase in equity (other than increases resulting from contributions by owners).

Income elasticity of demand A measure of the responsiveness of demand to changes in income, defined as the percentage change in quantity demanded divided by the percentage change in income.

Income tax paid The actual amount paid for income taxes in the period; not a provision, but the actual cash outflow.

Income tax payable The income tax owed by the company on the basis of taxable income.

Income trust A type of equity ownership vehicle established as a trust issuing ownership shares known as units.

Increasing marginal returns When the marginal product of a resource increases as additional units of that input are employed.

Increasing returns to scale When a production process leads to increases in output that are proportionately larger than the increase in inputs.

Incremental cash flow The cash flow that is realized because of a decision; the changes or increments to cash flows resulting from a decision or action.

Indenture Legal contract that describes the form of a bond, the obligations of the issuer, and the rights of the bondholders. Also called the *trust deed*.

Independent With reference to events, the property that the occurrence of one event does not affect the probability of another event occurring.

Independent projects Independent projects are projects whose cash flows are independent of each other.

Independently and identically distributed (IID) With respect to random variables, the property of random variables that are independent of each other but follow the identical probability distribution.

Index-linked bond Bond for which coupon payments and/or principal repayment are linked to a specified index.

Index of Leading Economic Indicators A composite of economic variables used by analysts to predict future economic conditions.

Indexing An investment strategy in which an investor constructs a portfolio to mirror the performance of a specified index.

Indifference curve A curve representing all the combinations of two goods or attributes such that the consumer is entirely indifferent among them.

Indirect format With reference to cash flow statements, a format for the presentation of the statement which, in the operating cash flow section, begins with net income then shows additions and subtractions to arrive at operating cash flow. Also called *indirect method*.

Indirect method See *indirect format*.

Indirect taxes Taxes such as taxes on spending, as opposed to direct taxes.

Industry A group of companies offering similar products and/or services.
Industry analysis The analysis of a specific branch of manufacturing, service, or trade.
Inelastic Said of a good or service when the magnitude of elasticity is less than one. Insensitive to price changes.
Inferior goods A good whose consumption decreases as income increases.
Inflation The percentage increase in the general price level from one period to the next; a sustained rise in the overall level of prices in an economy.
Inflation-linked bond Type of index-linked bond that offers investors protection against inflation by linking the bond's coupon payments and/or the principal repayment to an index of consumer prices. Also called *linkers*.
Inflation premium An extra return that compensates investors for expected inflation.
Inflation rate The percentage change in a price index—that is, the speed of overall price level movements.
Inflation Reports A type of economic publication put out by many central banks.
Inflation uncertainty The degree to which economic agents view future rates of inflation as difficult to forecast.
Information cascade The transmission of information from those participants who act first and whose decisions influence the decisions of others.
Information-motivated traders Traders that trade to profit from information that they believe allows them to predict future prices.
Informationally efficient market A market in which asset prices reflect new information quickly and rationally.
Initial coin offering An unregulated process whereby companies raise capital by selling crypto tokens to investors in exchange for fiat money or another agreed-upon cryptocurrency.
Initial margin The amount that must be deposited in a clearinghouse account when entering into a futures contract.
Initial margin requirement The margin requirement on the first day of a transaction as well as on any day in which additional margin funds must be deposited.
Initial public offering (IPO) The first issuance of common shares to the public by a formerly private corporation.
Input productivity The amount of output produced by workers in a given period of time—for example, output per hour worked; measures the efficiency of labor.
Intangible assets Assets lacking physical substance, such as patents and trademarks.
Interbank market The market of loans and deposits between banks for maturities ranging from overnight to one year.
Interbank money market The market of loans and deposits between banks for maturities ranging from overnight to one year.
Interest Payment for lending funds.
Interest coverage A solvency ratio calculated as EBIT divided by interest payments.
Interest-only mortgage A loan in which no scheduled principal repayment is specified for a certain number of years.
Interest rate A rate of return that reflects the relationship between differently dated cash flows; a discount rate.
Interest rate swap A swap in which the underlying is an interest rate. Can be viewed as a currency swap in which both currencies are the same and can be created as a combination of currency swaps.
Intergenerational data mining A form of data mining that applies information developed by previous researchers using a dataset to guide current research using the same or a related dataset.
Intermarket analysis A field within technical analysis that combines analysis of major categories of securities—namely, equities, bonds, currencies, and commodities—to identify market trends and possible inflections in a trend.
Internal rate of return (IRR) The discount rate that makes net present value equal 0; the discount rate that makes the present value of an investment's costs (outflows) equal to the present value of the investment's benefits (inflows).
Internet of Things A network arrangement of structures and devices whereby the objects on the network are able to interact and share information.
Interpolated spread The yield spread of a specific bond over the standard swap rate in that currency of the same tenor.
Interquartile range The difference between the third and first quartiles of a dataset.
Interval With reference to grouped data, a set of values within which an observation falls.
Interval scale A measurement scale that not only ranks data but also gives assurance that the differences between scale values are equal.
Intrinsic value See *exercise value.*
Inventory blanket lien The use of inventory as collateral for a loan. Though the lender has claim to some or all of the company's inventory, the company may still sell or use the inventory in the ordinary course of business.
Inventory investment Net change in business inventory.
Inventory turnover An activity ratio calculated as cost of goods sold divided by average inventory.
Inverse demand function A restatement of the demand function in which price is stated as a function of quantity.
Inverse floater A type of leveraged structured financial instrument. The cash flows are adjusted periodically and move in the opposite direction of changes in the reference rate.
Investing activities Activities associated with the acquisition and disposal of property, plant, and equipment; intangible assets; other long-term assets; and both long-term and short-term investments in the equity and debt (bonds and loans) issued by other companies.
Investment banks Financial intermediaries that provide advice to their mostly corporate clients and help them arrange transactions such as initial and seasoned securities offerings.
Investment opportunity schedule A graphical depiction of a company's investment opportunities ordered from highest to lowest expected return. A company's optimal capital budget is found where the investment opportunity schedule intersects with the company's marginal cost of capital.
Investment policy statement (IPS) A written planning document that describes a client's investment objectives and risk tolerance over a relevant time horizon, along with constraints that apply to the client's portfolio.
Investment property Property used to earn rental income or capital appreciation (or both).
January effect Calendar anomaly that stock market returns in January are significantly higher compared to the rest of the months of the year, with most of the abnormal returns reported during the first five trading days in January. Also called *turn-of-the-year effect.*
Joint probability The probability of the joint occurrence of stated events.

Joint probability function A function giving the probability of joint occurrences of values of stated random variables.

Just-in-time (JIT) method Method of managing inventory that minimizes in-process inventory stocks.

Key rate duration A method of measuring the interest rate sensitivities of a fixed-income instrument or portfolio to shifts in key points along the yield curve.

Keynesians Economists who believe that fiscal policy can have powerful effects on aggregate demand, output, and employment when there is substantial spare capacity in an economy.

Kondratieff wave A 54-year long economic cycle postulated by Nikolai Kondratieff.

Kurtosis The statistical measure that indicates the combined weight of the tails of a distribution relative to the rest of the distribution.

Labor force The portion of the working age population (over the age of 16) that is employed or is available for work but not working (unemployed).

Labor productivity The quantity of goods and services (real GDP) that a worker can produce in one hour of work.

Laddering strategy A form of active strategy which entails scheduling maturities on a systematic basis within the investment portfolio such that investments are spread out equally over the term of the ladder.

Lagging economic indicators Turning points that take place later than those of the overall economy; they are believed to have value in identifying the economy's past condition.

Laspeyres index A price index created by holding the composition of the consumption basket constant.

Law of demand The principle that as the price of a good rises, buyers will choose to buy less of it, and as its price falls, they will buy more.

Law of diminishing marginal returns The observation that a variable factor's marginal product must eventually fall as more of it is added to a fixed amount of the other factors.

Law of diminishing returns The smallest output that a firm can produce such that its long run average costs are minimized.

Law of one price The condition in a financial market in which two equivalent financial instruments or combinations of financial instruments can sell for only one price. Equivalent to the principle that no arbitrage opportunities are possible.

Lead underwriter The lead investment bank in a syndicate of investment banks and broker–dealers involved in a securities underwriting.

Leading economic indicators Turning points that usually precede those of the overall economy; they are believed to have value for predicting the economy's future state, usually near-term.

Legal tender Something that must be accepted when offered in exchange for goods and services.

Lender of last resort An entity willing to lend money when no other entity is ready to do so.

Leptokurtic Describes a distribution that has fatter tails than a normal distribution.

Lessee The party obtaining the use of an asset through a lease.

Lessor The owner of an asset that grants the right to use the asset to another party.

Letter of credit Form of external credit enhancement whereby a financial institution provides the issuer with a credit line to reimburse any cash flow shortfalls from the assets backing the issue.

Level of significance The probability of a Type I error in testing a hypothesis.

Leverage In the context of corporate finance, leverage refers to the use of fixed costs within a company's cost structure. Fixed costs that are operating costs (such as depreciation or rent) create operating leverage. Fixed costs that are financial costs (such as interest expense) create financial leverage.

Leveraged buyout A transaction whereby the target company's management team converts the target to a privately held company by using heavy borrowing to finance the purchase of the target company's outstanding shares.

Liabilities Present obligations of an enterprise arising from past events, the settlement of which is expected to result in an outflow of resources embodying economic benefits; creditors' claims on the resources of a company.

Life-cycle stage The stage of the life cycle: embryonic, growth, shakeout, mature, declining.

LIFO layer liquidation With respect to the application of the LIFO inventory method, the liquidation of old, relatively low-priced inventory; happens when the volume of sales rises above the volume of recent purchases so that some sales are made from relatively old, low-priced inventory. Also called *LIFO liquidation.*

LIFO method The last in, first out, method of accounting for inventory, which matches sales against the costs of items of inventory in the reverse order the items were placed in inventory (i.e., inventory produced or acquired last are assumed to be sold first).

LIFO reserve The difference between the reported LIFO inventory carrying amount and the inventory amount that would have been reported if the FIFO method had been used (in other words, the FIFO inventory value less the LIFO inventory value).

Likelihood The probability of an observation, given a particular set of conditions.

Limit down A limit move in the futures market in which the price at which a transaction would be made is at or below the lower limit.

Limit order Instructions to a broker or exchange to obtain the best price immediately available when filling an order, but in no event accept a price higher than a specified (limit) price when buying or accept a price lower than a specified (limit) price when selling.

Limit order book The book or list of limit orders to buy and sell that pertains to a security.

Limit up A limit move in the futures market in which the price at which a transaction would be made is at or above the upper limit.

Limitations on liens Meant to put limits on how much secured debt an issuer can have.

Limited partners Partners with limited liability. Limited partnerships in hedge and private equity funds are typically restricted to investors who are expected to understand and to be able to assume the risks associated with the investments.

Line chart In technical analysis, a plot of price data, typically closing prices, with a line connecting the points.

Linear interpolation The estimation of an unknown value on the basis of two known values that bracket it, using a straight line between the two known values.

Linear scale A scale in which equal distances correspond to equal absolute amounts. Also called *arithmetic scale.*

Linker See *inflation-linked bond.*

Liquid market Said of a market in which traders can buy or sell with low total transaction costs when they want to trade.

Liquidation To sell the assets of a company, division, or subsidiary piecemeal, typically because of bankruptcy; the form of bankruptcy that allows for the orderly satisfaction of creditors' claims after which the company ceases to exist.

Liquidity The ability to purchase or sell an asset quickly and easily at a price close to fair market value. The ability to meet short-term obligations using assets that are the most readily converted into cash.

Liquidity premium An extra return that compensates investors for the risk of loss relative to an investment's fair value if the investment needs to be converted to cash quickly.

Liquidity ratios Financial ratios measuring the company's ability to meet its short-term obligations.

Liquidity risk The risk that a financial instrument cannot be purchased or sold without a significant concession in price due to the size of the market.

Liquidity trap A condition in which the demand for money becomes infinitely elastic (horizontal demand curve) so that injections of money into the economy will not lower interest rates or affect real activity.

Load fund A mutual fund in which, in addition to the annual fee, a percentage fee is charged to invest in the fund and/or for redemptions from the fund.

Loan-to-value ratio The ratio of a property's purchase price to the amount of its mortgage.

Lockbox system A payment system in which customer payments are mailed to a post office box and the banking institution retrieves and deposits these payments several times a day, enabling the company to have use of the fund sooner than in a centralized system in which customer payments are sent to the company.

Locked limit A condition in the futures markets in which a transaction cannot take place because the price would be beyond the limits.

Lockup period The minimum holding period before investors are allowed to make withdrawals or redeem shares from a fund.

Logarithmic scale A scale in which equal distances represent equal proportional changes in the underlying quantity.

London interbank offered rate (Libor) Collective name for multiple rates at which a select set of banks believe they could borrow unsecured funds from other banks in the London interbank market for different currencies and different borrowing periods ranging from overnight to one year.

Long The buyer of a derivative contract. Also refers to the position of owning a derivative.

Long-lived assets Assets that are expected to provide economic benefits over a future period of time, typically greater than one year. Also called *long-term assets.*

Long position A position in an asset or contract in which one owns the asset or has an exercisable right under the contract.

Long-run average total cost The curve describing average total cost when no costs are considered fixed.

Longitudinal data Observations on characteristic(s) of the same observational unit through time.

Look-ahead bias A bias caused by using information that was unavailable on the test date.

Loss aversion The tendency of people to dislike losses more than they like comparable gains.

Loss severity Portion of a bond's value (including unpaid interest) an investor loses in the event of default.

Losses Asset outflows not directly related to the ordinary activities of the business.

Lower bound The lowest possible value of an option.

M^2 A measure of what a portfolio would have returned if it had taken on the same total risk as the market index.

M^2 alpha Difference between the risk-adjusted performance of the portfolio and the performance of the benchmark.

Macaulay duration The approximate amount of time a bond would have to be held for the market discount rate at purchase to be realized if there is a single change in interest rate. It indicates the point in time when the coupon reinvestment and price effects of a change in yield-to- maturity offset each other.

Machine learning Computer based techniques that seek to extract knowledge from large amounts of data by "learning" from known examples and then generating structure or predictions. ML algorithms aim to "find the pattern, apply the pattern."

Macroeconomics The branch of economics that deals with aggregate economic quantities, such as national output and national income.

Maintenance covenants Covenants in bank loan agreements that require the borrower to satisfy certain financial ratio tests while the loan is outstanding.

Maintenance margin The minimum amount that is required by a futures clearinghouse to maintain a margin account and to protect against default. Participants whose margin balances drop below the required maintenance margin must replenish their accounts.

Maintenance margin requirement The margin requirement on any day other than the first day of a transaction.

Management buy-ins Leveraged buyout in which the current management team is being replaced and the acquiring team will be involved in managing the company.

Management buyout A leveraged buyout event in which a group of investors consisting primarily of the company's existing management purchase at least controlling interest in its outstanding shares. At the extreme, they may purchase all shares and take the company private.

Management fee A fee based on assets under management or committed capital, as applicable, also called a *base fee.*

Manufacturing resource planning (MRP) The incorporation of production planning into inventory management. A MRP analysis provides both a materials acquisition schedule and a production schedule.

Margin The amount of money that a trader deposits in a margin account. The term is derived from the stock market practice in which an investor borrows a portion of the money required to purchase a certain amount of stock. In futures markets, there is no borrowing so the margin is more of a down payment or performance bond.

Margin bond A cash deposit required by the clearinghouse from the participants to a contract to provide a credit guarantee. Also called a *performance bond.*

Margin call A request for the short to deposit additional funds to bring their balance up to the initial margin.

Margin loan Money borrowed from a broker to purchase securities.

Marginal cost The cost of producing an additional unit of a good.

Marginal probability The probability of an event *not* conditioned on another event.

Marginal product Measures the productivity of each unit of input and is calculated by taking the difference in total product from adding another unit of input (assuming other resource quantities are held constant).

Marginal propensity to consume The proportion of an additional unit of disposable income that is consumed or spent; the change in consumption for a small change in income.

Marginal propensity to save The proportion of an additional unit of disposable income that is saved (not spent).

Marginal revenue The change in total revenue divided by the change in quantity sold; simply, the additional revenue from selling one more unit.

Marginal value curve A curve describing the highest price consumers are willing to pay for each additional unit of a good.

Mark to market The revaluation of a financial asset or liability to its current market value or fair value.

Market anomaly Change in the price or return of a security that cannot directly be linked to current relevant information known in the market or to the release of new information into the market.

Market bid–ask spread The difference between the best bid and the best offer.

Market-capitalization weighting An index weighting method in which the weight assigned to each constituent security is determined by dividing its market capitalization by the total market capitalization (sum of the market capitalization) of all securities in the index. Also called *value weighting*.

Market discount rate The rate of return required by investors given the risk of the investment in a bond; also called the *required yield* or the *required rate of return*.

Market float The number of shares that are available to the investing public.

Market liquidity risk The risk that the price at which investors can actually transact—buying or selling—may differ from the price indicated in the market.

Market model A regression equation that specifies a linear relationship between the return on a security (or portfolio) and the return on a broad market index.

Market multiple models Valuation models based on share price multiples or enterprise value multiples.

Market-on-close An execution instruction specifying that an order can only be filled at the close of trading.

Market order Instructions to a broker or exchange to obtain the best price immediately available when filling an order.

Market-oriented investors With reference to equity investors, investors whose investment disciplines cannot be clearly categorized as value or growth.

Market rate of interest The rate demanded by purchasers of bonds, given the risks associated with future cash payment obligations of the particular bond issue.

Market risk The risk that arises from movements in interest rates, stock prices, exchange rates, and commodity prices.

Market value The price at which an asset or security can currently be bought or sold in an open market.

Marketable limit order A buy limit order in which the limit price is placed above the best offer, or a sell limit order in which the limit price is placed below the best bid. Such orders generally will partially or completely fill right away.

Markowitz efficient frontier The graph of the set of portfolios offering the maximum expected return for their level of risk (standard deviation of return).

Matching principle The accounting principle that expenses should be recognized in the same period in which the associated revenue is recognized.

Matching strategy An active investment strategy that includes intentional matching of the timing of cash outflows with investment maturities.

Matrix pricing Process of estimating the market discount rate and price of a bond based on the quoted or flat prices of more frequently traded comparable bonds.

Maturity premium An extra return that compensates investors for the increased sensitivity of the market value of debt to a change in market interest rates as maturity is extended.

Maturity structure A factor explaining the differences in yields on similar bonds; also called *term structure*.

Mean absolute deviation With reference to a sample, the mean of the absolute values of deviations from the sample mean.

Mean–variance analysis An approach to portfolio analysis using expected means, variances, and covariances of asset returns.

Measure of central tendency A quantitative measure that specifies where data are centered.

Measure of value A standard for measuring value; a function of money.

Measurement scales A scheme of measuring differences. The four types of measurement scales are nominal, ordinal, interval, and ratio.

Measures of location A quantitative measure that describes the location or distribution of data; includes not only measures of central tendency but also other measures such as percentiles.

Median The value of the middle item of a set of items that has been sorted into ascending or descending order; the 50th percentile.

Medium of exchange Any asset that can be used to purchase goods and services or to repay debts; a function of money.

Medium-term note A corporate bond offered continuously to investors by an agent of the issuer, designed to fill the funding gap between commercial paper and long-term bonds.

Menu costs A cost of inflation in which businesses constantly have to incur the costs of changing the advertised prices of their goods and services.

Mesokurtic Describes a distribution with kurtosis identical to that of the normal distribution.

Mezzanine financing Debt or preferred shares with a relationship to common equity resulting from a feature such as attached warrants or conversion options. Mezzanine financing is subordinate to both senior and high-yield debt but is senior to equity. It is referred to as "mezzanine" because of its location on the balance sheet.

Microeconomics The branch of economics that deals with markets and decision making of individual economic units, including consumers and businesses.

Minimum efficient scale The smallest output that a firm can produce such that its long-run average total cost is minimized.

Minimum-variance portfolio The portfolio with the minimum variance for each given level of expected return.

Minority shareholders A particular shareholder or block of shareholders holding a small proportion of a company's outstanding shares, resulting in a limited ability to exercise control in voting activities.

Minsky moment Named for Hyman Minksy: A point in a business cycle when, after individuals become overextended in borrowing to finance speculative investments, people start realizing that something is likely to go wrong and a panic ensues leading to asset sell-offs.

Mismatching strategy An active investment strategy whereby the timing of cash outflows is not matched with investment maturities.

Modal interval With reference to grouped data, the most frequently occurring interval.

Mode The most frequently occurring value in a set of observations.

Modern portfolio theory (MPT) The analysis of rational portfolio choices based on the efficient use of risk.

Modified duration A measure of the percentage price change of a bond given a change in its yield-to-maturity.

Momentum oscillators A graphical representation of market sentiment that is constructed from price data and calculated so that it oscillates either between a high and a low or around some number.

Monetarists Economists who believe that the rate of growth of the money supply is the primary determinant of the rate of inflation.

Monetary policy Actions taken by a nation's central bank to affect aggregate output and prices through changes in bank reserves, reserve requirements, or its target interest rate.

Monetary transmission mechanism The process whereby a central bank's interest rate gets transmitted through the economy and ultimately affects the rate of increase of prices.

Monetary union An economic union in which the members adopt a common currency.

Money A generally accepted medium of exchange and unit of account.

Money convexity For a bond, the annual or approximate convexity multiplied by the full price.

Money creation The process by which changes in bank reserves translate into changes in the money supply.

Money duration A measure of the price change in units of the currency in which the bond is denominated given a change in its yield-to-maturity.

Money market The market for short-term debt instruments (one-year maturity or less).

Money market securities Fixed-income securities with maturities at issuance of one year or less.

Money market yield A yield on a basis comparable to the quoted yield on an interest-bearing money market instrument that pays interest on a 360-day basis; the annualized holding period yield, assuming a 360-day year.

Money multiplier Describes how a change in reserves is expected to affect the money supply; in its simplest form, 1 divided by the reserve requirement.

Money neutrality The thesis that an increase in the money supply leads in the long-run to an increase in the price level, while leaving real variables like output and employment unaffected.

Money-weighted return The internal rate of return on a portfolio, taking account of all cash flows.

Moneyness The relationship between the price of the underlying and an option's exercise price.

Monopolistic competition Highly competitive form of imperfect competition; the competitive characteristic is a notably large number of firms, while the monopoly aspect is the result of product differentiation.

Monopoly In pure monopoly markets, there are no substitutes for the given product or service. There is a single seller, which exercises considerable power over pricing and output decisions.

Monte Carlo simulation An approach to estimating a probability distribution of outcomes to examine what might happen if particular risks are faced. This method is widely used in the sciences as well as in business to study a variety of problems.

Moral principles Beliefs regarding what is good, acceptable, or obligatory behavior and what is bad, unacceptable, or forbidden behavior.

Mortgage-backed securities Debt obligations that represent claims to the cash flows from pools of mortgage loans, most commonly on residential property.

Mortgage loan A loan secured by the collateral of some specified real estate property that obliges the borrower to make a predetermined series of payments to the lender.

Mortgage pass-through security A security created when one or more holders of mortgages form a pool of mortgages and sell shares or participation certificates in the pool.

Mortgage rate The interest rate on a mortgage loan; also called *contract rate* or *note rate*.

Moving average The average of the closing price of a security over a specified number of periods. With each new period, the average is recalculated.

Moving-average convergence/divergence oscillator (MACD) A momentum oscillator that is constructed based on the difference between short-term and long-term moving averages of a security's price.

Multi-factor model A model that explains a variable in terms of the values of a set of factors.

Multi-market indexes Comprised of indexes from different countries, designed to represent multiple security markets.

Multi-step format With respect to the format of the income statement, a format that presents a subtotal for gross profit (revenue minus cost of goods sold).

Multilateral trading facilities See *alternative trading systems*.

Multinational corporation A company operating in more than one country or having subsidiary firms in more than one country.

Multiplication rule for probabilities The rule that the joint probability of events A and B equals the probability of A given B times the probability of B.

Multiplier models Valuation models based on share price multiples or enterprise value multiples.

Multivariate distribution A probability distribution that specifies the probabilities for a group of related random variables.

Multivariate normal distribution A probability distribution for a group of random variables that is completely defined by the means and variances of the variables plus all the correlations between pairs of the variables.

Municipal bonds A type of non-sovereign bond issued by a state or local government in the United States. It very often (but not always) offers income tax exemptions.

Munis A type of non-sovereign bond issued by a state or local government in the United States. It very often (but not always) offers income tax exemptions.

Mutual fund A comingled investment pool in which investors in the fund each have a pro-rata claim on the income and value of the fund.

Mutually exclusive projects Mutually exclusive projects compete directly with each other. For example, if Projects A and B are mutually exclusive, you can choose A or B, but you cannot choose both.

n Factorial For a positive integer n, the product of the first n positive integers; 0 factorial equals 1 by definition. n factorial is written as $n!$.

Narrow money The notes and coins in circulation in an economy, plus other very highly liquid deposits.

Nash equilibrium When two or more participants in a non-coop-erative game have no incentive to deviate from their respective equilibrium strategies given their opponent's strategies.

National income The income received by all factors of production used in the generation of final output. National income equals gross domestic product (or, in some countries, gross national product) minus the capital consumption allowance and a statistical discrepancy.

Natural language processing Computer programs developed to analyze and interpret human language.

Natural rate of unemployment Effective unemployment rate, below which pressure emerges in labor markets.

Negative screening An ESG investment style that focuses on the exclusion of certain sectors, companies, or practices in a fund or portfolio on the basis of specific ESG criteria.

Neo-Keynesians A group of dynamic general equilibrium models that assume slow-to-adjust prices and wages.

Net book value The remaining (undepreciated) balance of an asset's purchase cost. For liabilities, the face value of a bond minus any unamortized discount, or plus any unamortized premium.

Net exports The difference between the value of a country's exports and the value of its imports (i.e., value of exports minus imports).

Net income The difference between revenue and expenses; what remains after subtracting all expenses (including depreciation, interest, and taxes) from revenue.

Net operating cycle An estimate of the average time that elapses between paying suppliers for materials and collecting cash from the subsequent sale of goods produced.

Net present value (NPV) The present value of an investment's cash inflows (benefits) minus the present value of its cash outflows (costs).

Net profit margin An indicator of profitability, calculated as net income divided by revenue; indicates how much of each dollar of revenues is left after all costs and expenses. Also called *profit margin* or *return on sales*.

Net realisable value Estimated selling price in the ordinary course of business less the estimated costs necessary to make the sale.

Net revenue Revenue after adjustments (e.g., for estimated returns or for amounts unlikely to be collected).

Net tax rate The tax rate net of transfer payments.

Neural networks Computer programs based on how our own brains learn and process information.

Neutral rate of interest The rate of interest that neither spurs on nor slows down the underlying economy.

New classical macroeconomics An approach to macroeconomics that seeks the macroeconomic conclusions of individuals maximizing utility on the basis of rational expectations and companies maximizing profits.

New Keynesians A group of dynamic general equilibrium models that assume slow-to-adjust prices and wages.

No-load fund A mutual fund in which there is no fee for investing in the fund or for redeeming fund shares, although there is an annual fee based on a percentage of the fund's net asset value.

Node Each value on a binomial tree from which successive moves or outcomes branch.

Nominal GDP The value of goods and services measured at current prices.

Nominal rate A rate of interest based on the security's face value.

Nominal risk-free interest rate The sum of the real risk-free interest rate and the inflation premium.

Nominal scale A measurement scale that categorizes data but does not rank them.

Non-accelerating inflation rate of unemployment Effective unemployment rate, below which pressure emerges in labor markets.

Non-agency RMBS In the United States, securities issued by private entities that are not guaranteed by a federal agency or a GSE.

Non-cumulative preference shares Preference shares for which dividends that are not paid in the current or subsequent periods are forfeited permanently (instead of being accrued and paid at a later date).

Non-current assets Assets that are expected to benefit the company over an extended period of time (usually more than one year).

Non-current liabilities Obligations that broadly represent a probable sacrifice of economic benefits in periods generally greater than one year in the future.

Non-cyclical A company whose performance is largely independent of the business cycle.

Non-deliverable forwards Cash-settled forward contracts, used predominately with respect to foreign exchange forwards. Also called *contracts for differences.*

Non-financial risks Risks that arise from sources other than changes in the external financial markets, such as changes in accounting rules, legal environment, or tax rates.

Non-participating preference shares Preference shares that do not entitle shareholders to share in the profits of the company. Instead, shareholders are only entitled to receive a fixed dividend payment and the par value of the shares in the event of liquidation.

Non-recourse loan Loan in which the lender does not have a shortfall claim against the borrower, so the lender can look only to the property to recover the outstanding mortgage balance.

Non-renewable resources Finite resources that are depleted once they are consumed, such as oil and coal.

Non-sovereign bonds A bond issued by a government below the national level, such as a province, region, state, or city.

Non-sovereign government bonds A bond issued by a government below the national level, such as a province, region, state, or city.

Nonconventional cash flow In a nonconventional cash flow pattern, the initial outflow is not followed by inflows only, but the cash flows can flip from positive (inflows) to negative (outflows) again (or even change signs several times).

Nonparametric test A test that is not concerned with a parameter, or that makes minimal assumptions about the population from which a sample comes.

Nonsystematic risk Unique risk that is local or limited to a particular asset or industry that need not affect assets outside of that asset class.

Normal distribution A continuous, symmetric probability distribution that is completely described by its mean and its variance.
Normal goods Goods that are consumed in greater quantities as income increases.
Normal profit The level of accounting profit needed to just cover the implicit opportunity costs ignored in accounting costs.
Notching Ratings adjustment methodology where specific issues from the same borrower may be assigned different credit ratings.
Note rate See *mortgage rate.*
Notice period The length of time (typically 30–90 days) in advance that investors may be required to notify a fund of their intent to redeem some or all of their investment.
Notional principal An imputed principal amount.
Number of days of inventory An activity ratio equal to the number of days in a period divided by the inventory ratio for the period; an indication of the number of days a company ties up funds in inventory.
Number of days of payables An activity ratio equal to the number of days in a period divided by the payables turnover ratio for the period; an estimate of the average number of days it takes a company to pay its suppliers.
Number of days of receivables Estimate of the average number of days it takes to collect on credit accounts.
Objective probabilities Probabilities that generally do not vary from person to person; includes a priori and objective probabilities.
Off-the-run Seasoned government bonds are off-the-run securities; they are not the most recently issued or the most actively traded.
Offer The price at which a dealer or trader is willing to sell an asset, typically qualified by a maximum quantity (ask size).
Official interest rate An interest rate that a central bank sets and announces publicly; normally the rate at which it is willing to lend money to the commercial banks. Also called *official policy rate* or *policy rate.*
Official policy rate An interest rate that a central bank sets and announces publicly; normally the rate at which it is willing to lend money to the commercial banks.
Oligopoly Market structure with a relatively small number of firms supplying the market.
On-the-run The most recently issued and most actively traded sovereign securities.
One-sided hypothesis test A test in which the null hypothesis is rejected only if the evidence indicates that the population parameter is greater than (smaller than) θ_0. The alternative hypothesis also has one side.
One-tailed hypothesis test A test in which the null hypothesis is rejected only if the evidence indicates that the population parameter is greater than (smaller than) θ_0. The alternative hypothesis also has one side.
Open economy An economy that trades with other countries.
Open-end fund A mutual fund that accepts new investment money and issues additional shares at a value equal to the net asset value of the fund at the time of investment.
Open interest The number of outstanding contracts in a clearinghouse at any given time. The open interest figure changes daily as some parties open up new positions, while other parties offset their old positions.
Open market operations The purchase or sale of bonds by the national central bank to implement monetary policy. The bonds traded are usually sovereign bonds issued by the national government.
Operating activities Activities that are part of the day-to-day business functioning of an entity, such as selling inventory and providing services.
Operating breakeven The number of units produced and sold at which the company's operating profit is zero (revenues = operating costs).
Operating cash flow The net amount of cash provided from operating activities.
Operating cycle A measure of the time needed to convert raw materials into cash from a sale; it consists of the number of days of inventory and the number of days of receivables.
Operating efficiency ratios Ratios that measure how efficiently a company performs day-to-day tasks, such as the collection of receivables and management of inventory.
Operating lease An agreement allowing a lessee to use some asset for a period of time; essentially a rental.
Operating leverage The use of fixed costs in operations.
Operating profit A company's profits on its usual business activities before deducting taxes. Also called *operating income.*
Operating profit margin A profitability ratio calculated as operating income (i.e., income before interest and taxes) divided by revenue. Also called *operating margin.*
Operating risk The risk attributed to the operating cost structure, in particular the use of fixed costs in operations; the risk arising from the mix of fixed and variable costs; the risk that a company's operations may be severely affected by environmental, social, and governance risk factors.
Operational independence A bank's ability to execute monetary policy and set interest rates in the way it thought would best meet the inflation target.
Operational risk The risk that arises from inadequate or failed people, systems, and internal policies, procedures, and processes, as well as from external events that are beyond the control of the organization but that affect its operations.
Operationally efficient Said of a market, a financial system, or an economy that has relatively low transaction costs.
Opportunity cost The value that investors forgo by choosing a particular course of action; the value of something in its best alternative use.
Option A financial instrument that gives one party the right, but not the obligation, to buy or sell an underlying asset from or to another party at a fixed price over a specific period of time. Also referred to as *contingent claim* or *option contract.*
Option-adjusted price The value of the embedded option plus the flat price of the bond.
Option-adjusted spread OAS = Z-spread – Option value (in basis points per year).
Option-adjusted yield The required market discount rate whereby the price is adjusted for the value of the embedded option.
Option contract See *option.*
Option premium The amount of money a buyer pays and seller receives to engage in an option transaction.
Order A specification of what instrument to trade, how much to trade, and whether to buy or sell.

Order-driven markets A market (generally an auction market) that uses rules to arrange trades based on the orders that traders submit; in their pure form, such markets do not make use of dealers.

Order precedence hierarchy With respect to the execution of orders to trade, a set of rules that determines which orders execute before other orders.

Ordinal scale A measurement scale that sorts data into categories that are ordered (ranked) with respect to some characteristic.

Ordinary annuity An annuity with a first cash flow that is paid one period from the present.

Ordinary shares Equity shares that are subordinate to all other types of equity (e.g., preferred equity). Also called *common stock* or *common shares.*

Organized exchange A securities marketplace where buyers and seller can meet to arrange their trades.

Other comprehensive income Items of comprehensive income that are not reported on the income statement; comprehensive income minus net income.

Out-of-sample test A test of a strategy or model using a sample outside the time period on which the strategy or model was developed.

Out of the money Options that, if exercised, would require the payment of more money than the value received and therefore would not be currently exercised.

Outcome A possible value of a random variable.

Over-the-counter (OTC) markets A decentralized market where buy and sell orders initiated from various locations are matched through a communications network.

Overbought A market condition in which market sentiment is thought to be unsustainably bullish.

Overcollateralization Form of internal credit enhancement that refers to the process of posting more collateral than needed to obtain or secure financing.

Overfitting An undesirable result from fitting a model so closely to a dataset that it does not perform well on new data.

Overlay/portfolio tilt An ESG investment style that focuses on the use of certain investment strategies or products to change specific aggregate ESG characteristics of a fund or investment portfolio to a desired level (e.g., tilting an investment portfolio toward a desired carbon footprint).

Oversold A market condition in which market sentiment is thought to be unsustainably bearish.

Own price The price of a good or service itself (as opposed to the price of something else).

Own-price elasticity of demand The percentage change in quantity demanded for a percentage change in good's own price, holding all other things constant.

Owners' equity The excess of assets over liabilities; the residual interest of shareholders in the assets of an entity after deducting the entity's liabilities. Also called *shareholders' equity* or *shareholders' funds.*

Paasche index An index formula using the current composition of a basket of products.

Paired comparisons test A statistical test for differences based on paired observations drawn from samples that are dependent on each other.

Paired observations Observations that are dependent on each other.

Pairs arbitrage trade A trade in two closely related stocks involving the short sale of one and the purchase of the other.

Panel data Observations through time on a single characteristic of multiple observational units.

Par curve A sequence of yields-to-maturity such that each bond is priced at par value. The bonds are assumed to have the same currency, credit risk, liquidity, tax status, and annual yields stated for the same periodicity.

Par value The amount of principal on a bond.

Parallel shift A parallel yield curve shift implies that all rates change by the same amount in the same direction.

Parameter A descriptive measure computed from or used to describe a population of data, conventionally represented by Greek letters.

Parametric test Any test (or procedure) concerned with parameters or whose validity depends on assumptions concerning the population generating the sample.

Pari passu On an equal footing.

Partial duration See *key rate duration.*

Participating preference shares Preference shares that entitle shareholders to receive the standard preferred dividend plus the opportunity to receive an additional dividend if the company's profits exceed a pre-specified level.

Pass-through rate The coupon rate of a mortgage pass-through security.

Passive investment A buy and hold approach in which an investor does not make portfolio changes based on short-term expectations of changing market or security performance.

Passive strategy In reference to short-term cash management, it is an investment strategy characterized by simple decision rules for making daily investments.

Payable date The day that the company actually mails out (or electronically transfers) a dividend payment.

Payback period the number of years required to recover the original investment in a project. The payback is based on cash flows.

Payment date The day that the company actually mails out (or electronically transfers) a dividend payment.

Payments system The system for the transfer of money.

Peak The highest point of a business cycle.

Peer group A group of companies engaged in similar business activities whose economics and valuation are influenced by closely related factors.

Pennants A technical analysis continuation pattern formed by trendlines that converge to form a triangle, typically over a short period.

Per capita real GDP Real GDP divided by the size of the population, often used as a measure of the average standard of living in a country.

Per unit contribution margin The amount that each unit sold contributes to covering fixed costs—that is, the difference between the price per unit and the variable cost per unit.

Percentiles Quantiles that divide a distribution into 100 equal parts.

Perfect competition A market structure in which the individual firm has virtually no impact on market price, because it is assumed to be a very small seller among a very large number of firms selling essentially identical products.

Perfectly elastic When the quantity demanded or supplied of a given good is infinitely sensitive to a change in the value of a specified variable (e.g., price).

Perfectly inelastic When the quantity demanded or supplied of a given good is completely insensitive to a change in the value of a specified variable (e.g., price).

Performance bond See *margin bond.*

Performance evaluation The measurement and assessment of the outcomes of investment management decisions.

Performance fee Fees paid to the general partner from the limited partner(s) based on realized net profits.

Period costs Costs (e.g., executives' salaries) that cannot be directly matched with the timing of revenues and which are thus expensed immediately.

Periodicity The assumed number of periods in the year, typically matches the frequency of coupon payments.

Permanent differences Differences between tax and financial reporting of revenue (expenses) that will not be reversed at some future date. These result in a difference between the company's effective tax rate and statutory tax rate and do not result in a deferred tax item.

Permissioned networks Networks that are fully open only to select participants on a DLT network.

Permissionless networks Networks that are fully open to any user on a DLT network.

Permutation An ordered listing.

Perpetual bonds Bonds with no stated maturity date.

Perpetuity A perpetual annuity, or a set of never-ending level sequential cash flows, with the first cash flow occurring one period from now. A bond that does not mature.

Personal consumption expenditures All domestic personal consumption; the basis for a price index for such consumption called the PCE price index.

Personal disposable income Equal to personal income less personal taxes.

Personal income A broad measure of household income that includes all income received by households, whether earned or unearned; measures the ability of consumers to make purchases.

Plain vanilla bond Bond that makes periodic, fixed coupon payments during the bond's life and a lump-sum payment of principal at maturity. Also called *conventional bond.*

Platykurtic Describes a distribution that has relatively less weight in the tails than the normal distribution.

Point and figure chart A technical analysis chart that is constructed with columns of X's alternating with columns of O's such that the horizontal axis represents only the number of changes in price without reference to time or volume.

Point estimate A single numerical estimate of an unknown quantity, such as a population parameter.

Point of sale (POS) Systems that capture transaction data at the physical location in which the sale is made.

Policy rate An interest rate that a central bank sets and announces publicly; normally the rate at which it is willing to lend money to the commercial banks.

Population All members of a specified group.

Population mean The arithmetic mean value of a population; the arithmetic mean of all the observations or values in the population.

Population standard deviation A measure of dispersion relating to a population in the same unit of measurement as the observations, calculated as the positive square root of the population variance.

Population variance A measure of dispersion relating to a population, calculated as the mean of the squared deviations around the population mean.

Portfolio company In private equity, the company in which the private equity fund is investing.

Portfolio demand for money The demand to hold speculative money balances based on the potential opportunities or risks that are inherent in other financial instruments.

Portfolio planning The process of creating a plan for building a portfolio that is expected to satisfy a client's investment objectives.

Position The quantity of an asset that an entity owns or owes.

Positive screening An ESG investment style that focuses on the inclusion of certain sectors, companies, or practices in a fund or portfolio on the basis of specific minimum ESG criteria.

Posterior probability An updated probability that reflects or comes after new information.

Potential GDP The level of real GDP that can be produced at full employment; measures the productive capacity of the economy.

Power of a test The probability of correctly rejecting the null—that is, rejecting the null hypothesis when it is false.

Precautionary money balances Money held to provide a buffer against unforeseen events that might require money.

Precautionary stocks A level of inventory beyond anticipated needs that provides a cushion in the event that it takes longer to replenish inventory than expected or in the case of greater than expected demand.

Preference shares A type of equity interest which ranks above common shares with respect to the payment of dividends and the distribution of the company's net assets upon liquidation. They have characteristics of both debt and equity securities. Also called *preferred stock.*

Preferred stock See *preference shares.*

Premium In the case of bonds, premium refers to the amount by which a bond is priced above its face (par) value. In the case of an option, the amount paid for the option contract.

Prepaid expense A normal operating expense that has been paid in advance of when it is due.

Prepayment option Contractual provision that entitles the borrower to prepay all or part of the outstanding mortgage principal prior to the scheduled due date when the principal must be repaid. Also called *early repayment option.*

Prepayment penalty mortgages Mortgages that stipulate a monetary penalty if a borrower prepays within a certain time period after the mortgage is originated.

Prepayment risk The uncertainty that the timing of the actual cash flows will be different from the scheduled cash flows as set forth in the loan agreement due to the borrowers' ability to alter payments, usually to take advantage of interest rate movements.

Present value (PV) The present discounted value of future cash flows: For assets, the present discounted value of the future net cash inflows that the asset is expected to generate; for liabilities, the present discounted value of the future net cash outflows that are expected to be required to settle the liabilities.

Present value models Valuation models that estimate the intrinsic value of a security as the present value of the future benefits expected to be received from the security. Also called *discounted cash flow models.*

Pretax margin A profitability ratio calculated as earnings before taxes divided by revenue.

Price elasticity of demand Measures the percentage change in the quantity demanded, given a percentage change in the price of a given product.

Price index Represents the average prices of a basket of goods and services.

Price limits Limits imposed by a futures exchange on the price change that can occur from one day to the next.

Price multiple A ratio that compares the share price with some sort of monetary flow or value to allow evaluation of the relative worth of a company's stock.

Price priority The principle that the highest priced buy orders and the lowest priced sell orders execute first.

Price relative A ratio of an ending price over a beginning price; it is equal to 1 plus the holding period return on the asset.

Price return Measures *only* the price appreciation or percentage change in price of the securities in an index or portfolio.

Price return index An index that reflects *only* the price appreciation or percentage change in price of the constituent securities. Also called *price index*.

Price stability In economics, refers to an inflation rate that is low on average and not subject to wide fluctuation.

Price takers Producers that must accept whatever price the market dictates.

Price to book value A valuation ratio calculated as price per share divided by book value per share.

Price to cash flow A valuation ratio calculated as price per share divided by cash flow per share.

Price to earnings ratio (P/E ratio or P/E) The ratio of share price to earnings per share.

Price to sales A valuation ratio calculated as price per share divided by sales per share.

Price value of a basis point A version of money duration, it is an estimate of the change in the full price of a bond given a 1 basis point change in the yield-to-maturity.

Price weighting An index weighting method in which the weight assigned to each constituent security is determined by dividing its price by the sum of all the prices of the constituent securities.

Priced risk Risk for which investors demand compensation for bearing (e.g. equity risk, company-specific factors, macroeconomic factors).

Primary bond markets Markets in which issuers first sell bonds to investors to raise capital.

Primary capital markets (primary markets) The market where securities are first sold and the issuers receive the proceeds.

Primary dealers Financial institutions that are authorized to deal in new issues of sovereign bonds and that serve primarily as trading counterparties of the office responsible for issuing sovereign bonds.

Primary market The market where securities are first sold and the issuers receive the proceeds.

Prime brokers Brokers that provide services that commonly include custody, administration, lending, short borrowing, and trading.

Principal The amount of funds originally invested in a project or instrument; the face value to be paid at maturity.

Principal–agent relationship A relationship in which a principal hires an agent to perform a particular task or service; also known as an *agency relationship*.

Principal amount Amount that an issuer agrees to repay the debt holders on the maturity date.

Principal business activity The business activity from which a company derives a majority of its revenues and/or earnings.

Principal value Amount that an issuer agrees to repay the debt holders on the maturity date.

Principle of no arbitrage See *arbitrage-free pricing*.

Prior probabilities Probabilities reflecting beliefs prior to the arrival of new information.

Priority of claims Priority of payment, with the most senior or highest ranking debt having the first claim on the cash flows and assets of the issuer.

Private equity fund A hedge fund that seeks to buy, optimize, and ultimately sell portfolio companies to generate profits. See *venture capital fund*.

Private equity securities Securities that are not listed on public exchanges and have no active secondary market. They are issued primarily to institutional investors via non-public offerings, such as private placements.

Private investment in public equity (PIPE) An investment in the equity of a publicly traded firm that is made at a discount to the market value of the firm's shares.

Private placement Typically, a non-underwritten, unregistered offering of securities that are sold only to an investor or a small group of investors. It can be accomplished directly between the issuer and the investor(s) or through an investment bank.

Probability A number between 0 and 1 describing the chance that a stated event will occur.

Probability density function A function with non-negative values such that probability can be described by areas under the curve graphing the function.

Probability distribution A distribution that specifies the probabilities of a random variable's possible outcomes.

Probability function A function that specifies the probability that the random variable takes on a specific value.

Producer price index Reflects the price changes experienced by domestic producers in a country.

Production function Provides the quantitative link between the levels of output that the economy can produce and the inputs used in the production process.

Productivity The amount of output produced by workers in a given period of time—for example, output per hour worked; measures the efficiency of labor.

Profession An occupational group that has specific education, expert knowledge, and a framework of practice and behavior that underpins community trust, respect, and recognition.

Profit The return that owners of a company receive for the use of their capital and the assumption of financial risk when making their investments.

Profit and loss (P&L) statement A financial statement that provides information about a company's profitability over a stated period of time. Also called the *income statement*.

Profit margin An indicator of profitability, calculated as net income divided by revenue; indicates how much of each dollar of revenues is left after all costs and expenses.

Profitability index (PI) For a simple project, the PI is the present value of a project's future cash flows divided by the initial investment.

Profitability ratios Ratios that measure a company's ability to generate profitable sales from its resources (assets).

Project sequencing To defer the decision to invest in a future project until the outcome of some or all of a current project is known. Projects are sequenced through time, so that investing in a project creates the option to invest in future projects.

Promissory note A written promise to pay a certain amount of money on demand.

Property, plant, and equipment Tangible assets that are expected to be used for more than one period in either the production or supply of goods or services, or for administrative purposes.

Prospectus The document that describes the terms of a new bond issue and helps investors perform their analysis on the issue.

Protective put An option strategy in which a long position in an asset is combined with a long position in a put.

Proxy contest Corporate takeover mechanism in which shareholders are persuaded to vote for a group seeking a controlling position on a company's board of directors.

Proxy voting A process that enables shareholders who are unable to attend a meeting to authorize another individual to vote on their behalf.

Pseudo-random numbers Numbers produced by random number generators.

Public offer See *public offering.*

Public offering An offering of securities in which any member of the public may buy the securities. Also called *public offer.*

Pull on liquidity When disbursements are paid too quickly or trade credit availability is limited, requiring companies to expend funds before they receive funds from sales that could cover the liability.

Pure discount bonds See *zero-coupon bonds.*

Pure-play method A method for estimating the beta for a company or project; it requires using a comparable company's beta and adjusting it for financial leverage differences.

Put An option that gives the holder the right to sell an underlying asset to another party at a fixed price over a specific period of time.

Put–call–forward parity The relationship among puts, calls, and forward contracts.

Put–call parity An equation expressing the equivalence (parity) of a portfolio of a call and a bond with a portfolio of a put and the underlying, which leads to the relationship between put and call prices.

Put/call ratio A technical analysis indicator that evaluates market sentiment based upon the volume of put options traded divided by the volume of call options traded for a particular financial instrument.

Put option An option that gives the holder the right to sell an underlying asset to another party at a fixed price over a specific period of time.

Putable bonds Bonds that give the bondholder the right to sell the bond back to the issuer at a predetermined price on specified dates.

Quantile A value at or below which a stated fraction of the data lies. Also called *fractile.*

Quantitative easing An expansionary monetary policy based on aggressive open market purchase operations.

Quantity equation of exchange An expression that over a given period, the amount of money used to purchase all goods and services in an economy, $M \times V$, is equal to monetary value of this output, $P \times Y$.

Quantity theory of money Asserts that total spending (in money terms) is proportional to the quantity of money.

Quartiles Quantiles that divide a distribution into four equal parts.

Quasi-fixed cost A cost that stays the same over a range of production but can change to another constant level when production moves outside of that range.

Quasi-government bonds A bond issued by an entity that is either owned or sponsored by a national government. Also called *agency bond.*

Quick assets Assets that can be most readily converted to cash (e.g., cash, short-term marketable investments, receivables).

Quick ratio A stringent measure of liquidity that indicates a company's ability to satisfy current liabilities with its most liquid assets, calculated as (cash + short-term marketable investments + receivables) divided by current liabilities.

Quintiles Quantiles that divide a distribution into five equal parts.

Quota rents Profits that foreign producers can earn by raising the price of their goods higher than they would without a quota.

Quotas Government policies that restrict the quantity of a good that can be imported into a country, generally for a specified period of time.

Quote-driven market A market in which dealers acting as principals facilitate trading.

Quoted interest rate A quoted interest rate that does not account for compounding within the year. Also called *stated annual interest rate.*

Quoted margin The specified yield spread over the reference rate, used to compensate an investor for the difference in the credit risk of the issuer and that implied by the reference rate.

Random number An observation drawn from a uniform distribution.

Random number generator An algorithm that produces uniformly distributed random numbers between 0 and 1.

Random variable A quantity whose future outcomes are uncertain.

Range The difference between the maximum and minimum values in a dataset.

Ratio scales A measurement scale that has all the characteristics of interval measurement scales as well as a true zero point as the origin.

Real GDP The value of goods and services produced, measured at base year prices.

Real income Income adjusted for the effect of inflation on the purchasing power of money. Also known as the *purchasing power of income.* If income remains constant and a good's price falls, real income is said to rise, even though the number of monetary units (e.g., dollars) remains unchanged.

Real interest rate Nominal interest rate minus the expected rate of inflation.

Real risk-free interest rate The single-period interest rate for a completely risk-free security if no inflation were expected.

Realizable (settlement) value With reference to assets, the amount of cash or cash equivalents that could currently be obtained by selling the asset in an orderly disposal; with reference to liabilities, the undiscounted amount of cash or cash equivalents expected to be paid to satisfy the liabilities in the normal course of business.

Rebalancing Adjusting the weights of the constituent securities in an index.

Rebalancing policy The set of rules that guide the process of restoring a portfolio's asset class weights to those specified in the strategic asset allocation.

Recession A period during which real GDP decreases (i.e., negative growth) for at least two successive quarters, or a period of significant decline in total output, income, employment, and sales usually lasting from six months to a year.

Recognition lag The lag in government response to an economic problem resulting from the delay in confirming a change in the state of the economy.

Recourse loan Loan in which the lender has a claim against the borrower for any shortfall between the outstanding mortgage balance and the proceeds received from the sale of the property.

Redemption yield See *yield to maturity.*

Redemptions Withdrawals of funds by investors, as allowed by the notice period and other terms in the partnership agreement.

Refinancing rate A type of central bank policy rate.

Registered bonds Bonds for which ownership is recorded by either name or serial number.

Relative/best-in-class screening An ESG investment style that focuses on sectors, companies, or projects selected for ESG performance relative to industry peers.

Relative dispersion The amount of dispersion relative to a reference value or benchmark.

Relative frequency With reference to an interval of grouped data, the number of observations in the interval divided by the total number of observations in the sample.

Relative price The price of a specific good or service in comparison with those of other goods and services.

Relative strength analysis A comparison of the performance of one asset with the performance of another asset or a benchmark based on changes in the ratio of the securities' respective prices over time.

Relative strength index A technical analysis momentum oscillator that compares a security's gains with its losses over a set period.

Renewable resources Resources that can be replenished, such as a forest.

Rent Payment for the use of property.

Reorganization Agreements made by a company in bankruptcy under which a company's capital structure is altered and/or alternative arrangements are made for debt repayment; US Chapter 11 bankruptcy. The company emerges from bankruptcy as a going concern.

Replication The creation of an asset or portfolio from another asset, portfolio, and/or derivative.

Repo A form of collateralized loan involving the sale of a security with a simultaneous agreement by the seller to buy the same security back from the purchaser at an agreed-on price and future date. The party who sells the security at the inception of the repurchase agreement and buys it back at maturity is borrowing money from the other party, and the security sold and subsequently repurchased represents the collateral.

Repo margin The difference between the market value of the security used as collateral and the value of the loan. Also called *haircut.*

Repo rate The interest rate on a repurchase agreement.

Repurchase agreement A form of collateralized loan involving the sale of a security with a simultaneous agreement by the seller to buy the same security back from the purchaser at an agreed-on price and future date. The party who sells the security at the inception of the repurchase agreement and buys it back at maturity is borrowing money from the other party, and the security sold and subsequently repurchased represents the collateral.

Repurchase date The date when the party who sold the security at the inception of a repurchase agreement buys the security back from the cash lending counterparty.

Repurchase price The price at which the party who sold the security at the inception of the repurchase agreement buys the security back from the cash lending counterparty.

Required margin The yield spread over, or under, the reference rate such that an FRN is priced at par value on a rate reset date.

Required rate of return See *market discount rate.*

Required yield See *market discount rate.*

Required yield spread The difference between the yield-to-maturity on a new bond and the benchmark rate; additional compensation required by investors for the difference in risk and tax status of a bond relative to a government bond. Sometimes called the *spread over the benchmark.*

Reserve accounts Form of internal credit enhancement that relies on creating accounts and depositing in these accounts cash that can be used to absorb losses. Also called *reserve funds.*

Reserve funds See *reserve accounts.*

Reserve requirement The requirement for banks to hold reserves in proportion to the size of deposits.

Resistance In technical analysis, a price range in which selling activity is sufficient to stop the rise in the price of a security.

Responsible investing The practice of identifying companies that can efficiently manage their financial, environmental, and human capital resources to generate attractive long-term profitability; often synonymous with *sustainable investing.*

Restricted payments A bond covenant meant to protect creditors by limiting how much cash can be paid out to shareholders over time.

Retracement In technical analysis, a reversal in the movement of a security's price such that it is counter to the prevailing longerterm price trend.

Return-generating model A model that can provide an estimate of the expected return of a security given certain parameters and estimates of the values of the independent variables in the model.

Return on assets (ROA) A profitability ratio calculated as net income divided by average total assets; indicates a company's net profit generated per dollar invested in total assets.

Return on equity (ROE) A profitability ratio calculated as net income divided by average shareholders' equity.

Return on sales An indicator of profitability, calculated as net income divided by revenue; indicates how much of each dollar of revenues is left after all costs and expenses. Also referred to as *net profit margin.*

Return on total capital A profitability ratio calculated as EBIT divided by the sum of short- and long-term debt and equity.

Revaluation model Under IFRS, the process of valuing long-lived assets at fair value, rather than at cost less accumulated depreciation. Any resulting profit or loss is either reported on the income statement and/or through equity under revaluation surplus.

Revenue The amount charged for the delivery of goods or services in the ordinary activities of a business over a stated period; the inflows of economic resources to a company over a stated period.

Reversal patterns A type of pattern used in technical analysis to predict the end of a trend and a change in direction of the security's price.

Reverse repo A repurchase agreement viewed from the perspective of the cash lending counterparty.

Reverse repurchase agreement A repurchase agreement viewed from the perspective of the cash lending counterparty.

Reverse stock split A reduction in the number of shares outstanding with a corresponding increase in share price, but no change to the company's underlying fundamentals.
Revolving credit agreements The strongest form of short-term bank borrowing facilities; they are in effect for multiple years (e.g., 3–5 years) and may have optional medium-term loan features.
Rho The sensitivity of the option price to the risk-free rate.
Ricardian equivalence An economic theory that implies that it makes no difference whether a government finances a deficit by increasing taxes or issuing debt.
Risk Exposure to uncertainty. The chance of a loss or adverse outcome as a result of an action, inaction, or external event.
Risk averse The assumption that an investor will choose the least risky alternative.
Risk aversion The degree of an investor's inability and unwillingness to take risk.
Risk budgeting The establishment of objectives for individuals, groups, or divisions of an organization that takes into account the allocation of an acceptable level of risk.
Risk exposure The state of being exposed or vulnerable to a risk. The extent to which an organization is sensitive to underlying risks.
Risk factor/risk premium investing An ESG investment style that focuses on the inclusion of ESG information in the analysis of systematic risks as, for example, in smart beta and factor investment strategies (similar to size, value, momentum, and growth strategies).
Risk governance The top-down process and guidance that directs risk management activities to align with and support the overall enterprise.
Risk management The process of identifying the level of risk an organization wants, measuring the level of risk the organization currently has, taking actions that bring the actual level of risk to the desired level of risk, and monitoring the new actual level of risk so that it continues to be aligned with the desired level of risk.
Risk management framework The infrastructure, process, and analytics needed to support effective risk management in an organization.
Risk-neutral pricing Sometimes said of derivatives pricing, uses the fact that arbitrage opportunities guarantee that a risk-free portfolio consisting of the underlying and the derivative must earn the risk-free rate.
Risk-neutral probabilities Weights that are used to compute a binomial option price. They are the probabilities that would apply if a risk-neutral investor valued an option.
Risk premium An extra return expected by investors for bearing some specified risk.
Risk shifting Actions to change the distribution of risk outcomes.
Risk tolerance The amount of risk an investor is willing and able to bear to achieve an investment goal.
Risk transfer Actions to pass on a risk to another party, often, but not always, in the form of an insurance policy.
Robo-adviser A machine-based analytical tool or service that provides technology-driven investment solutions through online platforms.
Robust The quality of being relatively unaffected by a violation of assumptions.
Rule of 72 The principle that the approximate number of years necessary for an investment to double is 72 divided by the stated interest rate.
Running yield See *current yield.*
Safety-first rules Rules for portfolio selection that focus on the risk that portfolio value will fall below some minimum acceptable level over some time horizon.
Safety stock A level of inventory beyond anticipated needs that provides a cushion in the event that it takes longer to replenish inventory than expected or in the case of greater than expected demand.
Sales Generally, a synonym for revenue; "sales" is generally understood to refer to the sale of goods, whereas "revenue" is understood to include the sale of goods or services.
Sales risk Uncertainty with respect to the quantity of goods and services that a company is able to sell and the price it is able to achieve; the risk related to the uncertainty of revenues.
Sales-type leases Under US GAAP, a type of finance lease, from a lessor perspective, where the present value of the lease payments (lease receivable) exceeds the carrying value of the leased asset. The revenues earned by the lessor both a selling profit at inception and financing (interest) revenues.
Sample A subset of a population.
Sample excess kurtosis A sample measure of the degree of a distribution's kurtosis in excess of the normal distribution's kurtosis.
Sample kurtosis A sample measure of the degree of a distribution's peakedness.
Sample mean The sum of the sample observations, divided by the sample size.
Sample selection bias Bias introduced by systematically excluding some members of the population according to a particular attribute—for example, the bias introduced when data availability leads to certain observations being excluded from the analysis.
Sample skewness A sample measure of degree of asymmetry of a distribution.
Sample standard deviation The positive square root of the sample variance.
Sample statistic A quantity computed from or used to describe a sample.
Sample variance A sample measure of the degree of dispersion of a distribution, calculated by dividing the sum of the squared deviations from the sample mean by the sample size minus 1.
Sampling The process of obtaining a sample.
Sampling distribution The distribution of all distinct possible values that a statistic can assume when computed from samples of the same size randomly drawn from the same population.
Sampling error The difference between the observed value of a statistic and the quantity it is intended to estimate.
Sampling plan The set of rules used to select a sample.
Say on pay A process whereby shareholders may vote on executive remuneration (compensation) matters.
Say's law Named for French economist J.B. Say: All that is produced will be sold because supply creates its own demand.
Scatter plot A two-dimensional plot of pairs of observations on two data series.
Scenario analysis Analysis that shows the changes in key financial quantities that result from given (economic) events, such as the loss of customers, the loss of a supply source, or a catastrophic event; a risk management technique involving examination of the performance of a portfolio under specified situations. Closely related to stress testing.

Screening The application of a set of criteria to reduce a set of potential investments to a smaller set having certain desired characteristics.

Seasoned offering An offering in which an issuer sells additional units of a previously issued security.

Second-degree price discrimination When the monopolist charges different per-unit prices using the quantity purchased as an indicator of how highly the customer values the product.

Second lien A secured interest in the pledged assets that ranks below first lien debt in both collateral protection and priority of payment.

Secondary bond markets Markets in which existing bonds are traded among investors.

Secondary market The market where securities are traded among investors.

Secondary precedence rules Rules that determine how to rank orders placed at the same time.

Sector A group of related industries.

Sector indexes Indexes that represent and track different economic sectors—such as consumer goods, energy, finance, health care, and technology—on either a national, regional, or global basis.

Secured bonds Bonds secured by assets or financial guarantees pledged to ensure debt repayment in case of default.

Secured debt Debt in which the debtholder has a direct claim—a pledge from the issuer—on certain assets and their associated cash flows.

Securitization A process that involves moving assets into a special legal entity, which then uses the assets as guarantees to secure a bond issue.

Securitized assets Assets that are typically used to create asset-backed bonds; for example, when a bank securitizes a pool of loans, the loans are said to be securitized.

Security characteristic line A plot of the excess return of a security on the excess return of the market.

Security market index A portfolio of securities representing a given security market, market segment, or asset class.

Security market line (SML) The graph of the capital asset pricing model.

Security selection The process of selecting individual securities; typically, security selection has the objective of generating superior risk-adjusted returns relative to a portfolio's benchmark.

Self-investment limits With respect to investment limitations applying to pension plans, restrictions on the percentage of assets that can be invested in securities issued by the pension plan sponsor.

Sell-side firm A broker/dealer that sells securities and provides independent investment research and recommendations to their clients (i.e., buy-side firms).

Semi-strong-form efficient market A market in which security prices reflect all publicly known and available information.

Semiannual bond basis yield An annual rate having a periodicity of two; also known as a *semiannual bond equivalent yield*.

Semiannual bond equivalent yield See *semiannual bond basis yield*.

Semideviation The positive square root of semivariance (sometimes called *semistandard deviation*).

Semilogarithmic Describes a scale constructed so that equal intervals on the vertical scale represent equal rates of change, and equal intervals on the horizontal scale represent equal amounts of change.

Semivariance The average squared deviation below the mean.

Seniority ranking Priority of payment of various debt obligations.

Sensitivity analysis Analysis that shows the range of possible outcomes as specific assumptions are changed.

Separately managed account (SMA) An investment portfolio managed exclusively for the benefit of an individual or institution.

Serial maturity structure Structure for a bond issue in which the maturity dates are spread out during the bond's life; a stated number of bonds mature and are paid off each year before final maturity.

Settlement The process that occurs after a trade is completed, the securities are passed to the buyer, and payment is received by the seller.

Settlement date Date when the buyer makes cash payment and the seller delivers the security.

Settlement price The official price, designated by the clearinghouse, from which daily gains and losses will be determined and marked to market.

Share repurchase A transaction in which a company buys back its own shares. Unlike stock dividends and stock splits, share repurchases use corporate cash.

Shareholder activism Strategies used by shareholders to attempt to compel a company to act in a desired manner.

Shareholder engagement The process whereby companies engage with their shareholders.

Shareholders' equity Assets less liabilities; the residual interest in the assets after subtracting the liabilities.

Sharpe ratio The average return in excess of the risk-free rate divided by the standard deviation of return; a measure of the average excess return earned per unit of standard deviation of return.

Shelf registration Type of public offering that allows the issuer to file a single, all-encompassing offering circular that covers a series of bond issues.

Short The seller of an asset or derivative contract. Also refers to the position of being short an asset or derivative contract.

Short position A position in an asset or contract in which one has sold an asset one does not own, or in which a right under a contract can be exercised against oneself.

Short-run average total cost The curve describing average total cost when some costs are considered fixed.

Short selling A transaction in which borrowed securities are sold with the intention to repurchase them at a lower price at a later date and return them to the lender.

Shortfall risk The risk that portfolio value will fall below some minimum acceptable level over some time horizon.

Shutdown point The point at which average revenue is equal to the firm's average variable cost.

Simple interest The interest earned each period on the original investment; interest calculated on the principal only.

Simple random sample A subset of a larger population created in such a way that each element of the population has an equal probability of being selected to the subset.

Simple random sampling The procedure of drawing a sample to satisfy the definition of a simple random sample.

Simple yield The sum of the coupon payments plus the straight-line amortized share of the gain or loss, divided by the flat price.

Simulation Computer-generated sensitivity or scenario analysis that is based on probability models for the factors that drive outcomes.

Simulation trial A complete pass through the steps of a simulation.

Single-step format With respect to the format of the income statement, a format that does not subtotal for gross profit (revenue minus cost of goods sold).

Sinking fund arrangement Provision that reduces the credit risk of a bond issue by requiring the issuer to retire a portion of the bond's principal outstanding each year.

Situational influences External factors, such as environmental or cultural elements, that shape our behavior.

Skewed Not symmetrical.

Skewness A quantitative measure of skew (lack of symmetry); a synonym of skew.

Small country A country that is a price taker in the world market for a product and cannot influence the world market price.

Smart beta Involves the use of simple, transparent, rules-based strategies as a basis for investment decisions.

Smart contract A computer program that is designed to self-execute on the basis of pre-specified terms and conditions agreed to by parties to a contract.

Socially responsible investing An investment approach that excludes investments in companies or industries that deviate from an organization's beliefs and sometimes includes investments with favorable environmental or social profiles.

Solvency With respect to financial statement analysis, the ability of a company to fulfill its long-term obligations.

Solvency ratios Ratios that measure a company's ability to meet its long-term obligations.

Solvency risk The risk that an organization does not survive or succeed because it runs out of cash, even though it might otherwise be solvent.

Sovereign A bond issued by a national government.

Sovereign bond A bond issued by a national government.

Sovereign yield spread An estimate of the country spread (country equity premium) for a developing nation that is based on a comparison of bonds yields in country being analyzed and a developed country. The sovereign yield spread is the difference between a government bond yield in the country being analyzed, denominated in the currency of the developed country, and the Treasury bond yield on a similar maturity bond in the developed country.

Spearman rank correlation coefficient A measure of correlation applied to ranked data.

Special dividend A dividend paid by a company that does not pay dividends on a regular schedule, or a dividend that supplements regular cash dividends with an extra payment.

Special purpose entity A non-operating entity created to carry out a specified purpose, such as leasing assets or securitizing receivables; can be a corporation, partnership, trust, limited liability, or partnership formed to facilitate a specific type of business activity. Also called *special purpose vehicle* or *variable interest entity*.

Special purpose vehicle See *special purpose entity*.

Specific identification method An inventory accounting method that identifies which specific inventory items were sold and which remained in inventory to be carried over to later periods.

Speculative demand for money The demand to hold speculative money balances based on the potential opportunities or risks that are inherent in other financial instruments. Also called *portfolio demand for money*.

Speculative money balances Monies held in anticipation that other assets will decline in value.

Split coupon bond See *deferred coupon bond*.

Sponsored A type of depository receipt in which the foreign company whose shares are held by the depository has a direct involvement in the issuance of the receipts.

Spot curve A sequence of yields-to-maturity on zero-coupon bonds. Sometimes called *zero* or *strip curve* because coupon payments are "stripped" off of the bonds.

Spot markets Markets in which assets are traded for immediate delivery.

Spot prices The price of an asset for immediately delivery.

Spot rates A sequence of market discount rates that correspond to the cash flow dates; yields-to-maturity on zero-coupon bonds maturing at the date of each cash flow.

Spread In general, the difference in yield between different fixed income securities. Often used to refer to the difference between the yield-to-maturity and the benchmark.

Spread over the benchmark See *required yield spread*.

Spread risk Bond price risk arising from changes in the yield spread on credit-risky bonds; reflects changes in the market's assessment and/or pricing of credit migration (or downgrade) risk and market liquidity risk.

Spurious correlation A correlation that misleadingly points toward associations between variables.

Stackelberg model A prominent model of strategic decision making in which firms are assumed to make their decisions sequentially.

Stagflation When a high inflation rate is combined with a high level of unemployment and a slowdown of the economy.

Staggered boards Election process whereby directors are typically divided into multiple classes that are elected separately in consecutive years—that is, one class every year.

Stakeholder management The identification, prioritization, and understanding of the interests of stakeholder groups, and managing the company's relationships with these groups.

Stakeholders Individuals or groups of individuals who may be affected either directly or indirectly by a decision and thus have an interest, or stake, in the decision.

Standard deviation The positive square root of the variance; a measure of dispersion in the same units as the original data.

Standard normal distribution The normal density with mean (μ) equal to 0 and standard deviation (σ) equal to 1.

Standardizing A transformation that involves subtracting the mean and dividing the result by the standard deviation.

Standards of conduct Behaviors required by a group; established benchmarks that clarify or enhance a group's code of ethics.

Standing limit orders A limit order at a price below market and which therefore is waiting to trade.

Stated annual interest rate A quoted interest rate that does not account for compounding within the year. Also called *quoted interest rate*.

Statement of changes in equity (statement of owners' equity) A financial statement that reconciles the beginning-of-period and end-of-period balance sheet values of shareholders' equity; provides information about all factors affecting shareholders' equity. Also called *statement of owners' equity*.

Statement of financial condition The financial statement that presents an entity's current financial position by disclosing resources the entity controls (its assets) and the claims on those resources (its liabilities and equity claims), as of a particular point in time (the date of the balance sheet).

Statement of financial position The financial statement that presents an entity's current financial position by disclosing resources the entity controls (its assets) and the claims on those resources (its liabilities and equity claims), as of a particular point in time (the date of the balance sheet).

Statement of operations A financial statement that provides information about a company's profitability over a stated period of time.

Statistic A quantity computed from or used to describe a sample of data.

Statistical inference Making forecasts, estimates, or judgments about a larger group from a smaller group actually observed; using a sample statistic to infer the value of an unknown population parameter.

Statistically significant A result indicating that the null hypothesis can be rejected; with reference to an estimated regression coefficient, frequently understood to mean a result indicating that the corresponding population regression coefficient is different from 0.

Statutory voting A common method of voting where each share represents one vote.

Step-up coupon bond Bond for which the coupon, which may be fixed or floating, increases by specified margins at specified dates.

Stock dividend A type of dividend in which a company distributes additional shares of its common stock to shareholders instead of cash.

Stock-out losses Profits lost from not having sufficient inventory on hand to satisfy demand.

Stock split An increase in the number of shares outstanding with a consequent decrease in share price, but no change to the company's underlying fundamentals.

Stop-loss order See *stop order*.

Stop order An order in which a trader has specified a stop price condition. Also called *stop-loss order*.

Store of value The quality of tending to preserve value.

Store of wealth Goods that depend on the fact that they do not perish physically over time, and on the belief that others would always value the good.

Straight-line method A depreciation method that allocates evenly the cost of a long-lived asset less its estimated residual value over the estimated useful life of the asset.

Straight voting A shareholder voting process in which shareholders receive one vote for each share owned.

Strategic analysis Analysis of the competitive environment with an emphasis on the implications of the environment for corporate strategy.

Strategic asset allocation The set of exposures to IPS-permissible asset classes that is expected to achieve the client's long-term objectives given the client's investment constraints.

Strategic groups Groups sharing distinct business models or catering to specific market segments in an industry.

Street convention Yield measure that neglects weekends and holidays; the internal rate of return on cash flows assuming payments are made on the scheduled dates, even when the scheduled date falls on a weekend or holiday.

Stress testing A specific type of scenario analysis that estimates losses in rare and extremely unfavorable combinations of events or scenarios.

Strong-form efficient market A market in which security prices reflect all public and private information.

Structural (or cyclically adjusted) budget deficit The deficit that would exist if the economy was at full employment (or full potential output).

Structural subordination Arises in a holding company structure when the debt of operating subsidiaries is serviced by the cash flow and assets of the subsidiaries before funds can be passed to the holding company to service debt at the parent level.

Structured financial instruments Financial instruments that share the common attribute of repackaging risks. Structured financial instruments include asset-backed securities, collateralized debt obligations, and other structured financial instruments such as capital protected, yield enhancement, participation and leveraged instruments.

Subjective probability A probability drawing on personal or subjective judgment.

Subordinated debt A class of unsecured debt that ranks below a firm's senior unsecured obligations.

Subordination Form of internal credit enhancement that relies on creating more than one bond tranche and ordering the claim priorities for ownership or interest in an asset between the tranches. The ordering of the claim priorities is called a senior/subordinated structure, where the tranches of highest seniority are called senior followed by subordinated or junior tranches. Also called *credit tranching*.

Substitutes Said of two goods or services such that if the price of one increases the demand for the other tends to increase, holding all other things equal (e.g., butter and margarine).

Sunk cost A cost that has already been incurred.

Supervised learning A machine learning approach that makes use of labeled training data.

Supply shock A typically unexpected disturbance to supply.

Support In technical analysis, a price range in which buying activity is sufficient to stop the decline in the price of a security.

Support tranche A class or tranche in a CMO that protects the PAC tranche from prepayment risk.

Supranational bonds A bond issued by a supranational agency such as the World Bank.

Surety bond Form of external credit enhancement whereby a rated and regulated insurance company guarantees to reimburse bondholders for any losses incurred up to a maximum amount if the issuer defaults.

Survey approach An estimate of the equity risk premium that is based upon estimates provided by a panel of finance experts.

Survivorship bias The bias resulting from a test design that fails to account for companies that have gone bankrupt, merged, or are otherwise no longer reported in a database.

Sustainable growth rate The rate of dividend (and earnings) growth that can be sustained over time for a given level of return on equity, keeping the capital structure constant and without issuing additional common stock.

Sustainable investing The practice of identifying companies that can efficiently manage their financial, environmental, and human capital resources to generate attractive long-term profitability; often synonymous with *responsible investing*.

Sustainable rate of economic growth The rate of increase in the economy's productive capacity or potential GDP.

Swap contract An agreement between two parties to exchange a series of future cash flows.

Syndicated loans Loans from a group of lenders to a single borrower.

Syndicated offering A bond issue that is underwritten by a group of investment banks.

Systematic risk Risk that affects the entire market or economy; it cannot be avoided and is inherent in the overall market. Systematic risk is also known as non-diversifiable or market risk.

Systematic sampling A procedure of selecting every kth member until reaching a sample of the desired size. The sample that results from this procedure should be approximately random.

***t*-Test** A hypothesis test using a statistic (t-statistic) that follows a t-distribution.

Tactical asset allocation The decision to deliberately deviate from the strategic asset allocation in an attempt to add value based on forecasts of the near-term relative performance of asset classes.

Target balance A minimum level of cash to be held available—estimated in advance and adjusted for known funds transfers, seasonality, or other factors.

Target capital structure A company's chosen proportions of debt and equity.

Target independent A bank's ability to determine the definition of inflation that they target, the rate of inflation that they target, and the horizon over which the target is to be achieved.

Target semideviation The positive square root of target semivariance.

Target semivariance The average squared deviation below a target value.

Tariffs Taxes that a government levies on imported goods.

Tax base The amount at which an asset or liability is valued for tax purposes.

Tax expense An aggregate of an entity's income tax payable (or recoverable in the case of a tax benefit) and any changes in deferred tax assets and liabilities. It is essentially the income tax payable or recoverable if these had been determined based on accounting profit rather than taxable income.

Tax loss carry forward A taxable loss in the current period that may be used to reduce future taxable income.

Taxable income The portion of an entity's income that is subject to income taxes under the tax laws of its jurisdiction.

Taxable temporary differences Temporary differences that result in a taxable amount in a future period when determining the taxable profit as the balance sheet item is recovered or settled.

Technical analysis A form of security analysis that uses price and volume data, which is often displayed graphically, in decision making.

Technology The process a company uses to transform inputs into outputs.

Tender offer Corporate takeover mechanism which involves shareholders selling their interests directly to the group seeking to gain control.

Tenor The time-to-maturity for a bond or derivative contract. Also called *term to maturity*.

Term maturity structure Structure for a bond issue in which the bond's notional principal is paid off in a lump sum at maturity.

Term structure See *maturity structure*.

Term structure of credit spreads The relationship between the spreads over the "risk-free" (or benchmark) rates and times-to-maturity.

Term structure of yield volatility The relationship between the volatility of bond yields-to-maturity and times-to-maturity.

Terminal stock value The expected value of a share at the end of the investment horizon—in effect, the expected selling price. Also called *terminal value*.

Terminal value The expected value of a share at the end of the investment horizon—in effect, the expected selling price.

Terms of trade The ratio of the price of exports to the price of imports, representing those prices by export and import price indexes, respectively.

Text analytics The use of computer programs to analyze and derive meaning from typically large, unstructured text- or voice-based datasets.

Thematic investment An ESG investing style that focuses on investing in themes or assets specifically relating to ESG factors, such as clean energy, green technology, or sustainable agriculture.

Third-degree price discrimination When the monopolist segregates customers into groups based on demographic or other characteristics and offers different pricing to each group.

Time-period bias The possibility that when we use a time-series sample, our statistical conclusion may be sensitive to the starting and ending dates of the sample.

Time-series data Observations of a variable over time.

Time tranching The creation of classes or tranches in an ABS/MBS that possess different (expected) maturities.

Time value The difference between the market price of the option and its intrinsic value.

Time value decay Said of an option when, at expiration, no time value remains and the option is worth only its exercise value.

Time value of money The principles governing equivalence relationships between cash flows with different dates.

Time-weighted rate of return The compound rate of growth of one unit of currency invested in a portfolio during a stated measurement period; a measure of investment performance that is not sensitive to the timing and amount of withdrawals or additions to the portfolio.

Tokenization The process of representing ownership rights to physical assets on a blockchain or distributed ledger.

Top-down analysis An investment selection approach that begins with consideration of macroeconomic conditions and then evaluates markets and industries based upon such conditions.

Total comprehensive income The change in equity during a period resulting from transaction and other events, other than those changes resulting from transactions with owners in their capacity as owners.

Total cost The summation of all costs, for which costs are classified as fixed or variable.

Total factor productivity A scale factor that reflects the portion of growth that is not accounted for by explicit factor inputs (e.g. capital and labor).

Total fixed cost The summation of all expenses that do not change as the level of production varies.

Total invested capital The sum of market value of common equity, book value of preferred equity, and face value of debt.

Total probability rule A rule explaining the unconditional probability of an event in terms of probabilities of the event conditional on mutually exclusive and exhaustive scenarios.

Total probability rule for expected value A rule explaining the expected value of a random variable in terms of expected values of the random variable conditional on mutually exclusive and exhaustive scenarios.

Total return Measures the price appreciation, or percentage change in price of the securities in an index or portfolio, plus any income received over the period.

Total return index An index that reflects the price appreciation or percentage change in price of the constituent securities plus any income received since inception.

Total return swap A swap in which one party agrees to pay the total return on a security. Often used as a credit derivative, in which the underlying is a bond.

Total variable cost The summation of all variable expenses.

Tracking error The standard deviation of the differences between a portfolio's returns and its benchmark's returns; a synonym of active risk.

Tracking risk The standard deviation of the differences between a portfolio's returns and its benchmarks returns. Also called *tracking error*.

Trade creation When regional integration results in the replacement of higher cost domestic production by lower cost imports from other members.

Trade credit A spontaneous form of credit in which a purchaser of the goods or service is financing its purchase by delaying the date on which payment is made.

Trade diversion When regional integration results in lower-cost imports from non-member countries being replaced with higher-cost imports from members.

Trade payables Amounts that a business owes to its vendors for goods and services that were purchased from them but which have not yet been paid.

Trade protection Government policies that impose restrictions on trade, such as tariffs and quotas.

Trade surplus (deficit) When the value of exports is greater (less) than the value of imports.

Trading securities Under US GAAP, a category of debt securities held by a company with the intent to trade them. Also called *held-for-trading securities*.

Traditional investment markets Markets for traditional investments, which include all publicly traded debts and equities and shares in pooled investment vehicles that hold publicly traded debts and/or equities.

Transactions money balances Money balances that are held to finance transactions.

Transactions motive In the context of inventory management, the need for inventory as part of the routine production–sales cycle.

Transfer payments Welfare payments made through the social security system that exist to provide a basic minimum level of income for low-income households.

Transparency Said of something (e.g., a market) in which information is fully disclosed to the public and/or regulators.

Treasury Inflation-Protected Securities A bond issued by the United States Treasury Department that is designed to protect the investor from inflation by adjusting the principal of the bond for changes in inflation.

Treasury stock method A method for accounting for the effect of options (and warrants) on earnings per share (EPS) that specifies what EPS would have been if the options and warrants had been exercised and the company had used the proceeds to repurchase common stock.

Tree diagram A diagram with branches emanating from nodes representing either mutually exclusive chance events or mutually exclusive decisions.

Trend A long-term pattern of movement in a particular direction.

Treynor ratio A measure of risk-adjusted performance that relates a portfolio's excess returns to the portfolio's beta.

Triangle patterns In technical analysis, a continuation chart pattern that forms as the range between high and low prices narrows, visually forming a triangle.

Trimmed mean A mean computed after excluding a stated small percentage of the lowest and highest observations.

TRIN A flow of funds indicator applied to a broad stock market index to measure the relative extent to which money is moving into or out of rising and declining stocks.

Triple bottoms In technical analysis, a reversal pattern that is formed when the price forms three troughs at roughly the same price level; used to predict a change from a downtrend to an uptrend.

Triple tops In technical analysis, a reversal pattern that is formed when the price forms three peaks at roughly the same price level; used to predict a change from an uptrend to a downtrend.

Trough The lowest point of a business cycle.

True yield The internal rate of return on cash flows using the actual calendar including weekends and bank holidays.

Trust deed The governing legal credit agreement, typically incorporated by reference in the prospectus. Also called *bond indenture*.

Trust receipt arrangement The use of inventory as collateral for a loan. The inventory is segregated and held in trust, and the proceeds of any sale must be remitted to the lender immediately.

Turn-of-the-year effect Calendar anomaly that stock market returns in January are significantly higher compared to the rest of the months of the year, with most of the abnormal returns reported during the first five trading days in January.

Two-fund separation theorem The theory that all investors regardless of taste, risk preferences, and initial wealth will hold a combination of two portfolios or funds: a risk-free asset and an optimal portfolio of risky assets.

Two-sided hypothesis test A test in which the null hypothesis is rejected in favor of the alternative hypothesis if the evidence indicates that the population parameter is either smaller or larger than a hypothesized value.

Two-tailed hypothesis test A test in which the null hypothesis is rejected in favor of the alternative hypothesis if the evidence indicates that the population parameter is either smaller or larger than a hypothesized value.

Two-week repo rate The interest rate on a two-week repurchase agreement; may be used as a policy rate by a central bank.

Type I error The error of rejecting a true null hypothesis.

Type II error The error of not rejecting a false null hypothesis.

Unanticipated (unexpected) inflation The component of inflation that is a surprise.

Unconditional probability The probability of an event *not* conditioned on another event.

Underemployed A person who has a job but has the qualifications to work a significantly higher-paying job.

Underlying An asset that trades in a market in which buyers and sellers meet, decide on a price, and the seller then delivers the asset to the buyer and receives payment. The underlying is the asset or other derivative on which a particular derivative is based. The market for the underlying is also referred to as the *spot market*.

Underwriter A firm, usually an investment bank, that takes the risk of buying the newly issued securities from the issuer, and then reselling them to investors or to dealers, thus guaranteeing the sale of the securities at the offering price negotiated with the issuer.

Underwritten offering A type of securities issue mechanism in which the investment bank guarantees the sale of the securities at an offering price that is negotiated with the issuer. Also known as *firm commitment offering*.

Unearned revenue A liability account for money that has been collected for goods or services that have not yet been delivered; payment received in advance of providing a good or service. Also called *deferred revenue* or *deferred income*.

Unemployed People who are actively seeking employment but are currently without a job.

Unemployment rate The ratio of unemployed to the labor force.

Unexpected inflation The component of inflation that is a surprise.

Unit elastic An elasticity with a magnitude of negative one. Also called *unitary elastic*.

Unit labor cost The average labor cost to produce one unit of output.

Unit normal distribution The normal density with mean (μ) equal to 0 and standard deviation (σ) equal to 1.

Units-of-production method A depreciation method that allocates the cost of a long-lived asset based on actual usage during the period.

Univariate distribution A distribution that specifies the probabilities for a single random variable.

Universal owners Long-term investors, such as pension funds, that have significant assets invested in globally diversified portfolios.

Unlimited funds An unlimited funds environment assumes that the company can raise the funds it wants for all profitable projects simply by paying the required rate of return.

Unsecured debt Debt which gives the debtholder only a general claim on an issuer's assets and cash flow.

Unsponsored A type of depository receipt in which the foreign company whose shares are held by the depository has no involvement in the issuance of the receipts.

Unsupervised learning A machine learning approach that does not make use of labeled training data.

Up transition probability The probability that an asset's value moves up.

Validity instructions Instructions which indicate when the order may be filled.

Valuation allowance A reserve created against deferred tax assets, based on the likelihood of realizing the deferred tax assets in future accounting periods.

Valuation ratios Ratios that measure the quantity of an asset or flow (e.g., earnings) in relation to the price associated with a specified claim (e.g., a share or ownership of the enterprise).

Value at risk (VaR) A money measure of the minimum value of losses expected during a specified time period at a given level of probability.

Value investors With reference to equity investors, investors who are focused on paying a relatively low share price in relation to earnings or assets per share.

VaR See *value at risk*.

Variable costs Costs that fluctuate with the level of production and sales.

Variance The expected value (the probability-weighted average) of squared deviations from a random variable's expected value.

Variation margin Additional margin that must be deposited in an amount sufficient to bring the balance up to the initial margin requirement.

Veblen goods Goods that increase in desirability with increasing price.

Vega A measure of the sensitivity of an option's price to changes in the underlying's volatility.

Venture capital Investments that provide "seed" or startup capital, early-stage financing, or later-stage financing (including mezzanine-stage financing) to companies that are in early development stages and require additional capital for expansion or preparation for an initial public offering.

Venture capital fund A hedge fund that seeks to buy, optimize, and ultimately sell portfolio companies to generate profits. See *private equity fund*.

Vertical analysis Common-size analysis using only one reporting period or one base financial statement; for example, an income statement in which all items are stated as percentages of sales.

Vertical demand schedule Implies that some fixed quantity is demanded, regardless of price.

Volatility As used in option pricing, the standard deviation of the continuously compounded returns on the underlying asset.

Voluntarily unemployed A person voluntarily outside the labor force, such as a jobless worker refusing an available vacancy.

Voluntary export restraint A trade barrier under which the exporting country agrees to limit its exports of the good to its trading partners to a specific number of units.

Vote by proxy A mechanism that allows a designated party—such as another shareholder, a shareholder representative, or management—to vote on the shareholder's behalf.

Warehouse receipt arrangement The use of inventory as collateral for a loan; similar to a trust receipt arrangement except there is a third party (i.e., a warehouse company) that supervises the inventory.

Warrant Attached option that gives its holder the right to buy the underlying stock of the issuing company at a fixed exercise price until the expiration date.

Weak-form efficient market hypothesis The belief that security prices fully reflect all past market data, which refers to all historical price and volume trading information.

Wealth effect An increase (decrease) in household wealth increases (decreases) consumer spending out of a given level of current income.

Weighted average cost method An inventory accounting method that averages the total cost of available inventory items over the total units available for sale.

Weighted average cost of capital A weighted average of the aftertax required rates of return on a company's common stock, preferred stock, and long-term debt, where the weights are the fraction of each source of financing in the company's target capital structure.

Weighted average coupon rate Weighting the mortgage rate of each mortgage loan in the pool by the percentage of the mortgage outstanding relative to the outstanding amount of all the mortgages in the pool.

Weighted average life A measure that gives investors an indication of how long they can expect to hold the MBS before it is paid off; the convention-based average time to receipt of all principal repayments. Also called *average life*.

Weighted average maturity Weighting the remaining number of months to maturity for each mortgage loan in the pool by the amount of the outstanding mortgage balance.

Weighted mean An average in which each observation is weighted by an index of its relative importance.

Wholesale price index Reflects the price changes experienced by domestic producers in a country.

Winsorized mean A mean computed after assigning a stated percent of the lowest values equal to one specified low value, and a stated percent of the highest values equal to one specified high value.

Working capital The difference between current assets and current liabilities.

Working capital management The management of a company's short-term assets (such as inventory) and short-term liabilities (such as money owed to suppliers).

World price The price prevailing in the world market.

Yield The actual return on a debt security if it is held to maturity.

Yield duration The sensitivity of the bond price with respect to the bond's own yield-to-maturity.

Yield to maturity Annual return that an investor earns on a bond if the investor purchases the bond today and holds it until maturity. It is the discount rate that equates the present value of the bond's expected cash flows until maturity with the bond's price. Also called *yield-to-redemption* or *redemption yield*.

Yield to redemption See *yield to maturity*.

Yield-to-worst The lowest of the sequence of yields-to-call and the yield-to-maturity.

Zero-coupon bonds Bonds that do not pay interest during the bond's life. It is issued at a discount to par value and redeemed at par. Also called *pure discount bonds*.

Zero volatility spread (Z-spread) Calculates a constant yield spread over a government (or interest rate swap) spot curve.